THE WELL-TRAINED MIND

ALSO BY SUSAN WISE BAUER

The Art of the Public Grovel: Sexual Sin and Public Confession in America
(Princeton University Press, 2008)

The Complete Writer: Writing with Ease
(Peace Hill Press, 2008)

The History of the Ancient World: From the Earliest Accounts to the Fall of Rome
(W. W. Norton, 2007)

The Well-Educated Mind: A Guide to the Classical Education You Never Had
(W. W. Norton, 2003)

The Story of the World: History for the Classical Child (Peace Hill Press)
Volume I: Ancient Times, rev. ed. (2006)
Volume II: The Middle Ages, rev. ed. (2007)
Volume III: Early Modern Times (2004)
Volume IV: The Modern World (2005)

ALSO BY JESSIE WISE

First Language Lessons for the Well-Trained Mind
(Peace Hill Press, 2002)

The Ordinary Parent's Guide to Teaching Reading
(Peace Hill Press, 2004)

THE WELL-TRAINED MIND

A Guide to Classical Education at Home

Third Edition

SUSAN WISE BAUER

JESSIE WISE

W. W. Norton & Company

New York London

For information about special discounts for bulk purchases, please contact W. W. Norton Special Sales at specialsales@wwnorton.com or 800-233-4830

Manufacturing by RR Donnelley, Harrisonburg
Production manager: Julia Druskin

Library of Congress Cataloging-in-Publication Data
Bauer, S. Wise.
The well-trained mind : a guide to classical education at home / Susan Wise Bauer, Jessie Wise. — 3rd ed.
p. cm.
Includes bibliographical references and index.
ISBN 978-0-393-06708-8 (hardcover)
1. Home schooling—United States—Handbooks, manuals, etc.
2. Education, Humanistic—United States—Handbooks, manuals, etc.
3. Education—Parent participation—United States—Handbooks, manuals, etc.
I. Wise, Jessie. II. Title.
LC40.B39 2009
371.04'20973—dc22

2009000708

W. W. Norton & Company, Inc., 500 Fifth Avenue, New York, N.Y. 10110
www.wwnorton.com

W. W. Norton & Company Ltd., Castle House, 75/76 Wells Street, London W1T 3QT

1 2 3 4 5 6 7 8 9 0

For Christopher, Benjamin,

and Daniel.

And also for Emily.

CONTENTS

PART I. THE GRAMMAR STAGE: KINDERGARTEN THROUGH FOURTH GRADE

PART III. THE RHETORIC STAGE: NINTH GRADE THROUGH TWELFTH GRADE

APPENDICES

ACKNOWLEDGMENTS FOR THE FIRST EDITION

I am grateful to Amelia and Luther Morecock—Meme and Uncle Luther—for adopting me, teaching me to read before I went to school, and requiring me to be diligent. The credit for any academic or professional success I have enjoyed begins with them. My introduction to phonics materials came from a York, Maine, first-grade teacher in whose class *every* child learned to read. She showed me her systematic phonics program and told me how to order it, with the result that I taught my children how to read and started down the path to home education. I am immensely thankful that, when I took my "misfit" children to the Henrico Mental Clinic in Henrico, Virginia, I met a perceptive and encouraging psychologist, Jeffrey C. Fracher. Dr. Fracher told me to teach my children at home, an idea that had never occurred to me. I'm grateful to my children, Bob, Deborah, and Susan, for learning with me and for continuing to study and learn as adults. Working with Susan on this book has been a challenging, rewarding task. When she was a child, I nudged her beyond her intellectual comfort zone, and she is now continually doing the same for me. Finally, my husband of forty years, Jay, has been in the midst of all of this since our college years. He has encouraged and supported me at every turn.

—Jessie Wise

I am immensely grateful to my husband, Peter, for educating, caring for, and parenting our three sons. His willingness to take on half the burden of home education has made it possible for me to put the necessary hours into writing this book. Douglas Wilson and Gene Edward Veith have helped me understand the theory and practice of classical education; Beth Ferguson has provided invaluable guidance in the area of mathematics; Peggy Ahern kindly shared her expertise in college application and allowed us to quote her at length. Anne Miller and the Home Educators Association of Virginia made it possible for us to present these ideas to a wide spectrum of home schoolers. The home schoolers who told us what does and doesn't work at home include Diane Montgomery, Beth Galvez, and Traci Winyard; thanks to you and to all those we've talked to at conferences, at workshops, and by e-mail. The Williamsburg Public Library reference librarians cheerfully looked up long lists of citations for us, even in the middle of an ice storm. Thanks also to my agent, Richard Henshaw, for his expert advice and stellar work on our behalf; to Starling Lawrence for giving us confidence in our own words and ideas; to Patricia Chui for seeing us through a thousand pages of manuscript and a nine-day power outage right before the final deadline; and to Carol Flechner for the suggestions that helped us clarify and present our ideas. Finally, I'd like to thank my parents, Jay and Jessie Wise, for investing all the time and care it took to train my mind. I love you both, and I'm more grateful than I can say.

—Susan Wise Bauer

ACKNOWLEDGMENTS FOR THE REVISED EDITION

We would never have finished these revisions without the cheerful help of the Peace Hill Press staff. Thanks to Peter Buffington, Charlie Park, Sara Buffington, Sarah Park, and Sherrill Fink for their noble efforts in checking addresses, phone numbers, prices, availability, and web addresses.

Thanks also to the hundreds of dedicated and knowledgeable parents who have posted their experiences, curricula likes and dislikes, and great discoveries on the Well-Trained Mind Message Boards (www.welltrained mind.com/forums). We have learned as much from them as they have from us.

ACKNOWLEDGMENTS FOR THE THIRD EDITION

This third edition builds on the support and encouragement of all those who helped with the first and second editions—and we remain immensely grateful to them for their assistance.

In addition, we'd like to thank Kim Norton, who freed us up to research and write by taking on the administrative duties at Peace Hill Press; Suzanne Hicks, who managed our conference appearances and took care of all those annoying details; Madelaine Wheeler, who did such a wonderful job of checking phone numbers, addresses, websites, prices and all those other details; Diane Wheeler, who not only let Madelaine come and stay with us (a real sacrifice on her part) but who came out to the East Coast and helped finish up the job; Heather Hawkins Wise, who took over all the jobs Susan couldn't (or wouldn't) do; and Bob Wise, who helped overcome our technical deficiencies (there were many). Thanks as well to the kind, patient, and generous folks at W. W. Norton who have done so much to help us over the past decade: not just Starling Lawrence but also (among others) Dosier Hammond, Bill Rusin, Jenn Chan, Golda Rademacher, Deidre Dolan, and the sales reps who have so ably worked on our behalf.

WHAT *THE WELL-TRAINED MIND* DOES: AN OVERVIEW

If you're fortunate, you live near an elementary school filled with excellent teachers who are dedicated to developing your child's skills in reading, writing, arithmetic, history, and science. These teachers have small classes—no more than ten students—and can give each student plenty of attention. The elementary school sits next to a middle school that is safe (no drugs, guns, or knives). This school also has small classes; the teachers train their students in logic, critical thinking, and advanced writing. Plenty of one-on-one instruction is offered, especially in writing. And in the distance (not too far away) is a high school that will take older students through world history, the classics of literature, the techniques of advanced writing, high-level mathematics and science, debate, art history, and music appreciation (not to mention vocational and technical training, résumé preparation, and job-hunting skills).

This book is for the rest of us.

After a combined total of forty years in education—Jessie as elementary and middle-school teacher and administrator in both public and private schools, Susan as student, graduate student, and college teacher—we have come to one simple conclusion: if you want your child to have an excellent education, you need to take charge of it yourself. You don't have to reform your entire school system. All you have to do is teach your own child.

Never mind educational rhetoric about the years of specialized training necessary for teachers. Forget everything you've heard about the need for classes in child development and educational psychology. These things are indeed necessary for the teacher faced with thirty squirming first graders or twenty-five turned-off adolescents. But you have an entirely different task: the education of your own child, one-on-one.

You probably feel that you don't have the skills to teach your child at home. You aren't alone; every home-schooling parent has felt this way (see Chapter 1). But we have consulted with scores of parents—some college-educated, some without high-school diplomas—who have successfully guided their children's education. At conferences and seminars, we've met hundreds more. Home-education magazines overflow with stories of parent-taught teens who excel at reading, writing, science, and math.

All you need to teach your child at home is dedication, some basic knowledge about how children learn, guidance in teaching the particular skills of each academic subject, and lots of books, tapes, posters, kits, and other resources. This book will provide you with everything except the dedication.

The Well-Trained Mind is a parent's guide to a do-it-yourself, academically rigorous, comprehensive education—a *classical* education.

What is classical education?

It is language-intensive—not image-focused. It demands that students use and understand words, not video images.

It is history-intensive, providing students with a comprehensive view of human endeavor from the beginning until now.

It trains the mind to analyze and draw conclusions.

It demands self-discipline.

It produces literate, curious, intelligent students who have a wide range of interests and the ability to follow up on them.

The Well-Trained Mind is a handbook on how to prepare your child to read, write, calculate, think, and *understand.* In the Prologue, we'll outline what a classical education is and tell you about our own experience with classical education and with various forms of school at home.

You may decide to remove your child from school; you may decide to leave her in regular classes. Either way, this book will give you the tools you need to teach her at home or to supplement and reinforce what she's learning in the classroom. We have heard from parents all over the world who are choosing to "afterschool" their children—to work with them individually in the evenings and weekends and over summers, either to remediate or enrich their classroom educations.

Part I tells you how to lay the foundations of academic excellence, from kindergarten through fourth grade. Part II outlines a program that will train the maturing mind of a middle-school child—grades 5 through 8. Part III covers high-school skills. Even if you're starting with an older child, though, you should read through the earlier sections so that you understand the basic principles of classical education. Each section includes a grade-by-grade summary so that you can see at a glance what each school year should include.

Part IV is dedicated to the issues surrounding full-time home education—socialization, grade keeping, standardized testing, getting into college, athletics, and other home-schooling matters. If you want to keep your child in school but do remedial work in grammar or math, you can use the curricula and methods we suggest in the evenings or during breaks. If your child wants to go above and beyond what she's learning in history or science, she can pursue on her own time the at-home programs we outline.

A word about resources. We find huge lists of resources overwhelming. When Susan goes looking for a book about ancient Egypt for her second grader, she doesn't have time to sort through an extensive list of recommended books—she just wants two or three of the best choices. For this reason, we've sorted through available resources and listed our top picks. There are many books, programs, and resources that are compatible with the goals of classical education, and we have made no effort to list them all here. The resources that appear in this book are those that combine academic excellence, ease of use for the parent, clarity, and (when possible) affordability. Other excellent programs may not be listed because they duplicate material in a program we've listed; because they seem unnecessarily complicated, especially for beginners; because they have grown hard to find; or because they are (in our opinion) overpriced. But you can substitute with confidence wherever needed.

Some of our recommendations have changed since 1999, when *The Well-Trained Mind* was first published. In some cases, the original materials simply went out of print, forcing us to find new titles to replace them. But in many cases, curricula developed in the ten years between the first and third editions have (in our opinion) superseded our earlier recommendations. For those who wonder why recommendations from the 1999 and 2004 editions didn't make the cut, we have provided Appendix 5, Previous Recommendations.

For those who want to explore all available options, Chapter 46, "More Stuff: The Annotated Catalog List," will give you a place to start. Visit www.welltrainedmind.com for updates, Parents' Forum, and further information.

PRACTICAL CONSIDERATIONS: USING *THE WELL-TRAINED MIND* WITHOUT LOSING YOUR OWN

This is a very big book. *The Well-Trained Mind* provides information on teaching all the subjects in the classical curriculum for all twelve grades—literature, writing, grammar, history, science, math, Latin, modern languages, art, music, debate, and more.

It's a rare parent who will follow this program exactly. The freedom to tailor an academic program to your child's particular interests and needs is one of home education's greatest advantages. We've explained the general philosophy that governs each part of the curriculum, but our specific schedules, texts, and programs are just *illustrations* of how to put this philosophy into practice. We think the texts and programs we've settled on are the best available, but you should always feel free to substitute, to pick and choose. For example, in Chapter 16 we recommend that middle-grade history students outline their history lessons, and we demonstrate this process by quoting from the *Kingfisher History Encyclopedia,* our recommended text. But if you've found another book of world history that you love, you can certainly use it instead. (See page xxiii for more about our selection criteria.)

You can follow one part of the program, but not another. If, for example, you've found a math curriculum that works well for your sixth grader, you can use the language resources we suggest without feeling as though you've got to convert to the math books we like. If your high-school student already has a literature list he's reading his way through, you can still use our writing and grammar suggestions without adopting our reading list.

It's a rare child who will do *all* the work we suggest—especially in the early grades, when learning to read, write, and do sums may take most of the child's study time. Many students have extracurricular activities (soccer, music lessons, serious hobbies, clubs, skills courses such as accounting or typing) that may bump art appreciation or French from your schedule. In the classical curriculum, reading, writing, grammar, and math are the center of the curriculum. History and science become more and more important as the child matures. Foreign languages are immensely valuable, but shouldn't crowd out these basic skill areas. And music and art are wonderful when you can manage them.

After you read through Parts I, II, and III, you should have a good grasp of the principles that guide a classical education. As you put them into effect, take seriously our constant direction toward texts and curricula that are systematic and rigorous. Remember that a child *must* have a thorough grounding in the basic skills of grammar, spelling, and writing before he can proceed to more complex analytical work (more on this in Part I). But when you teach your child at home, *you* make the final decision on which books you'll use and how much time you'll spend on schoolwork. Our suggestions are simply that, suggestions, meant to guide you as you plan your child's education at home.

SUPPLEMENTING YOUR CHILD'S EDUCATION: *THE WELL-TRAINED MIND* AND FULL-TIME SCHOOL

Not everyone who uses this book will want to join the ranks of full-time home schoolers. Although much in this book (and most of the information in Part IV) will be useful to parents who are educating their children completely at home, the information on teaching each subject and the resource lists that follow each chapter will help you supplement the education of a child who's already in school.

Every involved parent is a home educator. If you're checking your child's compositions, talking him through his history homework, or drilling him in math, you're already teaching him. In this case, you're acting as a teacher's aide—helping to teach and reinforce material that has already been presented in the classroom.

You may find, though, that you want to move beyond this role and take on the job of organizing and presenting new material yourself. Your child may need extra tutoring and practice in a subject in order to master it. Or he may be so interested in a subject that he wants to go beyond the prescribed curriculum.

Either way, we suggest that you read Chapters 1 and 2, which explain our basic theory of classical education, and the chapters that deal with each stage of the mind's development: Chapter 3, "The Parrot Years"; Chapter 13, "The Argumentative Child"; and Chapter 24, "Speaking Your Mind." These will give you an overview of the process of learning, no matter what age your child is. We also suggest that you call for the catalogs listed in Chapter 46, "More Stuff," which will give you some idea of the immense wealth of supplementary materials available.

Encourage your child toward absorption in grades 1 through 4, critical thought in grades 5 through 8, and expression in grades 9 through 12. He must have good, phonics-based reading skills. Use one of the phonics programs that we recommend to teach beginning reading skills; make sure he does plenty of extra reading in the early grades; and use the Critical Thinking Press books recommended throughout Part II to help him think critically about middle-grade history, science, and math. In the high-school years, use as reference works Anthony Weston's *A Rulebook for Argumentation* (see Chapter 24) and *Writing Exposition* (see Chapter 25) to help the upper-grade student write and argue with fluency. Also consider using the *Writing Strands* program (described in Chapters 5, 17, and 25) as a summer project, continuing with it until the student finishes level 7. Writing is a difficult skill to teach in a group setting, and most students need extra practice and individual attention to write well.

If you want to encourage your child to go beyond the classroom, use the information we present, and adapt it to his school schedule. For example, in Chapter 18, "Making Deductions," we describe a science program for fifth through eighth grade that requires the student to complete experiments, write reports, and sketch diagrams. You can use the science kits we recommend and key the child's study to what he's learning in the classroom. If he's studying fifth-grade biology and wants to know more, use our biology resource sections to provide your child with supplementary learning.

You can also use these chapters to guide a course of summer study. But bear in mind that a twelve-week summer course can't cover all the material listed in these chapters, which are designed to provide a school year's worth of study at home.

If you want to make sure that your child masters a skill area that's giving him trouble, you can use the books and programs we describe as systematic and drill-oriented. You shouldn't try to key these to classroom work since each skill builds on what has already been taught. Instead, devote an appropriate amount of time to pursuing the additional study as an extracurricular activity.

If you're particularly unhappy with the way one subject is being taught, consider asking your school system whether your child can study that particular material with a tutor. Many schools will allow this as long as the child shows steady progress. You can then substitute one of the programs we outline, either acting as tutor yourself or hiring someone to work one-on-one with your child (see Chapters 42 and 43 for information on approaching your local school and finding reliable tutors). It sometimes happens that an excellent teacher and a bright student are unable to connect in the classroom because their learning styles conflict. And many children need one-on-one instruction in order to do their best work.

For we let our young men and women go out unarmed in a day when armor was never so necessary. By teaching them to read, we have left them at the mercy of the printed word. By the invention of the film and the radio, we have made certain that no aversion to reading shall secure them from the incessant battery of words, words, words. They do not know what the words mean; they do not know how to ward them off or blunt their edge or fling them back; they are a prey to words in their emotions instead of being the masters of them in their intellects. . . . We have lost the tools of learning, and in their absence can only make a botched and piecemeal job of it.

—Dorothy L. Sayers, "The Lost Tools of Learning"

THE WELL-TRAINED MIND

PROLOGUE

THE STORY OF A CLASSICAL HOME EDUCATION

1

UNCHARTED TERRITORY: JESSIE

The first day I taught my three children at home, I cleaned up the playroom and set up three desks. I hung an American flag at the front of the room and led them in the Pledge of Allegiance. I was shaking with nervousness.

It was 1973, and my husband, Jay, and I had just done something radical. We had removed our children from school.

I was terrified, which was ridiculous. After all, I was a state-certified teacher. I'd taught public school for six years; I'd taken postgraduate courses in education from Tulane University, the College of William and Mary, and the University of Virginia. One year, I'd managed thirty-eight second graders from dawn till dusk—no lunch break, no recess break, and no teacher's aide.

Yet I was completely intimidated by those three little children, certain that I couldn't do an adequate job of teaching them myself. All my teacher education had brainwashed me. I was convinced that parents couldn't possibly teach their own children—certainly not at home. It had to be done in an institutional setting, run by professionals, with their resources and specialized training and expertise.

Unfortunately, the professionals had let us down.

I wasn't a stranger to failures in the system. The last year I taught public school, I had in my sixth-grade class two sixteen-year-old boys who had not yet learned to read. I'd never even heard of home schooling, but I remember thinking: If I ever have a child, he will know how to read before he goes to school. I will not have my son sitting in sixth grade, unable to read.

So when my oldest child turned four, I said to him one day, "Bob, would you rather take a nap, or would you like to learn how to read?" He chose reading (not surprisingly), and I started him on the old-fashioned phonics I'd been taught when I was a child. I'd lie down with him on his little bed after lunch and work on his letters (since I also had a two year old and a thirteen month old, I was always glad to lie down). We practiced vowels and consonants, and sounded out new words that year. We called it "doing kindergarten." By the time my middle child was three, she wanted in. "My do kindergarten, too," she'd say, and I would boost her up and let her repeat the sounds after me.

I was proud of myself. I was preparing my children for school. Kindergarten, when it came, was uneventful and purely social. Bob loved to play at school. At home, I went on reading to him and teaching him his language and number skills.

But when Bob reached first grade, he didn't fit in. He already knew the material, and he was bored. The school—a well-regarded private school—was cooperative and moved him into second grade. He was bored there, too. The class was working on early reading skills, and we'd already done that. The second graders didn't like him because he was a little upstart invading their turf. The administration moved him back to first grade, but now the first graders were hostile. He was a big shot who'd been thought worthy of second grade, and they wouldn't play with him. They were jealous because he was well prepared.

So here he was, in first grade, already feeling that doing well in school made him unpopular. He started to change. He had been an excited, exuberant, curious child. Now he was a behavior problem. He stopped doing well in school. His papers had always been meticulously done, but suddenly his writing became sloppy. The teacher complained to us that Bob was always questioning her in class. And the bus ride to school was horrendous: the older kids made the younger ones sit on the floor, stole their lunches, and dirtied their clothes so they'd get demerits from the teachers at school. Every day, Bob got off the school bus with a handful of bad papers, and he was either fighting mad or crying.

At this point, Jay and I realized that we were spending most of our time with this child trying to undo what was happening to him when he was at school. And we were afraid that our second child, Susan, would go through the same metamorphosis. Susan had just started kindergarten, and the teacher was already protesting to us that she would be a social misfit because she wanted to read during free time instead of playing. We were experiencing firsthand the terrific leveling pressure applied in so many schools: the effort to smooth out the bumps by bringing well-prepared kids down to the level of the rest.

This still happens in some schools. Just this year, the best private preschool in our area agreed to stop teaching four year olds beginning reading skills. Kindergarten teachers in the local public schools had complained that the children turned out by this preschool were bored in kindergarten because they already knew the material. The schools demanded that the preschool quit turning out such well-prepared five year olds so that all the kindergartners would start at the same level of ignorance. I was appalled when the preschool buckled and went back to teaching colors and "social skills."

Back in 1973, no one had told me to stop teaching phonics to my preschoolers. And we didn't know what to do with these academic misfits I had managed to produce. So we took our two school-age children to a psychologist in the local mental-health system. He tested both of them, and I found out what my careful preparation for kindergarten had done: Bob, the second grader, was reading on a seventh-grade level; Susan, the kindergartner, was reading fifth-grade material. The psychologist called us into his office afterward. "Listen," he said, "if you keep those children in school, they are going to become nonlearners. They're bored to death. You've got a teacher's certificate. Why don't you take them out of school and teach them yourself?"

This had never occurred to us. After all, education was the domain of schools . . . and these were *our* children! We didn't know anyone else who was home-schooling. The whole idea was odd and radical, and we weren't sure it was even legal; Virginia law was fuzzy on this point.

But we had no other choice. The local public school was a terrible environment socially, and test scores ranked our county at the bottom of the state year after year. The private school had been our solution. So, quaking in my boots, I set up the desks and the American flag and started to teach my children at home. I worried the whole time. I worried that my children weren't going to get into college. I worried that the school system was going to come and take them away from us for neglect and truancy. I worried that their social development would suffer.

I could tell you the stories of all three children, but I want to focus on my older daughter, Susan, because we've had the chance to work and speak together, and to reflect on what I did right—and wrong—in her education. As I write this, Susan is happily married and the mother of four (three boys and a girl). She went to college at seventeen on a full scholarship, awarded to her for being a National Merit finalist. She worked summers for a good salary as secretary for a legal firm. Her college chose her to spend a term at Oxford as a visiting student. After college, she completed a Master of Divinity—a three-year theological degree—and then a Master of Arts in English literature. She reads Hebrew, Greek, Latin, Aramaic, and French. She has a thriving career as a writer; she has published novels and nonfiction books, she writes for several journals and periodicals, and she has started her own small press. She has earned her doctoral degree in American studies, and teaches literature and writing at the College of William and Mary in Virginia.

As I look back on the education I gave her, I can see that it follows a pattern that has mostly disappeared from public education. To begin with, I filled her head with facts when she was small. I taught her to read early and kept books everywhere in the house; we had books for presents and rewards, and I was known at the local public library as "the lady with the laundry basket" because I took my children in every week and filled a laundry basket with their books. On each library visit, I had them check out the following books: one science book, one history book, one art or music appreciation book, one practical book (a craft, hobby, or "how-to"), a biography or autobiography, a classic novel (or an adaptation suited to age), an imaginative storybook, a book of poetry. They were allowed to choose the titles, but I asked them to follow this pattern. And they were also allowed to check out other books on any topic they pleased. Furthermore, I made Susan memorize. She could recite multiplication tables, lists of linking verbs, dates, presidents, and Latin declensions.

As her thought processes matured, I taught her how to fit her knowledge into logical structures. I spent a lot of time with her in one-on-one discussion and interaction. We learned spelling rules, mathematics, and basic logic; we followed an unfashionably strict grammar book and diagrammed sentences of increasing complexity; we kept science notebooks and time lines so that we could organize her growing knowledge of facts into logical and chronological order. I taught her how to organize a paragraph, an essay, a research paper. She learned Latin grammar. She learned how to discipline herself to follow a custom-made schedule, balancing academics and personal interests like music and creative writing. And she continued to read every spare moment.

As she moved into high school, I spent more time working on her skills in writing and expression. She wrote papers, book reports, and stories; she had a particular bent for this and also wrote two novels, although that wasn't a part of my curriculum. My plan *did* include allowing her to develop a specialty, some area in which she could deepen her knowledge in preparation for college and a career. She became interested in early British history and literature, and taught herself Welsh and Gaelic (certainly nothing I would have come up with). She loved practicing the piano. She also started working part-time. And we spent an hour every day studying for her SATs, using test-preparation books to review reading skills, logical constructs, English vocabulary, and mathematics. She scored 740 on the verbal section of the SATs, 630 on the math (and this was before the new, adjusted scoring came in). Our mailbox was filled with college catalogs. She finally chose a school where she'd been offered a Presidential Scholarship based on her standardized scores. In her freshman year, she was given the chance to test out of several survey courses by taking the College Level Examination Program examinations. She took the whole battery, just for fun, and was awarded over thirty hours of college credit. After college she made a perfect score on the verbal section of the Graduate Record Exam and did her graduate work at William and Mary on full scholarship.

I didn't know until later that I had followed the pattern of classical education called the trivium. I did know that what I was doing worked.

Susan will write about the trivium in the next chapter; it's the classical theory of education, which organizes learning around the maturing capacity of the child's mind. It no longer exists in public education. *I* didn't learn by this method when I was educated in the county public schools back in the forties and fifties. But I was raised by elderly relatives who had been taught by classical methods popular before the turn of the century. Meme, as I called her, had only finished eighth grade in a one-room schoolhouse, and Uncle Luther hadn't even gone that far. But by eighth grade, Meme had learned Latin and algebra, and Uncle Luther had learned advanced practical mathematics and how to think and write. They taught me to read before I ever went to school. The first-grade teacher was our neighbor, and when she heard that Meme was drilling me in phonics, she made a special trip over to warn us that I'd be ruined for life if Meme used such an outdated method. Meme was undaunted, and when I did enter school I was put straight into second grade because of the skills I'd already acquired.

When I came home from school in the evenings, Meme and Uncle Luther sat me down and made me learn. Meme would point at the lists in the books—multiplication tables, parts of speech—and say, "Memorize those."

"But the teacher said we don't have to memorize them," I protested. "We just have to be able to use them."

"I don't care what the teacher says," Meme insisted. "These are things you have to know."

I had been trained to be obedient and disciplined, so I memorized the lists, even though memorization was difficult for me. I learned my algebra and grammar. I went on to college and a professional position; I was the only girl in my high-school class to graduate from college. When I had children of my own, I used Meme's method and found that the three-part process of memorization, logical organization, and clear expression put them far above their peers.

In the middle of this century, Dorothy Sayers, author and creator of Lord Peter Wimsey, told an audience at Oxford University that education had given up on the trivium and was now running on what she called the "educational capital." We no longer teach our children the process of memorization, organization, and expression—the *tools* by which the mind learns.

The leftover remnants of those methods have carried us through several decades of schooling without catastrophe; I made it through public school at the top of my class because my guardians taught me from *what they had learned.* But sooner or later, the capital gets used up. My own children were faced with teachers who brought them down to the level of the class; teachers who thought it was more important to teach social skills than academic subjects; textbooks that had abandoned grammatical rules and mathematical logic in favor of scattershot, incidental learning. They were surrounded by peers who considered anyone good at learning to be a geek. They spent seven hours every day sitting in desks, standing in lines, riding buses, and doing repetitive seatwork so that their classmates could learn what they already knew.

I wanted something better for them. As I've watched home education develop over the last two decades, I've become convinced that any dedicated parent can do what I did. My own education didn't stretch to Latin or Gaelic or calculus or computer science or art, but my children learned all of these things. With the help of resources and support groups now in place throughout the country—and with the principles we'll give you in this book—you can provide your child with a classical education at home, even if you've never glanced at Latin or logic.

You can do what my guardians did and, on your own time, teach your child the basic skills she may not be learning at school. Your young student may need particular help in math, science, reading, or writing. Even the best and most diligent teacher (I speak from experience) is often prevented from giving necessary individual attention by the growing size of her class. If you use the resources we've collected in this book and invest in some one-on-one time with your child, you are capable of educating him.

When I taught school, I was convinced that parents couldn't teach their own children. But twenty-five years later, I can look back and say: The experiment was a success. I was the best teacher my children could possibly have had *because* I was their parent.

I happened to have a teacher's certificate. But during my years of home schooling, I learned more academic material, more about how to manage individual relationships with children, and more about how to teach than I did in any of my teacher-education courses. Teacher-education courses gave me a great deal of good information on how to manage large groups of children. I needed that in schools, but a parent doesn't need it to teach at home.

I happened to have a college degree. But in the twenty-five years since I first became involved with the home-education movement, I've seen parents who only finished high school lead their children successfully through twelfth grade, and I've watched those children thrive in college.

You shouldn't be afraid to take your child out of school, if necessary. This is a radical step for most parents; it means a change in schedule, in priorities, in lifestyle. And apart from academic concerns, many parents ask, "What about my child's social development? Doesn't he need peers?" Children need friends. Children do *not* need to be surrounded by large groups of peers who inevitably follow the strongest personality in the crowd. The question for any parent is: Do I want my child to be like his peers? Or do I want my child to rise above them?

Finally, if you're accustomed to sending your child to school every morning and allowing the professionals to worry about what he learns and how he learns it, the idea of supervising an entire education may overwhelm you. I sympathize. When I started, I was convinced I could never do it. But if you feel your child is being shortchanged in school, we can give you a plan to fix that. In this book, not only will we introduce you to the trivium method, but we'll give you resources to carry it out and a plan for the entire twelve years of school.

I discovered that home education has a great advantage I knew nothing about when I started. Home education teaches children to *learn* and eventually to teach themselves. By the time my children were twelve or so, I did less and less actual teaching. I supervised; I discussed content with them; I held them accountable; I graded; I bought books and organized coursework. But by early high school, they had been trained in the methods of learning. From this point, they began the process of educating themselves, with some help from tutors and correspondence courses. As adults, they continue to educate themselves, to widen their intellectual horizons. Certainly, this should be the first goal of education.

2

A PERSONAL LOOK AT CLASSICAL EDUCATION: SUSAN

I loved going to school at home. As a high-school student, I would get up in the morning, practice the piano for two hours, do my math and grammar lessons, finish off my science, and then devote the rest of my school day to my favorite subjects—history, ancient languages, and writing. Once a week, we all piled into the car and drove around to music lessons, math tutoring sessions, library visits, college classes. On weekends, we went to athletic meets—my brother's bicycle races, the horse shows my sister and I trained for and rode in.

But I was nervous when I went away to college. Although I'd done well on standardized exams, I'd never really sat in a regular classroom, facing inflexible deadlines. I was used to taking tests from my mother.

I shouldn't have worried. I tested out of thirty hours' worth of college courses; by my second semester, I was taking 400-level courses. I had a host of strange skills: I could diagram sentences; I could read Latin; I knew enough logic to tell whether an assertion was true or faulty. And I was surrounded by eighteen year olds who couldn't write, didn't want to read, and couldn't reason.

I worked in the Peer Tutoring Center for two years, tutoring English composition and Greek grammar. I found myself teaching fifth-grade grammar to college students. My peers came in because they were getting failing grades in composition; I discovered that they couldn't tell the difference between fragments and run-on sentences. Students of Greek came in because they were having trouble translating; they couldn't identify nouns and verbs or tell me what the difference was.

This college was small and nonexclusive, but the problem is universal. Ten years later, I taught my first semester of university classes at the College of William and Mary in Virginia. William and Mary, which still holds to the model of classical education, *is* selective about admissions. The students in my literature classes had high grades, high test scores, lots of extracurricular credits. I had sixty students my first year and taught two sections of Major British Writers, Eighteenth and Nineteenth Centuries: Jonathan Swift to Arthur Conan Doyle in one fell swoop.

I spent the beginning of the semester teaching remedial English to these freshmen. My first hint of trouble came when I assigned Wordsworth's "Ode: Intimations of Immortality" and gave a reading quiz. As I collected the test, I saw that Wordsworth's title had been thoroughly mangled: "Intemmitions," "Intimmations," "Inntemisions."

"Didn't any of you learn phonetic spelling?" I asked. Most of them shook their heads. Well, I already knew that phonics tends to be unfashionable, so I decided to be merciful. After all, I thought, they can always run a spell checker on their papers. I told them to write a four- to six-page paper comparing two of the poems we'd covered or comparing one of the poems to a modern work—no footnotes necessary, no research into scholarly articles required. Almost at once, the e-mail started to flood into my electronic mailbox:

> Professor Bauer, I never wrote a paper on a poem before and I don't know where to start.

> Professor Bauer, I want to write on "The Rime of the Ancient Mariner," but I don't think I can say enough about it to fill up four pages.

("The Rime of the Ancient Mariner" has enough metaphor and philosophy in it to provide material for a doctoral thesis.)

> While thinking about my paper topic, I have realized that I have no clue as to what I should write on.
>
> Professor Bauer, I'm completely lost, I only have dillusions of correct paper topics.

The papers, when finally turned in, contained a few gems, but the majority were badly written, illogical, and full of grammatical errors. And, with a few exceptions, my privately educated students struggled right along with the public-school graduates. They labored to put a thesis into words. They sweated and complained and groaned, trying to prove it. And they didn't know whether they'd proved it or not when they got to the end of their paper.

I spend time talking to these freshmen and sophomores in my office. They're bright, lively, energetic, interesting kids. They have ideas and passions and philosophical problems and social concerns and creative aspirations. But they've been done a great disservice. Their schools gave them few tools; their minds are filled with the raw materials needed for success, but they're having to dig with their hands.

I was ahead of them when I was their age—not because of superior mental abilities, but because I'd been equipped with a closetful of mental tools. My mother taught us the way she'd been taught at home. Our education was language-centered, not image-centered; we read and listened and wrote, but we rarely watched. She spent the early years of school giving us facts, systematically laying the foundation for advanced study. She taught us to think through arguments, and *then* she taught us how to express ourselves.

This is the classical pattern of the trivium, the three-part process of training the mind.

The first years of schooling are called the "grammar stage"—not because you spend four years doing English, but because these are the years in which the building blocks for all other learning are laid, just as grammar is the foundation for language. In the elementary-school years—grades 1 through 4—the mind is ready to absorb information. Since children at this age actually find memorization fun, during this period education involves not self-expression and self-discovery, but rather the learning of facts: rules of phonics and spelling, rules of grammar, poems, the vocabulary of foreign languages, the stories of history and literature, descriptions of plants and animals and the human body, the facts of mathematics—the list goes on. This information makes up the "grammar" for the second stage of education.

By fifth grade, a child's mind begins to think more analytically. Middle-school students are less interested in finding out facts than in asking "Why?" The second phase of the classical education, the "logic stage," is a time when the child begins to pay attention to cause and effect, to the relationships among different fields of knowledge, to the way facts fit together into a logical framework.

A student is ready for the logic stage when the capacity for abstract thought begins to mature. During these years, the student learns algebra and logic, and begins to apply logic to all academic subjects. The logic of writing, for example, includes paragraph construction and support of a thesis; the logic of reading involves the criticism and analysis of texts, not simple absorption of information; the logic of history demands that the student find out why the War of 1812 was fought, rather than simply reading its story; the logic of science requires the child to learn the scientific method.

The final phase of a classical education, the "rhetoric stage," builds on the first two. At this point, the high-school student learns to write and speak with force and originality. The student of rhetoric applies the rules of logic learned in middle school to the foundational information learned in the early grades and expresses her conclusions in clear, forceful, elegant language. The student also begins to specialize in whatever branch of knowledge attracts her; these are the years for art camps, college courses, foreign travel, apprenticeships, and other forms of specialized training.

A classical education is more than just a pattern of learning, though. First, it is *language-focused:* learning is accomplished through words, written and spoken, rather than through images (pictures, videos, and television).

Why is this important? Language learning and image learning require very different habits of thought. Language requires the mind to work harder; in reading, the brain is forced to translate a symbol (words on the page) into a concept. Images, such as those on videos and television, allow the mind to be passive. In front of a video screen, the brain can "sit back" and relax; faced with the written page, the mind is required to roll its sleeves up and get to work.

Second, a classical education follows a specific three-part pattern: the mind must be first supplied with facts and images, then given the logical tools for organization of those facts and images, and finally equipped to express conclusions.

Third, to the classical mind, all knowledge is interrelated. Astronomy, for example, isn't studied in isolation; it's learned along with the history of scientific discovery, which leads into the church's relationship to science and from there to the intricacies of medieval church history. The reading of the *Odyssey* allows the student to consider Greek history, the nature of heroism, the development of the epic, and humankind's understanding of the divine.

This is easier said than done. The world is full of knowledge, and finding the links between fields of study can be a mind-twisting task. A classical education meets this challenge by taking history as its organizing outline, beginning with the ancients and progressing forward to the moderns in history, science, literature, art, and music.

We suggest that the twelve years of education consist of three repetitions of the same four-year pattern: the ancients (5000 B.C.–A.D. 400), the medieval period through the early Renaissance (400–1600), the late Renaissance through early modern times (1600–1850), and modern times (1850–present). The child studies these four time periods at varying levels—simple for grades 1 through 4, more difficult in grades 5 through 8 (when the student begins to read original sources), and taking an even more complex approach in grades 9 through 12, when the student works through these time periods using original sources (from Homer to Hitler) and also has the opportunity to pursue a particular interest (music, dance, technology, medicine, biology, creative writing) in depth.

The other subject areas of the curriculum are linked to history studies. The student who is working on ancient history will read Greek and Roman mythology, the tales of the *Iliad* and *Odyssey,* early medieval writings, Chinese and Japanese fairy tales, and (for the older student) the classical texts of Plato, Herodotus, Virgil, Aristotle. She'll read *Beowulf,* Dante, Chaucer, Shakespeare the following year, when she's studying medieval and early Renaissance history. When the eighteenth and nineteenth centuries are studied, she starts with Swift *(Gulliver's Travels)* and ends with Dickens; finally, she reads modern literature as she is studying modern history.

The sciences are studied in a four-year pattern that roughly corresponds to the periods of scientific discovery: biology, classification, and the human body (subjects known to the ancients); earth science and basic astronomy (which flowered during the early Renaissance); chemistry (which came into its own during the early modern period); and basic physics and computer science (very modern subjects).

The Study of Science

Name of period	Years covered	Scientific subjects	Studied during grades . . .
Ancients	5000 B.C.–A.D. 400	Biology Classification Human body	1, 5, 9
Medieval–early Renaissance	400–1600	Earth science Astronomy	2, 6, 10
Late Renaissance–early modern	1600–1850	Chemistry	3, 7, 11
Modern	1850–present	Physics Computer science	4, 8, 12

This pattern lends coherence to the study of history, science, and literature—subjects that are too often fragmented and confusing. The pattern widens and deepens as the student matures and learns. For example, a first grader listens to you read the story of the *Iliad* from one of the picture-book versions available at any public library. (Susan's experience has been that first graders think the *Iliad* is a blast, especially when Achilles starts hauling Hector's body around the walls of Troy.) Four years later, the fifth grader reads one of the popular middle-grade adaptations—Olivia Coolidge's *The Trojan War,* or Roger L. Green's *The Tale of Troy.* Four more years go by, and the ninth grader—faced with Homer's *Iliad* itself—plunges right in, undaunted. She already knows the story. What's to be scared of?

In the chapters that follow, we'll show you how to follow this pattern for each subject, list the resources you'll need, and tell you where to find these resources.

Classical education is, above all, systematic—in direct contrast to the scattered, unorganized nature of so much secondary education. Rigorous, systematic study has two purposes. Rigorous study develops virtue in the student: the ability to act in accordance to what one knows to be right. Virtuous men (or women) can force themselves to do what they know is right, even when it runs against their inclinations. Classical education continually asks a student to work against her baser tendencies (laziness or the desire to watch another half hour of TV) in order to reach a goal—mastery of a subject.

Systematic study allows the student to join what Mortimer J. Adler calls the "Great Conversation": the ongoing conversation of great minds down through the ages. Much modern education is so eclectic that the student has little opportunity to make connections between past events and the flood of current information. "The beauty of the classical curriculum," writes classical schoolmaster David Hicks, "is that it dwells on one problem, one author, or one epoch long enough to allow even the youngest student a chance to exercise his mind in a scholarly way: to make connections and to trace developments, lines of reasoning, patterns of action, recurring symbolisms, plots, and motifs."[1]

My mother struggled hard to give us the benefits of a classical education. She began to teach us at home in a day when few materials existed for home-educating parents; she had to create her own curriculum. We're going to lay out a whole plan of study for you—not just theory, but resources and textbooks and curricula.

It's still hard work. We don't deny it. We'll give you a clear view of the demands and requirements of this academic project. But a classical education is worth every drop of sweat—I can testify to that. I am constantly grateful to my mother for my education. It gave me an immeasurable head start, the independence to innovate and work on my own, confidence in my ability to compete in the job market, and the mental tools to build a satisfying career.

In fifteen years, I believe that my own children will say the same to me.

[1]David Hicks, *Norms and Nobility: A Treatise on Education* (New York: Praeger, 1981), p. 133.

PART I

THE GRAMMAR STAGE

Kindergarten through Fourth Grade

3

THE PARROT YEARS

So far (except, of course, for the Latin), our curriculum contains nothing that departs very far from common practice. The difference will be felt rather in the attitude of the teachers, who must look upon all these activities less as "subjects" in themselves than as a gathering-together of material for use in the next part of the *Trivium*.

—Dorothy Sayers, "The Lost Tools of Learning"

Houses rest on foundations. Journalists gather all the facts before writing their stories; scientists accumulate data before forming theories; violinists and dancers and defensive tackles rely on muscle memory, stored in their bodies by hours of drill.

A classical education requires a student to collect, memorize, and categorize information. Although this process continues through all twelve grades, the first four grades are the most intensive for fact collecting.

This isn't a fashionable approach to early education. Much classroom time and energy has been spent in an effort to give children every possible opportunity to express what's inside them. There's nothing wrong with self-expression, but when self-expression pushes the accumulation of knowledge offstage, something's out of balance.

Young children are described as sponges because they soak up knowledge. But there's another side to the metaphor. Squeeze a dry sponge, and nothing comes out. First the sponge has to be filled. Language teacher Ruth Beechick writes, "Our society is so obsessed with creativity that people want children to be creative before they have any knowledge or skill to be creative with."[1] Your job, during the elementary years, is to supply the knowledge and skills that will allow your child to overflow with creativity as his mind matures.

That doesn't mean that your first grader has to learn about complex subjects in depth or that you're going to force him to memorize long lists of details. In the first four years of learning, you'll be filling your child's mind and imagination with as many pictures, stories, and facts as you can. Your goal is to supply mental pegs on which later information can be hung.

Think of an experience most adults have had. You read about a minor movie star, and suddenly you see his name everywhere. You learn a new vocabulary word and instantly notice it sprinkled through all sorts of different texts. You happen across the name of a tiny, obscure foreign country and in the next few days notice a dozen news items about it.

You might remark to your spouse, "What a coincidence!" Usually, though, that information has surrounded you all along. The movie star's name, the new word, the foreign country were already in the magazines and newspapers at the checkout line, but because the information was unfamiliar to you, your eyes passed over it without recognition. Once the information entered your memory, you recognized it and began to accumulate more and more details.

This is what you'll be doing with your elementary-school child. You might read a book about the planet Mars to your second grader. If it's the first time he's heard about Mars, he probably won't grasp all the information you're giving him. But he may hear on the news that night the most recent information from the Mars space probe, and suddenly something that would have passed by him clicks in his mind. You'll tell him, in history, about the Roman god Mars, the father of Romulus and Remus, and he'll hang this detail on the peg you provided when you read that book about the planets. When he runs across the word *martial* and asks what it means, you can tell him that it means *warlike* and comes from the name Mars, god of war—and the information will stick.

[1]Ruth Beechick, *A Strong Start in Language: Grades K–3* (Pollock Pines, Calif.: Arrow Press, 1993), p. 6.

The whole structure of the trivium recognizes that there is an ideal time and place for each part of learning: memorization, argumentation, and self-expression. The elementary years are ideal for soaking up knowledge.

A classical education assumes that knowledge of the world past and present takes priority over self-expression. Intensive study of facts equips the student for fluent and articulate self-expression later on. Too close a focus on self-expression at an early age can actually cripple a child later on; a student who has always been encouraged to look inside himself may not develop a frame of reference, a sense of how his ideas measure up against the thoughts and beliefs of others.

So the key to the first stage of the trivium is content, content, content. In history, science, literature, and, to a lesser extent, art and music, the child should be accumulating masses of information: stories of people and wars; names of rivers, cities, mountains, and oceans; scientific names, properties of matter, classifications; plots, characters, and descriptions. The young writer should be memorizing the nuts and bolts of language—parts of speech, parts of a sentence, vocabulary roots. The young mathematician should be preparing for higher math by mastering the basic math facts.

NOW OR NEVER

Why are the first four grades a particularly fruitful time to concentrate on content?

This is the first time your child will encounter Egyptian embalming rites or the atmosphere of Venus; this is the first time he will understand what light is made of or why Americans rebelled against the British. He will never get a second chance to read *The Lion, the Witch, and the Wardrobe,* or hear *The Hobbit* read aloud for the first time. Seize this early excitement. Let the child delve deep. Let him read, read, read. Don't force him to stop and reflect on it yet. Don't make him decide what he likes and doesn't like about ancient Rome; let him wallow in gladiators and chariot races. He wants to find out how things work, how ancient people lived, where Mount Vesuvius is located, and what Pompeii looked like, covered with volcanic ash. This thirst for sheer accumulation won't ever die completely, but it is more easily satisfied later on. And the wonder of that first encounter with a strange civilization will never come again.

The immature mind is more suited to absorption than argument. The critical and logical faculty simply doesn't develop until later on. The typical second grader will take great joy in singing the latest television commercials to you word for word but will stare at you slack-jawed if you ask him why the advertiser wants him to buy the product, or what the merits of the product are, or whether it's reasonably priced. There is nothing wrong with a child accumulating information that he doesn't yet understand. It all goes into the storehouse for use later on.

Susan recalls that somewhere around second grade she learned to chant the entire list of helping verbs. The uses of a helping verb weren't clear to her until much later on. But she finds that list popping into her mind whenever she's checking her own writing for grammatical errors or learning a foreign language.

Finally, there's the enjoyment factor. Children *like* lists at this age. They like rattling off rote information, even if they don't understand it. They enjoy the accomplishment, the look on the face of an adult when they trot out their stored knowledge, and the sounds of the syllables rolling off their tongues. As adults, we may tend to "protect" our children from memory work because *we* find it difficult and tedious. But most young children enjoy repetition and delight in the familiarity of memorized words. How many times have you read *Green Eggs and Ham* to a four year old who already knows the entire book by heart?

HOW TO TEACH THE POLL-PARROT STAGE

As your child's teacher, you'll serve as a source of information. In the early grades, you'll be telling your child stories, reading to him from history and science books, teaching him math facts. And you'll expect him to be able to repeat back to you the stories and facts he's heard. This process—which we'll outline in detail for each area of the curriculum—will train him to grasp facts and express them in his own words.

Don't make K–4 students dig for information. Fill their mind and imagination with images and concepts, pictures and stories. Spread knowledge out in front of them, and let them feast.

PRIORITIES

Schools struggle to make time for all the subjects students need and want—grammar, writing, reading, math, history, science, art, music, religion, typing, sex ed, and so forth.

Part of the school dilemma results from the school's assertion of a parental role; since you're already filling that position, you won't have to decide between sex ed and mathematics. But home schoolers also struggle with the mass of material that *could* be covered. There are so many good history books, science experiments, works of classic literature, piano pieces, violin concerti, art techniques. How do you pick and choose?

In the elementary grades, we suggest that you prioritize reading, writing, grammar, and math. History and science are important. But if you don't cover all of biology in first grade, it doesn't matter: the child's going to get biology at least twice more before he goes to college. If you skimp on reading or writing, though, you're likely to hamper the child's educational progress. History and science are reading-dependent. A child who reads and writes well will pick up surprising amounts of history and science as he browses. A child who has difficulty reading and writing will struggle with every subject.

In first grade especially, the child's mind is busy with new skills. You spend an immense amount of time in one-on-one tutoring. Language skills and math will take up most of that time. If you do history and science two or three times a week, that's fine. If you don't start music until second or third grade, the sky won't fall. If you don't do art until fourth or fifth grade, nothing drastic will happen. Don't feel that you must teach every subject in depth.

Remember, classical education teaches a child *how* to learn. The child who knows how to learn will grow into a well-rounded—and well-equipped—adult . . . even if he didn't finish his first-grade science book.

4

UNLOCKING THE DOORS: THE PRESCHOOL YEARS

> Very soon after I went to live with Mr. and Mrs. Auld, she very kindly commenced to teach me the A, B, C. After I had learned this, she assisted me in learning to spell words of three or four letters. . . . I had no regular teacher [but] . . . the first step had been taken. Mistress, in teaching me the alphabet, had given me the inch, and no precaution could prevent me from taking the ell. The plan which I adopted, and the one by which I was most successful, was that of making friends of all the little white boys whom I met in the street. As many of these as I could, I converted into teachers. With their kindly aid, obtained at different times and in different places, I finally succeeded in learning to read.
>
> —Frederick Douglass, *Narrative of the Life of Frederick Douglass, an American Slave, Written by Himself*

SUBJECT: Preparation for reading, writing, and math; birth–age 5
TIME REQUIRED: Start with 10 minutes a day for each subject, gradually increasing to about 30 minutes a day by age 5

When you educate your child at home, you don't have to draw a line between parenting and teaching. Teaching—preparing the child for the twelve formal years of classical education—begins at birth.

PRESCHOOL: BIRTH TO THREE

The best early teaching you can give your child is to immerse her in language from birth.

Reading

Turn off the television—half an hour per day is plenty for any child under five. Talk, talk, talk—adult talk, not baby talk. Talk to her while you're walking in the park, while you're riding in the car, while you're fixing dinner. Tell her what you're doing while you're doing it. ("Now I'm going to send a fax. I put the paper in face down and punch in the telephone number of the fax machine I'm calling . . . and then the paper starts to feed through like this." "I spilled flour on the floor. I'm going to get out the vacuum cleaner and plug it in. I think I'll use this brush—it's the furniture brush, but the flour's down in the cracks, so it should work better than the floor brush.") This sort of constant chatter lays a verbal foundation in your child's mind. She's learning that words are used to plan, to think, to explain; she's figuring out how the English language organizes words into phrases, clauses, and complete sentences. We have found that children from silent families ("We never really talk much during the day," one mother told us) struggle to read.

Read, read, read. Start reading chunky books to your baby in her crib. Give her sturdy books that she can look at alone. (A torn book or two is a small price to pay for literacy.) Read picture books, pointing at the words with your finger. Read the same books over and over; repetition builds literacy (even as it slowly drives you insane). Read longer books without pictures while she sits on your lap or plays on the floor or cuts and pastes and colors. Read books onto tapes, along with the child's comments, so that she can listen to you read over and over again. Get an infant-proof tape recorder so that she can listen to you reading, singing, talking, telling stories, and reciting poems while she plays in her crib.

After you read to your toddler, ask her questions about the story. What did the gingerbread boy do when the old woman tried to eat him? When the dogs got to the top of the tree at the end of *Go, Dog, Go*, what did they find? What happened after Bananas Gorilla stole all the bananas?

As soon as your child begins to talk (which will be early if she's this immersed in language), teach her the alphabet. Sing the alphabet song whenever you change her diaper (often). Stencil alphabet letters, both capital letters and lowercase letters, to the wall, or put up a chart. Read alphabet rhymes and alphabet books.

When she knows the names of the letters, tell her that each letter has a sound, just as each animal makes a sound—"Pigs say *oink*"; "Dogs say *woof*"; and "*B* says *b, b, b* as in *baby*." Start with the sounds of the consonants (that's everything except *a, e, i, o,* and *u*). Tell her that *b* is the sound at the beginning of *bat, ball,* and *Ben;* say, "*T, t, tickle*" and "*M, m, mommy*" and "*C, c, cat.*"

Then tell her that the vowels *(a, e, i, o, u)* are *named A, E, I, O,* and *U*. Sing, "Old McDonald had a farm, A, E, I, O, U." Then teach her that each vowel has a sound, just as each animal makes a sound—"*A* as in *at,*" "*E* as in *egg,*" "*I* as in *igloo,*" "*O* as in *octopus,*" and "*U* as in *umbrella.*" These are the *short sounds* of the vowels, the only vowel sounds you should teach at first. All of this is *prereading.*

Prereading preparation works. Susan was reading on a fifth-grade level in kindergarten. Her son Christopher was checking out fourth- and fifth-grade books halfway through his first year of school at home. We've seen these results duplicated by other home schoolers. If you create a language-rich home, limit TV and videos, and then teach systematic phonics, you will produce readers.

Writing

Very young children (under two) will pick up a pencil and imitate scribbling. Teach a child from the beginning to hold the pencil correctly. Draw lots of circles and loops *in a counterclockwise direction.* Most printed letters use counterclockwise circles; although many children naturally want to draw circles clockwise, this habit will make cursive handwriting difficult later on. Make snowmen, Slinkies™, smoke from a train, car wheels, and so forth counterclockwise.

Let the child practice making letters without using a regular pencil. A young child lacks fine-motor maturity, but she can form letters and numbers by writing in rice or sand with her finger. Or, if she wants to use a writing tool, she can use chalk on a big chalkboard or a crayon or pencil on large sheets of paper. Regular-diameter short pencils are often easier for small fingers to handle than fat "preschool" pencils. Teach your three year old basic dot-to-dot skills by drawing your own dot-to-dot picture (a house, a smiley face) using four or five big dots, then guiding the child's crayon from dot to dot so that she can see the picture emerge. Continual drawing and making counterclockwise circles will prepare the preschooler for kindergarten writing.

Math

Start to make your child "mathematically literate" in the toddler years. Just as you read to the toddler, surrounding her with language until she understood that printed words on a page carried meaning, you need to expose her to mathematical processes and language continually. Only then will she understand that mathematical symbols carry meaning.

Bring numbers into everyday life as often as possible. Start with counting: fingers, toes, eyes, and ears; toys and treasures; rocks and sticks. Play hide-and-seek, counting to five and then to ten, fifteen, or twenty together. Count by twos, fives, and tens before shouting, "Coming, ready or not!" Play spaceship in cardboard boxes, and count backward for takeoff. Read number books together. Once the child is comfortable counting, you can start working on simple math sums—usually during the K–4 and K–5 years.

General Preschool Learning

In addition to teaching your child prereading and beginning math skills, you can prepare her for kindergarten work by using June R. Oberlander's *Slow and Steady, Get Me Ready.* It's a birth-to-age-5 activity book that provides a new, developmentally appropriate activity for each week of life. Week 1 begins with exercising the newborn's arms and legs; age 5, week 52, ends with learning to pack an overnight bag. In between, Oberlander (a kindergarten teacher) covers everything from playing peekaboo and learning "in" and "out" through tying shoes, memorizing telephone numbers, bouncing balls, and singing the alphabet while making a different body movement for each letter. It's a complete preschool in one volume. You may not feel you need this resource, but by combining the prereading instruction of the

Oberlander book with lots of active play, you'll have the at-home equivalent of an excellent preschool program.

KINDERGARTEN YEARS: FOUR AND FIVE

We have mixed feelings about formal kindergarten programs for four and five year olds. A kindergarten program that combines beginning reading and writing with lots of artwork and active play can be productive. But it's a rare five year old who's ready to do very much paper-and-pencil work at a desk, and a six year old who hasn't done a formal kindergarten program can easily begin first-grade work.

"I can always tell the children who've been to kindergarten from the ones who haven't," a first-grade teacher told Susan.

"Are they that much further ahead?" Susan asked.

"No," she said, "but they already know how to stand in line."

Kindergarten *does* teach five year olds to stand in line, to wait to go to the bathroom, to raise their hand when they want to ask a question, and to walk through a cafeteria without spilling their food. But if you're teaching your child at home, these aren't the survival skills she has to have right away.

Kindergarten for four year olds accomplishes even less. Most four year olds have microscopic attention spans, immature hand-eye coordination, and a bad case of the wiggles. And normal four year olds differ widely in their maturity levels: one might be ready to read but be completely disinterested in writing; another might enjoy drawing and handwork but show no desire to read; a third might like to play endless games of Uno but reject anything having to do with letters and words.

We feel that there's little point in following a formal, academic K–4 or K–5 curriculum at home. Rather, the first four or five years of a child's life should be spent in informal teaching—preparing the child for first-grade work. In about thirty minutes per day, plus informal teaching as you go about your family life, you can easily teach your child beginning reading, writing, and math concepts, all without workbooks or teacher's manuals.

If you're already teaching an older child at home, your four year old may beg to "do school" as well. At the end of the chapter, we'll recommend several reading and math programs that will keep a kindergartner occupied at one end of the table while her big sister does second-grade math at the other end. But try not to think of these curricula as schoolwork, or you may find yourself pushing a reluctant preschooler to "just finish that page" when her attention span has long since expired.

Rather, you should aim to teach reading and math in the same way that you taught the child to speak, to tie her shoes, to dress, to clean up after herself—by demonstrating the basic skills yourself, practicing them for a few minutes each day, and talking about them as you go through the routines of life. ("There are four of us. How many spoons should you put on the table so that we can each have one?" "Can you get me the can that says *Tomato* on it? You'll recognize the *T* that says *t, t, tomato.*")

You can use charts, tapes, games, workbooks, and stickers if you want to. But you don't need them.

Reading

A classical education relies heavily on the written word. As a parent-educator, your number one goal should be to have your child reading fluently when she starts first-grade work.

Here's the good news: Reading is simple.

We'll repeat that: Reading is simple.

One more time: Reading is simple.

Unfortunately, the First Commandment of American Education seems to be "Thou shalt be an expert before attempting to teach reading." It isn't true. Forget everything you've ever heard about decoding, phonemic awareness, and comprehension skills. If a five year old can master beginning reading, you can master it as well.[1]

[1]However, don't be surprised if you are discouraged by some professional educators. I [Jessie] was verbally accosted twenty-five years ago when I went to a reading professor to find readers for Susan. He demanded, "*What* do you think you are doing, teaching your child to read yourself?" I was so intimidated that I never went back to him for help. In contrast, a first-grade teacher who was successfully teaching *all* her first graders to read directed me to the phonics material she was using so that I could get it for myself. Alas, the material has now been revised beyond recognition.

Reading is simple. Frederick Douglass, as well as Abraham Lincoln, Benjamin Franklin, and thousands of eighteenth-century pioneer children, learned to read with the alphabet and a few good books. Douglass learned his ABC's from an adult and obtained the rest of his reading competency skills from street urchins. I [Jessie] learned to read from a set of alphabet blocks. Between the ages of four and six, most children who have been read to since toddlerhood and are not suffering from an organic disorder can learn to read. And any reasonably literate adult (which includes anyone who can read this book) can serve as tutor for basic phonics skills.[2]

You should continue to immerse four and five year olds in language, just as you've been doing since birth. Read with them in the "real world": billboards, store names, bumper stickers, cereal boxes in the grocery store, banners at the gas station.

Get them books on tape—not the fifteen-minute children's tapes with all the bells and whistles designed to keep children occupied, but real books read in their entirety without sound effects. Most public libraries have shelves of books on tape in the children's sections. Children can listen to and enjoy books that are far, far above their vocabulary level; in one year, Susan's three year old and five year old listened to all of Kipling's *Just So Stories,* the original *Jungle Book,* all of Edith Nesbit's books, *The Chronicles of Narnia,* Barrie's densely written *Peter Pan,* E. B. White's *Charlotte's Web* and *The Trumpet of the Swan,* Frances Hodgson Burnett's *A Little Princess,* the unabridged *Christmas Carol* by Dickens. Books on tape stock a child's mind with the sounds of thousands of words. When children start sounding out words later on, they'll progress much more quickly if they recognize the words.

Read yourself. Turn off the TV, and read a book, do a crossword puzzle, buy the *New York Times.*

Keep on reading together. Start to ask slightly more complex questions about the stories. "What was Wilbur afraid of in *Charlotte's Web*?" "Why was Fern's mother worried when Fern told her that the animals were talking to her?"

By the age of four, the average child should know her alphabet and the sounds that each letter makes. Continue to work on letter names and sounds. Lowercase magnetic refrigerator letters are a good way to do this.

[2]Many parents have been told by a reading teacher that phonics will somehow "ruin" their child's reading skills. See pages 221–225 for a brief discussion of the phonics–whole language debate.

You can give the child a *d* magnet and say, *"D, d, d, dog"*; you can say, "Mary, go get me the letter that says *t, t, t,"* and Mary will go over to the refrigerator and decide which letter makes that sound.

Sometime around age four or five, most children are ready to start reading. Sit down with a simple primer that teaches phonics—the sounds that letters make when they're combined together into words. *The Ordinary Parent's Guide to Teaching Reading,* by Jessie Wise, contains clear step-by-step instructions on how to teach reading from the very beginning stages, starting with letter sounds and moving systematically through blending sounds into reading real words and sentences. This primer is designed to get children—even very young children—reading quickly and confidently; handwriting and spelling can be delayed until the child has enough fine motor coordination to write without frustration. (In the earlier edition of this book, we recommended *Phonics Pathways* as our first choice for a beginning primer; this is still a good choice, but contains less step-by-step instruction for the parent.)

Progress systematically through the primer. Go slowly, with plenty of repetition; reread the lessons until your child is completely comfortable with the sounds and their combination into words. Do this for five minutes to start with; work up to ten or fifteen minutes per session.

At some other time during the day, sit down with the child and a "real book," and let her read it. At the end of this chapter, you'll find a list of books that can be read with relative ease, even by a child who's only learned consonants and one or two vowel sounds. (The first few Bob Books and Modern Curriculum Press's early readers use only the *a* vowel sound, so you can start on a "real book" right after the first few lessons!) Don't forget that you've already done your drill. Give the child a good chance to sound words out, but if she gets stuck, sound it out for her and move on. If you get to a word that uses a rule she hasn't used yet, simply tell her what the rule is and keep going.

CHILD: Ann went to the steps and went —— *(Sticks on the word "down.")*
YOU: That says "down." *O* and *w* together say "ow." *D-ow-n.*
CHILD: —— down.

If you don't know the rule yourself, tell the child the word and move on. (Look the rule up later.)

Although *The Ordinary Parent's Guide to Teaching Reading* is our first choice because it is a thorough phonics program that provides clear and explicit instruction for the parent, you can follow this process with any systematic phonics program.[3]

In beginning reading instruction, it is best to stay with supplementary readers that are strictly phonetic (see suggested "Beginning Readers" in the Resources at the end of this chapter). But as your child becomes more confident in his ability to sound out words, he will want to read easy books that contain "sight" words that don't follow phonetic rules (and that he will need to recognize on "sight"). Such words used frequently in beginning story books include: *are, build, busy, buy, come, do, does, done, eye, father, gone, have, love, mother, of, oh, one, there, they, to, two, was, were, where, you. Could, should,* and *would,* although phonetic, appear in many early readers before they are taught in systematic programs, and may be treated as sight words. Make flashcards for these words and teach them a few at a time as you see them occur in your child's books. Do not teach these in isolation! Wait until they occur in the beginning readers. Reading is best taught in the context of meaningful content. And you don't want your beginning reader to memorize whole words as a habit, rather than sounding out the phonetic elements in each word.

Start with five minutes of drill and five minutes of reading in an easy book every day. Work up to fifteen minutes of each. Don't ask, "Do you want to do your reading now?" (They always say no.) Plan it as matter-of-factly as you would plan toothbrushing and bedmaking. You'll be astounded at the speed with which children begin to sound out words on their own.

The advantage of this method is that you're not limited in what you read with the child; if you sound out words that are beyond the child's "drill level," together the two of you can read practically anything in the "easy reading" or "beginning reader" section of the library. And you'll often find that your child has already absorbed a rule by the time you get to it in the primer. If you say enough times, while reading, "The *e* on the end makes the *a* say its name—that's the difference between *hat* and *hate*," your little reader will greet that rule when you arrive at it with a shrug and "I already knew that."

And that's it. Remember: Reading is simple.

Reading is simple.

Reading is simple.

[3]*Reading Reflex,* by Carmen and Geoffrey McGuinness (New York: Fireside, 1999), is an excellent source for remedial reading for older students; see page 344 in Chapter 17.

Don't you need songs, drills, exercises, workbooks, and charts? We don't think so, for several reasons.

In the first place, lots of people who teach a four or five year old to read also have a toddler or newborn. (Susan had both when her oldest son was five.) Sorting through charts and songs and trying to follow a program with lots of aids make teaching more complicated than it needs to be. With our method, all you need is a primer and lots of books.

Second, all those reinforcements and aids create extra mental steps for the learner. If you're teaching a child to sing the song "*A* is for apple, *b* is for bear, . . . ," you're teaching her to see an *a,* think "apple," and then think the sound of short *a.* If you have a flash card with a *b* and a picture of a bird on it, the picture—not the letter—becomes a signal to the child to say the *b* sound. The child goes through an extra step in associating the sound with the letter. Instead of looking at a *b* and forming the *b* sound, the mental process becomes "*B* . . . bird . . . *b.*" This is slow, and in many cases the child stays slow because she becomes dependent on the clue. Without the clue, she has no idea how to "break" the code of the word. There's an easier way. Just point to the *a* and say "*A, a, a*" (that's the short *a* sound as in *at*); point to the *b* and say, "*B, b, b.*" Even two and three year olds love this game, and they learn these associations much faster than you might expect.

Third, most reinforcements—even though they may be advertised and produced for a home-education setting—were originally designed for a classroom of children. A teacher teaching a whole group of students to read can't sit down with each one and teach her to pronounce each letter correctly whenever she sees it on the page. That's an intensive, one-on-one process. The teacher has to resort to the second-best method: reinforcing the correct sound through secondary aids in a nonreading context. You don't have to do that.

Fourth, you're not teaching your four or five year old the exhaustive elements of the English language. Beginning in first grade, your child will receive a more thorough grounding in the rules of spelling, which are simply phonics rules applied to writing. (We'll recommend resources for doing this in Chapter 5.) During the K–4 and K–5 years, your goal is simply to get the child reading as quickly and fluently as possible. A kindergartner doesn't need to be able to list from memory all the different ways a long-*e* sound can be spelled; she just needs to be able to pronounce *meal, field,* and *teeth* when she sees them.

If you prefer a workbook approach and have a coordinated preschooler who doesn't have trouble with writing skills, or if you have a younger child who's anxious to do workbooks in imitation of an older sibling, you might consider investing in Modern Curriculum Press's Phonics Program. This has lots of fun stuff for young learners: playing Alphabet Hopscotch, making "consonant cans," finding hidden pictures, and so on. None of this is necessary, but you might enjoy using it. A few words of caution. This phonics program ties reading and writing together, which we think can be frustrating for the very young child and can retard reading skills. Many children are ready to read before they are ready to write. Ignore the writing sections if you don't think your child is ready to do them. It's probably best used as an activity supplement to *The Ordinary Parent's Guide to Teaching Reading.* Modern Curriculum Press's kindergarten-level book (*Level K*) seems more appropriate for home-taught three and early four year olds; *Level A*, the first-grade book, can be done at home in kindergarten. You don't need to buy the expensive teacher's manuals, which are heavy on classroom supplements and suggestions for teaching these skills to children for whom English is a second language. Another supplementary workbook program used successfully by many parents is the *Explode the Code* series, published by Educators Publishing Service. These books offer activities and writing exercises to go along with systemic phonics learning. Again, don't tie these exercises to the child's phonics learning if he's not yet ready to do pencil work.

What if my child isn't ready to read? If you've read to your preschooler since she could stare at a page, you can start this process at age four and take a couple of years to go through it. Or you can start at age five and do it in less time. Second and third children, who've watched older brothers and sisters learn to read, are likely to want to start sooner. If your four year old asks you for a reading lesson, oblige her. I [Jessie] taught Susan to read at three because every time I sat down with her five-year-old brother to do a phonics lesson, she wanted to be included.

Reading readiness (like everything else in this chapter) isn't complicated. A child is ready to learn to read when she collects her stuffed animals and a picture book and tells them a story; or when she picks up a book, sits on the sofa, and pretends she's reading to you; or when she constantly asks you, "What does this say?" All of these activities show that she understands that printed words carry a message.

Most five year olds are capable of learning to read, which doesn't mean that they'll want to do it. A child who squirms, complains, and protests every time you produce the primer isn't demonstrating "reading unreadiness." She's simply being five. It's a rare child who wants to do something unfamiliar that involves work; as a matter of fact, we've yet to meet a five year old who could be convinced to set her eyes on long-range goals.[4] If the child doesn't want to learn to read, tell her that you're going to do five minutes per day anyway.

The beginning stage, when you're teaching the child to sound out three-letter words for the first time, is the most difficult. Persist until you can start the child on the Bob Books, the Flyleaf Books to Remember, or the first Modern Curriculum Press readers (see the list of resources at the end of this chapter). Most children will swell up with pride over being able to read a "whole book all alone." Once they've started putting sentences together, they'll tell you they don't need to do the drill anymore; they just want to read. That's a good sign, but insist on the ten minutes of drill every day until you've covered all the pages in *The Ordinary Parent's Guide to Teaching Reading.*

But use common sense. If you've started on three-letter words, doing a faithful ten minutes per day for three or four weeks, and the child shows no comprehension, she hasn't made the connection between print and sounds yet. Drop it for a month or two, and then come back to it.

[4]We are not impressed by "child-led" education (waiting until the child brings you a book and begs for a reading lesson) for the same reasons that we don't let our elementary-school children eat exactly what they want: young children do not realize that spinach is not only better for them than Twinkies, but actually more satisfying in the long run. A typical learning-to-read-at-home dialogue sounds like this:

PARENT: Don't you want to learn to read? If you work on these lists of rules for a year, you can read books to yourself!

CHILD: *(Eyeing twenty pages of rules and reasoning that the parent reads books to her anytime she wants anyway.)* I don't like it.

PARENT: But you haven't even tried yet.

CHILD: But I don't like it anyway.

This exchange ought to sound familiar to anyone who's served a child a new food:

PARENT: These are fresh strawberries. You'll love them.

CHILD: *(Eyeing the strawberries.)* I don't like them.

PARENT: But you've never eaten a strawberry.

CHILD: I don't like them anyway.

The reasonable response is: Eat one every time I serve them, and you'll learn to like them. Reading is no different.

Writing

Many of the phonics programs we examined insist that you combine writing with reading. In other words, teach the child the consonants and the sound of *a,* but don't go on to the next step until the child is able both to read and write *sat, cat, fat, bat.*

We think this tends to frustrate very young readers (see page 36). Remember, you want the child to read quickly, easily, and early. Many children are ready to read long before they have the muscular coordination to write. Why delay reading until the muscles of the hand and eye catch up?

So do your reading and writing drills separately during your child's fourth and fifth years. When she is able to hold the pencil comfortably and has some control over it, then move on to formal writing instruction. Get her a beginning writing workbook that has large-ruled lines and patterns for forming each letter (see pages 47–48 for ordering information). Teach only one letter (always do a capital and small letter together) or one number at a time until you've gone through the entire alphabet and the numbers 1 through 100. You can either follow the suggested workbook sequence or teach the letters in the order presented in *The Ordinary Parent's Guide to Teaching Reading.* The writing workbooks have arrows and numbers to show the exact way that letters should be written: the circle for a small *a* is always drawn counterclockwise; the straight edge of a capital *D* is always drawn first, with the curve of the letter drawn second. *This is important!* Make sure you teach the child to write the letter properly, and for the first few months supervise her carefully so that she doesn't fall into bad habits.

The best resources for teaching writing are from Zaner-Bloser, which publishes colorful learn-to-write workbooks using the "continuous-stroke alphabet." In traditional ball-and-stick writing, the student continually lifts her hand—if she writes a small *d,* for example, she draws a circle, picks up her pencil, and then connects a line to the circle. In the continuous-stroke alphabet, the letter is written in one motion. This simplifies writing and makes for an easier transition into cursive. Start with the kindergarten-level book, and let the child progress forward at her own rate. The books don't give a lot of practice space, so you'll want to order some extra writing paper (see the ordering information on page 48).

An alternative for children who are very challenged in the area of muscular coordination is the *Handwriting Without Tears* series. This program emphasizes using short pencils of regular diameter rather than fat preschool pencils, since the small pencils are easier for children to manipulate. The program also has the child do manipulative work before he actually writes. When he does begin to copy letters, instead of writing a whole line of letters (as most penmanship books suggest), he writes fewer letters at a time but concentrates on writing them as perfectly as possible. Each lesson involves fifteen minutes of penmanship time: ten minutes of instruction and five minutes of carefully supervised practice. The student does less work than in traditional penmanship books, but what he does is as perfect as he can make it. The workbooks have many model letters per line, so the child doesn't write a line of one letter, consistently getting worse and worse as he goes (children tend to copy the last letter *they* made, rather than looking back at the correct model). Although this program offers many excellent insights for teaching writing, it isn't our first recommendation because the script itself is not as attractive as the Zaner-Bloser script; the focus is on legibility rather than beauty. However, a child who is struggling will benefit greatly from this program.

When you've worked through the entire alphabet, let the child begin to copy words that you write out for her—family names are a good place to start. Eventually, ask her to copy very short sentences: "I love you." "Ben is smart!" "Do you like to write?" In this way, the five year old not only practices writing, but begins to learn the conventions of written language: capitals for names and the beginnings of sentences, spaces between words, periods and exclamation points. In first and second grades, you'll progress to dictation, where she will write without a model in front of her. But for now, write out the sentences for her to copy, and let her refer to your models as often as needed. Ten minutes per day, three to five times per week, is sufficient. Frequency and consistency bring quicker results than prolonged sessions.

A word about cursive writing. A great debate is on about when to introduce cursive penmanship. Some educators say that children should begin with cursive and skip manuscript printing; others recommend beginning cursive anywhere between first and fourth grade. We have always chosen to teach printing until the child is writing quickly and well, and then begin cursive penmanship, usually in the middle of second grade. This seems easier for most children. *Handwriting Without Tears* begins cursive work in third grade, which is also acceptable.

Math

Now that the child can count, continue to do "daily" math by adding and subtracting in the context of everyday family life. Setting the table is a great math exercise: ask your child to figure out how many plates, knives, forks, and spoons are necessary. Add and subtract in the grocery store ("Look, Mike. I'm picking up four tomatoes and then one more tomato—that makes five!"). Cook together—recipes are full of fractions and measures. When you cut a sandwich in half or quarters, say, "Look, I cut this in half!" or "I cut this into fourths!"

Play games that use numbers. Uno™ is a classic—it teaches both number and color matching. Simple card games such as Battle and Go Fish require children to remember which numbers are higher and which are lower.

Do lots of addition and subtraction with manipulatives (beans, buttons, pencils, chocolate chips). Practice counting to one hundred—by twos, fives, and tens. Learn about money, tell time, and name geometric figures—circles, squares, triangles, rectangles. Learn to write the numbers (but don't expect the written numbers to mean very much to the child at this point).

Your public library should have a colorful selection of kindergarten-level math books—easy problems worked out with photographed objects. Get a book every week, and read through it with your child.

If you do this, your child will be ready for first-grade math. Susan's oldest had no difficulty with first-grade Saxon math (see Chapter 6), even though we had never done a formal kindergarten math program. As in reading, though, younger children may enjoy having a math program to work on along with an older brother or sister; many kindergarten math programs are fun and full of manipulatives. Again, think of a kindergarten math program as a game, not as an academic pursuit. If the child gets tired after five or ten minutes, don't force her to finish the lesson.

General Kindergarten Learning

If you'd like to do kindergarten science projects with your preschooler, two elementary science books will provide you with plenty of fun science activities: *Mudpies to Magnets,* by Robert A. Williams, and *Everybody Has a Body,* by Robert Rockwell. Both books offer clear instructions and experiments that use common household items. You can supplement beginning reading, writing, and math by doing a science experiment once or twice a week; more formal science study isn't necessary at this stage.

RESOURCES

For publisher and catalog addresses, telephone numbers, and other information, see Sources (pages 751–778). Where noted, resources are listed in chronological order (the order you'll want to use them in). Books in series are listed together.

General Learning

Oberlander, June R. *Slow and Steady, Get Me Ready*. 4th ed. Longwood, Fla.: Xulon Press, 2002.

$22.99. Order from Rainbow Resource Center or from Amazon.com.

Reading Skills

Explode the Code. Cambridge, Mass.: Educators Publishing Service, 2003.

Order from EPS. Each workbook drills a particular phonetic sound. The "½" books provide additional practice. The student books are $7.60 each. If you find an answer key is necessary, they are available for each book and are priced at $7.55.

Book 1. Consonants, short vowels.

Book 1 ½.

Book 2. Blends

Book 2 ½.

Book 3. Beginning long vowels, consonant digraphs, diphthongs.

Book 3 ½.

Book 4. Compound words, common endings, syllables.

Book 4 ½.

Book 5. Word families, three-letter blends.

Book 5 ½.

Book 6. Vowels plus r, diphthongs.

Book 6 ½.

Book 7. Soft *c* and *g*, silent consonants, *ph*.

Book 8. Suffixes and irregular endings.

Modern Curriculum Press Plaid Phonics Program. Published by Modern Curriculum Press, a division of Pearson Learning. Lebanon, Ind.: Pearson Learning, 2003.

Order from Modern Curriculum Press. The student editions range from $7.95 to $11.95; the teacher's resource guides, which you don't really need (they contain classroom information), are $53.95 each. MCP also offers Levels D, E, and F, but these books shift from phonics instruction to word study. Since they overlap substantially with the spelling and writing program you'll be following in first and second grade, there's no need to follow the program through to its end. If you're starting with an older child, start with Level B.

Level K, Student Edition. For ages 3–4.
Level A, Student Edition. For ages 4–5.
Level B, Student Edition. For ages 5–6.
Level C, Student Edition. For ages 6–7.

Wise, Jessie. *The Ordinary Parent's Guide to Teaching Reading.* Charles City, Va.: Peace Hill Press, 2004.
$29.95. Order from Peace Hill Press.

Beginning Readers

Books to Remember series. Lyme, N.H.: Flyleaf Publishing.
$7.95. Order from Flyleaf Publishing or check your local library. These decodable readers progress from short vowels up through diphthongs and more difficult words. The program flyer gives an exact description of the skills required to read each book (they are listed in increasing order of difficulty below).

Reading Series One, by Laura Appleton-Smith, 1999:
The Sunset Pond.
Jen's Best Gift Ever.
Meg and Jim's Sled Trip.
Lin-Lin and the Gulls.
Just a Box.
It Is Halloween.
Winter, Spring, Summer, Fall.
My Vivid Town.
Reading Series Two, by Laura Appleton-Smith, 2001:
Frank the Fish Gets His Wish.
Marvin's Trip to Mars.
Mr. Sanchez and the Kick Ball Champ.
The Twins THIS and THAT.

A Sled Dog Morning.
Mister Mole's Stove.
My Summertime Camping Trip.
Tracking With Uncle Joe.
The Case of Jake's Escape.
Queen Bee Needs to Be Free.
Reading Series Three, by Laura Appleton-Smith, 2001:
Shep the Sheep of Caladeen.
Bon-Bon the Downtown Cow.
Pearl Learns a Lesson.
Snail Hits the Trial.
Oh, My! It Must Be the Sky!

Little Books 1–10. Pensacola, Fla.: A Beka Book, 1995.
$7.00. Order from A Beka Book. Ten small storybooks that begin with only short vowel words and progress through blends, words, and simple sentences. Includes pages to color.

Little Owl Books. Pensacola, Fla.: A Beka Book, 1990.
$7.00. Order from A Beka Book. A set of eight full-color booklets, phonetically progressing from three-letter words to words with long vowel sounds.

Maslen, Bobby Lyn. Bob Books series. Illus. John R. Maslen. New York: Scholastic, 2006.
$16.99 for each boxed set. The sets contain eight small paperbacks inside each box. These are the first books your child will be able to read alone; children love them because they can start on the Bob Books after only a few weeks of phonics lessons. The experience of reading an entire book independently right at the beginning of the learning process provides young readers with immense encouragement. *Highly recommended.* Most libraries carry them; but the books are in high demand, and you may have trouble getting them (and keeping them for more than a couple of weeks). If you plan to teach more than one child how to read, they're worth buying because older children can help younger siblings sound them out. Order from a bookstore, from Rainbow Resource Center, or directly from Scholastic.
Bob Books, Set 1: Beginning Readers.
Bob Books, Set 2: Advancing Beginners.
Bob Books, Set 3: Word Families.

Bob Books, Set 4: Compound Words.
Bob Books, Set 5: Long Vowels.

Modern Curriculum Press Phonics Practice Readers. Published by Modern Curriculum Press, a division of Pearson Learning. Lebanon, Ind.: Pearson Learning, n.d.

Order from Modern Curriculum Press. Sets of beginning readers, with each book designed to drill one particular rule. The books are marked with the rule they are meant to reinforce. (The first two books in each series, for example, are "short *a*" books and use *only* short-a words—"Max the cat sat." This allows you to match the books with the appropriate lessons in *The Ordinary Parent's Guide to Teaching Reading.*) Each series contains two books each for short *a, i, u, o,* and e; two books each for five different types of consonant blend; and two books each for the sounds *th, wh, sh, ch,* and *ng/ck* (these are called "digraphs). If cost is a problem, consider splitting the bill with a friend or neighbor. Each set of ten different books is $26.50.

Series A.
Set 1: Short Vowels.
Set 2: Long Vowels.
Set 3: Blends.
Set 4: Digraphs.

Series B. The same skills taught in Series A, but different stories.
Set 1: Short Vowels.
Set 2: Long Vowels.
Set 3: Blends.
Set 4: Digraphs.

Series C. The same skills taught in Series A and B, but different stories.
Set 1: Short Vowels.
Set 2: Long Vowels.
Set 3: Blends.
Set 4: Digraphs.

Beginning Story Books: "Easy Readers"

The "Easy Reader" category is confusing because most of these books are geared to whole language teaching and not to phonetic instruction. They have just a few words on the page, but a beginning reader cannot read some of these books unless he memorizes whole words. A number of companies publish these interesting books. If there are many sight words or words the child has not yet encountered in his phonics instruction, I would either read these books *to* the child, pointing to the pictures, or wait until the child has been taught to read phonetically.

The beginning readers sections of libraries and bookstores include many more titles than those listed below. Also look for the Little Bear series by Elsie Minarik; anything by Arnold Lobel (*Owl at Home,* the *Frog and Toad* books); the Henry and Mudge books by Cynthia Rylant; and the Dial Easy-to-Read books. A particular favorite of ours is *"Stand Back," Said the Elephant, "I'm Going to Sneeze,"* by Patricia Thomas, illustrated by Wallace Tripp (New York: Lothrop, Lee & Shepard, 1990). The rhyming story contains many vowel combinations that look different but sound the same (for example, *bear, fair, declare* all in a row).

The I Can Read Book series. New York: HarperTrophy.
Progress through Level 1, Level 2, etc. Titles include *Oliver* by Syd Hoff, *Detective Dinosaur* by James Skofield, and many others.

The Step Into Reading series. New York: Random House.
Titles include *I Like Bugs* by Margaret Wise Brown, *Hot Dog* by Molly Coxe, and many others.

Eastman, P. D. *Go, Dog, Go!* New York: Random House, 1961.

Geisel, Theodore Seuss (Dr. Seuss). *Dr. Seuss's A.B.C.* New York: Random House, 1996.

———. *The Foot Book.* New York: Random House, 1988.

———. *Hop On Pop.* New York: Random House, 1963.

———. *One Fish, Two Fish, Red Fish, Blue Fish.* New York: Random House, 1981.

———. *There's a Wocket in my Pocket.* New York: Random House, 1974.

The Hello Reader series. New York: Scholastic.
Progress through Level 1, Level 2, etc. Titles include *One Snowy Day* by Jeffrey Scherer, *Whales and Dolphins* by Peter Roop, Connie Roop, and Carol Schwartz, and many others.

The I Can Read It All By Myself Beginner Books series. New York: Random House.

Titles include *Snow* by P. D. Eastman, *A Fish Out of Water* by Helen Palmer, and many others.

Books on Tape

Many books are worth listening to. Here are a few favorites. Check these out of your local library, and listen with your preschooler or kindergartner. Many different versions of these classics have been made. Make sure you look for tapes marked "unabridged"; abridged versions often aren't marked at all.

Barrie, J. M. *Peter Pan.*

Carroll, Lewis. *Alice in Wonderland.*

———. *Through the Looking-Glass and What Alice Found There.*

Kipling, Rudyard. *The Jungle Books,* I and II.

———. *Just So Stories.*

Lawson, Robert. *Rabbit Hill.*

Lewis, C. S. *The Chronicles of Narnia.*

McDonald, George. *The Princess and Curdie.*

Nesbit, Edith. *The Complete Book of Dragons.*

———. *The Railway Children.*

White, E. B. *Charlotte's Web.*

———. *Stuart Little.*

———. *The Trumpet of the Swan.*

Look for versions read by E. B. White himself, which are very pleasant listening.

Books on tape tend to be expensive, but if you're interested in buying them (or simply finding out what's on tape) you can call the following companies for catalogs or visit them online. All produce unabridged versions:

Blackstone Audiobooks, 800-729-2665, blackstoneaudio.com.

Blackstone has an extensive catalog and a marvelous rental program; they ship the tapes in resealable, prepared-for-return boxes.

Books in Motion, 800-752-3199, booksinmotion.com.

Recorded Books Productions, Inc., 800-638-1304, recordedbooks.com.

Audiobooks in MP3 format can be purchased and downloaded from Blackstone Audiobooks (blackstoneaudio.com), Books in Motion (books inmotion.com), Audible (audible.com, now partnered with Amazon.com), Audiobooks Alive (audiobooksalive.com), and Simply Audiobooks (simply audiobooks.com). This gives you the option to burn the files onto your own CDs and replace them when they get scratched. Although some MP3s are coded so that you can only burn one copy, a phone call to customer service will often get you permission to make more than one CD (you just need to explain that you're a home educator making a replacement for a destroyed disk).

Read-Aloud Books

We have too many favorites to list here. But a good guide to reading aloud is *The Read-Aloud Handbook,* 6th ed., by Jim Trelease (New York: Penguin Books, 2006). You can check it out of the library, or any bookstore can order it for you.

Writing

Olsen, Jan Z. *Handwriting Without Tears* program. Cabin John, Md.: Handwriting Without Tears.

Order from Handwriting Without Tears. The books below are listed in progressive order.

Letters and Numbers for Me (K). $6.35.

Handwriting Without Tears Teacher's Guide. $6.35. Provides an overview of the program and tips on teaching.

My Printing Book (First grade). $6.35.

1st Grade Printing Teacher's Guide. $6.35.

Printing Power (Second grade). $6.35.

2nd Grade Printing Teacher's Guide. $6.35.

Double Line Notebook Paper. Designed specifically to go along with the skills taught in this program.

Wide (K–1). 100 sheets. $2.95.
Wide (K–1). 500 sheets. $10.00.
Regular (2–3). 100 sheets. $2.95.
Regular (2–3). 500 sheets. $10.00.

Zaner-Bloser Handwriting series. Columbus, Ohio: Zaner-Bloser, 2008. Order from Zaner-Bloser. This is the Zaner-Bloser continuous-stroke alphabet method. Since the child doesn't have to lift her hand as she forms the letters, the transition into cursive is simpler. Also, some capital letters in the cursive alphabet have been simplified so that they look more like the printed versions. Start with *K Student Book* and progress forward. The manuscript lines become smaller with each book. The teacher editions are not necessary.

Handwriting with Continuous-Stroke Alphabet series. $10.69 each.
Grade K Student Book.
Grade 1 Student Book.

Zaner-Bloser Handwriting Paper. $8.99 per ream.
Order these packs of writing paper for extra handwriting practice from Zaner-Bloser. One ream per year is plenty. The ruled lines on these sheets narrow each year. A child who is having difficulty with handwriting will sometimes improve if you move to a paper with narrower lines.

Grade K paper (1⅛" wide).
Grade 1 paper (⅝" wide).
Grade 2 paper (½" wide).

Math

Wooden Pattern Blocks. Rowley, Mass.: Didax Educational Resources. $22.95. Order from Rainbow Resource Center or from Didax. One of the most useful preschool manipulative sets; each 250-piece set of 1-cm-thick blocks contains 25 yellow hexagons, 25 orange squares, 50 green triangles, 50 red trapezoids, 50 blue parallelograms, and 50 tan rhombuses. Stack them, count them, make pictures with them, wallow in them.

Check your local library or bookstore for these math story books and make them part of your reading routine:

Anno, Mitsumasa. *Anno's Mysterious Multiplying Jar*. New York: Paper Star, 1999.

Axelrod, Amy. *Pigs Will Be Pigs: Fun with Math & Money.* New York: Aladdin, 1997.

Burns, Marilyn. *Greedy Triangle*. New York: Scholastic, 2008.

———. *Spaghetti and Meatballs for All: A Mathematical Story*. New York: Scholastic, 2008.

Jonas, Ann. *Splash!* New York: Mulberry Books, 1997.

MacKain, Bonnie. *One Hundred Hungry Ants*. Boston: Houghton Mifflin, 1999.

Miranda, Anne. *Monster Math*. New York: Harcourt, 2002.

Mogard, Sue. *Gobble Up Math: Fun Activities to Complete and Eat for Kids in Grades K–3*. Huntington Beach, Calif.: Learning Works, 1994.

Murphy, Stuart J. *Divide and Ride*. New York: HarperTrophy, 1997.

Myllar, Rolf. *How Big Is a Foot?* New York: Yearling, 1991.

Neuschwander, Cindy. *Sir Cumference and the First Round Table: A Math Adventure*. Watertown, Mass.: Charlesbridge Publishing, 2002. Also look for Sir Cumference's four additional adventures.

Schwartz, David M. *How Much Is a Million?* New York: 20th Anniversary Edition. HarperTrophy, 2004.

Scieska, Jon, and Lane Smith. *Math Curse*. New York: Viking Children's Books, 2007.

Tang, Greg. *Math for All Seasons*. New York: Scholastic, 2005.

Science

Rockwell, Robert E., et al. *Everybody Has a Body: Science from Head to Toe*. Mt. Ranier, Md.: Gryphon House, 1992.

Williams, Robert A. *Mudpies to Magnets*. Mt. Ranier, Md.: Gryphon House, 1987.

Williams, Robert A. *More Mudpies to Magnets*. Mt. Ranier, Md.: Gryphon House, 1990.

5

WORDS, WORDS, WORDS: SPELLING, GRAMMAR, READING, AND WRITING

> For their Studies, First they should begin with the chief and necessary rules of some good Grammar. . . . Next to make them expert in the usefullest points of Grammar, and withall to season them, and win them early to the love of vertue and true labour, ere any flattering seducement, or vain principle seize them wandering, some easie and delightful Book of Education would be read to them.
>
> —John Milton, "Of Education"

SUBJECT: Spelling, grammar, reading, and writing
TIME REQUIRED: 60–110 minutes per day (by fourth grade)

Your goal, in grades 1 through 4, is to make the proper use of language second nature to your child. In the logic and rhetoric stages of classical education (grades 5 through 8 and 9 through 12, respectively), the student will need to use language to reason, argue, and express ideas. He can't do this as long as he's still struggling with the how-tos of written and verbal expression.

The first four years of formal classical education are called the grammar stage because the student spends them learning the conventions and basic facts—the "grammar"—of each academic subject. In a way, the grammar of language is the foundation on which all other subjects rest. Until a student reads without difficulty, he can't absorb the grammar of history, literature, or science; until a student writes with ease, he can't express his growing mastery of this material.

Acquiring the "grammar" of language involves practice in four separate disciplines: spelling (the "grammar" of individual words—how each one is put together), English grammar itself (the way those words fit together into sentences), reading (through which the student's mind will be filled with images, stories, and words), and writing (the way in which sentences are assembled into stories and essays). Because language skills are the cornerstone of classical education, the student will spend more time on reading and writing than on any other task.

HOW TO DO IT

When you act as your child's teacher, you need a way to organize and store all of the child's work. We recommend that you keep a three-ringed notebook for each major subject: spelling, grammar, reading, writing, history, and science.[1] Soon you'll have a fat stack of books, each showing the student's growing comprehension of a subject. These notebooks will also be useful for evaluation at testing time (see Part IV for more on testing for home schoolers).

Begin the academic year with three-ringed notebooks (3-inch rings are best), a three-hole punch, and lots of paper, both lined and plain. Also lay in a boxful of art supplies: glue, scissors, construction paper, colored pencils (good artist-quality ones like Sanford Prismacolor), stickers, and anything else that strikes the child's (or your) fancy. Bring the art box out only at "notebook time."

For language skills, use one notebook. Divide the language skills notebook into four divisions, and label them "Spelling," "Grammar," "Reading," and "Writing." (You'll probably want to start a fresh notebook each year.)

[1]Math and foreign-language curricula come with their own workbooks, so you won't need to keep additional notebooks for these subjects. For art and music, the elementary student does very little writing; but if you wish to keep drawings in a portfolio, you can do so (see Chapter 12).

GENERAL INSTRUCTIONS FOR GRADES 1 THROUGH 4

In the early years of school, children vary so widely in their development that assigning a child to a particular "grade" can be extremely difficult. Normal children can begin first grade reading "first grade" books and writing comfortably, reading "third grade" books and writing reasonably well, or reading "sixth grade" books and hardly writing at all. For this reason, much of the material we recommend isn't divided into grades, but rather into levels. You should always spend as much time on one level as you need and progress on to the next level only when your child has mastered the first level, whether that comes before or after the "normal" age.

Adjust the time you spend on each subject so that you can concentrate on weaker areas. Your goal will be to bring the child up to fourth-grade level in each area—spelling, grammar, reading, and writing—by the end of fourth grade (ages 10 to 11).

You should aim to begin first-grade work when your child has gone almost through *The Ordinary Parent's Guide to Teaching Reading* primer (or another phonics-based primer), has covered most of the major rules of phonics, and is reading simple books without reluctance. By the beginning of first grade, the student should also know how to form his letters. He does *not* need to write with ease; many bright children (especially boys) struggle with handwriting, and it's common for letter reversal (*p* and *q*, *b* and *d*) to persist through first grade. This is not necessarily a sign of dyslexia. We recommend beginning cursive penmanship in second grade, but if letter reversal is a consistent problem, you might consider starting cursive early (it's impossible to reverse cursive letters).

Spelling

Spelling is the first step in writing. Before you can put a word on paper, you have to know what letters to use.

We recommend that you get at least halfway through *The Ordinary Parent's Guide to Teaching Reading* primer before beginning spelling. In the primer, your child has already encountered basic spelling rules. For example, the reading rule "The silent *e* at the end of a word makes the vowel say its name" is also a spelling rule; it tells you that a word such as *late,* where *a* says its name, must have a silent *e* at the end. Now it's time for the child to apply those rules of reading to words he wants to write. Spelling, then, is a matter of transforming rules of reading into rules of writing.

The best set of workbooks we've found for this is Modern Curriculum Press's Spelling Workout. As the student progresses through these books, he'll learn rules of spelling ("The sound /*oi*/ can be spelled *oy* or *oi,* as in *toy* and *oil*"), the proper names for letter combinations ("A *consonant digraph* is two consonants that come together to make just one sound"), and the phonetic symbols used in dictionaries ("/*ar*/ makes the sound in *farm*"). The *Spelling Workout* series even teaches basic proofreading marks.

Begin first grade with the first workbook, *Spelling Workout A*. This workbook is the most basic one: it reviews the letters of the alphabet, asks children to connect pictures of objects that begin or end with the same letter, and then has the children write three-letter words. These exercises teach beginning spellers to hear the individual sounds in words and translate those sounds into written symbols. Most first-grade students who are reading well will find this book easy. Don't skip anything, though; the books build valuable skills and confidence through repetition.

Start by spending ten minutes per day on spelling lessons—one to three workbook pages. As the lessons get harder, you'll progress to fifteen minutes per day—aim to do fifteen minutes per day by the middle of the first-grade year. Most first graders can finish *Spelling Workout A* by the middle of the first year and continue on to *Spelling Workout B*. If spelling is a weak area, the student may not move on to *B* until later.

When you reach *Spelling Workout B,* you'll begin to see more rules, which appear at the head of the page in a little box headed "Pep Talk." Whenever the child is having trouble applying one of these rules, he should copy it on a sheet of notebook paper and place it in the front of the Spelling section of the notebook. (You may have to help him write these in first grade; by second grade, however, he should be able to copy the rules himself.)

For example, an early second-grade "Pep Talk" reads:

> The long *a* sound is the vowel sound you hear in <u>save</u> **and** <u>sail</u>. Each List Word has the long *a* sound spelled in one of these ways: *a*_*e* or *ai*.

You would help the second grader write on his Spelling Rules page:

The long *a* sound can be spelled *a_e* or *ai*.

He should also keep a page of "Trouble Words"—a running list of words that the child consistently misspells. Two or three times per week, review the rules and trouble words at the beginning of his spelling lesson.

Do spelling exercises, and write down difficult rules and trouble words for fifteen minutes a day all the way through grade 4. Aim to finish at least level *D* by the end of the fourth-grade year. The student who is able to finish *E* or *F* by the end of the fourth-grade year will be exceptionally well prepared for the logic stage (grades 5 through 8).

A good alternative resource for students who dislike Spelling Workout (or who continue to misspell after using it) is *Spelling Power*, published by Castlemoyle Press. This one-volume spelling resource is designed for use in any grade. Rather than taking a workbook approach to spelling, *Spelling Power* is list-focused; it teaches students to visualize and trace words in the air before writing them, and is particularly good for visual learners. It does require a little more time on the part of the teacher, since you have to prepare the lessons yourself before teaching them.

Grammar

You'll begin oral grammar lessons in first grade, transitioning slowly into a more writing-intensive course. Writing done in the course of grammar study will be placed in the Grammar section of the language notebook.

In the elementary years, grammar involves learning the names of the parts of speech ("A noun is the name of a person, place, thing, or idea"), the proper relationships between these parts of speech ("Singular nouns take singular verbs"), and the mechanics of the English language (indenting paragraphs, using quotation marks, and so on).

Many language arts programs fold the study of grammar into complex programs that require too much writing and often do not present grammar clearly and sequentially. We recommend that you use Jessie's elementary grammar series *First Language Lessons for the Well-Trained Mind*. These scripted texts include grammar, memorization assignments, picture study, and narration exercises (these encourage the child to express thoughts in complete sentences), poem memorization assignments, and copywork and narration exercises designed to reinforce grammar learning. Review of all concepts and memory work is built into the lessons. First-grade lessons are primarily oral, with optional enrichment exercises that involve writing; second-grade lessons begin to require slightly more writing from the student. You'll use the first book in the series, *First Language Lessons, Levels One and Two,* two or three times a week during the first- and second-grade years, filing all copy-work and narration exercises in the grammar section of the language notebook.

Narration is a way to develop the child's understanding and storytelling skills. The process is simple: the child tells you what he's just heard or read. You started this process in preschool, when you asked your child questions about the stories you were reading together. In first grade, you begin to ask the child to summarize the plots of short simple stories: *First Language Lessons* uses Aesop's fables and other familiar tales. Read the child the story, close the book, and ask, "What was the story about?" (More specific questions, such as, "What happened to Goldilocks at the end of the story?" or "What did the littlest Billy Goat Gruff say to the troll?" are just fine; do encourage the child to answer in complete sentences, though, even if you have to rephrase his answer and have him repeat it back to you.) Write down the child's narration, and then read it back to him.

Narration lets you know how much a child retains and understands. It also develops vocabulary and powers of expression, and lays the foundation for good writing later on. A short essay is a cinch for a child who's become accustomed to narration.

You can supplement the narration exercises in *First Language Lessons* with your own exercises—choose a book of Aesop's fables, short tales, or familiar fairy stories. Record the child's answers in your own handwriting, and put these papers into the grammar section of the language notebook.

When you finish the first volume of *First Language Lessons*, your child will have a good basic grounding in punctuation, types of sentences, word use, elementary parts of speech, and beginning writing. Now it's time for a more formal approach to grammar (one that involves more actual writing).

By the end of fourth grade, the child should learn the proper names and usages of all the parts of speech, the rules of punctuation and capitalization, dictionary use, and the proper forms for letters, reports, and other common pieces of writing. Until these basic skills are mastered, he won't be able to exercise language with the mastery that the logic stage demands.

The *First Language Lessons* series continues into third and fourth grade with Level 3 and Level 4. The instructor's guide for both levels is scripted for the parent's use, like the first volume in the series, but Levels 3 and 4 also include student workbooks; these workbooks cover all of the topics necessary to prepare the student for logic-stage work, and also introduce diagramming in a gentle manner.

Parents who do not wish to continue with the scripted style of *First Language Lessons* can instead use the textbook series published by Rod & Staff. The third-grade book is called *Beginning Wisely: English 3*, the fourth-grade book is called *Building with Diligence: English 4*, and the series is unabashedly Christian (Rod & Staff is a Mennonite publisher).

These texts provide an excellent, rigorous, thorough grounding in grammar and composition. Remember, though, that this program was originally designed for a classroom, and there's enough repetition in the exercises to keep a roomful of students busy. Don't feel that you need to complete every exercise if the child understands the concept. The books are nonconsumable and the student is expected to copy out each exercise, be very careful how much physical writing you require of a third- or fourth-grade student, and feel free to do as many exercises orally as you think appropriate. Finally, if the student finds the writing exercises in Rod & Staff to be overwhelming, simply skip them. Young students who are naturally gifted writers may enjoy them, but students whose fine motor skills and writing abilities are still developing can be easily frustrated by the limited amount of guidance provided in the text. These students should follow the writing recommendations in the next section instead.

Our choice for those looking for a less sectarian and unscripted approach to grammar is Voyages in English, a series originally designed by Loyola Press for Catholic schools and reissued in a nonsectarian version. The rules are clearly stated and the exercises are adequate; the program is not quite as rigorous or complete as the Rod & Staff program, and the writing exercises are not useful in building expository writing skills and should be skipped (see the Writing section in this chapter).

If you're undecided, know that we prefer *First Language Lessons* or the Rod & Staff books; they demand more from the student. Whichever program you choose, continue to file written exercises in the appropriate section of the language notebook ("grammar" for grammar excercises, "writing" for composition assignments). For third- and fourth-grade writing, use paper ruled for third and fourth grades (see ordering information at the end of this section).

If you're just beginning the study of grammar with a second-grade student, go ahead and work through the first volume of *First Language Lessons*, skipping lessons that seem too repetitious, and then move on to grade-level work in *First Language Lessons 3*, Rod & Staff, or Voyages in English. A third- or fourth-grade student can go into any one of these programs at grade level, since each one reviews the previous year's work before moving on. If the student seems frustrated or overwhelmed, simply back up one year.

Reading

We strongly feel that "reading texts" (books with snippets of stories and poems followed by comprehension exercises) turn reading into a chore. Books, even in the early grades, ought to be sources of delight and information, not exercises to be mastered. A good classical education instills a passion for books in the student. "Reading texts" mutilate real books by pulling sections out of context and presenting them as "assignments." Even worse are textbooks that provide selections designed especially for textbook use, which means that your child spends his time reading generic prose produced by textbook writers instead of stories written by masters.

During the first four years of education, you have two purposes: to get the child to read quickly, well, and habitually; and to fill his mind with stories of every kind—myths, legends, classic tales, biographies, great stories from history. In the reading notebook, you and the child will make a record of these stories. Divide the Reading section of the language notebook into two sub-sections: "My Reading" and "Memory Work."

We suggest that reading follow the same pattern as history studies:

First grade	Ancients (5000 B.C.–A.D. 400)
Second grade	Medieval–early Renaissance (400–1600)
Third grade	Late Renaissance–early modern (1600–1850)
Fourth grade	Modern (1850–present)

See Chapter 7 for a full explanation of these divisions. (Once you've read Chapter 7, the following will make more sense.)

Every day, the child reads or (at first) is read to. Begin with twenty to thirty minutes of reading in first grade; you'll want to work up to forty-five minutes to an hour by fourth grade.

The principle is simple: try to give the child simplified versions of the original literature that he'll be reading in the higher grades, or introduce him (through stories or biographies) to a writer he'll encounter later.

How do you do this with elementary-aged students?

At the end of this chapter, you'll find a list of major authors for each period. Search in the children's section of the library for books about the lives of these writers and paraphrases of their works. We've supplied you with a list of some of our favorite resources: retellings of ancient myths, of the *Iliad* and *Odyssey,* of Shakespeare and Dickens. First graders who are working with the Ancients can begin on the fairy tales of ancient China and Japan, stories of the Bible, myths of Rome and Greece, Aesop's fables, stories about Plato and Aristotle, and simplified versions of Homer. Susan and her husband, Peter, spent six weeks reading through a lavishly illustrated child's version of the *Iliad* with their six and four year old. Since the children hadn't learned to be frightened of the classics, they were enthralled and eventually put on a puppet show with their stuffed animals: *The Fall of Troy,* starring a stuffed bear as Ajax.

Don't overlook books on tape as a supplement to (not a replacement for) reading. Most fourth graders, for example, can't read Shakespeare independently but will listen to a dramatized version of *As You Like It* (or the *Odyssey,* or *Oliver Twist,* or Robert Frost reading his own poetry). The biographies listed in the history resources can also be read. (You should find history and reading assignments overlapping quite a bit. Generally, put imaginative literature—stories, myths, fairy tales, poems, novels—in the reading notebook. Put factual books and biographies in the history notebook. See Chapter 7 for a full explanation.)

Don't limit the student's reading to works on a first- or second-grade level. Even though he should be doing some independent reading, you should continue to read more difficult books to him, especially during the first- and second-grade years. For example, we've recommended several interesting and beautifully illustrated versions of the *Odyssey* for first-grade reading. These books will be well beyond most first graders' reading ability. But try reading them aloud; first graders are fascinated by the adventures of Odysseus and will listen openmouthed.

The My Reading section of the language notebook should be a record of books (imaginative literature) that the child has read and enjoyed or that you have read to him. Although you shouldn't make him report on every book, you should ask him at least twice a week to tell you, in two to four sentences, something about the plot of the book you have just read. Younger students will need you to ask them specific questions about the book: "What was the most exciting thing that happened in the book?" or "Who was your favorite character, and what did he do?" are two useful questions that help the child narrow in on the book's central theme. Some third and fourth graders will be able to answer the more general question "What was the book about?" while others will still need more guidance. In either case, help the child narrow the answer down to under five sentences. Learning how to identify one or two items about a book as *more* important than the rest is a vital first step in learning to write; a young writer will flounder as long as he cannot pick out one or two of the ideas in his mind as *central* to his composition. For first grade, you write the narration down, have the child read it back to you, and then place it under My Reading. Most first graders will enjoy drawing crayon pictures to illustrate these narrations. You can also copy out favorite poems to file under My Reading, letting the child decorate the pages with stickers and glitter.

Narration removes the need for "comprehension exercises." Instead of learning to complete fill-in-the-blank questions, the child uses all his mental faculties to understand, remember, and relate the main points of a story.

Not all reading should be linked to the history outline, however. And not all reading should be narrated back to the teacher. In addition to the reading time spent on assembling the reading notebook, the child should have a set time every day to read for fun. Begin with half an hour for first graders, and build up to an hour of reading time daily. We've listed some "read for fun" resources at the end of this chapter.

This is an important part of the child's education: it improves his reading skills, teaches him the habit of sitting still with a book, and reminds him that reading is fun. Remember: this doesn't *replace* the half hour spent in "assigned" reading. The reading you do for the reading notebook ought to be difficult because the child is building reading skills; the free reading time ought to be spent on literature at or slightly below the child's present reading level so that he can simply enjoy himself. The easier reading will also help him increase his speed.

However, if the child leaps off the sofa and runs to you, book in hand, shouting, "We've got to make a page for this in my notebook!" go right ahead.

Every two or three weeks, the child should also memorize a poem and recite it to you. Memorization and recitation of poetry is an important part of the reading process; it exercises the child's memory, stores beautiful language in his mind, and gives him practice in speaking aloud (early preparation for the rhetoric stage). Aim for memorization of at least four to eight short poems during each school year. Pick poems that the child has read and enjoyed, either during his "assigned" reading or his "free" reading. These poems don't have to be tied to the progression of literature from ancient to modern; let him memorize anything that he likes. Have him read it several times onto a tape, and then allow him to listen to the tape over and over again. When he can recite the poem along with the tape, turn the tape recorder off and ask him to stand up and recite it for you.

Most children don't like this—not because they can't memorize, but because they don't like to be watched while they recite. Let them practice in front of the mirror or in front of their stuffed animals. Then have them stand up and, with their hands and feet still, recite the poem in front of you. When they can do that, bring in an extra audience member: your spouse, a grandparent, a neighbor. You're now building public-speaking skills.

When a poem has been memorized and recited to your satisfaction, write it out (or have the child write it out, if his skills are up to the job) and place it in the Memory Work section of the language notebook along with the date of recitation. This will serve as a reward—visual proof of the child's accomplishment—as well as a reminder to review the memory work every few weeks.

You'll follow this basic pattern during second, third, and fourth grades as well. Second-grade students should spend at least thirty minutes per day reading literature from the Middle Ages and early Renaissance: simple tales from Chaucer and Shakespeare, written for children; books about Shakespeare's life; stories of King Arthur and the Knights of the Round Table. We've supplied a resource list at the end of this chapter. As in first grade, you can read aloud anything that's beyond the child's reading level.

Continue making notebook pages two or three times a week and filing them under My Reading in the language notebook. By second grade, most children can dictate short narrations to you and then copy these narrations themselves. The second-grade notebook should contain less of your writing and more of the child's.

Also continue to give the child thirty minutes to an hour of free reading time every day. This reading should be done on the sofa or somewhere else comfortable, but we recommend that you keep an eye on the child to make sure he's actually reading.

Continue to memorize poetry and any speeches that the child finds and likes in his reading. Aim to memorize eight to twelve pieces during the second-grade year. If possible, expand the audience to include grandparents and friends.

Your third grader will spend thirty minutes per day reading writers from the late Renaissance–early modern period, which includes John Bunyan (the simplified *Pilgrim's Progress*) and Charles Dickens (abridged versions), along with the simpler poetry of Wordsworth and Blake. We provide a full list at the end of this chapter. By third grade, you should be encouraging the child to read all by himself; read to him only if you want him to read an original text instead of an abridgment (*A Christmas Carol* is a good book to read aloud in its entirety), or if he is still struggling with the mechanics of reading. Don't be afraid to assign the child abridged and simplified versions of the classics. In grades 5 through 8, he'll cycle through the ancient, medieval, Renaissance, and modern eras again. If he's already read *Great Expectations* in a simplified form, he'll know the basic outline of the plot and won't be intimidated by the original.

Continue to make notebook pages at least twice a week, summarizing the books the child is reading. By third grade, your student should be able to narrate the plot back to you and write it down himself without the intermediate step of dictating and then copying. In short, he'll have gradually worked his way up to doing book reports.

Aim to memorize and recite twelve to fifteen poems and speeches during the third-grade year. Third-grade history, like third-grade reading, covers the years 1600 to 1850, a period during which great American documents and speeches (the preamble to the Constitution, the Declaration of Independence, and Patrick Henry's "Give Me Liberty" speech, among others) abound. Third grade isn't too early to memorize many of these foundational American works.

The fourth grader will read and make notebook pages for literature of the modern period, 1850 to the present. We've listed a few reading suggestions at the end of the chapter, but children vary widely in reading ability by fourth grade. Your best bet would be to consult with your local children's librarian. Also, don't neglect poetry; Carl Sandburg, T. S. Eliot, Walter de la Mare, and other great poets of the modern period wrote much that can be enjoyed by young children.

A fourth grader's written summary of a book should fill three-quarters of a notebook page or more.

By fourth grade, your child should be spending at least an hour in free reading every day. Do *not* require any sort of reporting on this reading. Library visits should be a weekly or biweekly part of your schedule. Help your child check out many different books—don't leave the selection entirely up to ten-year-old discretion—but let him choose anything from that stack that he wants to read during his free hour. And never force your child to finish something that he has no taste for.

A word about beginning readers. Your child is already doing two types of reading: the books you choose for his literature study, and the books you help him select for his free hour. The reading done during the free hour should not be difficult for him, but we do recommend that you avoid lightweight series such as the *Goosebumps, Sweet Valley High,* or *Bionicles* books. These books are the literary equivalent of TV cartoons; their short sentences, easy vocabulary, uncomplicated paragraphs, and shallow plots do not help the student develop a taste for good reading. Comic books and graphic novels, like cartoons, are image-centered entertainment—they do *not* qualify as "books" for free reading time.

However, outside of the free reading hour, let the child read what he pleases. You should, of course, censor books for content that may be too mature—that's part of your job as a parent. But don't worry if a young student wants to read the same easy books over and over again for fun. The quality literature read during the free hour will slowly develop his taste for better books.

Oral Reading

Even after your child has completed a phonics program and is reading independently, continue to have him read aloud to you periodically through about sixth grade. In this way, you will catch errors before they become a habit, discourage guessing, and help the child practice word attack skills for new words.

You can choose a paragraph from your child's history, science, or literature reading, or from a vintage McGuffey Eclectic reader; the McGuffey reading selections are perfect length for oral reading. Begin the oral reading with the *Third Eclectic Reader* after finishing your phonics program. (If you choose to use McGuffey, make sure to get the originals republished by John Wiley & Sons, rather than the reworked version published by Eerdmans.)

In addition to preventing errors from becoming habits, oral reading develops fluency, which takes time and practice. Fluency is best developed by repeated reading aloud of the same passage. Once a week is plenty to practice reading for fluency. When developing fluency, follow this pattern:

1. Model fluency by reading a specific passage aloud for the child (not the whole selection).
2. Have the child read the passage to you four times as you offer guidance. Practice only on passages that are easy for the child. If he misreads more than one out of every twenty words, he'll focus on word recognition rather than fluency as he reads.

You can also improve fluency by reading prose or poetry aloud in unison with the child. Books on tape can also help develop this skill. Have the child listen to a passage on tape, following along in his copy of the book and pointing to each word as the reader reads it. Next, have the student read the passage out loud along with the tape. Then ask the child to read the passage out loud independently.

Writing

Writing is a difficult skill because it requires the child to express content at the same time that he is learning the tools of expression. For this reason, early writing should not involve a great deal of original content. Early writing instruction should involve copywork, dictation, and the retelling of passages from history, science, or literature.

At the beginner level, writing is simply penmanship practice. As the child is able, work up from five to fifteen minutes per day, using a handwriting book, such as one from the Zaner-Bloser or Handwriting Without Tears series (see Chapter 4 for details).

Once he's writing well, your child should begin to do simple copying exercises. *First Language Lessons* provides copywork assignments that reinforce grammar learning. In addition, your child should copy sentences from good writers three or four times per week. Pick sentences from good literature (E. B. White, C. S. Lewis, Lynn Reid Banks), from the child's history, or from science. Aim to work up from five-word sentences to longer and more complex sentences. Write these sentences out (in your best handwriting) on first-grade manuscript paper (see the ordering information on pages 85–86). Put the paper in front of the child and ask him to copy the sentence. At this stage, it's best to sit with the child and correct him when he begins to make a mistake. There is no point in allowing him to copy incorrectly. He should always use a pencil, so that he can erase and correct if necessary. Encourage him to compare his work frequently with the model. Praise him when he's finished! File this copywork in the language notebook under Writing. This copywork, along with the oral narration recommended for reading, history, and science, is sufficient for first-grade writing.

Does this stifle creativity?

No—it builds the skills the child needs in order to be truly creative. When a first grader copies a sentence from *Charlotte's Web,* he's learning spelling, mechanics (punctuation and so forth), basic grammar (subject-verb agreement, adjective use), and vocabulary from a master of English prose. He'll need all this information in order to write down the sentences he forms in his own head. Jack London learned to write by copying literature in the San Francisco Public Library; Benjamin Franklin learned to write by copying essays from *The Spectator.* The classical pupil learns to write by copying great writers.

If your first grader has a sudden desire to write a story, poem, or letter to a friend (or to Santa Claus), by all means put the copying away and help him do it. Put the stories and poems in the language notebook. If at all possible, photocopy the letter before you send it, and keep the copy.

But the next day, get the copying work back out. You're laying the groundwork for dictation (second grade), which in turn will develop the skills needed for original writing (third and fourth grades . . . and the rest of the child's life).

Traditionally, children transition into cursive writing in second grade. If you are using the Zaner-Bloser handwriting program recommended in Chapter 4, you'll begin the Zaner-Bloser *Grade 2C Student Book* around the beginning of the second grade year; this book begins with practice of manuscript letters and then moves on to cursive handwriting. The Handwriting

Without Tears program introduces cursive later (closer to third grade). Either way, until the child is comfortable with all cursive letters, he can continue to print his spelling and writing assignments (*Spelling Workout B* begins the transition to cursive halfway through the book). Spend a few minutes each day practicing cursive writing one letter at a time. And make sure you order second-grade paper at the beginning of the second-grade year—the lines are slightly narrower than those on first-grade paper (see the ordering information on pages 85–86).

Once your child is copying sentences easily, move on to dictation. This usually happens around the beginning of the second-grade year.

The process is simple. Dictate a short sentence slowly to the child as he writes. Choose sentences from your phonics primer, history, science, or literature. If the child makes a mistake, stop him and have him write the word correctly. Give him all necessary help with punctuation and spelling. Make sure that he uses a pencil so he can erase and correct as he goes. Remind him of proper spacing as he writes. That's all there is to it.

At first, this will take a lot of time. Start with simple words in very short sentences, three or four words maximum ("The cat sat up"). You'll have to help the child sound the letters out, reminding him of his phonics (and telling him the answers if he's stuck). Don't frustrate him, especially at the beginning. "What letters make the *th* sound? *T* and *h,* remember? Now write a *t* and an *h.* Do you remember what letter comes at the end of the word *the*? You don't? It's an *e. The. Cat.* Do you remember what letters make a *k* sound? Does a *k* or a *c* come at the beginning of *cat*? Now what letter makes that middle sound?" The child who's spent first grade copying will already have a visual memory of common words. But during the transition from copying to dictation, you'll need to help him develop the skills of sounding out and writing down words without looking at a model. When he's finished writing, praise some aspect of his work.

Like any new skill, this is difficult at first. But do it for a brief time—three days per week. Ten to twenty minutes per day on a regular basis will result in a rapid improvement in writing skills.

When these short sentences become easy, progress to dictating sentences from literature—any ten- to fifteen-word sentence from the child's books. Susan likes E. B. White's books: *Charlotte's Web, Stuart Little,* and *The Trumpet of the Swan.* White's books are full of amusing sentences, and he's a wonderful stylist. C. S. Lewis's *Chronicles of Narnia* are another good source for dictation.

File dictation exercises in the Writing section of the language notebook. This will allow your child to look back over his work and see how he's improved or what areas of punctuation and form continue to trip him up.

Dictation is a tool that develops a number of language skills: phonics, spelling, handwriting, grammar, and punctuation. By writing sentences from high-quality writers, the child learns—almost subconsciously—the rules of good style and expression.

Also during second grade, ask your child at least once a month to write a letter to a friend or relative. Photocopy these letters, and file them under Writing. Letter writing is an important part of language development. As soon as possible, the child should begin to use his writing skills by composing short letters (thank-you notes for gifts are a marvelous starting place) to relatives and friends.

Although you should encourage any creative impulses, we don't think you should require the child to be creative during the grammar stage of education. He's still absorbing and taking in. If he's naturally creative, fine. If not, demanding creativity will only be counterproductive.

If the child does have a bent toward storytelling, you can follow the same pattern you're using for narration: write down the stories that the first grader tells, and put them in the notebook; write down the stories that the second grader tells, and have the child copy them in his own writing; help a third or fourth grader write his own stories and poems without a written model.

But don't force this skill. In many cases, creativity will develop later, once the child is comfortable with writing skills. And some children may never become creative writers. That's fine; they'll still have the essay- and letter-writing skills they need.

By third grade, encourage the child to do all formal work using cursive writing. Continue to practice penmanship. Require all work to be done neatly; don't be afraid to tell a third grader to recopy something that's carelessly done. Order third-grade paper for all writing exercises (see the ordering information on page 86).

Third graders should continue to do dictation exercises three times per week. Most third graders can now progress to complex sentences or two or three sentences at a time.

In first and second grade, the student's "writing program" consists of copywork, dictation, and oral narration in literature, history, and science (see Chapters 5, 7, and 8). You've been writing these oral narrations down as the student speaks them. In second grade, you should begin to encourage the student to write down at least the first sentence of his oral narration, even if you then need to complete the rest of it.

In third and fourth grade, the student should continue to do dictation twice a week. Third-grade dictation should involve longer and more complex sentences; by the end of fourth grade, the student should be able to write a short paragraph from dictation, inserting punctuation marks such as quotation marks and semicolons where appropriate. The student will also begin to write his own summaries in history and science (see Chapters 7 and 8).

If an elementary student is doing regular copywork, dictation, narration, and summary-writing in history, science, and literature, he is learning the basics of writing. Parents who are comfortable with the writing process do not necessarily need a separate "writing program" in the elementary years. But if you are an uncertain writer yourself, have a pencil-phobic student, or are schooling more than one child, you can use one of the following curricula to make sure that the student's training is thorough.

Note that if you are using any of the following programs along with Rod & Staff grammar, you should probably *not* also complete the Rod & Staff composition assignments; this is too much writing for most young students.

The Complete Writer: Writing with Ease
Strong Fundamentals

Susan has laid out a complete program based on these principles in *The Complete Writer: Writing with Ease*. The core text, *Strong Fundamentals*, gives a detailed overview of the skills that should be developed during the elementary, middle, and high-school years; outlines a complete four-year progression of copywork, dictation, and narration for elementary students, complete with weekly lesson plans; and provides trouble-shooting for common writing problems. The core text allows the parent to plan out the four years of elementary writing and to choose the majority of the copywork, dictation, and narration exercises independently.

Parents who would prefer to have each day's lesson spelled out can use the accompanying workbooks. *The Complete Writer: Level 1 Workbook* lays out an entire year's worth of copywork and narration exercises, all based on classic literature, and provides a script for the instructor to follow. The *Level 2*, *Level 3*, and *Level 4* workbooks each cover one year of elementary writing, progressing from copywork into dictation and more complex narration exercises.

Writing Strands

Students who do not struggle with the writing process may instead enjoy *Writing Strands*, a seven-book series that begins with simple descriptions and progresses through paragraph construction, tense use, narrative voice, dialogue, reports, interviews, and short stories. Two additional books cover exposition and fiction on the high-school level. Since *Writing Strands* contains creative writing exercises as well, it should not be used with young students who find imaginative writing or journaling difficult.

Do not begin *Writing Strands* until third grade; for grades one and two, spend time instead on copywork, narration, and dictation (as described above).

In third grade, begin work on a *Writing Strands* assignment twice a week. When you start *Writing Strands* work, reduce dictation from three days per week to two (but no more!).

The first *Writing Strands* book is really a prewriting book. It describes word games you can play with your child to prepare him for writing. You can read through it for ideas, but there's no need to go through it systematically; a child who's done narration and dictation will be ready to go straight into *Writing Strands* 2. According to the National Writing Institute, book 2 is written for second graders. However, if it seems too simple, skip to the third book.

File the *Writing Strands* exercises in the language notebook. As you move on into book 3, the child will learn to organize paragraphs and will begin to write longer and longer compositions. (The *Writing Strands* books also give you pages on which to list words that are consistently misspelled; we suggest that you ignore these pages and continue to put this list in the spelling section.)

One caution. The *Writing Strands* books declare that no one ever learned to write by studying grammar. While this is true, there's a strong flavor of "Therefore, nobody needs to study grammar" throughout the books. *Grammar is necessary.* So is writing. Contractors should be able to draw up plans *and* hammer nails; young writers should know their grammar rules and be able to put them to use in compositions.

In fourth grade, the student will write from dictation twice a week and do *Writing Strands* exercises twice a week. Use fourth-grade paper (see the ordering information on page 85).

You should choose short paragraphs for fourth-grade dictation. By this time, most children are capable of writing from dictation such paragraphs as this:

> The house was really a small castle. It seemed to be all towers; little towers with long pointed spires on them, sharp as needles. They looked like huge dunce's caps or sorcerer's caps. And they shone in the moonlight and their long shadows looked strange on the snow! Edmund began to be afraid of the house.[2]

The fourth grader who writes this from dictation is practicing spelling and punctuation (semicolons and exclamation points); he's learning vocabulary (What is a dunce cap?); and he's working on spelling *(sorcerer, moonlight, afraid)*. Most of all, he's learning what a vivid, evocative description sounds like.

Aim to finish book 4 of *Writing Strands* by the end of the fourth-grade year. Books 3 and 4 deal with paragraph construction, composition organization, and other elements of style—voice, tense, person, descriptive technique, dialogue, and so on. Book 5 begins dealing with the logical development of arguments; although you can start book 5 if you finish book 4 early, it really takes the student into the logic stage. But if you do finish book 4 before the end of fourth grade, consider using the extra time to catch up on another subject or to write history or science compositions, extra letters to friends and grandparents, or stories and poems.

Fourth graders should continue to write letters several times per month.

Institute for Excellence in Writing

The Institute for Excellence in Writing (IEW) takes a very different approach. Whereas the *Writing Strands* lessons break the process of writing down into small "chunks" and give the student direction on how to perform each step, the Institute for Excellence in Writing is a writing seminar for parents that teaches *how* to teach writing: sentence structure, making and using key-word outlines, and writing summaries, three-paragraph and longer compositions, and critiques. It also includes three taped student workshops (for grades 2 to 4, grades 5 to 7, and grades 8 and up). The pro-

[2]C. S. Lewis, *The Lion, the Witch, and the Wardrobe* (New York: Macmillan, 1978), pp. 88–89.

gram, *Teaching Writing: Structure and Style*, comes on DVD and video, with a notebook that summarizes the main points covered in the lectures. At various points during the tapes, viewers are instructed to stop and complete a practicum.

There are nine units in the program. Generally you would go through the units each year with the student, increasing the complexity of the writing each year (IEW provides suggestions on how to use the units with each level of student). IEW is designed to be used along with the rest of the child's curriculum; although you do teach the child skills directly in a "writing session," he is then supposed to use these skills when writing compositions in other subjects. (IEW also pays a great deal of attention to style; Susan would prefer to see parents deemphasize this aspect of the program in favor of allowing young writers to develop their own style. She also feels that, for expository writing, plain and simple *is* good style.)

Which program you choose will depend on your child's needs (and your preferences). *The Complete Writer* is designed for children who need direct, careful instruction in order to get words down on paper; it is particularly suited to young writers who are easily frustrated or overwhelmed. *Writing Strands* works well for students who can already get words down on paper without difficulty, but who need the writing process broken down into small steps; it also suits students who prefer to work independently. IEW works well for parents who are willing to go through the lessons themselves and direct students in writing. (Note that IEW also provides a supplementary Student Writing Intensive, which is a DVD seminar targeted directly to the student. However, parent involvement remains high and the nine-unit *Teaching Writing* program is still required.)

Samples can be viewed on the publishers' websites: www.peachhill press.com, www.writingstrands.com, and www.excellenceinwriting.com.

OVERVIEW OF LANGUAGE WORK

Daily Schedule

		First Grade
Spelling	10–15 minutes	Finish reading primer; begin *Spelling Workout A.*
Grammar	15–20 minutes	*First Language Lessons, Levels 1 & 2.*
Reading	20–30 minutes	Structured reading (schedule 30–60

		minutes at another time for fun reading); focus on ancient myths and legends.
Writing	5–20 minutes	Begin with penmanship practice; progress to copying short sentences two or three days per week, or use Level 1 of *The Complete Writer*.
		Second Grade
Spelling	10–15 minutes	Go on to *Spelling Workout B* and *C*.
Grammar	20 minutes	*First Language Lessons, Levels 1 & 2*.
Reading	30 minutes	Structured reading (schedule 30–60 minutes at another time for fun reading); focus on stories of the Middle Ages.
Writing	10–20 minutes	Begin cursive penmanship. Write from dictation three days per week and do regular narrations from history, science, and literature; or use Level 2 of *The Complete Writer*; or begin the lowest level of IEW.
		Third Grade
Spelling	15 minutes	Go on to *Spelling Workout C* and *D*.
Grammar	20–30 minutes	Use Rod & Staff, Voyages in English, or *First Language Lessons 3*.
Reading	30 minutes	Structured reading (schedule 30–60 minutes at another time for fun reading); read literature of the late Renaissance to early modern eras.
Writing	20–30 minutes	Continue cursive penmanship. Write from dictation three days per week and do regular narrations from history, science, and literature; or use *Level 3* of *The Complete Writer*; or continue with the lower levels of IEW; or begin *Writing Strands 2*.
		Fourth Grade
Spelling	15 minutes	Continue with *Spelling Workout D* and *E* (or *E* and *F*).

Grammar	20 minutes	Rod & Staff or Voyages in English.
Reading	30–45 minutes	Structured reading (schedule 60 minutes at another time for fun reading); focus on modern works.
Writing	20–30 minutes	Practice penmanship. Write from dictation two or three days per week and do regular narrations from history, science, and literature; or use *Level 4* of *The Complete Writer*; or continue with the lower levels of IEW; or continue with *Writing Strands*.

RESOURCES

For publisher and catalog addresses, telephone numbers, and other information, see Sources (pages 751–778). Most books can be obtained from any bookstore or library; where we know of a mail-order option, we have provided it. Where noted, resources are listed in chronological order (the order you'll want to use them in). Books in series are listed together.

Spelling

Adams-Gordon, Beverly L. *Spelling Power,* 4th ed. Pomeroy, Wash.: Castlemoyle Press, 2006.

$64.95. Order from Castlemoyle Press.

Modern Curriculum Press Spelling Workout series, revised ed. Lebanon, Ind.: Modern Curriculum Press (Pearson Learning Group), 2002.

$10.95 for each student edition, $11.50 for each *Teacher's Edition* (you probably won't need these until you're into the fourth or fifth book at the earliest). Order from Modern Curriculum Press. We've listed the entire series for your reference, but most children won't get past *E* or *F* by fourth grade. The grade levels are approximate, but will give you a guide as to where to begin with an older student.

Spelling Workout A (first-grade level).
Teacher's Edition A.
Spelling Workout B (second-grade level).
Teacher's Edition B.

Spelling Workout C (third-grade level).
Teacher's Edition C.
Spelling Workout D (fourth-grade level).
Teacher's Edition D.
Spelling Workout E (fifth-grade level).
Teacher's Edition E.
Spelling Workout F (sixth-grade level).
Teacher's Edition F.
Spelling Workout G (seventh-grade level).
Teacher's Edition G.
Spelling Workout H (eighth-grade level).
Teacher's Edition H.

Grammar

Beechick, Ruth. *A Strong Start in Language.* Pollock Pines, Calif.: Arrow Press, 1993.
$4.00. Most bookstores can order this for you (or you can buy it through Amazon.com). It's a good resource for technique in dictation and for tips on teaching reading skills.

Rod & Staff Grammar and Composition.
Beginning Wisely: English 3. Crockett, Ky.: Rod & Staff, 1991.
Order from Rod & Staff.
Pupil Textbook. $12.00.
Worksheets (additional practice). $2.95.
Teacher's Manual. $15.25.
Test Booklet. $1.95.

Building with Diligence: English 4. Crockett, Ky.: Rod & Staff, 1992.
Order from Rod & Staff.
Pupil Textbook. $14.90.
Worksheets (additional practice). $2.95.
Teacher's Manual. $20.20.
Test Booklet. $1.95.

Voyages in English. Chicago, Ill.: Loyola Press, 2006.
Order from Loyola Press.
Voyages in English, Grade 3, Student Edition. $44.95.

Voyages in English, Grade 3, Student Edition, Extra Practice Workbook. $8.95.

Voyages in English, Grade 3, Teacher Guide. $75.95.

Voyages in English, Grade 4, Student Edition. $44.95.

Voyages in English, Grade 4, Student Edition, Extra Practice Workbook. $8.95.

Voyages in English, Grade 4, Teacher Guide. $75.95.

Wise, Jessie. *First Language Lessons for the Well-Trained Mind.* Charles City, Va.: Peace Hill Press.

Order from Peace Hill Press.

First Language Lessons for the Well-Trained Mind, Levels 1 & 2 (2003). $18.95 softcover, $24.95 hardcover.

First Language Lessons for the Well-Trained Mind, Level 3 (2007). $29.95.

First Language Lessons, Level 3 Student Workbook. $18.95.

First Language Lessons for the Well-Trained Mind, Level 4 (2008). $29.95.

First Language Lessons, Level 4 Student Workbook. $19.95.

Reading

This is listed in order of use. Remember, you don't have to read all of these. But you can choose reading assignments from among the following names. Note that this list—especially the early-modern and modern sections—is merely a starting place. There are many other authors and books worth reading, and you'll discover them as you explore your library. Rather than organizing these books and authors alphabetically, we have listed them in chronological order, and we suggest that you read them in this order. In most cases, you can use any version of these stories. We have suggested a few specific editions that we particularly like.

Ancients, 5000 B.C.–A.D. 400 (First Grade)

Work through these books and authors in the following order. Many other literature selections that correspond to history are provided in the activity guide to *The Story of the World,* recommended for history study. (See Chapter 7.)

Stories and poems by, about, or from . . .

The Bible

Homer

Clement-Davies, David. *Trojan Horse.* New York: Dorling Kindersley, 1999.

A DK Reader for beginners, this retells the story of the siege of Troy with clear print and colorful pictures.

McCaughrean, Geraldine. *The Odyssey.* Illus. Victor G. Ambrus. New York: Puffin, 1997.

At most public libraries; worth asking for on interlibrary loan. Too difficult for first graders, but a wonderful read-to over several weeks (one chapter per session). Geraldine McCaughrean manages to keep the poetic flow of the original.

Sutcliffe, Rosemary. *Black Ships Before Troy: The Story of the Iliad.* Illus. Alan Lee. New York: Bantam, 1993.

Find at any bookstore or library. Another read-aloud with beautiful illustrations.

Greek and Roman Myths

Aliki. *The Gods and Goddesses of Olympus.* New York: HarperTrophy, 1997.

An age-appropriate set of tales.

Burleigh, Robert. *Pandora.* Illus. Raul Colon. New York: Silver Whistle, 2002.

Artwork inspired by Greek sculptures and paintings in this picture-book retelling.

Climo, Shirley. *Atalanta's Race: A Greek Myth.* Illus. Alexander Koshkin. New York: Clarion Books, 2000.

D'Aulaire, Ingri, and Edgar Parin D'Aulaire. *D'Aulaires' Book of Greek Myths.* New York: Delacorte Books for Young Readers, 1992.

Demi. *King Midas: The Golden Touch.* New York: Margaret K. McElderry, 2002.

Spectacular illustrations in this picture-book retelling.

Mayer, Marianna. *Pegasus.* Illus. Kinuko Y. Craft. New York: Harper Collins, 1998.

Verniero, Joan C., and Robin Fitsimmons, eds. *An Illustrated Treasury of Read-Aloud Myths and Legends: More than 40 of the World's Best-Loved Myths and Legends Including Greek, Roman, Celtic, Scandinavian, Indian, Mexican, and Many More.* New York: Black Dog & Leventhal, 2004.

Osborne, Mary Pope. *Favorite Greek Myths*. New York: Scholastic, 1991.
A read-aloud collection that retells stories from Ovid in an age-appropriate manner.

Aesop's fables
Plato
Aristotle

Egyptian myths
Barker, Henry. *Egyptian Gods and Goddesses*. New York: Grosset & Dunlap, 1999.
From the All Aboard Reading series; some young students will be able to read this independently.

Indian folktales
Shephard, Aaron. *Savitri: A Tale of Ancient India*. Illus. Vera Rosenberry. Morton Grove, Ill.: Albert Whitman & Co., 1992.

African folktales
Arkhurst, Joyce Cooper. *The Adventures of Spider: West African Folktales.* Illus. Jerry Pinkney. New York: Little, Brown & Co., 1992.

Confucius

Chinese and Japanese folktales
Bishop, Claire. *The Five Chinese Brothers*. New York: Paper Star, 1996.
Try your local library. This favorite folktale is available in several different versions.

Ancient Chinese and Japanese poetry
Cicero
Virgil

English, Irish, and Welsh fairy tales
Stephens, James. *Traditional Irish Fairy Tales.* Illus. Arthur Rackham. New York: Dover, 1996.
Read-aloud fairy tales with classic illustrations.

Medieval/Early Renaissance, 400–1600 (Second Grade)

Work through these books and authors in the following order.

Stories and poems by, about, or from . . .

Saint Augustine

Beowulf

Szobody, Michelle L. *Beowulf: Grendel the Ghastly,* illus. Justin Gerard. Greenville, S.C.: Portland Studios, 2008.

Sir Gawain and the Green Knight

Geoffrey Chaucer, *Canterbury Tales*

McCaughrean, Geraldine. *The Canterbury Tales.* Illus. Victor G. Ambrus. New York: Puffin, 1997.

The Junior Bookshelf calls this "one of the very finest interpretations of Chaucer for the young." A read-to for most second graders. Well worth the effort of ordering on interlibrary loan.

Edmund Spenser, *The Fairie Queene*

Hodges, Margaret. *Saint George and the Dragon.* Illus. Trina Schart Hyman. New York: Little, Brown, 1990.

A Caldecott Medal winner; retells the story of Saint George from Edmund Spenser's *Fairie Queene.* Beautiful illustrations, and Hodges retains some of Spenser's original poetry. At most libraries.

William Shakespeare, all the plays

A Shakespeare Coloring Book. Santa Barbara, Calif.: Bellerophon, 1995.

$4.95. Order from Greenleaf Press. Historical illustrations of famous scenes from Shakespeare's plays.

Burdett, Lois. The Shakespeare Can Be Fun series.

Designed for ages 6–8, these books retell the plays in rhyming couplets, illustrated by children's drawings. Order from any bookstore or from the Writing Company.

Hamlet for Kids. Toronto: Firefly Books, 2000.
Macbeth for Kids. Buffalo, N.Y.: Black Moss Press, 1996.
Much Ado About Nothing for Kids. Toronto: Firefly Books, 2002.
Romeo and Juliet for Kids. Toronto: Firefly Books, 1998.
Twelfth Night for Kids. Buffalo, N.Y.: Black Moss Press, 1995.

Coville, Bruce. *William Shakespeare's A Midsummer Night's Dream.* Illus. Dennis Nolan. New York: Penguin, 2003.

A beautiful picture-book version.

———. *William Shakespeare's Macbeth.* Illus. Gary Kelley. New York: Dial, 2004.

A picture-book retelling, dark but not unnecessarily gory.

———. *William Shakespeare's Romeo and Juliet.* Illus. Dennis Nolan. New York: Dial, 1999.

Another lovely picture-book retelling.

Garfield, Leon. *Shakespeare Stories.* Boston: Houghton Mifflin, 1998.

__________. *Shakespeare Stories II.* Boston: Houghton Mifflin, 2000.

Read-aloud tales, fairly detailed; for slightly older readers.

Lamb, Charles, and Mary Lamb. *Tales from Shakespeare.* New York: Puffin Classics, 1995.

$4.99. Order from the Writing Company. These classic retellings of Shakespeare's stories use the original words wherever possible. Sixth-grade reading level. A read-to for grammar-stage students.

Dante, *The Inferno*

Thomas Malory, *Morte d'Arthur*

Translated, this means the "death of Arthur." Look for retellings of the Arthur legend, most of which are based on Malory.

Gross, Gwen. *Knights of the Round Table.* Stepping Stone series. Illus. Norman Green. New York: Random House, 1985.

The Stepping Stone series adapts classic stories to a second- to third-grade level.

Hodges, Margaret. *The Kitchen Knight: A Tale of King Arthur.* Illus. Trina Schart-Hyman. New York: Holiday House, 1990.

Erasmus

Martin Luther

John Calvin

Sir Thomas Wyatt

Wyatt, a poet in his own right, sometimes shows up as a secondary character in stories about Henry VIII and Anne Boleyn.

John Knox
René Descartes

Late Renaissance/Early Modern, 1600–1850 (Third Grade)

Work through these book and authors in the following order.

Stories and poems by, about, or from . . .

John Milton

French fairy tales
Many were collected by Charles Perrault, 1628–1703.

Daniel Defoe, *Robinson Crusoe*

Jonathan Swift, *Gulliver's Travels*
Riordan, James. *Gulliver's Travels*. Illus. Victor G. Ambrus. New York: Oxford University Press, 1998.
Wonderful pictures, and a decent adaptation of Swift's prose; most third graders should be able to read the text. You may need to order this by interlibrary loan.

John Bunyan, *Pilgrim's Progress*

Victor Hugo
Hugo, Victor, and Marc Cerasini. *The Hunchback of Notre Dame*. Bullseye Step into Classics series. New York: Random House, 1995.
Adapted to a second- to third-grade reading level.

Hugo, Victor, and Monica Kulling. *Les Miserables*. Stepping Stone series. New York: Random House, 1995.
Adapted to a second- to third-grade reading level.

Alexandre Dumas
Dumas, Alexandre, and Deborah G. Felder. *The Three Musketeers*. Stepping Stone series. New York: Random House, 1994.
Adapted to a second- to third-grade reading level.

William Blake, *Songs of Innocence*
William Wordsworth, collected poems

Jane Austen
Alfred, Lord Tennyson
Robert Browning, *The Pied Piper of Hamelin*
Elizabeth Barrett Browning
Jacob and Wilhelm Grimm, *Grimms' Fairy Tales*

Charles Dickens

Dickens, Charles, *A Christmas Carol.* Illus. Dean Morrissey. New York: HarperTrophy, 2004.

A beautiful picture-book version.

Dickens, Charles, and Monica Kulling. *Great Expectations.* Stepping Stone series. New York: Random House, 1996.

Adapted to a second- to third-grade reading level.

Dickens, Charles, Les Martin, and Jean Zallinger. *Oliver Twist.* Stepping Stone series. New York: Random House, 1990.

Adapted to a second- to third-grade reading level.

Edward Lear, the nonsense poems
Christina Rossetti, children's poems
Lewis Carroll, *Alice in Wonderland* and *Through the Looking-Glass*

Mark Twain, all the stories

Twain, Mark, and Deidre S. Laikin. *The Adventures of Tom Sawyer: Great Illustrated Classics.* Edina, Minn.: Abdo Publishing Company, 2002.

Adapted to a third- to fourth-grade reading level.

James Fenimore Cooper, all the novels

Jules Verne, all the novels

Verne, Jules, and Judith Conaway. *20,000 Leagues Under the Sea.* Illus. Gino D'Achille. Stepping Stone series. New York: Random House, 1983.

Norwegian folktales

Asbjrnsen, Peter, et al. *Norwegian Folk Tales.* New York: Pantheon, 1982.

This book is an affordable version of the original 1849 collection.

Herman Melville, *Moby-Dick*

Melville, Herman, and Allan Drummond. *Moby Dick.* New York: Farrar, Straus, & Giroux, 1997.

An abridged, illustrated telling that uses lines from the novel itself.

Modern, 1850–Present (Fourth Grade)

Tell the children's librarian at your local library that you're looking for classic literature from 1850 to the present, on your child's reading level, and follow up on his or her suggestions. (Librarians may differ in their ideas about what's suitable for fourth graders, so glance through all the recommendations.) We also suggest the following (work through these books and authors in the following order).

Stories and poems by, about, or from . . .

Robert Louis Stevenson, all the novels

Stevenson, Robert Louis. *A Child's Garden of Verses.* Illus. Tasha Tudor. Rev. ed. New York: Simon & Schuster, 1999.

Stevenson, Robert Louis. *Kidnapped.* Narrated by John Sessions. Franklin, Tenn.: Naxos Audiobooks, 1997.

Although this is an abridged audiobook, *Kidnapped* can be difficult to follow, and this version is worth checking out; it makes the storyline clear, and Sessions is a wonderful narrator.

Arthur Conan Doyle

Doyle, Sir Arthur Conan, and Judith Conaway. *Mysteries of Sherlock Holmes.* Stepping Stone series. New York: Random House, 1982.

Adapted to a second- to third-grade reading level.

Johanna Spyri, *Heidi*

Carlo Collodi, *Pinocchio*

Collodi, Carlo. *The Adventures of Pinocchio: Story of a Puppet.* Illus. Robert Ingpen. New York: Purple Bear Books, 2005.

Avoid the Disney version, which changes both the plot and the original moral message of the story.

H. G. Wells, all the novels

Wells, H. G., and Malvina G. Vogel. *War of the Worlds: Great Illustrated Classics.* Edina, Minn.: Abdo Publishing Company, 2005.

Adapted to a third- to fourth-grade reading level.

Louisa May Alcott, all the novels

Andrew Lang, collected tales

Lang, Andrew. *The Blue Fairy Book.* New York: Dover, 1965.

———. *The Orange Fairy Book*. New York: Dover, 1968.
———. *The Lilac Fairy Book*. New York: Dover, 1968.

Frances Hodgson Burnett, all the novels

Kenneth Grahame, *The Wind in the Willows*
Grahame, Kenneth. *The Wind in the Willows*. New York: Signet Classics, 2006.

James Barrie, *Peter Pan* and all the plays
Barrie, James, and Cathy East Dubowski. *Peter Pan*. Illus. Jean Zallinger. Stepping Stone series. New York: Random House, 1991.
Adapted to a second- to third-grade reading level.

Rudyard Kipling, *Just So Stories* and *The Jungle Books*
Kipling, Rudyard. *How the Camel Got His Hump*. Illus. Lisbeth Zwerger. New York: North South Books, 2003.
A picture-book retelling.

———. *The Jungle Book*. Illus. Robert Ingpen. Bath, U.K.: Palazzo Editions, 2007.

———. *Rikki-Tikki-Tavi*. Illus. Lambert Davis. New York: Harcourt, 1992.
A picture-book retelling.

Beatrix Potter, all the stories
Laura Ingalls Wilder, all the novels
Walter de la Mare, collected poems
Carl Sandburg, collected poems

John Ciardi, collected poems
Ciardi, John. *You Read to Me, I'll Read to You*. Illus. Edward Gorey. New York: HarperTrophy, 1987.
Order from Greenleaf Press. An award-winning book of poetry designed for parents and children to read to each other.

T. S. Eliot, *Old Possum's Book of Practical Cats*

Recordings to Supplement Readings

Storyteller Jim Weiss retells classic stories for children and sells them through Greathall Productions. These audiotapes and compact discs are wonderful listening; they won't replace reading, but they will serve as a valuable supplement. You can order them from Greathall Productions. Many libraries also stock them. The list below is only partial; visit Greathall Productions at www.greathall.com for a full list. Very highly recommended for building knowledge of the classics and improving general literacy! Titles include:

Arabian Nights.
A Christmas Carol and Other Favorites.
Greek Myths.
The Jungle Book.
King Arthur and His Knights.
Rip Van Winkle/Gulliver's Travels.
Shakespeare for Children.
She and He: Adventures in Mythology.
Sherlock Holmes for Children.
Tales from Cultures Far and Near.
Tales from the Old Testament.
Three Musketeers/Robin Hood.

Imaginative Reading

There are hundreds of good books and collections of poetry available to a child who is reading on a first- through fourth-grade level. The children's librarian at your local library or the children's books manager at a larger bookstore can direct you toward award-winning stories, novels, and poetry on your child's reading level. Also consider the following resources:

Hirsch, E. D., Jr., and John Holdren. *Books to Build On: A Grade-By-Grade Resource Guide for Parents and Teachers.* New York: Delta, 1996.
Recommended titles divided by curricular areas: language arts, history, visual arts, music, science, math.

Lipson, Eden Ross. *The New York Times Parent's Guide to the Best Books for Children.* 3d ed. New York: Three Rivers Press, 2000.
An annotated list of books in six age ranges, from "wordless books" for babies all the way up to young adults.

Perfection Books Catalog, Grades PreK–8. Logan, Iowa: Perfection Learning Corporation.

This catalog lists literally hundreds of children's titles on all subjects and provides short descriptions. Readers on all levels, fairy tales and fables, stories of ancient times, stories of other nations, poetry, science titles, biographies, Newbery and Caldecott winners, and even audio books, all coded for reading level and interest level. You'll use this catalog as a resource for finding titles and as a source for placing orders. Visit them at www.perfectionlearning.com, or call 800-831-4190, tell them you're teaching your child at home, and ask for a catalog.

Wilson, Elizabeth L., and Susan Schaeffer Macaulay. *Books Children Love: A Guide to the Best Children's Literature*. Wheaton, Ill.: Crossway Books, 2002.

Oral Reading

McGuffey, William Holmes. *Eclectic Reader.* New York: John Wiley, 1997.
$10.95 each. Order from any bookstore.

McGuffey's Third Eclectic Reader.
McGuffey's Fourth Eclectic Reader.
McGuffey's Fifth Eclectic Reader.
McGuffey's Sixth Eclectic Reader.

Writing

Bauer, Susan Wise. *The Complete Writer*. Charles City, Va.: Peace Hill Press, 2008.

Order from Peace Hill Press.

Writing with Ease: Strong Fundamentals. $29.95.
Level 1 Workbook for Writing with Ease. $34.95.
Level 2 Workbook for Writing with Ease. $34.95.
Level 3 Workbook for Writing with Ease. $36.95.
Level 4 Workbook for Writing with Ease. $36.95.

Institute for Excellence in Writing series. Atascadero, Calif.: Institute for Excellence in Writing.

Order from IEW.

Teaching Writing: Structure and Style. $169.00.

Video seminar instructs parents on how to teach writing. The package includes 10 DVDs and a workbook/syllabus.

Student Writing Intensive, Level A. $99.00.

Optional DVD seminar directed at the student.

Olsen, Jan Z. Handwriting Without Tears program, rev. ed. Cabin John, Md.: Handwriting Without Tears.

Order from Handwriting Without Tears. The books below are listed in progressive order.

My Printing Book (First grade). $6.35.

1st Grade Printing Teacher's Guide. $6.35.

Printing Power (Second grade). $6.35.

2nd Grade Printing Teacher's Guide. $6.35.

Cursive Handwriting (Third grade). $6.35.

3rd Grade Cursive Teacher's Guide. $6.35.

Cursive Success (Fourth grade). $6.35.

4th Grade Cursive Teacher's Guide. $6.35.

Double Line Notebook Paper. Designed specifically to go along with the skills taught in this program.

Regular (2–3). 100 sheets. $2.95.

Regular (2–3). 500 sheets. $10.00.

Narrow (4+). 100 sheets. $2.95.

Narrow (4+). 500 sheets. $10.00.

Writing Strands: Challenging Writing Programs for Homeschoolers series. Niles, Mich.: National Writing Institute, revised edition.

The Writing Strands program can be purchased directly from the National Writing Institute or, at a small discount, from Rainbow Resource Center. The books aren't consumable; you do all the assignments on notebook paper, so you can reuse these books for another child.

Writing Strands 2. $20.00.

Writing Strands 3. $20.00.

Writing Strands 4. $20.00.

Writing Strands 5. $20.00.

Zaner-Bloser Handwriting series. Columbus, Ohio: Zaner-Bloser, 2008.

$10.69 each. Order from Zaner-Bloser. This is the Zaner-Bloser continuous-stroke alphabet method. See Chapter 4, Resources, for the first two books in the series (Grades K–1).

Handwriting: Grade 2C Student Book.

This book provides the transition into cursive writing. Use for second or third grade.

Handwriting: Grade 3 Student Book.

More practice in cursive writing.

Handwriting: Grade 4 Student Book.

Handwriting: Grade 5 Student Book.

Handwriting: Grade 6 Student Book.

Zaner-Bloser Handwriting Paper.

$8.99 per ream except for Grade 5 paper. Order these packs of writing paper for extra handwriting practice from Zaner-Bloser. A typical student uses one ream of writing paper per year. The ruled lines on these sheets narrow each year. See Chapter 4, Resources, for K–1 paper.

Grade 2 paper (½" wide).

Grade 3 paper (½" wide).

Grade 4 paper (⅜" wide).

Grade 5 paper (⅜" wide without red baseline), $11.99.

6

THE JOY OF NUMBERS: MATH

Let no one ignorant of mathematics enter here.
—Plato (inscription written over the entrance to the Academy)

SUBJECT: Elementary mathematics
TIME REQUIRED: 30–60 minutes per day

The four years of elementary math—first through fourth grade—lay the foundation for the high-level abstract thinking required by algebra, trigonometry, and calculus later on. And foundation laying is what the grammar stage is all about.

The job of laying a mathematical foundation should be taken seriously. Basic mathematics—the skills of addition and subtraction, multiplication and division, the knowledge of basic geometrical shapes and patterns, the ability to think through word problems, a firm grasp of the relationships between numbers—is as vital to high-level mathematical achievement as an understanding of punctuation and sentence structure is to high-level language use.

In fact, mathematics *is* a language because it uses symbols and phrases to represent abstract realities. For most children, it's a foreign language because they don't grow up hearing it all around them.

Before a child can master the much touted "higher-level thinking skills" so necessary to mathematics, she must learn the language of mathematics. Higher-level thinking skills can never be substituted for mathematical literacy; rather, those thinking skills are dependent on the child's knowledge of basic mathematical operations. In this chapter, we'll explain how to make your grammar-stage student mathematically literate so that she can master those higher-level thinking skills when the time is right.

THE WAY CHILDREN THINK

As you teach math to your first grader, you'll use the same process we described in the language chapter. When you taught the child to write, the first step was to put a concrete model—a written word or sentence—in front of the child so that she could copy it. Only when she mastered copying did you take away the concrete model and ask her to write from dictation. Only after copying from a written model was she able to form a mental picture of the spoken sentence.

This first step is necessary because young children tend to think in concrete terms. They don't do mathematical operations in their heads; if you ask a first grader to add 3 and 2, she'll look around for spoons, fingers, apples, or pennies to count so that she can find the answer. Just as you asked the beginning writer to copy a visible model, you'll ask the beginning mathematician to do arithmetic using "manipulatives"—objects that she can see, touch, and move around.

Math companies sell boxed manipulatives (see Resources at the end of this chapter), but you can also use beans, pennies, blocks, or chocolate chips. Toothpicks work well when you get to place value—you can move a bundle of 10 toothpicks from the 1s column to the 10s column to illustrate adding two-digit numbers, or you can break the bundles open to illustrate "borrowing." Every time you teach a new math skill, have the child work the problems out with real objects until the concept makes sense to her.

YOU: Put these three beans in one pile. Put these two beans in another pile. Now push them together. That's addition. How many do you have?

CHILD: *(Carefully counts the beans.)* Five.

Or . . .

YOU: Let's add thirty-six and twenty-seven. For thirty-six, we have three bundles of ten toothpicks—that's thirty—plus six extra toothpicks. For twenty-seven we have two bundles of ten, plus seven extra. How many bundles of toothpicks do we have?

CHILD: *(Counts the bundles.)* Five.

YOU: How many is that all together?

CHILD: Fifty.

YOU: That's the number that goes in the tens column. How many ones—single toothpicks—do we have?

CHILD: *(Groups the six toothpicks with the seven.)* Thirteen.

YOU: Can we write that in the ones column? No, because it won't fit. Where can we put the extra toothpicks?

(The child sees that she can bundle together ten of the thirteen and put them with the five bundles she already has. Now she has six groups of ten and three left over—sixty-three in all. She's just learned how to carry.)

Even older children may revert to this mode when learning a new skill; fractions, for example, may require division of an apple pie before they make sense.

When the concept is mastered on this concrete level, it is time to move on to mental arithmetic, where the child can picture the items in her mind instead of having actual apples, pennies, beans, or toothpicks in front of her.[1] Mental arithmetic requires abstract thinking because numerals now stand for concrete objects: 3 and 2 represent 3 beans and 2 beans; the number 27 represents 2 bundles plus 7 single toothpicks. But don't push the child to dispense with her manipulatives until she's ready. Children's minds mature at different rates; if you require a child to do addition with

[1]Educators refer to this as moving from the *manipulative* or *preoperational* stage to the *mental image* or *concrete operational* stage.

numerals alone (no objects) before she's ready, the result will be math frustration.

Children aged 5 through 7 usually need concrete objects; children aged 8 through 10 shift into "mental image" mode. Ask a five year old how many people are in her family, and she'll turn around and count everyone present. Ask an eight year old the same question, and you'll see her summon a mental image of each person to mind and count the images: "Me, Mom, Dad, Jeremy. That's four."

True abstract thinking—the ability to use the symbols $5 + 7$ or 27×2 without using or picturing concrete objects—is the third stage of mental development. Abstract thinking begins around age nine or ten, which coincides with the beginning of the logic stage. And the logic stage is the time to teach "higher-order critical thinking skills."

The goal of early elementary mathematics is to move the child from manipulating real objects to picturing those objects mentally. You achieve this through lots of practice with real objects. In later elementary mathematics (third or fourth grade), you'll begin to nudge the child, through much repetition, toward early symbolic thinking so that she can use written numbers and understand what those numbers represent.

You can't force a child to develop abstract thinking. Instead, lay the foundation for it with practice. You've got four years to get there. Take your time, and the child will have a strong foundation on which to build those higher-order skills.[2]

MATH TABLES: A DEFENSE

We think that the memorization of mathematical facts—addition and subtraction facts, the multiplication and division tables—is essential in building a strong foundation. We feel that much of the protest over learning the math tables by rote arose because children were being taught to skip that

[2]The concept of "higher-order skills" may seem to imply that "lower-order skills" (such as the knowledge of addition or division facts) are somehow inferior, less important, or unnecessary. But "higher" simply means "coming after." The tenth story of a building is "higher" than the foundation, but no one would argue that the foundation is less important simply because it is "lower."

important mental-image step of thinking. If a child goes straight from manipulative mode to symbolic mode, the symbols $2 + 4 = 6$ don't mean anything to her. She's never practiced them with beans. If she's forced to memorize a whole sheet of these meaningless symbols ($2 + 1 = 3$, $2 + 2 = 4$, $2 + 3 = 5$), she's memorizing gobbledygook. That's rote learning at its worst, and, of course, it isn't productive.

But after you've practiced addition with manipulatives (2 beans and 1 bean equal 3 beans, 2 beans and 2 beans equal 4 beans, 2 beans and 3 beans equal 5 beans) and then practiced these same sums with imaginary beans, the child understands the concept of addition. At this point, the memorization of the math tables reinforces and strengthens the concept that the child comprehends.

The memory work also moves the child's mind toward abstract, symbolic thinking. Thorough knowledge of math facts leads to an instinctive understanding of math relationships. Consider, for example, the 9 times table:

$9 \times 2 = 18$
$9 \times 3 = 27$
$9 \times 4 = 36$
$9 \times 5 = 45$
$9 \times 6 = 54$

When you multiply a number by 9, the first digit of the resulting number is always one less than the number you began with:

$9 \times 2 = 1\_$
$9 \times 3 = 2\_$
$9 \times 4 = 3\_$
$9 \times 5 = 4\_$
$9 \times 6 = 5\_$

And the second digit of the resulting number, when added to the first digit, always adds up to 9.

$9 \times 2 = 18$ $(1 + 8 = 9)$
$9 \times 3 = 27$ $(2 + 7 = 9)$
$9 \times 4 = 36$ $(3 + 6 = 9)$

$9 \times 5 = 45$ $(4 + 5 = 9)$
$9 \times 6 = 54$ $(5 + 4 = 9)$

This little mental trick for remembering the 9 times table also reveals an important mathematical relationship: because 9 is 1 less than 10, multiplying a number (like 6) by 9 will never produce a number that has a 6 in the 10s column:

$$\begin{array}{r} 6 \\ \times\, 9 \\ \hline 54 \end{array} \qquad \begin{array}{r} 6 \\ \times\, 10 \\ \hline 60 \end{array}$$

There's also a practical aspect to math-facts memorization: math facts protect you from being suckered. Yes, you could carry a calculator around with you all the time to compute grocery prices, taxi tips, and the totals of restaurant meals. Most people don't. It's much easier to memorize the math facts in grades 1 through 4, when the mind is naturally receptive.

Mastering basic facts now lays the foundation for true understanding later on. One of Jessie's eighth-grade relatives goes to a well-regarded private school nearby. Instead of being required to memorize his math facts, he has been allowed to use a calculator for math since a very early grade. He's now doing algebra. He can work rote problems—problems that exactly follow the pattern in the textbook—but he lacks a true understanding of basic mathematical relationships. When more difficult or innovative problems appear, he's helpless. The machine has done his computation for too many years.

This leads us to a firm principle of elementary mathematics: *no calculators.* No child who has not already memorized her mathematical facts should be allowed to use a calculator. We recommend the use of calculators beginning in seventh grade and not before.

HOW TO DO IT

We've found several different math curricula that are both rigorous and systematic, introducing new concepts only after earlier ones have been thoroughly mastered. No math system is perfect, but we recommend that you choose one of the following.

Saxon Math

Saxon—which originally created material for classroom use—now sells *Home Study Kits* that contain student workbooks, a teacher's manual that explains the concepts to the parent and tells her/him how best to teach them, and something called the *Daily Meeting Book*, which takes the parent through practical skills like measuring, telling time, reading charts, and so on. Saxon Math has plenty of activities as well: playing story, measuring rooms, graphing the ages of everyone the child knows, and so on.

The *Home Study Kits* are expensive but complete—well worth the cost. Saxon also provides help via an 800 number and website. The manuals recommend that the young child study math for short periods twice per day: for the first session, explain the concept using manipulatives, and complete one side of a work sheet; later in the day, have the child review the material by completing the other side of the sheet. Many home schoolers (Susan included) find one session per day (and one side of the work sheet) to be plenty, though. You don't have to buy the manipulative kit sold separately. But if you don't, be sure to read ahead so that you can prepare; the lessons are often structured around a particular type of manipulative.

Saxon Math is graded K, 1, 2, and 3 for kindergarten through third-grade students. After third grade, the textbooks switch to "skill level" rather than "grade level." Thus, Math 3 is followed by Math 5/4, which is for advanced fourth graders who have finished the Math 3 book or for average fifth graders who took two years to get through the Math 3 book. The second digit is for quick workers; the first is supposed to represent the "average" student level. Math 5/4 is followed by 6/5, 7/6, 8/7 (general math for those who need extra practice), and then Algebra 1/2 (see Chapter 5). Ideally, you go from Math 7/6 straight to Algebra 1/2.

Saxon works only if you (the parent) take the job of teaching it seriously. It is not a self-teaching program. You *must* explain the concepts thoroughly, or the child will be confused—the text alone won't do the job. Parents who are not seriously math-phobic can teach Saxon math successfully.

Math-U-See

This program takes a very different approach; it is suited to parents who are intimidated by the idea of teaching math, and to children who are very hands-on or visual in their learning styles. The Math-U-See program is based on a series of teaching videos in which concepts are demonstrated using manipulatives; the student also works with these manipulatives when completing workbook exercises.

Rather than providing grade-by-grade texts, the Math-U-See Elementary Curriculum is divided into levels. The *Primer* level, for preschool and kindergarten, can probably be skipped by most students unless you feel a gentle introduction to formal math is necessary. Otherwise, progress through the six books of the Elementary Curriculum in order: *Alpha* (single-digit addition and subtraction), *Beta* (multiple-digit addition and subtraction), *Gamma* (multiplication), *Delta* (division), *Epsilon* (fractions), and *Zeta* (decimals and percentages). This progression will take you through fifth or sixth grade. (This description reflects the 2004 revision of the Math-U-See program; if you buy secondhand materials published in 2003 or before, you'll find the curriculum divided into *Foundations of Mathematics,* which covers first-, second-, and third-grade material, and *Intermediate Mathematics,* which covers fourth, fifth, and sixth grades.)

Each level includes DVDs or videos, a student text and teacher manual, a test booklet, manipulatives, and various memory aids. Be sure that you purchase additional practice sheets if necessary, so that students will have plenty of opportunity to solidify their knowledge of the math facts.

A Beka Math

A Beka Book, a long-time publisher of home-school materials, supplies a very comprehensive math program. A Beka's general philosophy is to review previously taught concepts over and over again. A student who's been through A Beka math *knows* math.

The downside of A Beka is that the books provide too much drill. You'll want to pick and choose among the problems so that the child won't be overwhelmed. Since A Beka is a conservative Christian publisher, an occasional Bible verse crops up at the bottom of the workbooks' pages, along with quotes from Jefferson, Franklin, Milton, and others.

Developmental Math

Another option, less "classroom" in feel, is the Developmental Math program published by Mathematics Programs Associates. This set of twenty workbooks begins with counting and ends with Algebra 2. It is much less complicated than the other programs listed in this chapter, and the child works at her own pace instead of sticking to a daily lesson plan.

The drawback to this program is that, although it is sold as a complete math system, there is very little drill and problem solving. Once you do the workbook page, you're finished. It seems to us that Developmental Math is best used along with another program; it would be an excellent choice for a child who attends regular school but is struggling and in need of supplemental work. Because the books are divided by skill and are affordable, you could also use them for extra work in a particular area where a student simply needs much more practice.

Singapore Primary Math

A relatively recent import to America, Singapore Math is the program used in Singapore's schools. The program has become popular here in large part because of the high scores earned by Singapore's children on international math tests. Singapore Math is also attractive because its focus is on teaching mathematical thinking from the very beginning; "mental math" puzzles are assigned as soon as children learn to count. Because the goal of the Singapore program is to produce an understanding of the way mathematical processes work, skills are introduced differently than in American programs. Multiplication and division are begun very early (right at the beginning of second grade), so that the student is aware of the relationship between multiplication/addition and subtraction/division.

Each semester of the Singapore Primary Math program (for grades K–6) consists of one course book and two workbooks. The books are colorful, with cartoon-like illustrations and pictures showing each new concept worked out with actual objects (very important for grammar-stage students). The accompanying workbooks are consumable.

Singapore is not as concrete and fact-oriented as Saxon, A Beka, or Math-U-See. Many children flourish with it, but others simply need a less abstract approach in the early years. The Singapore method leads children into "logic stage" thinking much earlier than other programs. If you try Singapore and your child is frustrated, this may signal a maturity gap; stick with another program for a couple of additional years. There are no manipulatives; parents using this program will need to supply their own so that young students can do some hands-on working out of the problems. Also, remember that this program produces high marks in Singapore because it is part of a math-oriented culture that provides plenty of additional reinforcement. The coursebooks and workbooks alone do not provide enough practice; invest in the additional resources the program offers, such as the *Extra Practice* and *Challenging Word Problems* books.

Calvert Math

The Calvert Math program, offered as an independent correspondence course (Calvert's other programs are part of their entire grade package), is a solid traditional mathematics course for grades 1–8. Taking it by correspondence provides you with daily lesson plans and good teacher support from Calvert tutors (the "Advisory Teaching Service"). Calvert also supplies all manipulatives and supplies, along with tests and quizzes; Calvert awards the grade and keeps an official transcript.

If you feel that you need additional help to teach math, as well as grading support, this program is a very good choice that will build excellent math understanding.

Right Start Math

Right Start Math is a hands-on program based on Montessori principles. The program, which makes heavy use of an abacus and manipulatives and deemphasies worksheets, is well designed for students who struggle with fine motor skills; learning is not tied to the student's ability to write multiple sets of numbers.

The elementary program is divided into levels, not grades; Level A is preliminary, kindergarten-type preparation, and most first-grade students can progress directly into Level B. The Right Start website, wwww.alabacus.com, provides a placement test. Completion of Levels B through E should bring the student to the end of fourth grade; see Chapter 15, page 255, for thoughts about the transition out of Right Start into another math program.

Other Useful (Fun) Stuff

For an entirely different approach to math, consider investing in the Life of Fred series to complement your math course. Written by teacher Stanley

Schmidt, the series provides a *narrative* survey of mathematics. It is entertaining and highly nontraditional, and it can help the student avoid the math doldrums (that period of time after the first excitement of "doing school" wears off, when math lessons can easily become repeated drill sessions with no end in sight). You can begin the first Life of Fred volume, *Fractions*, as soon as the student has gotten through long division—usually sometime between third and fifth grade. The series gives even young students the opportunity to look at mathematics from another angle, and to think again about *why* numbers work as they do.

In the Resources section at the end of this chapter, we have listed several tools that can be used with any program: math games; the Times Tales memory system, a nontraditional method for mastering the multiplication tables; Fraction Stax, a particularly useful manipulative tool for learning fractions; Math on the Level activity books, which provide extra practice in money and decimals, measurements, and other topics; and a few more. We also highly recommend the website LivingMath.net, established by a home educator who dislikes the way that traditional curricula "isolate" math learning from all other subjects. Here, you can find multiple reviews of many different math programs, games, teaching ideas, a forum, and much more.

CHOOSING PROGRAMS

Pick a program, and start on it. If the child thrives, stick with it; if she doesn't do well, switch to another program. Sometimes a child's mind simply is not in sync with a particular math program. She may flounder with Saxon and sail through A Beka or vice versa.

Once you find a workable program, though, try to stick with it. All math programs build on what's been taught the year before. The more often you change systems, the more chances you have to confuse the student.

Many parents agonize over choosing the correct math program. But each of the math programs we list here is a good choice. Choosing a math program shouldn't cause you to stay awake at night.

If your child cries when you bring out the math book, switch programs, no matter how good everyone else tells you the program is. If your child is flourishing, stick with the program, even if everyone else in your home school support group switches to something else.

If you want to check that your child *understands* what she's learning (rather than simply doing it by formula, with no comprehension of the principles involved), simply take a lesson or two from another math program and ask her to complete it. (Developmental Math and Singapore Math, both fairly inexpensive, are good for this purpose.) Make sure you pick lessons that involve material the child has covered several months before, since it takes time for math concepts to "sink in." If the child can do lessons from another program, she's understanding her work; she is able to take concepts from one program and transfer them to another. If she seems lost, she may be learning by formula—figuring out how to "plug in" answers that a particular math program requires, without really knowing why. If this happens, try another program.

SCHEDULES

Math is best done daily, especially in the early grades. (And most home schoolers schedule math first thing in the morning.) A typical school year is 36 weeks, or 180 days, although you can arrange your school year to fit your family situation (see Chapter 38 for more details). Count the lessons in whichever curriculum you've chosen. Then decide if you want to do math five days a week or four days a week (saving one day for field trips or library visits).

The Saxon first-grade home-study kit, for example, has 130 lessons, which means that you can do four lessons per week and save a day for something else, or four lessons per week with the option of doing a lesson or two over two days (some of the lessons are longer than others), or five lessons per week and take a week off from math now and then. When Susan's oldest was in first grade, he loved the playing-store lessons, so we would stretch those over a couple of days. We also took a week off from math now and then and did some special history or science project: building a model of the Great Wall of China; assembling a nature notebook; planting a flower garden; going to the science museum.

Remember, in first and second grades especially, you won't want to take more than a week off at a time from math. Unfamiliar math concepts are easily forgotten.

Sample Schedules

	First Grade	
30–40 minutes per day	M, T, W, TH	Math lesson
	F	Project/library day
	Second Grade	
40–60 minutes per day	M, T, W, TH	Math lesson
	F	Project/library day
	Third Grade	
40–60 minutes per day	M, T, W, TH	Math lesson
	F	Project/library day
	Fourth Grade	
40–60 minutes per day	M, T, W, TH	Math lesson
	F	Project/library day

RESOURCES

For publisher and catalog addresses, telephone numbers, and other information, see Sources (pages 751–778). We suggest that you contact these publishers of math materials and examine their catalogs closely before deciding on a curriculum. Most will aid you in assigning your child to the appropriate level.

Math Curricula

A Beka Book Traditional Arithmetic series. Pensacola, Fla.: A Beka Book. Order from A Beka Book. A Beka Book also offers a wide range of mathematics teaching aids. Ask for a copy of their Home School Catalog.

Arithmetic 1. $13.25.

Arithmetic 1 Teacher Edition. $22.25.

Student Speed Drills and Tests. $5.25.

Teacher Speed Drills/Test Key. $9.65.

Arithmetic 2. $13.25.

Arithmetic 2 Teacher Edition. $22.25.
Student Speed Drills and Tests. $5.25.
Teacher Speed Drills/Test Key. $9.65.
Arithmetic 3. $13.25.
Arithmetic 3 Answer Key. $18.95.
Student Speed Drills and Tests. $5.25.
Teacher Speed Drills/Test Key. $9.65.
Arithmetic 4. $13.25.
Arithmetic 4 Teacher Key. $22.25.
Student Speed Drills and Tests. $5.25.
Teacher Speed Drills/Test Key. $9.65.

Calvert Math. Baltimore, MD: The Calvert School.
$125.00 per course. Order directly from Calvert. Each math course includes a textbook, a workbook, and a lesson manual to help you administer the lessons. Manipulatives are additional.
Calvert Math Grade 1.
Calvert Math Grade 2.
Calvert Math Grade 3.
Calvert Math Grade 4.

Developmental Mathematics: A Self-Teaching Program. Halesite, N.Y.: Mathematics Programs Associates.
Each level includes a workbook and teacher's edition and costs $14.00. Buy from Mathematics Programs Associates, or at a small discount from Rainbow Resource Center. A full description of the twenty levels available can be obtained by calling 631-643-9300 or visiting www.greatpyramid.com.
Level 1. Ones: Concepts and Symbols.
Level 2. Ones: Addition Concepts and Basic Facts.
Level 3. Ones: Subtraction Concepts and Basic Facts.
Level 4. Tens Concept: Addition and Subtraction of Tens.
Level 5. Two-Digit Numbers: Addition and Subtraction without Regrouping.
Level 6. Tens & Ones: Adding and Grouping.
Level 7. Tens & Ones: Subtracting with Exchange.
Level 8. Multiplication: Concepts and Facts.
Level 9. Division: Concepts and Facts.

Level 10. Hundreds and Three-Unit Numbers: Concepts, Addition and Subtraction Skills.

Level 11. Three-Unit Numbers: Multiplication and Division Skills.

Level 12. Thousands and Large Numbers: Concepts and Skills.

Level 13. Decimals, Fractions, and the Metric System: Concepts and Basic Skills.

Level 14. Fractions: Concepts and Skills.

Level 15. Fractions: Advanced Skills.

Math-U-See.

This program has a number of different levels and workbook/video/manipulative combinations. For prices, explanatory material, and brochures, call the Math-U-See national number (888-854-6284; 800-255-6654 from Canada), which will transfer you to a local representative; or visit the website at www.mathusee.com. Teacher kits include a manual and the instruction video or DVD; student kits include text and test booklet.

Manipulative Blocks. $30. These are necessary for all levels.

Primer (preschool and kindergarten).

Teacher Kit. $25.00.

Student Kit. $15.00.

Alpha (single-digit addition and subtraction).

Teacher Kit. $35.00.

Student Kit. $20.00.

Beta (multiple-digit addition and subtraction).

Teacher Kit. $35.00.

Student Kit. $20.00.

Gamma (multiplication).

Teacher Kit. $35.00.

Student Kit. $20.00.

Delta (division).

Teacher Kit. $35.00.

Student Kit. $20.00.

Epsilon (fractions).

Teacher Kit. $35.00.

Student Kit. $20.00.

Fraction Overlays. $30.00.

Zeta (decimals and percentages).
Teacher Kit. $35.00.
Student Kit. $20.00.
Algebra/Decimal Inserts. $20.00.

Right Start Mathematics. Hazelton, N.D.: Activities for Learning, Inc.
Order from Right Start Mathematics. Like Math-U-See, this program sells different combinations of manipulatives, worksheets, and instructor's manuals. Visit the Right Start website at www.alabacus.com to see all options; the kits listed below contain the essentials.
Level A Starter Kit (optional). $129.00.
Level B Starter Kit. $186.50.
Level C Starter Kit. $225.50.
Level D Starter Kit. $219.00.
Level E Starter Kit. $214.00.

Saxon Homeschool Mathematics. Orlando, Fla.: Harcourt Achieve.
Order from Saxon. The Saxon home study catalogs include a diagnostic test to help you with placement. Request a catalog and test from Saxon Publishers at 800-284-7019, or visit their website at www.saxonhomeschool.harcourtachieve.com.
Homeschool Math 1. $96.50.
Homeschool Math 2. $96.50.
Homeschool Math 3. $96.50.
Homeschool Math Manipulative Kit. $69.50.
Contains all manipulatives required for K–3.
Homeschool Math 5/4. $75.50.
For fourth-grade students.

Singapore Math, U.S. edition.
$8.70 for each textbook and workbook. Singapore Math workbooks and textbooks can be ordered from Singapore Math (an independent dealer, not the program publisher), or from Rainbow Resource Center. The U.S. edition uses American weights and money (the previous edition for sale in the U.S. did not). These prices are for the U.S. editions.
Primary Math Textbook 1A.
Primary Math Workbook 1A.

Primary Math Home Instructor's Guide 1A. $16.50.
Primary Math Textbook 1B.
Primary Math Workbook 1B.
Primary Math Home Instructor's Guide 1B. $16.50.
Primary Math Textbook 2A.
Primary Math Workbook 2A.
Primary Math Home Instructor's Guide 2A. $16.50.
Primary Math Textbook 2B.
Primary Math Workbook 2B.
Primary Math Home Instructor's Guide 2B. $16.50.
Primary Math Textbook 3A.
Primary Math Workbook 3A.
Primary Math Home Instructor's Guide 3A. $16.50.
Primary Math Textbook 3B.
Primary Math Workbook 3B.
Primary Math Home Instructor's Guide 3B. $16.50.
Primary Math Textbook 4A.
Primary Math Workbook 4A.
Primary Math Home Instructor's Guide 4A. $16.50.
Primary Math Textbook 4B.
Primary Math Workbook 4B.
Primary Math Home Instructor's Guide 4B. $16.50.
Extra Practice for Primary Math 1. $14.50.
Extra Practice for Primary Math 2. $14.50.
Extra Practice for Primary Math 3. $7.80.
Extra Practice for Primary Math 4. $7.80.
Challenging Word Problems 2. $8.20.
Challenging Word Problems 3. $8.20.
Challenging Word Problems 4. $8.20.

Other Useful (Fun) Stuff

Audio Memory Songs. Newport Beach, Calif.: Audio Memory. $9.95 each for cassette, $12.95 for CD; each includes a workbook. Order from AudioMemory. These tapes and CDs contain the addition, subtraction, multiplication, and division facts, put to music. Play them in the car, and learn all your math facts.

Addition Songs.
Subtraction Songs.
Multiplication Songs.
Division Songs.

Fraction Stax.
$22.99. Order from School Specialty Publishing. 51 stacking pieces allow the student to form halves, thirds, fourths, fifths, sixths, eighths, tenths, and twelfths.

Learning Wrap-Ups.
$8.99 each. Order from The Book Peddler. As you go through the facts printed on the front of each card, wrap the attached string through the notches of the correct answers to form a pattern.
Addition.
Division.
Fractions.
Multiplication.
Subtraction.

Life of Fred. Reno, Nev.: Polka Dot Publishing.
Order from Polka Dot Publishing. You can begin the Life of Fred series as soon as the student has begun long division.
Fraction. $19.00.
Decimals and Percents. $19.00.

Math on the Level.
Order from Math on the Level. Each book covers a different topic with plenty of hands-on work and practical application. Note that this is sold as its own complete curriculum; it is a new program, so it is untested as a full math program.
Operations. $90. A parent guide to teaching the major K–8 topics.
Geometry and Measurements. $65.
Money and Decimals. $50.
Fractions. $65.00
Math Adventures. $65.00. Math in daily life.
9's Down Math Facts: Addition and Subtraction. $45.00. Practice sheets.
9's Down Math Facts: Multiplication and Division. $45.00. Practice sheets.

Pizza Party.
$16.99. Order from School Specialty Publishing. A fun fractions game.

Times Tales Deluxe.
$19.95. Order from Trigger Memory Systems. A nontraditional memory system for the multiplication tables, based on pictures and a simple narrative.

Timed Math Drills.
$6.99 or $24.99 for all four. Order from Rainbow Resource Center. Each book has 28 pages of drill on a specific skill.
Addition.
Multiplication.
Subtraction.
Division.

7

SEVENTY CENTURIES IN FOUR YEARS: HISTORY AND GEOGRAPHY

The history of the world is but the biography of great men.

—Thomas Carlyle

SUBJECT: History and geography

TIME REQUIRED: An average of 3 hours per week, about 60 minutes per day, three days per week or 1½ hours per day, two days per week

Documentary filmmaker Ken Burns appeared at the National Press Club in early 1997 to plug his latest project (the life of Thomas Jefferson). Afterward, he took questions. One questioner pointed out that an astronomical percentage of high-school graduates saw no purpose in studying history and asked for a response.

Ken Burns answered: History is the study of everything that has happened until now. Unless you plan to live entirely in the present moment, the study of history is inevitable.

History, in other words, is not *a* subject. History is *the* subject. It is the record of human experience, both personal and communal. It is the story of the unfolding of human achievement in every area—science, literature, art, music, and politics. A grasp of historical facts is essential to the rest of the classical curriculum.

When you first introduce the elementary student to history, you must keep one central fact in mind: *history is a story.*

The logical way to tell a story is to begin (as the King said to Alice) at the beginning and go on till you come to the end. Any story makes less sense when learned in bits and pieces. If you were to tell your five year old the story of Hansel and Gretel, beginning with the house made of candy and cookies (because that's likely to be the most interesting part of the story to the child), then backing up and telling about the woodchopper's unfortunate second marriage, then skipping to the witch's demise, and then scooting backward again and relating the story of Hansel and Gretel's walk in the woods, the story isn't going to form a coherent whole in the child's mind. Even if he listens to the end, you may have lost him long before that.

History is no different. Yet it's too often taught unsystematically—as a series of unrelated bits and pieces: American history this year, ancient history the next, eighteenth-century France the year after that. Think back. By the time you graduated high school or college, you'd studied King Tut and the Trojan War and the Bronze Age; you probably learned about the end of the Athenian monarchy and the rise of the city-state; you may have been taught about the Exodus and the conquest under Joshua or the early history of Ethiopia. Chances are you studied these subjects in different years, in different units, out of different textbooks. You probably have difficulty fitting them together chronologically.

Furthermore, you probably started with American history (which is pretty near the end of the story as we know it) and then spent at least twice as much time studying American history as you did studying the rest of the world. Yes, American history is important for Americans, but this myopic division of the curriculum does the Founding Fathers a disservice. Children who plunge into the study of the American Revolution with no knowledge of the classical models used by Jefferson, Washington, and their colleagues can achieve only a partial understanding of American government and ideals. And American history ought to be kept in perspective: the history curriculum covers seventy centuries; America occupies only five of them.

A common assumption found in history curricula seems to be that children can't comprehend (or be interested in) people and events distant from their own experience. So the first-grade history class is renamed Social Studies and begins with what the child knows: first, himself and his family, followed by his community, his state, his country, and only then the rest of the world.

This intensely self-focused pattern of study encourages the student of history to relate everything he studies to himself, to measure the cultures and customs of other peoples against his own experience. And that's exactly what the classical education fights *against*—a self-absorbed, self-referential approach to knowledge. History learned this way makes *our* needs and wants the center of the human endeavor. This attitude is destructive at any time, but it is especially destructive in the present global civilization.

The goal of the classical curriculum is multicultural in the true sense of the word: the student learns the proper place of his community, his state, and his country by seeing the broad sweep of history from its beginning and then fitting his own time and place into that great landscape. The systematic study of history in the first four years lays the foundation for the logic stage, when the student will begin to understand the relationships between historical events—between Egypt and Greece, Greece and Rome, Rome and England, England and America.

From a practical point of view, starting the curriculum with ancient history makes sense. First graders are fascinated by ancient times—the mummies of Egypt, the myths of Greece, the great wars of Rome, the armies of China. The average first grader would much rather read about the embalming process than go on a field trip to his local center of government.

SEVENTY CENTURIES IN FOUR YEARS

Where's the text that supplies this comprehensive survey of history from its beginnings?

Well, there isn't one. The trivium in general steers away from "texts"—predigested historical facts, analyzed and reduced by someone else—and requires the student to tackle original sources. In the years to come, your history student will read Herodotus, not a textbook version of his histories; *The Federalist,* not a simplified explanation of the relationship between the states and the federal government.

Of course, students aren't reading at this level in first through fourth grades. But instead of limiting your elementary student to a text, you'll use a basic history survey to anchor your study. Armed with a library card, you'll study history using the fascinating, inventive, colorful history books published for young children.

Over the four years of the grammar stage, you'll progress from 5000 B.C. to the present, accumulating facts the whole way. These four years will be an exploration of the *stories* of history: great men and women of all kinds; battles and wars; important inventions; world religions; details of daily life and culture; and great books.

As a base text—a book that will serve as your "spine," or jumping-off point, for the study of history—you'll need a simple, chronological world history. We recommend *The Story of the World: History for the Classical Child,* a four-volume series written by Susan especially to provide a narrative story that connects events around the world in a way that grammar-stage children can grasp. You can supplement this "spine" with a grammar-stage reference book: *The Usborne Internet-Linked Encyclopedia of World History,* a colorful illustrated encyclopedia that contains illustrations, important dates, and additional information (as well as links to Internet resources that can supplement your history study). The *Usborne* encyclopedia is written on a third- to fifth-grade reading level; *The Story of the World* is designed to be read aloud to first and second graders, while many third-grade readers will be able to read it independently.

For the logic stage, you'll be using a more difficult text: the *Kingfisher History Encyclopedia.* If possible, buy this book now; the memorization assignments we suggest are neatly outlined in its appendix.

World history is divided into four segments, one segment per year of study. In first through fourth grades, the child will study history from 5000 B.C. through the present day. In fifth through eighth grades (the logic stage), he'll study it again, concentrating on cause-and-effect and chronological relationships. In grades 9 through 12, he'll repeat it yet again, this time studying original sources and writing thoughtful essays about them.

The classical method leans heavily on original sources. Because these increase as time goes on, the centuries aren't divided evenly among the four years of study (see the table). This breakdown, however, does allow for a fairly even division of labor from year to year. It takes notice of the fact that an immense amount of great literature was produced between the years 1600 and 1850, and that scientific discovery and technological changes accelerated at a tremendous rate between 1850 and the present day.

The Study of History

Period	**Years**	**Studied during grades . . .**
Ancients	5000 B.C.–A.D. 400 (5,400 years)	1, 5, 9
Medieval–early Renaissance	400–1600 (1,200 years)	2, 6, 10
Late Renaissance–early modern	1600–1850 (250 years)	3, 7, 11
Modern	1850–present (150 years)	4, 8, 12

WHAT IF YOU'RE STARTING IN THE MIDDLE?

If you're beginning to home-school a second or third grader, remember that history is a story and that you should usually start at the beginning. Most of the resources we recommend can be used and enjoyed by students between grades 1 and 6. No matter what grade you begin in, progress to the moderns over four years; when the student reaches fifth grade (the "logic stage"), supplement his study with the *Kingfisher History Encylopedia,* a time line, and the teaching techniques suggested in Chapter 16 (see Chapter 16, "Starting in the Middle," for more details).

If you're teaching more than one child, you can certainly adjust your history lessons so that both students are covering the same period. Grammar skills, spelling, writing, and math should be taught individually, but both a first and third grader could study ancient history. Expect more writing, more discussion, and more outside reading from the third grader. When your third-grade student reaches fifth grade, incorporate the suggestions found in Chapter 16 into his study of history, no matter what *period* of history he is studying at that point.

HOW TO DO IT

To study history and geography, you'll need a 3-inch three-ring notebook with lots of paper, a three-hole punch, art supplies, *The Story of the World*, the *Usborne Internet-Linked Encyclopedia*, geography resources (a globe, a wall map of the world, and maps to color—see Resources for ordering information), and a library card.

The history notebook will contain your child's pictures, compositions, and narrations about history, and will organize the child's history study for grades 1 through 4.

Make four dividers:

Ancients, 5000 B.C.–A.D. 400
Medieval/Early Renaissance, 400–1600
Late Renaissance/Early Modern, 1600–1850
Modern, 1850–Present Day

In Chapter 5, we introduced you to narration, reading to the child (or giving the child a reading assignment), and then asking him to tell you what he's just read. You'll be using this technique extensively in the study of history.

When you open *The Story of the World,* you'll find that each chapter is divided into sections and that each section tells a "story" about a civilization, an event, or a place. For each story in this history book, you'll follow the same basic pattern:

1. Make a narration page. After your first or second grader tells you about what you've just read, write his version down on notebook or drawing paper for him (by the end of second grade or the beginning of third grade, children should be starting to write down their own narrations).
2. Ask the child to illustrate what he's just read (and help him make a caption), or let him color a picture related to the story.
3. Find the geographical area under discussion on a globe and on a wall-map, and color the appropriate black-line map.
4. Go to the library to find out more about the subject.

Although you can assemble your own maps, illustrations, and reading lists, using the suggestions we provide here, each volume of *The Story of the World* can be ordered with an accompanying activity book (see Resources at the end of this chapter), which contains comprehension questions and answers, sample narrations for each section (to give you some idea of the appropriate level of detail you hope to hear from the child), both nonfiction and fiction library lists for additional reading, black-line maps and exercises for each chapter, coloring pages, project instructions (for hands-on learning), and review cards for children to color, cut out, and use to remind themselves of the basic facts they've learned.

First Grade: Ancients (5000 B.C.–A.D. 400)

During first grade, aim to spend at least three hours per week on history.

Use common sense. History is important, but the first grader is learning all sorts of foundational skills from scratch: reading, writing, putting sentences together, keeping track of the dates, telling time, adding, subtracting, and so forth. If the child misses some ancient history in first grade, he'll pick it up in fifth grade, or in ninth grade, or in independent reading. If he doesn't learn to read, write, and do basic mathematical operations, he'll be hampered for years. So in the early grades, give priority to reading, grammar, spelling, writing, and math. History and science follow on these basic abilities.

Ideally, you'll do history three days per week for an hour each day, or two days for a slightly longer period; or you'll do math, grammar, writing, and reading four days a week and devote the fifth to history and science. (See the Epilogue, "The Grammar Stage at a Glance," pages 215–218, for several sample schedules.)

Sit down on the sofa with your first grader and read a section of *Ancient Times* (volume one of *The Story of the World*) aloud to him. Let him ask questions. When you've finished the section, move to a writing surface (a desk or the kitchen table). Get out a sheet of notebook paper, and give it the same title as the section you've just read ("The First Writing," for example, or "Making Mummies"). Then ask the child to tell back to you the most important or most interesting thing that you just read. Prompt him with questions, if necessary.[1] Write his narration down in your neatest printing

[1]See Chapter 5, page 55, for a discussion of the narration method. You'll progress, over the first- and second-grade years, from writing what the child dictates to you, to writing

—you want him to be able to read it. When this page is finished, ask the child to read it back to you. Then put it into the child's history notebook. Continue this process for each section until you reach the end of the chapter (most chapters contain two related sections).

Now ask the child to complete a coloring page related to the history lesson (provided in the activity book or taken from one of the historical coloring books listed in the Resources at the end of this chapter), or to draw a picture of something from the lesson that strikes his fancy. Although the child should have fun, don't let him do unnecessarily sloppy work; encourage him to draw or color carefully (this will help to improve fine motor skills). When the coloring page or illustration is finished, write a caption for the page. By the end of first grade, you should write out the caption on another sheet of paper, and ask the child to copy it onto the drawing; by the end of second grade, he should be writing his own captions. Then put this drawing in the notebook as well. Keep these pages in chronological order. By the end of the year, this notebook will contain the child's own story of ancient history. (*Note:* Work done for the notebook should be carefully done; handwriting, cut edges, labels, and coloring should all be the child's best effort.)

Once the child has finished the narration and coloring page, look together at the map at the beginning of the chapter. Find the location of the map on your globe. Most children enjoy putting their finger on their own location and then traveling to the ancient country under discussion. Then go to the wall map, which is larger and more detailed than the globe, and find the location there. Finally, ask the child to color a black-line map of the area, either from the accompanying activity book or from one of the resources listed at the end of this chapter. Punch holes in the black-line map and put it into the notebook as well.

You may wish to finish all of this work in one long session; you may want to stretch it out over two. (Alternately, you can read an entire chapter in your first session, and then use your second session to do one nar-

---

his words out and asking him to copy part of the narration out in his own writing, to helping the child write his own original sentences without a written model in front of him. The *Activity Book* that goes along with *The Story of the World* provides both "prompting questions" and sample narrations.

ration, coloring page, and map exercise to cover the whole chapter.) Once you've completed the process of read/narrate/color/map, it's time to go to the library. Find books in the children's section about anything in the lesson that interests the child. Your children's librarian can help you; most libraries have reference works that will help the librarian find, for example, picture books set in ancient Egypt. We have included a few recommended titles at the end of this chapter (you can use this either as a library list or as a shopping list if you decide to buy the books instead); the activity book that accompanies *The Story of the World* has much more detailed library lists for each chapter. Check these books out, and read them at home.

Then, move on to the next topic in the history book.

As you continue, you'll find that some topics provide very little opportunity for extra reading (so far as we know, there's no first-grade guide to Ur on your library shelves), while others will lead you to scads of wonderful books (ancient Egypt probably occupies an entire library shelf of its own). Use your common sense. You don't have to make a library visit for every chapter, or labor to find books on obscure topics; just do a narration, a coloring page, and move on. If, on the other hand, the child's interest is sparked by the invention of writing, mummification, or the Hanging Gardens of Babylon, take as much time as you please to investigate it thoroughly. History should be a delight-centered activity for the grammar-stage child. Allow him to explore, do activities and projects, and have fun; you can always hurry over (or skip) later chapters without injury.

In place of library visits, you can also use the *Usborne Internet-Linked Encyclopedia* to explore some topics; visual learners will enjoy looking at the pictures.

Keep the following tips in mind as you study history:

Don't limit yourself to books the child can read on his own. Most children's history books are written on a third- to seventh-grade reading level. Check them out, and read them to your young student. Soon he'll be reading them on his own.

You'll never read every good book in the library, so don't even try. At the beginning, you may find it easier to go to the library on your own and bring books home. By second grade, however, you'll want to take your child with you at least part of the time so that he can learn to find books in the catalog and then locate them on the shelf. (A children's librarian will be glad to show him—and you—how the catalog works.)

Use hands-on projects as well as books. We've recommended several resources for history projects: treasure chests with Egyptian beads inside, ancient Chinese games, books that tell you how to make Greek clothing or Roman food. The activity book that accompanies each volume of *The Story of the World* provides simple projects—from making bricks to playing the "Ransom Caesar" game—that help hands-on learners enjoy history study.

You'll want the child to make notebook pages about some of the library books and projects he does. Use your judgment. As with reading, don't make him do a page for every book, or the fun of discovery will quickly become drudgery.

A tip for recording history projects. Veteran home schoolers continually wonder what to do with all the maps, projects, crafts, and activities their children produce. We suggest that when you finish a project, you take a picture of it, tape the picture to a notebook page, and record the date. The project has thus been immortalized. Eventually, you can disassemble it or throw it away.

Pay special attention to biographies. Try to make a page for all the great men and women you encounter (Sargon, Moses, Hammurabi, Hatshepsut, Tutankhamen, Alexander the Great, Julius Caesar, . . . the list goes on). These biographies can be wonderful "pegs" on which to hang the progression of history. You may not remember much about ancient history, but you probably remember that Alexander cried when he found no more worlds to conquer. We've supplied a list of great men and women at the end of this chapter, for your reference.

Again, don't feel that you have to read a biography of every historical figure. The elementary years are not the time to develop comprehensive knowledge, but to see how history progresses. First graders are not only learning how to record information, but the information itself, so you'll move slowly at first. If you spend a lot of time on the first Olympic games and end up skipping the Scythians, nothing dreadful will happen. Your child will come across this period again in fifth grade, when he's reading and writing well.

Remember, file all these pages in the history notebook chronologically. By the end of fourth grade, the history notebook will be crammed with fas-

cinating information; the student's first trip through the entire expanse of world history, organized and recorded in his own hand (and yours).[2]

What about testing?

Formal testing is unnecessary at this level. If the child can tell you what you've read to him, he's been listening. If he reads several books on the same subject, the information will be fixed in his mind. Once a month, sit down with the child and read through the pages he's already done so that he can review the history he's covered.

Memorization

The history notebook should be accompanied by a certain amount of memorization. Dates, personalities, and wars serve as pegs on which to hang incoming information. (Alexander Graham Bell invented the telephone in 1876. Quick: Was this before or after the Civil War?)[3]

You can pick your own "pegs." Almost any series of major events or personalities will do, but these "mental pegs" will be most useful if they correspond to the child's interest. In first grade, people and events will probably be more meaningful than dates. A first grader could memorize the pharaohs of Egypt and the first twenty emperors of Rome. (Any six year old who can say tyrannosaurus can learn to say Amenhotep or Pertinax.)[4] The *Kingfisher History Encyclopedia* has a "Ready Reference" section in the back of the book that lists names of Egyptian dynasties, principal pharaohs, Chinese dynasties, kings of Rome, and emperors of the Roman Empire. Aim to memorize at least two of these lists by the end of the first-grade year. A first grader who reads a list out loud every day will have it memorized within weeks.

Suggested Schedule

A good rule of thumb is to cover one chapter (two related sections) of *The Story of the World* per week (although nothing bad will happen if you fall behind). If you're studying history on Mondays, Wednesdays, and Fridays, consider one of the following schedules:

[2]The notebooks are also useful for evaluation at testing time (see Part IV for more on testing).

[3]After. The Civil War was fought from 1861 through 1865.

[4]Memorization tip: read the names onto a tape, and have the child listen to the taped list every morning; he'll have them down in no time.

Monday — Read one section from *The Story of the World.* Ask the child to make a narration page, and put it in the history notebook. Complete a coloring page or illustration and put this in the notebook as well. Go over memory work.

Wednesday — Read one section from *The Story of the World.* Ask the child to make a narration page, and put it into the history notebook. Find the location on the globe and wall map; color a black-line map and put it into the history notebook.

Friday — Read one to three library books on the subject out loud together. (It's usually best to select these books ahead of time, either on last week's library trip with the child or on your own.) Or read corresponding pages from the *Usborne Internet-Linked Encyclopedia.* Optional: do a history project or activity.

Or:

Monday — Read an entire chapter from *The Story of the World.* Ask the child to make a narration page and put it into the history notebook. Complete a coloring page or illustration. Go over memory work.

Wednesday — Find the location on the globe and wall map; color a black-line map and put it into the history notebook. Read an additional library book, or consult the *Usborne Internet-Linked Encyclopedia.*

Friday — Read additional library books; complete a history project or activity.

If you're studying history on Tuesdays and Thursdays:

Tuesday — Read a chapter from *The Story of the World.* Ask the child to make a narration page and put it into the history notebook. Complete a coloring page or illustration. Find the location on the globe and wall map; color a black-line map and put it into the history notebook.

Thursday — Read additional library books or consult *The Usborne Internet-*

Linked Encyclopedia. Optional: do a history project or activity. Go over memory work.

Second Grade: Medieval–Early Renaissance (400–1600)

Using narration, coloring pages, map work, and library trips, the second grader (or the student in the second year of history) will study history from about 400 to 1600 (the period of time covered in *The Story of the World,* Volume II: *The Middle Ages*). You'll follow the same basic procedure, but you'll find many more on-topic library books for this historical period.

At the beginning of second grade, write half of the child's narration, and ask him to write (or copy from your model) the other half. Aim to have him writing his own narrations by the end of the year. Again, don't do these narrations for all the books he reads; this would tie his reading skills to his writing skills, which are typically slower to develop. If he writes the narration for the *Story of the World* pages, he can dictate other narrations to you (or draw pictures).

Don't forget to review once a month, and look back at those first-grade pages several times during the year.

Memorization

A second-grader could memorize the rulers of England from Egbert through Elizabeth I, along with each ruler's family allegiance (Saxon, Dane, Norman, Plantagenet, Lancaster, York, Tudor); this information is found in the back of the *Kingfisher History Encyclopedia.* Other options, depending on the child's interest and background, are the rulers of Scotland from Malcolm II through James VI, the later Holy Roman Emperors, or the rulers of other medieval countries—France, Spain, Japan, Russia. Second graders could also memorize the major wars and major discoveries (listed at the back of the *Kingfisher* book). Aim for two lists: the rulers of England plus one other set of rulers, wars, or discoveries. Second graders can also memorize a Shakespeare sonnet (Sonnet 18, "Shall I compare thee to a summer's day?" is probably the most familiar; see shakespeare-online.com for all of the sonnets) and a selection from *Macbeth* (retold in *The Story of the World,* Volume II: *The Middle Ages;* the activity book reprints Macbeth's "Tomorrow, and tomorrow, and tomorrow" speech from Act V, Scene V for this purpose) or some other Shakespeare play.

Suggested Schedule

Aim to spend a week on each chapter. If you find yourself getting behind, you can skip a few library visits; the history book itself is stuffed with information. You'll want to follow the same daily schedule as in first grade. But don't forget to add map coloring to the day that you do your globe work.

Third Grade: Late Renaissance–Early Modern (1600–1850)

Third graders (or students in the third year of history study) will cover the years from 1600 to 1850, the period covered in *The Story of the World,* Volume III: *Early Modern Times.* Continue on with narration (these narrations should now contain more detail, and should begin to resemble one- to two-paragraph compositions; see Chapter 5 for more details), coloring pages, map work, library readings, and projects. By third grade, some children are ready to begin to make several written pages per week for the history notebook; aim for this if writing has become easier for the student.

Memorization

During the third-grade year, the student should memorize at least the beginning of the Declaration of Independence (most children can master the entire document, given enough time and repetition). The third grader should also memorize the first twelve presidents of the United States and the major wars for the period 1600 to 1850 (these lists are in the back of the *Kingfisher History Encyclopedia*). You can assign other lists—rulers of other countries, important discoveries and explorations—at your own discretion.

Suggested Schedule

The third grader can follow the same basic weekly schedule as the first- or second-grade student; he should be reading more books independently, but you should still plan to read aloud those books that may be over your child's reading level.

The third-grade student, who will probably have a longer attention span than his first-grade counterpart, may enjoy doing all of his history work in one morning; you could schedule (for example) Friday morning as "history day." On this day, you could do history for three hours, perhaps from 9:30 until lunch: reading from *The Story of the World,* either aloud or independently, preparation of a narration (two paragraphs or so in length), a drawing or coloring page, a project or activity, and the reading of two or three relevant books.

Fourth Grade: Modern (1850–Present)

The fourth grader will use *The Story of the World,* Volume IV: *The Modern Age* for his study. Follow the same pattern: narration (now short compositions of two or three paragraphs), illustrations or coloring pages, maps, and library visits. Even more library resources will be available for the student on contemporary topics, so don't feel obliged to read even a fraction of the supplemental books available; let the child pick the subjects that interest him for further reading.

The fourth grader should use additional map resources to learn the fifty states of the United States of America. Use one of the coloring or geography resources listed in Resources under "Modern, 1850–Present (Fourth Grade)" at the end of this chapter. By the end of the year, the fourth grader should be able to locate each state on a map of the United States.

Also plan to spend several weeks (three to six, depending on the emphasis your state places on state history) studying the history of your own state. Your public library should carry several series of books about the states. Look for the From Sea to Shining Sea series, published by Children's Book Press; each state has its own heavily illustrated book with easy-to-read text on history, geography, and culture. You can also order the individual titles (for example, *Hawaii: From Sea to Shining Sea*) from any bookstore. Use the same basic procedure to study these books: read, have the child complete a narration, and then look for additional library resources on subjects that interest you. Children's Book Press also publishes a more advanced series, called America the Beautiful, that will challenge advanced fourth graders; these books are also suitable for older students.

Memorization

Fourth graders should know the Preamble to the Constitution, the Gettysburg Address, and the purpose (if not the exact words) of the amendments to the Constitution. Also, plan to finish memorizing the list of presidents from 1850 to the present, the dates of the major wars since 1850 (this list is in the *Kingfisher History Encyclopedia*), and the capitals of the fifty states. At the end of this chapter, we've suggested songs, games, flash cards, and coloring books to help with this memory work.

Suggested Schedule

As in third grade, you can follow a Monday-Wednesday-Friday schedule, a Tuesday-Thursday schedule, or do all your history study on one morning. For state history, spend this time reading through your selected state history book; stop at the end of each chapter to make a narration page. Make time to color the state flag and the state map (see Resources for more information). You might also plan some time for field trips to historic locations nearby. Making a scrapbook of your own state could be an interesting project for weekends or summer afternoons; state chambers of commerce and places of historical interest will often mail you colored brochures to cut and paste.

RESOURCES

For publisher and catalog addresses, telephone numbers, and other information, see Sources (pages 751–778). Most books can be obtained from any bookstore or library; where we know of a mail-order option, we have provided it. The titles we list are only a few of the many available. Plan on exploring library and bookstore shelves for yourself.

During first and second grades, you should plan on reading many of these biographies and histories aloud. We have suggested a few simple books that young children can read alone.

Basic texts for the four-year grammar stage are listed first. A supplementary list is provided for each year of study. The first section for each year lists books that provide general information about the historical period, including coloring books and other project resources. The second section lists some of the most useful biographies alphabetically by subject.

Because biographies are often the most useful supplemental reading for young children, we have supplied chronological lists of famous people to help you in your search for library titles. For third and fourth grade, when children are better able to understand historical "topics," we have also supplied a list of major historical events that the student can explore.

Basic Texts

Bauer, Susan Wise. *The Story of the World: History for the Classical Child.* Vol. I *Ancient Times,* rev. ed. Charles City, Va.: Peace Hill Press, 2006.

$16.95. Order from Peace Hill Press or from any bookstore. A hardcover is available for $24.95. Covers history 5000 B.C.–400 A.D.

Bauer, Susan Wise, ed. *The Story of the World Activity Book I: Ancient Times,* 3rd ed. Charles City, Va.: Peace Hill Press, 2006.

$34.95. Order from Peace Hill Press or from any bookstore. Contains comprehension questions and answers, sample narrations, cross-references to the Usborne and Kingfisher history encyclopedias, maps and map exercises, coloring pages, reading lists, history activities, and review cards.

———. *The Story of the World: History for the Classical Child.* Vol. II, *The Middle Ages,* rev. ed. Charles City, Va.: Peace Hill Press, 2007.

$16.95. Order from Peace Hill Press or from any bookstore. Covers history 400–1600.

———. *The Story of the World Activity Book II: The Middle Ages,* rev. ed. Charles City, Va.: Peace Hill Press, 2008.

$34.95. Order from Peace Hill Press or from any bookstore. See description above.

———. *The Story of the World: History for the Classical Child.* Vol. III, *Early Modern Times.* Charles City, Va.: Peace Hill Press, 2004.

$16.95. Order from Peace Hill Press or from any bookstore. Covers history 1600–1850.

———. *The Story of the World Activity Book III: Early Modern Times.* Charles City, Va.: Peace Hill Press, 2004.

$32.95. Order from Peace Hill Press or from any bookstore.

———. *The Story of the World: History for the Classical Child.* Vol. IV, *The Modern Age.* Charles City, Va.: Peace Hill Press, 2004.

$16.95. Order from Peace Hill Press or from any bookstore. Covers history 1850–present.

———. *The Story of the World Activity Book IV: The Modern Age.* Charles City, Va.: Peace Hill Press, 2004.

$32.95. Order from Peace Hill Press or from any bookstore. See description above.

Bingham, Jane, Fiona Chandler, and Sam Taplin. *The Usborne Internet-Linked Encyclopedia of World History.* Tulsa, Okla.: E.D.C. Publishing, 2003.
$19.99 for the paperback version; a hardback version, dated 2001 and priced at $39.99, is also available. Order from any bookstore.

The Kingfisher History Encyclopedia. New York: Kingfisher, 2004.
$29.95. Order from any bookstore. You'll use this for the logic stage, but buy it now if possible for the memory lists; it also contains time lines, short biographies, maps, and illustrations.

Basic Geography Resources

Up-to-date globes and wall maps can be found at the National Geographic online map store (maps.nationalgeographic.com).

Johnson, Terri. *Blackline Maps of World History: The Ancients (5000 B.C.–500 A.D.).* Boring, Ore.: Knowledge Quest Maps.
$14.90. "Historical" rather than "geographical," these maps reflect ancient national boundaries. Order from Knowledge Quest.

———. *Blackline Maps of World History: The Middle Ages (500–1600 A.D.).* Boring, Ore.: Knowledge Quest Maps.
$14.90. From the dark ages of Europe to the spread of the black death. Twenty-four maps with lesson plans included. Order from Knowledge Quest.

———. *Blackline Maps of World History: The Age of Exploration (1492–1850).* Boring, Ore.: Knowledge Quest Maps.
$14.90. From the discovery of the New World to the California Gold Rush. Twenty-six maps with lesson plans included. Order from Knowledge Quest. Knowledge Quest Maps.

———. *Blackline Maps of World History: The Modern World (1850–The Present).* Boring, Ore.: Knowledge Quest Maps.
$14.90. From the Crimean and Civil and World Wars to the present day. Twenty-seven maps with lesson plans included. Order from Knowledge Quest.

———. *Blackline Maps of World History CD-ROM.* Boring, Ore.: Knowledge Quest Maps.

$29.95. All four sets of maps listed above on CD, so that you can print multiple copies from your computer. Order from Knowledge Quest.

Petty, Kate. *The Amazing Pop-Up Geography Book.* Illus. Jennie Maizels. New York: Dutton, 2000.

$22.99. Order from any bookstore. Designed for elementary students, this fascinating book uses flaps, wheels, tabs, pop-ups, and an expandable globe to explain continents, oceans, rivers, mountains, and much more. A good resource for arousing enthusiasm.

Wiggers, George and Hannah. *Uncle Josh's Outline Map Book.* Nancy, Ky.: Geography Matters, 2000.

$19.95. Order from Geography Matters. Contains 44 black-line maps of the world for coloring; also includes ten regional U.S. maps and all state maps. The CD, available for $26.95 from Geography Matters, makes it possible for you to print multiple copies of each map (and also includes 21 additional maps, including more detailed Canadian territories). Necessary for U.S. geography study.

Ancients, 5000 B.C.–A.D. 400 (First Grade)

List of Great Men and Women to Cover

Cheops, pharaoh of Egypt (2700–2675 B.C.)
Abraham (c. 2100 B.C.)
Hammurabi (c. 1750 B.C.)
Queen Hatshepsut of Egypt (c. 1480 B.C.)
Moses (c. 1450 B.C.)
Tutankhamen (c. 1355 B.C.)
Nebuchadnezzar (1146–1123 B.C.)
King David (c. 1000 B.C.)
Homer (c. 800 B.C.)
Romulus (753–716 B.C.)
Sennacherib (705–681 B.C.)
Lao-tse (Chinese philosopher, b. 604 B.C.)
Pythagoras (581–497 B.C.)

Confucius (K'ung Fu-tsu) (551–479 B.C.)
Buddha (Siddhartha Gautama) (550–480 B.C.)
Socrates (470–399 B.C.)
Plato (427–347 B.C.)
Aristotle (384–322 B.C.)
Alexander the Great (356–323 B.C.)
Hannibal (fought with Rome c. 218–207 B.C.)
Cicero (106–43 B.C.)
Julius Caesar (100–44 B.C.)
Virgil (70–19 B.C.)
Caesar Augustus (c. 45 B.C.–A.D. 14)
Jesus Christ (c. 4 B.C.–A.D. 33)
Saint Paul (c. A.D. 45)
Nero (died A.D. 68)
Constantine the Great (ruled A.D. 306–337)

General Information

Ancient China Treasure Chest. Philadelphia: Running Press, 1996.
$22.95. Order from Running Press or Amazon. A small treasure chest containing a brush and ink set, lessons on how to draw Chinese characters, coins, a fan, charts, stickers, and a booklet about Taoism, Chinese dynasties, and archaeological discoveries. First-grade students will need help with some activities.

Ancient Egypt Treasure Chest. Philadelphia: Running Press, 1994.
$22.95. Order from Running Press or Amazon. A small treasure chest containing (among other things) Egyptian jewelry, hieroglyphic stamps, papyrus, and a board game. Some of the work is difficult for first graders, so plan on helping out.

Broida, Marian. *Ancient Egyptians and Their Neighbors: An Activity Guide.* Chicago: Chicago Review Press, 1999.
$16.95. Order from any bookstore. Includes information and activities about Mesopotamians, Nubians, and Hittites, as well as the more popular Egyptians.

Carlson, Laurie. *Classical Kids: An Activity Guide to Life in Ancient Greece and Rome.* Chicago: Chicago Review Press, 1998.

$14.95. Order from any bookstore. Information and hands-on activities about these two ancient cultures.

Chisholm, Jane. *Who Built the Pyramids?* Tulsa, Okla.: E.D.C. Publishing, 1996.

$4.99. Order from an Usborne representative or from Rainbow Resource Center. On a first- to third-grade reading level.

A Coloring Book of Ancient Egypt. Santa Barbara, Calif.: Bellerophon Books, 1988.

$4.95. Order from any bookstore. Museum-shop-quality coloring book with designs and images from Egyptian tombs and monuments.

A Coloring Book of Ancient Greece. Santa Barbara, Calif.: Bellerophon Books, 1988.

$4.95. Order from any bookstore. Museum-shop-quality coloring book with designs and images from Greek pottery, frescoes, temples, and tombs.

A Coloring Book of Ancient India. Santa Barbara, Calif.: Bellerophon Books, 1989.

$4.95. Order from Bellerophon Books or from any bookstore. Scenes drawn from ancient Indian paintings and carvings show everyday life as well as pictures from myth and legend.

A Coloring Book of Ancient Rome. Santa Barbara, Calif.: Bellerophon Books, 1988.

$4.95. Order from any bookstore. Museum-shop-quality coloring book with Roman art depicting Caesars, senators, chariot races, and other scenes from Roman life.

A Coloring Book of the Near East. Santa Barbara, Calif.: Bellerophon Books, 1983.

$4.95. Order from any bookstore. Illustrations drawn from carvings, temple paintings, and other primary Near Eastern sources.

Cox, Phil Roxbee. *Who Were the Romans?* Tulsa, Okla.: E.D.C. Publishing, 2002.

$4.95. Order from an Usborne representative or from any bookstore. First- to third-grade reading level.

Green, John. *Life in Ancient Egypt.* New York: Dover, 1989.

$3.95. Order from Dover. An artist's detailed drawings of Egyptian life.

———. *Life in Ancient Greece.* New York: Dover, 1993.

$3.95. Order from Dover. An artist's detailed drawings of Greek life.

———. *Life in Ancient Rome.* New York: Dover, 1997.

$3.95. Order from Dover. An artist's detailed drawings of Roman life.

———. *Life in Old Japan.* New York: Dover, 1994.

$3.95. Order from Dover. An artist's detailed drawings of ancient Japanese life.

Guerber, H. A. *The Story of the Greeks.* 3d ed. Fort Collins, Colo.: Nothing New Press, 2003.

$21.95. Order from Nothing New Press or from Curriculum Connection. An engaging narrative history, broken into small, readable sections, first published in the late nineteenth century; a great reference book to have on hand for extra reading through the year.

———. *The Story of the Romans.* 3d ed. Fort Collins, Colo.: Nothing New Press, 2002.

$21.95. Order from Nothing New Press or from Curriculum Connection. An engaging narrative history, broken into small, readable sections, first published in the late nineteenth century; a great reference book to have on hand for extra reading through the year.

Lawrence, Michelle. *Ancient Egypt Jigsaw Book.* London: Usborne Books, 2006.

$14.99. Order from any bookstore. Good for tactile learners, the Jigsaw Books require students to assemble pictures and spot important details.

Mann, Elizabeth. *The Great Pyramid.* New York: Mikaya Press, 2006.

$9.95. Order from any bookstore. A lavishly illustrated guide to the construction of this wonder of the ancient world, with fold-out sections.

———. *The Great Wall.* New York: Mikaya Press, 2006.

$9.95. Order from any bookstore. Another beautiful book, covering the history and extent of the Great Wall of China, with a fold-out scene of an attack on the wall's center.

Payne, Elizabeth. *The Pharaohs of Ancient Egypt.* New York: Random House, 1998.

$5.99. Order from any bookstore. Each chapter tells about one pharaoh. Fourth- to fifth-grade reading level but easily read aloud. Covers Egypt's history from the beginning to its conquest by Greece and Rome.

Queen Nefertiti Coloring Book. Santa Barbara, Calif.: Bellerophon Books, 1992.

$3.50. Order from Amazon. Museum-shop-quality coloring book with actual images from tombs and monuments in Egypt.

Reid, Struan. *Ancient Romans Jigsaw Book.* London: Usborne Books, 2007.

$14.99. Order from any bookstore. Good for tactile learners, the Jigsaw Books require students to assemble pictures and spot important details.

Sanders, Nancy I. *Old Testament Days: An Activity Guide.* Chicago: Chicago Review Press, 1995.

$14.95. Order from any bookstore. Activities and information about near eastern lands during ancient times.

Smith, A. G. *Building the Pyramids Sticker Book.* New York: Dover, 1998.

$4.95. Order from any bookstore. Use stickers to fill in scenes of ancient Egyptian life and work.

Tagholm, Sally. *Everyday Life in the Ancient World: A Guide to Travel in Ancient Times.* New York: Kingfisher, 2002.

$15.95. Order from any bookstore. Ties together the ancient worlds of the Mediterranean and the Americas.

Biographies

The Historical Biography series. Barrington, Ill.: Heinemann Library, 2002.

$7.99 each. Order from any bookstore. One of the very few biography series designed for elementary students that covers ancient times, the Historical Biography series offers 32-page, easy-reader, heavily illustrated biographies.

Reid, Struan. *Cleopatra.*

———. *Julius Caesar.*

Williams, Brian. *Aristotle.*

———. *Tutankhamen.*

Alexander the Great

Langley, Andrew. *Alexander the Great: The Greatest Ruler of the Ancient World.* Oxford: Oxford University Press, 1997.

$12.95. Order from any bookstore. A biography for beginning readers, with large illustrations and simple text.

Cleopatra

Stanley, Diane, and Peter Vennema. *Cleopatra.* New York: HarperTrophy, 1997.

$6.99. Order from any bookstore. The picture-book format makes this biography attractive to young readers, but you'll need to read the text aloud.

Eratosthenes

Lasky, Kathryn. *The Librarian Who Measured the Earth.* New York: Little, Brown & Co., 1994.

$17.99. Unfortunately available only in an expensive library binding; check your library. This picture book tells the story of the ancient Greek librarian who managed to measure the earth's circumference, using the shadows cast by the sun.

Tutankhamen

Sabuda, Robert. *Tutankhamen's Gift.* Glenview, Ill.: Scott Foresman, 1997.

$7.99. Order from any bookstore. This picture-book biography tells about Tutankhamen's life, not just his tomb.

Medieval/Early Renaissance, 400–1600 (Second Grade)

List of Great Men and Women to Cover

Saint Augustine (writing c. 411)
Attila the Hun (c. 433–453)
King Arthur (probably killed in 537 at the Battle of Camlan)
Mohammed (570–632)
Charlemagne (ruled 768–814)
Alfred the Great (849–899)
Leif Ericsson (discovered America c. 1000)
Edward the Confessor (1042–1066)
Genghis Khan (b. 1155)

Dante Alighieri (1265–1321)
Geoffrey Chaucer (c. 1340–1400)
Jan van Eyck (c. 1390–1441)
Johannes Gutenberg (c. 1396–1468)
Christopher Columbus (1451–1506)
Leonardo da Vinci (1452–1519)
Amerigo Vespucci (1454–1512)
Nicolaus Copernicus (1473–1543)
Michelangelo (1475–1564)
Ferdinand Magellan (1480–1521)
Martin Luther (1483–1546)
Raphael (1483–1520)
Nostradamus (1503–1566)
John Calvin (1509–1564)
Hernando Cortés (entered Mexican capital, 1519)
Tycho Brahe (1546–1601)
Walter Raleigh (1554–1618)
William Shakespeare (1564–1616)
Galileo Galilei (1564–1642)

General Information

Adkins, Jan. *What If You Met a Knight?* New York: Roaring Brook Press, 2006.
$16.95. Order from any bookstore. A realistic and entertaining portrait of what knighthood in the Middle Ages was like.

Aliki. *A Medieval Feast.* New York: Harper, 1998.
$6.99. Order from any bookstore. A colorful account of the journey of a medieval king, and the preparations made for his arrival.

Braman, Arlette N. *The Inca: Activities and Crafts from a Mysterious Land.* San Francisco, Calif.: Jossey-Bass, 2003.
$12.95. Order from any bookstore. From the Secrets of Ancient Cultures series, this book offers hands-on activities, projects, and games.

Braman, Arlette N., and Michele Nidenoff. *The Maya: Activities and Crafts from a Mysterious Land.* San Francisco, Calif.: Jossey-Bass, 2003.
$12.95. Order from any bookstore. From the Secrets of Ancient Cultures series, this book offers hands-on activities, projects, and games.

Carlson, Laurie. *Days of Knights and Damsels: An Activity Guide.* Chicago: Chicago Review Press, 1998.

$14.95. Order from any bookstore. Activities and information about the Middle Ages, designed for elementary students.

Chisholm, Jane. *Who Were the Vikings?* Tulsa, Okla.: E.D.C. Publishing, 2002.

$4.95. Order from an Usborne distributor or from any bookstore. First- to third-grade reading level.

Chrisp, Peter. *The Middle Ages: My World.* Chanhassen, Minn.: Two-Can Publishing, 2000.

$14.95. Order from any bookstore. Clothing, food, and occupations from the Middle Ages, explained so that young children can reproduce them.

A Coloring Book of the Middle Ages. Santa Barbara, Calif.: Bellerophon Books, 1985.

$4.95. Order from Bellerophon Books. Pictures from actual medieval drawings and paintings, showing daily life, worship, knights, kings, monks, and warfare.

Copeland, Peter F. *Exploration of North America.* New York: Dover, 1990.

$3.95. Order from any bookstore.

———. *Indian Tribes of North America.* New York: Dover, 1990.

$3.95. Order from any bookstore.

Cox, Phil Roxbee. *What Were Castles For?* Tulsa, Okla.: E.D.C. Publishing, 1995.

$4.99. Order from an Usborne distributor or from any bookstore. First- to third-grade reading level.

Green, John. *Life in a Medieval Castle and Village Coloring Book.* New York: Dover, 1991.

$3.95. Order from The Book Peddler.

Knights Treasure Chest. Philadelphia: Running Press, 1985.

$22.95. Order from any bookstore. The treasure chest contains heraldic insigna—sealing rings, seals and clay, stencils, and a coat of arms—as well as a model catapult, a Gothic window craft, and more.

Macdonald, Fiona. *How Would You Survive in the Middle Ages?* New York: Orchard Books, 1997.

$7.95. Order from Rainbow Resource Center. Helps children imagine their lives in various strata of medieval society.

Manning, Mick, and Brita Granstrom. *Viking Longship.* London: Frances Lincoln Children's Books, 2006.

$15.95. Order from any bookstore. An interactive and entertaining guide to Viking life, from the well-done Fly on the Wall series.

Miller, Christine, H. A. Guerber, and Charlotte M. Yonge. *The Story of the Middle Ages.* 3d ed. Fort Collins, Colo.: Nothing New Press, 2002.

$27.95. Order from Nothing New Press or from Curriculum Connection. An engaging narrative history, broken into small, readable sections, that reworks two nineteenth-century texts into a chronicle of events and colorful personalities.

Olmon, Kyle, and Tracy Sabin. *Castle: Medieval Days and Knights.* London: Orchard Books, 2006.

$19.99. Order from any bookstore or through the Metropolitan Museum Store. Designed by paper engineers Robert Sabuda and Matthew Reinhart, this pop-up book lets you into a wonderfully detailed castle complete with prisoners, jousting, and a drawbridge.

Paper Soldiers of the Middle Ages: 100 Years' War. Santa Barbara, Calif.: Bellerophon, 1992.

$3.95. Order from Bellerophon.

Paper Soldiers of the Middle Ages: The Crusades. Santa Barbara, Calif.: Bellerophon, 1992.

$4.95. Order from Bellerophon.

Polin, C. J. *The Story of Chocolate.* New York: Dorling Kindersley, 2005.

$3.99. Order from any bookstore. A DK Reader designed for second and third graders, this history of chocolate gives details about its use in the Aztec world and in medieval times—a fun way to connect ancient America to the present day.

Queen Elizabeth I: Paper Dolls to Color. Santa Barbara, Calif.: Bellerophon, 1985.

$4.95. Order from Bellerophon. Paper dolls of Elizabeth I, Sir Walter Raleigh, the earl of Essex, and others, with outfits and some text written by Queen Elizabeth herself.

The Renaissance Coloring Book. Santa Barbara, Calif.: Bellerophon, 1985.
$4.95. Order from Bellerophon. Images from Renaissance paintings, engravings, and frescoes.

Shakespeare Fandex Family Field Guide. New York: Workman Publishing, 2003.
$9.95. Order from the Metropolitan Museum Store. Fifty cards, held together in an easy-reference fan shape, with plenty of color illustrations and fascinating facts about Shakespeare, his plays, and his times.

Smith, A. G. *Castles of the World Coloring Book.* New York: Dover, 1986.
$3.95. Order from Dover. Medieval castles not only from England and France, but from Spain, Portugal, Japan, and other countries.

———. *Knights and Armor Coloring Book.* New York: Dover, 1985.
$3.95. Order from Dover. Drawings of knights and armor at different periods in history.

———. *Life in Celtic Times Coloring Book.* New York: Dover, 1997.
$3.95. Order from Dover.

———. *Story of the Vikings Coloring Book.* New York: Dover, 1998.
$3.95. Order from Dover. Tells the story of the Viking presence in Europe as well as in Russia and other countries.

Vikings. Rio Rancho, N. Mex.: Rio Grande Games.
$34.95. Order from Amazon or through Rio Grande Games. A family game for up to four players; lead a Viking band, discover islands, build settlements, and conquer your neighbors.

Biographies

Christopher Columbus

DeKay, James T. *Meet Christopher Columbus.* New York: Random House, 2001.

$3.99. Order from Greenleaf Press. A Landmark Biography on a second- to fourth-grade reading level.

Foster, Genevieve. *The World of Columbus and His Sons.* Sandwich, Mass.: Beautiful Feet Books, 1998.

$15.95. Order from American Home-School Publishing. A read-aloud biography of Columbus and his sons, interwoven with other biographies: Erasmus, Copernicus, Richard III, and others.

Wade, Mary Dodson. *Christopher Columbus: A Rookie Biography.* San Francisco, Calif.: Children's Book Press, 2003.

$4.95. Order from any bookstore. One of the books in the wonderful Rookie Biography series for first- to third-grade readers.

Elizabeth I

Stanley, Diane. *Good Queen Bess.* New York: HarperCollins, 2001.

$16.95. Order from American Home-School Publishing.

Galileo

Sis, Peter. *Starry Messenger.* New York: Farrar, Straus & Giroux, 1996.

$6.95. Order from any bookstore. Tells the story of Galileo's discoveries, with illustrations based on Galileo's own journals and records.

Joan of Arc

Stanley, Diane. *Joan of Arc.* New York: HarperCollins, 2002.

$7.99. Order from Greenleaf Press.

Leif Ericsson

d'Aulaire, Ingri, and Edgar Parin. *Leif the Lucky.* Sandwich, Mass.: Beautiful Feet Books, 1994.

$13.95. Order from American Home-School Publishing.

Marco Polo

Herbert, Janis. *Marco Polo for Kids.* Chicago: Chicago Review Press, 2001.

$16.95. Order from Greenleaf Press. A biography of Marco Polo that includes activities and projects.

Strathloch, Robert. *Marco Polo.* Barrington, Ill.: Heinemann Library, 2002.

$7.99. Order from Rainbow Resource Center. One of the Historical Biography series designed especially for grades 2–4.

Montezuma

Reid, Struan. *Montezuma.* Barrington, Ill.: Heinemann Library, 2002.

$7.99. Order from Rainbow Resource Center. One of the Historical Biography series designed especially for grades 2–4.

Who in the World Biography Series. Charles City, Va.: Peace Hill Press.

$9.50 each. Order from any bookstore or from Peace Hill Press. This series, designed especially for second- to fourth-grade readers, meshes with Volume II of *The Story of the World.* Accompanying audiobooks, read by Jim Weiss, are also available on CD for $12.95.

Beckman, Robert. *Who in the World Was the Secretive Printer? The Story of Johannes Gutenberg*. 2005.

Clark, Connie. *Who in the World Was the Unready King? The Story of Ethelred*. 2005.

Lambert, Loreen. *Who in the World Was the Forgotten Explorer? The Story of Amerigo Vespucci*. 2005.

Phillips, Robin. *Who in the World Was the Acrobatic Empress? The Story of Theodora*. 2006.

Late Renaissance/Early Modern, 1600–1850 (Third Grade)

List of Historical Topics to Cover

Your children's librarian can point you to third-grade-level books exploring these major events (listed chronologically):

the *Mayflower*
early American settlements
Russia under Peter the Great and his successors
Prussia in the eighteenth century
the Enlightenment
the agricultural revolution
Native American cultures
the British in India
the French Revolution
British-French conflict in Canada
the American Revolution
the Napoleonic Wars
the industrial revolution
Simón Bolívar's fight for independence in South America
the siege of the Alamo
the California gold rush
Australia's beginnings as a penal colony.

List of Great Men and Women to Cover

Mary Stuart (Mary Queen of Scots) (1542–1587)
Tokugawa Ieyasu (1543–1616)

James I of England (1566–1652)
Queen Nzinga of Angola (1582–1644)
Shah Jahan (1592–1666)
Oliver Cromwell (1599–1658)
Charles I (1600–1649)
Rembrandt (1606–1669)
John Milton (1608–1674)
Robert Boyle (1627–1691)
Louis XIV of France (1638–1715)
Isaac Newton (1642–1747)
William Penn (1644–1718)
Peter I (Peter the Great) (1672–1725)
Yoshimune (1684–1751)
Johann Sebastian Bach (1685–1750)
Frederick William I (Frederick the Great) (1688–1740)
Benjamin Franklin (1706–1790)
Qianlong (1711–1795)
Maria Theresa (1717–1780)
Catherine the Great (1729–1796)
George Washington (1732–1799)
Franz Joseph Haydn (1732–1809)
Thomas Jefferson (1743–1826)
Betsy Ross (1752–1836)
Phyllis Wheatley (1753–1784)
Louis XVI (1754–1793)
Marie Antoinette (1755–1793)
Wolfgang Amadeus Mozart (1756–1791)
George III of England (1760–1820)
Eli Whitney (1765–1825)
Captain James Cook (1768–1771)
Tecumseh (1768–1813)
Napoleon (1769–1821)
Ludwig van Beethoven (1770–1827)
Meriwether Lewis (1774–1809) and William Clark (1770–1838)
Simón Bolívar (1783–1830)
Shaka Zulu (1787–1828)
Sacagawea (c. 1788–1812)
Nat Turner (1800–1831)

General Information

Benchley, Nathaniel. *George the Drummer Boy.* New York: HarperTrophy, 1987.

$3.99. Order from Rainbow Resource Center. Historical fiction on a second- to fourth-grade reading level about the battles at Lexington and Concord.

———. *Sam the Minuteman.* New York: HarperTrophy, 1987.

$3.99. Order from Rainbow Resource Center. Historical fiction on a second- to fourth-grade reading level about a Revolutionary War soldier.

Bliven, Bruce. *The American Revolution.* New York: Random House, 1981.

$5.99. Order from any bookstore. Part of the excellent Landmark series.

Brill, Ethel. *Madeleine Takes Command.* South Bathgate, N.D.: Bethlehem Books, 1997.

$12.95. Order from any bookstore. A read-aloud that corrects the U.S.-centered focus of most books written about this time period by telling the story of a French Canadian heroine.

Copeland, Peter F. *Early American Trades Coloring Book.* New York: Dover, 1980.

$3.50. Order from Amazon. Drawings of the different occupations in Colonial America.

———. *Life in Colonial America Coloring Book.* New York: Dover, 2002.

$3.95. Order from The Book Peddler.

———. *The Story of the American Revolution Coloring Book.* New York: Dover, 1988.

$3.95. Order from The Book Peddler.

Daugherty, James. *The Landing of the Pilgrims.* New York: Random House, 1981.

$5.99. Order from Children's Books.

The French Revolution: Paper Dolls to Cut Out. Santa Barbara, Calif.: Bellerophon Books, 1993.

$5.95. Order from Bellerophon. Biographies of historical figures (in French and in English) from Lafayette to Robespierre accompany these paper dolls.

Guerber, H. A. *The Story of the Great Republic.* Edited by Christine Miller. Fort Collins, Colo.: Nothing New Press, 2002.

$23.95. Order from Nothing New Press or from Curriculum Connection. An engaging narrative history, broken into small, readable sections, first published in the late nineteenth century. The first half of the book deals with America before the Civil War.

———. *The Story of the Thirteen Colonies.* Fort Collins, Colo.: Nothing New Press, 2002.

$23.95. Order from Nothing New Press or from Curriculum Connection. An engaging narrative history, broken into small, readable sections, first published in the late nineteenth century; a great reference book to have on hand for extra reading through the year.

Harness, Cheryl. *They're Off! The Story of the Pony Express.* New York: Aladdin, 2002.

$6.99. Order from Rainbow Resource Center. The story of communications between the east and west coasts in the mid-1800s, written on a third- to fourth-grade reading level.

King, David C., and Bobbie Moore. *Colonial Days: Discover the Past with Fun Projects, Games, Activities, and Recipes.* New York: Wiley, 1997.

$12.95. Order from any bookstore.

———. *Pioneer Days: Discover the Past with Fun Projects, Games, Activities, and Recipes.* New York: Wiley, 1997.

$12.95. Order from any bookstore.

Maestro, Betsy and Giulio. *A More Perfect Union: The Story of Our Constitution.* Paramus, N.J.: Pearson, 1990.

$7.99. Order from any bookstore. The simplest and clearest introduction to the Constitution and its history, written for grades 2–4.

Moore, Kay. *If You Lived at the Time of the American Revolution.* New York: Scholastic, 1998.

$5.99. Order from Greenleaf Press. Part of the Scholastic series written for young children; covers both daily life and history in an entertaining way.

Morley, Jacqueline. *You Wouldn't Want to Be an American Colonist.* New York: Franklin Watts, 2004.

$9.95. Order from any bookstore. Leads young students step-by-step through the perils of life in the early American colonies.

San Souci, Robert, and N. C. Wyeth. *N. C. Wyeth's Pilgrims.* San Francisco: Chronicle Books, 1996.

$6.95. Buy from any bookstore or from Greenleaf Press. Simple text accompanies N. C. Wyeth's wonderful full-color paintings of pilgrims. Generally informative, but ignore the page that explains how the first settlers threw a Thanksgiving feast to thank the *Indians*(!).

Tierney, Tom. *American Family of the Colonial Era: Paper Dolls in Full Color.* New York: Dover, 1987.

$6.95. Order from Dover Publications. Large, historically accurate paper dolls.

———. *American Family of the Pilgrim Period: Paper Dolls in Full Color.* New York: Dover, 1987.

$5.95. Order from Dover Publications.

Wingate, Philippa. *Who Were the First North Americans?* Tulsa, Okla.: Usborne Publishing, Ltd., 2003.

$4.99. Order from any bookstore or from an Usborne distributor. This Starting Point History title is designed for grades 1–3.

Biographies

Adams, Abigail

Wagoner, Jean Brown. *Abigail Adams: Girl of Colonial Days.* New York: Aladdin, 1992.

$5.99. Order from any bookstore. Written on a third- to fifth-grade level, these imaginative biographies in the Childhood of Famous Americans series focus on the childhood of each subject. Highly recommended.

Adams, John

Benge, Janet. *John Adams: Independence Forever*. Lynnwood, Wash.: Emerald Books, 2002.

$8.99. Order from any bookstore. One of the Heroes of History series, written on an entertaining fourth- to fifth-grade level.

Hopkinson, Deborah. *John Adams Speaks for Freedom*. Illus. Craig Orback. New York: Aladdin, 2005.

$3.99. Order from any bookstore. One of the Read-to-Read series, this is ideal for students reading on a second- to third-grade level (much simpler than the Heroes of History biography above).

Attucks, Crispus

Millender, Dharathula H. *Crispus Attucks: Black Leader of Colonial Patriots*. New York: Aladdin, 1986.

$5.99. Order from any bookstore. A Childhood of Famous Americans biography.

Bach, Johann Sebastian

Celenza, Anna Harwell. *Bach's Goldberg Variations*. Illus. Joann E. Kitchel. Watertown, Mass.: Charlesbridge Publishing, 2005.

$21.95. Order from any bookstore. Not a traditional biography of Bach, but an account of the composition of the Goldberg Variations, along with a CD; plenty of historical detail.

Beethoven, Ludwig van

Rachlin, Ann. *Beethoven*. Hauppage, N.Y.: Barron's, 1994.

$7.95. Order from any bookstore. One of the Famous Children series.

Boone, Daniel

Stevenson, Augusta. *Daniel Boone: Young Hunter and Tracker*. New York: Aladdin, 1986.

$5.99. Order from any bookstore. A Childhood of Famous Americans biography.

Buffalo Bill

Stevenson, Augusta. *Buffalo Bill: Frontier Daredevil*. New York: Aladdin, 1991.

$5.99. Order from any bookstore. A Childhood of Famous Americans biography.

Crockett, Davy

Parks, Eileen Wells. *Davy Crockett: Young Rifleman*. New York: Aladdin, 1986.

$5.99. Order from any bookstore. A Childhood of Famous Americans biography.

Franklin, Benjamin

Cousins, Margaret. *Ben Franklin in Old Philadelphia.* New York: Random House, 2004.

$5.99. Order from Greenleaf Press. One of the Landmark Biography series.

Giblin, James Cross. *The Amazing Life of Benjamin Franklin.* Illus. Michael Dooling. New York: Scholastic, 2006.

$7.99. Order from any bookstore. A well-written picture-book biography with plenty of additional information about Franklin's times.

Harness, Cheryl. *The Remarkable Benjamin Franklin.* National Geographic Children's Books, 2008.

$7.95. Order from any bookstore. Another fine, highly illustrated biography suitable for readers in grades 3–5.

Handel, George Frideric

Venezia, Mike. *George Handel.* Chicago, Ill.: Children's Press, 1995.

$6.95. Order from any bookstore. Part of the readable junior series Getting to Know the World's Greatest Composers.

Henry, Patrick

Adler, David A. *A Picture Book of Patrick Henry.* New York: Holiday House, 2001.

$6.95. Order from Greenleaf Press. A simple and interesting guide to Patrick Henry's life.

Fritz, Jean. *Where Was Patrick Henry on the 29th of May?* Illus. Margot Tomes. New York: Putnam, 1997.

$6.99. Order from any bookstore. A classic children's book, covering the history of the early Revolution as it tells the story of Patrick Henry.

Jackson, Andrew

Venezia, Mike. *Andrew Jackson: Seventh President, 1829–1837.* Chicago, Ill.: Children's Press, 2005.

$7.95. Order from any bookstore. A simpler read than the Jackson biography listed below, this is part of the Getting to Know the U.S. Presidents series.

Stanley, George Edward. *Andrew Jackson: Young Patriot.* New York: Aladdin, 2003.

$5.99. Order from any bookstore. One of the Childhood of Famous Americans series

Jefferson, Thomas

Barrett, Marvin. *Meet Thomas Jefferson.* New York: Knopf, 2001.

$4.99. Order from The Book Peddler. A Landmark Biography.

Giblin, James Cross. *Thomas Jefferson: A Picture Book Biography.* New York: Scholastic, 2006.

$5.99. Order from any bookstore. A simple biography with attractive color illustrations.

Lafayette, Marquis de

Fritz, Jean. *Why Not Lafayette?* Illus. Ronald Himler. New York: Putnam, 2001.

$5.99. Order from any bookstore. A fourth- to fifth-grade level biography of the Marquis; this would also make an entertaining read-aloud for younger students.

Monroe, James

Venezia, Mike. *James Monroe: Fifth President, 1817–1825.* Chicago, Ill.: Children's Press, 2005.

$7.95. Order from any bookstore. Part of the Getting to Know the U.S. Presidents series.

Mozart, Wolfgang Amadeus

Rachlin, Ann. *Mozart.* Hauppage, N.Y.: Barron's, 1992.

$7.99. Order from any bookstore. One of the Famous Children series of biographies.

Pocahontas

Penner, Lucille Rech. *The True Story of Pocahontas.* New York: Random House, 1994.

$3.99. Order from Greenleaf Press. A Step Into Reading biography, written on a second-grade level.

Revere, Paul

Stevenson, Augusta. *Paul Revere: Boston Patriot.* New York: Aladdin, 1984.

$5.99. Order from any bookstore. One of the Childhood of Famous Americans series.

Ross, Betsy

Greene, Stephanie. *Betsy Ross and the Silver Thimble.* New York: Aladdin, 2002.

$3.99. Order from American Home-School Publishing. A Step Into Reading easy reader for beginners.

Sacagawea

Seymour, Flora Warren. *Sacagawea: American Pathfinder.* New York: Aladdin, 1991.

$5.99. Order from any bookstore. One of the Childhood of Famous Americans series.

Sitting Bull

Stevenson, Augusta. *Sitting Bull: Dakota Boy.* New York: Aladdin, 1996.

$5.99. Order from any bookstore. One of the Childhood of Famous Americans series.

Squanto

Bulla, Clyde Robert. *Squanto, Friend of the Pilgrims.* New York: Scholastic, 1990.

$4.99. Order from Greenleaf Press.

Tecumseh

Collier, James Lincoln. *The Tecumseh You Never Knew*. Illus. Greg Copeland. Chicago, Ill.: Children's Press, 2004.

$25.50. Order from any bookstore. This well-illustrated picture-book biography is more difficult than the biography listed below.

Mayer, Cassie. *Tecumseh*. Portsmouth, N.H.: Heinemann, 2007.

$5.99. Order from any bookstore. A First Biography, written on a very simple reading level.

Washington, George

Cross, James. *George Washington: A Picture Book Biography.* New York: Scholastic, 1998.

$5.99. Order from Greenleaf Press. A simple biography with colorful illustrations.

Harness, Cheryl. *George Washington*. Des Moines, Iowa: National Geographic Children's Books, 2006.

$7.95. Order from any bookstore. Large illustrations, straightforward text on a third- to fifth-grade level.

Heilbroner, Joan. *Meet George Washington.* New York: Random House, 2001.

$4.99. Order from The Book Peddler. A Step-Up Biography.

Washington, Martha

Wagoner, Jean Brown. *Martha Washington: America's First First Lady.* New York: Aladdin, 1986.

$5.99. Order from any bookstore. One of the Childhood of Famous Americans series.

Wheatley, Phillis

Weidt, Maryann. *Revolutionary Poet: A Story about Phillis Wheatley.* Minneapolis, Minn.: Lerner Publishing, 1997.

$6.95. Order from any bookstore.

Modern, 1850–Present (Fourth Grade)

List of Historical Topics to Cover

Your children's librarian can point you to fourth-grade level books exploring these major events (listed chronologically). For state history, also write your state's Chamber of Commerce and request materials to study your state's history, geography, and commerce.

Africa under European control
the Indian mutinies
the Crimean War
the Victorian era
the War between the States (Civil War)
exploration of the American West
Euro-American conflict with the Native American tribes
the Boxer Rebellion
World War I
the Russian Revolution
the Soviet Union
the Great Depression
the New Deal

civil war in Spain
the Axis and the Allies
World War II
Nazi Germany/Hitler
the Holocaust
Zionism/the Jews' return to Palestine
apartheid/South African segregation
China under Mao
the Korean War
the civil-rights movement
the Vietnam War
landing on the moon

List of Great Men and Women to Cover

Andrew Jackson (1767–1845)
Louis Joseph Papineau (1786–1871)
Samuel Morse (1791–1872)
Commodore Matthew Perry (1794–1858)
Santa Anna (1794–1876)
Robert E. Lee (1807–1870)
Abraham Lincoln (1809–1865)
David Livingstone (1813–1873)
Otto von Bismarck (1815–1898)
Elizabeth Cady Stanton (1815–1902)
Karl Marx (1818–1883)
Queen Victoria (1819–1901)
Victor Emmanuel II (1820–1878)
Susan B. Anthony (1820–1906)
Florence Nightingale (1820–1910)
Harriet Tubman (1820–1913)
Ulysses S. Grant (1822–1885)
Catewayo of the Zulus (1826–1884)
Sitting Bull (1831–1890)
Samuel Clemens (Mark Twain) (1835–1910)
George Custer (1839–1876)
Claude Monet (1840–1926)

Alexander Graham Bell (1847–1922)
Thomas Edison (1847–1931)
Mutsuhito (emperor of Japan) (1852–1912)
Theodore Roosevelt (1858–1919)
Henry Ford (1863–1947)
Wilbur Wright (1867–1912) and Orville Wright (1871–1948)
Mahatma Gandhi (1869–1948)
Vladimir Lenin (1870–1924)
Winston Churchill (1874–1965)
Josef Stalin (1879–1953)
Franklin D. Roosevelt (1882–1945)
Benito Mussolini (1883–1945)
Adolf Hitler (1889–1945)
Dwight D. Eisenhower (1890–1969)
Charles de Gaulle (1890–1970)
Francisco Franco (1892–1975)
Mao Zedong (1893–1976)
Czar Nicholas II (1895–1917)
Amelia Earhart (1897–1932)
Albert Einstein (1897–1955)
Charles Lindbergh (1902–1974)
John F. Kennedy (1917–1963)
Nelson Mandela (1918–)
Margaret Thatcher (1925–)
Martin Luther King, Jr. (1929–1968)
Neil Armstrong (1930–)
Saddam Hussein (1937–2006)
Bill Gates (1955–)

General Resources

Both *The Story of the World* and the *Usborne Internet-Linked Encyclopedia* cover world history; the *Story of the World Activity Book* suggests many library books and resources to reinforce this learning. Since most states suggest that students spend fourth grade studying American history, the following resources focus on American history so that you can prepare for any possible testing. Use them at the appropriate chronological point in the study of world history, in order to cover the basics of American history while still placing it into its larger context.

Archambault, Alan. *Black Soldiers in the Civil War Coloring Book.* Santa Barbara, Calif.: Bellerophon, 1995.

$3.95. Order from Bellerophon. A museum-shop-quality coloring book of Civil War-era images.

———. *Civil War Heroes: A Coloring Book.* Santa Barbara, Calif.: Bellerophon, 1991.

$4.95. Order from Bellerophon. A museum-shop-quality coloring book of contemporary Civil War portraits.

Bernhard, Annika. *State Birds and Flowers Coloring Book.* New York: Dover, 1990.

$3.95. Order from Dover.

Bunting, Eve. *The Wall.* Boston: Houghton Mifflin, 1992.

$5.95. Order from any bookstore. A little boy is taken to find his grandfather's name on the Vietnam Veterans Memorial.

Carey, Charles W. *The Emancipation Proclamation.* Chanhassen, Minn.: Child's World, 1999.

$28.50. Part of the Journey Into Freedom series, this informative book for young students is (unfortunately) only available in an expensive library binding, but is well worth borrowing through Interlibrary Loan if necessary.

A Coloring Book of Our Presidents, Washington through Clinton. Santa Barbara, Calif.: Bellerophon, 1988.

$4.95. Order from Bellerophon. Contemporary portraits of each president.

Copeland, Peter F. *Civil War Uniforms Coloring Book.* New York: Dover, 1980.

$3.95. Order from Greenleaf Press.

———. *Famous Women of the Civil War Coloring Book.* New York: Dover, 1999.

$3.95. Order from Dover.

———. *From Antietam to Gettysburg Coloring Book.* New York: Dover, 1983.

$3.95. Order from Dover.

———. *Story of the Civil War Coloring Book.* New York: Dover, 1991.
$3.95. Order from Dover.

Douglas, Lloyd G. *The White House.* Chicago, Ill.: Children's Press, 2003.
$4.95. Order from any bookstore. A simple introduction to the history of the president's home.

DuBoise, Muriel L. *The U.S. House of Representatives.* Mankata, Minn.: Capstone Press, 2000.
$6.95. Order from any bookstore. Simple and heavily illustrated guide.

———. *The U.S. Presidency.* Mankata, Minn.: Capstone Press, 2000.
$6.95. Order from any bookstore. Simple and heavily illustrated guide to one of the three branches of government.

———. *The U.S. Senate.* Mankata, Minn.: Capstone Press, 2000.
$6.95. Order from any bookstore. Simple and heavily illustrated guide.

———. *The U.S. Supreme Court.* Mankata, Minn.: Capstone Press, 2000.
$6.95. Order from any bookstore. Simple and heavily illustrated guide.

Fit-a-State Puzzle. Smetheport, Pa.: Lauri Toys.
$19.99. Order from Rainbow Resource Center. This 11½ × 17-inch puzzle has the name and capital of each state beneath its puzzle pieces.

Flags of the U.S.
Blackline coloring pages of all fifty state flags can be printed out at enchantedlearning.com/usa/flags.

Foster, Genevieve. *Abraham Lincoln's World.* Sandwich, Mass.: Beautiful Feet Books, 2000.
$17.95. Order from Greenleaf Press. Tells the story not only of Lincoln, but also of other men and women whose lives intersected his.

Fradin, Dennis Brindell. From Sea to Shining Sea series. Danbury, Conn.: Children's Book Press.
This series includes one title for each state and is written on a simple second- to fourth-grade reading level.

Geography Songs Kit. Newport Beach, Calif.: AudioMemory, 1999.
$19.95 for tape, $22.95 for CD. Order from AudioMemory. Thirty-three

songs cover continents, oceans, planets, and 225 countries; includes 23 maps to label.

Guerber, H. A. *The Story of the Great Republic.* Edited by Christine Miller. Fort Collins, Colo.: Nothing New Press, 2002.

$23.95. Order from Nothing New Press. An engaging narrative history, broken into small, readable sections, first published in the late nineteenth century; a great reference book to have on hand for extra reading through the year. The last half of the book deals with the Civil War and afterward.

Heinrichs, Ann. America the Beautiful series. New York: Scholastic.

This series includes one title for each state and is slightly more difficult than the From Sea to Shining Sea series.

Holling, Holling C. *Minn of the Mississippi.* Boston: Houghton Mifflin, 1978.

$11.95. Order from American Home-School Publishing. The history of the Mississippi told through the adventures of a snapping turtle.

———. *Paddle-to-the-Sea.* Boston: Houghton Mifflin, 1980.

$11.95. Order from American Home-School Publishing. A Caldecott-winning story about an Indian boy's toy canoe and its journey from the Great Lakes to the Atlantic.

———. *Tree in the Trail.* Boston: Houghton Mifflin, 1990.

$11.95. Order from American Home-School Publishing. The history of the Great Plains and Santa Fe Trail, centered on a cottonwood tree.

King, David C. *Civil War Days: Discover the Past with Exciting Projects, Games, Activities, and Recipes.* New York: Jossey-Bass, 1999.

$12.95. Order from Rainbow Resource Center. Follows the lives of two families, one white and one black, through daily activities; plenty of suggestions for hands-on learning.

———. *World War II Days: Discover the Past with Exciting Projects, Games, Activities, and Recipies.* New York: Jossey-Bass, 2000.

$12.95. Order from The Book Peddler. Explore the culture of American in the thirties and forties.

Krull, Kathleen. *A Kids' Guide to America's Bill of Rights: Curfews, Censorship, and the 100-Pound Giant.* Illus. Anna Divito. New York: HarperCollins, 1999.

$16.99. Order from any bookstore. Younger students may need help with this text, but good readers will be able to follow the development of the ten amendments.

Levine, Ellen. *If You Lived at the Time of Martin Luther King*. New York: Scholastic, 1994.

$5.99. Order from any bookstore. Simple reading about the civil rights movement.

Lincoln, Abraham. *The Gettysburg Address.* Illus. Michael McCurdy. New York: Houghton Mifflin, 1998.

$6.95. Order from any bookstore. Each sentence of the Gettysburg Address stands in large type above a woodcut illustration; this book will bring the famous speech to life.

Moore, Kay. *If You Lived at the Time of the Civil War.* New York: Scholastic, 1994.

$5.99. Order from any bookstore. Simple reading level.

Murphy, Jim. *The Boys' War.* Boston: Clarion Press, 1993.

$8.95. Order from any bookstore. Boys as young as 11 and 12 fought in the Civil War; this book tells their stories in their own words.

United States Map. Torrance, Calif.: Frank Schaffer Publications, 1988.

$15.99. Order from School Specialty Publishing. A large floor puzzle, with each state a separate piece.

Presidents of the United States Pocket Flash Cards.

$2.99. Order from Rainbow Resource Center. All the presidents on cards: portraits, signatures, brief biographies, and trivia.

The Presidents Songs. Animaniacs, 1995.

The catchiest memory aid around; Wakko and friends sing the first forty-three presidents. The song can be purchased as part of the Animaniacs series, Season 3, Episode 75, first aired on November 11, 1995; you can also find it on youtube.com.

Rickman, David. *Cowboys of the Old West Coloring Book.* New York: Dover, 1990.

$3.95. Order from The Book Peddler. A detailed coloring book.

Smith, A. G. *Civil War Paper Soldiers in Full Color.* New York: Dover, 1986.
$6.95. Order from Greenleaf Press. One hundred small soldiers, from both sides.

———. *Confederate Army Paper Soldiers.* New York: Dover, 1995.
$5.95. Order from Greenleaf Press. Twenty-four large soldiers.

———. *Plains Indian Punch-Out Panorama.* New York: Dover, 1994.
$6.95. Order from Rainbow Resource Center. A modeling project that needs no scissors!

———. *Union Army Paper Soldiers.* New York: Dover, 1995.
$6.95. Order from Greenleaf Press. Twenty-four large soldiers.

States and Capitals Flash Cards.
$2.99. Order from Rainbow Resource Center. This pack of 50 cards drills all sorts of information—date of statehood, flower, nickname, bird, industries, and more.

States and Capitals Songs. Newport Beach, Calif.: AudioMemory, 1998.
$9.95 for tape, $12.95 for CD. Order from AudioMemory. The kit includes the tape or CD with states and capitals songs, plus a map to color.

West, Delno C. and Jean M. *Uncle Sam and Old Glory: Symbols of America.* New York: Atheneum, 2000.
$17.99. Order from any bookstore. Gives the stories behind fifteen American symbols, from the American flag and the bald eagle to Smokey the Bear.

Biographies

Alcott, Louisa May
Meigs, Cornelia. *Invincible Louisa: The Story of the Author of Little Women.* New York: Scholastic, 1995.
$7.99. Order from Greenleaf Press. A 1937 Newbery winner.

Anthony, Susan B.
Monsell, Helen Albee. *Susan B. Anthony: Champion of Women's Rights.* New York: Aladdin, 1986.

$5.99. Order from any bookstore. One of the Childhood of Famous Americans series, imaginative biographies written on a third- to fifth-grade level that focus on the childhood of each subject. Highly recommended.

Barton, Clara.

Stevenson, Augusta. *Clara Barton: Founder of the American Red Cross.* New York: Aladdin, 1986.

$5.99. Order from any bookstore. One of the Childhood of Famous Americans series.

Bethune, Mary McLeod

Greenfield, Eloise. *Mary McLeod Bethune.* New York: HarperCollins, 1994.

$6.99. Order from any bookstore. A simple biography of the famous educator born as the fifteenth child of former slaves.

Blackwell, Elizabeth

Henry, Joanne Landers. *Elizabeth Blackwell: Girl Doctor.* New York: Aladdin, 1996.

$5.99. Order from any bookstore. One of the Childhood of Famous Americans series.

Carver, George Washington

Moore, Eva. *The Story of George Washington Carver.* Illus. Alexander Anderson. New York: Scholastic, 1990.

$4.99. Order from any bookstore. This Scholastic Biography is written for good third- to fifth-grade readers.

Chavez, Cesar

Krull, Kathleen. *Harvesting Hope: The Story of Cesar Chavez.* New York: Harcourt, 2003.

$17.00. Order from any bookstore. A fascinating picture-book account of Cesar Chavez's childhood and his rise to activism.

Darwin, Charles

Hopkinson, Deborah. *Who Was Charles Darwin?* Illus. Nancy Harrison. New York: Grosset & Dunlap, 2005.

$4.99. Order from any bookstore. A thorough but simple biography, written on about a fourth-grade level.

Douglass, Frederick

Adler, David A. *A Picture Book of Frederick Douglass.* New York: Holiday House, 1997.

$6.95. Order from any bookstore. A simple illustrated guide to Douglass's life.

Earhart, Amelia

Henderson, Meryl. *Amelia Earhart: Young Aviator.* New York: Aladdin, 2000.

$5.99. Order from any bookstore. One of the Childhood of Famous Americans series.

Edison, Thomas

Guthridge, Sue. *Thomas Edison: Young Inventor.* New York: Aladdin, 1986.

$5.99. Order from any bookstore. One of the Childhood of Famous Americans series.

Edmonds, Emma

Reit, Seymour. *Behind Rebel Lines.* New York: Gulliver Books, 2001.

$6.95. Order from any bookstore. The true story of a Civil War–era girl who posed as a boy, became a soldier, and then became a spy.

Einstein, Albert.

Hammontree, Marie. *Albert Einstein: Young Thinker.* New York: Aladdin, 1986.

$5.99. Order from any bookstore. One of the Childhood of Famous Americans series.

Eisenhower, Dwight D.

Hudson, Wilma J. *A Picture Book of Dwight David Eisenhower.* New York: Holiday House, 2004.

$6.95. Order from any bookstore. A simple illustrated account of Eisenhower's accomplishments.

Ford, Henry

Aird, Hazel B. *Henry Ford: Young Man with Ideas.* New York: Aladdin, 1986.

$5.99. Order from any bookstore. One of the Childhood of Famous Americans series.

Gandhi, Mohandas

Demi. *Gandhi.* New York: Margaret K. McElderry, 2001.

$21.99. Order from any bookstore. A biography that most elementary students can read independently.

Hughes, Langston

Walker, Alice. *Langston Hughes: American Poet.* Illus. Catherine Deeter. New York. Amistad, 2005

$7.99. Order from any bookstore. This picture-book biography also contains several of Hughes's poems.

Keller, Helen

Davidson, Margaret. *Helen Keller.* Illus. Wendy Watson. New York: Scholastic, 1989.

$5.99. Order from any bookstore. This Scholastic Biography is written for good third- to fifth-grade readers.

Kennedy, John F.

Frisbee, Lucy Post. *John F. Kennedy: America's Youngest President.* New York: Aladdin, 1986.

$5.99. Order from any bookstore. One of the Childhood of Famous Americans series.

King, Martin Luther, Jr.

Millender, Dharathula H. *Martin Luther King, Jr.* New York: Aladdin, 1986.

$5.99. Order from any bookstore. One of the Childhood of Famous Americans series.

Lee, Robert E.

Monsell, Helen Albee. *Robert E. Lee: Young Confederate.* New York: Aladdin, 1986.

$5.99. Order from any bookstore. One of the Childhood of Famous Americans series.

Lincoln, Abraham

Freedman, Russell. *Lincoln: A Photobiography.* Paramus, N.J.: Pearson, 1989.

$8.95. Order from Greenleaf Press. This Newbery Award winner shows the changes in Lincoln over time.

Harness, Cheryl. *Abe Lincoln Goes to Washington, 1837–1863*. Des Moines, Iowa: National Geographic Children's Books, 2003.

$7.95. Order from any bookstore. Simple and well-illustrated biography covering the most important years in Lincoln's life.

Marshall, Thurgood

Adler, David A. *A Picture Book of Thurgood Marshall.* New York: Holiday House, 1999.

$6.95. Order from Rainbow Resource Center. A simple illustrated guide to Marshall's accomplishments.

Parks, Rosa

Mara, Will. *Rosa Parks*. Chicago, Ill.: Children's Press, 2007.

$4.95. Order from any bookstore. A very simple Rookie Biography.

Pasteur, Louis

Alphin, Elaine Marie. *Germ Hunter: A Story About Louis Pasteur.* Illus. Elaine Verstrate. New York: Carolrhoda Books, 2003.

$6.95. Order from any bookstore. Part of the Creative Minds Biography series, this book is written with an almost novelistic tone—enjoyable reading for grades 3–5.

Pitcher, Molly

Stevenson, Augusta. *Molly Pitcher: Young Patriot*. New York: Aladdin, 1983.

$5.99. Order from any bookstore. One of the Childhood of Famous Americans series.

Roosevelt, Eleanor

Weil, Ann. *Eleanor Roosevelt: Fighter for Social Justice*. New York: Aladdin, 1989.

$4.99. Order from Greenleaf Press. One of the Childhood of Famous Americans series.

Roosevelt, Franklin D.

Mara, Will. *Franklin D. Roosevelt*. Chicago, Ill.: Children's Press, 2004.

$4.95. Order from any bookstore. A very simple Rookie Biography.

Roosevelt, Theodore

Mara, Will. *Theodore Roosevelt*. Chicago, Ill.: Children's Press, 2007.

$4.95. Order from any bookstore. A very simple Rookie Biography.

Ruth, Babe

Burleigh, Robert. *Home Run: The Story of Babe Ruth.* Illus. Mike Wimmer. San Diego, Calif.: Silver Whistle, 1998.

$7.00. Order from any bookstore. This picture-book biography combines a simple narrative with beautiful illustrations.

Stanton, Elizabeth Cady

Fritz, Jean. *You Want Women to Vote, Lizzie Stanton?* New York: Paper Star, 1999.

$6.99. Order from Rainbow Resource Center. An entertaining account of Stanton's life.

Tubman, Harriet

McDonough, Yona. *Who Was Harriet Tubman?* New York: Grosset & Dunlap, 2002.

$4.99. Order from any bookstore. A thorough but simple biography, written on about a fourth-grade level.

Twain, Mark

Mason, Miriam E. *Mark Twain: Young Writer.* New York: Aladdin, 1991.

$5.99. Order from any bookstore. One of the Childhood of Famous Americans series.

Wright, Wilbur and Orville

Schulz, Walter A. *Will and Orv.* New York: Carolrhoda Books, 2003.

$6.95. Order from Greenleaf Press. An easy-reader account of the day when the airplane first flew.

Stevenson, Augusta. *Wilbur and Orville Wright: Young Fliers.* New York: Aladdin, 1986.

$5.99. Order from any bookstore. One of the Childhood of Famous Americans series.

8

MAKING SENSE OF THE WORLD: SCIENCE

All the world is a laboratory to the enquiring mind.
—Martin H. Fischer

SUBJECT: Beginning science
TIME REQUIRED: An average of 2 to 3 hours per week, 60–90 minutes twice per week

For the next four years, the beginning science student gets to explore the physical world: animals and people (biology), the earth and the sky (earth science and astronomy), the way the elements work together (chemistry), and the laws that govern the universe (physics).

We divide the four years of science into subjects that roughly correspond to the history periods. First graders, who are studying the ancients, learn about those things that the ancients could see—animal life, the human body, and plants. They make collections, take nature walks, and sprout beans in jars.

Second graders collect facts about the earth and sky, a division designed to go along with the medieval–early Renaissance period, when Copernicus and Tycho Brahe observed the heavens.

Third graders work on basic chemistry—atoms and molecules, what elements are and how they interact. They're also reading history from the period spanning 1600 to 1850, the years when the first great chemists lived—Robert Boyle, Georg Ernst Stahl, Antoine Lavoisier, John Dalton.

Fourth graders, studying modern times, learn basic physics and are introduced to the elements of computer science.

These divisions—the study of life, the study of earth and sky, the study of chemistry, the study of physics—correspond to the child's growing ability to think abstractly. A six year old can collect and examine plants and animals; a seven year old, who is a little more mature, can understand something about the vastness of space; an eight year old can comprehend atoms, even though she can't see them; and a nine year old can begin to understand what light and sound are made of.

Don't forget—these are years to explore. As usual, we'll recommend some memory work. But don't be afraid to take off on tangents. There's no way you're going to cover the entire animal kingdom or every chemical reaction in one year's study, let alone the entire scope of physics. The foundation you lay now has to do with basic facts (the differences between insects and spiders, the names of constellations, the way different chemicals interact, the parts of an atom). But it also involves *enthusiasm.* Have fun.

PRIORITIES

The classical education is organized around reading and writing, arithmetic skills, and history. Especially in the early years, science tends to take a secondary place. A second grader who doesn't finish learning her constellations won't be permanently hampered later on. But a second grader who doesn't grasp the concept of writing complete sentences instead of fragments will be hobbled until she figures this out.

Some classical academies go so far as to leave science out of the poll-parrot stage altogether. We don't think this is a good idea. Grades 1 through 4 are a time of discovery—why leave science out of the equation?

But it's true that the elementary student—especially a first or second grader—will spend a large percentage of her time and energy on basic skills.

Because of this, you'll want to schedule science study only one or two days per week, and you may want to introduce science for the first time several weeks into the first-grade year, after the six year old has settled into her reading, writing, and math routine.

TEXTBOOKS

The only books more boring than basic history textbooks are standard science textbooks. And, on the whole, science textbooks lack coherence. They cover, in hit-or-miss fashion, everything from rain forests to diet and nutrition in no particular order. And they never devote more than six weeks or so to any one topic before moving on to the next. The basic idea seems to be that the child will encounter the same subjects at each grade level for a short time and at slightly greater depth.

Every elementary science textbook we examined leaped from subject to subject in six-week chunks. It takes time for a child to develop interest in a new subject, to understand its boundaries and its purposes, and to see what new fields of exploration it opens up. If you use a standard science textbook, you'll move on to the next unit just as this is beginning to take place. A better plan is to cover the basic sciences thoroughly, one year at a time, without jumping around from subject to subject. A classical education is, above all, orderly.

Instead of using a single text, then, we suggest that you use encyclopedia-type works or "spines" as guides and supplement them with a number of different science books designed to make science clear and interesting for children. To organize your study, you'll need four science notebooks (one for each subject), notebook paper, a three-hole punch, and art supplies—construction paper, colored pencils, stickers, glue. You'll be making notebook pages on the information you read and the observations you make.

Note: The following four-year plan gives you a great deal of freedom and flexibility—but also requires that you pull together the elements of science study yourself. For those who prefer a pre-planned science curriculum, we have suggested two alternative programs at the end of this chapter (pages 174–175).

HOW TO DO IT

First Grade: Life Science (Animals, Human Beings, Plants)

For first grade, label your three-ringed notebook "Life Science," and divide it into three sections: "Animals," "The Human Body," and "Plants."

Your basic "texts" for this year should be colorful, large-print guides to the natural world that you can use as jumping-off points for further investigation. We like Dorling Kindersley's *DK First Animal Encyclopedia, The Kingfisher First Human Body Encyclopedia,* and Laurie Carlson's *Green Thumbs* as science spines for the grammar-stage years.

This year, you and your six year old will be studying living things—animals, humans, and plants. Your job will be to help the child *examine* and *describe* living things. In a thirty-six-week school year, you'll spend approximately twenty weeks on the animal kingdom, ten weeks on the human body, and the last six weeks (or so) on the plant kingdom.

The process is simple: You'll read aloud to the child from the science book and then ask her to narrate—to tell back to you in her own words two or three important facts that she's learned (see Chapter 5 for a description of the narration process). You'll write this narration down (or ask the child to write it, if her skills permit). If the child shows interest, you'll find additional library books on the topic. And if not, you'll move on to the next topic.

Important Instructions. As you work through first-grade science, don't forget that you can stop at any time and dig deeper into a subject. If the child develops a sudden devouring interest in mushrooms or guinea pigs or the skeleton, that's fine. Spend three weeks collecting pictures, checking books out of the library, and making detailed pages. *The purpose of the first-grade notebook is not to "complete" the study of life on earth somehow.* It's to develop the child's curiosity, as well as her observation, reading, and writing skill, and her concentration span. Your goal is simple: when biology comes around again in fifth grade, you want to hear your child say, "Oh, good. I *love* biology!"

The Animal Kingdom

Choose twenty topics from the *First Animal Encyclopedia* (see page 162) and plan on spending about a week on each one. Begin by reading the one-page topic to the child, and then ask her to narrate the information back to you while you write. *Note:* The best way to prompt a science narration at this level is to say, "Can you tell me two things that you learned about this animal?" or "What was the most interesting thing we read about this animal?"

Then, go to the library and browse through the juvenile science books. You'll find plenty of titles with colorful pictures and clear, simple text. Read a few of these titles together. You don't have to make a narration page for every book, but try to make a narration page from an outside source every two weeks or so. The child can illustrate the narration pages with pictures she's drawn, photocopied, or cut out of magazines.

Narration pages should be kept in the science notebook. We've recommended several coloring books in our Resources list; you can punch holes in these pages and put them into the science notebook as well.

If weather and your surroundings permit, you can also do outside observation (perhaps as an occasional substitute for library visits). Go outside and hunt for worms, butterflies, or spiders. Put the specimens in a jar or bug-house. Ask the child to draw a picture of the specimen. Then, write down the answers to the following questions:

Does it have a backbone?
Does it have fur?
Does it have wings?
What does its skin feel like?
How many feet does it have? What do its feet look like?
How many legs does it have? What do the legs look like?
What does its body look like?
What does it eat?
Where does it live?
How big is it?
What do its babies look like?
Is it domesticated (tamed by man) or wild?
Is it endangered?

For a worm observation, the questions and answers might look like this:

Does it have a backbone? The worm has no backbone.
Does it have fur? The worm has no fur.
Does it have wings? The worm has no wings.
What does its skin feel like? The skin feels soft and slimy.
How many feet does it have? What do its feet look like? The worm has no feet.

How many legs does it have? What do the legs look like? The worm has no legs.
What does its body look like? The body is round and soft, with segments.
What does it eat? The worm eats soil.
Where does it live? It lives in dirt all over the world.
How big is it? [Measure the worm.]
What do its babies look like? We don't know. [Where can we find out?]
Is it domesticated (tamed by man) or wild? [Have you ever seen a tame worm?]
Is it endangered? [Ask the child how many earthworms she's seen. Are they in any danger of disappearing from the earth?]

This process introduces the scientific method—the child is *observing* the animal in an attempt to answer certain questions about it and deducing from what she sees.

Choosing Topics

The twenty weeks you'll spend studying the animal kingdoms isn't nearly long enough to get through the entire *First Animal Encyclopedia*. Instead, you'll want to pick and choose. Plan on covering one topic (one page) per week, along with additional reading (and if the child develops a passion for armadillos or rattlesnakes, don't hold yourself to this schedule). You might want to read through the table of contents with your six year old and allow her to pick twenty animals that she wants to study.

The *First Animal Encyclopedia* is organized alphabetically, not by classification. We think this is appropriate for first-grade students, who (in most cases) aren't yet ready to sort and classify the world; classification is more likely to benefit the fifth-grade student who is moving into the logic stage of study. However, if you would prefer to group animals together by phylum, use this simple chart and study animals in the same phylum and class at the same time:

The Animal Kingdom

Phylum	Class	Animals
Mollusca		Octopus, squid, slug, snail
Annelida		Earthworm
Echinodermata		Starfish, ray
Cnidaria		Jellyfish

Chordates		
	Amphibia	Frog and toad, newt, amphibian
	Reptilia	Lizard, all snakes, turtle and tortoise, alligator and crocodile, chameleon, komodo dragon and iguana
	Chondroichthyes	Shark
	Osteichthyes	Eel, salmon and trout, fish, goldfish, seahorse, swordfish
	Aves	All birds, chicken and turkey, duck and goose
	Mammalia	Aardvark, anteater, antelope, armadillo, baboon, badger, bat, bear, beaver, bison and musk ox, buffalo, camel, cat, chimpanzee, cow and bull, deer, dog, dolphin, donkey, elephant, elk, fox, giraffe, goat, gorilla, guinea pig, hedgehog, hippopotamus, horse, hyena, kangaroo and wallaby, killer whale, koala, wombat and opossum, lemur, leopard, lion, llama, meerkat, mole, monkey, mouse, orangutan, otter, panda, pig, polar bear, porcupine, puma, rabbit and hare, racoon, rat, reindeer, rhinoceros, sea cow, seal and sea lion, sheep, skunk, sloth, squirrel, tiger, walrus, weasel, whale, wolf, yak, zebra
Arthropoda		
	Chilopoda	Centipede
	Arachnida	Spider, scorpion

	Insecta	Ant and termite, bee and wasp, beetle, butterfly and moth, cricket and grasshopper, dragonfly and damselfly, fly
Crustacea (subphylum of arthropoda)		
	Malacostraca	Crab, lobster and crayfish, shrimp and prawn

If you decide to introduce classification to the young student, you should begin by explaining what classification is. *Classification is organizing things into groups.* For an example, use types of stores: grocery stores, hardware stores, toy stores, and clothes stores all sell different kinds of things. Help the child think through the differences between groceries, hardware, toys, and clothes. Then explain that the *kingdoms* (animal and plant) are like stores for organizing different types of living things—animals and plants.

You can play this game with your house as well. Why do you keep certain things in the bedroom, certain things in the kitchen, and certain things in the living room? Each room can represent a kingdom, where different types of household items are kept.

Go on to explain that within each kingdom, things are divided into smaller groups. The grocery store is the food kingdom. But the grocery store doesn't just put all the food into one big heap—meat is in one place, cereal in another, fresh vegetables in another. Use your next grocery trip as a classification exercise, and see if the two of you can figure out why food is classified as it is: Why do eggs, milk, and cheese all belong together?

Once the child understands this concept, you can explain the different *groups* (phyla) within the animal kingdom. When you read the section on worms, explain that earthworms are in the annelid group because they have bodies divided into segments, but that flatworms belong to another group because they have no segments. Explain that insects have bodies divided into three parts (head, thorax, and abdomen), six legs, and wings; spiders, therefore, aren't insects because they have only two body parts (head and abdomen), eight legs, and no wings. (Don't worry—all this information is clearly laid out in the book.) As you make your narrative pages, try to note the group (phylum) to which each animal belongs. You'll probably want to begin each grouping by reading the topic page ("Mammal," "Insect," "Amphibian") that describes the phylum or class under study.

If you're doing science two days a week, your schedule might look like this:

Tuesday	Read the *First Animal Encyclopedia* page together. Talk about the reading. Ask the child to narrate back to you as you write.
Thursday	Read additional library books, and/or take an observation walk outside. (Optional: make a narration page on one of the outside readings.)

If you decide to do science only once a week, you'll want to make a trip to the library ahead of time so that you can offer the child several library books to look at as soon as you've finished the narration.

The Human Body

After twenty weeks (or so) on the animal kingdom, you'll move on to the study of the human body. For this, we suggest The *Kingfisher First Human Body Encyclopedia,* which is colorful and simple but offers enough detail to satisfy curiosity. (This book does cover reproduction, so you may want to pre-read before handing it over to your child.)

As with the *First Animal Encyclopedia,* you can pick and choose which topics you'd like to cover over the next ten weeks. You're not trying to cover all body systems, just those that interest the child. Continue on with the same process: read each topic, make a narration page, do any experiment and make an Experiment Page, and then do additional library reading. Your schedule will continue as above.

You may want to invest in a few of the recommended resources at the end of this chapter (such as *The Magic School Bus: Inside the Human Body* or the *Human Body: Hidden World*), so that you can occasionally read more about a body system without having to make a library trip.

The Plant Kingdom

We've saved the plant kingdom for last so that its study will coincide with spring. Learning the difference between monocotyledons and dicotyledons doesn't seem to inspire most six year olds. A better approach to botany is a hands-on nature-study approach: Grow plants and see what happens.

We suggest using *Green Thumbs: A Kid's Activity Guide to Indoor and Outdoor Gardening.* This simple project book explains the basic facts about seeds, plants, and trees, and offers both inside and outside gardening projects. Pick one project per week, do it together, and then record the results. Library reading is optional; plant books for first graders don't tend to be all that interesting, but we've made a few suggestions in the Resources list at the end of this chapter. Remember that this is simply a very basic introduction to botany. The student is not expected to master the basics of this scientific field until fifth grade. Have fun!

Summary

Animal kingdom	20 weeks	Dorling Kindersley's *DK First Animal Encyclopedia*
Human body	10 weeks	*The Kingfisher First Human Body Encyclopedia*
Plant kingdom	6 weeks	*Green Thumbs: A Kid's Activity Guide to Indoor and Outdoor Gardening*

Second Grade: Earth Science and Astronomy

Now that your child has studied life on earth, she's ready to move on to the study of the planet itself.

As before, you should plan on doing science two days per week for an hour to an hour and a half per day. For second-grade science, get a new science notebook and divide it into two sections: "The Earth" and "Sky and Space." You'll spend half the year (eighteen weeks) on earth science, the other half on astronomy.

For base texts, use *The Usborne Internet-Linked First Encyclopedia of Our World* and *The Usborne Internet-Linked First Encyclopedia of Space.* As in first grade, pick and choose your topics; don't expect to cover everything in these books. Follow the student's interest. Your aim is simply to introduce the study of earth science and astronomy (and to enjoy it).

The *Usborne First Encyclopedias* cover each topic ("Volcanoes," "The Moving Sky") in colorful double-page spreads. Choose eighteen (or so) topics to cover in each book. Each week, read the appropriate pages from the *Usborne First Encyclopedia* aloud to the student. Encourage her to begin to read portions of the text aloud to you, if she's able. After reading, ask her to narrate back to you what she's just heard; use the prompting questions "Can you tell me two or three things that you learned?" and "What was the most interesting thing we just read?" to encourage her. This narration should be written down and put in the science notebook. Most second graders will still need to dictate to you as you write, but some children may be ready to write their own narrations. You can also encourage the second grader to write the first sentence of the narration and then finish it for her.

Then do additional reading. Again, use library visits; we've recommended a few excellent earth and space titles in our Resources list, and a search of the library catalog will provide others. Since the *First Encyclopedias* are Internet-linked, appropriate websites are provided for some topics; you can also use these for additional reading (although you certainly shouldn't do *all* your outside reading from the computer). Aim to make a narration page for at least one additional source.

When possible, try to also complete an activity. The *First Encyclopedias* don't offer experiments, but we recommend *More Mudpies to Magnets* and the *Night Sky Spotter's Guide* as activity resources. For each project or activity that you select, make an Experiment Page that answers the following questions:

What Did We Use?
What Did We Do?
What Happened?
What Did We Learn?

When studying earth science, you can use experiments from "Digging in the Dirt: Earth Explorations" (seventeen projects) and "How Hot, How Cold, How Windy, How Wet: Weather Watchers" that correspond to the section you're studying in *The Usborne Internet-Linked First Encyclopedia of Our World.* For astronomy, you can use the "Aerial Acrobatics: Flight and Space" experiments from *More Mudpies to Magnets* while studying through *The Usborne Internet-Linked First Encyclopedia of Space,* but it is more important to schedule stargazing with the help of the *Night Sky Spotter's Guide.* Stargazing can be difficult in urban areas. If you're surrounded by light pollution, plan a nighttime trip out of the city and away from city lights. Most major cities have astronomy clubs that sponsor star parties, with telescopes set up and resident experts on hand. Watch for these in your local newspaper, or call your local museum and ask for information.

We also recommend using a wonderful book called *Glow-In-The-Dark Constellations: A Field Guide for Young Stargazers,* which offers brief retellings of the legends behind the constellations, descriptions and diagrams of each constellation, and, across from each diagram, a glow-in-the-dark picture of the sky so that you can practice finding a constellation in the dark before you go outside. If you're going stargazing, also consider investing in *The Stargazer's Guide to the Galaxy,* a small and economical paperback that offers plenty of extra help in locating constellations at different locations and all seasons of the year.

If the student shows interest, you can spend several weeks on the constellations and do notebook pages on the legends behind his favorite constellations.

If you do science two days a week, your daily schedule might look like this:

Tuesday	Read a double-page spread from the appropriate *First Encyclopedia.* Ask the child to tell you two or three important facts she's learned. Write these down on a notebook page (perhaps asking the child to write the first sentence herself) and put it in the science notebook. Read one additional picture book on the topic, or follow the Internet link to find out more.
Thursday	Read another picture book and ask the student to complete a narration page describing one or two additional facts learned. OR do an activity or project based on *More Mudpies to Magnets* or the *Night Sky Spotter's Guide,* and create an Experiment Page.

Important Instructions. Don't try to cover every detail on every page of either *First Encyclopedia.* Pick out the topics that excite your second grader; don't attempt to catalog the earth and sky. If she gets excited about volcanoes or the sun, let her spend weeks in the library, discovering everything she can. Don't hurry her along! Remember: *You are not giving the child an exhaustive course in earth science and astronomy.* The goal of classical education is to teach the student to *enjoy* investigation and learning. If you can successfully introduce her to astronomy, you'll find her checking out books about the planets and stars—and reading them on her own time.

Summary

Earth science	18 weeks	*The Usborne Internet-Linked First Encyclopedia of Our World*
		More Mudpies to Magnets
Astronomy	18 weeks	*The Usborne Internet-Linked First Encyclopedia of Space*
		Night Sky Spotter's Guide
		Supplemental
		Glow-In-The-Dark Constellations: A Field Guide for Young Stargazers
		The Stargazer's Guide to the Galaxy

Third Grade: Chemistry

Most elementary science texts ignore chemistry altogether. In fact, no simple, easy-to-follow chemistry text exists for elementary students. But several good chemistry experiment books *do* exist. So in third grade, you'll want to use a chemistry experiment book and a science encyclopedia.

For chemistry experiments, we recommend *Adventures with Atoms and Molecules,* chemistry experiment books that increase in difficulty as you go along. The first two books are well within the abilities of most third graders, providing the children have adult supervision and help. Since the aim of authors Robert C. Mebane and Thomas R. Rybolt is to teach principles of chemistry through experimentation, your third grader will be learning chemistry through experimentation.

Get a fresh notebook for chemistry, and make two dividers. Mark one "Definitions" and the other "Experiments." The Mebane and Rybolt books contain a total of sixty experiments; thus, the student should aim to do two experiments per week—one per science period. This gives you five weeks of flexibility, which you may spend on experiments that are complicated. (And if two experiments a week stress either you or the child, cut back to one.)

Every time the child does an experiment, she should record it on a notebook page in the Experiments section, answering the following questions:

What Did We Use?
What Did We Do?
What Happened?
What Did We Learn?

This Experiment Page is the first part of her chemistry lesson. The second part involves definitions. All chemical terms in the experiment books are underlined. After doing the science experiment, the student should look up these underlined terms in a science encyclopedia. She should then make a Definition Page that contains the term (or terms), its definition, and a drawing or diagram that makes the term clear.

Most third graders will enoy using *The Usborne Internet-Linked First Encyclopedia of Science* as their primary reference work. This encyclopedia is written for third-grade readers; it's not intimidating (we feel that *not* frustrating your beginning chemist should be a very high priority) and is heavily illustrated. However, it doesn't cover all of the terms (and third graders who are reading on an unusually advanced level may find it too elementary). So you'll probably do best to purchase it along with *The Usborne Internet-Linked Science Encyclopedia,* which is written for early middle-grade students. Both are available in paperback, and you'll use both again next year.

Your daily schedule, then, might look like this:

Tuesday and Thursday	Do a chemistry experiment from *Adventures with Atoms and Molecules*. Answer all four questions on the Experiment Page. Make a Definition Page for the underlined words, using the *First Encyclopedia of Science* or, if necessary, referring to the higher-level *Science Encyclopedia.*

The student's first chemistry lesson will involve an unusual amount of definition writing, since the terms *atom, electrons, protons, neutrons, chemical reactions, molecules, water,* and *polymers* appear as underlined terms in the Introduction (and are briefly defined), and since later experiments assume that the student understands these terms. Read through the Introduction together, and then help the child to write out these words and look up their definitions in the science encyclopedia. This will probably take two or three sessions. If the third-grade student is still a reluctant writer, go ahead and write out some of the definitions for him as he dictates (always an acceptable way to help young students learn). Since there are so many terms in this first lesson, don't require the child to draw diagrams to illustrate; he'll come back and do this when he encounters these terms in the lessons.

Once these definition pages are completed, turn to the first experiment: "Do Molecules Move?" The child will use food coloring and a glass of water to observe colored molecules spreading through the clear molecules of water. He'll then complete an Experiment Page, which will look something like this:

Experiment Page
Do Molecules Move?

What Did We Use? We used food coloring and a glass of water.
What Did We Do? We dropped one drop of food coloring into the water and did not move the glass.
What Happened? The color spread out through the water even though the glass was still.
What Did We Learn? This showed us that the molecules in the water were moving.

The student has now learned from experimentation a basic principle of chemistry: molecules are in constant motion. *Adventures with Atoms and Molecules* confirms this, explaining that molecules in solids move very slowly within a small space, molecules in liquids move slowly throughout a larger space, and gas molecules move very fast.

There were no underlined words in this particular experiment, since the Introduction covered the definition of *molecule,* but the student could now go back and draw a diagram of a molecule. (When he encounters the other introductory terms in experiments, he can do the same.)

Further on in the book, an experiment with yeast explores whether molecules can be broken into smaller molecules. The experiment contains several underlined words: *enzymes, yeast,* and *fermentation.* After doing the experiment, the child writes *enzyme* on a blank notebook page, along with the definition in the book: "Enzymes are complex molecules made by living organisms." When she looks up *enzymes* in the appropriate *Science Encyclopedia,* she will find a fuller explanation plus diagrams and pictures. With your help, she uses this information to make her notebook page and then places it in Definitions.

On the one hand, we wish all this information had been published neatly in one book; on the other, the child is practicing how to look up and record information—a very scientific endeavor. Even if you're science-challenged, don't worry—all these texts are written in plain, easy-to-understand language with lots of pictures.

Don't forget the library. Chemistry books as such are difficult to find, but if the child shows an interest, you can locate simple books on individual topics: atoms, molecules, yeast, fermentation, acids. This isn't a requirement. The two experiment books and the *Science Encyclopedia* are adequate resources for a first chemistry course.

Don't worry if the third grader doesn't finish both experiment books. Even if she only completes the thirty experiments in Book I, she'll know more chemistry than 98 percent of American third graders.

Fourth Grade: Physics

Chemistry is the study of the way molecules react to each other to form different substances. Physics is the study of how those substances act in the universe.

Physics is simply the study of the physical world and how it works. The way sound travels, magnetism, the laws of electricity, energy, and motion—these are the concepts of physics.

Like third-grade chemistry, fourth-grade physics is experiment-focused. A good and very simple physics handbook for fourth graders, comparable to the Adventures with Atoms and Molecules series, is *Physics Experiments for Children,* by Muriel Mandell. This small paperback, first published in 1959, has been republished by Dover Books for $4.95. It contains 113 experiments divided into seven chapters: Matter: Air; Matter: Water; Mechanical Energy and Machines; Heat; Sound; Light; and Magnetism and Electricity.

Keep a physics notebook, and divide it in half as you did the chemistry notebook: this year, the two divisions will be "Experiments" and "Finding Out More." You'll want to aim for two experiments per week this year, so begin the year by sitting down and settling on nine experiments in each chapter. There's a fair amount of overlap between the experiments, so it isn't necessary for the student to do every single one; you can eliminate those that call for materials not found around your house, since one or two of the experiments use items more common in the fifties than today (a medicine bottle sealed with a cork?).

Plan on doing science twice a week. For each lesson, the student should perform the experiment, and fill out an Experiment Page as in third grade. Then turn to the appropriate science encyclopedia (recommended in the previous section) to read more. After reading, the student should then write a three- or four-sentence narration, explaining one or two of the concepts covered.

For example, the student working on the experiments in the chapter "Mechanical Energy and Machines" might choose to do the "Why Do We Oil Machines?" experiment. He'll rub two blocks of wood against each other and then repeat the action after covering the blocks with soap or Vaseline. The text explains that the soap (or Vaseline) covers the surfaces of the wood so that the blocks are no longer actually touching, thus reducing friction.

After completing his Experiment Page, the student would then turn to the *First Science Encyclopedia* or the *Science Encyclopedia,* depending on his reading level, and read the section on "Friction." He would conclude his lesson by writing three or four sentences describing friction and its effects.

By the end of the fourth-grade year, your young student will have been introduced to basic concepts of physics.

More than that, over the four years of grammar-stage science, she'll have learned something about each kind of scientific endeavor. She'll have basic knowledge of scientific principles and lots of hands-on experience. And she'll have four notebooks filled with information that she's collected and experiments she's done—concrete proof of her scientific accomplishments.

Note: We examined a number of physics experiment books designed for children, and settled on this one, despite its black-and-white format and slightly dated drawings, because it covered all seven major topics in physics in one book—and because the experiments are *simple* (and likely to work on the first try). Most elementary students need a gentle introduction to physics, and since many are still working to master the basic skills of reading and writing, we don't want to frustrate and overwhelm.

However, if you'd prefer a more challenging physics course, you can follow the basic procedure outlined above with the following books:

Starting with Science: Solids, Liquids, and Gases, by Louise Osborne
Starting with Science: Simple Machines, by Deborah Hodge
Electricity and Magnetism, by Margaret Whalley
Sound and Light, by David Glover
Energy and Power, by Rosie Harlow

These five books cover the basics of physics with more complex experiments and more detailed explanations. Together, they form a good "curriculum" for the parent who wants to place more emphasis on science in the fourth-grade year.

Starting in the Middle

The order described here (life science, earth science, astronomy, chemistry, physics) moves from most concrete to most abstract; when studied along with the history periods described in Chapter 7, it also provides links between science study and the times when scientists lived. However, in the grammar stage, this link is not all that strong (you're not going to find too many biographies of Robert Boyle written on a third-grade level). Don't strain to keep science and history together if you're coming into this progression later than first grade; there's no reason why the third grader shouldn't study ancient history and chemistry at the same time. If you'd like to choose the science subject that piques the child's interest, or that coordinates with another child's study, go right ahead.

Other Curricula Options

In recent years, two home-school science programs have been developed that seem to us compatible with the classical approach; they have been used with success by many home-school parents. Real Science-4-Kids, designed by molecular biologist Rebecca Keller, offers Pre-Level 1 Chemistry and Pre-Level 1 Biology; each curriculum provides one year of study and is designed for use by K–3 students. A teacher's manual, student text, and student workbook are included. The parent must assemble experiment materials, which are generally common household objects (rubber bands, marshmallows, antacid tablets, white grape juice, etc.). Chemistry is studied first, followed by biology, so if you decide to use this program, you should feel free to tinker with our suggested order of study.

Great Science Adventures, written by Dinah Zike and Susan Simpson, has an entirely different approach. As students progress through the lessons, they cut, fold, draw, and glue paper handouts into mini-books and construct paper models. The program is designed for teaching students of different ages together; each lesson provides three different projects on three different levels of difficulty. Most elementary students would do only the first and easiest project; some may be ready to progress to the second. The program is well organized and interesting, but it may frustrate students (and parents) who don't like to cut and paste.

Each GSA book provides 24 lessons and should take 8–12 weeks to complete. We suggest the following pattern:

First grade	*The World of Vertebrates* *The World of Plants* *Discovering the Human Body and Senses* Optional: *The World of Insects and Arachnids*
Second grade	*Discovering Atoms, Molecules, and Matter*
Third grade	*The World of Space* *Discovering Earth's Atmosphere and Weather* *Discovering Earth's Landforms and Surface Features* Optional: *Discovering the Ocean*
Fourth grade	*The World of Tools and Technology* *The World of Light and Sound*

If you use GSA, you will need to supplement the second- and fourth-grade years with additional materials.

Both authors have designed their programs to avoid any discussion of origins, which means that the curricula tend to draw fire from critics on both sides of the origins debate. You can read overviews and sample lessons at the Real Science-4-Kids website, www.gravitaspublications.com, and at the Common Sense Press website, www.commonsensepress.com. Ordering information can be found at the end of the Resources section for this chapter.

RESOURCES

For publisher and catalog addresses, telephone numbers, and other information, see Sources (pages 751–778). Most books can be obtained from any bookstore or library; where we know of a mail-order option, we have provided it. Each year's resources are divided into basic texts and optional supplementary materials; these are further divided by subject (human body, earth science, astronomy, and so forth) in the order you'll encounter them during the school year.

Life Science: Animals, Human Beings, and Plants (First Grade)

Basic Texts

Arlon, Penelope. *DK First Animal Encyclopedia.* New York: Dorling Kindersley, 2004.

$15.99. Order from any bookstore.

Carlson, Laurie. *Green Thumbs: A Kid's Activity Guide to Indoor and Outdoor Gardening.* Chicago: Chicago Review Press, 1995.

$12.95. Order from any bookstore.

Walker, Richard, and Roy Palmer. *The Kingfisher First Human Body Encyclopedia.* New York: Kingfisher, 1999.

$16.95. Order from any bookstore.

Supplementary Resources

Animals

Audubon, J. J., and Paul E. Kennedy. *Audubon Birds of America Coloring Book.* New York: Dover, 1974.

$3.95. Order from Rainbow Resource Center. Includes instructive captions and color pictures on the inside covers.

Bernath, Stefen. *Tropical Fish Coloring Book.* New York: Dover, 1978.

$3.95. Order from Rainbow Resource Center. Includes instructive captions and color pictures on the inside covers.

Green, John. *Wild Animals Coloring Book.* New York: Dover, 1987.

$3.95. Order from Rainbow Resource Center. Includes instructive captions and color pictures on the inside covers.

Green, John, and Alan Weissman. *Birds of Prey Coloring Book.* New York: Dover, 1989.

$3.95. Order from Rainbow Resource Center. Includes instructive captions and color pictures on the inside covers.

Grow-A-Frog Kit.

$24.99. Order from Tobin's Lab. Raise a live hybrid frog with transparent skin (so that you can see its internal organs)!

Gundy, Samuel C., and Thomas C. Quirk, Jr. *Reptiles and Amphibians Coloring Book*. New York: Dover, 1990.

$3.95. Order from Rainbow Resource Center. Includes instructive captions and color pictures on the inside covers.

National Audubon Society Pocket Guides. New York: Knopf.

If you're able to go out and search for wildlife while making your life-science notebook, consider the National Audubon Society Pocket Guides. These are full of beautiful, clear color photographs with full descriptions; too difficult for six year olds, but a wonderful parent resource. Most libraries carry the field guides, or you can buy them through any bookstore for $19.95 each.

Familiar Birds of North America: Eastern Region. 1987.
Familiar Birds of North America: Western Region. 1987.
Familiar Birds of Sea and Shore. 1994.
Familiar Insects and Spiders of North America. 1988.
Familiar Mammals of North America. 1988.
Familiar Reptiles and Amphibians of North America. 1988.

Owen, John. *Horses of the World Coloring Book*. New York: Dover, 1978.

$3.95. Order from Rainbow Resource Center. Includes instructive captions and color pictures on the inside covers.

Sovak, Jan. *Butterflies Coloring Book*. New York: Dover, 1992.

$3.95. Order from Rainbow Resource Center. Includes instructive captions and color pictures on the inside covers.

———. *Insects Coloring Book*. New York: Dover, 1994.

$3.95. Order from Rainbow Resource Center. Includes instructive captions and color pictures on the inside covers.

———. *Snakes of the World Coloring Book*. New York: Dover, 1995.

$3.95. Order from Rainbow Resource Center. Includes instructive captions and color pictures on the inside covers.

Human Beings

16½-Inch Human Skeleton.

$23.99. Order from Tobin's Lab. A fully-assembled plastic skeleton on a stand with a moveable jaw and detachable limbs.

Cole, Joanna. *The Magic School Bus: Inside the Human Body.* New York: Scholastic, 1990.

$5.99. Order from any bookstore. A trip through all the major parts of the body!

Colombo, Luann. *Uncover the Human Body.* San Diego, Calif.: Silver Dolphin Books, 2003.

$18.95. Order from Fat Brain Toys. The thick pages allow you to construct and deconstruct a human body, one system at a time.

Human Anatomy Floor Puzzle. Wilton, Conn.: Melissa & Doug.

$9.95. Order from Fat Brain Toys. This 4-foot-tall two-sided floor puzzle has the skeletal system on the front and other body systems on the reverse.

Life-Size Skeleton Poster.

$35.00. Order from Anatomy Warehouse. A 6-foot poster of a human skeleton with bones and joints labelled.

Rookie Read About Science Series. San Francisco, Calif.: Children's Book Press.

$5.95 each. Order from any bookstore or check your library; many can also be ordered from Rainbow Resource Center. This beginning-reader series is heavily illustrated and has very brief, large-print text on each page. Excellent for encouraging young readers!

Blevins, Wiley. *Where Does Your Food Go?* 2004.

Curry, Don L. *How Do Your Lungs Work?* 2004.

———. *How Does Your Brain Work?* 2004.

———. *How Does Your Heart Work?* 2004.

Fowler, Allan. *A Look at Teeth.* 2000.

———. *Arms and Legs and Other Limbs.* 1999.

———. *Knowing About Noses.* 1999.

Somebody: Five Human Anatomy Games.

$25.00. Order from Fat Brain Toys. Play five different games of increasing complexity with this body-parts game—wonderful for teaching anatomy as well as organ function.

Plants

Arbel, Lil. *Favorite Wildflowers Coloring Book.* New York: Dover, 1991.

$3.95. Order from Rainbow Resource Center. Includes instructive captions and color pictures on the inside covers.

Bernath, Stefen. *Garden Flowers Coloring Book.* New York: Dover, 1978.
$3.95. Order from Rainbow Resource Center. Includes instructive captions and color pictures on the inside covers.

Miles, Lisa. *Flowers Sticker Book.* Tulsa, Okla.: Usborne Publishing, 2002.
$7.95. Order from Tobin's Lab or from an Usborne distributor.

National Audubon Society Pocket Guides. New York: Knopf.
If you're able to go out and search for plants while making your life-science notebook, consider the National Audubon Society Pocket Guides. These are full of beautiful, clear color photographs with full descriptions; too difficult for six year olds, but a wonderful parent resource. Most libraries carry the Pocket Guides, or you can buy them through any bookstore for $19.95 each.

Familiar Trees of North America: East. 1987.
Familiar Trees of North America: West. 1987.
Familiar Mushrooms. 1990.
Familiar Flowers of North America: East. 1987.
Familiar Flowers of North America: West. 1987.

Rookie Read About Science Series. San Francisco, Calif.: Children's Book Press.
$4.95 each. Order from any bookstore or check your library; many can also be ordered from Rainbow Resource Center. This beginning-reader series is heavily illustrated and has very brief, large-print text on each page. Excellent for encouraging young readers!

Fowler, Allan. *Cactuses.* 2002.
———. *It Could Still Be a Tree.* 1991.
———. *Maple Trees.* 2002.
———. *Plants That Eat Animals.* 2001.
———. *Pine Trees.* 2002.
———. *From Seed to Plant.* 2001.
Robinson, Fay. *Vegetables, Vegetables!* 1995.

Soffer, Ruth. *Coral Reef Coloring Book.* New York: Dover, 1996.
$3.95. Order from Rainbow Resource Center. Includes instructive captions and color pictures on the inside covers.

Earth Science and Astronomy (Second Grade)

Basic Texts

Brooks, Felicity. *The Usborne Internet-Linked First Encyclopedia of Our World.* Illus. David Hancock. Tulsa, Okla.: Usborne Publishing, 2002.
$9.99. Order from any bookstore or from an Usborne distributor.

Dowswell, Paul, et al. *The Usborne First Encyclopedia of Space.* Tulsa, Okla.: Usborne Publishing, 2003.
$9.99. Order from any bookstore or from an Usborne distributor.

Henbest, Nigel, and Stuart Atkinson. *Night Sky Spotter's Guide (Internet Linked).* Rev. ed. Tulsa, Okla.: E.D.C. Publications, 2006.
$5.99. Order from any bookstore or from an Usborne distributor.

Pearce, Q. L. *The Stargazer's Guide to the Galaxy.* Illus. Mary Ann Fraser. New York: Tor, 1991.
$6.99. Order from any bookstore.

Sherwood, Elizabeth A., et al. *More Mudpies to Magnets: Science for Young Children.* Beltsville, Md.: Gryphon House, 1990.
$16.95. Order from any bookstore.

Thompson, C. E. *Glow-In-The-Dark Constellations: A Field Guide for Young Stargazers.* Illus. Randy Chewning. New York: Grosset & Dunlap, 1999.
$9.99. Order from any bookstore.

Supplementary Resources

Earth Science

Burns, T. D. *Rocks and Minerals.* New York: Dover, 1995.
$3.95. Order from Dover Press. This is a high-quality coloring book with instructive captions and color illustrations on the inside covers.

Rocks and Minerals of the U.S. Collection.
Order from Rainbow Resource Center. These are the most economical rock collections around and include study guides.
$19.00. Basic Collection, 35 pieces.
$14.00. Reference Collection, 24 pieces.

Rookie Read-About Science series. San Francisco, Calif.: Children's Book Press.

$4.95 each. Order from any bookstore or check your library; many can also be ordered from Rainbow Resource Center. This beginning-reader series is heavily illustrated and has very brief, large-print text on each page. Excellent for encouraging young readers!

Fowler, Allan. *The Earth Is Mostly Ocean*. 1996.

———. *Icebergs, Ice Caps, and Glaciers*. 1998.

———. *The Top and Bottom of the World*. 1997.

Science in a Nutshell series. Nashua, N.H.: Delta Education.

$36.00. Order from Delta Education. These kits provide a complete science experiment and activity center, designed for grades 2–6. Consider sharing the cost with a neighbor, since the kits provide materials for two or three students.

Fossil Formations.

The kit includes six actual fossil samples, sand, plaster of Paris, modeling clay, an activity guide, and a journal.

Rock Origins.

Investigate the origins of 22 rock and mineral samples; includes actual samples.

Simon, Seymour.

$6.99. Simon's elementary science books, available through libraries and bookstores, have spectacular photographs and easy-to-follow text, written on a first- to third-grade reading level.

Earthquakes. New York: HarperCollins, 2006.

Hurricanes. New York: HarperCollins, 2007.

Icebergs and Glaciers. New York: HarperCollins, 1999.

Lightning. New York: HarperCollins, 2006.

Mountains. New York: HarperCollins, 1997.

Oceans. New York: HarperCollins, 2006.

Storms. New York: Mulberry Books, 1992.

Tornadoes. New York: HarperCollins, 2001.

Volcanoes. New York: HarperCollins, 2006.

Weather. New York: HarperCollins, 2006.

Volcano Poster.

$8.99. Order from Tobin's Lab. A cutaway volcano with plenty of detail and sidebars about faults and tremors.

Astronomy

3-D Solar System: Glow in the Dark. San Francisco, Calif.: Great Explorations.
$20.00. Order from Fat Brain Toys. Nine glow-in-the-dark planets, 200 glow-in-the-dark stars, and supplies to turn them into a mobile.

Cole, Joanna. *The Magic School Bus: Lost in the Solar System.* New York: Scholastic, 1992.
$5.99. Order from any bookstore.

Lafontaine, Bruce. *Constellations in the Night Sky.* New York: Dover, 2003.
$3.95. Order from Rainbow Resource Center. A coloring book of the constellations.

Ghez, Andrea Mia, and Judith Love Cohen. *You Can Be a Woman Astronomer.* New York: Cascade Press, 1995.
$6.00. Order from any bookstore. Dr. Ghez has extensive experience in astronomy, ranging from a stint at a Chilean observatory to work on the Hubble Space Telescope. This title is one of a series depicting real women in science and math careers.

Rey, H. A. *The Stars: A New Way to See Them.* Enlarged World-Wide Edition. New York: Houghton Mifflin, 1976.
$11.99. Order from any bookstore. The author of Curious George provides a way to picture the constellations that is much simpler than the classic drawings of Greek myths.

Simon, Seymour.
$6.99. Simon's elementary science books, available through libraries and bookstores, have spectacular photographs and easy-to-follow text, written on a first- to third-grade reading level.
Comets, Meteors, and Asteroids. HarperCollins, 1998.
Destination: Jupiter. New York: HarperCollins, 2000.
Destination: Mars. New York: HarperCollins, 2004.
Destination: Space. HarperCollins, 2006.
Galaxies. New York: HarperCollins, 1991.
Saturn. New York: HarperCollins, 1988.
Stars. New York: HarperCollins, 2006.
The Sun. New York: HarperCollins, 1989.

The Universe. New York: HarperCollins, 2006.

Uranus. New York: HarperCollins, 1990.

Venus. New York: HarperCollins, 1998.

Solar System Floor Puzzle. Wilton, Conn.: Melissa & Doug.
$12.00. Order from Fat Brain Toys. A 2 × 3-foot floor puzzle of the solar system and asteroid belt.

Chemistry (Third Grade)

Basic Texts

Firth, Rachel, et al. *The Usborne Internet-Linked First Encyclopedia of Science.* Tulsa, Okla.: Usborne Publishing, 2003.
$9.99. Order from any bookstore or from an Usborne distributor.

Mebane, Robert C., and Thomas R. Rybolt. *Adventures with Atoms and Molecules, Book I: Chemistry Experiments for Young People.* Springfield, N.J.: Enslow, 1998.
$11.93. Order from any bookstore.

———. *Adventures with Atoms and Molecules, Book II: Chemistry Experiments for Young People*. Springfield, N.J.: Enslow, 1998.
$9.95. Order from any bookstore.

Rogers, Kirsteen, and Peter Tachell. *The Usborne Internet-Linked Science Encyclopedia.* Tulsa, Okla.: Usborne Publishing, 2003.
$19.99 (paperback version). Order from any bookstore or from an Usborne distributor.

Supplementary Resources

Atom Chartlet.
$1.99. Order from Rainbow Resource Center. A 17 × 22-inch chart showing the parts of an atom.

Edom, Helen. *Science With Water.* Tulsa, Okla.: E.D.C. Publications, 2007.
$5.99. Order from any bookstore. One of the Usborne Science Activities series designed for grades 1–4; the experiments overlap with physics concepts.

Fizzy Foamy Science. Seattle, Wash.: Scientific Explorer.

$21.95. Order from Young Explorers. Safe kit of acids and bases and a set of experiments that foam and bubble.

Goose Eggs: Three In One Science Kits. Greensboro, N.C.: The Wild Goose Company.

$6.99 each. Order from Teaching Planet. These affordable minilabs contain three activities each, materials, and illustrated instructions.

Chemo-Electrio!

Zinc plating and electrical messages.

Growing Crystals!

Crystals.

Mysterious Fibers!

Paper and ink.

pH Fun!

Measure the pH of common household substances (including dog slobber).

Slippery Slime Time!

Colloids.

Super Bounce Putty!

Make polymers.

Wired!

Circuits.

Heddle, Rebecca. *Science in the Kitchen.* Rev. ed. Tulsa, Okla.: E.D.C. Publications, 2007.

$5.99. Order from any bookstore. One of the Usborne Science Activities series designed for grades 1–4; the experiments overlap with physics concepts.

My First Chemistry Kit. Seattle, Wash.: Scientific Explorer.

$20.00. Order from Fat Brain Toys. A chemistry set and microscope designed especially for elementary students.

Physics (Fourth Grade)

Basic Texts

Firth, Rachel, et al. *The Usborne Internet-Linked First Encyclopedia of Science.* Tulsa, Okla.: Usborne Publishing, 2003.

$9.99. Order from any bookstore or from an Usborne distributor.

Glover, David. *Sound and Light (Young Discoverers: Science Facts and Experiments)*. New York: Kingfisher, 2002.
$7.95. Order from any bookstore.

Harlow, Rosie. *Energy and Power (Young Discoverers: Environmental Facts and Experiments)*. New York: Kingfisher, 2002.
$7.95. Order from any bookstore.

Hodge, Deborah. *Starting with Science: Simple Machines*. Tonawanda, New York: Kids Can Press, 1997.
$6.95. Order from any bookstore.

Mandell, Muriel. *Physics Experiments for Children*. New York: Dover, 1968.
$4.95. Order from Dover or from any bookstore.

Osborne, Louise. *Starting With Science: Solids, Liquids, and Gases*. Tonawanda, New York: Kids Can Press, 1995.
$6.95. Order from any bookstore.

Rogers, Kirsteen, and Peter Tachell. *The Usborne Internet-Linked Science Encyclopedia*. Tulsa, Okla.: Usborne Publishing, 2002.
$19.99 (paperback version). Order from any bookstore or from an Usborne distributor.

Whalley, Margaret. *Electricity and Magnetism: The Book and Disk that Work Together*. Chanhassen, Minn.: Creative Publishing International, 2000.
$14.95. Order from any bookstore.

Supplementary Resources

Cassidy, John. *Explorabook: A Kid's Science Museum in a Book*. Palo Alto, Calif.: Klutz Press, 1992.
$21.95. Order from Klutz Press. One hundred pages on seven subjects like light-wave craziness, magnetism, hair-dryer science, and ouchless physics. Bound directly into the book are most of the tools needed: a mylar mirror, a magnet, two packets of agar growth medium, a diffraction grating, and a Fresnel lens.

Doherty, Paul, John Cassidy, and Martin Gardner. *Magnetic Magic*. Palo Alto, Calif.: Klutz Press, 1994.

$12.95. Order from Klutz Press. This spiral-bound book/kit, written by an MIT physicist and two magicians (one of whom is also a mathematician) includes ten magnets, a coin, and a guide to magical magnetic physics.

Macaulay, David, and Neil Ardley. *The New Way Things Work*, rev. ed. Boston: Houghton Mifflin, 1998.

$35. Order from any bookstore. A massive and fascinating book that will provide the curious with months of additional exploration, this book groups machines together by the principles that make them run. Gears, sound, magnetism, computer technology, and much, much more.

Newton's Antics. Salt Lake City, Utah: Be Amazing Toys.

$15.00. Order from Fat Brain Toys. Simple experiments in force and motion, with all materials included.

Our Amazing Bridges Architecture Kit. Plymouth, Mich.: Poof-Slinky, Inc.

$25.00. Order from Fat Brain Toys. Slightly more difficult than the other kits listed, but appropriate for fourth graders interested in the physics of bridges; build three different model bridges.

Science in a Nutshell series. Nashua, N.H.: Delta Education.

$36.00. Order from Delta Education. These kits provided a complete science experiment and activity center, designed for grades 2–6. Consider sharing the cost with a neighbor, since the kits provide materials for two or three students.

Bubble Science.

Variables affecting the size, shape, color, and durability of bubbles.

Charge It! Static Electricity.

Positive and negative charges, static electricity.

Electrical Connections.

Simple and complex circuits, current, batteries.

Energy and Motion.

Stored energy, motion; weights, marbles and ramps.

Gears at Work.

Gear systems and interaction.

Magnet Magic.

Magnetic materials, polar strength.

Sound Vibrations.

Sound waves and their interaction with various materials.

Work: Plane and Simple.

Inclined planes; force and friction.

Other Curricula Options

Great Science Adventures, by Dinah Zike and Susan Simpson. Melrose, Fla.: Common Sense Press.

Order from Common Sense Press. Each book is $24.00.

Discovering Atoms, Molecules, and Matter

Discovering Earth's Landforms and Surface Features

Discovering the Ocean

Discovering the Human Body and Senses

The World of Insects and Arachnids

The World of Light and Sound

The World of Plants

The World of Space

The World of Tools and Technology

The World of Vertebrates

Discovering Earth's Atmosphere and Weather

Real Science-4-Kids, by Rebecca Keller. Albuquerque, N.M.: Gravitas Publications, Inc.

Order from Gravitas Publications.

Pre-Level 1 Chemistry

Student Text. $27.95

Student Workbook. $21.95

Teacher's Manual. $23.95.

Student/Teacher Bundle (contains all of the above). $73.85

Pre-Level 1 Biology

Student Text. $27.95

Student Workbook. $21.95

Teacher's Manual. $23.95.

Student/Teacher Bundle (contains all of the above). $73.85

9

DEAD LANGUAGES FOR LIVE KIDS: LATIN (AND OTHER LANGUAGES STILL LIVING)

Docendo discitur.[1]
—Seneca

SUBJECT: Latin (and other foreign languages)
TIME REQUIRED: 3–4 hours per week, beginning in third or fourth grade.

As you've no doubt noticed, Latin is not the defining element of a classical education. Classical education has to do with setting up solid foundations, with learning how to learn, with mental discipline and intellectual curiosity and a willingness to grapple with the lessons of the past. All of this is much more important than a single foreign-language course.

But you still have to take Latin.

Elementary students are perfectly capable of studying Latin. In third

[1]"One learns by teaching" (something you'll have the opportunity to do as you go through Latin with your third grader).

and fourth grade, the students do basic memory work—vocabulary and parts of speech—and work on English derivations from Latin words.

We've discovered systematic, easy-to-follow Latin courses that you can teach to your third- or fourth-grade child. And you'll have the opportunity to learn along with him.

WHY LATIN?

Why bother with Latin? It is, after all, a dead language (a pejorative phrase)—no literature is being produced in it, no one's speaking it or doing business in it.

We bother with it for a number of reasons.

Latin trains the mind to think in an orderly fashion. Latin (being dead) is the most systematic language around. The discipline of assembling endings and arranging syntax (grammar patterns) according to sets of rules is the mental equivalent of a daily two-mile jog. And because Latin demands precision, the Latin-trained mind becomes accustomed to paying attention to detail, a habit that will pay off especially when studying math and science.

Latin improves English skills. The grammatical structure of English is based on Latin, as is about 50 percent of English vocabulary. The student who understands how Latin works is rarely tripped up by complicated English syntax or obscure English words. Susan attributes her high standardized test scores (740 in SAT verbal, 800 in GRE verbal) partly to her study of Latin, beginning in third grade.

Latin prepares the child for the study of other foreign languages: French, Spanish, and Italian are all related to Latin. Even non-Latinate languages can be more easily learned if Latin has already been studied. The child who has been drilled in Latin syntax understands the concepts of agreement, inflected nouns, conjugated verbs, and grammatical gender no matter what language these concepts appear in.

Latin guards against arrogance. The study of the language shows the young child that his world, his language, his vocabulary, and his way of expression are only one way of living and thinking in a big, tumultuous, complicated world. Latin forces the student to look at words and concepts anew:

What did this Latin word really mean?

Is this English word a good translation for it?

Doesn't the Latin word express something that English has no equivalent word for?

Does this reveal a gap in my own thinking?

A foreign language, as Neil Postman writes in *The End of Education,* "provides one with entry into a worldview different from one's own. . . . If it is important that our young value diversity of point of view, there is no better way to achieve it than to have them learn a foreign language."[2]

HOW DOES LATIN WORK?

The third-grade Latin course we suggest consists almost entirely of vocabulary memorization and word study. But some grammar is introduced toward the end of the course.

Here's what you have to know to get all the way through Leigh Lowe's *Prima Latina.*

To understand how Latin works, you have to remember that *word endings are more important than word order.*

If I want to say that my husband just planted his shoe in the dog's ribs, I say:

Peter kicked the dog.

(although he would never do such a thing). How do you know that the dog was the receiver of the kick and that Peter was the giver of the kick? Because Peter comes before the verb, and the dog comes after. This tells English speakers that the dog is the *object* (receiver) of the kick and that Peter is the *subject* (the doer) of the kick.

But Latin works slightly differently. Latin has special endings (called *inflections*) that tell the reader whether a noun is the subject or the object.

[2]Neil Postman, *The End of Education: Redefining the Value of Schools* (New York: Knopf, 1995), p. 147.

It's as though, in English, every noun acting as a subject had an *s* on the end and every noun acting as an object had an *o* on the end:

> Peter-s kicked the dog-o.

If English worked this way, we could reverse the sentence:

> The dog-o kicked Peter-s.

and the reader would still realize that Peter had done the kicking and that the dog had received it—because of the ending.

That's how Latin works. Case endings take the place of word order. Case endings tell you whether a word is being used as a subject, object, possessive, and so on.

You also need to know that Latin uses these word endings on verbs to take the place of pronouns. If I say:

> I kicked the dog

you know who did the action, because "I" comes before "kicked." But instead of using pronouns *before* verbs, Latin *conjugates* verbs by tacking the pronouns onto the ends of the verbs:

> Kicked-I the dog.

Now I could say "The dog kicked-I" and mean the same thing.

There's more to Latin than this, of course, but the above explanations will get you started.

There are several different ways to pronounce Latin: the so-called classical pronunciation (in which, for example, "v" is pronounced as "u" or "w") and the "Christian" or "ecclesiastical" pronunciation, used by choirs, are the two most common. We prefer not to worry overmuch about pronunciation. As Douglas Wilson explains,

> Because microphones were not thrust in Augustus Caesar's face . . . we are not exactly sure what his pronunciation was. . . . There are alternative approaches to Latin pronunciation [and the simplest method] is called

> the "Protestant," "Old," or "English" method. It follows out the bright idea of linking Latin pronunciation to the vernacular. In other words, say it as though it were English.[3]

The ecclesiastical pronunciation will be useful if the child ever gets to sing in Latin. Otherwise, though, don't get too sidetracked trying to master pronunciation.

HOW TO DO IT

If you decide to begin Latin in third or fourth grade (see Chapter 19 for other options), you'll take advantage of the child's most natural "window" for language learning. We suggest that you consider using either *Prima Latina*, published by Memoria Press, or *The Big Book of Lively Latin*. Both are gentle introductions to Latin, and neither requires that you have previous knowledge of the language.

Prima Latina, written by Leigh Lowe, consists of a student book, teacher manual, and pronunciation CD; you can also buy an instructional DVD and premade flashcards. The teacher's manual has a summary of Latin grammar in the front. Read it over, but don't let it confuse you. In the 25 lessons provided, you can learn the basic grammar needed along with your child.

You can begin *Prima Latina* in either third or fourth grade; the program will take a year or less to complete. When you complete this introduction to Latin, you can continue on to *Latina Christiana I*, which is put out by the same press and is designed to follow *Prima Latina*. Both of these programs are written for parents who do not know Latin and feature very clear instruction. The optional DVDs provide instruction from one of the program's authors, Leigh Lowe.

Latina Christiana introduces more complex Latin grammar, and in most cases students will need to be working on at least a fourth-grade level in English grammar before beginning it.

Prima Latina is ideal for beginning Latin with a student who is third grade or younger. If you are working with an advanced third grader or fourth grader, you may also consider using *The Big Book of Lively Latin*. Written by

[3]Douglas Wilson, Wesley Callihan, and Douglas Jones, *Classical Education and the Home School* (Moscow, Idaho: Canon Press, 1995), p. 32.

Latin teacher and home school parent Catherine Drown, the *Big Book* provides more supplementary material (historical background, activities and games, studies in mythology and Roman society) and moves a little faster than *Prima Latina*.[4] *The Big Book* is self-explanatory, intended for parents and students to work through together. After completing the *Big Book*, students can continue on to one of the programs suggested in Chapter 43.

Samples of both programs can be seen at the publishers' websites: www.memoriapress.com and www.livelylatin.com.

As you investigate Latin curricula, beware of "whole to parts"[5] Latin instruction. These two programs provide systematic, "parts to whole" instruction: children memorize vocabulary and then learn to use that vocabulary properly; conjugations and declensions are taught all at once rather than incidentally.

Here's what we mean. In Latin, every verb (such as *amo*, "I love") has a *root*, which carries the verb's basic meaning (*am-*, "love"), and *endings*, which serve as pronouns: *-o* means "I," *–as* means "you" singular, and so on. These pronoun endings are the same for every verb the child encounters in the first two years of study. So once the student learns the list of endings for *I*, *you* (singular), *he/she/it*, *we*, *you* (plural), *they* (the endings are *–o*, *-as*, *-at*, *-amus*, *-atis*, *-ant*), he can put them on any verb he wants:

amo	I love	*voco*	I call
amas	You love	*vocas*	You call
amat	He/she/it loves	*vocat*	He/she/it calls
amamus	We love	*vocamus*	We call
amatis	You love	*vocatis*	You call
amant	They love	*vocant*	They call

This is parts-to-whole instruction: first the student learns the parts, *then* he learns how to put them together to form a whole.

Whole-to-parts Latin primers, on the other hand, tell the child that the word *amamus* means "we love," never explaining that the word has both a root

[4]*Prima Latina* teaches the first declension; *Lively Latin* takes students through the second declension and also does Latin diagramming, more vocabulary, and more advanced verb work.

[5]See pages 221–225 for a further explanation of "whole to parts" versus "parts to whole" instruction.

and a personal ending. Later, the child will meet *vocamus* in a sentence and discover that this word means "we call"—again with no explanation. Sooner or later, he'll figure out that *-amus* means "we." Or he may get frustrated with this apparently patternless language and quit. Either way, he'll have wasted a great deal of time and energy trying to understand how Latin works.

But if he is simply given the list of personal endings to memorize, he will have the power to form any Latin verb he likes as well as the knowledge to decode the Latin words he encounters in his reading. Whole-to-parts Latin instruction is frustrating and counterproductive, and breaks down the very skill that systematic Latin lessons develop—the habit of systematic thinking.

SCHEDULES

Plan on spending about three to four hours per week on Latin. It's more productive to spend thirty minutes every day than to do one long session or even two shorter ones per week. Three days per week is an absolute minimum; four is better.

WHAT ABOUT OTHER LANGUAGES?

Why do we recommend beginning Latin when everyone knows that starting a modern foreign language at a young age is the best way to achieve fluency?

Well, we agree. The elementary grades *are* the best time to learn a modern foreign language—and at the end of this chapter we've recommended a couple of modern language programs suitable for home use. However, in our experience, *none* of these programs will get you speaking a foreign language. This only happens if you're able to *speak* the language (with a live person) at least twice a week. Conversation, which requires you to think in the language you're learning, is the only path to fluency.

If you speak a foreign language fluently and would like to teach it to your student, go ahead and do this during the third- and fourth-grade years, and save Latin until fifth or sixth grade. Or if you can arrange for a tutor (preferably a native speaker) to come in and converse with your child at least twice a week, go ahead and study a modern language now and save Latin until fifth or sixth grade. (We think every American child should learn to speak Spanish at some point, if possible.)

But if you can't arrange for modern-language conversation, make Latin central to your foreign language learning for right now. The study of Latin syntax and vocabulary will provide many of the same benefits as modern language study, as well as improving the child's general language skills. The student who has completed a Latin course will have much less difficulty when he encounters a modern foreign language later on. And since Latin isn't a spoken language, you won't need to worry about the conversational component.

As you study Latin, you may want to use one of the modern language programs listed below as an additional resource, perhaps adding it to your schedule once or twice a week. This will give the student exposure to a modern language and prepare him for later learning.

RESOURCES

Basic Texts

Latin

Drown, Catherine. *The Big Book of Lively Latin.* San Marcos, Calif.: Lively Latin, 2008.

$55.00 for the online PDF version, $79.00 for the PDF on a 2-CD set, $125.00 for the print version. Order from Lively Latin.

Lowe, Cheryl. *Latina Christiana I: An Introduction to Christian Latin.* Louisville, Ky.: Memoria Press, 2001.

$39.95 for the set. Order from Memoria Press.

Student Book. $15.00.

Teacher Manual. $20.00.

Pronunciation CD or Tape. $4.95.

Instructional DVDs. 5-DVD set, $55.00.

———. *Latina Christiana II. An Introduction to Christian Latin.* Louisville, Ky.: Memoria Press, 2001.

$39.95 for the set. Order from Memoria Press.

Student Book. $15.00.

Teacher Manual. $20.00.

Pronunciation CD or Tape. $4.95.
Instructional DVDs. 4-DVD set, $45.00.

Lowe, Leigh. *Prima Latina: An Introduction to Christian Latin,* 2d ed. Louisville, Ky.: Memoria Press, 2003.
$32.95 for the set. Order from Memoria Press.
Student Worktext. $14.00.
Teacher Manual. $14.00.
Pronunciation CD. $4.95.
Instructional DVDs. 3-DVD set, $45.00.

Latina Christiana/Prima Latina Flashcards. Louisville, Ky.: Memoria Press.
$14.95. Order from Memoria Press. Includes the vocabulary for both *Prima Latina* and *Latina Christiana.*

Modern Languages

Kraut, Julia, et al. *Spanish for Children.* Classical Academic Press, 2008.
Order from Classical Academic Press. The approach of this Spanish primer meshes well with Latin studies. An audio CD accompanies the student text. Samples can be viewed on the Classical Academic Press website; an instructional DVD and two more levels are in the works.
Spanish for Children, Primer A. $21.95.
Spanish for Children, Primer A, Answer Key. $12.95

La Clase Divertida. Holly Hills, Fla.: La Clase Divertida.
Order from La Clase Divertida. This Spanish program, developed by a home-school father with twenty years of Spanish teaching experience, is designed as a family learning project. The Rosetta Stone courses listed below are focused primarily on language learning; this program provides games, stories, cooking and project activities, and other resources along with video and audio cassette instruction, turning Spanish into something closer to a mini-unit study. Good for family fun. Each kit provides enough material (workbooks and craft supplies) for two students.
Level 1 Kit. $110.00.
Additional Student Packet. $15.00.
Level II Kit. $125.00.
Additional Student Packet. $25.00.

Rosetta Stone Language Learning: Homeschool Edition. Harrisonburg, Va. $219.00 for Level 1 (probably two to three years of study for a young student). Order from Rosetta Stone. An interactive computer-based language learning program which uses photos and graphics to encourage the student to think in a foreign language. Each Homeschool Edition Level 1 includes the CDs, a study guide, a consumable workbook plus answer key, a teacher handbook, and a program for keeping track of the student's progress. Many other languages are available at the Rosetta Stone website, www.RosettaStone.com.

Spanish Level 1.

French Level 1.

German Level 1.

Schultz, Danielle. *First Start French.* Louisville, Ky.: Memoria Press, 2008. Order from Memoria Press. This beginning French program takes the same approach as *Prima Latina.* The pronunciation CD features a native speaker. Each book offers one year of study. Samples can be viewed on the Memoria Press website.

Book One

Student Book. $17.50.

Teacher Book. $17.50.

Pronunciation CD. $4.95.

Book Two

Student Book. $17.50.

Teacher Book. $17.50.

Pronunciation CD. $4.95.

10

ELECTRONIC TEACHERS: USING COMPUTERS AND VIDEOS

> Anyone who tells you computers are more effective than anything else is either dumb or lying.
>
> —Larry Cuban[1]

You'll notice that we haven't recommended any videos or computer games in our Resources lists. Yes, we know they exist. We just don't think they ought to be used for teaching grammar-stage students.

Reading is mentally active.

Watching a video is mentally passive.

Writing is labor-intensive.

Clicking icons is effortless.

Print that stays still and doesn't wiggle, talk, or change colors makes the brain work hard at interpretation. Print that jumps up and sings a song (à la *Sesame Street*) doesn't make the brain work at all. Watch your

[1]Larry Cuban, quoted in Rumesh Ratnesar, "Learning by Laptop," *Time*, March 2, 1998, pp. 62–63. Stanford University professor Larry Cuban is an expert on technology in American education.

preschooler's face the next time you sit her in front of *Sesame Street*—the mouth hangs open, the eyes are glazed.

All children prefer ease to effort. It seems reasonable to us to limit their exposure to the easier way until the harder way has been mastered.

There's some scientific evidence to back us up on this. The brain activity created by reading and writing is significantly different from the brain activity created by image-based technologies. Jane Healy, Ph.D. in education psychology and the author of *Endangered Minds,* points out that while reading and writing depend on left-hemisphere brain development, children's television programming depends almost entirely on right-hemisphere stimuli—quickly changing visual images instead of stability; noises (booms, crashes, single-word exclamations) rather than complex sentences; bright colors, rapid movement, and immediate resolutions rather than logical sequencing of actions.[2]

In the early grades, the brain develops more quickly than at any other time. Connections are made. Neural pathways are established. The grammar stage is a particularly crucial time for verbal development: the brain is mapping out the roads it will use for the rest of the child's life. (This is why foreign languages acquired during early childhood are almost always completely fluent, while languages learned later are never as natural.) It is vital that the child become fluent in reading and writing during the elementary years—and the brain development required for this fluency is markedly different from that used for comprehending video and computer images.

Both software programs and videos are image-centered, not word-centered. "In print culture," Neil Postman writes in *The End of Education,* "we are apt to say of people who are not intelligent that we must 'draw them pictures' so that they may understand. Intelligence implies that one can dwell comfortably without pictures, in a field of concepts and generalizations."[3] Indeed, the higher stages of the classical education require the child to think without pictures—to be so comfortable with nonvisual con-

[2]See Jane Healy, *Endangered Minds: Why Our Children Don't Think and What We Can Do about It* (New York: Touchstone, 1990), ch. 10 ("TV, Video Games, and the Growing Brain"), esp. p. 211.

[3]Neil Postman, *The End of Education: Redefining the Value of School* (New York: Knopf, 1995), p. 25.

cepts such as responsibility, morality, and liberty that she can ponder their meanings in widely different circumstances.

Word-centered education requires the student to interact with the material—to comprehend it, interpret it, and talk about it. Videos and software don't engage the brain in the same way. A student must be *actively* involved in the learning process in order to benefit; this is why we lay such stress on reading history and science and then writing about the knowledge gained. Videos and software are designed to entertain, not to engage. They promote passive, not active, learning.

Video and software images replace the child's own imagination. Susan once checked out a copy of the children's classic *The Lion, the Witch, and the Wardrobe* for her six-year-old son, Christopher. We'd read the book aloud together, and although he enjoyed the video, he heaved a big sigh when it was over.

"What's wrong?" Susan asked.

"Mommy," he said, "I had another picture of Lucy in my head, and that girl didn't look *anything* like her."

"Well, you can still think of her in your head however you want."

"No," he said. "Now that picture's in my head and I can't get it out."

Should you ban all videos and computer games?

No, of course not. You should limit their use. You should supervise content. As much as possible, steer away from highly visual, quickly changing programs with a constant barrage of sound effects. (Yes, this means *Sesame Street.*) When you have the flu, or when you're trying to teach fractions to your third grader while your four year old sprints around and around the kitchen, or when company's coming and the bathroom hasn't been cleaned, put on a video.

But always ask yourself: What am I giving up? If I didn't put this on, would the kids go play basketball out back, or drag out Chutes and Ladders out of sheer boredom? Would they read a book? Would I be forced to give the four year old a math lesson to keep him happy, too? If my twelve year old doesn't watch this movie, will he go build a model? If my ten year old is told she can't play this computer game, will she wander off and read fairy tales?

As entertainment, educational software beats Nintendo hollow. Just be aware that *software is entertainment*. There's nothing wrong with a computerized phonics program, but it can't replace your work with the child and her primer. It's a game, not school.

Use computer software solely as a supplement to your print-based curriculum. For elementary students, computer time should be classified with TV watching and candy eating as treats that must be limited in order to be enjoyed.

Educational videos can be useful in science. We've enjoyed the spectacular photography of the *Eyewitness* science videos, and we watch National Geographic specials with rapt attention (lava flowing down a mountain has to be seen to be believed). But we view videos in the evening—curled up with a bowl of popcorn—not during schooltime. During schooltime, we read books, do experiments, and write about what we're learning. It's hard work, but the more the student reads and writes, the more natural reading and writing become.

Unfortunately, the same is true of TV viewing and computer game playing. The brain becomes expert at whatever it does the most of during the formative years. So limit the young child's lessons with the "electronic teacher." We guarantee you that she won't have any trouble catching up later on.

11

MATTERS OF FAITH: RELIGION

Man is by his constitution a religious animal.

—Edmund Burke, *Reflections on the Revolution in France*

The old classicists called theology the "queen of sciences" because it ruled over all other fields of study. Theology still does, either in its presence or its absence. In its most honest form, the debate over the teaching of creation and evolution in public-school science classes is not about whether the species evolved over unimaginable years or were created in the span of one word. Because evolution is often taught as an undirected, random process, the debate is over the presence or absence of a Creator. This presence or absence has immense implications for every area of the curriculum: Are we animals or something slightly different? Do math rules work because of the coincidental shape of space and time or because God is an orderly being, whose universe reflects His character? Is a man who dies for his faith a hero or a fool?

Public schools, which have the impossible task of teaching children of many different faiths, must proclaim neutrality. *We don't deal in matters of faith,* the teachers explain. *We're neutral.*

Think about this for a minute. Arguing for the presence of God is generally considered "biased." Assuming His absence is usually called "neutral." Yet both are statements of faith; both color the teacher's approach to any subject; both make a fundamental assumption about the nature of men and women.

To call this neutrality is intellectually dishonest.

Education cannot be neutral when it comes to faith: it is either supportive or destructive. The topic of education is humanity, its accomplishments, its discoveries, its savage treatment of its own kind, its willingness to endure self-sacrifice. And you cannot learn—or teach—about humanity without considering God.

Let's take biology as an example. Mammals are characterized by, among other things, their tendency to care for and protect their young. Do mothers love their babies because of sheer biological imperative? If so, why do we come down so hard on fathers who neglect their children? It's a rare male mammal that pays much attention to its young. Do fathers love their babies because of the urge to see their own genetic material preserved or because fathers reflect the character of the father God? How should a father treat a defective child? Why?

We don't blame the public schools for sidestepping these sorts of questions. In most cases, it's the only strategy they can adopt.

Yet this separation of religious faith from education yields an incomplete education. We're not arguing that religion should be "put back" into public schools. We'd just like some honesty: an education that takes no notice of faith is, at the very least, incomplete.

Since you're teaching your child yourself, you can rectify this situation. Don't ignore instruction in (at the bare minimum) the facts of the world's major religions. Do try to relate the child's studies to your own faith, to your own religious heritage.

Your child will probably start asking the tough questions in the logic stage (something to look forward to): Why did the Crusades take place? Isn't it wrong to try to change people's religion by forcible means? Well, how about peaceful means? Was the pope wrong to put all of England under an interdict? Why would a medieval scholar risk excommunication? Why did Newton believe in God? And what about that father and his defective child?

The elementary-level student won't be thinking on this level, so you can relax for a few years. But now is the time to understand the basics of the faiths that have shaped both history and science. Explain Islam and Buddhism and Hinduism and ancestor worship. Discuss the elements of Christianity and Judaism. Teach the Exodus and the Conquest and the Exile and the birth of Christ right along with ancient history. Show how these world religions have collided—why, for example, the English ruling India were so appalled over suttee (widow burning) while the Indians considered it an honorable act. Don't be afraid of America's Puritan and Dissenter past. And don't fall into the "Thanksgiving trap."[1]

If you don't do this now, your child will reach the logic stage badly equipped—unable to understand fully the events of history and why they have unfolded in their present pattern. Religion plays a major role in the formation of any culture. For this reason, it is imperative that the continuing education of the child include how religion has influenced art, music, literature, science, and history itself.

We believe that religion's role in both past and present cultures is best taught by the parents from the strength of their own faith. I (Susan) don't *want* my six year old taught religion in school. That's my job. It is my responsibility to teach my children what I believe, why I believe it, and why it makes a difference.

RESOURCES

For the teaching of religion, use family resources or check with your own religious community for suggestions.

[1]Many elementary-school history texts, unwilling to run the risk of lawsuits, tell third graders that the Pilgrims gave thanks at Thanksgiving but never mention God. One particularly bad text informs children that the Pilgrims gave thanks to the Indians.

12

FINER THINGS: ART AND MUSIC

Oh, the world is so full of a number of things.
—Robert Louis Stevenson

SUBJECT: Art and music
TIME REQUIRED: 1–4 hours per week

One of the distinctive traits of classical education is the attention it pays to basics. Classical education takes great care in laying the proper foundations for reading, writing, math, history, and science.

Laying foundations is time-consuming. If you learn these subjects thoroughly and well, you may find that you don't have a great deal of time for other areas of study at this level.

In the science chapter (Chapter 8), we told you not to try to cover all of the animal kingdom or all of astronomy. The purpose of the elementary years is to accumulate knowledge, yes; but the focus of your teaching should not be sheer amount of material covered. Rather, your child ought to be learning how to *find* information, how to *fit* information together, and how to *absorb* information through narration, notebook pages, and memorization.

What is true for science holds true for the entire elementary curriculum. You will never be able to cover every subject taught in elementary schools. Resist the temptation to spread your instruction too thin. Give the academic basics your best time and teaching energy during these early years.

Having said that, we now go on to say that art and music have great value for elementary students. Instruction in drawing and art appreciation improves muscle coordination and perception skills. Recent studies have shown that piano lessons improve the reasoning skills of preschool children.

We suggest that you try to schedule at least one block of time (an hour or two) per week for art and music appreciation. If you can manage two blocks of time during the week, do art appreciation one day and music appreciation another. If you can only cope with one more teaching period per week, alternate—art appreciation one week, music the next.

ART

Art for elementary students should involve basic training in two areas: learning about art techniques and elements (drawing, color, and so forth) and about great artists.

You can alternate actual art projects and reading books about great artists. For art projects, we recommend Mona Brookes's *Drawing with Children*. This is a book for you and your child to use together; you'll be surprised at how much *you* learn about drawing.

Alternate art projects with picture study, the method used by Charlotte Mason, the educator who originated narration as a teaching tool. Like narration, picture study requires the student to take in information and then repeat it back to the teacher.

Using the children's art books we've recommended in Resources, ask the child to look intently at a painting for a while—two or three minutes for younger children, up to ten for fourth graders. Then take the picture away, and ask the student to tell you about it.

At first, you may have to ask leading questions. "What color is ———?" "What is the man at the side doing?" With practice, though, the student will start to notice more and more details and retain them longer and longer.

Many home-schooling parents combine picture study and hands-on art by using *Artistic Pursuits*, a nine-book program that combines art appreciation and art history with art instruction. Each lesson gives a simple description of a style or the work of a particular artist, and follows this with a related art project. For example, a simple story about the medieval fresco painter Giotto di Bondone leads into the close examination of a Giotto painting, and then into an elementary fresco project. Art supplies must be purchased separately. Sample lessons and a scope and sequence can be found on the publisher's website, www.artisticpursuits.com.

MUSIC

As with other subjects, music in grades 1 through 4 is a matter of accumulation—getting familiar with what's out there. You can require the child, twice a week, to spend half an hour or so listening to classical music. Most public libraries have a fairly extensive classical music selection available for checkout. Start with music designed for children, such as *Peter and the Wolf*, and then explore together. You can also use the Classical Kids series described in Resources, which will familiarize children not only with great music, but also with the lives of well-known composers and some of their minor works.

The first time the child listens to a piece of music, have her listen to it two or three times in a row. Then make sure she plays it again at the beginning of her next listening period. Familiarity breeds enjoyment. She can do handwork such as Play-Doh™ or coloring books about the composer she is listening to (see Resources at the end of this chapter) but nothing that involves words; her attention should be focused on what she hears, not on what she reads.

There's no easy way to "narrate" symphonies. Asking the child how the music made her feel is of dubious value; asking her to hum the melody only works if she can hum and the melody is uncomplicated. We suggest that you simply make sure she listens to the piece at least twice.

Just as math and reading are easier for children who've heard sums and stories all their lives, so music appreciation comes more naturally to children whose parents play music in the house. The best way to follow up on the child's music-appreciation lesson is to play the piece yourself a couple of weeks later and listen to it as a family. Playing lively classical music while doing housework and playing quiet classical music during meals are two ways to have your family become familiar with classical music.

If you can afford them, piano lessons are good. I (Jessie) feel that every child should take two years of piano (all of mine did). My experience has been that if they showed no interest in it after two years of study, keeping them at it was a waste of time and energy, counterproductive to their love and appreciation of music.

If you want to try music lessons at home, we recommend *John Thompson's Modern Course for the Piano*, a series of books and CDs that slowly introduce note reading and piano playing for children (and parents) with no musical experience.

Another resource for ages eight and up is the Piano Adventures series, which is a self-teaching course that doesn't require any parental knowledge or skill.

Finally, we recently found a most intriguing (and impressive) set of books designed for home-school families who want to try the violin at home. Developed by a concert violinist and experienced teacher, The Violin Book series is the only learn-at-home violin series we've run across! Visit www.theviolinbook.com for a look at the series and at the student violins offered.

RESOURCES

Pick and choose from among these books and tapes in order to familiarize children with a wide range of art and music skills and styles. Most of these titles (and some of the tapes and CDs) will be at your local library or bookstore. Where we know of a mail-order option, we have supplied it.

Art Appreciation

Artistic Pursuits: The Curriculum for Creativity. Rev. ed. Arvada, Colo.: Artistic Pursuits, 2008.

Order from Artistic Pursuits. The books are $42.95 each.

Grades K–3 Book One: An Introduction to the Visual Arts

Grades K–3 Book Two: Stories of Artists and Their Art

Grades K–3 Book Three: Modern Painting and Sculpture

Grades 4–6 Book One: Elements of Art and Composition

Art supplies can be purchased from one of several art supply companies (links and lists for each book are provided on the Artistic Pursuits website) or in a pre-assembled kit.

Supply Kit Grades K–3 Kit 1. $76.00
Supply Kit Grades K–3 Kit 2. $92.00
Supply Kit Grades K–3 Kit 3. $81.00
Supply Kit Grades 4–6 Kit 1. $45.00

Dover Art Postcards. New York: Dover.

Order from Rainbow Resource Center. These sets of art postcards (24 each) provide a simple way to study paintings. $6.95 each.

Chagall.
Dalí.
Degas Ballet Dancers.
Gauguin.
Great Impressionists and Post-Impressionist Paintings.
Masterpieces of Flower Painting.
Mary Cassatt.
Picasso.
Renoir.
Van Gogh.

Martin, Mary, and Steven Zorn. *Start Exploring Masterpieces Coloring Book.* Philadelphia: Running Press, 2000.

$9.95. Sixty famous paintings to color, along with the stories behind them.

Muhlberger, Richard. *What Makes a . . .* New York: Viking.

$16.99 each. This series from the Metropolitan Museum of Art has beautiful illustrations and explains the technical distinctions of each artist's work in a way young children can understand.

What Makes a Degas a Degas? 2002.
What Makes a Monet a Monet? 2002.
What makes a Van Gogh a Van Gogh? 2002.

Venezia, Mike. *Getting to Know the World's Greatest Artists.* Chicago: Children's Press.

$6.95 each. Order from Rainbow Resource Center or check your library. These short, 32-page children's books provide an entertaining introduction to some of the most important artists of the Renaissance along with very nice reproductions of paintings. The text is written on a third- to fourth-grade level.

Botticelli. 1994.
Bruegel. 1994.
Mary Cassatt. 1994.
Paul Cézanne. 1998.
Dalí. 1994.
Da Vinci. 1994.
Gauguin. 1994.
Francisco Goya. 1994.
Edward Hopper. 1994.
Paul Klee. 1994.
Henri Matisse. 1997.
Michelangelo. 1991.
Monet. 1994.
O'Keeffe. 1994.
Picasso. 1994.
Pollock. 1994.
Rembrandt. 1994.
Renoir. 1996.
Diego Rivera. 1995.
Toulouse-Lautrec. 1995.
Van Gogh. 1994.
Grant Wood. 1996.

Wolf, Aline D. *How to Use Child-size Masterpieces.* Hollidaysburg, Penn.: Parent Child Press, 1996.

$12.00. Order from Parent Child Press or from Rainbow Resource Center. This instruction manual tells the parent how to use the postcard-sized art reproductions listed below; children are encouraged to match, pair, and group paintings, to learn the names of artists and their works, to learn about schools of art, and finally to place paintings on a time line.

Child-size Masterpieces. $10.95 each. Each book below has postcard-sized reproductions of paintings for you to remove and use in picture study. Use these three books to match and group paintings and artists:

Child-size Masterpieces, Easy Level.
Child-size Masterpieces, Intermediate Level.
Child-size Masterpieces, Advanced Level.

Use the next three books to learn names of paintings and artists:

Child-size Masterpieces, Step 4.
Child-size Masterpieces, Step 5.
Child-size Masterpieces: Black Images.

Use the final book (priced at $14.00) to learn about the chronology of paintings:

Child-size Masterpieces for Step 8: Using a Time Line.

Art Skills

Artistic Pursuits. See page 208.

A Book of Artrageous Projects. Palo Alto, Calif.: Klutz Press, 2000.
$19.95. Order from Emmanuel Books or from Klutz Press. A hands-on art museum in a book: paint, draw, emboss, stain glass. A fun project book to do together.

Brookes, Mona. *Drawing with Children.* New York: Jeremy P. Tarcher/Putnam, 1996.
$15.95. Order from any bookstore. This has become a modern classic.

Press, Judy, and Loretta Trezzo Braren. *The Little Hands Art Book: Exploring Arts and Crafts with 2- to 6-Year-Olds.* Charlotte, Vt.: Williamson Publishing, 2003.
$12.95. Order from Rainbow Resource Center. For younger children, art (glue, paint, paper, crayons, markers) and crafts (clothespins, popsicles, paper bags, etc.) projects that are simple to do (and use common household items).

Usworth, Jean. *Drawing Is Basic.* Parsippany, N.J.: Dale Seymour Publications, 2000.
$23.93 each. Order from Rainbow Resource Center. For the busy parent who wants to do art but can't find the time, these books offer fifteen-minute "drawing breaks" for you to guide the student in; these breaks teach beginning skills and grow a little more demanding with each year.

Drawing Is Basic: Grade 1.
Drawing Is Basic: Grade 2.
Drawing Is Basic: Grade 3.
Drawing Is Basic: Grade 4.

Music Appreciation

Beethoven's Wig. Cambrige, Mass.: Rounder Records.

$12.98. Order from any music store or from iTunes. A favorite at the Bauer household, this puts (silly) words to great music, builds familiarity, and reveals the underlying structure of symphonies and other music forms.

Sing-Along Symphonies. 2002.

Vol. 2: More Sing-Along Symphonies. 2004.

Vol. 3: Many More Sing-Along Symphonies. 2006.

Vol. 4: Dance-Along Symphonies. 2008 ($14.98).

Brownell, David. *A Coloring Book of Great Composers: Bach to Berlioz*. Santa Barbara, Calif.: Bellerophon.

$4.95. Order from Bellerophon. Portraits to color along with biographical sketches for fifteen composers.

Vol. One: Bach to Berlioz.

Vol. Two: Chopin to Tchaikovsky.

Vol. Three: Mahler to Stravinsky.

American Composers.

Hammond, Susan, producer. Classical Kids series. Toronto: Children's Group.

$16.98. Order from any music store, from Rainbow Resource Center, or check your library. These tapes combine music with history and dramatic storytelling to familiarize children with great composers and their works. Very highly recommended.

Beethoven Lives Upstairs. 2000.

A young boy learns about Beethoven's life through letters to his uncle.

Hallelujah Handel. 2000.

The composer gets involved in a fictional plan to help an orphan boy who sings but won't speak.

Mozart's Magic Fantasy: A Journey Through "The Magic Flute." 2000.

A young girl is magically transported into the middle of *The Magic Flute*.

Mr. Bach Comes to Call. 1999.

An eight year old practicing the Minuet in G is startled when Bach shows up in her living room. Includes over twenty excerpts from Bach's works.

Tchaikovsky Discovers America. 2000.

The composer arrives in New York in 1891 for the opening of Carnegie Hall.

Vivaldi's Ring of Mystery. 1994.

An orphaned violinist tries to find out more about her family in Vivaldi's Venice. Over twenty-four Vivaldi works are included.

Masters of Classical Music series. Los Angeles: Delta, 1990.

$17.98, or $9.99 from iTunes. Each 60-minute recording includes excerpts from major works of each composer. Excerpts are a good way to get young children "hooked" on classical music; they're usually the most tuneful and attractive parts of longer, more complicated works.

Volume 1: Mozart.

Volume 2: Bach.

Volume 3: Beethoven.

Volume 4: Strauss.

Volume 5: Wagner.

Volume 6: Tchaikovsky.

Volume 7: Vivaldi.

Volume 8: Chopin.

Volume 9: Schubert.

Volume 10: Verdi.

Tomb, Eric. *Early Composers Coloring Book.* Illus. Nancy Conkle. Santa Barbara, Calif.: Bellerophon, 1988.

$3.95. Order from Greenleaf Press. From Palestrina through Corelli, with a biographical note and a portrait (to color) of each.

Music Skills

John Thompson's Modern Course for the Piano.

Order from J. W. Pepper.

Teaching Little Fingers to Play: A Book for the Earliest Beginner. $4.95.

First Grade: Book/CD. $16.95.

Popular Piano Solos, First Grade: Book/CD. $10.95.

Piano Adventures. Fort Lauderdale, Fla.: FJH Music Company, Inc.
Order from J. W. Pepper.
Primer Level
Lesson Book. $6.95.
Theory Book. $6.50.
Technique and Artistry. $6.50.
Performance Book. $6.50.
Level One
Lesson Book. $6.95.
Theory Book. $6.50.
Technique and Artistry. $6.50.
Performance Book. $6.50.

The Violin Book Series. Clearwater, Fla.: Ebaru Publishing.
Order from Ebaru Publishing. Eden Vaning, a concert violinist and violin teacher, developed this series of self-teaching books for parents who want to bring children up to youth-orchestra level on the violin. Learn more (and order both books and student violins) at her website, www.theviolinbook.com. Beginning levels are listed below.
The Violin Book
Book 0: Let's Get Ready for Violin. $11.95.
Book 1: Beginning Basics. $20.95.
Book 1 Practice & Performance CD. $14.95.
Book 2: The Left Hand. $20.95.
Book 2 Practice & Performance CDs. $19.95.
Student violins (see website).

PART I

EPILOGUE

The Grammar Stage at a Glance

Guidelines to how much time you should spend on each subject are general; parents should feel free to adjust schedules according to child's maturity and ability.

Kindergarten (Ages Four and Five)

Reading	Spend time every day reading out loud, as much time as you can afford. Learn basic phonics for fluent reading. Begin with 10 minutes, gradually working up to 30 minutes. Practice reading easy books.
Writing	Practice printing. Work up to 10 minutes per day. Copy short sentences from a model.
Mathematics	Learn to count from 1 to 100. Use actual objects to understand what numbers mean, 1 to 100. Be able to write the numbers from 1 to 100. Practice skip-counting by 2s, 5s, and 10s. Teach about math as you go about life. If you use a kindergarten math program, plan on 30 minutes a day.

First Grade

Language	*Do Spelling Workout A* for 10 to 15 minutes per day; begin *First Language Lessons* for 15 to 20 minutes per day; spend 30 minutes per day reading and making the notebook

page. Spend at least 30 minutes per day reading "fun books." Practice penmanship.

Writing Work on simple letters to relatives and friends twice a week. Copy short sentences two or three days per week for 5 minutes each day, working up to 20 minutes each day.

Mathematics Work on the math lesson (either learning a concept or doing a drill) for 30 to 40 minutes per day.

History Study ancient times (5000 B.C.–A.D. 400). Read biographies and easy history books to the child; ask the child to tell you what you've just read; make notebook pages together for the history notebook. Do this for 3 hours per week.

Science Study animals, the human body, and plants, twice a week for 60 minutes each session.

Religion Learn about world religions through the study of history; learn the basics of the family's faith for 10 to 15 minutes per day as part of "family time."

Art Do art projects or picture study once or twice a week.

Music Spend 1 hour per week listening to classical music; begin the study of an instrument, if possible.

Second Grade

Language Do *Spelling Workout B* or *C* for 10 to 15 minutes per day; begin cursive penmanship; spend 30 minutes per day reading or making the notebook page; do *First Language Lessons* for 20 minutes per day; spend 10 minutes per day on memory work. Spend 30 to 60 minutes per day reading "fun books" quietly to self.

Writing Work on simple letters to relatives and friends twice a week. Write from dictation 3 days per week for 10 to 20 minutes each day.

Mathematics Work on the math lesson (either learning a concept or doing a drill) for 40 to 60 minutes per day.

History Study medieval–early Renaissance times (400–1600). Read biographies and easy history books to the child; ask the child to tell you what you've just read; make notebook pages together for the history notebook. The child should begin to do more writing (instead of telling the parent

	what to write). Do this for 3 hours per week.
Science	Study basic earth science and astronomy twice a week for 60 minutes each session.
Religion	Learn about world religions through the study of history; learn the basics of the family's faith for 10 to 15 minutes per day as part of "family time."
Art	Spend 1 hour per week doing picture study, using recommended art books for elementary students; or do art projects.
Music	Spend 1 hour per week listening to classical music; begin or continue the study of an instrument, if possible.

Third Grade

Language	Do *Spelling Workout C* or *D* for 15 minutes per day; spend 30 minutes reading or making the notebook page; do formal grammar for 20 to 30 minutes per day; spend 10 minutes per day on memory work. Spend 30 to 60 minutes per day reading "fun books" quietly to self. Continue penmanship.
Writing	Work on longer letters to relatives and friends once a week. Write from dictation 3 days per week. Begin a writing program twice per week for 20 to 30 minutes each day.
Mathematics	Work on the math lesson (either learning a concept or doing a drill) for 40 to 60 minutes per day.
History	Study late Renaissance–early modern times (1600–1850). Read history books to the child; assign easy biographies and histories for the child to read; ask the child to tell you what you've just read; make notebook pages together for the history notebook. The child should be doing his own writing now. Do this for 3 hours per week.
Science	Study basic chemistry twice a week for 60 to 90 minutes each session.
Latin	Memorize vocabulary; study language daily.
Religion	Learn about world religions through the study of history; learn the basics of the family's faith for 10 to 15 minutes per day as part of "family time."
Art	Spend 1 hour per week doing picture study, using

	recommended art books for elementary students; or do art projects.
Music	Spend 1 hour per week listening to classical music; begin or continue the study of an instrument, if possible.

Fourth Grade

Language	Do *Spelling Workout D, E,* or *F* for 15 minutes per day; spend 30 to 45 minutes per day reading or making the notebook page; study your grammar textbook for 20 minutes per day; spend 10 minutes per day on memory work. Spend 60 minutes per day reading "fun books" quietly to self. Continue penmanship.
Writing	Work on letters to relatives and friends once every two weeks. Write from dictation two or three days per week. Do your writing program two days per week for 20 to 30 minutes each day.
Mathematics	Work on the math lesson (either learning a concept or doing a drill) for 40 to 60 minutes per day.
History	Study modern times (1850–present). Read history books to the child; assign easy biographies and histories for the child to read; ask the child to tell you what you've just read; make notebook pages together for the history notebook. The child should be doing own writing. Do this for 3 hours per week.
Science	Study basic physics twice a week for 90 minutes each session.
Latin	Learn vocabulary and the basic rules of syntax for 45 minutes per day.
Religion	Learn about world religions through the study of history; learn the basics of the family's faith for 10 to 15 minutes per day as part of "family time."
Art	Spend 1 hour per week doing picture study, using recommended art books for elementary students; or do art projects.
Music	Spend 1 hour per week listening to classical music; begin or continue the study of an instrument, if possible.

Notebook Summary, Grades 1 through 4

Language (use a different notebook for each grade)
This notebook contains four sections:

1. *Spelling.* Use for rules that the child is having difficulty with, and for a list of "Trouble Words" that he consistently misspells.
2. *Grammar.* Use to file any grammar exercises that the child completes on his own paper.
3. *Reading.*
   a. *My Reading.* Use for summaries or illustrations of books from the reading lists in Chapter 5.
   b. *Memory Work.* All pieces learned by heart and recited in front of family or friends.
4. *Writing.* Use for copywork assignments, dictation, composition assignments, letters, and other writings.

History (use the same notebook for grades 1–4)
This notebook contains four divisions; each has pictures, compositions, and historical narrations, arranged in chronological order.

1. *Ancients*
2. *Medieval–early Renaissance*

3. *Late Renaissance–early modern*
4. *Modern*

Science (use a new notebook each year)
The life-science notebook (first grade) has three divisions:

1. *Animals*
2. *The Human Body*
3. *Plants*

The earth-science notebook (second grade) has two divisions:

1. *The Earth*
2. *Sky and Space*

The chemistry notebook (third grade) has two divisions:

1. *Definitions*
2. *Experiments*

The physics notebook (fourth grade) has two divisions:

1. *Definitions*
2. *Experiments*

Whole Language and Phonics: Whole to Parts versus Parts to Whole

Using phonics—the method of teaching children the sounds of letters and combinations of letters—is the best way to teach reading. "Whole language" instruction, popular in many classrooms, is based on an innovation of the 1930s—the so-called "look-say" method.

The inventors of look-say reading thought that teaching children the sounds of letter combinations (phonics) required lots of drill and memorization, resulting in tedium. Couldn't this unnecessary step be eliminated? After all, good readers don't sound a word out from beginning to end; good readers glance at a word and take it all in in one gulp. Children ought to learn this from the start. So a new method of reading took over: "whole word" or "look-say." Instead of learning letter combinations and sounding words out, children were taught each word separately and in isolation.

Whole-word teaching, meant to preserve children from the drudgery of drill, actually increased the amount of drill needed. It also prevented children from reading anything that contained words they hadn't yet learned, which is why it took Theodore Geisel (Dr. Seuss) almost a year to write *The Cat in the Hat*. "That damned *Cat in the Hat* took nine months until I was satisfied," Geisel later wrote. "I did it for a textbook house and they sent me . . . two hundred and twenty-three words to use in this book. I read the list three times and I almost went out of my head." Children taught that same list could read *The Cat in the Hat* and practically nothing else.

And parents weren't able to teach whole-word reading.[1] Look-say required expert teachers. You couldn't just start teaching a child words; you had to teach the words in a particular order so that the child could read his lessons. And you had to reinforce this memory work with a complex system of drills and word games.

Look-say is generally acknowledged to have been a disaster. It's true that some children—those whose subconsciouses were very well stocked with words and sounds because they came from homes where print was important—were able to figure the process out. But many more simply gave up. Whole-word reading might have died a quick and ignoble death but for the phonics teachers, who had been laboring to turn phonics into a science. Instead of learning how to pronounce the alphabet, six year olds in phonics classrooms were taught phonetic notation and drilled on individual sounds for months before they were allowed to read actual sentences.

Eventually, both "scientific phonics" and look-say reading gave way to the "whole language" classroom, where students—rather than being taught to sound out words—are "immersed" in language. Teachers read stories, point to words, talk to the children, and generally surround them with words, as we suggest you do during the preschool years.

Unfortunately, illiteracy is still soaring in states where whole-language classrooms dominate. There are several reasons for this. First, many whole-language teachers, while insisting that their methods differ from look-say, are still using look-say drills. They read texts over and over again, pointing to each word and encouraging the children to join in. Children eventually learn to recognize many of the words through sheer repetition. This, of course, does nothing to teach them how to read real literature, which might contain words they haven't seen in the classroom.

Second, most whole-language teachers will insist that they don't rely on look-say alone; they also teach something called "incidental phonics." If, for example, the child has seen the words *smile, smoke, small, smog,* and *smith* over and over again, the teacher will finally point out that *sm* makes the

[1]This antiparent mood still has a voice in many "whole language" classrooms, expressed in such phrases (encountered by us in our research) as "No parent should tutor a child without the teacher's knowledge," "Maybe the parent shouldn't be tutoring the child," and "Reading instructional material is not designed for parents." If a teacher has ever told you not to tutor your child in phonics, you've experienced this legacy.

same sound *every time.* Incidental phonics teaches the connections between words and sounds *only* as the child runs across them in texts. Which means that a child who doesn't encounter many words ending in *-ough* could get to sixth grade or so before finding out that *-ough* can make an *f* sound.

This guessing game is labeled "developing phonemic awareness." It's also called "whole-to-parts phonics instruction" because the student is given the "whole" (the entire word) and only later is told about the "parts" (the letter sounds) that make it up. Granted, it's an improvement on pure look-say, which never lets on that there's any connection between words and the letters that make them up. But whole-language teaching still encourages children to guess. They see a familiar combination of letters, but they haven't learned the letters that come after. They see a word that starts with *in-*, but then they have to use *context* to figure out whether the word is *incidental, incident, inside, incite,* and so forth. And unless a teacher is standing over them to help, they have no tools to read the rest of the word.[2]

But why force the children to guess? Why not simply put them in a systematic phonics program and give them the rules?

A good systematic phonics program does just that—it tells children the rules up front. This is called "parts-to-whole" instruction because the student is taught the parts of words and then shown how they fit together. A good phonics program has the children reading books as soon as possible. Most phonics-taught children can read picture books with easy text after a few weeks. Many move on to chapter books after only a few months of instruction.[3]

Whole-language teachers want to saturate children with language; the classical education requires it. Yet whole-language philosophy collides with the philosophy of classical education. Whole-language teachers put the highest priority on the child's mental process, not on the information that is on the page. If the child is constructing *a* meaning while reading, that's

[2]The whole-language method is infamous for suggesting that it doesn't really matter whether the child reads *incite* or *incident* as long as the sentence makes sense to the child.

[3]And, yes, English *is* a phonetic language. Rudolph Flesch writes, "About 13 per cent of all English words are partly irregular in their spelling. The other 87 per cent follow fixed rules. Even the 13 per cent are not 'unphonetic,' as Dr. Witty calls it, but usually contain just one irregularly spelled vowel: *done* is pronounced 'dun,' *one* is pronounced 'wun,' *are* is pronounced 'ar,' and so on" (Rudolph Flesch, *Why Johnny Can't Read and What You Can Do about It* [New York: Harper & Row, 1985], p. 13).

good enough. It doesn't matter if the meaning may not correspond to what's in front of them. Guessing (whole-language teachers prefer to call this "predicting by context") is perfectly all right. Ken Goodman, professor of education at the University of Arizona and a whole-language proponent, says that "accuracy is not an essential goal of reading."[4]

This attitude is one of the most troubling aspects of whole-language reading. A classical education tries to equip a child to join the Great Conversation, to understand and analyze and argue with the ideas of the past. Those *ideas* are important. Those *words* are important. Aristotle chose his terms with care; the reader must struggle to understand why, not substitute another phrase to simplify matters.

Furthermore, whole-language rejects all drill and repetitive memory work. Granted, drill can be overdone (and has been in many phonics-based classrooms). But the goal of classical education is to show a child how subjects—reading, writing, science, history—are assembled, from the most basic elements to the finished structure. And drill is important because it equips a child's mind with the most basic tools needed for understanding language.

Teaching reading by a pure whole-language approach is like trying to train a house builder by showing him a manor house, explaining to him how to construct those parts that catch his interest—a chimney here, a porch front there—and then leaving him to figure out the rest on his own. A classical approach first explains the properties of brick, wood, concrete, plaster, and steel; then teaches the prospective builder to read a plan; and only then sets him on the task of house building. A builder who knows his work from the bottom up can fix a leak or a sagging floor, instead of staring helplessly at the problem and wondering what went wrong.

In the early grades, all teaching should be parts to whole, rather than whole to parts. Parts-to-whole teaching gives the student all the facts—the building blocks—and then lets him assemble them into a meaningful structure. Whole-to-parts instruction presents the child with the entire structure and then pulls bits and pieces out and explains them, one at a time, as the child encounters them.

Parts-to-whole teaching tells the young historian about the gods and

[4]Art Levine, "Education: The Great Debate Revisited," *Atlantic Monthly*, December 1994, 41.

goddesses of ancient Rome and explains how the Romans used omens and auguries to tell the future. Whole-to-parts teaching gives the child stories about Roman religious customs and asks, "What gods did the Romans worship? Why? How is this like modern religion in America? How is this like your own experience with religion?"

Parts-to-whole science informs the budding entomologist that insects have five different types of leg and foot (swimming leg, digging leg, jumping leg, pollen-carrying leg, and food-tasting brush foot), and then asks the student to place the insects he finds into these categories. Whole-to-parts science lays out a trayful of insects and asks, "What differences do you see between these legs and those legs?"

What's the matter with whole-to-parts instruction? Nothing, except that it's immensely frustrating for children who are at the poll-parrot stage. Whole-to-parts instruction requires analytical thought, an ability that is developed later (in our experience, around fourth or fifth grade). And whole-to-parts teaching assumes a certain knowledge base that untaught children don't yet have. Examine the instances above. The history example requires the immature mind to reflect on religious practices about which it knows very little. And the whole-to-parts science assignment can't be done unless the student knows that different insects do different things with their legs.

Learning through deduction and analysis is a valuable method—but *in the second stage of the trivium,* the logic years, when the student has the accumulated knowledge of the poll-parrot years to build on. Trying to instruct children by deduction and analysis without first laying the foundation of good, solid, systematic knowledge is like building a house from the top down. Many popular school texts are whole to parts in the elementary grades; when you recognize whole-to-parts instruction, avoid it.

PART II

THE LOGIC STAGE

Fifth Grade through Eighth Grade

13

THE ARGUMENTATIVE CHILD

> The Pert age . . . is characterized by contradicting, answering back, liking to "catch people out" (especially one's elders); and by the propounding of conundrums. Its nuisance-value is extremely high.
>
> —Dorothy Sayers, "The Lost Tools of Learning"

Somewhere around fourth grade, the growing mind begins to switch gears. The child who enjoyed rattling off her memorized spelling rules now starts noticing all the awkward exceptions. The young historian says, "But *why* did Alexander the Great want to conquer the whole world?" The young scientist asks, "What keeps the earth in orbit around the sun?" The mind begins to generalize, to question, to analyze—to develop the capacity for abstract thought.

In the second stage of the trivium, the student begins to connect all the facts she has learned and to discover the relationships among them. The first grader has learned that Rome fell to the barbarians; the fifth grader asks why and discovers that high taxes, corruption, and an army made up entirely of mercenaries weakened the empire. The second grader has learned that a noun names a person, place, thing, or idea; the sixth grader discovers that gerunds, infinitives, and noun clauses can also act as nouns.

The third grader has learned how to multiply two-digit numbers together to produce an answer; the seventh grader asks, "What if I have only one two-digit number and an answer? Can I discover the missing number if I call it *x*?"

Now it's time for critical thinking.

"Critical thinking skills" has become the slogan of educators from kindergarten through high school. Critical-thinking books, software, and curricula abound. Catastrophe is predicted for children who miss out on this vital training. "Are you going to wait until schools teach thinking directly?" asks the back cover of one critical-thinking tome. "That may be too late for your children."

But what are these "critical thinking skills," and how are they to be taught?

A quick look through education materials reveals certain phrases popping up again and again: "higher-order thinking," "problem solving," "metacognitive strategies." All these boil down to one simple concept: critical thinking means that the student stops absorbing facts uncritically and starts to ask "Why?": "Why do you multiply the tops and bottoms of fractions?" "Why did the North and South really go to war?" "Why do scientists believe that nothing can go faster than the speed of light?" "Why do words that begin with *pre-* all have to do with something that comes 'before'?" "How do we know that water boils at two hundred twelve degrees Fahrenheit?"

The student who has mastered "higher-order thinking" and "problem-solving techniques" doesn't simply memorize a formula. ("To find the area of a square, multiply the length of a side by itself.") Instead, she memorizes the formula and then figures out why it works. ("Hmmm . . . the sides of a square are the same, so the area inside the square is always going to measure the same horizontally and vertically. That's why I multiply the side by itself.") Once she knows why the formula works, she can extrapolate from it to cover other situations. ("How would I find the area of a triangle? Well, this triangle is like half a square . . . so if I multiply this side by itself, I'll get the area of a square . . . and then if I take half of that, I'll know how much area the triangle covers. The area of a triangle is this side, times itself, times one-half.")

Some critical-thinking advocates suggest that "thinking skills" can somehow replace the acquisition of specific knowledge. "Traditional teaching" is referred to, with scorn, as "mere fact assimilation" or "rote memorization," an outdated mode of learning that should be replaced with classes in "learning to think." The popular teacher's journal *Education Week* defines critical thinking as "the mental process of acquiring information, then evaluating it to reach a logical conclusion or answer," and adds, "Increasingly, educators believe that schools should focus more on *critical* thinking than on memorization of facts."[1]

But you shouldn't consider critical thinking and fact gathering to be mutually exclusive activities. Critical thinking can't be taught in isolation (or "directly," as the above quote from a critical-thinking manual suggests). You can't teach a child to follow a recipe without actually providing butter, sugar, flour, and salt; piano skills can't be taught without a keyboard. And your new focus on the whys and wherefores doesn't mean that your child will no longer learn facts. A math student can't think critically about how to find the area of a triangle unless she already knows the formula for finding the area of a square. A fifth grader can't analyze the fall of Rome until she knows the facts about Rome's decay.

So we won't be simply recommending workbooks that claim to develop isolated "critical-thinking skills." Instead, as we cover each of the subjects—math, language, science, history, art, music—we'll offer specific instructions on how to teach your middle schooler to evaluate, to trace connections, to fit facts into a logical framework, and to analyze the arguments of others. The middle-grade student still absorbs information. But instead of passively accepting this information, she'll be interacting with it—deciding on its value, its purpose, and its place in the scheme of knowledge.

BUILDING ON THE FOUNDATION

The poll-parrot stage has prepared the middle-grade student for the logic stage in two important ways. First, the middle-grade student should no longer be struggling with the basic skills of reading, writing, and arithmetic. A child must read fluently and well before entering the logic stage; the student who still battles her way through a sentence cannot concentrate on what that sentence means. The logic-stage student will write exten-

[1]"Critical Thinking," *Education Week on the Web,* www.edweek.org.

sively as she evaluates, analyzes, and draws conclusions; the study of grammar and punctuation will continue through high school, but the basic mechanics of spelling, comma placement, capitalization, and sentence construction should no longer act as barriers to expression. The middle-grade child will begin to think of mathematics in terms of concepts and ideas; she can't do this unless the basic facts of arithmetic are rock solid in her mind.

Second, the student has already been exposed to the basics of history, science, art, music, and other subjects. Now she has a framework of knowledge that will allow her to think critically.

On pages 221–225, we discussed the differences between parts-to-whole and whole-to-parts instruction. When you taught bugs in first grade, you used parts-to-whole instruction. You got out all the pictures of bugs (or used actual bugs) and described the five different types of legs and feet. Then you asked the child to tell you what she just heard, to point out the different types of legs, to write a sentence or draw a picture. In other words, you taught the bits of information—the parts—to the child and then helped her to assemble them into a whole.

The middle grader has already learned something about bugs, though. And her mind has matured and developed beyond the need for spoon-feeding. In the middle grades, you'll move toward a whole-to-parts method of teaching—presenting the student with a piece of information or a phenomenon and asking her to analyze it. When you study biology with a fifth grader, you lay out a trayful of insects and ask: "What differences do you see between these legs and those?" "How would you describe each leg?" "What function does each have?"

In the following chapters, we'll guide you through this type of teaching in the middle-grade curriculum.

LOGIC AND THE TRIVIUM

A classical education isn't a matter of tacking logic and Latin onto a standard fifth-grade curriculum. Rather, logic trains the mind to approach every subject in a particular way—to look for patterns and sets of relationships in each subject area.

But *formal logic* is an important part of this process. The systematic study of logic provides the beginning thinker with a set of rules that will help her to decide whether or not she can trust the information she's receiving. This logic will help her ask appropriate questions: "Does that conclusion follow the facts as I know them?" "What does this word really mean? Am I using it accurately?" "Is this speaker sticking to the point, or is he trying to distract me with irrelevant remarks?" "Why is this person trying to convince me of this fact?" "Why don't I believe this argument—what do *I* have at stake?" "What other points of view on this subject exist?"

These are questions that very young minds cannot grapple with. A seven year old has difficulty in understanding that (for example) a public figure might twist the facts to suit himself, or that a particular text might not be trustworthy because of the writer's bias, or that newspaper reports might not be accurate. But in the expanding universe of the middle-grade child, these questions will begin to make sense.

You may find yourself indebted to formal logic as well. Any parent of a fifth grader should be able to point out such logical fallacies as the *argumentum ad nauseam* (the incorrect belief that an assertion is likely to be accepted as true if it is repeated over and over again) and the *argumentum ad populum* (if everyone's doing it, it must be okay).

LOGIC IN THE CURRICULUM

In language, the logic-stage student will begin to study syntax—the logical relationships among the parts of a sentence. She'll learn the art of diagramming (drawing pictures of those relationships). The grammar-stage student wrote compositions that summarized information—how the Egyptians wrote, the important battles of the Civil War, the life of George Washington. Now, compositions will begin to focus on questions of motivation, of historical development, of debated fact. How did picture language such as hieroglyphics develop into written language? What were the real causes of the Civil War? Why did George Washington keep slaves? Logic-stage students will also begin to read literature more critically, looking for character and plot development.

Properly speaking, grammar-stage math is concerned with *arithmetic*—adding, subtracting, multiplying, and dividing actual numbers. Arithmetic isn't theoretical. Arithmetic problems can be worked out in apples and oranges and pieces of bread. But in the second stage of the trivium, the student begins mathematics proper—the study of the many different relationships between numbers, both real and theoretical (negative numbers, for example). In other words, arithmetic is the foundation for mathematics proper.

History in the logic stage will take on a new character. The student will still be responsible for dates and places, but you'll encourage her to dig deeper into the motivations of leaders, into the relationships between different cultures that existed at the same time, into forms of government and causes of war. Morality should become a matter of discussion as well. Was this action (this war, this threat) justified? Why?

The study of art and music at this point will become synchronized with the study of history. The student will learn about broad developments in society and culture, and will try to understand how these are reflected in the creative works of the times.

HOW TO TEACH THE LOGIC STAGE

For you, the teacher, the teaching process will change slightly. In first through fourth grades, your focus was on memorization—on the learning of rules, dates, stories, and scientific facts. You *told* the student what she needed to learn, either by reading to her or by giving her a little lecture, and you expected her to be able to repeat that information back to you. You used narration and notebook pages to bring this about.

Now, you won't be feeding the child with a spoon. You'll be asking her to dig a little deeper, to do more discovering on her own. Instead of lecturing, you'll concentrate on carrying on a dialogue with your child, a conversation in which you guide her toward the correct conclusions, while permitting her to find her own way. You'll allow the child to disagree with your conclusions, if she can support her points with the facts. And you'll expect her not simply to repeat what she's read, but to rework the material to reflect her own thoughts. Once she's done this, she'll have learned the material once and for all.

Here, one-to-one tutoring has an obvious advantage over the large public-school classroom. Classrooms encourage children to answer questions set to them; one-on-one instruction encourages children to formulate their own questions and then pursue the answers. Even the most dedicated teacher can't allow a class of thirty to dialogue their way to comprehension—the noise would be overwhelming.

As the logic stage progresses, you'll be using more and more original sources, steering away from "textbooks." Many textbooks are boring. And most present information in a way that's actively incompatible with the intent of the logic stage. History, for example, is often given as a series of incontrovertible facts. As Neil Postman observes, there is usually "no clue given as to who claimed these are the facts of the case . . . no sense of the frailty or ambiguity of human judgment, no hint of the possibilities of error."[2] A textbook leaves nothing for the child to investigate or question; it leaves no connections for the student to discover.

How do you guide this journey toward discovery?

Start with logic. In the next chapter, we'll introduce you to the formal study of logic. In the chapters that follow, we'll guide you in applying the categories and structures of logic to the various subjects.

We cover logic and mathematics first; then, since the middle-grade humanities curriculum is structured around the logic of history, we present history before continuing on to reading, writing, grammar, science, foreign languages, art, and music.

PRIORITIES

The logic-stage student is doing much more independent work than the grammar-stage student and is requiring much less one-on-one attention from you. Home-educated students typically spend an hour in self-directed work for every ten minutes of parental tutoring.

Because of this new time economy, and because the student has now mastered the most basic elements of reading, writing, and math, you'll find that you're able to cover more material. Language, mathematics, logic, history, and science are staples of the logic stage; art and music should be pursued, if possible.

While you won't need to do as much one-on-one teaching with the student, maintain close supervision. Every home-schooling parent has made

[2]Neil Postman, *The End of Education: Redefining the Value of Schools* (New York: Knopf, 1995), p. 115.

the mistake of handing a textbook off to a seemingly mature seventh grader only to find at Christmas that two lessons had been completed. Check assignments on a weekly basis.

By the middle grades, students will often develop a particular fondness for one subject (or a loathing for another). Because home education is flexible, you can structure your academic day to allow a child to follow an interest. If, for example, your seventh grader acquires a passion for King Arthur, let her follow the knights of the Round Table throughout literature and history for several months; don't insist that she move to the Reformation right on schedule. At the same time, though, do insist that the student keep up in each subject area. Don't let math slide for history, or foreign language for math. It's too early for the child to develop a speciality; she still hasn't been exposed to the full range of possibilities.

14

SNOW WHITE WAS IRRATIONAL: LOGIC FOR THE INTUITIVE

"Captain, that is an illogical conclusion."
—Mr. Spock

SUBJECT: Formal logic and puzzle solving, grades 5–8
TIME REQUIRED: 3 hours per week

How do you teach logic when you've never studied it?

If you can read, you can understand the logic texts we recommend: Memoria Press's *Traditional Logic*, *The Art of Argument* from Classical Academic Press, and resources from the Critical Thinking Company. None require any previous knowledge of logic.

You'll start the actual study of logic in seventh grade. The fifth- and sixth-grade years will serve as a warm-up for the study of formal logic. A student entering into formal logic must have a good grasp on the parts of speech; if he can't tell a subject from a predicate, he won't be able to construct a syllogism. In Chapter 17, we recommend middle-grade language curricula that will thoroughly prepare him for formal logic.

As he's learning the grammar needed for formal logic, the student will also be learning the beginning stages of critical thought. Before he begins a logic course, he should be accustomed to reasoning his way through problems, rather than simply accepting the solutions you offer him. We recommend that during the fifth- and sixth-grade years, you spend three teaching periods (an hour at a time) per week first doing logic puzzles, and then moving on to study critical thinking directly. This will shape and strengthen the child's capacity for abstract problem solving and familiarize both of you with basic logical categories.

The Critical Thinking Company offers several different logic warm-ups. The *Building Thinking Skills* books walk students through problem-solving in several different verbal and mathematical areas: vocabulary, pattern recognition, sequencing, and more. Try starting with Level 2; if the child struggles, back up to Level 1. After Level 2, choose either *Level 3 Figural* (for visual or mathematically inclined students) or *Level 3 Verbal* (for eager readers).

The *Mind Benders* books take a slightly different approach to the same skills: the puzzles are primarily verbal, excellent for highly word-focused students. There are eleven books in the series, but you do not have to complete a set number over the course of the year; instead, simply progress through them at a natural pace, spending three to four hours per week on the problems.

After a year of problem-solving, turn to an introduction to logic: *Critical Thinking, Book One* and *Critical Thinking, Book Two*. These books introduce basic logical categories and apply the logic to newspapers, ads, speeches, and so on, with interesting real-life examples and exercises. The logic itself focuses on fallacies, rather than on a systematic explanation of logical structures. However, working through these texts in sixth grade will prepare the student to begin formal logic in seventh grade.

You can teach formal logic using Memoria Press's *Traditional Logic*, by Martin Cothran. This text comes with a student workbook, teacher key, and lectures on DVD; the lectures are highly recommended unless you are already comfortable with logic.[1] Plan on completing *Traditional*

[1]The 2004 edition of *The Well-Trained Mind* did not recommend *Traditional Logic* for middle school because the material seemed a little too difficult for parents to teach in junior high; this problem was solved when the DVD lectures by Mr. Cothran became available.

Logic I in the seventh-grade year. Mastery of logic follows on mastery of grammar. If your student is still struggling with grammar in seventh grade, don't frustrate him; spend another year using the Critical Thinking Company materials, and delay logic until the eighth- and ninth-grade years.

A second option: if your seventh grader is not quite ready for traditional logic, you can spend the seventh-grade year studying *The Art of Argument*, from Classical Academic Press. This entertaining guide to logical fallacies helps students apply critical thinking to advertisements, news reports, and other real-world situations. It is not a systematic guide to logic, though, and students should then go on to complete *Traditional Logic I* during the eighth-grade year.

The second year of the program, *Traditional Logic II*, takes the student deeper into the thickets of formal logic. It is valuable, but not necessary for all students; you can certainly continue on into rhetoric (see Chapter 24) after completing *Traditional Logic I*.

For both years of study, you may wish to consider enrolling the student in Memoria Press's Online Academy, which provides chat-based tutorials. For more information, visit www.memoriapress.com/onlineschool.

HOW TO DO IT

You'll want to spend three teaching periods of one hour each per week on the study of logic. Consider one of the following schedules:

Grade 5	60 minutes per day, MWF	*Mind Benders* or *Building Thinking Skills*
Grade 6	60 minutes per day, MWF	*Critical Thinking, Book 1* and *Book 2*
Grade 7	60 minutes per day, MWF	*Traditional Logic I*
Grade 8	60 minutes per day, MWF	*Traditional Logic II*

A slightly slower progression:

Grade 5	60 minutes per day, MWF	*Mind Benders* or *Building Thinking Skills*

Grade 6	60 minutes per day, MWF	*Critical Thinking, Book 1* and *Book 2*
Grade 7	60 minutes per day, MWF	*The Art of Argument*
Grade 8	60 minutes per day, MWF	*Traditional Logic I*
(Optional)		
(Grade 9	60 minutes per day, MWF	*Traditional Logic II*)

FOR THE LOGICALLY CHALLENGED

What is logic, anyway? Logic is the study of rules of reasoning. Think of the study of logic as a road map that keeps you driving in the correct direction. The road map has no control over where you start, just as the rules of logic won't automatically guarantee that an argument begins with the correct assumptions. If you begin an argument about affirmative action, for example, by stating that one race is naturally inferior to another, logic won't prevent you from arriving at a bigoted conclusion. But if you have your facts straight, the rules of logic will guide you to the correct destination.

Logic has a three-part structure, used to help you examine an argument:

1. the *premise,* the facts you start with—statements
2. the *argument,* the deductions you make from these facts
3. the *conclusion,* your final deduction—another statement

A *fallacy* is a flaw in the process: a lousy premise, an incorrect argument, or an irrelevant statement in the middle.

Let's demystify this with the help of Snow White and the Seven Dwarfs (the Brothers Grimm version). At the beginning of the story, a queen is sitting at her ebony window, looking out at the falling snow. She pricks her finger, and blood falls on the snow. "Ah," she sighs, "I wish I had a child as white as snow, as red as blood, and as black as ebony." Some (unspecified) time later, this does indeed happen. The queen names the baby Snow White and dies immediately after her birth.

Already we've got material to work with here. The story contains a number of *statements,* sentences that tell us something that can be true or false.

The first lesson of logic is that statements (which are the foundation of logical arguments) must be distinguished from other types of sentences.

Was the queen happy with her baby?

This isn't a statement. It doesn't give us information, and it can't be classified as true or false, so it can't be used as part of an argument. Neither can a command, such as

Finish reading the story.

Only sentences that give information can be used in a logical argument.

The queen pricked her finger.
The queen wished for a white, red, and black baby.
Snow White was born after the queen's wish.
The queen died after Snow White's birth.

All of these sentences give information, so they pass the test: they're statements (as opposed, say, to questions or commands). Now we have to decide on their *truth value.*

The queen pricked her finger.

is true.

The queen didn't want a baby.

is false.

A valid argument is made up of two types of statements: true statements called *premises,* and a statement of *conclusion.*

Premise A: The queen wished for a white, red, and black baby.
Premise B: Afterward, the queen had a white, red, and black baby.
Conclusion: Therefore, the queen got her wish.

This is a valid argument. The premises are true, and the conclusion comes directly from information contained in the premises.

But it's unexpectedly easy to trip up. Consider this:

Premise A:	The queen wished for a white, red, and black baby.
Premise B:	Afterward, the queen had a white, red, and black baby.
Conclusion:	Therefore, the queen's wish was granted.

What's the problem? Well, the premises don't say anything about the wish being *granted.* Just because one event follows another event in time (the baby came after the wish), we can't assume that the first event *caused* the second. This fallacy has a nice Latin tag—the *post hoc, ergo propter hoc*—and shows up all the time in politics.

Premise A:	I was elected in 1997.
Premise B:	The economy began to improve in 1998.
Conclusion:	My policies caused economic improvement.

Notice that both the premises are true, but the conclusion isn't valid because it doesn't come directly from the premises.

This kind of fallacy is called an *inductive fallacy*—the conclusion might be true, but you just don't have enough information in the premises to be sure. Inductive fallacies show up when you make a conclusion (an "induction") on insufficient evidence.

Another type of inductive fallacy is the *hasty generalization:*

Premise A:	Snow White's stepmother was wicked.
Premise B:	Cinderella's stepmother was wicked.
Premise C:	Hansel and Gretel's stepmother was wicked.
Conclusion:	All fairy-tale stepmothers are wicked.

This could well be true (I can't think of any exceptions offhand), but unless you do an exhaustive survey of fairy-tale stepmothers, you can't be sure.

To continue. Snow White's father, misguided man, marries a witch who can't bear any rival to her beauty. Every morning she asks her magic mirror, "Mirror, mirror on the wall, who is the fairest of them all?" And the mirror, which never lies, replies, "You are the fairest of them all." But one day, Snow White surpasses the witch in beauty, and the mirror informs the witch, "You, my queen, have beauty rare, but Snow White is beyond compare." The queen, unable to live with this competition, tells her chief huntsman to take Snow White into the forest, kill her, and bring back her lungs and liver.

The huntsman agrees but has an attack of conscience in the forest and lets Snow White go. He brings back the lungs and liver of a boar as proof that Snow White is dead. According to the Brothers Grimm, the wicked queen then eats the organs for dinner (with salt).

Notice the queen's logic here:

Premise A: Snow White is more beautiful than I am.
Premise B: I believe that I cannot live if anyone is more beautiful than I am.
Conclusion: I cannot let Snow White live.

Is this a valid argument?

Well, let's start with the premises. After all, one of the first rules of logic is: Be sure of your premises because false premises will always yield a false conclusion.

Premise A: The earth is a flat surface.
Premise B: It is possible to fall off the edge of a flat surface.
Conclusion: It is possible to fall off the edge of the earth.

That's an impeccably valid argument in form, but since the first premise is wrong, the conclusion is useless.

How does the queen's argument look? Premise B is fine; it's called a *self-supporting statement*—a statement that has to be accepted as true. There are three types of self-supporting statements: those that have to be true because they cover all the possibilities ("Snow White is either alive or dead"), those that have to be true because they contain their own definitions ("The mirror reflects"), and those that have to do with personal belief (called "self-reports"). To say "I believe that the sun is blue" has to be accepted as logically valid, even by those who don't agree. I can prove to you that the sun is yellow, but I have to accept as fact that you *believe* it's blue. Premise B is a self-report—it has to do with the queen's feelings. Logically, it's valid.

But notice. We've already encountered one limit of logic. Is it morally acceptable to believe that you have to be the most beautiful person on earth? No, of course not. But logic is concerned with the form of the argument, not its content. You can always discount a valid conclusion if you disagree with one of its premises.

Let's apply this to history for a moment. A typical sixth-grade history-book account of the Civil War might proceed in this way:

Premise A: Lincoln believed that it was necessary for the federal government to stop slavery.
Premise B: Only a civil war could stop slavery.
Conclusion: It was necessary for the federal government to fight a civil war.

Case closed? Not for the classically trained student, who has learned in his formal-logic class to be wary of self-reports when they show up as premises of arguments. Recast this argument without a self-report as premise A, and the argument appears quite different:

Premise A: It was necessary for the federal government to stop slavery.
Premise B: Only a civil war could stop slavery.
Conclusion: It was necessary for the federal government to fight a civil war.

This is still a valid conclusion, but now that premise A is no longer a self-report, the student cannot automatically accept it as valid. Was it truly necessary for the federal government to stop slavery? This statement has now ceased to be self-supporting and is now a *supported statement:* outside evidence has to be brought in to support it. Premise B is a supported statement as well. Before the sixth grader can accept this argument, he has to investigate other remedies for slavery and conclude that they were inadequate. And once he's done that, he'll understand the Civil War in a new and vivid way.

Now back to Snow White and the egomaniacal stepmother.

If we allow the wicked queen her self-report in premise B, we still have to deal with premise A: "Snow White is more beautiful than I am." This isn't a self-supporting statement: it doesn't cover all the possibilities

("Snow White is either beautiful or not beautiful") or contain its own definition ("Snow White is snow white"), and it doesn't have to do with personal belief. So this statement is a supported statement. There's a hidden argument in this premise:

Premise A: The mirror always tells the truth.
Premise B: The mirror says Snow White is more beautiful than I am.
Conclusion: Snow White is more beautiful than I am.

Because the mirror is magical, premise A is true and the conclusion is valid.

Snow White flees through the forest until she finds the house of the seven dwarfs, where she dines on leftovers and falls asleep in one of the dwarf's beds. The dwarfs come home, discover their things in disarray, and exclaim, "Who's been eating our food? Who's been sitting in our chairs?" in an echo of the Three Bears. When they find Snow White, they decide she can stay as long as she cooks and cleans for them.

Meanwhile, the wicked queen discovers (with the help of her magical mirror) that Snow White is still alive. She disguises herself as an old peasant woman and arrives at the dwarfs' cottage with a poisoned apple—half red, half white, and magically constructed so that all the poison is in the red half. The dwarfs have warned Snow White not to let anyone in while they're at the mines, but Snow White really wants that apple.

"Look here," says the disguised queen. "I'll cut it in half and eat half myself." She eats the white half. And when Snow White sees that the apple seems harmless, she lets the woman in, takes a bite from the red half, and falls down dead. Eventually, a prince comes along and carries her body away, which jolts her so that the poisoned apple falls from her throat, and she wakes up, marries him, and lives happily ever after.

Now, there are any number of logical fallacies—statements that sound like valid arguments but aren't—implied in this story:

- *anecdotal evidence fallacy*—using a personal experience to prove a point. "I've met peasant women before, and none of them ever poisoned me."
- *argumentum ad hominem*—an attack on the speaker rather than on the argument itself. "Did the dwarfs tell you not to let anyone in? They

just want you to keep on cooking their meals and scrubbing their floors."

- *argumentum ad misericordiam*—appeal to pity. "I'm just a poor peasant woman trying to earn a penny for my sick children, so you have to let me in."
- *argumentum ad verecundiam*—appeal to authority; it uses the name of a famous person in support of an assertion. "I just sold an apple to the king, and he said it was the best apple he ever ate!" (Unless the king is a noted apple connoisseur, this is irrelevant.)
- *argumentum ad lazarum*—the assumption that a poor person is automatically more virtuous than a rich person. "I'm just a simple beggar woman, so I'd never hurt you."

Once you've studied these and a host of other logical fallacies, you'll find them everywhere: policy speeches, ad campaigns, election slogans, newspaper editorials, and junior-high history textbooks.

As logic continues, the student will begin to learn that all statements can be placed into one of four categories—the *universal affirmative* ("All stepmothers are witches"), the *universal negative* ("No princes are villains"), the *particular affirmative* ("Some dwarfs are miners"), and the *particular negative* ("Some fairy-tale heroines are not intelligent"). These are known as *categorical statements.*

The *syllogism* is a type of logical argument used for evaluating categorical statements. Snow White's syllogism probably went something like this:

My stepmother is a witch.
This peasant woman is not a witch.
Therefore, this peasant woman is not my stepmother.

Syllogisms have particular rules. For one thing, the first statement in the syllogism

My stepmother is a witch.

ought to describe the last phrase of the conclusion, the so-called *major term*—in this case, "my stepmother."

Also, the second statement in the syllogism

This peasant woman is not a witch.

ought to describe the first phrase of the conclusion, the *minor term*—"this peasant woman."

Furthermore, the syllogism has to have a *middle*—a term that appears in both of the premises, but not in the conclusion. The *middle* in Snow White's syllogism is "witch." So far, so good.

But Snow White's middle has problems. In a syllogism, the middle has to refer to *every member of its class* in at least one of the premises (this is called a *distributed middle*). Snow White never makes a sweeping statement (a *universal* categorical statement) about witches. She has committed the fallacy of the *undistributed middle,* which always yields a false conclusion.

If she had constructed this syllogism properly, it would have looked like this:

My stepmother is a witch.
No peasant woman is a witch.
Therefore, this peasant woman is not my stepmother.

In this syllogism, the statement "No peasant woman is a witch" has a *distributed middle* because it says something about *all* witches (none of them is a peasant woman). But if Snow White had made this argument—which is logically valid—she might have hesitated over that middle premise. How does she *know* that no peasant women are witches? Has she met them all?

Snow White pays for her muddled thought: she chokes to death on the apple. Fortunately, she lives in an enchanted forest and so revives and lives happily ever after—something that violates *all* known laws of logic.

RESOURCES

For publisher and catalog addresses, telephone numbers, and other information, see Sources (pages 751–778). These texts can be obtained directly from the publishers;

where we know of a mail-order option, we have provided it. Books in series are listed together in the order you'll want to use them.

Building Thinking Skills. Pacific Grove, Calif.: Critical Thinking Press.
$29.99 per book. Order directly from the Critical Thinking Company. Each book contains its own answer guide.
Building Thinking Skills, Level 1 (optional).
Building Thinking Skills, Level 2.
After completing Level 2, choose one of the following:
Building Thinking Skills, Level 3 Figural.
Building Thinking Skills, Level 3 Verbal.

Cothran, Martin. *Traditional Logic.* Louisville, Ky.: Memoria Press.
Order directly from Memoria Press.
Traditional Logic I
Student Text and Teacher Key. $31.90.
DVD Set. $45.00.
Traditional Logic II
Student Text and Teacher Key. $31.90
DVD Set. $45.00.

Critical Thinking. Pacific Grove, Calif.: Critical Thinking Press.
Order directly from the Critical Thinking Company. All four books can be bundled together for $59.99.
Critical Thinking Book One. $21.99.
Critical Thinking Book One: Instruction/Answer Guide. $9.99.
Critical Thinking Book Two. $24.99.
Critical Thinking Book Two: Instruction/Answer Guide. $9.99.

Larsen, Aaron, and Joelle Hodge. *The Art of Argument: An Introduction to the Informal Fallacies.* Camp Hill, Pa.: Classical Academic Press.
Order directly from Classical Academic Press.
Student Text. $21.95.
Teacher's Edition. $9.95.

Mind Benders. Pacific Grove, Calif.: Critical Thinking Press.
$9.99 per book. Order directly from the Critical Thinking Press.
Mind Benders A1.
Mind Benders A2.

Mind Benders A3.

Mind Benders A4.

Mind Benders B1.

Mind Benders B2.

Mind Benders B3.

Mind Benders B4.

Mind Benders C1.

Mind Benders C2.

Mind Benders C3.

15

THE LANGUAGE OF REASON: MATH

Mathematics possesses not only truth, but supreme beauty—a beauty cold and austere, like that of a sculpture.

—Bertrand Russell

SUBJECT: Mathematics and algebra, grades 5–8
TIME REQUIRED: 45 to 60 minutes per day

During the logic stage, the study of mathematics goes from *arithmetic* (mathematical operations such as adding, subtracting, dividing, multiplying, and so on) to *mathematics* (understanding how numbers relate and why).

The child's mind also makes the transition from the *mental image* mode (picturing objects to go along with numerical symbols) to the *symbolic* mode (using numerals alone). Until this transition is complete, the abstract operations demanded by pre-algebra and algebra are impossible. A problem such as 9×2 simply requires you to picture two sets of nine objects. But a problem such as $-5x = -15$ requires you to deal with symbols that have no easily pictured reality behind them. If I don't know what *x* is, how can I picture it? And what mental image can I make of a negative number?

In math, the fifth- and sixth-grade years complete the transition to symbolic thinking. During these years, the student solidifies her grasp of mathematical operations (addition, subtraction, multiplication, and division). She will also be introduced to more abstract concepts: negative numbers, percentages, probabilities, and decimals. She'll begin to do more complex word problems, ones that will require both logic *and* abstract mathematical reasoning.

The fifth- and sixth-grade math curricula should involve plenty of practice and no use of hand-held calculators. Until the transition to the symbolic mode of thought is complete, the student must continue to practice math operations.

We suggest that you also do some practical, hands-on math work during these years. The middle-grade student grows easily impatient with material that doesn't seem to have any logical connection to real life, which is why the National Council of Teachers of Mathematics suggests that middle-grade math curricula place "math in the context of students' everyday lives . . . giving students hands-on activities"[1] and real-life problems to solve.

Most math curricula can be finished in a year if you do four lessons per week and set aside one extra day to do testing, consumer math, a real-life math problem, or math games. We've suggested a few consumer math and math game books at the end of this chapter. Real-life problems might include

- figuring out the family's grocery budget for a week (or a month), or finding the best buys at the grocery store
- figuring out expenses and profits for a kid-run home business—grass cutting, pet tending, baby-sitting, baking
- balancing a checkbook (better now than in college)
- figuring out the monthly and yearly interest on a credit-card debt (ditto)
- calculating the area of a room, a wall, or the entire house for wallpapering, carpeting, or another home project
- figuring out the cost of driving the car to and from a special event

[1]Debra Viadero, "Math Texts Are Multiplying," *Education Week on the Web*, May 8, 1996, www.edweek.org.

- figuring out how much a restaurant meal would cost if it were cooked at home
- calculating the cost in work hours of movie tickets, concert passes, or other types of entertainment
- altering a recipe so that it serves a different number of people—for example, reducing a six-person dish so that it will now serve two or (more complicated) rewriting a four-person recipe so that it will now serve nine or eleven
- working out the itinerary for a family trip, complete with routes, timetables, and scheduled stops

Your own family life will yield plenty of additional problems. Try to stay alert for those times you use numbers, measurements, or calculations, and then ask yourself whether this problem is within the reach of your young math student.

HOW TO DO IT: FIFTH AND SIXTH GRADES

Somewhere in the logic stage, you may find yourself stymied as you teach your child mathematics. Math, unlike history or reading, requires the mastery of the language of symbols. If you feel uncomfortable speaking this language, you won't be able to guide your child in its use.

Unless you decide to use the Math-U-See program, with its teaching videos, or the Calvert correspondence course, you may eventually need a mathematics tutor. In Chapter 43, we discuss the numerous tutoring options available to home-school parents: home-school co-ops, local college students, online tutorials, and more.

Whether you use a tutor or teach the material yourself, you'll need to choose a curriculum and supervise overall progress. For fifth and sixth grades, we recommend one of the following:

Saxon Math

In the middle grades, the Saxon texts continue to teach mathematics incrementally, introducing new concepts one at a time, with plenty of drill and application. The middle-grade home study kits include the texts, an answer key for you, and examinations (with answers) that you can give the child throughout the year. The examinations start with *Math 5/4,* which is typically used in fourth grade; in grades 1 through 3, students complete oral and written assessments that are not formally graded. Home-schooled students need to practice taking examinations without "peeking," begging you for extra help, or getting up for chocolate milk. Without this practice, the transition into college work will be unnecessarily difficult.

Saxon is systematic, simple to teach, and mathematically excellent. The Saxon publishing company cultivates the home-school market, providing help for home schoolers via e-mail, a website, and an 800 number. If you used Saxon for grades 1 through 4, you probably finished *Math 5/4* at the end of the fourth-grade year. Continue with *Math 6/5,* the fifth-grade book, and *Math 7/6,* the sixth-grade book. If you haven't used Saxon before, request the home-study catalog. A diagnostic test is bound into the center of the catalog; the score card will tell you which Saxon level is right for your child.

Math-U-See

The Math-U-See program is based on a series of teaching videos in which concepts are demonstrated using manipulatives; the student also works with these manipulatives when completing workbook exercises. If you've been using Math-U-See, you're probably over halfway through the Elementary Curriculum; the last three levels of this curriculum, *Delta* (division), *Epsilon* (fractions), and *Zeta* (decimals and percentages), will take you through the fifth- or sixth-grade year, depending on how quickly your student moves through the levels. After finishing *Zeta,* Math-U-See moves to a standard progression: pre-algebra, first-year algebra, geometry, second-year algebra, trigonometry. You'll want to begin pre-algebra in seventh or eighth grade and continue on through the progression.

A Beka Math

A Beka Book is used by many home schoolers. The program is comprehensive and drill-intensive. As we've noted before, don't try to do all the problems. You must pick and choose among the A Beka lessons as well if you want to spend one day per week doing real-life math, as we suggest. *Note:* A Beka is a Christian publishing house, so you'll find Psalms interspersed with some lessons.

Developmental Math

The Developmental Math program, published by Mathematics Programs, provides a simple math option, in which the child works at her own pace instead of sticking to a daily lesson plan. However, there's just not enough practice in this program (used alone) to produce mastery, especially in the important early middle-grade years. Developmental Math is best used along with another program; it would be an excellent choice for a child who attends regular school but is struggling and in need of supplemental work. Because the books are divided by skill and are affordable, you could also use them for extra work in a particular area where a student simply needs much more practice.

Singapore Math

Singapore Math, described in detail in Chapter 6, is a program that focuses on teaching mathematical thinking. The fifth- and sixth-grade years of the Singapore Primary Math program consist of one course book and two workbooks for each half of the year; the program focuses on math concepts and on teaching problem-solving and application. Students just beginning Singapore should usually begin with the B book of the semester preceding their grade year.

The coursebook and workbooks alone will not provide enough drill for most students to master thoroughly the facts needed to lay a foundation for upper-level math; invest in the *Extra Practice* and *Challenging Word Problems* books as well, or supplement with drill from another program.

Calvert Math

The Calvert math program, offered as an independent correspondence course (Calvert's other programs are part of their entire grade package), is a solid traditional mathematics course for grades 5 through 8. Taking it by correspondence provides you with daily lesson plans and good teacher support from Calvert tutors (the "Advisory Teaching Service"). Calvert also supplies all manipulatives and supplies, along with tests and quizzes; Calvert awards the grade and keeps an official transcript.

If you feel that you need additional help to teach math, as well as grading support, this program is a very good choice that will build excellent math understanding.

Right Start Math

The elementary levels of Right Start Math end with Level E, which should finish out the fourth-grade year. The next level of the course, Intermediate Mathematics, acts as the transition between arithmetic and mathematics; students are intended to progress from the end of Intermediate Mathematics on into a pre-algebra course.

Many students should be able to transition from Intermediate Math into one of the courses listed in the Upper-Level Math section that follows. However, we would offer one caution: the Intermediate Mathematics course takes less than two years to finish, so a student who begins it in fifth grade will be finished in mid-sixth grade. This is young to begin a pre-algebra course. Although some children will be ready to move on to more abstract work, many more need an extra year (or more) of maturity before starting an upper-level program.

You can use Intermediate Mathematics and then plan on going into the sixth-grade year of one of the programs that then progresses on into pre-algebra: Saxon, A Beka, Singapore, or Teaching Textbooks (perhaps moving a little more quickly than usual so as to finish up the sixth-grade year on time). Alternatively, you can go directly from Level E of Right Start Math into the fifth-grade level of any of these programs.

Teaching Textbooks

Teaching Textbooks is a relatively new program that combines texts and software to provide a tutorial experience for the student: the courses are designed for independent study in grades 5 and up. Students read the text lesson, watch a DVD lecture, work practice problems, watch a DVD explanation of the solutions to the practice problems, complete a problem set, and then watch a final solutions lecture: this back-and-forth method allows the student multiple opportunities to understand the material. Teaching Textbooks is not yet a tried-and-true method, but response from the home-schooling community has been very positive and test scores seem to be high. Teaching Textbooks is not dependent on parent expertise, and offers a seamless transition from arithmetic on into high-school level mathematics.

Other Useful (Fun) Stuff

As a supplement, consider the entertaining narrative math series Life of Fred (discussed in Chapter 6, pages 96–97). The arithmetic volumes, *Fractions* and *Decimals and Percents,* are followed by *Beginning Algebra, Geometry,* and more advanced topics.

In the Resources section at the end of this chapter, we have listed several resources for real-life math; we strongly recommend making use of at least one or two during grades 5, 6, and 7. The website LivingMath.net can continue to be of use as you evaluate your student's progress.

Schedules

Schedule formal math lessons four days per week, allotting one day to real-life math or math games. Math is generally best done first thing in the morning or at the beginning of your scheduled schooltime.

Sample Schedules

Fifth Grade

45–60 minutes per day	M, T, W, TH	Math lesson
60 minutes or more	F	Real-life math

Sixth Grade

45–60 minutes per day	M, T, W, TH	Math lesson
60 minutes or more	F	Real-life math

THE SHIFT TO UPPER-LEVEL MATH

Seventh grade begins the real journey into symbolic mathematics. College-bound students (and seventh grade is too early to cut off the possibility of college) should plan on taking—*as a minimum*—pre-algebra, geometry, and two years of algebra. Most students should try to continue their math studies with a pre-calculus/trigonometry course. The mathematically inclined can then, in their senior year, take an advanced elective such as calculus.

A mastery of algebra has implications that go far beyond successful college admissions. Algebra, even at its most basic level, requires the student to work with unknowns, which means that she cannot memorize set answers and fill them in mechanically. Instead, she must analyze each problem, discover its central point, and then apply knowledge already acquired to its solution. Algebra, like logic, teaches the mind to think straight. It demands not only the memorization of information, but also the ability to apply that information in a number of different situations. *That* is higher-order thinking.

We can't emphasize enough that higher-order thinking requires mastery of those lower-order skills. Calculators in seventh grade are fine, but only if the student has already comprehended basic mathematical operations. Again, we depart from the opinion of the National Council of Teachers of Mathematics, which recommends the use of calculators beginning in fourth grade—a standard that inevitably produces seventh graders with little intuitive understanding of mathematics.

The student who's still shaky on fundamentals should use the summer before seventh grade to review them. Saxon Publishers offers *Saxon Middle Grade Basic Facts,* which should ground any student in the operations necessary for a successful move into pre-algebra.

Once the basic operations are mastered, it's time to prepare for algebra.

Comparing Math Programs

Of the programs we've described, all but Calvert and Right Start extend through the twelfth grade. Since Calvert doesn't offer a high school program, you'll want to switch over to another program in seventh grade to assure a smooth pre-algebra-to-algebra transition. (See page 255 for information on Right Start.)

Of the other programs, A Beka and Saxon are time-tested and well-used, both by home schools and private schools. Developmental Math does not offer enough practice in applying concepts to stand alone as a high school preparatory program, although it may still be valuable as a reinforcement course to take alongside another program. Singapore Math, which progresses from Primary Math (grades 1 through 6) into New Elementary Math (junior and senior high school), and Teaching Textbooks, a young company, are less "traditional" (not as strongly schoolroom oriented) in their approaches and have a much shorter track record. The same is true of Chalk Dust Math (see page 263). That doesn't mean that you should avoid these programs; only that you should take seriously the task of checking the student's progress. Frequently, ask him to complete a lesson from a different program (always one covering material he already knows), to see how well he's able to transfer his math knowledge from one context to another. And pay attention to his yearly standardized scores.

Each one of these programs prepares the student for the transition into algebra. The seventh grade A Beka text, *Basic Mathematics I,* reviews all arithmetic topics and provides plenty of drill in application of math to daily life. The eighth-grade book, *Pre-Algebra,* introduces basic algebra concepts and continues to drill the student in word problems. The student who struggles with arithmetic and isn't ready to begin pre-algebra in seventh grade (as the Saxon program does) will do well with A Beka. As we've mentioned before, the A Beka program provides more drill than most students need; don't feel that you need to do every problem in every set.

For seventh and eighth grade, Math-U-See begins its advanced sequence with pre-algebra (seventh or eighth grade) and then moves on to first-year algebra (eighth or ninth grade). The program presents concepts on video or DVD before the student completes his workbook assignments; the program also includes teacher's manuals and manipulatives. This is a good course for a visual or hands-on learner, and the videos provide plenty of teacher support.

The Singapore Math books for seventh and eighth grades, *New Elementary Mathematics 1* and *New Elementary Mathematics 2*, are the first two of a four-year series that continues on into grades 9 and 10. Each chapter contains explanations, a class activity which you'll need to adapt to home use, several different sets of exercises, a chapter review, and a challenge for advanced students. Notes on the history of mathematics occasionally appear in sidebars. According to the publisher, NEM 1 is the equivalent of introductory algebra and geometry, while NEM 2 is intermediate algebra and geometry; all four books are the equivalent of American first- and second-year algebra, geometry, and trigonometry.

Saxon Math introduces algebra a year earlier than A Beka and slightly later than NEM. The pre-algebra book, *Algebra 1/2* , is excellent preparation for the *Algebra I* book.

The only problem with the Saxon program is that it doesn't have a separate geometry book; the geometry is "integrated" into each year's study. Proofs are introduced in *Algebra II,* and the study of geometry concludes with *Advanced Mathematics,* the book that comes after *Algebra II.* There's nothing wrong with the geometry material itself, but to get the equivalent of a full geometry course, students must stick with Saxon all the way through and in a sequence that differs from standard geometry-separate high-school mathematics (see the table "Comparing Mathematics Programs," below). Math-U-See follows the standard pattern.

Comparing Mathematics Programs: Saxon versus Standard

Grade	Saxon	Standard
Seventh	*Algebra 1/2*	Pre-algebra
Eighth	*Algebra I*	Algebra I
Ninth	*Algebra II*	Geometry
Tenth	*Advanced Mathematics*	Algebra II
Eleventh	*Calculus*	Pre-calculus
Twelve	Elective	Calculus

As you can see, Saxon advances the student an entire year by combining geometry with the rest of mathematics. If the student is able to stay with Saxon Math, she'll have more math earlier than if she were involved with other programs. This allows mathematically gifted students to progress further in high-school math. Also, a student going through the Saxon sequence will have completed *Advanced Mathematics* by the time she takes her PSATs and SATs, which will give her a chance at a much higher score.

A problem arises when you deal with students who need to progress more slowly. In recognition that many seventh graders won't be ready to start pre-algebra *(Algebra 1/2),* Saxon provides *Math 8/7* to serve as a bridge between *Math 7/6* (the sixth-grade book) and *Algebra 1/2.* If your sixth grader is still stumbling over the concepts in *Math 7/6,* don't push her into *Algebra 1/2;* use Saxon's alternate sequence (see the table "The Saxon Program," below). *Either sequence is perfectly acceptable for a middle-grade student.* Pushing a child who struggles with math into pre-algebra before she's ready is counterproductive. The child won't "catch up"; she'll get frustrated and develop a long-lasting hatred for math.

The Saxon Program: Regular versus Alternate

Grade	**Regular Saxon sequence**	**Alternate Saxon sequence**
Fifth	*Math 6/5*	*Math 6/5*
Sixth	*Math 7/6*	*Math 7/6*
Seventh	*Algebra 1/2*	*Math 8/7*
Eighth	*Algebra I*	*Algebra 1/2*

The only caution we have about the alternate sequence is that if the student sticks with Saxon throughout, she won't finish geometry until the end of eleventh grade. Standardized tests—PSATs and SATs—are geometry-intensive. PSATs are taken in the fall of the eleventh-grade year, and a good score can bring multiple offers of financial aid—from National Merit Scholarships to in-house offers made by individual schools. It's been our experience that students who take a focused geometry course in tenth grade and then finish Algebra II in eleventh grade test better. (See Chapter 27 for the suggested high-school sequence.) If your child isn't comfortable with arithmetic by the end of sixth grade and isn't ready to begin Algebra 1/2 in seventh grade, you may want to choose A Beka or Math-U-See instead.

The Singapore NEM program, like Saxon, has integrated geometry (this is more common in European and Asian countries than in America). The student who takes *New Elementary Mathematics* in grades 7 through 10 will have finished all geometry, algebra, and trigonometry before standardized testing. However, we suspect that many students won't be ready for this highly accelerated pace. If you're using Singapore and don't plan to be finished with NEM 3 before standardized testing, you will run into the same complication: the student will not have finished a full geometry course and may score lower than average. In this case, consider switching to a program with a standard Algebra 1/Geometry/Algebra 2 progression.

Finally: Two more curriculum options, both of which offer DVD lectures, are Teaching Textbooks and Chalk Dust Math. Teaching Textbooks, described on page 255, progresses from Math 5 and Math 6 to Math 7 and Pre-algebra (eighth grade). A placement test on the website, teachingtext books.com, is meant to help you decide whether the student is ready for pre-algebra; students who are just beginning the program in seventh grade should take the test to decide whether Math 7 or Pre-algebra is a better starting place.

Like Teaching Textbooks, Chalk Dust Math offers textbook-based courses accompanied by teaching DVDs, intended for students to use independently. Whereas the Teaching Textbooks texts are original, the Chalk Dust texts are derived from standard Houghton Mifflin texts. Teaching Textbooks appears to offer a more interactive process (the Chalk Dust DVD lectures are accompanied by Complete Solution Guides rather than additional solution lectures). Chalk Dust begins pre-algebra in seventh grade and does not have a course for students who need to move slightly slower, while Teaching Textbooks gives you the option of completing a seventh-grade year before moving on into pre-algebra. Samples of both programs can be viewed at the publishers' websites, www.chalkdust.com and www.teachingtextbooks.com.

If you're looking far ahead, Teaching Textbooks offers courses only through pre-calculus, while Chalk Dust also offers calculus and trigonometry.

One of these math programs will certainly match your student's learning style. If you intend to use a tutor or are comfortable with high-school math, Saxon, A Beka, or Singapore may suit you; if you need a course that provides the student with more tutorial support, Math-U-See, Teaching Textbooks, or Chalk Dust may be a better fit. Pick a program, try it, and if the student remains frustrated, try another instead. (Borrow from a friend before investing, if possible, or buy used: Sale and Swap boards are located at welltrainedmind.com/forums, and a Google search for used curricula will bring up more options.)

Schedules

Advanced math is best done five days per week, first thing in the morning or at the beginning of your scheduled schooltime. You can divide the number of lessons in the course (Saxon's pre-algebra, for example, has 137 lessons) by the number of days in your school year (35 weeks or around 180 days on average). Use the extra days for extra drill, testing, or stretching a difficult lesson over two days. And use common sense. If your child flies through pre-algebra, start her on algebra—there's no reason to make her wait.

Seventh Grade

50–60 minutes per day	M, T, W, TH, F	Selected math program

Eighth Grade

60 minutes per day	M, T, W, TH, F	Selected math program

RESOURCES

For publisher and catalog addresses, telephone numbers, and other information, see *Sources (pages 751–778).* *We suggest that you contact these publishers of math materials and examine their catalogs closely before deciding on a curriculum. Most will aid you in placing your child in the most appropriate level. We have listed basic curricula first and supplementary materials second.*

Math Curricula

A Beka Book Traditional Arithmetic series. Pensacola, Fla.: A Beka Book.

Order from A Beka Book. A Beka Book also offers a wide range of mathematics teaching aids. Ask for a copy of their home-school catalog. Parents don't need the curriculum/lesson-plan books for each level; these give tips for classroom teaching.

Arithmetic 5. $13.25.

Arithmetic 5, Teacher Edition. $22.25.

Student Speed Drills and Tests. $5.25.

Teacher Speed Drills/Test Key. $9.65.

Arithmetic 6. $13.25.

Arithmetic 6, Teacher Edition. $22.25.

Student Speed Drills and Tests. $5.25.

Teacher Speed Drills/Test Key. $9.65.

Basic Mathematics I (seventh grade). $19.00.

Basic Mathematics I, Teacher Edition. $25.00.

Solution Key. $21.75.

Student Test and Quiz Book. $6.75.

Teacher Test/Quiz Key. $9.50.

Pre-Algebra (eighth grade). $20.25.

Pre-Algebra, Teacher Key. $25.00.

Student Test and Quiz Book. $6.75.

Teacher Test/Quiz Key. $9.50.

Calvert Math. Baltimore, Md.: The Calvert School.

Order directly from Calvert. Each math course includes a textbook, a workbook, and a lesson manual to help you administer the lessons.

Calvert Math Grade 5. $115.00.

Calvert Math Grade 6. $125.00.

Chalk Dust Math. Sugar Land, Tex.: Chalk Dust Company.
Order from Chalk Dust Company.
Prealgebra Traditional. 10 DVDs, textbook, and solutions guide. $399.00.
Algebra 1. 6 DVDs, textbook, and solutions guide. $354.00.

Developmental Math: A Self-Teaching Program. Halesite, N.Y.: Mathematics Programs Associates.
Each level includes a workbook and Instruction Guide. Buy from Mathematics Programs Associates, or at a small discount from Rainbow Resource Center. A full description of the twenty levels available can be obtained by calling 631-643-9300 or visiting www.mathplace.com.
Level 11. Three-Unit Numbers: Multiplication and Division Skills. $20.00.
Level 12. Thousands and Large Numbers: Concepts and Skills. $20.00.
Level 13. Decimals, Fractions, and the Metric System: Concepts and Basic Skills. $20.00.
Level 14. Fractions: Concepts and Skills. $20.00.
Level 15. Fractions: Advanced Skills. $20.00.
Level 16. Special Topics: Ratio, Percent, Graphs and More. $20.00.
Level 17. Algebra 1: Signed Numbers. $20.00.
Level 18. Algebra 2: Equations. $20.00.
Level 19. Geometry 1: Foundations of Geometry. $30.00.
Level 20. Geometry 2: Two-Dimensional Figures. $30.00.

Math-U-See.
This program has a number of different levels and workbook/video/manipulative combinations. For prices, explanatory material, and brochures, call the Math-U-See national number (888-854-6284), which will transfer you to a local representative; or visit the website at www.mathusee.com. Each teacher kit includes an instructional video or DVD and a manual; each student kit contains a text and test booklet.
Finishing up elementary mathematics in grades 5–6:
Delta (division).
Teacher Kit. $35.00.
Student Kit. $20.00.
Manipulative Blocks. $30.00.
Epsilon (fractions).
Teacher Pack. $35.00.

Student Kit. $20.00.

Fraction Overlays. $30.00.

Zeta (decimals and percentages).

Teacher Pack. $35.00.

Student Kit. $20.00.

Algebra/Decimal Inserts. $20.00.

Beginning advanced mathematics in grades 7–8 (requires the same *Manipulative Blocks* and *Algebra/Decimal Inserts* listed above):

Pre-Algebra.

Teacher Pack. $50.00.

Student Kit. $20.00.

Algebra 1.

Teacher Pack. $50.00.

Student Kit. $20.00.

Right Start Mathematics. Hazelton, N.D.: Activities for Learning, Inc. Order from Right Start Mathematics. Like Math-U-See, this program sells different combinations of manipulatives, worksheets, and instructor's manuals. Visit the Right Start website at www.alabacus.com to see all options; the kit listed below contains the essentials.

Intermediate Level: RightStart Starter Kit, Geometric Approach. $115.00.

Saxon Middle and Secondary Mathematics. Orlando, Fla.: Harcourt Achieve. Order from Saxon Homeschool. The Saxon home-study catalogs include a diagnostic test; you can also obtain the middle-grade placement test at their website. Request a catalog and test from Saxon Publishers at 800-284-7019, or visit their website at www.saxonhomeschool.harcourtachieve.com.

Homeschool Math 5/4 (fourth grade). 2005. $55.75.

Homeschool Math 6/5 (fifth grade). 2005. $56.75.

Homeschool Math 7/6 (sixth grade). 2005. $57.75.

Homeschool Math 8/7. 2005. $59.75.

This is the transitional book for seventh-grade students who aren't ready to begin pre-algebra. If your sixth grader went through *Math 7/6* without unusual difficulty, you can skip *Math 8/7* and go straight into *Algebra* 1/2.

Algebra 1/2, 2000. $65.00.

Pre-algebra for seventh grade; also used by eighth graders who did the *Math 87* book in seventh grade.

Algebra 1, 1998. $67.00.

For eighth grade; also used by ninth graders who did *Algebra 1/2* in eighth grade.

Singapore Math, U.S. edition.

Singapore Math workbooks and textbooks can be ordered from Singapore Math (an independent dealer, not the program publisher), or from Sonlight. The U.S. edition uses American weights and money (the previous edition for sale in the U.S. does not).

Primary Mathematics 4A.

Textbook. $8.70.

Workbook. $8.70.

Home Instructor's Guide. $16.50.

Primary Mathematics 4B.

Textbook. $8.70.

Workbook. $8.70.

Home Instructor's Guide. $16.50.

Primary Mathematics 5A.

Textbook. $8.70.

Workbook. $7.70.

Home Instructor's Guide. $16.50.

Primary Mathematics 5B.

Textbook. $8.70.

Workbook. $7.70.

Home Instructor's Guide. $16.50.

Primary Mathematics 6A.

Textbook. $8.70.

Workbook. $7.70.

Home Instructor's Guide. $16.50.

Primary Mathematics 6B.

Textbook. $8.70.

Workbook. $7.70.

Home Instructor's Guide. $16.50.

New Elementary Mathematics 1 (seventh grade).

Textbook. $21.50.

Workbook. $8.30.

Teacher's Guide. $29.00.

Solution Manual. $27.00.

New Elementary Mathematics 2 (eighth grade)
Textbook. $21.50.
Workbook. $8.30.
Teacher's Guide. $29.00.
Solution Manual. $27.00.

Teaching Textbooks. Oklahoma City, Okla.: Teaching Textbooks.
Order from Teaching Textbooks.
The Math 5 Teaching Textbook. $119.90.
The Math 6 Teaching Textbook. $149.90.
The Math 7 Teaching Textbook. $149.90.
The Pre-Algebra Teaching Textbook. $184.90.

Other Useful (Fun) Stuff

For drill, consumer math, and hands-on math.

Checkbook Math: Detailed Exercises for Learning to Manage a Checkbook. Scottsdale, Ariz.: Remedia Publications.
$8.99. Order from Remedia Publications. Students learn to write checks, keep a register, and balance a checkbook.

Learning Wrap-Ups.
$8.99 each. Order from The Book Peddler. An innovative drill tool; as you go through the facts printed on the front of each card, wrap the attached string through the notches of the correct answers to form a pattern.
Addition.
Division.
Fractions.
Multiplication.
Subtraction.

Life of Fred. Reno, Nev.: Polka Dot Publishing.
Order from Polka Dot Publishing.
Fractions. $19.00.
Decimals and Percents. $19.00.
Beginning Algebra. $29.00.

Math on the Menu. Berkeley, Calif.: GEMS, 1999.
$18.00. Order from the Lawrence Hall of Science Museum Store.

Developed by teachers Jaine Kopp and Denise Davila, this 144-page math unit will lead you through a real-life math scenario: the Rosada family is opening and then expanding their Mexican restaurant, and they need help pricing the menu, combining ingredients, analyzing costs, opening a second location, and more.

Menu Math: Market Math and Extra Price Lists. Scottsdale, Ariz.: Remedia Publications.

$17.99. Order from Remedia Publications. A colorful grocery price list and real-life math problems for students to solve: comparing prices and quantities, using coupons, and more.

Moneywise Kids. Ann Arbor, Mich.: Aristoplay, 1994.

$12.00. Order from Aristoplay. Two games that require kids seven and up to budget and dispose of a hypothetical paycheck.

Scratch Your Brain: Clever Math Ticklers. Pacific Grove, Calif.: Critical Thinking Press.

Order from the Critical Thinking Company. A critical-thinking series designed to help with the transition to higher-level math; progress through the books in order.

Scratch Your Brain A1. $16.99.
Scratch Your Brain B1. $16.99.
Scratch Your Brain C1. $16.99.
Scratch Your Brain Geometry. $19.99.
Scratch Your Brain Algebra. $19.99.

Stanmark, Jean, et al. *Family Math.* Berkeley, Calif.: Equals, 1996.

$19.95. Order from a bookstore, Rainbow Resource Center, or the Lawrence Hall of Science Museum Store. Published by the Family Math program at the Lawrence Hall of Science, this series is designed for use by the entire family (K–6 especially). It contains hands-on math activities, games, and reference charts. A good guide to real-life math problems.

Thompson, Virginia, et al. *Family Math: The Middle School Years, Algebraic Reasoning and Number Sense.* Berkeley, Calif.: Equals, 1998.

$20.95. Order from a bookstore or from the Lawrence Hall of Science Museum Store. The sequel to *Family Math,* this book provides more family-oriented math activities, including some that reinforce algebra skills.

16

WHY 1492? HISTORY AND GEOGRAPHY

All things from eternity are of like forms and come round in a circle.
—Marcus Aurelius, *Meditations* II.14

SUBJECT: History and geography, grades 5–8
TIME REQUIRED: 3 hours of intensive study, 90 minutes per day, two days per week, or 60 minutes per day, three days per week, plus as much additional time as possible to be spent in free reading and investigation.

ORGANIZING THE MATERIAL

During the logic stage, the student learns how to find connections. In formal logic, he discovers connections between a set of propositions and a conclusion. In math, he's taught the connections between the parts of an equation.

In history, he'll concentrate on finding connections between world events. Instead of simply reading the story of Rome's fall, the fifth grader will look at what happened before that fall—the events that led to the empire's destruction. Instead of studying the Revolutionary War as a single event, the seventh grader will read about the early days of the colonies and ask: What happened to make Americans discontent? What happened after the war that allowed America to stay independent as a nation? In the logic stage, history changes from a set of stories into one long, sequential story filled with cause and effect.

Beginning in the logic stage, the study of history becomes the backbone of classical education. Reading, art, music, and even science to some degree are organized around the outline provided by history. History is the training ground where the student learns how to organize and evaluate information. And that's the goal of the classical education—to produce an adult who can take in new knowledge, evaluate its worth, and then discard it or put it to good use.

In Part I, we referred to the mind of an elementary student as a storeroom that must be stocked with all sorts of images and words. Imagine what would happen to that storeroom if you kept cramming in more and more stuff without ever stopping to organize it. Greek history, Chinese fairy tales, biological classifications, the life of Bach, the concentration camps of the Third Reich—all lie stacked together. The student who can't get beyond this point will never realize that the laws of Hammurabi, the Magna Carta, and the Bill of Rights are linked. The information will remain jumbled together and ultimately unusable. And unless the student is given the mental skills to sort through and classify all this knowledge, he'll become an adult with (in the words of classical schoolmaster David Hicks) a "cluttered, disorderly mind—helpless to make the fundamental connections between basic ideas, or to . . . participate intelligently in the public debate over the great issues confronting his nation and his times."[1]

How does the student sort through and classify all this material?

He'll still make up history notebooks as he did in the elementary grades. But the study of history will now incorporate four elements:

1. creating a time line
2. outlining

[1]David Hicks, *Norms and Nobility: A Treatise on Education* (New York: Praeger, 1981), p. 132.

3. using and evaluating primary sources
4. organizing this information using the history notebook

Each of these activities has a separate role in the mind's development. Creating a time line teaches the student to trace chronological connections; outlining trains the student to look past rhetorical smoke and mirrors in order to find the "bare bones" argument of a speech or essay; the use of primary sources teaches the student to interpret material himself instead of relying on "experts"; organizing information into the divisions of the history notebook helps the student to classify similar events and historical trends together.

The Time Line

The time line is simply a piece of paper long enough to stretch along one (or more) walls of the student's room. (Hallways are also good places for time lines.) You can tape sheets of oversized construction paper together or use a commercial time line (see Resources section for ordering information).

Time lines help the student make visual connections between events. A young historian could study the conquests of Genghis Khan, Francis of Assisi's founding of the Franciscan order, and the death of Richard the Lionhearted without realizing that these events all occurred within the same decade[2]—until he saw them marked on a time line.

The time line should begin with a reasonable date in ancient history. We suggest 5000 B.C.,[3] when farming begins in earnest in China, Mesopotamia, and the Nile River valley. Make the time line as long as you can, measure it, and divide it by the number of centuries you'll be studying that year. You'll be repeating the divisions you used during the grammar stage:

[2]Richard the Lionhearted was killed in France in 1199. He was succeeded by King John. Genghis Khan defeated his greatest rival in 1203 and was crowned chief prince of the Mongols in 1206. John himself was excommunicated in 1209, the same year that the Franciscan order was founded.

[3]Western civilization has traditionally divided time into the centuries before Christ's birth (B.C.) and the centuries after Christ's birth (A.D., or *anno domini*—the "year of our Lord"). Some people prefer to use the abbreviations C.E. ("Christian Era" or "Common Era") and B.C.E. ("before the Christian Era" or "before the Common Era"). As Westerners, we're accustomed to B.C. and A.D.

Ancients	5000 B.C.–A.D. 400
Medieval–early Renaissance	400–1600
Late Renaissance–early modern	1600–1850
Modern	1850–present

During the first year of logic-stage history, since you'll be covering fifty-four centuries, you'll want to divide the time line into 54 equal parts and label each one. Don't forget that years B.C. run backward, while A.D. years run forward:

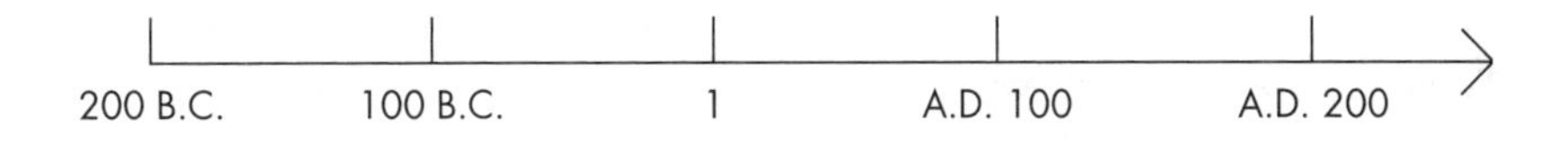

(A peculiarity of chronology: there's no year 0. Dating goes from 1 B.C. to A.D. 1 without a break.)

Try to make the century divisions as long as possible. There's not much going on between 5000 and 3000 B.C., but resist the temptation to make the early centuries short just to save space—*the time line must be kept in proportion.* Each year's time line should have centuries of equal length. The 3500–3400 B.C. space may remain bare, compared with the crowded space between 300 and 200 B.C. But part of the time line's purpose is to give some sense of the quickening pace of recorded history.

The time line can be simple (birth and death dates recorded in red pencil, political events in green, scientific discoveries in purple, and so forth). Or it can be as complicated as the student likes (adorned with drawings and cutout pictures: notebook-paper-sized inserts hung above or below a particular date to allow for expansion—for example, a month-by-month account of the Civil War or a year-by-year description of the Arab conquests of the seventh century). You can purchase published time lines, but avoid those with dates and events already printed on them. Writing up the dates is part of the learning process.

We suggest that you leave two spaces at the beginning of the Ancients time line, one marked "before 9000 B.C." and the other marked "9000–5000 B.C." You can put in these two spaces the small amount of information provided about very early civilizations and ages or your religious teachings about origins.

The time line will not only be an at-a-glance reference tool, but it will also act as a synthesizer of areas of knowledge. Birth and death dates of great writers, scientific advances made in biology and chemistry, dates of symphonies, paintings, and cathedrals—all will be recorded on the time line. Astronomers, poets, kings, wars, discoveries, and publication dates will appear, breaking down the walls between science, history, and literature. Since the stories of the Old Testament have influenced so much of Western thought, you may want to integrate them with recorded secular history. The history texts we recommend place Old Testament events in the flow of ancient history.

The Outline

You'll use outlining as an exercise at least once a week. In the elementary grades, the student created narrations—at first telling you what he'd just read while you wrote it down, and then writing the narration down himself. This process developed the student's comprehension skills and taught him how to tell the difference between irrelevant details and important elements of plots or argument.

But as texts grow more complex, the simple narration process will no longer be adequate. Instead of doing narrations, the student will begin to outline what he's read. Eventually, he'll be able to pick out the central idea from a chapter in any book and distinguish it from supporting ideas. This is an invaluable skill for note taking during college lectures; it also prepares the student to do advanced research. Once he can write a good, succinct précis of a scholarly work, he'll be ready to tackle the research paper without thrashing around in masses of unnecessary information.

Outlining simply involves finding the main ideas of a work and listing the supporting ideas beneath it. In fifth grade, the student will begin to develop this skill by simply summarizing each paragraph he reads. By eighth grade, he'll be able to condense a book chapter into Roman-numeral outline form. He'll also learn to use these outlines as the basis for short original compositions. We lay out the how-tos of outlining for each grade in the sections that follow.

For logic-stage history study, the student should use a core text that outlines the events in world history, but does not give predigested interpretations. Depending on your student's reading skills and maturity level, consider choosing one of the following:

- *The Usborne Internet-Linked Encyclopedia of World History.* The simplest of the four resources recommended here, *The Usborne Internet-Linked Encyclopedia* (also recommended in Chapter 7) is written on an advanced elementary level and is appropriate for average fifth-grade readers or older students who struggle with reading.
- The Dorling Kindersley *History of the World.* Also recommended as a simple supplement for high school study (see Chapter 26), this is written on a sixth- to eighth-grade level.
- *National Geographic Almanac of World History.* Instead of being organized as a series of short paragraphs, the *Almanac* provides short essays, which is most useful for students reading on a strong seventh- to eighth-grade level or higher. The chronological survey of history begins with the second section, "Major Eras."
- *History: The Definitive Visual Guide.* Published by Dorling Kindersley, this is a visually beautiful book, but the reading level is quite difficult; for advanced students only.

Unless you decide to use *History: The Definitive Visual Guide* (the most complete of the four volumes), you may want to supplement the core text with a time line that provides additional information on more obscure cultures, times, and people. We recommend either the simpler *Timelines of World History,* published by Dorling Kindersley, or the more complex *National Geographic Concise History of the World: An Illustrated Time Line.*

Primary Sources

In the logic stage, the child will still use paraphrases of difficult works such as the *Aeneid,* the *Odyssey,* and *The Canterbury Tales.* But he'll also begin to explore *primary source material*—original letters, reports, engravings, journals, and essays. Use of primary sources is vital to logic-stage history; the student can't evaluate historical events unless he has firsthand knowledge of them.

In the Resources at the end of this chapter, we've listed ways to find primary sources for each historical period. A primary source is anything that has its origins in the actual time under study. The *Epic of Gilgamesh,* for example, is a primary source if you read it in a good translation (a retelling in picture-book form wouldn't be a primary source because the story has been substantially changed and simplified). The Magna Carta, the poetry of Henry VIII, Martin Luther's journals, the Declaration of Independence, and the letters of Civil War soldiers are all primary sources. (A book about the Magna Carta, a biography of Henry VIII or Martin Luther, or the story of the creation of the Declaration would be a secondary source.)

Whenever the student encounters a primary source, he needs to evaluate it. As he studies history, he will develop his own ways of evaluating primary sources. To start, we suggest that the student go through the following checklist whenever he finishes reading a primary source:

What does this source say? (Content)
Who is the author? (Social position, profession, political affiliations, age, any other relevant personal detail)
What is the writer's purpose?
What does he/she have to lose or gain by convincing others of his/her position?
What events led to this piece of writing?
What happened as a result of this writing?

For each primary source, have the student head a sheet of notebook paper with the name of the source ("The First Amendment to the Constitution") and answer the above questions. In this way, he will learn how to ask critical questions of historical documents. File these sheets of paper in the history notebook.

The Notebook

Logic-stage history involves both *synthesis* (fitting information into one overall framework) and *analysis* (understanding individual events). The time line will be the student's tool for synthesis. To help in analysis, he'll be creating another history notebook—a fat three-ring binder full of notebook paper. Label this notebook with the period under study (for example, "Ancients: 5000 B.C. to A.D. 400"), and divide it into ten sections:

1. Facts
2. Great Men and Women
3. Wars, Conflicts, and Politics
4. Inventions and Technology
5. Religion
6. Daily Life
7. Cities and Settlements
8. Primary Sources
9. The Arts and Great Books
10. Outlines

Basic resources for the logic stage of history are the core text you've chosen, a wall map, a globe, and an atlas. Consider having two atlases on hand: a simple "student" atlas as well as a regular atlas. We like the *National Geographic Family Reference Atlas* (2d ed.) and the simpler *National Geographic World Atlas for Young Explorer* (3d ed.); fifth and sixth graders will probably be fine with the *Young Explorers* atlas alone, but older students will appreciate the more detailed information in the *Family Reference Atlas.* Be sure to look for the most recent edition of each (see the Resources list at the end of this chapter) since political boundaries change so frequently. History and geography fall naturally together; every time you study an event or person, you'll want to look up the location on the globe, on the wall map, and in the atlas (which will give you not only political borders, but also a brief history of the region). *Note:* Don't neglect the use of a globe—all wall maps and atlases distort land masses by laying them out flat.

Encyclopedias are expensive, but consider investing in a set for your middle-grade student; the encyclopedia is an invaluable first stop for research. The standards are *World Book* and *Britannica. World Book* is readable and nicely illustrated; *Encyclopaedia Britannica* is more complex but also more comprehensive.

Now the student is ready to begin. For the next four years, he'll follow the same basic pattern. He will

1. read a section from the core text and list important facts.
2. mark all dates on the time line.
3. find the region under study on the globe, on the wall map, and in the atlas.

4. do additional reading from the library or from the Resources list.
5. prepare summaries of information on one or more of the above topics and file them in the history notebook.
6. practice outlining one to four pages of text, once per week.

Additional Help for Parents

The student who does history using the methods described below will learn by using three basic study skills: reading, outlining, and summarizing. He'll then follow his interests to learn more with additional history books, hands-on projects, models, detailed coloring books, and more resources (listed at the end of this chapter).

The student who reads well and who has been following a good standard grammar and composition course in the grammar stage of education shouldn't have too much trouble with the methods we're about to suggest. However, some students need additional practice—either to build confidence, or to reinforce basic skills. So consider using one of the following additional resources if your student finds reading and outlining difficult:

For basic reading skills: Scholastic publishes *Teaching Students to Read Nonfiction,* an easy-to-use review of the reading skills necessary for successful history study; it teaches strategies for comprehension, gives tips on how to study maps, time lines, and other elements of history texts, and provides plenty of practice. You could work your way through the fifteen lessons in this book before beginning history study, if necessary—or return to it if the student begins to have difficulty.

For outlining skills: The two-book series *Note Taking & Outlining,* a straightforward two-workbook series published by Frank Schaffer Publications, builds basic skills in outlining. *Note Taking & Outlining Grades 3–5* introduces outlining skills and is an excellent first guide for students with no exposure to the subject; if your student has already been given the basics of outlining, you can go straight to *Note Taking & Outlining, Grades 6–8.*

Practice in more advanced outlining skills is provided in the high-school level text *Study Skills Strategies: Outlining,* published by Walch Education (also recommended in Chapter 24 for high-school students). For ordering information, see Resources for Teaching Skills on page 304.

STARTING IN THE MIDDLE (OR WITH MORE THAN ONE)

We describe a pattern of study that takes the student through four years of history chronologically, once in the grammar stage (grades 1–4) and again in the logic stage (grades 5–8). However, you can certainly adapt this progression for a student who doesn't begin the history cycle neatly in first or fifth (or ninth) grade. Pick one of the strategies below.

1. Start with the ancients and progress forward more quickly so that the student finishes the modern age by the end of eighth grade and begins the high school progression with the ancients in ninth grade. Hit the "high points" of history rather than attempting to cover it all (which you'll never manage to do in any case); do less outside reading.
2. Start with the period of history your student would fall into if you'd begun the progression in fifth grade: Medieval/early Renaissance for sixth grade, late Renaissance/early modern for seventh, modern for eighth. Go forward from that point. After all, the student is going to start over again with the ancients when you reach high school.
3. Start in whatever period of history you please, progress forward at a normal rate, and transition into the Great Books study recommended for high school when the student reaches ninth grade—no matter what *period* the student has reached. For example, a student who begins chronological history study in seventh grade might follow this pattern:

Seventh grade	Ancients. Keep a timeline, do outlining, and use the resources recommended for fifth grade (most of the books listed in the Resources section at the end of this chapter are appropriate for use anytime between grades 5 and 8).
Eighth grade	Medieval/early Renaissance. Keep a time line, do outlining, and use the resources recommended for sixth grade.
Ninth grade	Begin Great Books study with the late Renaissance/early modern period.
Tenth grade	Modern Great Books.

Eleventh grade	Ancient Great Books.
Twelfth grade	Medieval/early Renaissance Great Books.

The chronological progression forward provides the student with coherence, even if you choose a later starting point. (As a matter of fact, there can be a useful trade-off in doing the Great Books in this way: The ancient and medieval lists are technically very challenging, and the student will meet them with more mature reading skills. However, the subject matter of the modern list is disturbing, although the work itself is technically easier; it is usually best to encounter these books at tenth grade or later.)

If you're doing history with several children, follow the same basic principle: do the same year of history with all of them, so that you're not trying to keep up with two or three historical periods simultaneously—a sure path to burnout. When each student reaches fifth grade, begin the logic-stage process of outlining and and keeping a time line, no matter what period of history you're in; whenever the student reaches modern times, he can then go back to the Ancients and start filling in the beginning of the time line. When each student reaches ninth grade, begin the transition into Great Books study (see Chapter 26 for more detail).

If you are using the *Story of the World* series for younger children as well as educating older students, you can read the chapter from *The Story of the World* with all of the children together. Then ask the older students to (1) read the pages from the more difficult core text that correspond to the topic in *The Story of the World,* and (2) complete the other work described below.

HOW TO DO IT

Fifth Grade: Ancients (5000 B.C.–A.D. 400)

Let's assume that your fifth grader has chosen *The Usborne Internet-Linked Encyclopedia of World History* for this year's history text, and opens it to the section entitled "Traders from Phoenicia" (pages 144–145). These two pages contain brief paragraphs covering basic information about the Phoenicians, a map of the Mediterranean, illustrations, and a box with a brief list of important dates.

(1) The student will begin his assignment by reading the section (both pages) and making a list of six to eight important facts about the

Phoenicians. This list does not need to include every fact on the page (the student can choose the facts that he finds most interesting), and should be in the form of complete sentences. The text in the section reads:

> **Traders from Phoenicia.** The Phoenicians were descended from the Canaanites, who lived at the eastern end of the Mediterranean Sea (see page 140). From around 1200 BC, they became the most successful traders in the ancient world.
> **Cities by the sea.** The main Phoenician trading ports were the cities of Tyre, Sidon and Byblos. The cities were protected by strong walls and each one had its own king, who lived in a luxurious palace.
> **Ships and sailing.** The Phoenicians were expert sailors. Their sturdy trading ships sailed all over the Mediterranean and beyond, probably even reaching the British Isles. One expedition sailed all the way around Africa.
> **Crafts.** Skilled craftworkers made objects for traders to sell abroad. The Phoenicians were known for their fine ivory carvings and their beautiful glass bottles and beads.
> **Purple people.** The Phoenicians used a shellfish, called a murex, to make an expensive purple dye. The name "Phoenicians" comes from a Greek word meaning "purple men."
> **The city of Carthage.** Merchants set up trading posts and colonies around the Mediterranean. The most famous one was Carthage on the north coast of Africa. It was set up by a Phoenician princess called Dido, who tricked the local African ruler into giving her enough land to build a city.
> **Writing.** The Phoenicians invented a simple alphabet with just 22 letters. It gradually developed into the alphabet we use today.
> **The end of the Phoenicians.** Although the Phoenicians became part of the mighty empires of Assyria, Babylon, and Persia, their way of life survived until they were conquered by Alexander the Great in 332 BC. The city of Carthage remained powerful for another 200 years, but was totally destroyed by the Romans in 146 BC.

The student's list of facts might look like this:

1. The ancestors of the Phoenicians came from Canaan.
2. The cities of Tyre, Sidon, and Byblos were the main trading posts.
3. The Phoenicians sailed around Africa.

4. They made purple dye from shellfish.
5. They invented an alphabet with 22 letters.
6. They were conquered by Alexander the Great.
7. Carthage was destroyed by the Romans.

Remember that the list of facts is not intended to be exhaustive; it should be a record of the information the student finds most interesting. Place the list of facts in the history notebook under Facts (the first section), where it will serve as a running summary of information learned.

(2) Now it's time to mark dates on the time line. The Important Dates box in the book contains five dates:

c. 1200–1000 B.C.	The Phoenicians become rich and powerful
c. 814 B.C.	Carthage is built
c. 701 B.C.	Phoenicia is conquered by the Assyrians
332 B.C.	Phoenicia is conquered by Alexander the Great
146 B.C.	Carthage is destroyed by the Romans

Each of these dates should go on the time line, along with the accompanying caption.

(3) Once these dates have been placed on the time line, the student should compare the map of the Mediterranean found in the book with his globe, wall map, and atlas. Make sure he can find the modern locations of ancient cities. For example, the map depicting Phoenican travel routes shows Carthage in northern Africa; when the student looks up northern Africa in his atlas, he'll find that this area is now known as Tunis. He should also color the appropriate map from the *Geography Coloring Book* (see Resources at the end of this chapter).

(4 and 5) Now the student is ready to do extra reading. *The Usborne Internet-Linked Encyclopedia of World History* mentions the following topics in the text we've reprinted:

The port cities of Tyre, Sidon, and Byblos
Phoenician expeditions to the British Isles and Africa
Ivory carvings
Glass bottles and beads
Purple dye

Phoenician trading posts and colonies
Carthage
The Phoenician princess Dido
The Phoenician alphabet
Conquest by Assyria, Babylon, and Persia
Conquest by Alexander the Great
Destruction of Carthage by the Romans

The captions of the illustrations also mention:

Salt from North Africa
Ivory from Egypt
Copper from Cyprus
Phoenician cedarwood
The warship known as a *bireme*

The student should choose at least one topic, do outside reading, and then use his outside reading to prepare a notebook page giving more information about that topic.

At first, you may need to read through the section and help the student pick out these topics, but fifth graders will soon be able to do this independently.

The student can begin his investigation in the encyclopedia, with any of the resources listed at the end of this chapter, or in the library stacks. If, for example, he's interested in Phoenician crafts, he can look for books on ancient dyes and glasswork. And he can search the library's catalog—the children's librarian will be glad to help.[5]

After the student has done additional reading, ask him to write several sentences (a minimum of three; five to six is better) about how the Phoenicians built warships or first began to blow glass.[6] If he has trouble extracting the relevant facts, glance through his book with him and ask ques-

[5]The classically educated student learns library skills as he researches—hands-on training in research is one of the benefits of the classical method.

[6]The writing programs recommended in Chapters 5 and 17 will help prepare the student to do this sort of short composition.

tions: Where did the murex come from? How did the Phoenicians get the dye out? What did it smell like? Was the process difficult to do? Remember, in the logic stage, conversation becomes your primary teaching tool. *Talk* to the student about what he's reading; encourage him to talk to you.

Pay special attention to biographies. Try to make a page for all the great men and women you encounter (personalities act as memorable "pegs" on which to hang the progression of history). Actual names will be in short supply at first. But by the time you get to 3000 B.C., you'll be finding many great individuals (mostly men). For the centuries between 3000 and 2500, for example, you'll have the pharaohs Zoser, Cheops (Khufu), and Khafre (the sphinx was built to guard Khafre's pyramid) as well as Gilgamesh, who reigned in Sumer around 2700 B.C.

As in the early grades, some topics (Egyptian pharoahs and life in ancient Rome) will turn up dozens of useful library books, while others will produce nothing. Don't waste time digging for obscure details. If our resource list is silent and the library catalog yields no useful titles, move on.

For primary source work, we suggest using the Jackdaws resource packs—portfolios of primary source material coupled with study guides, activities, and topics for further research (see page 306). Take at least a week (preferably two) to study each Jackdaw Portfolio. For fifth grade, we recommend several: *Tutankhamun and the Discovery of the Tomb; Ancient Athletic Games: Heracles and the Olympics; Inspirational Women: Muses and Women in Antiquity; Many Faces of the Hero: Odysseus, Theseus and Jason; China: A Cultural Heritage*. Choose your favorite, and do one (or more) at the appropriate time in your history study. Be sure to file in the Primary Sources section of the notebook any extra work inspired by the Jackdaw Portfolios. You can also use the Internet to find primary sources archived online; a particularly good website, the Internet Ancient History Sourcebook, can be found at www.fordham.edu/halsall/ancient/asbook.html.

The Arts and Great Books section of the notebook will be filled with pages done during language study and art study. Whenever you run across a writer, musician, or artist—Homer, Virgil, Cicero, Praxiteles—make a biographical page listing his or her works and details about his or her life. Although these pages will be filed under Great Men and Women, those notebook pages covering the books, paintings, and compositions themselves will be created outside of the history lesson (see Chapters 17 and 21 for further details).

By the end of fifth grade, the student will have created two historical resources: a time line that synthesizes all of his knowledge about historical events, personalities, and achievements; and a notebook that shows him at a glance the development of specific areas of human endeavor. He can flip through the Wars, Conflicts, and Politics section of his notebook and see the progression of conflict from the war uniting Upper and Lower Egypt, through the Greek siege of Troy, all the way to the wars of Alexander the Great and the Punic Wars. Or he can trace world religions from Osiris and Ra through the spread of Christianity.

(6) Ask the student to choose one page of text (approximately 250 to 300 words, or five to six paragraphs) from the most interesting history resource he's read during the week. He should outline this page of text on his own notebook paper.

This outlining practice will begin to prepare the student for more advanced composition. As he moves into high school, he'll need to know how to write his own history essays from an outline. Before he can do this, however, he needs to study the outlines of *other* writers. The best and simplest way to do this is to create an outline from a finished piece of writing.

The fifth grader needs to master the most basic element of the outline: the main point. Ask him to boil down each paragraph into one sentence by asking, "What is the most important statement in this paragraph?" This statement should be put into his own words, and each statement should be given a Roman numeral:

I. Main point of first paragraph
II. Main point of second paragraph
III. Main point of third paragraph

and so on. See "How to Outline" on pages 297–301 for more detailed direction.

This outline should be placed in the Outlines section of the history notebook. (The student can do this outlining practice either before or after completing the summary; choose whichever sequence seems more natural.)

Suggested Schedule

The suggested texts begin with a section on prehistory and then move into recorded history (beginning around 5000 B.C.). Since prehistory overlaps with science study, you can either start the first year of history study with prehistory, or else skip over these introductory topics and begin with the first civilizations of the Fertile Crescent.

This choice will affect how quickly you'll move through the history topics. In *The Usborne Internet-Linked Encyclopedia of World History,* prehistory is covered in the first hundred pages and ancient history in pages 104–195. If you decide to begin with prehistory, you'll need to cover approximately three two-page sections per week to finish in a thirty-six week school year; if you begin with ancient history instead, you'll only need to cover one or two sections per week (giving yourself much more time for outside reading).

If you choose to use the slightly more advanced Dorling Kindersley *History of the World,* you'll see that prehistory is covered in the first thirty pages, while ancient history begins on page 32 and ends on page 96. The text is denser, and each topic tends to be covered on a single page. If you include prehistory in your year of study, you'll need to cover two or three pages and topics per week; if not, you can slow down to one or two topics per week.

Just remember that your goal is to teach the student *how* to study history, not to do an exhaustive survey of all possible history topics! If you get behind, skip sections. (Nothing terrible will happen if the student doesn't study the Hittites.) Or take a week now and then to spend history time doing nothing but reading (no compositions, outlines, or outside reading) in order to catch up.

If you're studying history Mondays, Wednesdays, and Fridays:

Monday	Complete the week's reading from the core history resource. Make a list of facts and place in the history notebook. Mark all dates on the time line; find locations on the globe, the wall map, and in the atlas.
Wednesday	Do additional reading on one or two chosen topics, using library books or books recommended in the Resources list. Pick one resource and outline one page (five to six paragraphs). Place the outline in the history notebook.
Friday	Prepare a written summary of the information on the chosen topic and file it in the appropriate section of the history notebook.

If you're studying history on Tuesdays and Thursdays:

Tuesday — Complete the week's reading from the core history resource. Make a list of facts and place in the history notebook. Mark all dates on the time line; find locations on the globe, the wall map, and in the atlas. Begin additional reading on one or two chosen topics, using library books or books recommended in the Resources list.

Thursday — Finish additional reading. Pick one resource and outline one page (five to six paragraphs). Place the outline in the history notebook. Prepare a written summary of the information on the chosen topic and file it in the appropriate section of the history notebook.

A note to busy parent-teachers: Logic-stage history involves a great deal of reading and writing. The classical curriculum is centered around reading and writing as the primary means of knowledge. If you're wondering how time-consuming all this is, note that you'll be spending several hours per week helping the child find topics and locating library books, in addition to providing assistance in composition and checking over the finished work. But home schoolers inevitably find that the time parents need to spend in one-on-one instruction decreases dramatically in the middle grades. Your fifth grader may spend an hour reading history on Wednesdays, but that's not time-intensive on your part; you'll spend ten minutes at the beginning of the period giving directions and guidance, and ten minutes at the end talking to him about what he's read so that he can put the facts down in a composition.

Sixth Grade: Medieval–Early Renaissance (400–1600)

For the years 400 to 1600, you'll be following the same basic pattern as you did in the fifth grade (see pages 278–285).

The List of Facts

The sixth grader will read his history pages and make his list of six to eight important facts to place in the history notebook.

If you choose to use the Dorling Kindersley *History of the World,* which is more difficult than the Usborne history, the student should treat each single page as a separate section. Remind him to choose the most *important* facts rather than just listing the first six or eight he encounters. Let's take as an example the Dorling Kindersley page on Cambodia and Japan between A.D. 800 and 1000. There are two main paragraphs of text on this page:

> **802. Khmer empire founded.** The Khmer people of Cambodia built their first state on the southern Mekong river. Called Funan, and much influenced by India, it was overrun in the late 500s by another Khmer state, Chenla. In 802 the young king Jayavarman II founded the Angkorian dynasty which he made the centre of Khmer life and religion. He and his successors were worshipped as gods and built cities with massive temple complexes. For many years the Khmer capital was at Roluos, until in about 900 Jayavarman's great-nephew built a new capital a short distance away which was named Angkor. The god-kings built advanced irrigation schemes, and created an empire which lasted until after 1300.
>
> **866. The regency of Yoshifusa.** In 858 a child, Seiwa, became Japanese emperor. Previously, a member of the royal family had been appointed regent for a child-emperor but Yoshifusa, a member of the powerful Fujiwara clan, wanted power. Although he was the child's grandfather he was not a member of the royal family. In 866 he removed his opponents and established himself as regent (sessho). He continued in power even after Seiwa came of age. Yoshifusa's nephew Mototsune succeeded him and became the first regent for an adult emperor and the first civil dictator (kampaku). From this time the imperial family retreated into isolation while the country was governed by successive administrations headed by military or civilian rulers.

In addition, there are five lengthy captions for illustrations:

> **Brahma.** This Khmer monument shows three of the four heads of the important Hindu god, Brahma.
>
> **Many gods.** In Cambodia, the religions of Buddhism and Hinduism, and worship of the king and his ancestors, co-existed peacefully.
>
> **Preah Ko.** The temple of Preah Ko was built near Roluous. There were two rows of towers, the front row devoted to the king's male ancestors and the back row to the female.

The Heian shrine. In 794, Heian-Kyoto became the capital of Japan. The Heian period saw a break away from Chinese influence. This shrine shows the Chinese-style palace buildings of the earlier period.

Enthronement of an emperor. Seiwa was only nine or ten years old when he became emperor, but still had to undergo the elaborate ritual of enthronement. The ceremony and even the clothes the emperor wears have changed little since Seiwa's day.

The section is focused on Cambodia and Japan, so the student should choose facts about both countries. His list of facts might look like this:

1. The first state of the Khmer people was called Funan.
2. Funan was conquered by Chenla in the late 500s.
3. The empire lasted until after 1300.
4. Seiwa became emperor of Japan in 858.
5. Seiwa's regent was a member of the Fujiwara clan.
6. The capital of Japan was Heian-Kyoto.
7. The emperors withdrew and civil dictators governed Japan.

The Time Line

The student should enter the dates found in the text on his time line. Begin the school year by creating a time line that covers the medieval–early Renaissance period—twelve centuries, or twelve equal divisions. You'll have much more space for each century, which is good—the centuries are crowded.

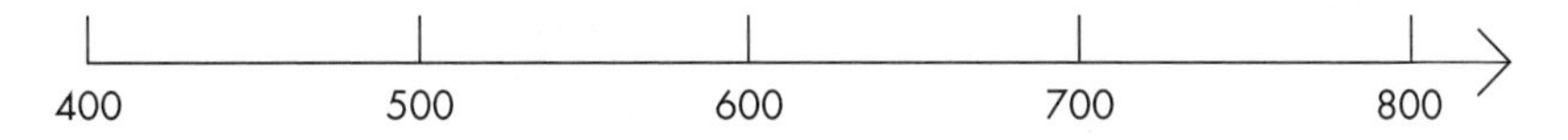

The Outline

The student should still choose pages from his additional reading to outline. But now, instead of simply condensing the reading into one sentence per paragraph, he'll identify one main point and two to four subpoints for each paragraph. These will be written out in proper outline form, using Roman numerals and uppercase letters. Even though he's already learned this in fifth-grade grammar (see Chapter 17), it bears repeating:

I. First main point
  A. First supporting point
  B. Second supporting point
II. Second main point
  A. First supporting point
  B. Second supporting point
  C. Third supporting point

and so on. In this type of outlining, two short paragraphs covering the same subject can be combined together; a long paragraph can be broken in half, if it begins a new thought halfway through. The goal: to create an outline that lays out the logical development of the text. In a good outline, each supporting point is related to the main point. See "How to Outline" on pages 297–301 for more detailed direction; note that, as the student grows more practiced, he should aim to outline up to two pages from his chosen resource.

In the passage above, the lives of the rulers Jayavarman II and Seiwa could be researched to create a notebook page for the Great Men and Women section; the practice of royal ancestor worship in Cambodia could provide material for a page to be filed in Religion; the city of Heian-Kyoto or the Cambodian capitals Roluos and Angkor could be covered for a page in Cities and Settlements. These short compositions will follow the rules for composition taught in the writing program which the student should be using concurrently (see Chapter 17). Aim for one-half to one full page for each composition (that is, 200–400 words). If the student does full-page compositions, don't expect more than one notebook page for history per week.

Primary Sources

The student will continue to use primary sources, evaluating them by asking himself the same questions he did in fifth grade (see page 274). Four Jackdaw Portfolios of primary sources are particularly good for the sixth-grade year: *Magna Carta* (study this along with thirteenth-century England), *Elizabeth I* (study this when you reach Tudor England), *Martin Luther* (use when studying the Reformation), and *Columbus and the Age of Explorers*. You wouldn't need to do all four; feel free to pick and choose. You will find a longer list of available resources in the Resources at the end of this chapter; substitute other topics if you wish. (You'll probably want to use a few more of these when you pass through medieval–early Renaissance history again in high school.) The student can also locate primary resources online; a particularly good Internet site for this is the Internet Medieval Sourcebook at www.fordham.edu/halsall/sbook.html.

Evaluating primary resources can take the place of outside reading and notebook-page creation for as long as necessary.

The Notebook

Using a new three-ring binder, label it "Medieval-Early Renaissance: 400–1600," and divide it into the same ten sections as in fifth grade (see page 275).[8] The student will complete the same five steps: reading and outlining, marking dates, finding locations, doing extra reading, filing summaries in the history notebook.

If you've chosen to use the Dorling Kindersley *History of the World,* you'll see that the years 400–1600 are covered in approximately a hundred pages, so you'll need to plan on reading two or three pages per week. The text is fairly dense, so the student will find plenty of additional topics for research. If you find yourself getting behind, skip a few pages; the text is a springboard, not a prison.[9]

On the other hand, if you've only progressed a hundred years from September to Christmas, you may need to reevaluate. Is the student dawdling? Does he need remedial writing or reading work? Do you need to drop back to the simpler history text for a while? Or are you letting other things—phone calls, jobs, visits from friends, housework—crowd out school? If so, you may need to adjust the child's daily schedule.

Suggested Schedule

If you choose to use the Dorling Kindersley *History of the World* for medieval–early Renaissance history, you'll need to cover to two to three

[8] Some parents choose to keep the same notebook for all four years, filing pages chronologically within each section, so that (for example) the "Famous Men and Women" sections would begin with an ancient hero and end with a modern person of note.

[9] This is one of the keys to successful home tutoring: You're the boss. You set the schedules. *Use common sense.* If the child spends three hours outlining his history lesson, you're doing too much. Start skipping sections. Or don't finish the book. How many textbooks did your teacher actually finish in high school or college?

pages per week; if you stick with the simpler Usborne encyclopedia, do one to two sections per week.

If you're studing history Mondays, Wednesdays, and Fridays:

Monday	Complete the week's reading from the core history resource. Make a list of facts and place in the history notebook. Mark all dates on the time line; find locations on the globe, the wall map, and in the atlas.
Wednesday	Do additional reading on one or two chosen topics, using library books or books recommended in the Resources list. Pick one resource and outline one or two pages (five to ten paragraphs). Place the outline in the history notebook.
Friday	Prepare a written summary of the information on the chosen topic and file it in the appropriate section of the history notebook.

If you're studying history on Tuesdays and Thursdays:

Tuesday	Complete the week's reading from the core history resource. Make a list of facts and place in the history notebook. Mark all dates on the time line; find locations on the globe, the wall map, and in the atlas. Begin additional reading on one or two chosen topics, using library books or books recommended in the Resources list.
Thursday	Finish additional reading. Pick one resource and outline one or two pages (five to ten paragraphs). Place the outline in the history notebook. Prepare a written summary of the information on the chosen topic and file it in the appropriate section of the history notebook.

Seventh Grade: Late Renaissance–Early Modern (1600–1850)

The List of Facts

As in the previous years, the seventh grader will read his history pages and make his list of six to eight important facts to place in the history notebook.

Although you can continue on with the same history core text used in sixth grade, very strong readers may wish to move on to a more difficult text such as the *National Geographic Almanac of World History*. The years 1600–1850 are covered in pages 174–259. Since this text is organized as a series of essays, rather than as illustrated one- or two-page sections, ask the student to read approximately two pages per week and to choose six or eight facts from each page.

For example, the first page of the essay "India under the British, 1757–1917" (page 234) reads:

> India splintered into many states in the 1700s as the Moguls who ruled the subcontinent began to lose power. While a dwindling Mogul Empire endured near Delhi, old provinces became independent kingdoms, a Hindu hill people called the Marathas spread out from central India, and Sikhs assumed control of the Punjab in the northwest. Meanwhile European trade with India flourished, with the British becoming the principal traders. To protect their economic interests, the British established armies composed mostly of local troops called sepoys. Armed and eqipped like the British Army, the sepoys were the most efficient fighters on the subcontinent.
>
> As businessmen, British traders wanted to acquire wealth, not territory. But over time, one aim led to the other. Calcutta, in the rich province of Bengal, was a prime center of British commerce. On June 20, 1756, the Indian ruler of Bengal seized Calcutta's British garrison for violations of local trading laws. As part of the takeover, scores of British prisoners were held overnight in a hot, poorly ventilated cell, later called the Black Hole of Calcutta. By morning, most had died. The incident—often retold with the numbers exaggerated—became a symbol to the British of Indian brutality. In January 1757 Col. Robert Clive retook Calcutta, then went on to seize all of Bengal.

The student's list of facts might look like this:

1. In the 1700s, the Moguls lost power and India divided into many states.
2. The Marathas and the Sikhs began to gain power.
3. Calcutta became the center of British trade.
4. The British kept local soldiers called sepoys.

5. In 1756, the Indian ruler of Bengal took the British in Calcutta prisoner.
6. The Black Hole of Calcutta was the cell where the prisoners were kept (most of them died).
7. The British recaptured Calcutta and then took the rest of the province of Bengal.

Remember that this text is quite difficult; many students will need to choose one of the simpler core texts instead.

The Time Line

For the years 1600 to 1850, you should create a new time line. Divide this one into ten twenty-five-year segments:

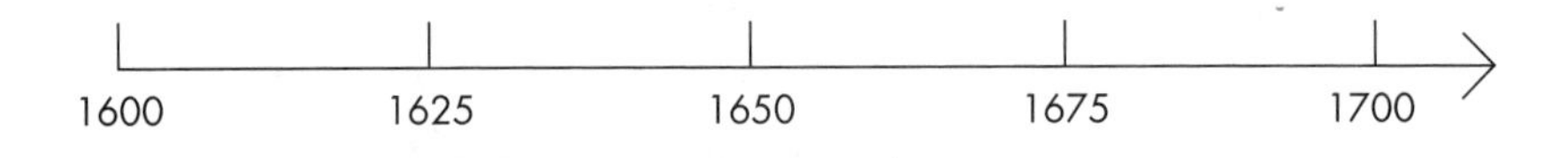

The Outline

The seventh grader should continue the sixth-grade method of outlining until he is comfortable with it. He can try to introduce yet more supporting points than before:

I. First main point
  A. First supporting point
    1. First subpoint
    2. Second subpoint
  B. Second supporting point
    1. First subpoint
    2. Second subpoint
II. Second main point
  A. First supporting point
  B. Second supporting point
  C. Third supporting point

The seventh grader should only begin to do this when the sixth-grade method has become easy. This point may be reached at any time during the seventh-grade year or at the beginning of the eighth-grade year.

Each subpoint must relate to the supporting point it follows. See "How to Outline" on pages 297–301 for more detailed direction; note that, as the student grows more practiced, he should aim to outline two to three pages from his chosen resource.

Primary Sources

Primary sources for this period include the Jackdaw Portfolios *The Mayflower and the Pilgrim Fathers, The American Revolution, The Making of the Constitution,* and *Lewis & Clark Expedition.* Or choose other topics from the list provided in the Resources section of this chapter. You can also visit the Internet Modern History Sourcebook at www.fordham.edu/halsall/mod/modsbook.html for online primary sources.

Primary resource evaluation, when done, can replace library reading and notebook-page creation. The student should continue to make evaluation pages for these primary sources (see pages 273–274) and file them in the Primary Sources section of the history notebook.

Critical-Thinking Resources

We strongly suggest that during the seventh-grade year you use the Critical Thinking in United States History series from Critical Thinking Press. Book One, *Colonies to Constitution,* and Book Two, *New Republic to Civil War,* supply the student with information about historical events and mysteries and ask him to draw conclusions. Did Pocahontas really rescue John Smith? What caused the Salem witch hysteria? What caused the American Revolution? Use these two books as supplements to the core history text; they are invaluable in helping the student evaluate historical evidence. Each book begins with a "Guide to Critical Thinking," which reviews the basics of logic: fallacies, proper use of sources, generalizations, and so on. The table of contents clearly identifies the historical event on which each lesson is based ("Was the Stamp Act Justified?" "Foreign Views of the Constitution"). Have the student complete these lessons when he reaches the corresponding historical event in the core history text.

The Notebook

Using a new three-ring binder, label it "Late Renaissance–Early Modern: 1600–1850," and divide it into the same ten sections as in fifth and sixth grades (see page 275).

This period is heavy on wars—the Glorious Revolution, the annexation of Ireland, the Great Northern War, the Seven Years' War, the American Revolution, the French Revolution, the Napoleonic Wars, the War of 1812, and more. You will find a great deal of material in the library on these topics, as well as on the creation of the Declaration of Independence and on the persons who defined early American political life. The Industrial Revolution also takes place during this period.

Memorization

American seventh graders should take time out during the year to memorize the Declaration of Independence and the Preamble to the Constitution.

Suggested Schedule

For late Renaissance–early modern history, you'll need to cover one to two sections or pages per week. Try to do two sections or pages when possible; this will give you extra time to work on the primary resources and the Critical Thinking Press books.

For Monday-Wednesday-Friday and Tuesday-Thursday schedules, see the sixth-grade year (page 290).

Eighth Grade: Modern (1850–Present)

Again, the student will read a section from the core text, prepare a list of facts, mark all dates on the time line, find locations on the globe/wall map/atlas, do additional reading, outline selected pages from one of the additional resources (eighth graders should aim to outline three or four pages), and prepare notebook pages.

The List of Facts

If the student has not already transitioned away from the Usborne history into a more difficult book, eighth grade is a good time to do so. If you are already using a more complex history core text, continue on as you have before.

Create a new time line. Divide this one into fifteen ten-year segments since you'll be recording a number of events that occur close together. In the case of World War II, for example, you may need to mark a series of events taking place over a matter of months. The time line should look like this:

The Outline

The student should make three-level outlines of selected pages from his additional resources. See “How to Outline” on pages 297–301 for more detailed guidance; note that, as the student grows more practiced, he should aim to outline three to four pages from his chosen resource.

Primary Sources

The best Jackdaw Portfolio for this period is *The Civil War,* a collection of posters, military documents, and letters. Use this with “The American Civil War.” Also look for some of the resources listed at the end of this chapter.

Since the Civil War was one of the earliest wars photographed, look in the adult nonfiction section of the library for books of Civil War photos. They bring the conflict to life as nothing else can.

We have listed a number of additional Jackdaw Portfolios in the Resources section. Other primary sources for the modern period are not difficult to find. Letters and speeches of world leaders—Queen Victoria, Abraham Lincoln, Winston Churchill, Benito Mussolini, Adolf Hitler, just to name a few—abound. Check the library for juvenile and young adult nonfiction on the great men and women of the modern age; many of these books will contain primary information. (We’ve listed a few suggestions in our Resources.) Whenever the student encounters a primary document such as the Gettysburg Address or Edward VIII’s abdication speech, he should fill out the primary-source evaluation and file it in Primary Sources.

As you move into the twentieth century, you should be making use of another type of primary source—oral history. Whenever the student encounters a major event in the twentieth century, make an effort to bring him into contact with someone who lived during that time. If you’re fortunate enough to have grandparents (or great-grandparents) and great-uncles or great-aunts nearby, send the child over to interview them. What was rationing like during World War II? Did you have to look out for airplanes? Did you get to eat chocolate? What were cars like in 1950? How much did you pay for rent in 1952? What music did you listen to? As you come closer to modern times, these recollections will become easier to find: friends may be willing to tell about tours of duty in Vietnam; older relatives and neighbors might recall the days of segregation; and most people born in the fifties will remember the first moon landing and where they were when they heard of Kennedy's assassination.

These oral histories should be written down and filed in Primary Sources (see "The Notebook," pages 274–276). If you can't find friends and relatives to fill in these accounts, you might consider a trip to a retirement community or nursing home; the staff should be able to direct you toward residents who can tell stories about the early twentieth century. Once you reach the 1930s and 1940s, try to conduct an oral-history interview at least twice per month, even if you have to sacrifice some library time to do so.

The oral-history project has two purposes. It develops the student's ability to "do" history by recording events and stories firsthand instead of relying on the written work of others. And it brings recent history to life—the student is able to connect the stories in books to real people's lives for the first time. Reading about the Holocaust is powerful; discovering that a nursing-home resident has a tattoo on her forearm is explosive.

We've supplied a list of questions at the end of this book (see Appendix 1, pages 721–723). Although the student can use these questions to give oral-history interviews direction, he shouldn't feel tied to them.

As in fourth grade, you should plan to take one to two weeks at the end of the year to read through the history of your own state (see Resources, page 331).

Critical-Thinking Resources

As in seventh grade, you should use the Critical Thinking Press series Critical Thinking in United States History—Book Three, *Reconstruction to Progressivism,* and Book Four, *Spanish-American War to Vietnam War.* The exercises, done when the student encounters the historical facts on which they are based, will help the student evaluate primary sources and draw conclusions.

The Notebook

Using a new three-ring binder, label it "Modern Times: 1850–Present," and divide it into the same ten sections as in fifth through seventh grades (see page 275). Add one additional section: Eyewitness Accounts.

Memorization

American eighth graders should take time during the year to memorize the Gettysburg Address. Optional memory work might be done on the Emancipation Proclamation, the amendments to the Constitution, the wartime speeches of Winston Churchill, the speeches of Martin Luther King, Jr., or anything else the student finds and likes.

Suggested Schedule

For Monday-Wednesday-Friday and Tuesday-Thursday schedules, see the sixth-grade year (page 290). As an alternative, you might take one week to do reading, outlining, and map work and then devote a full week to reading, research, and oral-history taking.

How to Outline

The student should begin to develop his outlining skills by finding the main idea in each paragraph and assigning it a Roman numeral. Remember that the goal is not to write a single sentence that incorporates *all* (or even most) of the information in the paragraph. Instead, the student should try to find the *topic sentence* in the paragraph—the one that summarizes the paragraph's central theme. Topic sentences are often found at the beginning or end of a paragraph. Remind the student to put the information into his own words.

It can be useful to ask the student two questions for each paragraph:

1. What is the main thing or person that the paragraph is about?
2. Why is that thing or person important?

For purposes of illustration, consider the following paragraph from *The Story of Canada,* by Janet Lunn and Christopher Moore.

> Five hundred years ago, 60 million bison—or buffalo, as they are more often called—roamed the grasslands of North America. They meant life itself to plains nations like the Blackfoot of what is now southern Alberta. The Blackfoot moved slowly across the land, following the herds and carrying with them everything they had. They hunted deer and antelope, they grew tobacco, and they gathered wild turnips and onion. But for centuries it was the buffalo that provided for the Blackfoot people. Buffalo

> hides made their tipis and their clothing. Buffalo sinews were their thread. Buffalo bones made clubs and spoons and needles. They even used dried buffalo dung as fuel for their campfires. To the Blackfoot, buffalo meat was "real" meat and nothing else tasted so good. They trusted the buffalo to keep them strong.

What is the main thing that the paragraph is about? Buffalo. Why is the buffalo important? Because the Blackfoot people used it for food, clothing, and other purposes. If the student combines these answers into one sentence, he will have his sentence:

I. The Blackfoot people used buffalo for food, clothing, and many other purposes.

The next paragraph in *The Story of Canada* reads:

> The Blackfoot had always gone on foot, using dogs to help carry their goods, for there were no horses in North America until Spanish colonists brought them in the 1500s. Soon after that, plains people captured animals that had gone wild, or stole them in raids. They traded the horses northward and early in the 1700s, horses came to the northern plains. Suddenly the Blackfoot were a nation on horseback. How exciting it was, learning to ride a half-wild mustang and galloping off to the horizon!

Ask the question: What is the main thing that the paragraph is about? Horses. Why are horses important? The Blackfoot tribe learned how to ride them in the 1700s.

II. The Blackfoot tribe learned to use horses in the 1700s.

You will have to remind the student continually that he is not trying to summarize the entire paragraph; he is finding the central idea in it. Leaving facts out is a difficult skill, and also involves a judgment call on the part of the student. As long as he can answer the two questions above with information that makes sense, don't agonize over whether he's chosen the "right" sentence for his outline.

Once the student is comfortable finding the main idea in each paragraph (something that can take the entire fifth-grade year), ask him to move on to a two-level outline. In this level of outlining, the main Roman-numeral point still provides the central idea of the paragraph, while each capital-letter subpoint should provide a specific piece of information that relates *directly* to the main idea.

After writing the main Roman-numeral point, the student should ask himself: What additional information does the paragraph give me about each of the people, things, or ideas in the main point? For the first paragraph above, the student would ask: What other important thing does the paragraph tell me about buffalo? There were 60 million buffalo in North America. What other important thing does the paragraph tell me about the Blackfoot's use of the buffalo? They relied on the buffalo to keep them strong.

The two-level outline of the paragraph would read:

I. The Blackfoot people used buffalo for food, clothing, and other purposes.
  A. There were 60 million buffalo in North America.
  B. The Blackfoot relied on the buffalo to keep them strong.

It is tempting for the sixth-grade student to use the capital letter subpoints to give specific details about the paragraph:

I. The Blackfoot people used buffalo for food, clothing, and other purposes.
  A. They hunted deer and antelope too.
  B. They made clothing from buffalo.
  C. They ate buffalo meat.
  D. They made clubs and spoons and needles from buffalo bones.

These are actually details about the extent to which the Blackfoot relied on the buffalo, so they would only appear in a three-level outline:

I. The Blackfoot people used buffalo for food, clothing, and other purposes.
  A. There were 60 million buffalo in North America.
  B. The Blackfoot relied on the buffalo to keep them strong.
    1. They made clothing from buffalo.
    2. They ate buffalo meat.

3. They made clubs and spoons and needles from buffalo bones.

(Note that the detail about deer and antelope is a random statement that doesn't fit into the outline at all.)

Before the student can do three-level outlines (which he'll begin in seventh grade), he needs to master the basic two-level outline; each capital-letter subpoint should make an independent statement relating directly to something in the main Roman-numeral point. This means that the student will need to work on the skill of eliminating unncessary detail, picking out only the central statements in each paragraph. A two-level outline of the second paragraph would answer the questions: What is the most important additional information that this paragraph gives me about the Blackfoot? What is the most important additional information that it gives me about the horses? An acceptable outline might look like this:

II. The Blackfoot tribe learned to use horses in the 1700s.
 A. They had always gone on foot before.
 B. The horses were brought to North America by Spanish colonists.

As the student grows more comfortable with two-level outlining, encourage him to outline up to two pages rather than merely outlining one.

Around seventh grade, the student can begin to construct three-level outlines. The third level of the outline uses Arabic numerals:

I. Main point.
 A. Additional information about the main point.
  1. Detail about that additional information.

Third-level details are relatively simple to find; the student merely needs to ask, "What else is important to know in this paragraph?" A full three-level outline of the two paragraphs above might look like this:

I. The Blackfoot people used buffalo for food, clothing, and other purposes.
 A. There were 60 million buffalo in North America.
  1. The buffalo are also called bison.

        2. They roamed North America 500 years ago.
    B. The Blackfoot relied on the buffalo to keep them strong.
        1. They made clothing from buffalo.
        2. They ate buffalo meat.
        3. They made clubs and spoons and needles from buffalo bones.
        4. They used buffalo dung for fuel.
II. The Blackfoot tribe learned to use horses in the 1700s.
    A. They had always gone on foot before.
        1. There were no horses in North America.
        2. They used dogs to carry their goods.
    B. The horses were brought to North America by Spanish colonists.
        1. The horses first came in the 1500s.
        2. Some of the horses escaped or were stolen.
        3. The horses came to the northern plains in the 1700s.

Once the student is reasonably comfortable with the three-level outline, encourage him to expand the number of pages that he outlines: up to three pages for seventh graders, three to four pages for eighth graders.

Developing outlining takes practice—and don't forget that this history outlining should be paired with a grammar program that teaches the basics of outlining skills. However, remember three things.

First, many guides to outlining will tell you that you should never have an A unless you have a B, and that you should never use 1 unless you use 2. While this might be a useful guide when you're constructing your own outlines to write from, it's not workable when you're outlining someone else's material; the writer might not have provided two subpoints per main point, and it's pointless to make one up to preserve some sort of ideal outline form.

Second, there may be several different ways to outline any given paragraph. If the student can give good reasons why he's chosen his main points and subpoints, don't worry about whether he's constructed the best possible outline.

Third, if the student struggles with outlining a particular resource, it is possible that the book itself is either badly written or written in "encyclopedic" form (many main points packed into single paragraphs of text). Put it away and try outlining from a different book.

RESOURCES

For publisher and catalog addresses, telephone numbers, and other information, see Sources (pages 751–778). Most books can be obtained from any bookstore or library; where we know of a mail-order option, we have provided it. The titles we list are only a few of the many available. Plan on exploring library and bookstore shelves for yourself.

Basic texts for the four-year logic stage are listed first, followed by basic geography resources. A three-part supplementary list is provided for each year of study. The first section for each year lists, in chronological order, great men and women (for grades 5 and 6) or major events (for grades 7 and 8) that you might want to cover during the year—this is simply a checklist to help you organize your history study. The second section lists primary sources—books and texts written during the period under study. The third section lists books that provide general information about the historical period, including coloring books and other project resources.

Many of the resources recommended in Chapter 7, such as the detailed Bellerophon coloring books, are still suitable for middle-grade students. Older students may also enjoy reading elementary-level biographies as a refresher. Check the Resources section at the end of Chapter 7 for details.

Basic Texts

Bingham, Jane, Fiona Chandler, and Sam Taplin. *The Usborne Internet-Linked Encyclopedia of World History.* London: Usborne Publishing, 2001.
$39.99. Order from any bookstore.

Daniels, Patricia, and Stephen G. Hyslop. *National Geographic Almanac of World History.* Washington, D.C.: National Geographic, 2006.
$24.00. Order from any bookstore.

Fry, Plantagenet Somerset. *History of the World,* 3d ed., rev. and updated. New York: Dorling Kindersley, 2007.
$39.99. Order from any bookstore.

Hart-Davis, Adam, ed. *History: The Definitive Visual Guide.* New York: Dorling Kindersley, 2007.
$50.00. Order from any bookstore.

National Geographic Concise History of the World: An Illustrated Time Line. Washington, D.C.: National Geographic, 2006.
$40.00. Order from any bookstore.

O'Reilly, Kevin. Critical Thinking in United States History series. Pacific Grove, Calif.: Critical Thinking Press, 1995.

$17.99 for each student book; the teacher's guides (which you'll find helpful) are $10.99 each. Order from the Critical Thinking Company.

Book One: Colonies to Constitution (seventh grade/third year of study).

Book Two: New Republic to Civil War (seventh grade/third year of study).

Book Three: Reconstruction to Progressivism (eighth grade/fourth year of study).

Book Four: Spanish-American War to Vietnam War (eighth grade/fourth year of study).

Teeple, John B. *Timelines of World History*. New York: Dorling Kindersley, 2006.

$30.00. Order from any bookstore.

Basic Geography Resources

Up-to-date globes and wall maps can be found at the National Geographic online map store (www.shopnationalgeographic.org) and at www.maps.com.

Hammond Historical World Atlas, Rev. and expanded. Duncan, S.C.: Hammond World Atlas Corporation, 2000.

$11.95. Order through any bookstore. A paperback atlas containing 118 chronological maps showing the rise and fall of empires, the territories of wars, and more worldwide.

Kapit, Wynn. *Geography Coloring Book*. 3d ed. Upper Saddle River, N.J.: Prentice-Hall, 2003.

$25.60. Order from The Book Peddler.

National Geographic Family Reference Atlas. 2d ed. Washington, D.C.: National Geographic Society, 2006.

$65.00 list price, but you can often find it discounted at the National Geographic online store or from other booksellers. Before buying, though, visit the National Geographic store for the most recent edition.

National Geographic World Atlas for Young Explorers. 3d ed. Washington, D.C.: National Geographic Society, 2007.

$24.95 list price, but you can often find it discounted at the National

Geographic online store or from other booksellers. Before buying, though, visit the National Geographic store for the most recent edition.

Wiggers, George and Hannah. *Uncle Josh's Outline Map Book.* Nancy, Ky.: Geography Matters, 2000.

$19.95. Order from Geography Matters. Contains 44 black-line maps of the world for coloring; also includes ten regional U.S. maps and all state maps. The CD, available for $26.95 from Geography Matters, makes it possible for you to print multiple copies of each map (and also includes 21 additional maps, including more detailed Canadian territories). Necessary for U.S. geography study.

Time-Line Resources

Blank Timeline Templates.

$5 for 10. Order from Rainbow Resource Center. These 22-inch time-line segments are each divided into twenty sections, which can be divided in numerous ways. Designate each section as one, five, ten, twenty, or more years; tape them together to form a custom time line.

Mark-It Timeline of World History. Nancy, Ky.: Geography Matters.

$10.95. Order from Geography Matters. Good for houses without a long hallway, this time line is set up on a 23 x 34-inch laminated poster; you can also cut it apart and tape it together for a 21-foot time line. One side is dated (4000 B.C.–2050 A.D.); the other is undated.

Resources for Teaching Skills

Boynton, Alice, and Wiley Blevins. *Teaching Students to Read Nonfiction.* Scholastic Teaching Strategies, Grades 4 and Up. New York: Scholastic, 2003.

$23.99. Order from any bookstore or from Social Studies School Service. Designed for grades 4–7, this book guides students through the basics of reading nonfiction, with an emphasis on history. A good way to build skills and confidence.

Mueller, Mary. *Study Skills Strategies: Outlining.* Portland, Maine: Walch Education, 2003.

$24.99. Order through any bookstore or from Walch Education (you can also read samples at www.walch.com). High-school skills.

Pearce, Q. L. *Note Taking & Outlining*. Grand Rapids, Mich.: Frank Schaffer Publications, 2003.

$6.99 for each book. Order from School Specialty Publishing. Each student will need her own book.

Note Taking & Outlining, Grades 3–5.

Note Taking & Outlining, Grades 6–8.

Ancients, 5000 B.C.–A.D. 400 (Fifth Grade)

List of Great Men and Women

Cheops, pharaoh of Egypt (2700–2675 B.C.)
Abraham (c. 2100 B.C.)
Hammurabi (c. 1750 B.C.)
Queen Hatshepsut of Egypt (c. 1480 B.C.)
Moses (c. 1450 B.C.)
Tutankhamen (c. 1355 B.C.)
Nebuchadnezzar (1146–1123 B.C.)
King David (c. 1000 B.C.)
Homer (c. 800 B.C.)
Romulus (753–716 B.C.)
Sennacherib (705–681 B.C.)
Lao-tse (Chinese philosopher, b. 604 B.C.)
Pythagoras (581–497 B.C.)
Confucius (K'ung Fu-tsu) (551–479 B.C.)
Buddha (Siddhartha Gautama) (550–480 B.C.)
Darius I of Persia (522–485 B.C.)
Socrates (470–399 B.C.)
Hippocrates (b. 460 B.C.)
Plato (427–347 B.C.)
Aristotle (384–322 B.C.)
Alexander the Great (356–323 B.C.)
Shi Huangdi (first emperor of unified China, 221–207 B.C.)
Hannibal (fought with Rome c. 218–207 B.C.)
Judas Maccabaeus (c. 168 B.C.)

Cicero (106–43 B.C.)
Julius Caesar (100–44 B.C.)
Virgil (70–19 B.C.)
Caesar Augustus (c. 45 B.C.–A.D. 14)
Jesus Christ (c. 4 B.C.–A.D. 33)
Caligula (died A.D. 42)
Saint Paul (c. A.D. 45)
Nero (died A.D. 68)
Marcus Aurelius (ruled A.D. 161–180)
Constantine the Great (ruled A.D. 306–337)

Primary Sources

The Internet Ancient History Sourcebook. www.fordham.edu/halsall/ancient/asbook.html.

Hosted by Fordham University, this invaluable website is an easy-to-navigate online archive of primary sources (translated into English) ranging from Sumer (artwork, Akkadian prayers, multiple translations of *Gilgamesh*, Sumerian king lists, and much more) to the third-century church (Pliny's letters, excerpts from the church fathers, official edicts, and more). Highly useful for the curious student.

Jackdaw Portfolios. Amawalk, N.Y.: Jackdaw Publications.

Various prices. Order from Jackdaw Publications or from Social Studies School Service. Jackdaws contain facsimiles of primary documents, essays (called Broadsheets) that combine relevant research into a single narrative; annotated notes about the background of each primary source; transcripts of anything that might be hard to read; and study guides with activities, vocabulary, writing activities, reading suggestions, debate and drama ideas. Pick and choose from among these portfolios (and visit www.jackdaw.com for even more choices):

Ancient Athletic Games: Heracles and the Olympics. $27.95.
China: A Cultural Heritage. $51.95.
The Development of Writing. $51.95.
Hadrian's Wall. $51.95.
Inspirational Women: Muses and Women in Antiquity. $27.95.
Major Temples and Famous Statues of Deities. $27.95.
Many Faces of the Hero: Odysseus, Theseus, and Jason. $27.95.

The Middle East: The Land and Its People. $51.95.
Oracles and Sibyls: Telling the Future in the Past. $27.95.
Tutankhamen and the Discovery of the Tomb. $51.95.

Lewis, Jon. *The Mammoth Book of How It Happened: Eyewitness Accounts of Great Historical Moments from 2700 BC to AD 2005*, Rev. and updated. Philadelphia, Pa.: Running Press, 2006.

$13.95. Order from any bookstore. Useful for study of ancient times through modern ages, this anthology assembles readable excerpts from primary sources describing central events in history.

Plato. *The Last Days of Socrates.* Trans. Hugh Tredennick. New York: Penguin, 2003.

$12.00. Order from any bookstore. For good readers, this primary source contains dialogues that you and your middle-grade student could read together; the dialogue is often funny, and ideas are thought-provoking. (Remember, this is a first introduction to ancient thought; the student doesn't need to understand every word!)

General Information

Aldred, Cyril. *A Coloring Book of Tutankhamun.* Santa Barbara, Calif.: Bellerophon, 1995.

$3.50. Order from Bellerophon. Uses actual images from the ancient world to tell the story of Tutankhamen's reign and burial. Detailed and challenging.

Amery, Heather, et al. *Rome and Romans.* Tulsa, Okla.: E.D.C. Publications, 1998.

$6.95. Order from Children's Books or from an Usborne distributor. Part of the Usborne Time-Traveler series, this is written at a lower reading level (approximately fourth grade) and would be good for students who find reading difficult.

Anderson, John. *Alexander the Great Coloring Book.* Santa Barbara, Calif.: Bellerophon, 1988.

$4.95. Order from Bellerophon. These illustrations of Alexander the Great are taken from Persian and Indian drawings as well as from the art of ancient Greece and medieval Europe. Includes biographical material.

Art, Suzanne Strass. *Ancient Times* and *Early Times* series.

Art, an ancient history teacher, wrote these series because she couldn't find history texts for fifth graders that covered the ancient world in a systematic way, while still providing plenty of interesting detail. These books are well worth having on hand for additional reading on topics covered briefly in the *Kingfisher History Encyclopedia*; they are clear and readable, cover civilizations and stories neglected in other texts, and include projects, maps, writing assignments, personality profiles, and suggested additional readings.

Ancient Times: The Story of the First Americans. Lincoln, Mass.: Pemblewick Press, 1999.

$14.95. Order from Pemblewick Press.

Early Times: The Story of Ancient Egypt. 2d ed. Concord, Mass.: Wayside Publishing, 1993.

$8.95. Order from Wayside Publishing.

Early Times: The Story of Ancient Greece. 2d ed. Concord, Mass.: Wayside Publishing, 1994.

$11.95. Order from Wayside Publishing.

Early Times: The Story of Ancient Rome. Concord, Mass.: Wayside Publishing, 1993.

$10.95. Order from Wayside Publishing.

The Story of Ancient China. Lincoln, Mass.: Pemblewick Press, 2001.

$14.95. Order from Pemblewick Press. From Neolithic times to the Tang dynasty; includes explanations of Taoism, Confucianism, and Buddhism.

West Meets East: The Travels of Alexander. Concord, Mass.: Wayside Publishing, 1996.

$11.50. Order from Wayside Publishing.

Ashman, Iain. *Make This Egyptian Mummy.* Tulsa, Okla.: E.D.C. Publications, 1999.

$9.95. Order from any bookstore. This kit contains a punch-out-and-assemble sarcophagus with nesting coffins and mummy.

———. *Make This Model Egyptian Mummy.* Tulsa, Okla.: E.D.C. Publications, 2003.

$9.95. Order from Greenleaf Press. A punch-out-and-assemble mummy with nesting cases.

Burrell, Roy, illus. Peter Connolly. *The Oxford First Ancient History.* Oxford: Oxford University Press, 1997.

$24.95 (paperback). Order from any bookstore. A beautiful, readable book that begins with prehistory and continues on through Mesopotamia, the Far East, and the Mediterranean. Color paintings and photographs recreate ancient art; the text includes interviews with imaginary characters (a Greek theater worker, a twelve year old who is learning to be a scribe, a Babylonian loyal to Hammurabi).

Calliope. Peterborough, N.H.: Cobblestone Publishing.

$33.95 for one year's subscription. Order from Cobblestone Publishing. A world history magazine for readers aged 9–12; each 52-page issue has a theme ("The City-States of Sumer," "Tang Dynasty") and includes articles, maps, art, and a question-and-answer feature about world history. Back issues can be ordered from Cobblestone individually (see www.cobblestonepub.com/pages/CalliopeArchives.html for a chronological listing).

Conkle, Nancy. *A Coloring Book of the Trojan War: The Iliad, Vol. 1.* Santa Barbara, Calif.: Bellerophon, 1995. (Also Knill, Harry. *A Coloring Book of the Trojan War: The Iliad, Vol. 2.* Santa Barbara, Calif.: Bellerophon, 1997.)

$3.95 each. Order from Bellerophon. Detailed drawings, taken from Greek sculpture and architecture, can be turned into works of art with careful coloring.

Connolly, Peter, and Hazel Dodge. *The Ancient City: Life in Classical Athens and Rome.* Oxford: Oxford University Press, 2000.

$24.95. Order from Greenleaf Press. Beautiful full-color illustrations of the buildings and famous places of Athens and Rome, with interesting text covering government, domestic life, entertainment, and more.

Connolly, Peter. *The Ancient Greece of Odysseus.* Oxford: Oxford University Press, 1999.

$12.95. Order from Greenleaf Press. A retelling of Homer that incorporates an enormous amount of information about the ancient world.

Diez-Luckie, Cathy. *Famous Figures of Ancient Times: Moveable Paper Figures to Cut, Color, and Assemble.* Oakland, Calif.: Figures In Motion, 2009.

$19.95. Great for kids who like crafts: detailed, colored figures from history, from Narmer to Augustine, to cut out and assemble. The figures are on cardstock with moveable joints. Good for decorating time lines (or just for fun).

Egyptians Game. Roseville, Minn.: Mindware.
$24.95. Order from Fat Brain Toys. A board game based on historical knowledge. Compete with three other players to become supreme ruler of ancient Egypt.

Eyewitness Books series. New York: Knopf.
$15.99 each. These books, designed by Dorling Kindersley, are available in libraries and bookstores; the pictures, designs, and layout will provide more information than you need. Consider keeping these on hand so that you can refer back to them as you progress through the time line.
Ayo, Yvonne, et al. *Africa.* 2000.
Farndon, John. *Mesopotamia.* 2007.
Hart, George, et al. *Ancient Egypt.* 2004.
James, Simon, et al. *Ancient Rome.* 2004.
Pearson, Anne, et al. *Ancient Greece.* 2007.
Putnam, James, et al. *Pyramid.* 2004.
Tubb, Jonathan N., et al. *Bible Lands.* 2000.

Grant, Neil. *The World of Odysseus.* Jersey City, N.J.: Parkwest Publications, 1992.
$14.95. Order from any bookstore. A BBC Fact Finder with quality illustrations and quotes from the ancients themselves.

Green, John. *Egyptian Stained Glass Coloring Book.* New York: Dover, 1999.
$5.95. Order from Rainbow Resource Center. Color on translucent paper with crayons or colored pencils and end up with a stained-glass effect. (You can also order the *Little Coloring Book* for $1.50 for little brother or sister.)

Langley, Andrew, et al. *The Roman News.* New York: Candlewick Press, 1999.
$6.99. Order from Greenleaf Press. Headline stories from ancient history, along with facts, quotes, news flashes, and even want ads. Entertaining and informative; written for fifth graders.

Macaulay, David. *City: A Story of Roman Planning and Construction.* Boston, Mass.: Houghton Mifflin, 1983.
$9.95. Order from Greenleaf Press. All the stages of construction in a

Roman city. Fascinating for the mechanically minded. Incorporates history and culture into descriptions of the building process.

———. *David Macaulay's World of Ancient Engineering.* Alexandria, Va.: PBS Home Video, 2000.

$24.99 each. Order from PBS (or try your local library). These splendid videos use both live action and animation to explore the engineering marvels of the ancient world.

Pyramid.

Roman City.

———. *Pyramid.* Boston, Mass.: Houghton Mifflin, 1982.

$9.95. Order from any bookstore. The book on which the video above was based, this offers incredibly detailed drawings and explanations of pyramid construction.

Morley, Jacqueline. *The Temple at Jerusalem.* Illus. John James. New York: Peter Bedrick Books, 2001.

$18.95. Order from any bookstore. One of the Magnifications series, this book provides illustrations of Solomon's temple, Herod's temple, and the temple site today, allowing readers to "zoom in" on certain aspects of the drawings to learn more detail.

———. *You Wouldn't Want to Be . . .* series. Illus. David Antram.

$9.95. Order from any bookstore. Entertaining history series reviewing the life styles of unfortunate people from ancient times, with plenty of historical detail.

You Wouldn't Want to Be a Pyramid Builder! 2004.

You Wouldn't Want to Be in Alexander the Great's Army! 2005.

You Wouldn't Want to Work on the Great Wall of China! 2006.

You Wouldn't Want to Be a Sumerian Slave! 2007.

Payne, Elizabeth. *The Pharaohs of Ancient Egypt.* New York: Random House, 1981.

$5.99. Order from any bookstore. Covers Egypt's history from the beginning until its conquest by Greece and Rome. Each chapter tells about one pharaoh; on a fifth-grade reading level.

Perspective: The Timeline Game.

$29.95. Order from Rainbow Resource Center. Each player challenges others to put cards bearing historical events into the proper order on a time line.

Powell, Anton, and Philip Steele. *The Greek News.* New York: Candlewick Press, 1999.

$6.99. Order from Greenleaf Press. Headline stories from ancient history, along with facts, quotes, news flashes, and even want ads. Entertaining and informative; written for fifth graders.

Prior, Natalie Jane. *The Encyclopedia of Preserved People: Pickled, Frozen, and Mummified Corpses from Around the World.* New York: Crown Publishing, 2003.

$14.95. Order from any bookstore. Revolting but fascinating; this book describes various "preserved people" from ancient cultures on every continent, and tells what they reveal about each culture.

Queen Nefertiti. Santa Barbara, Calif.: Bellerophon, 1992.

$3.50. Order from Bellerophon. The story of one of the great women of the ancient world, told through a coloring book that uses complex images from Egyptian art itself.

Roehrig, Catharine. *Fun with Hieroglyphs.* New York: Simon & Schuster, 2008.

$24.99. Order from any bookstore. Designed by the New York Metropolitan Museum of Art, this set includes rubber stamps, an ink pad, and a key.

Roman Arch Set. Hamburg, Germany: HABA Toys.

$35.00. Order from Fat Brain Toys. Wooden blocks make it possible to construct (and understand the dynamics of) a Roman arch.

Steedman, Scott, ed. *The Egyptian News.* New York: Candlewick Press, 2000.

$6.99. Order from any bookstore. Headline stories from ancient history, along with facts, quotes, news flashes, and even want ads. Entertaining and informative; written for fifth graders.

Walton, John. *Chronological and Background Charts of the Old Testament.* Grand Rapids, Mich.: Zondervan, 1994.

$19.99. Order from Greenleaf Press. A highly valuable resource that gives dates for Old Testament events, helping you to fit them into "secular" history; where there is controversy over a date, a brief note is provided.

Wiese, Jim. *Ancient Science: 40 Time-Traveling, World-Exploring, History-Making Activities for Kids.* Illus. Ed Shems. San Francisco, Calif.: Jossey-Bass, 2003. $12.95. Order from any bookstore. Hands-on experience with inventions across the ancient world, from ancient candy and kites to counting systems and compasses.

Medieval/Early Renaissance, 400–1600 (Sixth Grade)

List of Great Men and Women

This list includes a few early rulers of major countries up until about 1050. After Edward the Confessor, any ruler of England, Holy Roman Emperor, ruler of France, emperor of Japan, or emperor of China is worth making a notebook page on; we don't list them here (there are simply too many). Check the encyclopedia for complete listings.

Saint Augustine (writing c. 411)
Attila the Hun (c. 433–453)
King Arthur (probably killed in 537 at the Battle of Camlan)
Gregory of Tours (540–594)
Mohammed (570–632)
The Venerable Bede (672–735)
Charles Martel (688–741)
Charlemagne (ruled 768–814)
Alfred the Great (849–899)
Leif Ericsson (discovered America c. 1000)
Omar Khayyam (1027–1123)
Edward the Confessor (1042–1066)
Chrétien de Troyes (1144–1190)
Genghis Khan (b. 1155)
Thomas Aquinas (1225–1274)
Dante Alighieri (1265–1321)
Geoffrey Chaucer (c. 1340–1400)
Thomas à Kempis (1380–1471)
Jan van Eyck (c. 1390–1441)
Johannes Gutenberg (c. 1396–1468)
Sandro Botticelli (1444–1510)
Christopher Columbus (1451–1506)

Leonardo da Vinci (1452–1519)
Amerigo Vespucci (1454–1512)
Erasmus (1465–1536)
Nicolaus Copernicus (1473–1543)
Michelangelo (1475–1564)
Titian (1477–1576)
Thomas More (1478–1535)
Ferdinand Magellan (1480–1521)
Martin Luther (1483–1546)
Raphael (1483–1520)
Ignatius Loyola (1491–1556)
Correggio (1494–1534)
Giovanni Angelo de' Medici (1499–1565)
Thomas Wyatt (1503–1542)
Nostradamus (1503–1566)
John Knox (1505–1572)
John Calvin (1509–1564)
Hernando Cortés (entered Mexican capital, 1519)
Pieter Brueghel (1520–1569)
Palestrina, Giovanni Pierluigi da (1525–1594)
Tycho Brahe (1546–1601)
Philip Sidney (1551–1586)
Walter Raleigh (1554–1618)
William Shakespeare (1564–1616)
Galileo Galilei (1564–1642)
Jan Brueghel (1568–1625)
John Donne (1572–1631)
Inigo Jones (1573–1652)
René Descartes (1596–1650)

Primary Sources

The Internet Medieval Sourcebook. www.fordham.edu/halsall/sbook.html. Hosted by Fordham University, this invaluable website is an easy-to-navigate online archive of primary sources (translated into English) ranging from decrees of Justinian to the Ballad of Bosworth Field. Highly useful for the curious student.

Jackdaw Portfolios. Amawalk, N.Y.: Jackdaw Publications, various dates.

Order from Jackdaw Publications. Jackdaws contain facsimiles of primary documents, essays (called Broadsheets) that combine relevant research into a single narrative with photos; annotated notes about the background of each primary source; transcripts of anything that might be hard to read; and study guides with activities, vocabulary, writing activities, reading ideas, debate and drama suggestions, and more. You can pick and choose among these portfolios (more choices are found at jack daw.com):

1066. $51.95.
The Black Death. $51.95.
Byzantine Empire. $51.95.
Columbus and the Age of Explorers. $51.95.
Elizabeth I. $51.95.
Magna Carta. $51.95.
Martin Luther. $51.95.
The Northwest Passage. $27.95.
Alfred the Great. $27.95.
The Conquest of Mexico. $51.95.
The Vikings. $51.95.
Drake and the Golden Hinde. $51.95.

Lewis, Jon. *The Mammoth Book of How It Happened: Eyewitness Accounts of Great Historical Moments from 2700 BC to AD 2005*. Rev. and updated. Philadelphia, Pa.: Running Press, 2006.

$13.95. Order from any bookstore. This anthology assembles readable excerpts from primary sources describing central events in history.

General Resources

Art, Suzanne Strauss. *China's Later Dynasties*. Lincoln, Mass.: Pemblewick Press, 2002.

$14.95. Order from Pemblewick Press. Tells about China during the time of the Song, Yuan, Ming, and Qing dynasties.

———. *The Story of the Renaissance*. Lincoln, Mass.: Pemblewick Press, 1997.

$14.95. Order from Pemblewick Press. A readable guide to major developments in the West during the fourteenth to sixteenth centuries; a good reference work to have on hand for additional reading.

Ashman, Iain. *Make This Model Castle.* Tulsa, Okla.: E.D.C. Publications, 2000.

$9.95. Order from any bookstore. A twelfth-century cut-out-and-assemble castle with forty cut-out figures.

———. *Make This Viking Settlement.* Tulsa, Okla.: E.D.C. Publications, 2000.

$9.95. Order from any bookstore. The settlement includes forty cut-out figures.

Birmingham, Duncan. *The Maya, Aztecs, and Incas Pop-Up.* Jersey City, N.J.: Parkwest Publishing, 1985.

$10.25. Order from any bookstore. For budding paper engineers, this make-it-yourself pop-up offers interesting text and excellent pictures.

Calliope. Peterborough, N.H.: Cobblestone Publishing.

$33.95 for one year's subscription. Order from Cobblestone Publishing. A world history magazine for readers aged 9–12; each 52-page issue has a theme ("The Qu'ran," "Mary Queen of Scots") and includes articles, maps, art, and a question-and-answer feature about world history. Back issues can be ordered from Cobblestone individually (see www.cobble stonepub.com/magazine/CAL/).

Cathedral: The Game of the Medieval City. Pukekohe, New Zealand: Brightway Products, 1997.

$40.00. Order from Rainbow Resource Center. In this high-quality wooden game, players place their pieces ("buildings") inside a walled city, trying to claim enough space to rule the city and become its lord. *Cathedral* has become a classic strategy game, winning a *Games* magazine award twice.

Chorzempa, Rosemary A. *Design Your Own Coat of Arms: An Introduction to Heraldry.* New York: Dover, 1987.

$4.95. Explains the symbolism and history of coats of arms so that you can design your own.

Davis, Courtney. *Celtic Stained Glass.* New York: Dover, 1993.

$5.95. Order from Greenleaf Press. The Dover stained-glass coloring books reproduce medieval windows on translucent paper. Color them and put them against a window for a beautiful effect.

Deary, Terry. *Horrible Histories.* Illus. Martin Brown. London: Scholastic.
$7.50. Order from horriblebooks.com or (if you can stomach the exchange rate) from amazon.co.uk. This British series highlights the more disgusting aspects of medieval life and does a good bit of history along the way; a sure middle-grade hit.

The Angry Aztecs. 2008.
The Cut-throat Celts. 2008.
Dark Knights and Dingy Castles. 1997.
The Incredible Incas. 2008.
Knights. 2006.
The Measly Middle Ages. 2007.
The Smashing Saxons. 2000.
The Stormin' Normans. 2007.
The Terrible Tudors. 2007.
The Vicious Vikings. 2007.

Duncan, Deborah, and Keith Jones. *The Vikings: With Standup Scenes to Cut Out and Glue Together.* Jersey City, N.J.: Parkwest Publishing, 1997.
$14.00. Order from American Home-School Publishing. This British Museum Press Activity Book includes detailed drawings to color, cartoons, maps, mysteries, fashions, monsters, and weapons.

Eyewitness Books. New York: Dorling Kindersley.
$15.99. These books are available in libraries and bookstores. The pictures and designs are beautiful, and the books will give you more information than you'll ever need. Consider keeping these on hand for several months, referring back to them as you progress through the time line.

Baquedano, Elizabeth, et al. *Aztec, Inca, and Maya.* 2005.
Byam, Michelle, et al. *Arms and Armor.* 2004.
Cole, Alison, et al. *Renaissance.* 2000.
Gravett, Christopher, et al. *Castle.* 2004.
———. *Knight.* 2007.
Langley, Andrew, et al. *Medieval Life.* 2004.
Margeson, Susan M., et al. *Viking.* 2005.

Green, John. *Cathedrals of the World Coloring Book.* New York: Dover, 1995.
$3.95. Order from Greenleaf Press. Over forty great cathedrals; floor plans, overhead, interior, and exterior views.

Griffiths, David. *The Pop-Up Paris.* Jersey City, N.J.: Parkwest Publishing, 1986.
$9. Order from any bookstore. A challenging assemble-yourself pop-up book that covers the history of Paris since ancient times; much information about the city in medieval and Renaissance times.

Henry VIII and His Wives Coloring Book. New York: Bellerophon, 1989.
$4.95. Order from Bellerophon. Paper dolls to color; includes all six wives, with several outfits for Henry.

Hindley, Judy. *Knights and Castles.* Tulsa, Okla.: E.D.C. Publications, 2003.
$6.95. Order from Children's Books. Part of the Usborne Time-Traveler series, this is written at approximately fourth-grade level and would be good for students who find reading difficult.

Leon, Vicki. *Outrageous Women* series. San Francisco, Calif.: Jossey-Bass.
$12.95 each. Buy from any bookstore. Accurate, fascinating, and readable accounts of women who achieved great things and probably don't appear in your standard history texts—from Aud, the Viking adventurer, to the Irish pirate Grace O'Malley.

Outrageous Women of the Middle Ages. 1998.

Outrageous Women of the Renaissance. 1999.

Macaulay, David. *Castle.* Glenview, Ill.: Scott Foresman, 1982.
$9.95. Order from any bookstore or from Greenleaf Press. Macaulay's books are engrossing, with detailed drawings and explanations of how things work; particularly good for the mechanically minded. This book traces the social, cultural, and political role of a castle through its construction.

———. *Cathedral.* Boston, Mass.: Houghton Mifflin, 1981.
$9.95. Order from any bookstore or from Greenleaf Press. The story of a cathedral's construction, beginning in a French town in 1252.

———. *David Macaulay's World of Ancient Engineering.* Alexandria, Va.: PBS Home Video.

$24.99 each. Order from PBS (or try your local library). These splendid videos use both live action and animation to explore the engineering marvels of the medieval world.

Castle

Cathedral

———. *Ship*. Boston, Mass.: Houghton Mifflin, 1995.

$12.95. Order from any bookstore. A fifteenth-century Spanish wooden sailing ship is built, shipwrecked, and then discovered. The story switches from the present day to the fifteenth century and back again.

Macdonald, Fiona. *How Would You Survive in the Middle Ages?* New York: Orchard Books, 1997.

$7.95. Order from Rainbow Resource Center. Gives students several imaginary scenarios based on conditions in medieval times.

A Medieval Alphabet to Illuminate. New York: Bellerophon, 1985.

$4.95. Order from Bellerophon. Ornate capital letters from medieval alphabets. Each is a full-page drawing, ready to be colored.

Medieval Siege Engines. Victoria, B.C.: Pathfinders Design and Technology.

Order from Pathfinders. These historically accurate model kits can be put together with glue; the wooden pieces are pre-cut. Sturdy and fun.

Catapult. $17.00.

Siege Tower. $29.00.

Trebuchet (shoots over twenty feet!). $27.00.

Medieval World series. New York: Crabtree Publishing.

$8.95 each. Buy from any bookstore. Readable 32-page guides to different aspects of life in the Middle Ages.

Cels, Marc. *Life in a Medieval Monastery*. 2004.

———. *Life on a Medieval Manor*. 2004.

Eastwood, Kay. *The Life of a Knight*. 2003.

———. *Places of Worship in the Middle Ages*. 2003.

———. *Women and Girls in the Middle Ages*. 2003.

Elliot, Lynne. *Children and Games in the Middle Ages*. 2004.

———. *Clothing in the Middle Ages*. 2004.

———. *Food and Feasts in the Middle Ages*. 2004.

———. *Medieval Medicine and the Plague*. 2005.

———. *Medieval Towns, Trade, and Travel.* 2004.

Findon, Joanne. *Science and Technology in the Middle Ages.* 2004.

Groves, Marsha. *Manners and Customs in the Middle Ages.* 2005.

———. *Medieval Projects You Can Do!* 2005.

Nicole, David. *Paper Soldiers of the Middle Ages.* Santa Barbara, Calif.: Bellerophon, 1992.

Vol. 1: The Crusades.

$4.95. Order from Bellerophon. Approximately sixty detailed, two-sided figures to be colored; includes Byzantine, Mongol, and Iranian cavalry, Muslim soldiers, crusader knights, and even Richard the Lionhearted.

Vol. 2: The Hundred Years' War.

$3.95. Order from Bellerophon. Approximately sixty detailed, two-sided figures to be colored; includes knights, archers, kings, queens, and peasants.

Platt, Richard. *Castle Diary.* Cambridge, Mass.: Candlewick Press, 2003.

$6.99. Order from any bookstore. This fictionalized diary of a thirteenth-century page, filled with detailed illustrations, describes the daily routine of medieval life: hunts, tournaments, Latin lessons, doctor visits, feasts, and more.

Queen Elizabeth I. New York: Bellerophon, 1985.

$4.95. Order from Bellerophon. Paper dolls to color include Sir Walter Raleigh, the earl of Essex, and Mary, Queen of Scots.

Sansevere-Dreher, Diane. *Explorers Who Got Lost.* New York: Tor Books, 1994.

$8.99. Order from Rainbow Resource Center. A good survey of the achievements (often unintentional) of a whole range of medieval and Renaissance explorers, from da Gama to Henry Hudson.

Sibbet, Ed. *Cathedral Stained Glass.* New York: Dover, 1979.

$5.95. Order from Greenleaf Press. The Dover stained-glass coloring books reproduce medieval windows on translucent paper. Color them, and put them against a window for a beautiful effect.

Smith, A. G. *Cut and Assemble a Medieval Castle.* New York: Dover, 1984.

$8.95. Order from Dover Publications. A full-color model of Caernarvon Castle, built by Edward in 1283.

Wingate, Philippa, et al. *The Viking World.* Tulsa, Okla.: E.D.C. Publications, 2003.

$11.95. Order from Rainbow Resource Center. Part of the Usborne Illustrated World History series, this is an appealing reference book with pictures, maps, and charts; written for fifth grade and up.

Late Renaissance/Early Modern, 1600–1850 (Seventh Grade)

List of Topics to Explore

the *Mayflower*
early American settlements
Russia under Peter the Great and his successors
Prussia in the eighteenth century
the Enlightenment
the agricultural revolution
Native American cultures
the British in India
the French Revolution
British-French conflict in Canada
the American Revolution
The Napoleonic Wars
the industrial revolution
Simón Bolívar's fight for independence in South America
the siege of the Alamo
the California gold rush
the Lewis and Clark expedition
the U.S. acquisition of North American territories
Australia's beginnings as a penal colony

Primary Sources

The Internet Modern Sourcebook. www.fordham.edu/halsall/mod/modsbook.html.

Hosted by Fordham University, this invaluable website is an easy-to-navigate online archive of primary sources (translated into English). Highly useful for the curious student.

Jackdaw Portfolios. Amawalk, N.Y.: Jackdaw Publications, various dates.

$51.95 each. Order from Jackdaw Publications. Jackdaws contain facsimiles of primary documents, essays (called Broadsheets) that combine relevant research into a single narrative with photos; annotated notes about the background of each primary source; transcripts of anything that might be hard to read; and study guides with activities, vocabulary, writing activities, reading ideas, debate and drama suggestions, and more. You can pick and choose among these portfolios (more choices are found at jackdaw.com):

The American Revolution.
California Gold Rush—1849.
French Revolution.
Indians of North America.
Lewis and Clark Expedition: 1804–1806.
The Story of the Constitution.
The Mayflower and the Pilgrim Fathers.
Nat Turner's Slave Revolt—1831.
The Plague and Fire of London.
Rise of Napoleon.
Salem Village and the Witch Hysteria.
Slavery in the United States.
The Slave Trade and Its Abolition.
The War of 1812.

Lepore, Jill. *Encounters in the New World: A History in Documents.* Oxford: Oxford University Press, 2002.

$22.95. Order from any bookstore. A collection of first-person accounts, written between the fifteenth and eighteenth centuries, by Europeans and Africans arriving in the New World.

Lewis, Jon. *The Mammoth Book of How It Happened: Eyewitness Accounts of Great Historical Moments from 2700 BC to AD 2005.* Rev. and updated. Philadelphia, Pa.: Running Press, 2006.

$13.95. Order from any bookstore. This anthology assembles readable excerpts from primary sources describing central events in history.

General Resources

Anderson, J. K. *Castles to Cut Out and Put Together.* Santa Barbara, Calif.: Bellerophon, 1987.

$4.95. Order from Bellerophon. These are models of the Tower of London and Chateau Gaillard, with all the turrets, towers, and walls. They need to be colored before assembly.

Anderson, J. K., and Nick Taylor. *Castles of Scotland to Cut Out and Put Together.* Santa Barbara, Calif.: Bellerophon, 1990.

$5.95. Order from Bellerophon. Doune Castle and Caerlaverock Castle. To be colored and assembled.

Bliven, Bruce. *The American Revolution.* New York: Random House, 1987.

$5.99. Order from American Home-School Publishing. This history for young people was first published in 1958. It gives a very detailed account of the struggle for independence and of George III's misdeeds.

Blos, Joan W. *A Gathering of Days: A New England Girl's Journal 1830–32.* New York: Aladdin, 1990.

$5.99. Order from Greenleaf Press. This is a Newbery award-winning novel (not "history" as such), but provides a well-researched look into everyday life in colonial America. The story is told through the journal of a teenage girl in colonial New Hampshire.

Brownell, David, ed. *A Coloring Book of Kings and Queens of England.* Santa Barbara, Calif.: Bellerophon, 1985.

$4.95. Order from Bellerophon. Portraits in royal dress, with quotes from Shakespeare as a bonus.

Cobblestone. Peterborough, N.H.: Cobblestone Publishing.

$33.95 for one year's subscription. Order from Cobblestone Publishing. An American history magazine for readers aged 9–12; each 52-page issue has a theme ("Medicine," "The Constitution," "The Circus") and includes articles, maps, art, and a question-and-answer feature about history. Back issues can be ordered from Cobblestone individually (see www.cobblestonepub.com).

Copeland, Peter F. *Early American Crafts and Occupations Coloring Book.* New York: Dover, 1994.

$3.95. Order from Dover. Historically accurate, detailed drawings with interesting text.

———. *Everyday Dress of the American Colonial Period.* New York: Dover, 1976.

$3.95. Order from Dover.

———. *Indian Tribes of North America Coloring Book.* New York: Dover, 1990.
$3.95. Order from Dover.

———. *Lewis and Clark Expedition Coloring Book.* New York: Dover, 1983.
$3.95. Order from Dover.

———. *Western Pioneers Coloring Book.* New York: Dover, 1997.
$3.95. Order from Dover.

Daugherty, James. *The Landing of the Pilgrims.* New York: Random House, 2001.
$5.99. Order from American Home-School Publishing. First published in the 1950s, this Landmark Book is a classic young-adult text on the Pilgrims and their settlements.

Eyewitness Books. New York: Knopf.
$15.99. These books, designed by Dorling Kindersley, are available in libraries, bookstores (you may need to special-order them, but all are in print), and online bookstores. The pictures and designs are beautiful, and the books will give you more information than you'll ever need. Consider keeping these on hand for several months, referring back to them as you progress through the time line.
Cole, Alison, et al. *Renaissance.* 2000.
Holmes, Richard, et al. *Battle.* 2000.
Matthews, Rupert O., et al. *Explorer.* 2005.
Murdoch, David, et al. *North American Indian.* 2005.
Murray, Stuart, et al. *American Revolution.* 2005.
Platt, Richard, et al. *Pirate.* 2007.

Freedman, Russell. *Children of the Wild West.* New York: Clarion, 1990.
$9.95. Order from any bookstore. With well-written text and plenty of photographs, Freedman explores the lives of children travelling west in the 1840s.

Fritz, Jean. *Why Not Lafayette?* New York: Puffin Books, 2001.
$5.99. Order from any bookstore. A readable biography of the French hero of the American Revolution that also brings the French Revolution into view.

Ganeri, Anita. *Exploration Into India.* New York: Chelsea House, 2000.

$25.00. Order from Rainbow Resource Center. Covers the history of this country from ancient times up to the twentieth century, with plenty of information about the British takeover and its aftermath.

Hakim, Joy. A History of US series. 3d rev. ed. New York: Oxford University Press, 2007.

$15.95 each. Order from any bookstore. This series is readable, written in story format, and interesting.

Volume 1: The First Americans (Prehistory–1600).

Volume 2: Making Thirteen Colonies (1600–1740).

Volume 3: From Colonies to Country (1735–1791).

Volume 4: The New Nation (1789–1850).

History Songs Kit. Newport Beach, Calif.: AudioMemory, 1998.

$12.95 for book and tape, $15.95 for book and CD. Order from AudioMemory. Eleven songs teach major events and dates in American history from 1492–1991. A painless way to review!

Johnston, Robert D. *The Making of America: The History of the United States from 1492 to the Present.* Washington, D.C.: National Geographic, 2002.

$29.95. Order from any bookstore. This one-volume history of the United States is a good alternative to the Hakim series; it is brief but thorough, readable (on about a sixth- to seventh-grade reading level), and well-illustrated.

Knill, Harry, and Nancy Conkle. *A Coloring Book of the American Revolution.* Santa Barbara, Calif.: Bellerophon, 1987.

$4.95. Order from Bellerophon. Based on a set of eighteenth-century caricatures.

Macaulay, David. *Mill Times.* Alexandria, Va.: PBS Home Video, 2001.

$24.99. Order from PBS. This splendid DVD, which covers the construction and use of a nineteenth-century New England mill, uses both live action and animation.

———. *Mill.* Boston: Houghton Mifflin, 1989.

$9.95. Order from any bookstore. The *Mill Times* video is based on this book. Macaulay tells the story of a nineteenth-century New England mill, tracing its social, political, and cultural roles with detailed, fascinating drawings and eloquent text.

Made for Trade. Plainwell, Mich.: Aristoplay.
$25.00. Order from Fat Brain Toys. Players "shop" and barter in a colonial American town in this game for two to four players.

Petrillo, Valerie. *Sailors, Whalers, Fantastic Sea Voyages.* Chicago: Chicago Review Press, 2003.
$14.95. Order from Rainbow Resource Center. A hands-on, activity-centered guide to sea life, from China in the 1700s to the rise of the New England whaling trade. Cook ship's food, paint china, make a lighthouse, and more.

Smith, A. G. *Cut and Assemble the Mayflower.* New York: Dover, 1990.
$9.95. Order from any bookstore. This detailed paper-engineering project will occupy students for several hours (and give them a better idea of the dimensions of this tiny ship).

Spier, Peter. *The Star-Spangled Banner.* New York: Yearling Books, 1992.
$10.95. Order from Rainbow Resource Center. An illustrated national anthem, with historical notes and maps describing the War of 1812, as well as a history of the anthem's composition.

Waldman, Carl. *Encyclopedia of Native American Tribes.* Rev. ed. Illus. Molly Braun. New York: Facts on File, 2006.
$21.95. Order from any bookstore. The history and customs of over 150 North American Indian nations, readable and illustrated.

Waters, Kate. The Day series. Illus. Russ Kendall. New York: Scholastic.
The Kate Waters series on early American life uses reenactors and interpreters for photographic illustration. Excellent information.

Samuel Eaton's Day. 1996.
$6.99. Order from Rainbow Resource Center. A typical day for a young boy at Plymouth.

Sarah Morton's Day. 1993.
$6.99. Order from Rainbow Resource Center. The daily life of a young girl in Plymouth colony.

Tapenum's Day. 1996.
$16.95 (hardback only). Order from Rainbow Resource Center. The daily life of a Native American boy living near Plymouth.

Modern, 1850–Present (Eighth Grade)

List of Topics to Explore

Africa under European control
the Indian mutinies
the Crimean War
the Victorian era
the War between the States (Civil War)
exploration in the American West
Euro-American conflict with the Native American tribes
the Boxer Rebellion
World War I
the Russian Revolution
the Soviet Union
the Great Depression
the New Deal
civil war in Spain
the Axis and the Allies
World War II
Nazi Germany/Hitler
the Holocaust
Zionism/the Jews' return to Palestine
apartheid/South African segregation
China under Mao
the Korean War
the civil-rights movement
the Vietnam War
landing on the moon

Primary Sources

Aten, Jerry. *Our Living Constitution, Then and Now,* 2d ed. Carthage, Ill.: Good Apple Press, 2002.

$16.99. Order from Greenleaf Press. The original text of the Constitution in one column, interpretation in another column; also includes games and writing activities.

Frank, Anne. *Anne Frank: The Diary of a Young Girl.* Trans. B. M. Mooyaart. New York: Bantam, 1993.

$4.99. Order from any bookstore. This classic journal is a good place to begin discussions of the Holocaust.

The Internet Modern History Sourcebook. www.fordham.edu/halsall/mod/modsbook.html.

Hosted by Fordham University, this invaluable website is an easy-to-navigate online archive of primary sources (translated into English) ranging from an eyewitness account of the lives of plantation slaves in the American South to a report on the Pope's visit to Cuba in 1998. Highly useful for the curious student.

Jackdaw Portfolios. Amawalk, N.Y.: Jackdaw Publications, various dates.

$51.95 each. Order from Jackdaw Publications. Jackdaws contain facsimiles of primary documents, essays (called Broadsheets) that combine relevant research into a single narrative with photos; annotated notes about the background of each primary source; transcripts of anything that might be hard to read; and study guides with activities, vocabulary, writing activities, reading ideas, debate and drama suggestions, and more. You can pick and choose among these portfolios (more choices are found at jackdaw.com):

Atomic Bomb.
Black Voting Rights.
The Civil War.
The Cold War.
The Coming of War, 1939.
Computers.
The Depression.
Early Industrialization of America.
The Easter Rising: Dublin 1916. ($27.95)
The Holocaust.
The New Deal.
The 1920s: America Enters the Modern Age.
The Russian Revolution.
The Spanish-American War.
The Vietnam War.
World War I: 1914–1918.
World War II: The Home Front.

Lewis, Jon. *The Mammoth Book of How It Happened: Eyewitness Accounts of Great Historical Moments from 2700 BC to AD 2005*. Rev. and updated. Philadelphia, Pa.: Running Press, 2006.

$13.95. Order from any bookstore. Useful for study of ancient times through modern ages, this anthology assembles readable excerpts from primary sources describing central events in history.

Murphy, Jim. *The Boys' War: Confederate and Union Soldiers Talk about the Civil War.* New York: Clarion Books, 1993.

$8.95. Order from any bookstore. Journal entries and letters from boys sixteen and under who fought in the Civil War. Sepia photographs.

General Information

Allen, Thomas B. *Remember Pearl Harbor: American and Japanese Survivors Tell Their Stories.* Washington, D.C.: National Geographic Society, 2001.

$17.95. Order from any bookstore. An illustrated account of the attack that brings the Japanese perspective into view.

Archambault, Alan. *Black Soldiers in the Civil War Coloring Book.* Santa Barbara, Calif.: Bellerophon, 1995.

$3.95. Order from Bellerophon.

Archambault, Alan, and Jill Caron. *Civil War Heroes: A Coloring Book.* Santa Barbara, Calif.: Bellerophon, 1991.

$4.95. Order from Greenleaf Press. Twenty-four of the most important personalities from both sides, each with a full-page drawing and a one-page biography.

Bachrach, Susan D. *Tell Them We Remember: The Story of the Holocaust.* Boston: Little, Brown, & Co., 1994.

$15.99. Order from any bookstore. This oversized softcover book, produced by the United States Holocaust Memorial Museum, is a good middle-grade introduction. The black-and-white photographs are disturbing but not horrifying, and include many portraits of children and families who perished (rather than focusing on graphic descriptions of the camps themselves).

Beattie, Owen, et al. *Buried in Ice.* New York: Scholastic, 1993.

$5.95. Order from any bookstore. One of the Time-Quest series about historical mysteries, this book explores the mystery of a failed nineteenth-century expedition to find the Northwest Passage.

Bial, Raymond. *The Strength of These Arms: Life in the Slave Quarters.* Boston, Mass.: Houghton Mifflin, 1997.

$16.00. Order from any bookstore. Photos and text contrast the life of Southern plantation owners and their families with the lives of their slaves.

Blumenthal, Karen. *Six Days in October: The Stock Market Crash of 1929.* New York: Atheneum Books, 2002.

$17.95. Order from any bookstore. A lucid and readable account of the stock market crash; this valuable book will also give students (and parents) a good basic grasp of how the stock market works. Highly recommended.

Clare, John D., ed. *Growing Up in the People's Century: Children's Eyewitness Accounts of the Twentieth Century.* London: BBC Publishing, 1999.

$23.95. Order from any bookstore. First-person accounts of daily life during all the decades of this century.

Cobblestone. Peterborough, N.H.: Cobblestone Publishing.

$33.95 for one year's subscription. Order from Cobblestone Publishing. An American history magazine for readers aged 9–12; each 52-page issue has a theme ("Whaling," "The Great Depression," "The Korean War") and includes articles, maps, art, and a question-and-answer feature about history. Back issues can be ordered from Cobblestone individually (see http://cobblestonepub.com).

Coloring Book of Our Presidents. Santa Barbara, Calif.: Bellerophon, 1988.

$4.95. Order from Bellerophon. From George Washington to Bill Clinton; full-page portraits, each from a historical source (paintings, campaign posters, and so forth). Great memory aid.

Copeland, Peter F. *Naval Battles of the Civil War Coloring Book.* New York: Dover, 1996.

$3.95. Order from Dover Press. Detailed and historically accurate drawings along with a narrative.

Devaney, John. *The Vietnam War.* New York: Franklin Watts, 1993.

$6.95. Order from any bookstore. One of the First Book series; a 64-page introduction to the war, its causes, and its results.

Freedman, Russell. *Lincoln: A Photobiography.* Boston, Mass.: Houghton Mifflin, 1989.

$8.95. Order from any bookstore. The personal and public story of Abraham Lincoln, with a series of profiles that shows him aging during his terms in office. A Newbery Medal winner.

———. *Wilbur and Orville Wright: How They Invented the Airplane.* New York: Holiday House, 1994.

$14.95. Order from any bookstore. Uses the brothers' own photographs along with a readable account of their achievements. Lots of quotes from the Wrights' own writings.

Giblin, James Cross. *The Life and Death of Adolf Hitler.* New York: Clarion, 2002.

$21.00. Order from any bookstore. A very well-done biography, both detailed and appropriate for eighth-grade reading.

Hakim, Joy. A History of US series. 3d rev. ed. New York: Oxford University Press, 2007.

$15.95 each. Order from any bookstore. This series is immensely popular among history fans; it's readable, written in story format, and interesting.

Volume 5: Liberty For All? (1820–1860).
Volume 6: War, Terrible War (1855–1865).
Volume 7: Reconstruction and Reform (1865–1890).
Volume 8: An Age of Extremes (1880–1917).
Volume 9: War, Peace, and All That Jazz (1918–1945).
Volume 10: All the People (since 1945).

Heinrichs, Ann. America the Beautiful series. San Francisco, Calif.: Children's Book Press.

Order from any bookstore. This series includes one title for each state and will provide the eighth-grade student with a good basic review of state history (required by most state educational boards).

History Songs Kit. Newport Beach, Calif.: AudioMemory, 1998.

$12.95 for book and tape, $15.95 for book and CD. Order from

AudioMemory. Eleven songs teach major events and dates in American history from 1492–1991. A painless way to review!

Houston, Jeanne Wakatsuki, and James D. Houston. *Farewell to Manzanar: A True Story of Japanese American Experience During and After the World War II Internment*. New York: Bantam, 1983.
$6.99. Order from any bookstore. The true story of a Japanese family's experience in America during World War II; the author spent part of her childhood in a Japanese internment camp after the attack on Pearl Harbor.

Johnston, Robert D. *The Making of America: The History of the United States from 1492 to the Present*. Washington, D.C.: National Geographic, 2002.
$29.95. Order from any bookstore. This one-volume history of the United States is a good alternative to the Hakim series; it is brief but thorough, readable (on about a sixth- to seventh-grade reading level), and well-illustrated.

Krull, Kathleen. *A Kids' Guide to America's Bill of Rights: Curfews, Censorship, and the 100-Pound Giant*. New York: Avon Books, 1999.
$16.99. Order from any bookstore. A simple and readable guide to the Bill of Rights, with plenty of real cases used as illustration; written on a sixth- to seventh-grade level.

McGowen, Tom. *The Korean War*. New York: Franklin Watts, 1993.
$6.95. Order from any bookstore. One of the First Book series; a 64-page, simple explanation of the war and its stages.

McPherson, James M. *Fields of Fury: The American Civil War*. New York: Atheneum Books, 2002.
$22.95. Order from any bookstore. This history of the Civil War, heavily illustrated and full of maps, charts, and contemporary photographs and posters, was written by a Pulitzer Prize–winning historian for middle-grade readers. Highly recommended.

New York Times. *A Nation Challenged: A Visual History of 9/11 and Its Aftermath (Young Reader's Edition)*. New York: Scholastic, 2002.
$18.95. Order from any bookstore. This early book, which combines photographs with text taken from the ongoing *New York Times* coverage in the

weeks and months afterward, is an evocative record, with good factual information and little editorializing.

Our America: Growing Up . . . series. Minneapolis, Minn.: Lerner Publications, 2002.

$26.60 for each hardback; these are expensive, but the contrasts between modern adolescence and the middle-school experience in previous decades makes them well worth finding. Try your local library.

Josephson, Judith Pinkerton. *Growing Up in a New Century, 1890 to 1914.*

———. *Growing Up in Pioneer America, 1800 to 1890.*

———. *Growing Up in World War II, 1942 to 1945.*

Ruth, Amy. *Growing Up in the Great Depression, 1929–1941.*

Presidents: Fandex Family Field Guide. New York: Workman Publishing.

$9.95. Order from any bookstore (the ISBN for the set is 0-7611-1203-3). This set of Presidential fact cards, connected at the bottom so that you can fan them out, has portraits, dates, brief biographies, and interesting facts. Great for review and memorization.

Taylor, Theodore. *Air Raid–Pearl Harbor! The Story of December 7, 1941.* New York: Gulliver Books, 2001.

$6.00. Order from any bookstore. A vivid account of the attack, written for middle-grade readers.

Thimmesh, Catherine. *Girls Think of Everything: Stories of Ingenious Inventions by Women.* Boston: Houghton Mifflin, 2002.

$6.95. Order from any bookstore. A fun look at modern inventions, from Liquid Paper to spacecraft bumpers, invented by women; includes information for young women on how to get started inventing.

U.S. States and Capitals Flash Cards

$6.99. Order from Rainbow Resource Center. Fifty-one flash cards (one extra for Washington, D.C.) with maps and capitals, along with 57 fact cards covering not only capitals but also birds, flowers, trees, and other fun facts; these also cover U.S. territories. The cards can be used for games as well.

The World in Conflict series. Minneapolis, Minn.: Lerner Publications.

$25.26 each, due to the reinforced library binding (the only available format). You can buy them from any bookstore, but try checking your local library for these; your student may find them helpful in understanding some of the ongoing conflicts that continue to afflict the twenty-first century. Written on an eighth- to ninth-grade level.

Black, Eric. *Bosnia: Fractured Region.* 1998.

———. *Northern Ireland: Troubled Land.* 1998.

Bodnarchuk, Kari. *Rwanda: A Country Torn Apart.* 1999.

———. *Kurdistan: Region Under Siege.* 2000.

Kizilos, Peter. *South Africa: Nation in Transition.* 1998.

———. *Quebec: Province Divided.* 1999.

———. *Tibet: Disputed Land.* 2000.

McGuinn, Taro. *East Timor: Island in Turmoil.* 1998.

Streissguth, Thomas. *Cyprus: Divided Island.* 1998.

Turk, Mary C. *Haiti: Land of Inequality.* 1999.

Zwier, Lawrence J. *Sri Lanka: War-Torn Island.* 1998.

———. *Sudan: North Against South.* 1999.

17

THINKING STRAIGHT: SPELLING, GRAMMAR, READING, AND WRITING

> Grammar: The fundamental rules of each subject.
> Logic: The ordered relationship of particulars in each subject.
> Rhetoric: How the grammar and logic of each subject may be clearly expressed.
>
> —Douglas Wilson, *Recovering the Lost Tools of Learning*

SUBJECT: Spelling, grammar, reading, and writing, grades 5–8
TIME REQUIRED: 5 to 10 hours per week

In the grammar years, your child learned to spell, to name the parts of speech and assemble them into properly punctuated sentences, to gather information through reading, and to write simple compositions—letters, descriptive paragraphs, book reports. She absorbed the basic rules and skills of language use.

Now, in grades 5 through 8, she will shift focus. Acquiring information is still important, but instead of simply absorbing facts about language use, the middle-grade student will learn to *analyze* language. Now that she knows "the fundamental rules" of language, as Douglas Wilson puts it, she'll start to learn language's "ordered relationships"—the way the language fits together. She'll ask why, instead of simply memorizing rules.

She'll pull English apart and find out how it works. And when she's finished, she'll be prepared to use language with precision and eloquence—she'll be ready for rhetoric.

Grammar-stage language study was organized around four subjects: spelling, grammar, reading, and writing. In the logic stage, the student will make the transition from spelling (learning how words are put together) to word study (discovering why words are formed the way they are). She's already studied the names and qualities of parts of speech; now she'll concentrate on how those parts of speech are put together. She'll begin to look at her reading assignments with a more critical eye: Why did this character act the way he did? How did the writer construct this particular plot? Is the argument in this essay sound? And in writing, she'll begin to construct longer compositions—well-reasoned essays, stories with coherent plots.

Like the elementary student, the middle-grade student will spend a good part of her study time working with the English language. Plan on a minimum of an hour per day, with extra time allotted for writing at least twice a week (often this writing will overlap with history or science work) and a separate time for imaginative reading.

HOW TO DO IT

Organize the middle-grade student's work in a 3-inch three-ring English notebook.

Divide this notebook into six sections:

1. Spelling
2. Word Study
3. Grammar
4. Reading
5. Memory Work
6. Writing
7. Dictation

You'll still need plenty of art supplies, but as the child grows older, you'll shift away from stickers and glitter, and lean toward high-quality colored pencils, watercolors, and other "real art" materials.

As in the grammar stage, students may be at different levels in spelling and word study, grammar, reading, and writing. We'll discuss each language skill separately, providing a year-by-year schedule at the end of the chapter.

SPELLING AND WORD STUDY

Try to follow this pattern for spelling and vocabulary:

Fifth grade	*Spelling Workout F* and *G*
Sixth grade	*Spelling Workout G* and *H*
Seventh grade	*Vocabulary from Classical Roots A* and *B*
Eighth grade	*Vocabulary from Classical Roots C* and *D*

The fifth grader should already be familiar with the basic rules of spelling and the common exceptions. In the logic stage, she'll begin to study words that are unusual because they come from outside the English spelling system—they're derived from other languages. Spelling these words correctly requires an understanding of their meaning and origin.

At first, you'll continue with the *Spelling Workout* books, just as you did in fourth grade. By fifth grade, you should be doing (or be close to doing) *Spelling Workout F.* Spend fifteen minutes per day working through the lessons. Continue to keep a list of frequently misspelled words in the Spelling section of the notebook, along with a copy of any spelling rules that the child has trouble applying.

Be aware that many of the rules in the more advanced *Spelling Workout* books are concerned not with spelling, but with meaning. "The prefixes *em* and *en*," begins one rule in *Spelling Workout F,* "mean *in, into, cause to be,* or *to make*." Any fifth grader who's studied Latin already knows this; she can also figure out that *embitter* (one of the spelling words for this lesson) means "to make bitter."

Because of this, when you begin *Spelling Workout F,* start keeping a list of prefixes, suffixes, and their meanings in the Word Study section of the notebook. Entitle a notebook page "Prefixes and Suffixes," and structure your list like this:

Prefixes and Suffixes

Prefix	Suffix	Meaning/function	Language (if given)
contra-		opposite, against	Latin
	-able	makes an adjective out of a noun	
mal-		bad	Latin
pan-		all	Latin
myria-		countless	Greek

Spelling Workout G introduces Latin, French, and Spanish word roots; *Spelling Workout H* adds Greek roots and origins. List these as well, but on a separate page headed "Word Roots." Follow this pattern:

Word Roots

Root	Meaning	Language
functio	to perform	Latin
cedere	to go forward	Latin
polis	city	Greek
annu	year	Latin

Whenever you make a new English notebook, transfer the lists of spelling rules, the "Prefixes and Suffixes" list, and the "Word Roots" list into the Word Study section of the new notebook. And continue to fill out these lists of prefixes and suffixes and word roots with their meaning and language of origin.

Aim to get at least through *Spelling Workout F* by the end of the fifth-grade year; start on G if possible. Ideally, you'll finish *Spelling Workout H* by the end of the sixth-grade year, which will free up the seventh- and eighth-grade years for the study of advanced vocabulary and word roots. (But if you're still in *Spelling Workout H* in seventh grade, simply finish it before going on to the vocabulary-development series that comes next.)

As the student moves into *Spelling Workout G* and *H,* she'll be spending less time on spelling rules and more on word derivations. *Spelling Workout H* is more of a vocabulary workbook than a spelling manual, covering word roots, prefixes, and suffixes from Latin, Greek, and French.

When you finish *Spelling Workout H,* you'll have covered all the common spelling rules for English words. Now—somewhere around the seventh-grade year—vocabulary study will replace spelling as a formal subject. And the best way to build a good vocabulary is by reading a large variety of things. But while your seventh grader is reading, she should also study word origins and meanings to reinforce and sharpen her word skills.

The books in the *Vocabulary from Classical Roots* series, from Educators Publishing Service, are part reference book and part workbook; they use classical quotes, definitions, and exercises to build vocabulary skills. The core books in the series are Books A through E, and each is sixteen lessons long. If you do one lesson per week, you can easily complete two books per year. The series now has three preliminary books for grades 4, 5, and 6; if you are using *Spelling Workout*, these will duplicate the work in the later spelling exercises and are unnecessary.

The *Vocabulary from Classical Roots* series provides exercises, but they aren't extensive. Instead of doing word study for fifteen minutes a day, as you did for spelling, we suggest that you follow this pattern:

Monday	30–45 minutes	Read through the word roots, definitions, and sample sentences; make 3 × 5-inch flash cards for each Latin root and unfamiliar English word.
Tuesday–Thursday	5–10 minutes	Drill with flash cards.
Friday	10 minutes	Review flash cards; complete exercises; check.

Continue to list all new word roots provided on the Word Roots page in the Word Study section of the notebook.

Also, the student should still keep a list of frequently misspelled words in the Spelling section of the notebook. Apart from this, you won't be doing formal spelling; but transfer the Spelling Rules list into the seventh-grade English notebook to act as a ready reference.

Aim to do one lesson per week from *Vocabulary from Classical Roots.* If you're able to begin *Vocabulary from Classical Roots* in seventh grade, you'll complete *A* and *B* in the seventh-grade year, and *C* and *D* in the eighth-grade year. If you don't finish the *Spelling Workout* texts until the middle of the seventh grade (or later), just stick to this same pattern—one lesson per week.

As noted in Chapter 5, you can substitute *Spelling Power* for the Spelling Workout series if you wish. However, note that *Spelling Power* does not do nearly as much word study as Spelling Workout, so if you use this resource, you should plan to use the three preliminary books from the *Vocabulary from Classical Roots* series; plan on doing the grades 4, 5, and 6 books over the fifth- and sixth-grade years (it isn't necessary to begin them sooner) and move on to Book A in seventh grade.

GRAMMAR

The logic-stage student must use a formal grammar program to build the language skills so necessary for good writing. The fifth grader knows what elements make up a sentence (nouns, pronouns, verbs, adverbs, adjectives) and how to string them together (proper punctuation, capitalization, word use). Now she's ready to study relationships between words—how they combine into clauses and how those clauses relate to form sentences.

These relationships are governed by rules. And as the student encounters these rules, she should memorize them. She should also learn to draw a picture of the rule—through diagramming.

We don't think diagramming sentences ought to be optional. Sentence diagrams reveal the logic of sentence structure, just as syllogisms reveal the logic of arguments. Diagramming is a hands-on grammar activity. Visual learners will benefit from "seeing a picture" of grammatical structure, and drawing the diagram will help kinesthetic learners to understand the abstractions of grammar. Most importantly, diagramming prevents the child from simply parroting back rules that she doesn't fully understand. She may be able to quote the definition of a dependent clause, but if she can't properly diagram a sentence that contains dependent clauses, you'll know that she doesn't really comprehend how they work. And until she understands how dependent clauses work, she won't be able to use them as she writes and talks. The study of grammar has as its goal the creation of a clear, persuasive, forceful, fully equipped speaker and writer.

Don't be intimidated by diagramming. It starts simply—writing a subject and a verb on a horizontal line and drawing a vertical line between them. Each sentence part has its own place on the diagram. But both you and your fifth grader will get plenty of practice in identifying those parts before you start diagramming them. (And you'll have the teacher's book!)

In the middle grades, you should plan to spend forty to sixty minutes per day, working through a grammar text and its accompanying exercises.

Which grammar texts are best?

After reviewing a number of grammar texts, we think that the Rod & Staff grammar series, which now extends through tenth grade, is the most thorough. The fifth-grade book, *Following the Plan,* builds on the material taught in the fourth-grade book we recommended in Chapter 5. The student can continue on with *Progressing with Courage* (sixth grade), *Building Securely* (seventh grade), and *Preparing for Usefulness* (eighth grade). Each nonconsumable text contains clear explanations of grammatical concepts, plenty of exercises for practice, and well-constructed writing exercises that teach sentence construction, paragraph development, outlining, and writing short essays from outlines. (Sample essays and outlines are also provided in the teacher's manual, to help you evaluate your student's work.) These texts take a rigorous, systematic, old-fashioned, and very effective approach to building expository writing skills.

Although the writing exercises in the middle-grade books should be completed, don't feel that you have to complete every grammar exercise. If your child understands the concepts and is able to put it into practice, there's no need to be compulsive about finishing the page. In addition, you should feel free to adjust the topics of the assigned essays so that they match the student's history or science learning. (For example, the seventh-grade book asks students to develop a paragraph for the topic sentences, "The life cycle of a butterfly is a marvelous process," but if the student is working through an astronomy course, he could substitute, "The life cycle of a star is a marvelous process" and go on to describe the birth and death of a star.)

Rod & Staff is a Mennonite press, and the examples and exercises sometimes refer to Biblical passages and Christian theology. If you prefer a nonsectarian text, you can choose one of the following options instead:

(1) Voyages in English is a grammar text published by Loyola Press. Originally designed for Catholic schools, it was revised for use in all classrooms. It is not quite as thorough as Rod & Staff, and the writing exercises are not as strong in building expository writing skills. If you use Voyages

in English, you'll need to eliminate the writing exercises and use one of the writing programs recommended in the "Writing" section of this chapter.

(2) Shurley English: Homeschool is a grammar program originally designed for classroom use and adapted for home schooling parents. This program takes a very different approach than Rod & Staff or Voyages in English. Rather than using a textbook with written exercises, Shurley English is a scripted teacher's manual. The parent-teacher is instructed to write examples on a blackboard or on notebook paper, and is given a set of questions and answers to go through with the student. This "Question and Answer Flow" is designed to show students how to identify and use parts of speech. Shurley also provides memory jingles to help students memorize definitions.

Generally, we feel that grammar (which is a skill intended to help you *write* well) is best practiced in the context of written language—including plenty of written exercises. Also, Shurley Grammar does not use diagramming; instead, students are taught to label the parts of speech in sentences, which does not teach them relationships between words and phrases (an essential part of logic-stage learning). And the writing element of Shurley is weak, especially in building expository skills.

However, the script Shurley offers has been helpful to parents who have difficulty in teaching grammar using a textbook. If you have tried Rod & Staff or another good textbook grammar program, and your student still shows no understanding of grammatical concepts, Shurley can give you guidance in *explaining grammatical concepts clearly.*

If you do decide to use Shurley, you will need to use a separate writing program (as described above for Voyages in English). You'll also need to add an outlining program (such as the Frank Schaffer *Note Taking & Outlining* series recommended in Chapter 5, as well as Mary Mueller's *Study Skills Strategies: Outlining*) and a diagramming resource (such as *The First Whole Book of Diagrams* or the *Better Sentence Structure Through Diagraming* series listed in the Resources at the end of this chapter). In addition, you might want to ask another Shurley user to help you get started; the program setup can seem confusing to new users.

As you progress through your grammar program, have the student write down any grammar or punctuation rule that gives him particular trouble. (For example, "Periods and commas go inside the closing quotation marks.") Keep a list of these "Trouble Rules" in the Grammar section of the language notebook. Also use these sections to file grammar exercises done on notebook paper. Composition assignments should be filed in the Writing section of the notebook.

Grammar Choices: Summary

Grade	Option
Fifth	Rod & Staff English: *Following the Plan*
	A Beka: *God's Gift of Language B*
	Shurley English: *Level 4*
Sixth	Rod & Staff English: *Progressing with Courage*
	Voyages in English: *Grade 6*
	Shurley English: *Level 5*
Seventh	Rod & Staff English: *Building Securely*
	Voyages in English: *Grade 7*
	Shurley English: *Level 6*
Eighth	Rod & Staff English: *Preparing for Usefulness*
	Voyages in English: *Grade 8*
	Shurley English: *Level 7*

If you're just beginning formal grammar with an older student, you can simply start right at grade level, with one exception: Seventh- or eighth-grade students just beginning in Rod & Staff should start with the fifth-grade book, *Progressing with Courage.*

READING

Follow this schedule:

Fifth grade	Ancients (5000 B.C.–A.D. 400)
Sixth grade	Medieval–early Renaissance (400–1600)
Seventh grade	Late Renaissance–early modern (1600–1850)
Eighth grade	Modern (1850–present)

During the logic stage, plan to spend thirty to sixty minutes, four days per week, reading and creating narration pages and reports.[1]

As in the grammar stage, reading is keyed to the historical period being studied. The student should place narrations of historical novels and other imaginative literature in the Reading section of the notebook.

However, she can put narrations of any great books—original literature written *during* the historical period under study—in The Arts and Great Books section of the history notebook. If she reads a novel about the Borgia in seventh grade, she should put it in the English notebook under Reading. But if she reads *Gulliver's Travels,* she can put this in her history notebook. In a way, it's a primary source, written by an eyewitness to the history she's working on.

You shouldn't feel that you have to confine the child to stories during her reading time. Although the fifth grader should be reading tales from ancient Egypt, if she shows interest in a biography of Tutankhamen, let her read that, too. She needs to read a version of the *Iliad* and *Odyssey,* but she can also read nonfiction books about Homer or Socrates or the wars of Alexander the Great. Reading and history will inevitably overlap. Just try to keep a balance: at least one work of imagination for every biography or book of history. Historical novels are fine, but make sure that the child also reads versions of the classics, if not the classics themselves.

During the logic stage, you're preparing the child to think critically about literature by *conversing* with her about it—carrying on a dialogue about what is or isn't important in plots, about whether characters are heroes or villains, about the effects that books have on readers.

Does this mean you have to read the book yourself?

Yes.

We've done our best, in this book, to guide you toward books and work texts that don't demand unnecessary preparation. But if you're going to discuss books with your child, you must (at the very least) skim through the

[1]A fifth grader who reads extremely slowly or who struggles with the mechanics of reading may need a review of vital phonics rules; sometimes, reluctant readers are reluctant because they have been improperly taught and don't have the basic skills needed to decode written English. For older students, the best choice for remedial phonics work is *Reading Reflex*, by Carmen and Geoffrey McGuinness; this resource provides clear and age-appropriate reading instruction, suitable for students who may already have developed poor reading habits.

story yourself. (You don't have to do this with every book the child reads, just with those for the "structured reading" of language study.) During the logic stage, your conversations with the student will guide her as she begins, for the first time, to think critically about what she reads. (And think of all the great literature you'll catch up on.)

What questions should you ask?

There's nothing wrong with relying on the summaries and questions provided by *Cliffs Notes,* that great college standby (for a complete listing, call a local bookstore). Most fifth graders won't be reading on a *Cliffs Notes* level yet, but glancing through the review questions at the end of the booklets can help you formulate your own questions. You can also use any question from the following list to begin your dialogue. As you grow more comfortable with the process, you'll think of others.

For a novel or story:

Whom is this book about? (central character[s])
What do the central characters want?
What keeps them from getting it?
How do they get what they want?
Do they have an enemy or enemies? Is there a villain?
What does the villain want?
What do you think is the most important event in the story?
What leads up to this event?
How are the characters different after this event?
What is the most important event in each chapter?
How many different stories does the writer tell?

For a biography:

What kind of family did the subject come from?
What were his parents like?
Where did he go to school?
What did he want the most as a child? As a grown-up?
How did he go about getting it?
Name three or four important people in his life.
Did he get married? To whom? When?
Did they have children?

What was the most important event in his life?
Name three other important events in his life.
Did he get what he wanted in life? Why or why not?
Why do we still remember this person?

For evaluation:

What was the most exciting part of the book?
What was the most boring part of the book?
Did you like the character[s]? Why or why not?
Did you hope that she would get what she wanted?
Did any part of the book seem particularly real?
Did any part of the book seem unlikely to you?
Did you hope it would end in another way? How?
Would you read this book again?
Which one of your friends would enjoy this book?

You should aim to spend at least four days per week, thirty to sixty minutes per day, on reading—that is, reading the books, talking about them, constructing a narrative, and then writing up that narrative in the child's best handwriting.

It is normal for a fifth-grade student to struggle with these questions at first. Putting thoughts into words and articulating them clearly to someone else is hard work. However, students who show ongoing frustration, or who come into fifth grade without any experience in narration and summary writing, may need to do some structured catch-up work in reading and comprehension skills. A useful remedial series, *Basic Skills: Language Arts,* can be purchased from Frank Schaffer Publications. The reading selections in these workbooks are not wonderful literature, but the series provides direct instruction in genre recognition, understanding characters, setting, and point of view, distinguishing main ideas from details, and so on. We suggest that during the fifth-grade year, you complete the following books in this order:

Story Elements, Grades 5–6
Summarizing, Grades 5–6
Reading for Understanding, Grade 6
Reading for Understanding, Grades 7–8

(Don't be intimidated by the grade designations—the workbooks are short and the difficulty level low.)

In the meantime, the student should continue to read from the fifth-grade list that follows, but you can delay discussing the books with him until he has finished the Basic Skills workbooks.

Throughout the logic stage, don't forget to provide a full hour (at least) some other time during the day for free reading. Children need to be encouraged to read for fun on a regular basis—and they should *not* have to report on every book they read. Visit the library regularly (many home-schooling families make library visits a weekly school activity), and help your fifth grader choose good novels and nonfiction books on interesting subjects. Consider requiring your child to pick out two science books and two history books on each library trip.

We're strong believers in parental censorship. Realize that not all Caldecott or Newbery winners are suitable for all children. Skim through books you aren't familiar with; just because a book is recommended by a librarian doesn't mean that it will provide age-appropriate entertainment.

A good annotated list of books for young readers is found in *Books Children Love* by Elizabeth L. Wilson (Wheaton, Ill.: Crossway Books, 2002), available at most bookstores. Many libraries keep their own lists of recommended books for middle-grade readers; ask your librarian.

Fifth Grade: Ancients (5000 B.C.–A.D. 400)

The fifth grader returns to the Ancients. In first grade, you read myths and fairy tales to your beginning reader. Now she can read them for herself. She'll begin the year with tales of ancient Egypt and end the year with the works of the Romans. Plan on spending a minimum of thirty minutes—sixty is better—on reading. Since her history curriculum is also centered on the Ancients, the history and reading curricula will reinforce and strengthen each other.

As in the grammar stage, avoid "reading textbooks." Go to the library, and check out the many middle-grade versions of classic literature—myths, legends, the works of Plato and Confucius, the tales of Homer and Virgil. At the end of this chapter, we've listed a number of adaptations suitable for fifth graders. We've also listed historical novels that can give the student an excellent picture of the ancient world.

Don't limit yourself to our suggestions, though. Go to the library catalog or children's librarian with the following chronological list, suitable for fifth to eighth graders (adaptations, biographies, and historical novels):

Confucius
Chinese folktales
Japanese folktales
ancient Chinese poetry
ancient Japanese poetry
myths of ancient Egypt
tales of the pharoahs
the Bible
Moses
Abraham
David
Solomon
Esther
Ruth
Homer
Buddha
Socrates
Plato
Aristotle
Alexander the Great
Roman emperors
the *Iliad* and the *Odyssey*
Greek and Roman myths
Aesop's fables
Indian folktales
African folktales
Cicero
Virgil

The fifth grader should continue to write one-half-page to one-page summaries of each book read during reading time. As she moves on to longer and more complex books, she may take a week or so to read a single book and write a one-page summary. Try to enforce the one-page limit even though this is difficult for longer books (the child typically wants to include every detail in her summary). Before she writes, talk to her about the book. Ask her to tell you the story (or relate the information, in the case of a nonfiction book). Help her to evaluate each detail by asking questions: "Is that important later on?" "Would the story still make sense if you left that part out?" "Does that character show up again at the end of the book?" "What does he do?" "If you leave him out of your report, will the story end the same way?" Talk about the book together until the child has pinpointed the most important events and is able to weave them into a narration.

At the end of the narration, ask the child to write a one- or two-sentence evaluation of the book that includes *specific* reasons why she did or didn't like the book. "I liked the *Odyssey* because Odysseus came back home to Penelope and she didn't have to marry someone she hated" is acceptable; "I liked the *Odyssey* because it was interesting" is not. Again, talk through this paragraph with your child. Ask: "What was your favorite part?" "Who was your favorite character?" "Why?" "Did you find this boring?" "How could it have been more interesting?"

This process of selecting, evaluating, and criticizing will move the fifth grader from grammar-stage reading (where she simply repeats what she reads back to you) into logic-stage reading. During the logic stage, the student *thinks* about what she's read: "What makes it interesting?" "What parts of it are most important?" "Why do I react the way I do?"

As the logic stage continues, *Writing Strands* and other texts will help the child's developing critical faculties.

Sixth Grade: Medieval–Early Renaissance (400–1600)

In sixth grade, the student will concentrate on literature from and about the Middle Ages and early Renaissance, a period that coincides with her study of history. If she's a good reader, she can tackle a few originals this year (many sixth graders are capable of reading some Malory, Chaucer, and *Beowulf* in modern English translation as well as scenes from Shakespeare).

Sixth grade is the first year the student will actually complete a reading list. Aim to read the following works in the following chronological order:

1. Robert Nye, *Beowulf: A New Telling* (New York: Laurel Leaf, 1982).
   A good (and very exciting) adaptation for sixth graders.

2. *Sir Gawain and the Green Knight,* verse translation by J. R. R. Tolkien (New York: Del Rey, 1979).
   Not a scholarly standard, but wonderful verse.
3. Geoffrey Chaucer, *The Canterbury Tales,* retold by Geraldine McCaughrean, Oxford Illustrated Classics series (New York: Puffin, 1997).
   An accessible prose retelling.
4. Geoffrey Chaucer, "Prologue" to *The Canterbury Tales.*
   A good modern English version, easily available, is published by Penguin Classics (translated by Nevill Coghill), 2003. The explanatory notes, annoyingly, are at the back of the book.
5. Dante Alighieri, *Inferno,* Cantos I–V.
   The standard translation is Allen Mandelbaum's, but for reading aloud we like the new translation by former poet laureate Robert Pinsky (New York: Farrar, Straus and Giroux, 1997).
6. Edmund Spenser, *Saint George and the Dragon,* from *The Fairie Queene.*
   A fun edition is Margaret Hodges's retelling (New York: Little Brown, 1990), which is really too simple for sixth graders. But Geraldine McCaughrean's retelling is unfortunately out of print (check your library for it—you might get lucky).
7. Thomas Malory, a version of *Le Morte d'Arthur.*
   Malory himself is pretty thick even for high-school students, but choose one (or more) of the following:
   a. *The Boy's King Arthur: Sir Thomas Malory's History of King Arthur and His Knights of the Round Table,* edited by Sidney Lanier, original illustrations by N. C. Wyeth (New York: Dover, 2006). Pardon the sexist title, but this is a classic adaptation of Malory, and the Wyeth illustrations are spectacular.
   b. Rosemary Sutcliff, *The Sword and the Circle: King Arthur and the Knights of the Round Table* (New York: Puffin, 1994). Paperback retelling of Malory.
   c. T. H. White, *The Sword in the Stone* (New York: Philomel, 1993). This is the first in T. H. White's four-novel adaptation of Malory. All four are collected together into *The Once and Future King* (New York: Ace, 1987). A classic in its own right.
   d. *Le Morte d'Arthur,* abridged (Minneapolis, Minn.: Highbridge Company, 2005). This audiobook version, read by Derek Jacobi, is an excellent introduction to Malory.

8. Leon Garfield, *Shakespeare Stories* (Boston: Houghton Mifflin, 1998).
   These narrative retellings of twelve plays include much of the original dialogue.
9. *If your sixth grader is a good reader, also include a Shakespeare play.*
   Choose one of the following Shakespeare plays, using the Oxford School Shakespeare editions, Oxford University Press—wonderfully clear texts (see the discussion below on selecting the first Shakespeare play): *Macbeth, Henry V, A Midsummer Night's Dream.*

The above are excellent introductory texts. Try to find the editions we've specified (nothing turns a reader from Shakespeare faster than a wrinkled, tiny-print edition with no explanatory footnotes). Our recommended editions should be readily available at libraries and bookstores (see Resources for mail-order information).

For *Sir Gawain and the Green Knight,* the "Prologue" to *The Canterbury Tales,* and the introduction to the *Inferno,* we strongly recommend reading the texts aloud with your child (poems that seem obscure on the page come to life when read out loud). Also look for audiobook versions; the whole family might enjoy Derek Jacobi's reading of *Le Morte d'Arthur* on a long drive.

What about Shakespeare?

Sixth grade is the earliest that Shakespeare is taught. If you think your sixth grader is ready, try an original play. Otherwise, stick with the Garfield retellings, *Shakespeare Stories* (which should be read in any case). Rely on your own judgment, and don't force an unready sixth grader to read Shakespeare. The goal of early Shakespeare studies is to create love, not loathing.

When you tackle Shakespeare for the first time, follow this three-step process:

1. Read a summary of the play's plot. For each play, the Oxford School Shakespeare editions provide a synopsis, a summary of each act, and a character list.
2. Now that you know what's going on, go to or watch at least one staged production. Shakespeare was written to be watched. Rent a video, and eat popcorn.
3. Now read the text.

Which play should you choose?

Romeo and Juliet is the high-school standard, but the sexual elements make it unsuitable for many sixth graders, who will be either embarrassed or bored. We suggest you choose *Macbeth* (tragedy), *Henry V* (history), or *A Midsummer Night's Dream* (comedy). *A Midsummer Night's Dream* is the easiest of the comedies to follow, but the video versions are so-so. Good video versions of *Macbeth* and *Henry V* are available, and the plays are about equal in terms of difficulty. Both require a fair amount of background historical knowledge (provided in the Oxford School Shakespeare editions). Susan leans toward *Henry V* because the Kenneth Branagh movie is one of the best introductions to Shakespeare for any young student—it's got sword fighting, romance, comedy, and moral dilemmas.

Continue to discuss these books, as outlined under "Fifth Grade," and to prepare one-page summaries and evaluations. You can also use the Writing Strands method for book reports and evaluations (taught in Lesson 6 of book 6—see pages 350–360). Because these books actually originated in the time period under study, file the summaries and book reports in the history notebook under The Arts and Great Books.

Besides following the list above, you should explore the library. Consult the catalog or ask your librarian for sixth- to-eighth-grade books (adaptations, biographies, historical novels) by and about these writers and thinkers (listed chronologically):

Saint Augustine
Geoffrey Chaucer
Erasmus
Edmund Spenser
Sir Thomas More
John Donne
William Shakespeare
Martin Luther
Sir Thomas Wyatt (try stories of Henry VIII and Anne Boleyn)
Dante Alighieri
Sir Thomas Malory
John Knox
John Calvin
René Descartes

Search for adaptations or versions of these specific works:

Beowulf
Sir Gawain and the Green Knight
The Canterbury Tales
The Fairie Queene (including "Saint George and the Dragon")
Inferno
Le Morte d'Arthur ("The Death of Arthur") or anything based on this work
the plays of Shakespeare

In sixth grade, try to spend at least four days per week, forty to sixty minutes per day, on reading—reading the books, talking about them, writing about them. As in fifth grade, provide an extra full hour (at least) during the day for free reading of a work that the child chooses herself.

Seventh Grade: Late Renaissance–Early Modern (1600–1850)

The seventh grader will read literature from the late Renaissance through the early modern period.[2]

With an extra year under her belt, the seventh-grade student can read even more originals than she did in sixth grade, starting with the simpler novels of the writers she'll meet again in eleventh grade. Specific editions are important only where we've noted it; otherwise, an easily located edition such as a Penguin Classic or Dover Thrift will do. Try to complete the following reading list in order:

1. Miguel de Cervantes, *Don Quixote,* abridged.
   Try the *Dover Children's Thrift Classics: Adventures of Don Quixote* (New York: Dover, 1999).
2. Charles Perrault. *Perrault's Complete Fairy Tales*. Trans. A. E. Johnson (Hertfordshire, U.K.: Wordsworth Editions, 2004).

[2]Although some of the titles in this list were written after 1850, we've placed them in the early modern period if most of the author's life passed before mid-century.

3. Jonathan Swift, "A Voyage to Lilliput" and "A Voyage to Brobdingnag," from *Gulliver's Travels* (New York: Dover, 1996).
4. John Bunyan, *The Pilgrim's Progress.*
   Any edition is fine, but a decent paperback is put out by Barbour (1993). If your seventh grader finds Bunyan tough going, try *The Pilgrim's Progress: A Retelling,* by Gary D. Schmidt (Grand Rapids, Mich.: Eerdmans, 1994).
5. Daniel Defoe, *Robinson Crusoe* (Penguin Classic paperback, 2003).
   Or read the more expensive hardback with N. C. Wyeth's illustrations, published by Simon & Schuster (1983).
6. William Wordsworth, "We Are Seven," "Lines Written in Early Spring," "Lines Composed a Few Miles above Tintern Abbey," "Lucy Gray," "Composed upon Westminster Bridge, September 3, 1802," and "I Wandered Lonely As a Cloud," in *Favorite Poems* (New York: Dover, 1992).
7. Samuel Taylor Coleridge, "The Rime of the Ancient Mariner," in *The Rime of the Ancient Mariner and Other Poems* (New York: Dover, 1992).
8. Washington Irving, *The Legend of Sleepy Hollow and Rip Van Winkle* (New York: Dover, 1995).
9. Robert Browning, "The Pied Piper of Hamelin," in *My Last Duchess and Other Poems* (New York: Dover, 2003).
10. Jacob and Wilhelm Grimm, *Grimm's Fairy Tales* (New York: Puffin Classics, 1996).
11. Benjamin Franklin, "The Way to Wealth," in *Benjamin Franklin: The Autobiography and Other Writings* (New York: Penguin, 2003).
12. Christina Rossetti, "Goblin Market," "A Birthday," "Sister Maude," "No, Thank You, John," in *Selected Poems* (New York: Dover, 1994).
13. Lewis Carroll, *Alice's Adventures in Wonderland.*
    Any edition.
14. Jane Austen, *Pride and Prejudice.*
    Any edition.
15. Mark Twain, *The Adventures of Tom Sawyer.*
    Any edition.
16. Jules Verne, *20,000 Leagues under the Sea.*
    Any edition.
17. Charles Dickens, *A Christmas Carol* (New York: Dover, 1991).

18. Alfred, Lord Tennyson, "The Lady of Shalott" and "The Charge of the Light Brigade."
    Any edition.
19. Edgar Allan Poe, "The Raven."
    Any edition.
20. Peter Christen Asbjrnsen, *East o' the Sun and West o' the Moon: Fifty-nine Norwegian Folk Tales* (New York: Dover, 1970).
21. Frederick Douglass, *Narrative of the Life of Frederick Douglass, an American Slave, Written by Himself* (Clayton, Del.: Prestwick House, 2004).

Most seventh graders will find that this list ranges from fairly simple to extremely challenging. As always, use your common sense. If you glance over a book and think it's too difficult or if the student begins it and struggles for more than a couple of chapters, skip it and move on. Good readers can certainly go on to explore the more difficult works of Dickens, Austen, Twain, and any of the writers listed below. Slower readers can simply skip some of these titles.

Where a particularly affordable and/or readable edition exists, we've listed this as top option; you can also browse through the literature section of your local bookstore and pick up the edition that appeals to you. Keep an eye out for the Dover Thrift editions, which are cheap and readable (but minus scholarly footnotes, which no seventh grader really needs anyway) and cost only $1.00 to $3.00. Most bookstores carry a good selection and can order any title in the series.

Continue to discuss these books and to prepare one-page summaries and/or book reports. File the book reports in the history notebook under The Arts and Great Books. Also explore the library for seventh- to ninth-grade-level books, adaptations, biographies, and historical novels by and about these writers and thinkers listed here in chronological order:

Daniel Defoe
Jonathan Swift
John Bunyan
Alexander Pope
John Milton
William Blake

Alfred, Lord Tennyson
William Wordsworth
Robert Browning
Elizabeth Barrett Browning
Charles Dickens
Jane Austen
Edward Lear
Percy Bysshe Shelley
Mary Shelley
Christina Rossetti
Lewis Carroll
Mark Twain
James Fenimore Cooper
Frederick Douglass
Jules Verne
Herman Melville

This is a bare outline—any literary figure encountered during the student's exploration of the years 1600 through 1850 is acceptable. Aim to spend at least four days per week, forty to sixty minutes per day, on reading the books, talking about them, writing about them.

Continue to require a full hour (at least) of free reading (no video games or computer projects or anything other than print on a page).

Eighth Grade: Modern (1850–Present)

The eighth grader will read literature from the modern period. A complete reading list for this period would take a lifetime to work through, so consider the following a skeleton that you can clothe with any number of additional authors and books. The goal of the list is to introduce the student to a wide range of genres—adventure, poetry, mystery, science fiction, short stories—spanning a century and a half. Each list (fiction, poetry, and drama) is organized in chronological order. The more challenging works (and more difficult authors) of this period will be read in the senior year of high school, when the student encounters this period for the last time. We haven't suggested specific editions since these titles are so widely available, but we've provided several mail-order sources in Resources, at the end of this chapter.

Classical education demands a great deal of reading—ideally, the eighth grader will read every title on the list. But because the list is long, we've divided it into fiction, poetry, and drama. If you're unable to complete the entire list, make sure you select titles from each category.

Fiction

1. Robert Louis Stevenson, *Kidnapped* or *Treasure Island*
2. Edward E. Hale, "The Man without a Country"
3. Louisa May Alcott, *Little Women*
4. Arthur Conan Doyle, any of the Sherlock Holmes stories or *The Hound of the Baskervilles*
5. Rudyard Kipling, *The Jungle Book*
6. H. G. Wells, *The Time Machine* or *The War of the Worlds*
7. Jack London, *The Call of the Wild*
8. G. K. Chesterton, any of the Father Brown stories
9. Baroness Orczy, *The Scarlet Pimpernel*
10. O. Henry, any of the short stories
11. Lucy Maud Montgomery, *Anne of Green Gables*
12. Agatha Christie, *Murder on the Orient Express*
13. Dorothy Sayers, *Strong Poison*
14. Margaret Mitchell, *Gone with the Wind*
15. Marjorie Kinnan Rawlings, *The Yearling*

Poetry

1. Henry Wadsworth Longfellow, "The Song of Hiawatha"
2. Robert Frost, "The Road Not Taken" and other poems
3. E. E. Cummings, collected poems
4. Walter de la Mare, *Poems 1919–1934*, any selections
5. Langston Hughes, *The Dream Keeper and Other Poems* or *The Block: Poems*

Drama

1. Oscar Wilde, *The Importance of Being Earnest*
2. George Bernard Shaw, *Pygmalion*
3. Arthur Miller, *The Crucible*
4. Robert Bolt, *A Man for All Seasons*

Discuss these works with your student. After you've talked through them, ask her to prepare one- to two-page book reports, and file them under The Arts and Great Books in the history notebook.

Although this list ought to keep you busy all year, you can also look for biographies on and works by the following writers listed chronologically:

Beatrix Potter
Laura Ingalls Wilder
Frances Hodgson Burnett
J. D. Wyss
Gerard Manley Hopkins
Alexandre Dumas
Willa Cather
Wilfred Owen
Thomas Hardy
Carl Sandburg
A. A. Milne
W. Somerset Maugham
T. S. Eliot
Ezra Pound
F. Scott Fitzgerald
Sinclair Lewis
Amy Lowell
Ernest Hemingway
W. B. Yeats
Pearl S. Buck
Robert Lowell
Isaac Asimov
Isaac Bashevis Singer
Toni Morrison

The eighth grader should plan on spending an hour per day, four or five days per week, reading, discussing, and writing about literature.

Free reading should continue. This is a good time for the student to go on with the novels of Agatha Christie, Thomas Hardy, Isaac Asimov, or another newly discovered writer she enjoys.

Memory Work

Each year, ask the student to select and memorize three to five favorite poems or passages from her reading. She should recite these for you before the end of the school year. Keep a page entitled "Memory Work" at the back of her notebook; write down the names of the pieces she has memorized and the dates she recited them for you. Fifth graders can choose English translations of classical poems or dramatic passages; sixth graders, passages from Chaucer or Dante; seventh graders have a wide range of choices, including poems of Wordsworth, Rossetti, and Poe, as well as Lewis Carroll's "Jabberwocky"; eighth graders have the entire range of modern poetry to choose from. Allow flexibility—the student ought to be able to memorize something that interests and attracts her.

WRITING

The student has been practicing narration and dictation in the early grades, and during fifth grade you should continue to do dictation twice per week. Use more complex sentences, and progress to short paragraphs as soon as the student is able to write well-crafted complex sentences from your dictation. Choose sentences from the books she's reading, either novels or her history and science. File the completed assignments in the Writing section of the language notebook.

This dictation, along with narration, the writing of summaries, and the outlining recommended in the history and science chapters all work to build the student's writing ability. However, a formal writing program is also an important element of good writing instruction.

If you choose to use Rod & Staff, the composition exercises provided can fulfill the middle-grade student's need for a writing program. However, if you choose Voyages in English, or Shurley Grammar, you should select a writing program to use in place of the writing instruction found in these curricula. Consider one of the following. (And remember, as we mentioned in Chapter 5, that a perfectly good writing program may not suit a particular student's learning style; if a program consistently frustrates your child, try another one.)

(1) The Writing Strands program recommended in Chapter 5 focuses on

persuasive writing and is simple to use. If you used this program in the grammar stage, simply continue on with it now. The entire series consists of seven books: Levels 2 through 7 and the final book, *Writing Exposition*, which contains thirteen lessons that prepare the student for college-writing assignments (story analysis, reaction papers, term papers, evaluations). *Writing Exposition* also reviews logic in writing (propaganda technique), library use, comparison and contrast, use of the first person in formal writing, and the SAT II writing test. This is a course that can be used any time from eighth grade to senior high. The assignments are demanding, and the student can take three or four weeks per lesson to complete each one of the lessons.

The Writing Strands levels don't necessarily correspond to grade levels; progress through them at a pace natural to the student. If you're just beginning with the program, follow the guidelines below:

Fifth grade, reluctant writer	Level 3
Fifth grade, average writer	Level 4
Fifth grade, advanced writer	Level 5
Sixth grade, reluctant writer	Level 4
Sixth grade, average writer	Level 5
Sixth grade, advanced writer	Level 5
Seventh grade, reluctant writer	Level 5
Seventh grade, average writer	Level 5
Seventh grade, advanced writer	Level 6
Eighth grade, reluctant writer	Level 5
Eighth grade, average writer	Level 6
Eighth grade, advanced writer	Level 6

(2) The Institute for Excellence in Writing, also recommended for grammar stage, focuses on teaching the student to write using models; the primary purpose of the program is to teach *parents* how to guide children in writing across the curriculum. Many students who find Writing Strands a chore flourish with this approach. You'll progress through the nine-unit course each year, increasing the difficulty as the student matures. (See Chapter 5 for a fuller description.)

(3) The three-book Wordsmith series, published by Common Sense Press, is a particularly good choice for reluctant writers. The assignments are short and clear, broken down into easily understood stages. As a draw-

back, there's not a great deal of practice; once a skill is taught, the student rarely returns to it.

If you're beginning with a fifth- or sixth-grade student, do the three books (*Wordsmith Apprentice, Wordsmith,* and *Wordsmith Craftsman)* in order. A seventh- or eighth-grade student could begin with *Wordsmith* unless he is very writing-phobic, in which case he'd be better off with *Wordsmith Apprentice* (even if the newspaper-reporter theme of this book strikes him as childish).

(4) *Classical Writing,* developed by four home-school parents, is based on the classical *progymnasmata:* a set of exercises assigned by ancient and medieval teachers of rhetoric in order to develop their students' persuasive skills. The original *progymnasmata* exercises ranged in difficulty from retelling a narrative in your own words through much more complex assignments, such as arguing for the moral worth of a particular law. The *progymnasmata* were generally given to older students, and in fact serve as the basis of the rhetoric courses we recommend for high school (see Chapter 24). *Classical Writing* brings the methods of the *progymnasmata* down to the early grades; the program's authors suggest that the first level of the program can be taught to third or fourth graders. We think that most younger students are better off tackling the *progymnasmata* with a few more years of reading and grammar under their belts. However, you could certainly begin the program with a mature fifth or sixth grader. The first two years of the program, *Aesop* and *Homer,* are focused on the skills involved in retelling narratives.

Classical Writing has both pros and cons. The curriculum makes very effective use of classical teaching techniques; imitation of good writers is at the center of the method, students are encouraged to incorporate grammar learning, spelling, and editing skills into the daily lessons, and the program develops the specific writing skills needed to tackle Great Books study. However, the lessons are complex and require the parent to be comfortable with grammar, spelling, vocabulary, and writing; the parent is responsible for planning the sessions and directing the integration of grammar and vocabulary learning into the lessons.

Classical Writing is probably best suited to experienced home-school parents and parents who are competent writers. We suggest that you visit the Classical Writing website (classicalwriting.com). Read the first three sections (The Progymnasmata, The Method, and The Models), the description of the first year of writing *(Classical Writing: Aesop)*, and the sample pages from the *Aesop* curriculum. If you're intrigued and interested, the program is for you. If it doesn't excite you, choose one of the curricula above. But don't feel pressure to use this program simply because it seems to be the "most classical" of the middle-grade writing curricula; the *progymnasmata* will be encountered again in the rhetoric stage of learning.

SCHEDULES

Daily Schedule

Fifth Grade

Spelling/word study	15 minutes	Continue with the *Spelling Workout* books (by this time, you should be finishing up *E* or beginning *F* and *G*).
Grammar	40–60 minutes	Formal grammar.
Reading	30–60 minutes	Do structured reading for four days (schedule an hour for imaginative reading at another time); you are returning to ancient myths and legends, classics, and books about the ancient writers. Memorize and recite poems or passages, three to five for the year.
Writing	30–60 minutes	Do formal writing assignments two or three times per week, dictation twice per week, letters to friends and relatives at least twice per month.

Sixth Grade

Spelling/word study	15 minutes	Continue with the *Spelling Workout* books (by this time, you should be finishing up *F* or *G* and moving toward *H*).
Grammar	40–60 minutes	Formal grammar.
Reading	40–60 minutes	Do structured reading (schedule

		an hour for imaginative reading at another time); read medieval and Renaissance literature and begin to use some originals. Memorize and recite poems or passages, three to five for the year.
Writing	30–60 minutes	Do formal writing assignments three times per week, a history or science essay once per week, letters to friends and relatives at least twice per month.

Seventh Grade

Spelling/word study	45 minutes one day; review 5 minutes other days	Continue with the *Spelling Workout* books (aim to finish *H* by the end of this year); then go on to *Vocabulary from Classical Roots A*.
Grammar	40–60 minutes	Formal grammar.
Reading	40–60 minutes	Do structured reading (schedule an hour for imaginative reading at another time); read late Renaissance through early modern literature. Memorize and recite poems or passages, three to five for the year.
Writing	30–60 minutes	Do formal writing assignments three times per week, letters to friends and relatives at least twice per month.

Eighth Grade

Word study	45 minutes one day; review 5 minutes other days	Continue with *Vocabulary from Classical Roots B* and *C* or *C* and *D*.

Grammar	40–60 minutes	Formal grammar.
Reading	60 minutes	Do structured reading (schedule an hour for imaginative reading at another time); read literature from 1850 to the present. Memorize and recite poems or passages, three to five for the year.
Writing	45–60 minutes	Do formal writing assignments three times per week, letters to friends and relatives at least twice per month.

RESOURCES

For publisher and catalog addresses, telephone numbers, and other information, see Sources (pages 751–778). Most books can be obtained from any bookstore or library; where we know of a mail-order option, we have provided it. Where noted, resources are listed in chronological order (the order you'll want to use them in). Books in series are listed together.

Spelling/Word Study

Adams-Gordon, Beverly L. *Spelling Power.* 4th ed. Pomeroy, Wash.: Castlemoyle Press, 2006.
 $64.95. Order from Castlemoyle Press.

Fifer, Norma, and Nancy Flowers. Vocabulary from Classical Roots series. Cambridge, Mass.: Educators Publishing Service.
 Order from Educators Publishing Service.
 Vocabulary from Classical Roots, Grade 4. $10.80.
 Teacher's Guide and Answer Key 4. $18.75.
 Vocabulary from Classical Roots, Grade 5. $10.80.
 Teacher's Guide and Answer Key 5. $18.75.
 Vocabulary from Classical Roots, Grade 6. $10.80
 Teacher's Guide and Answer Key 6. $18.75.
 Vocabulary from Classical Roots A. $10.80.

Teacher's Guide and Answer Key A. $18.75.
Vocabulary from Classical Roots B. $10.80.
Teacher's Guide and Answer Key B. $18.75.
Vocabulary from Classical Roots C. $10.80.
Teacher's Guide and Answer Key C. $18.75.
Vocabulary from Classical Roots D. $11.55.
Teacher's Guide and Answer Key D. $18.75.
Vocabulary from Classical Roots E. $11.55.
Teacher's Guide and Answer Key E. $18.75.

Modern Curriculum Press Spelling Workout series. Upper Saddle River, N.J.: Modern Curriculum Press (Pearson Learning Group), 2002.
$10.95 for each student edition, $11.50 for each *Teacher's Edition*. Order from Pearson Learning. The grade levels are approximate, but will give you a guide as to where to begin with an older student.
Spelling Workout D (fourth-grade level).
Teacher's Edition D.
Spelling Workout E (fifth-grade level).
Teacher's Edition E.
Spelling Workout F (sixth-grade level).
Teacher's Edition F.
Spelling Workout G (seventh-grade level).
Teacher's Edition G.
Spelling Workout H (eighth-grade level).
Teacher's Edition H.

Grammar

Rod & Staff Grammar and Composition.
Following the Plan: English 5. Crockett, Ky.: Rod & Staff, 1991.
Order from Rod & Staff.
Pupil Textbook. $15.30.
Worksheets (additional practice). $2.95.
Teacher's Manual. $21.90
Test Booklet. $1.95
Progressing with Courage: English 6. Crockett, Ky.: Rod & Staff, 1992.
Order from Rod & Staff.

Pupil Textbook. $17.35.

Worksheets (additional practice). $2.95.

Teacher's Manual. $23.95.

Test Booklet. $1.95.

Building Securely: English 7. Crockett, Ky.: Rod & Staff, 1994.

Order from Rod & Staff.

Pupil Textbook. $17.45.

Worksheets (additional practice). $2.95.

Teacher's Manual. $23.95.

Test Booklet. $1.95.

Preparing for Usefulness: English 8. Crockett, Ky.: Rod & Staff, 1994.

Order from Rod & Staff.

Pupil Textbook. $18.05.

Worksheets (additional practice). $2.95.

Teacher's Manual. $23.95.

Test Booklet. $1.95.

Shurley English Homeschool Edition. Cabot, Ark.: Shurley Instructional Materials Inc., 2003.

$70.00 per kit (each kit includes a teacher's manual, student workbook, and audio CD). Order from Shurley Instructional Materials. Additional student workbooks are available for $12.00 each.

Level 4 Kit.

Level 5 Kit.

Level 6 Kit.

Level 7 Kit.

Voyages in English. Chicago, Ill.: Loyola Press, 2006.

Order from Loyola Press.

Voyages in English, Grade 5, Student Edition. $44.95.

Grade 5, Student Edition, Extra Practice Book. $8.95.

Grade 5, Teacher Guide. $75.95.

Grade 5, Answer Key, Extra Practice Book. $15.95.

Voyages in English, Grade 6, Student Edition. $49.95.

Grade 6, Student Edition, Extra Practice Book. $9.95.

Grade 6, Teacher Guide. $79.95.

Grade 6, Answer Key, Extra Practice Book. $18.95.

Voyages in English, Grade 7, Student Edition. $49.95.

Grade 7, Student Edition, Extra Practice Book. $9.95.

Grade 7, Teacher Guide. $79.95.

Grade 7, Answer Key, Extra Practice Book. $18.95.

Voyages in English, Grade 8, Student Edition. $49.95.

Grade 8, Student Edition, Extra Practice Book. $9.95.

Grade 8, Teacher Guide. $79.95.

Grade 8, Answer Key, Extra Practice Book. $18.95.

Supplementary Grammar Resources

Basic Skills: Language Arts. Grand Rapids, Mich.: Frank Schaffer Publications. $6.99 each. Order from School Specialty Publishing.

Better Sentence Structure Through Diagraming 1.

Better Sentence Structure Through Diagraming 2.

Daly, Mary. *The First Whole Book of Diagrams*, rev. ed. Garretson, S.D.: Hedge School, 2002.

$26.00. Order from the Hedge School or from Emmanuel Books. A wonderful, complete guide to diagramming every part of speech.

Elementary Diagramming Worktext. $10.00 when ordered along with the text above. Provides students with plenty of practice.

Mueller, Mary. *Study Skills Strategies: Outlining.* Portland, Maine: Walch Education, 2003.

$24.99. Order through any bookstore or from Walch Education (you can also read samples at www.walch.com). High-school skills.

Pearce, Q. L. *Note Taking & Outlining.* Grand Rapids, Mich.: Frank Schaffer Publications, 2003.

$6.99 for each book. Order from School Specialty Publishing. Each student will need her own book.

Note Taking and Outlining, Grades 3–5.

Note Taking and Outlining, Grades 6–8.

Reading Remediation

Basic Skills: Language Arts. Grand Rapids, Mich.: Frank Schaffer Publications. $6.99 each. Order from School Specialty Publishing.

Reading for Understanding, Grade 6.

Reading for Understanding, Grades 7–8.
Story Elements, Grades 5–6.
Summarizing, Grades 5–6.

McGuinness, Carmen, and Geoffrey McGuinness. *Reading Reflex: The Foolproof Phono-Graphix Method for Teaching Your Child to Read.* New York: Fireside, 1999.
$17.95. Order from any bookstore.

Reading

These are listed in order of use. Remember, you don't have to read all of these. But you can choose reading assignments from among the following names. Note that this list—especially the early-modern and modern sections—is merely a starting place. There are many other authors and books worth reading, and you'll discover them as you explore your library. Rather than organizing these books and authors alphabetically, we have listed them in chronological order, and we suggest that you read them in this order; we have also included a few historical novels where appropriate. In most cases, you can find various versions of these stories. We have suggested a few specific editions that we particularly like.

For fifth grade, we have provided a number of different retellings of Greek myths and stories; pick one or several. From sixth grade on, the lists are divided into two parts. The first part, the formal reading list that we describe in detail in the chapter itself, is listed in chronological order. The supplementary list, containing books and novels that you can use to support the reading list, is listed alphabetically by author.

Ancients, 5000 B.C.–A.D. 400 (Fifth Grade)

Work through these books and authors in the following order.

Green, Roger Lancelyn. *Tales of Ancient Egypt.* New York: Puffin, 1996.
$4.99. Order from any bookstore. A minor classic in its own right. Green's retelling is clear and vivid.

McGraw, Eloise Jarvis. *The Golden Goblet.* New York: Scholastic, 2000.
$6.99. A young Egyptian boy solves the mystery of a goblet stolen from the City of the Dead.

———. *Mara, Daughter of the Nile.* New York: Puffin, 1990.
$6.99 An Egyptian slave girl gets involved with rivals who battle over the throne.

Birch, Cyril. *Tales from China.* New York: Oxford University Press, 2001.
$12.95. Part of the Myths and Legends series. Engrossing and well-written stories.

McAlpine, Helen, and William McAlpine. *Tales from Japan.* New York: Oxford University Press, 2002.
$12.95. Part of the Myths and Legends series. Engrossing and well-written stories.

Gray, J. E. B. *Tales from India.* New York: Oxford University Press, 2001.
$12.95. Part of the Myths and Legends series. Engrossing and well-written stories.

Arnott, Kathleen. *Tales from Africa.* New York: Oxford University Press, 2000.
$12.95. Part of the Myths and Legends series. Engrossing and well-written stories.

Evslin, Bernard. *Heroes, Gods and Monsters of Greek Myths.* Illus. William Hofmann. New York: Bantam, 1984.
$6.50. Vivid retellings of the "greatest hits" of Greek myth.

Coolidge, Olivia. *Greek Myths.* Boston, Mass.: Houghton Mifflin, 2001.
$5.95. Order from American Home-School Publishing. A classic retelling.

Colum, Padraic. *The Golden Fleece and the Heroes Who Lived before Achilles.* New York: Aladdin, 2004.
$9.95. Order from American Home-School Publishing. A classic retelling.

Green, Roger Lancelyn. *Tales of Greek Heroes.* New York: Puffin, 2002.
$4.99. Order from American Home-School Publishing. A minor classic in its own right. Green's retelling is clear and vivid.

———. *The Tale of Troy.* New York: Puffin, 1995.
$4.99. Order from American Home-School Publishing. A minor classic in its own right. Green's retelling is clear and vivid.

Coolidge, Olivia. *The Trojan Wars*. Boston, Mass.: Houghton Mifflin, 2001.
$6.95. Order from American Home-School Publishing. A classic retelling.

Colum, Padraic. *The Children's Homer: The Adventures of Odysseus and the Tale of Troy*. Illus. Willy Pogany. New York: Aladdin, 2004.
$9.95. Order from any bookstore. A classic retelling.

Sutcliff, Rosemary. *Black Ships before Troy: The Story of the Iliad*. Illus. Alan Lee. New York: Delacorte Press, 1993.
$19.95. Order from any bookstore. An excellent retelling with eerie, vivid illustrations.

Lively, Penelope. *In Search of a Homeland: The Story of the Aeneid*. Illus. Ian Andrew. London: Frances Lincoln Children's Books, 2007.
$19.63. In print, but expensive; try your local library. This is one of the few retellings of the *Aeneid* available, and it's a good one, with excellent illustrations.

McGovern, Ann. *Aesop's Fables*. New York: Scholastic, 1990.
$4.50. Order from Greenleaf Press. A good retelling of sixty fables, illustrated.

Plato. *The Last Days of Socrates*. Trans. Hugh Tredennick. New York: Penguin, 2003.
$12.00. Order from any bookstore. Contains the two dialogues "On Piety" and "The Death of Socrates." Most fifth graders can read this if you take one of the parts.

Coolidge, Olivia. *Caesar's Gallic Wars*. North Haven, Conn.: Linnet Books, 1998.
$23.50. Based on Julius Caesar's Commentaries, the story of Caesar's wars in Gaul, 58–51 B.C. The only retelling of Caesar we've ever seen, difficult to find, but try your library.

Vennema, Peter. *Cleopatra*. Illus. Diane Stanley. New York: HarperTrophy, 1997.
$7.99. Well-researched and beautifully illustrated life of the Egyptian queen.

Speare, Elizabeth George. *The Bronze Bow*. Boston, Mass.: Houghton Mifflin, 1997.

$6.95. A Jewish rebel in first-century Galilee encounters the itinerant preacher Jesus. A Newbery Medal winner.

Sutcliff, Rosemary. *Outcast*. New York: Sunburst, 1995.
$7.95. A Roman infant is rescued from a shipwreck and raised in a British village.

———. *The Eagle of the Ninth*. New York: Sunburst, 1993.
$7.95. In A.D. 119, a Roman legion disappears in the wilds of Britain. Fifteen years later, the commander's son sets out to find the missing company.

———. *The Silver Branch*. New York: Sunburst, 1993.
$7.95. In the sequel to *The Eagle of the Ninth*, Saxons raid Britain, and the Roman provinces fight for their land.

Horowitz, Anthony. *Myths and Legends*. Illus. Francis Mosley. New York: Kingfisher, 2007.
$6.95. A useful and fun-to-read collection of ancient stories from China, Polynesia, North and South America, and other parts of the world, as well as the usual Greek and Roman retellings.

Medieval/Early Renaissance, 400–1600 (Sixth Grade)

Formal Reading List

Work through the list in this order. Titles can be ordered from any bookstore.

Nye, Robert. *Beowulf: A New Telling*. New York: Laurel Leaf, 1982.
$5.99. A good (and very exciting) adaptation for sixth graders.

Tolkien, J. R. R. *Sir Gawain and the Green Knight*. New York: Del Rey, 1988.
$6.99. Not a scholarly standard, but a wonderful verse translation of the original. Fans of Tolkien will enjoy echoes of *The Hobbit* and *The Lord of the Rings*.

McCaughrean, Geraldine. *The Canterbury Tales*. New York: Puffin, 1997.
$3.99.

Chaucer, Geoffrey. "Prologue" to *The Canterbury Tales*. Trans. Nevill Coghill. New York: Penguin, 2003.
$10.00. This edition is in modern English.

Alighieri, Dante. *The Inferno of Dante: A New Verse Translation.* Trans. Robert Pinsky. New York: Farrar, Straus and Giroux, 1997.

$20.00. We like this free translation by the former poet laureate. Another standard is Allen Mandelbaum's translation (New York: Bantam Books, 1992). Read Cantos I–V.

Philip, Neil. *Illustrated Book of Myths.* Illus. Nilesh Mistry. New York: Dorling Kindersley, 2007.

$12.99. A well-written and -researched collection of myths from different parts of the world, showing the common themes that stretch across cultures.

Colum, Padraic. *Nordic Gods and Heroes.* Illus. Willy Pogany. New York: Dover, 1996.

$10.95. Myths rewritten in the style of the Eddas, for young readers; excellent.

Hodges, Margaret. *Saint George and the Dragon.* New York: Little Brown, 1990.

$7.99. From Spenser's *The Fairie Queene.* A better rendition is Geraldine McCaughrean's retelling, but it is out of print and difficult to find.

Malory, Thomas. Versions of *Le Morte d'Arthur:*

Jacobi, Derek, narrator. *Le Morte d'Arthur,* abridged. Minneapolis, Minn.: Highbridge Company, 2005. $34.95.

Lanier, Sidney, ed. *The Boy's King Arthur: Sir Thomas Malory's History of King Arthur and His Knights of the Round Table.* Illus. N. C. Wyeth. New York: Dover, 2006. $14.95.

Sutcliff, Rosemary. *The Sword and the Circle: King Arthur and the Knights of the Round Table.* New York: Puffin, 1994. $6.99.

White, T. H. *The Sword in the Stone.* New York: Philomel, 1993.

$24.99. White's illustrated reworking of Malory is marvelous; a "must-read."

———. *The Once and Future King.* New York: Ace, 1987.

$7.99. The entire saga of the Round Table. For good, mature readers. Most students will want to read this in high school.

Garfield, Leon. *Shakespeare Stories.* Boston, Mass.: Houghton Mifflin, 1998.

$19.95. A good introduction to Shakespeare.

Shakespeare, William. Oxford School Shakespeare series. Ed. Roma Gill. New York: Oxford University Press.

$7.95 each.

A Midsummer Night's Dream. 2002.

Henry V. 2001.

Macbeth. 2002.

Supplementary Resources

The Chaucer Coloring Book. Santa Barbara, Calif.: Bellerophon Books, 1991.
$3.95. Order from Bellerophon Books. Contains the "Prologue" to *The Canterbury Tales* in the original Middle English, along with woodcuts from the earliest published editions. A nice introduction to Middle English.

Chute, Marchette Gaylord. *Stories from Shakespeare.* New York: Plume, 1959.
$15.00. Order from any bookstore. All 36 plays in story form; gives a straightforward plot summary along with famous lines from each play. Good for reading along with the plays themselves.

Columbus, Christopher. *First Voyage to America: From the Log of the Santa Maria.* Whitefish, Mont.: Kessinger Publications, 2007.
$18.95. The actual log, abridged for ages 9–12.

de Angeli, Marguerite. *The Door in the Wall.* New York: Laurel Leaf, 1998.
$5.50. A historical novel. The 1950 Newbery winner about a crippled boy who longs to be a knight.

de Trevino, Elizabeth Borton. *I, Juan de Pareja.* New York: Farrar, Straus and Giroux, 1987.
$6.95. A novel about the painter Velazquez and his African slave.

French, Allen. *The Story of Rolf and the Viking Bow.* Chapel Hill, N.C.: Yesterday's Classics, 2007.
$10.95. A classic novel (first published around 1900 and still in print) about a young Viking boy's search for justice and his murdered father.

Fritz, Jean. *Brendan the Navigator: A History Mystery about the Discovery of America.* New York: Putnam, 1999.
$6.99. Imaginative biography of the Irish monk who sailed to the New World in A.D. 590.

Gray, Elizabeth. *Adam of the Road.* New York: Puffin, 1987.
$7.99. In 1294, a young minstrel searches for his stolen dog—and his father. A Newbery Medal–winning novel.

Green, Robert Lancelyn. *The Adventures of Robin Hood.* New York: Puffin, 1995.
$4.99. Read this classic retelling when you study the Crusades in history.

Kelly, Eric P. *The Trumpeter of Krakow.* New York: Aladdin, 1992.
$5.99. A Newbery Medal winner about a young fifteenth-century Polish boy and a mysterious jewel.

Picard, Barbara Leonie. *Tales of the Norse Gods.* New York: Oxford University Press, 2001.
$11.95. Part of the Myths and Legends series. You can use this as imaginative reading when you study the Vikings in history.

Pyle, Howard.
Howard Pyle wrote a series of modern classics—young adult novels of Arthurian and medieval times. If you can't find them in a bookstore, you can order them from Greenleaf Press.
$9.95. *The Merry Adventures of Robin Hood.* New York: Dover, 1985.
$8.95. *Otto of the Silver Hand.* New York: Dover, 1976.
$10.95. *The Story of King Arthur and His Knights.* New York: NAL, 1991.
$13.95. *The Story of Sir Lancelot and His Companions.* New York: Dover, 1991.
$11.95. *The Story of the Champions of the Round Table.* New York: Dover, 1968.
$12.95. *The Story of the Grail and the Passing of Arthur.* New York: Dover, 1993.

Shakespeare Coloring Book. Santa Barbara, Calif.: Bellerophon Books, 1985.
$4.95. Order from Greenleaf Press. Historical illustrations of famous scenes. A good memory aid.

Sperry, Armstrong. *Call It Courage.* New York: Simon Pulse, 2008.
$5.99. A novel about Mafatu, the son of a Polynesian chief, who must prove that he isn't a coward.

Sutcliff, Rosemary. *The Lantern Bearers.* New York: Sunburst, 1994.
$6.95. A historical novel. In 450, a Roman soldier in Britain fights against invading Angles and Saxons.

Willard, Barbara. *Augustine Came to Kent.* Warsaw, N.D.: Bethlehem Books, 1996.
$12.95. Order from Greenleaf Press. A historical novel. The story of a Saxon boy who accompanies Augustine on his mission to England.

Late Renaissance/Early Modern, 1600–1850 (Seventh Grade)

Formal Reading List

Work through this in order. Unless otherwise noted, these are standard editions available at most bookstores or from Amazon.com. Many of the titles can be found in more than one edition. Prices will no longer be noted unless a book is unusually expensive or difficult to find.

Miguel de Cervantes, *Don Quixote,* abridged.
Dover Children's Thrift Classics: Adventures of Don Quixote. New York: Dover, 1999.

Perrault, Charles. *Perrault's Complete Fairy Tales.* Trans. A. E. Johnson. Hertfordshire, U.K.: Wordsworth Editions, 2004.

Swift, Jonathan. "A Voyage to Lilliput" and "A Voyage to Brobdingnag." From *Gulliver's Travels.*
The Dover Thrift edition (New York: Dover, 1996) is cheapest, but any edition will do.

Bunyan, John. *The Pilgrim's Progress.*
Any edition is fine, but a decent paperback is the Barbour 1993 edition. You can also use *The Pilgrim's Progress: A Retelling* by Gary D. Schmidt (Grand Rapids, Mich.: Eerdmans, 1994) if the original seems too difficult.

Defoe, Daniel. *Robinson Crusoe.* New York: Penguin, 2003.
You can also order the hardback with N. C. Wyeth's illustrations (New York: Simon and Schuster, 1983) from American Home-School Publishing for $27.00.

Wordsworth, William. *Favorite Poems.*
Try the Dover Thrift edition (New York: Dover, 1992).

Coleridge, Samuel Taylor. "The Rime of the Ancient Mariner."
Found in most collections. You can buy the Dover Thrift edition of this poem and other works (New York: Dover, 1992).

Irving, Washington. *The Legend of Sleepy Hollow and Rip Van Winkle.* Dover Thrift edition. New York: Dover, 1995.

Browning, Robert. "The Pied Piper of Hamelin."
This is contained in the Dover Thrift edition of Browning, *My Last Duchess and Other Poems* (New York: Dover, 1993).

Grimm, Jacob, and Wilhelm Grimm. *Grimm's Fairy Tales.* New York: Puffin Classics, 1996.

Franklin, Benjamin. "The Way to Wealth." In *Benjamin Franklin: The Autobiography and Other Writings*. New York: Penguin, 2003.

Rossetti, Christina. "Goblin Market," "A Birthday," Sister Maude," "No, Thank You, John."
All are contained in the Dover Thrift edition, *Selected Poems* (New York: Dover, 1994).

Carroll, Lewis. *Alice in Wonderland.*
Any edition.

Austen, Jane. *Pride and Prejudice.*
Any edition

Twain, Mark. *The Adventures of Tom Sawyer.*
Any edition.

Verne, Jules. *20,000 Leagues under the Sea.*
Any edition.

Dickens, Charles. *A Christmas Carol.*
Any edition. Make sure you don't get an abridged version by accident—this book is often abridged.

Tennyson, Alfred, Lord. "The Lady of Shalott" and "The Charge of the Light Brigade."
In any Tennyson collection.

Poe, Edgar Allan. "The Raven."
In any collection or anthology.

Asbjrnsen, Peter Christen. *East o' the Sun and West o' the Moon: Fifty-nine Norwegian Folk Tales.* New York: Dover, 1986.

Douglass, Frederick. *Narrative of the Life of Frederick Douglass, an American Slave, Written by Himself.* Clayton, Del.: Prestwick House, 2004.

Supplementary Resources

Brady, Esther Wood. *Toliver's Secret.* New York: Random House, 1993.
A teenaged girl disguises herself as a boy to carry a message from New York to the American rebels in New Jersey.

Brink, Carol Ryrie. *Caddie Woodlawn.* New York: Aladdin, 1990.
The novel of a pioneer girl and her family, who have to decide whether to stay in America or return to an inherited title in England.

Collier, James Lincoln. *My Brother Sam Is Dead.* New York: Scholastic, 2005.
The novel of a Connecticut family divided by the Revolutionary War.

Dalgliesh, Alice. *The Courage of Sarah Noble.* New York: Aladdin, 2003.
A Newbery Medal–winning novel about a young girl in the Connecticut wilderness, 1707.

Field, Rachel. *Hitty: Her First Hundred Years.* New York: Aladdin, 1998.
This Newbery winner tells the story of the first hundred years in a doll's life.

Forbes, Esther. *America's Paul Revere.* Boston, Mass.: Houghton Mifflin, 1990.
A novel of the life and adventures of Paul Revere by the Newbery Medal–winning author.

———. *Johnny Tremain.* New York: Laurel Leaf, 1987.
The classic story of a silversmith's apprentice caught in the Revolutionary War.

Speare, Elizabeth George. *Calico Captive.* Boston, Mass.: Houghton Mifflin, 2001.

The story of a young girl, captured by Indians in 1754 and sold to the French. Based on an actual eighteenth-century diary.

———. *The Sign of the Beaver.* New York: Yearling, 1984.
A novel about a boy who learns survival skills from Indians in eighteenth-century Maine.

———. *The Witch of Blackbird Pond.* New York: Laurel Leaf, 1978.
A Puritan girl in Connecticut makes friends with a suspected witch.

Vernon, Louise. *The Beggar's Bible.* Grand Rapids, Mich.: Herald Press, 1971.
The biography of Bible translator John Wycliffe.

——. *The Man Who Laid the Egg.* Scottsdale, Penn.: Herald Press, 2002.
The story of Renaissance scholar Erasmus.

Yates, Elizabeth. *Amos Fortune, Free Man.* New York: Puffin, 1989.
The 1951 Newbery Medal–winning novel about an African prince brought to the United States as a slave.

Modern, 1850–Present (Eighth Grade)

Formal Reading List

These are available in standard editions at bookstores or from Amazon.com. Read each section in the order listed.

Fiction

Stevenson, Robert Louis. *Kidnapped* or *Treasure Island.*
You can order the Puffin Classic editions of both (New York: Puffin, 1995 and 1994, respectively) from American Home-School Publishing.

Hale, Edward E. "The Man Without a Country."

Alcott, Louisa May. *Little Women.*
You can order the Puffin Classic edition (New York: Puffin, 1997) from American Home-School Publishing.

Doyle, Arthur Conan. Any of the Sherlock Holmes stories or *The Hound of the Baskervilles.*

Kipling, Rudyard. *The Jungle Book.*
You can order the Puffin Classic edition (New York: Puffin, 2002) from American Home-School Publishing.

Wells, H. G. *The Time Machine* or *The War of the Worlds.*
London, Jack. *The Call of the Wild.*
Chesterton, G. K. Any of the Father Brown stories.
Orczy, Baroness. *The Scarlet Pimpernel.*
Henry, O. Any of the short stories.

Montgomery, Lucy Maud. *Anne of Green Gables.*
You can order the Puffin Classic edition (New York: Puffin, 1996) from American Home-School Publishing.

Christie, Agatha. *Murder on the Orient Express.*
Sayers, Dorothy. *Strong Poison.*
Mitchell, Margaret. *Gone with the Wind.*
Rawlings, Marjorie Kinnan. *The Yearling.*

Poetry

Longfellow, Henry Wadsworth. "The Song of Hiawatha."
Frost, Robert. "The Road Not Taken."
Cummings, E. E. Collected poems.
de la Mare, Walter. *Poems 1919–1934.* Any selections.
Hughes, Langston. *The Dream Keeper and Other Poems.* New York: Knopf, 1996.

Drama

Wilde, Oscar. *The Importance of Being Earnest.*
Shaw, George Bernard. *Pygmalion.*
Miller, Arthur. *The Crucible.*
Bolt, Robert. *A Man for All Seasons.*

Supplementary Resources

Burnett, Frances Hodgson. *Little Lord Fauntleroy.* New York: Puffin, 1996.
A children's classic; worth reading.

———. *A Little Princess*. New York: Penguin, 2002.
Another much-loved classic.

Gipson, Fred. *Old Yeller*. New York: HarperTrophy, 1995.
A fourteen year old tries to run the family farm in Texas after the Civil War. (Much better than the movie.)

Hunt, Irene. *Across Five Aprils*. New York: Berkley, 2002.
Jethro Creighton comes of age during the turbulent years of the Civil War.

Keith, Harold. *Rifles for Watie*. New York: Harper, 1987.
A sixteen year old chooses sides in the Civil War.

Lowry, Lois. *Number the Stars*. New York: Yearling Books, 1990.
A Newbery award–winner. A Danish girl and her family work to save their Jewish friends and neighbors from the invading Nazis.

O'Dell, Scott. *Sing Down the Moon*. New York: Laurel Leaf, 1997.
The story of a Navajo girl captured by Spanish soldiers in 1864.

Taylor, Mildred D. *Roll of Thunder, Hear My Cry*. New York: Puffin, 2004.
A sharecropper's family deals with prejudice and poverty in Depression-era Mississippi.

ten Boom, Corrie. *The Hiding Place*. New York: Bantam, 1984.
The ten Boom family was arrested for hiding Jews. This is Corrie's first-person account of the concentration camps. May be too intense for some eighth graders.

Wyss, J. D. *The Swiss Family Robinson*. New York: Signet Classics, 2004.

More Imaginative Reading

Ask your local librarian for lists of recommended titles. But also look for these authors, who produced classic tales that have been loved by generations of young readers.

Aiken, Joan
Alexander, Lloyd
Brink, Carol Ryrie
Bulla, Clyde Robert
Burnett, Frances Hodgson

Carroll, Lewis
Cleary, Beverly
Cooper, Susan
de Angeli, Marguerite
Enright, Elizabeth
Estes, Eleanor
Fisher, Dorothy Canfield
George, Jean
Henry, Marguerite
Holling, Holling Clancy
Irving, Washington
Juster, Norton
Kipling, Rudyard
Kjelgaard, Jim
Lawson, Robert
L'Engle, Madeline
Lewis, C. S. (Narnia series)
Little, Jean
Norton, Mary
Nesbit, E.
O'Brian, Robert C.
O'Dell, Scott
Sewell, Anna
Sharp, Margery
Sobel, Donald J.
White, E. B.
Wiggin, Kate Douglas
Wilder, Laura Ingalls

Writing

Cheaney, Janie B. Wordsmith series. Melrose, Fla.: Common Sense Press.
Order from Rainbow Resource Center or The Book Peddler.
Wordsmith Apprentice (use anytime between grades 4–6). $16.00.
Wordsmith (use anytime between grades 6–8). $16.00.
Teacher's Guide. $7.00.
Wordsmith Craftsman (use anytime between grades 7–10). $16.00.

Classical Writing. The Classical Writing website provides an e-mail contact and message board, but no physical address or phone number. You can purchase texts from Classical Writing, through print-on-demand from Lulu.com, or from Rainbow Resource Center. The texts are listed below in order of use; each level is approximately one year's worth of work and consists of a core book and student workbooks or guides. The first two levels also require the purchase of a separate instructor's guide.

Aesop (grade 5 or older)

Aesop core book. $20.95.

Student Workbook A. $24.95.

Instructor's Guide A. $16.95.

Student Workbook B. $24.95.

Instructor's Guide B. $16.95.

Homer (grade 6 or older)

Homer core book. $34.95.

Student Workbook A. $26.95.

Instructor's Guide A. $16.95.

Student Workbook B. $26.95.

Instructor's Guide B. $16.95.

Diogenes: Maxim (grade 7 or older)

Diogenes: Maxim core book. $26.96.

Student Guide. $26.95.

Diogenes: Chreia (grade 8 or older)

Visit the Classical Writing website for pricing information.

Diogenes: Chreia core book.

Student Guide.

Institute for Excellence in Writing series. Atascadero, Calif.: Institute for Excellence in Writing.

Order from IEW. Visit the website, www.excellenceinwriting.com, for additional options.

Teaching Writing: Structure and Style.

Video seminar instructs parents on how to teach writing and provides a syllabus. The package includes nine units, the syllabus, and a student workshop/demo class.

Complete Set (for those teaching grades 2–11). $169.00.

Writing Strands. Challenging Writing Programs for Homeschoolers series. Niles, Mich.: National Writing Institute.

$20.00 for each book. The Writing Strands program can be purchased directly from the National Writing Institute or at a small discount from Rainbow Resource Center. The books aren't consumable; you do all the assignments on notebook paper, so you can reuse these books for another child.

Writing Strands 5.

Writing Strands 6.

Writing Strands 7.

Writing Exposition.

Evaluating Writing.

This booklet for parents/teachers reviews common problems and how to fix them. A good parent resource.

18

MAKING DEDUCTIONS: SCIENCE

1. State the question.
2. Form a hypothesis.
3. Test the hypothesis through experimentation.
4. Draw conclusions.

—The scientific method

SUBJECT: Science: biology, astronomy and earth science, chemistry, physics
TIME REQUIRED: 3 hours per week—90 minutes per day, two days per week—plus additional time working on independent experimentation

In logic-stage science, the student begins to make connections—among the branches of science, between science and history, between the scientific method and the rules of logic. The middle-grade student will begin to mark scientific discoveries and the birth and death dates of scientists on his time line, bringing history and science closer together. He'll use the logic of the scientific method, testing his new knowledge through experiments.

Grammar-stage science was a time of discovery. During the logic stage, the young scientist digs below the surface of the discoveries made in the earlier grades. The first grader learned about animals; the fifth grader will learn about the cells that make up an animal's body. The second grader memorized the constellations; the sixth grader will learn about the birth and death of stars. The third grader experimented with food coloring and water; the seventh grader will study the atoms and molecules that make up water itself. The fourth grader did experiments with weights and planes; the eighth grader will learn about the laws of motion and the journey from Newton to Einstein.

YOUR GOALS

We warned you in the grammar stage against attempting a systematic study of any field of science. Scientific discovery hurtles forward while students pick their way carefully through new material. Middle-grade students have more maturity and better reading and writing skills than elementary students, but they still can't be stuffed with an exhaustive knowledge of science.

Your goal in the early grades was to foster enthusiasm for science and to expose the child to basic facts about each field. In the middle grades, your goal is to teach the young student to think critically about *doing* science. He'll learn how scientists in each field—biology, earth science, astronomy, chemistry, physics—use experimentation to confirm their theories. And through experimentation, he'll practice using the scientific method himself.

This experiment-focused study will help the student learn the basics of each scientific field.

In biology, the student can learn about cells and their functions; about the physical systems that bring living things nutrients and air; about the ways living creatures reproduce; and about the different characteristics that divide the animal and plant kingdoms into phyla, classes, orders, and families.

The student of astronomy and earth science can learn about the makeup of earth and space; about the different types of materials that constitute the earth, the types of objects found in space, and their composition; about the way the earth behaves and the rules that govern planetary motion. He should learn about the earth's relationship to the moon, the solar system, and the rest of the universe.

The young chemist should discover more about the basic elements of the physical universe and how they interact. He should be able to relate this knowledge to biology, astronomy, and earth science. What elements make up living things? the earth? the stars?

The beginning physicist should start to understand how that matter behaves in different circumstances (heated, chilled). He should explore how molecules behave, how the four forces (gravity, electromagnetism, weak and strong nuclear forces) affect matter. He should learn the basic properties of light. Most of all, the young scientist should enjoy doing hands-on science and learning through experimentation.

TEXTS

The logic-stage student will study science by doing an experiment, recording the results, and then by reading and writing more about his discovery. He'll also sketch important diagrams—the parts of a cell, the structure of an atom, the order of the planets—and label them.

In order to do this, you'll need a science program that offers plenty of interesting experiments and also gives the student a chance for deeper investigation. As in the grammar stage, you'll want to stay on one area of science for an entire year, giving the student the opportunity to fit his newly acquired knowledge into a pattern. However, most fifth- and sixth-grade science programs still hold to a spiral sequence that leaps from topic to topic—and although some seventh- and eighth-grade curricula do begin to focus in on particular topics, textbook presentation is too often dry, focused on memorization rather than on discovery.

For three of the four middle-grade years, we recommend replacing a science textbook with fascinating kits and projects. In the pages that follow, we will describe several different ways to approach middle-grade science—all of them focused on discovery and experimentation.

In addition, you'll need two or three science encyclopedias on hand for reference. The *Usborne Internet-Linked Science Encyclopedia* (also recommended for grammar-stage science) is a good resource for most fifth and sixth graders; the *Dorling Kindersley Visual Encyclopedia of Science* will provide an excellent second source for reports. Sixth graders and up will also benefit from the *Kingfisher Science Encyclopedia*, a slightly more advanced reference work, and the *Usborne Illustrated Dictionary of Science: Physics, Chemistry and Biology Facts*, a work approaching high-school level.

For each year, we also suggest books you might want to keep on hand—either purchased by you or borrowed from the library (although you might have to return them before you're done with them). If you're on a budget, you'll need to plan ahead, glancing over your student's science text several weeks in advance so that you can have the right library books on hand.

Remember, once again: Your goal for middle-grade science is *not* mastery of the principles that undergird biology, chemistry, astronomy, earth science, and physics. Those foundations will be laid in a systematic manner in the high-school courses. Your goal is to lead the student in understanding and using the scientific method across all of these scientific fields—to teach her *how* to do science.

As in the elementary years, remember that the biology/earth science-astronomy/chemistry/physics sequence is a convenient way to link history and science—but can always be rearranged if another sequence suits you better.

SCHEDULE

Plan on doing science two days per week for around an hour to an hour and a half per day. The student will spend the first science period performing experiments, recording the results, and making any appropriate sketches; he'll spend the second preparing a report and recording any important dates. He should also plan on spending an occasional afternoon or evening working on additional science-fair type projects.

Your weekly schedule for each year, then, will look like this:

Day 1 Spend around ninety minutes doing experiments, recording results, and completing any sketches.

Day 2 Spend around ninety minutes preparing the science report, using the science encyclopedias as resources and recording any dates.

THE NOTEBOOK

Because you'll be using a number of different resources over the course of each year, use the science notebook to pull all of your study together in one place. Divide the notebook into six sections:

1. Experiments
2. Sketches
3. Reports
4. Dates
5. Memory Work
6. Extra Activities

Experiments

In all the sciences, the student will do experiments, using the scientific method to test and confirm his newfound knowledge.

Experiments should be recorded on a page following this pattern:

1. *What question am I trying to answer?* (state the question)
2. *What could the answer be?* (form a hypothesis)
3. *How will I test this answer?* (the steps of the experiment)
4. *What result did I get?*
5. *Does this agree with the answer I thought I would get? If not, what answer should I give instead?*

Sketches

Any models or diagrams (such as cell structure, molecules, planetary rings or moons) encountered in the experiment materials should be carefully reproduced, with colored pencils, and with all the parts labeled in clear print. Place these in the second section of the science notebook.

Reports

Reports will grow progressively more complicated. The fifth grader will write science reports of two to three paragraphs; the sixth grader, a page; the seventh and eighth grader, up to two pages.

Dates

In this section of the science notebook, place four sheets of paper. At the top of each sheet, write one of the divisions from history: "Ancients (5000 B.C.–

A.D. 400)," "Medieval–Early Renaissance (400–2600)," "Late Renaissance-Early Modern (1600–1850)," and "Modern (1850–Present)." Whenever the student encounters dates of important scientific discoveries or events and the birth and death dates of scientists, he should write them on the appropriate sheet.

In addition, the student should enter on his history time line any scientific dates that fall within the period he's studying in history.

Memory Work

It isn't necessary to test at this level. The student is constantly reading, writing, and experimenting; and all of these activities will serve to fix the new knowledge in his mind.

At the end of the description for each grade, though, we've listed some information that the student should memorize, if possible. Set some time aside once every couple of weeks to review these lists.

Extra Activities

As time and interest permit, periodically plan extra activities and "field trips" to science museums or local science exhibits. Many areas also have science clubs (nature, astronomy, computer, and so forth) that welcome student and family participation. When possible, coordinate the activity with the subject under study each year.

Participating in a science fair is a great motivator for young science students. As a home schooler, you have two options: (1) to call your local school system and ask whether home schoolers can participate in the local school fair (in many cases, the answer will be yes); or (2) to call your state home-school organization and ask what exhibition opportunities are available for home schoolers. Organizations such as 4-H and the Boy or Girl Scouts also give students opportunities to show off science projects. And don't forget national science competitions (listed in Appendix 3). At the end of this chapter, we've suggested several science-project idea books to get the creative juices flowing.

Keep track of the activities in the notebook. You can simply write:

1. Visited science museum. Saw special history of machines exhibit, September 10.

2. Attended computer club, October 11.
3. Went on nature walk in park to identify trees, October 15.
4. Entered Science Fair with my project, "The Orbit of Jupiter," November 12.

and so on.

HOW TO DO IT

Fifth Grade: Biology

You'll want to plan on doing about thirty-six weeks of biology. Each week, the student will spend the first day of science doing experiments. Choose from the following science kits and complete the experiments in each kit at the student's natural pace; he can do as many (or as few) experiments as he can complete, record, and sketch during the ninety-minute experiment session. On the second day of science, allow the student to pick one topic (a concept, a new vocabulary item, a discovery) related to one of the finished experiments, research it briefly, and then write a short report. Two or three paragraphs is plenty. The student will learn more about research *and* writing by completing a brief weekly composition than by doing longer, less frequent papers. If the student develops a deep interest in one particular topic, adjust the science schedule—do more experiments in that area (skipping others if necessary), and allow him to research and write more detailed reports. Flexibility is one of the great advantages to home learning.

We suggest that you begin with Sally Stenhouse Kneidel's *Creepy Crawlies and the Scientific Method: Over One Hundred Hands-On Science Experiments for Children*. This book leads students through the five steps of the scientific method, giving valuable instruction to those who are just starting to think critically about science. Spend three to five weeks, picking and choosing from the experiments in this book on the first day of study; ask the student to write his report on a related topic on the second.

Once you're comfortable following the steps of the scientific method, you can begin to pick and choose from the following experiment kits. Begin with projects from the Intermediate list and then move on to the Advanced list. (Ordering information is in the Resources section at the end of this chapter.)

Intermediate

Owl Pellet Dissection Kit (1–2 weeks)
Three pellets and tools for identifying the owl's meal.

Bug Hunt Kit (1–3 weeks)
Build four traps, catch bugs, identify them, document the process. Length of use depends on the time of year, and how many insects live in your area.

Carnivorous Creations Terrarium Kit (1 week to establish, return to the kit for 2–4 weeks over the course of the year)
Grow and feed carnivorous plants.

Smithsonian Bio Dome Habitat (2–3 weeks to establish, return to the kit for 3–5 weeks over the course of the year)
Build and manage a frog "rainforest," an aquarium, a bug habitat, and an ant-hill.

Basic 5 Animals Dissection Kit (5–8 weeks)
Beginner dissection kit: crayfish, earthworm, starfish, frog, grasshopper, all tools, and a dissection manual/guide.

Blood Typing Kit (1 week)
Discover and document your blood type.

Fingerprint Kit (1–3 weeks)
Learn to collect and identify fingerprints as the unique markers they are.

Mind's Eye: Optical Illusions & Human Perception (8–12 weeks)
Learn how the human eye handles depth, perspective, shape, motion, and more. Experiment manual included with 94 different experiments.

Advanced

Botanical Discoveries Science Fair Kit (1 week to establish, return to the kit for 4–7 weeks over the course of the year)
Comes with experiment guide; students learn about germination, phototropism, photosynthesis, root structures, and more.

Microscope & Biology Kit (8–16 weeks)
Twenty-five directed experiments using microscope and slides: learn how to use the microscope, prepare slides, and investigate specimens.

Fetal Pig Anatomy Lab (3–5 weeks)

Fetal pig, dissection mats, and anatomy guide (you'll need to complete the Basic 5 Animals Dissection Kit above first).

In our Resources section, we've suggested several additional experiment books, science-project resources, and biology resources for you to consider.

Memory Work Choose among the following information:

- The basic phyla of the animal kingdom and their characteristics (Chordata, Echinodermata, Arthropoda, Mollusca, Annelida, Nematoda, Platyhelminthes, Coelenterata, Porifera).
- Plant-kingdom memory work, which should include lists of important structures—for example, the parts of a flower (receptacle, petals, sepals, nectaries, stamens, pistil); the types of compound leaves (palmate, trifoliate, ternate, pinnate, bipinnate); the types of root (taproot, fibrous root, adventitious root, aerial root, prop root). Keep your eyes open for other lists as you study.
- Human-body memory work, which could include the body systems (skin, skeletal system, muscular system, digestive system, respiratory system, circulatory system, urinary system, reproductive system, endocrine system, and nervous system); major bones (cranium, mandible, clavicle, scapula, rib cage, ulna, radius, pelvis, carpus, femur, patella, fibula, tibia); the components of blood and what each does (red blood cells carry oxygen, white blood cells fight disease, platelets stop bleeding); the types of teeth (incisors, premolars, molars, wisdom teeth).

Extra Activities Record all field trips, club activities, and so forth.

Sixth Grade: Astronomy and Earth Science

In sixth grade, the student will revisit astronomy and earth science, first studied in second grade. You'll want to plan on doing about eighteen weeks of earth science and eighteen weeks of astronomy over the course of the year; you can alternate, or choose to divide the year in half between the two subjects. Each week, the student will spend the first day of science doing experiments. Choose from the following science kits and complete the experiments in each kit at the student's natural pace; he can do as many (or as few) experiments as he can complete, record, and sketch during the ninety-minute experiment session. On the second day of science, allow the student to pick one topic (a concept, a new vocabulary item, a discovery) related to one of the finished experiments, research it briefly, and then write a short report. Three-quarters of a page to one full page is long enough; remember that the student will learn more about research *and* writing by completing a brief weekly composition than by doing longer, less frequent papers. If the student develops a deep interest in one particular topic, adjust the science schedule—do more experiments in that area (skipping others if necessary), and allow him to research and write more detailed reports. Flexibility is one of the great advantages to home learning.

Pick and choose from the following experiment kits. (Ordering information is in the Resources section at the end of this chapter.) Observation lessons such as stargazing may not allow the student to completely fill out the experiment sheet for the notebook.

Earth Science

National Geographic Earthquakes & Volcanoes Experiment Kit (5–6 weeks)
Six experiments in plate tectonics and seismograph use, along with an experiment manual.

Smithsonian Weather Center Science Kit (1 week to install, revisit for 3–5 weeks over the course of the year)
Set up this minature tower to measure and chart wind speed and direction, temperature, rainfall, cloud coverage, and other weather conditions.

Volcano: Power Tech Series
Make an erupting volcano and experiment with the properties of lava (3–5 weeks)

Crystal PRO Crystal Growing & Crystallography Kit (9–12 weeks)
Fourteen experiments in growing, measuring, and evaluating crystals.

Wind Power: Renewable Energy Science Kit (8–12 weeks)
Twenty experiments in wind energy: make a turbine and learn how wind interacts with the earth.

Astronomy

Primer for the Beginning Astronomer/Astromax Introductory Astronomy Binocular Kit (5–8 weeks)

Five detailed lessons in studying the sky, log sheets, sky charts, and high-powered binoculars for observation.

Space Exploration: The Planets, Moon, Stars, Solar System & Rockets (10–18 weeks)

Twenty-two experiments in rocket propulsion, telescope use, solar system modeling, moon exploration, and more.

Slooh Telescope Card and Book (1–2 weeks)

Computer card gives you fifty minutes of access to high-powered telescopes on the Canary Islands; use the observations to fill out the accompanying activity book.

Memory Work

- The planets of the solar system, in the proper order.
- The elements of the earth's crust (oxygen, silicon, aluminum, iron, calcium, sodium, potassium, magnesium).
- The parts of the earth (crust—oceanic and continental; mantle—lithosphere and asthenosphere; outer core; inner core).
- The continents.
- The plates (North American, Cocos, Caribbean, South American, Nazca, African, Eurasian, Indo-Australian, Pacific).
- Types of clouds.
- Types of stars and their characteristics (red giants, white dwarfs, variable stars, supernovas, pulsars, binary stars, black holes, neutron stars).

Extra Activities In the second half of the year, schedule a few additional stargazing evenings (see second-grade science for tips on how to do this). If you don't already have the second-grade astronomy guides on hand (*The Stargazer's Guide to the Galaxy* and *Spotter's Guide: The Night Sky*), invest in them now. Also, add a star wheel that helps you locate constellations at any time of year and night.

You can also visit available geographical sites—caverns, mountains, small islands, and so forth—and collect and classify rocks.

Seventh Grade: Chemistry

You'll want to plan on doing about thirty-six weeks of chemistry during this year. Each week, the student will spend the first day of science doing experiments. Choose from the following science kits and complete the experiments in each kit at the student's natural pace; he can do as many (or as few) experiments as he can complete, record, and sketch during the ninety-minute experiment session. On the second day of science, allow the student to pick one topic (a concept, a new vocabulary item, a discovery) related to one of the finished experiments, research it briefly, and then write a short report—one to one and a half pages long. Remember: the student will learn more about research *and* writing by completing a brief weekly composition than by doing longer, less frequent papers. If the student develops a deep interest in one particular topic, adjust the science schedule—do more experiments in that area (skipping others if necessary), and allow him to research and write more detailed reports. Flexibility is one of the great advantages to home learning.

We suggest that you invest in the Thames & Kosmos CHEM2000 chemistry kit, which comes with a 251-experiment manual covering the major topics in chemistry. Supplement this with experiments chosen (according to the student's interest) from *Mastering the Periodic Table: Exercises on the Elements*, by Linda Trombley and Thomas G. Cohn. For reference, we recommend an elements chart such as the Periodic Table of Elements Chartlet listed in the Resources section at the end of this chapter.

Alternative

Real Science-4-Kids, suggested for possible use in the grammar-school year, publishes a middle-school chemistry curriculum—one of the few that stays on topic for an entire year. The program includes experimentation, but is a more typical textbook-centered course. You can see samples of the RealScience curriculum at the publisher's website, www.gravitaspublications.com

If you decide to use Real Science-4-Kids, you may want to follow the Real Science recommended sequence of chemistry/biology/physics over grades 5–7, and do earth science and astronomy in eighth grade. Ordering information is found in the Resources section at the end of this chapter.

Chemistry

CHEM C2000 Chemistry Set (30–36 weeks)
This set and the accompanying manual from Thames & Kosmos provides material for 251 experiments that cover all of the major bases in beginning chemistry.

Linda Trombley and Thomas Cohn, *Mastering the Periodic Table: Exercises on the Elements.*

Periodic Table of Elements Chartlet.

In the Resources list, we've recommended several chemistry kits that you can add for a fun variation.

Memory Work At the very least, cover the following:

- Atom: the basic building blocks of all things; made up of a nucleus surrounded by electrons.
- Molecule: a combination of atoms, tightly bound together by electrical charges.
- Electron: small particle with a negative charge that spins around the nucleus.
- Proton: small particle in the nucleus; has a positive charge.
- Neutron: small particle in the nucleus; has no charge.
- Nucleus: the center of an atom; made up of protons and neutrons.

Also consider having the student memorize the basic makeup of common elements (water: H_2O) encountered in his study.

Extra Activities Along with science-fair projects, try to visit places where chemistry is at work: industrial plants that manufacture products, bakeries (we have a cookie factory near us), swimming pools (ask the staff how the chlorine and other chemicals are kept in balance), car-repair centers (ask how oil, used freon, and other chemicals are disposed of), and so forth.

Eighth Grade: Physics

You'll want to plan on doing about thirty-six weeks of physics (at this level, "physical science"—investigating force, motion, sound, light, and magnetism). Each week, the student will spend the first day of science doing experiments. Choose from the following science kits and complete the experiments in each kit at the student's natural pace; he can do as many (or as few) experiments as he can complete, record, and sketch during the ninety-minute experiment session. On the second day of science, allow the student to pick one topic (a concept, a new vocabulary item, a discovery) related to one of the finished experiments, research it briefly, and then write a report—one to two pages in length. If the student develops a deep interest in one particular topic, adjust the science schedule—do more experiments in that area (skipping others if necessary), and allow him to research and write more detailed reports. Flexibility is one of the great advantages to home learning.

Begin with projects from the Intermediate list and then move on to the Advanced list. (Ordering information is in the Resources section at the end of this chapter.)

Intermediate

Backyard Ballistics: Build Potato Cannons, Paper Match Rockets, Cincinnati Fire Kites, Tennis Ball Mortars, and More Dynamite Devices (4–8 weeks)

The only non-kit resource on this list, *Backyard Ballistics* is a guidebook to making projectiles with common household objects and investigating the physical principles behind their operation.

Physics Discovery (3–5 weeks)

An introduction to mechanical physics: build twelve models and learn about levers, pulleys, centripetal and centrifugal forces, gears.

Physics Workshop (10–14 weeks)

73 experiments based on 36 models: windmill, crane, centrifugal switch, and more; simple machines, planes, pulleys, and axles.

Physics Solar Workshop (6–10 weeks)

30 experiments based on twelve models: exploring motors, simple machines, the conversion of solar energy into electricity, fossil fuel use, and more.

Supercharged Science: Physics Kit (3–5 weeks)

Three categories of experiments: roller coaster experiments (force and motion), sonic vibrations, and simple machines. The kit comes with an instructional DVD, the "hard to find" materials (you supply some of the everyday ones, which will require a trip to the hardware store), and student workbook.

Supercharged Science: Electricity and Robotics Kit (3–5 weeks)
Electrical charges and currents, circuits and switches. The kit comes with an instructional DVD, student workbook, and most materials.

Supercharged Science: Laser Show Kit (3–5 weeks)
Experiments with lights: color, lenses, filters, prisms, and more. The kit comes with an instructional DVD, student workbook, and most materials.

Advanced

Introduction to Electronics (10–16 weeks)
Move from simple circuits through more complex systems with sensors, testers, timers, and more; 148 experiments, seven different categories of exploration.

Kite Dynamics (4–8 weeks)
Build different models of kites and test them to learn about the principles of flying: lift and drag, Bernoulli's principle, and more.

Physics Pro (15–20 weeks)
More complex experiments in statics and dynamics, building off lessons learned in the Physics Discovery, Physics Workshop, or Physics Solar Workshop kits above: fluid dynamics, oscillation, hydraulics, and pneumatics. Build first smaller models, then more difficult versions of real-life machines.

Alternatives

Real Science-4-Kids, suggested for possible use in the grammar-school year, publishes a middle-school physics curriculum—one of the few that stays on topic for an entire year. The program includes experimentation, but is a more typical textbook-centered course. You can see samples of the RealScience curriculum at the publisher's website, www.gravitaspublications.com.

If you decide to use the Real Science-4-Kids, you may want to follow the Real Science recommended sequence of chemistry/biology/physics over grades 5–7, and do earth science and astronomy in eighth grade. Ordering information is found in the Resources section at the end of this chapter.

A second alternative is the physical science course *Exploration Education: Intermediate Physical Science.* This engaging course, published on CD, is self-directing; the student progresses through the lessons on the computer (Windows or Mac), fills out a paper-and-pencil logbook, and completes a number of projects (supplies provided). The course is a good introduction to physical forces for most middle-grade students, but will be too elementary for advanced learners; they should stick to the more difficult physics projects listed above. Samples can be viewed on the publisher's website, www.explorationeducation.com.

Memory Work This memory work should center around physics facts collected by the student as he studies. These will differ, depending on which area of physics he's chosen to pursue. A few options:

- The speed of light.
- The speed of sound.
- The three gas laws.
- The boiling point of water, both Celsius and Fahrenheit.
- The laws of thermodynamics.
- Isaac Newton's three laws of motion.
- The definition of a solar day.
- The colors in the spectrum.
- Direct current versus alternating current.
- The definitions of *ampere, ohm, volt,* and *watt.*

Extra Activities Visit physical-science exhibits at local museums. Spend extra time on the physics projects (building machines and so forth) found in the resources we recommend.

At the end of four years of logic-stage science, the student will have grasped the basic principles of experimentation in biology, earth science, astronomy, chemistry, and physics. Even more important: he'll have learned how to draw conclusions from an experiment, how to research those conclusions, and how to summarize the information in writing.

RESOURCES

For publisher and catalog addresses, telephone numbers, and other information, see Sources (pages 751–778). Most books can be obtained from any bookstore or library; where we know of a mail-order option, we have provided it. Each year's resources are divided into basic texts and optional supplementary materials; these are further divided by subject (human body, earth science, astronomy, and so forth) in the order you'll encounter them during the school year. You can still use many of the resources listed in Chapter 8, particularly the detailed Dover coloring books and the experiment kits.

Reference Materials for All Four Years

Note: If you choose the Microscope & Biology Kit from Thames & Kosmos as one of the fifth-grade biology projects, a microscope is included in the kit.

Blister Microscope. Minneapolis, Minn.: General Science Service Co.
$65.95. Order from Blister Microscope. This affordable microscope can be used with regular slides or with the custom-fitted Blister Slides, which have a small depression for the easy viewing of insects and small organisms in liquid. 100 slides come with the microscope.

Brock Magiscope. Maitland, Fla.: Brock Optical, Inc.
$119.00 and up. Order from Brock. If you want better optics than those provided by the $65.95 microscope above, use a Brock Magiscope—tough, reliable, easy to use, good magnification.

Dorling Kindersley Visual Encyclopedia of Science. New York: Dorling Kindersley, 2005.
$12.99. Hundreds of photographs and diagrams; fifth- to sixth-grade reading level.

Rogers, Kirsteen, et. al. *The Usborne Internet-Linked Science Encyclopedia.* Tulsa, Okla.: Usborne Publishing, 2003.
$19.99 (paperback version).

Stockley, Corinne, et al. *The Usborne Illustrated Dictionary of Science.* Tulsa, Okla.: Usborne Publishing, 2007.
$29.99. Detailed facts in physics, chemistry, and biology.

Taylor, Charles. *The Kingfisher Science Encyclopedia.* New York: Kingfisher, 2006.

$24.95. An excellent middle-grade reference.

Life Science: Animals, Human Beings, and Plants (Fifth Grade)

Basic Resources

Basic 5 Animals Dissection Kit.

$29.99. Order from Tobin's Lab.

Biological Inheritance & Genetic Engineering. Portsmouth, R.I.: Thames & Kosmos.

$34.95. Order from Thames & Kosmos.

Blood Typing Kit.

$7.99. Order from Tobin's Lab. Single-use kit.

Botanical Discoveries Science Fair Kit.

$24.99. Order from Discover This.

Bug Hunt. Plymouth, Mich.: Slinky Science.

$12.95. Order from Discover This.

Carnivorous Creations Terrarum Kit. Chagrin Falls, Ohio: DuneCraft.

$24.99. Order from Discover This.

Fetal Pig Anatomy Lab.

$39.99. Order from Tobin's Lab. (Sequel to the Basic 5 Animals Dissection Kit, which should be completed first.)

Fingerprint Kit. Plymouth, Mich.: Slinky Science.

$9.88. Order from Are You Game.

Kneidel, Sally Stenhouse. *Creepy Crawlies and the Scientific Method: Over One Hundred Hands-On Science Experiments for Children.* Golden, Col.: Fulcrum Publications, 1993.

$18.95. Shows parents how to teach children the five steps of the scientific method: question, hypothesis, methods, result, and conclusion.

Microscope & Biology Kit. Portsmouth, R.I.: Thames & Kosmos.
$119.95. Order from Thames & Kosmos.

Mind's Eye: Optical Illusions & Human Perception. Portsmouth, R.I.: Thames & Kosmos.
$69.95. Order from Thames & Kosmos.

Owl Pellet Dissection Kit.
$19.95. Order from Discover This.

Planetarium Garden Lab.
$24.95. Order from Discover This.

Smithsonian Bio Dome Habitat.
$32.50. Order from The Science Fair.

Supplementary Resources

Animals

Burnie, David. *Eyewitness: Bird.* New York: Dorling Kindersley, 2008.
$15.99. A good resource to have on hand for the study of birds.

Giant Ant Farm.
$24.99. Order from Tobins Lab. A good-sized ant farm with a coupon for live ants.

Greenway, Theresa, and Geoff Dann. *Eyewitness: Jungle.* New York: Dorling Kindersley, 2004.
$15.99. A good reference book to have on hand for the study of mammals.

Parker, Steve, and Dave King. *Eyewitness: Mammal.* New York: Dorling Kindersley, 2004.
$15.99. Another good reference book to have on hand for the study of mammals.

———. *Eyewitness: Seashore.* New York: Dorling Kindersley, 2004.
$15.99. A good reference book to have on hand for the study of freshwater fish and amphibians.

Parker, Steve, and Philip Dowell. *Eyewitness: Pond and River.* New York: Knopf, 2005.

$15.99. A good reference book to have on hand for the study of fish, amphibians, and reptiles.

Peterson, Roger Tory, et al. *Butterflies (Peterson Field Guide Color-In Books).* Boston, Mass.: Houghton Mifflin, 2003.

$7.95. This coloring book, based on the Peterson's Field Guide series, contains detailed drawings with information about each specimen.

———. *Reptiles and Amphibians (Peterson Field Guide Color-In Books).* Boston, Mass.: Houghton Mifflin, 2003.

$7.95. This coloring book, based on the Peterson's Field Guide series, contains detailed drawings with information about each specimen.

———. *Birds (Peterson Field Guide Color-In Books).* Boston, Mass: Houghton Mifflin, 2003.

$7.95. This coloring book, based on the Peterson's Field Guide series, contains detailed drawings with information about each specimen.

Science Fair Fun 5 Book Set: Life Science. San Francisco, Calif.: University Games.

$26.88. Order from Are You Game. Five books with all the science experiments in botany, ecology, the human body, microscopes, and measurement you'll ever need.

Van Cleave, Janice. *A+ Projects in Biology: Winning Experiments for Science Fairs and Extra Credit.* New York: Wiley, 1999.

$22.75. Includes experiments in both animal and plant science.

———. *Biology for Every Kid.* New York: Wiley, 1990.

$12.95.

Human Beings

Cumbaa, Stephen. *The Bones Book and Skeleton.* Illus. Kim La Fave. New York: Somerville House, 1998.

$16.95. Assemble a 12-inch, 25-piece plastic skeleton with moving joints.

Matt, Margaret, et al. *Human Anatomy Coloring Book.* New York: Dover, 1990.

$3.95. Order from The Book Peddler. Detailed, scientifically accurate drawings of body organs and systems, with charts listing names of body parts.

Pac-Man: Human Torso Model. Bensenville, Ill.: Pacific Science Supplies. $35.00. Order from Tobin's Lab. A plastic molded figure with anatomically correct organs that fit into it to show how the body's parts work together.

Science in a Nutshell series. Nashua, N.H.: Delta Education. $36.00 each. Order from Delta Education. These kits provide a complete science experiment and activity center; consider going in with a friend, since the kits provide material for two or three students.

Body Basics.
Kit includes materials for an overview of the human body, along with an activity guide and student journal.

The Human Machine.
Kit includes materials for the study of bones, muscles, and joints, along with an activity guide and student journal.

A Peek Inside You.
Respiration, digestion, and circulation.

Smell, Taste, and Touch.
The senses.

Vision and Hearing.
Experiments based on illusions in sight and sound.

Stark, Fred. *Gray's Anatomy: A Fact-Filled Coloring Book.* Philadelphia, Pa.: Running Press, 2001.
This simplified black-line version of *Gray's Anatomy* is more difficult and more interesting than the Dover coloring book listed above.

The Visual Dictionary of the Human Body. New York: Dorling Kindersley, 1991. $18.99. Big clear drawings, exploded views, cutaways and sections, all labeled with proper Latin names. A beautiful book.

Plants

Arbel, Ilil. *Medicinal Plants Coloring Book.* New York: Dover, 1993. $3.95.

Bernath, Stefen. *Herbs Coloring Book*. New York: Dover, 1977.
$3.95.

Burnie, David. *Eyewitness: Plant*. New York: Dorling Kindersley, 2004.
$15.99. A good resource to keep on hand during the study of the plant kingdom.

Peterson, Roger Tory, et al. *Wildflowers (Peterson Field Guide Color-In Books)*. Boston, Mass: Houghton Mifflin, 2003.
$7.95. Order from Rainbow Resource Center. This coloring book, based on the Peterson's Field Guide series, contains detailed drawings with information about each specimen.

Earth Science and Astronomy (Sixth Grade)

Basic Resources

Crystal PRO Crystal Growing & Crystallography Kit.
$29.95. Order from Discover This.

National Geographic Earthquakes & Volcanoes Experiment Kit.
$34.95. Order from Thames & Kosmos.

Primer for the Beginning Astronomer/Astromax Introductory Astronomy Binocular Kit.
$5.00 for the five-lesson primer, $99.00 for the high-powered binocular/star chart kit. Order from Astromax.

Slooh Telescope Card and Book.
$14.99. Order from Learning Express.

Smithsonian Weather Center Science Kit.
$29.98. Order from Are You Game.

Space Exploration: The Planets, Moon, Stars, Solar System & Rockets. Portsmouth, R.I.: Thames & Kosmos.
$34.95. Order from Thames & Kosmos.

Volcano: Power Tech Series. Wheeling, Ill.: Elenco, Inc.
$24.99. Order from Amazon.com.

Wind Power: Renewable Energy Science Kits. Portsmouth, R.I.: Thames & Kosmos.

$49.95. Order from Thames & Kosmos.

Supplementary Resources

Earth Science

Clayborne, Anna. *The Encyclopedia of Planet Earth.* Tulsa, Okla.: Usborne, 2003.

$19.95. Order from any bookstore or from an Usborne distributor. Less like an encyclopedia than like an atlas; seven sections cover climate, the earth's layers, weather, land and water, and much more. Beautiful illustrations.

Introductory Earth Science Collection.

$65.00. Order from Rainbow Resource Center. Seventy-five rock samples, along with a study guide and equipment for testing properties.

Science Fair Fun 5 Book Set: Earth Sciences. San Francisco, Calif.: University Games.

$26.88. Order from Are You Game. Five books with science experiments in geology, weather, and magnetism.

Science in a Nutshell series. Nashua, N.H.: Delta Education.

$36.00 each. Order from Delta Education. These kits provide a complete science experiment and activity center; consider going in with a friend, since the kits provide material for two or three students.

Fossil Formations.

Six fossil samples, sand, plaster of Paris, and modeling clay, along with an activity guide and student journal.

Rock Origins.

Twenty-two rock and mineral samples and materials for investigating their properties.

Van Cleave, Janice. *Earth Science for Every Kid.* Boston, Mass.: Jossey-Bass, 1991.

$12.95. 101 experiments.

———. Spectacular Science: Mind-Boggling Experiments You Can Turn Into Science Fair Projects series. New York: Wiley.

$10.95 each. These experiments are more complex (and interesting) than those in the Every Kid series. Suitable for exhibition.

Earthquakes. 1993.

Rocks and Minerals. 1995.

Volcanoes. 1995.

Weather. 1995.

Van Rose, Susanna. *Eyewitness: Earth.* New York: Dorling Kindersley, 2005.
$15.99. A good reference work for report writing.

Astronomy

Henbest, N., and E. Harris. *Spotter's Guide: The Night Sky.* Tulsa, Okla: E.D.C. Publications, 2006.
$5.99. Order from any bookstore or from an Usborne distributor.

Lafontaine, Bruce. *Exploring the Solar System Coloring Book.* New York: Dover, 1998.
$3.95. Order from Rainbow Resource Center.

Lippincott, Kirsten. *Eyewitness: Astronomy.* New York: Dorling Kindersley, 2008.
$15.99. Wonderful pictures.

Mars 2020. Dexter, Mich.: Aristoplay.
$30.00. In this family board game, a race to Mars teaches about space and space exploration.

Pearce, Q. L. *The Stargazer's Guide to the Galaxy.* Illus. Mary Ann Fraser. New York: Tor, 1991.
$6.99.

Planet Poster Set.
$13.99. Order from Tobin's Lab. Twelve posters (just under 12 × 12 inches) with every planet, the sun, the moon, and a galaxy. Facts listed for each.

Staal, Julius D. *The New Patterns in the Sky: Myths and Legends of the Stars.* Granville, Ohio.: McDonald & Woodward, 1996.
$24.95. For good readers, a complete guide to the myths behind the constellations from a number of different countries.

Styrofoam Solar System Kit

$16.99. Order from Rainbow Resource Center. Paint and construct a Styrofoam ball model of the solar system.

Van Cleave, Janice. *Constellations for Every Kid.* New York: Wiley, 1997.

$12.95. Straightforward astronomy experiments.

———. *Astronomy for Every Kid.* New York: Wiley, 1991.

$12.95.

Chemistry (Seventh Grade)

Basic Resources

CHEM C2000 Chemistry Kit. Portsmouth, R.I.: Thames & Kosmos.

$154.95. Order from Thames & Kosmos.

Periodic Table of Elements Chartlet

$1.99. Order from Rainbow Resource Center. A 17 × 22-inch reference chart of the table of elements.

Trombley, Linda, and Thomas G. Cohn. *Mastering the Periodic Table: Exercises on the Elements.* Portland, Me.: J. Weston Walch, 1985.

$22.99. Order from J. Weston Walch or from Rainbow Resource Center.

Supplementary Resources

Cooper, Christopher. *Eyewitness: Matter*. New York: Dorling Kindersley, 1999.

$15.99. Same series as the *Chemistry* book listed below; a look at the elements from a slightly different angle.

ElementO.

$34.95. Order from Rainbow Resource Center. In this Monopoly-type game, players collect elements and pay each other with proton and neutron certificates. Keep track with the Periodic Table of Elements in the middle of the board. A great way to memorize the basic properties of chemistry.

Elements series. Danbury, Conn.: Grolier.

Check your library; most will carry a few of these titles. The books contain clear and detailed explanations of the elements, so consider reading through at least a couple of them. They are listed here in the order they appear on the periodic table.

Hydrogen and the Noble Gases.
Sodium and Potassium.
Calcium and Magnesium.
Iron, Chromium, and Manganese.
Copper, Silver, and Gold.
Zinc, Cadmium, and Mercury.
Aluminum.
Carbon.
Silicon.
Lead and Tin.
Nitrogen and Phosphorus.
Oxygen.
Sulfur.
Chlorine, Fluorine, Bromine, and Iodine.
Uranium and Other Radioactive Elements.

Goose Eggs: Three in One Science Kits. Greensboro, N.C.: The Wild Goose Company.

$6.99 each. Order from Wild Goose. These affordable minilabs contain three activities each, materials, and illustrated instructions.

Chemo-Electro!
Zinc plating and electrical messages.

Growing Crystals!
Crystals.

pH Fun!
Measure the pH of common household substances (including dog slobber).

Super Bounce Putty!
Make polymers.

Newmark, Ann. *Eyewitness: Chemistry.* New York: Dorling Kindersley, 2005. $15.99.

Science Fair Fun 5 Book Set: Chemistry. San Francisco, Calif.: University Games.

$24.36. Order from Are You Game. Five books with science-fair level experiments in chemistry.

Van Cleave, Janice. *Chemistry for Every Kid: One Hundred Easy Experiments That Really Work*. Boston, Mass.: Jossey-Bass, 2002.
$12.95.

———. *Janice Van Cleave's A+ Projects in Chemistry: Winning Experiments for Science Fairs and Extra Credit*. Boston, Mass.: Jossey-Bass, 1993.
$12.95. These experiments, slightly more complex than those in the Every Kid series, are suitable for exhibition.

———. *Molecules: Mind-Boggling Experiments You Can Turn Into Science Fair Projects*. Boston, Mass.: Jossey-Bass, 1995.
$10.95.

Physics (Eighth Grade)

Basic Texts

Gurstelle, William. *Backyard Ballistics: Build Potato Cannons, Paper Match Rockets, Cincinnati Fire Kites, Tennis Ball Mortars, and More Dynamite Devices*. Chicago, Ill.: Chicago Review Press, 2001.
$16.95. Order from any bookstore or from MindWare.

Introduction to Electronics. Portsmouth, R.I.: Thames & Kosmos.
$109.95. Order from Thames & Kosmos.

Kite Dynamics. Portsmouth, R.I.: Thames & Kosmos.
$39.95. Order from Discover This.

Physics Discover. Portsmouth, R.I.: Thames & Kosmos.
$24.95. Order from Discover This.

Physics Pro. Portsmouth, R.I.: Thames & Kosmos.
$54.95. Order from Thames & Kosmos.

Physics Solar Workshop. Portsmouth, R.I.: Thames & Kosmos.
$64.95. Order from Thames & Kosmos.

Physics Workshop. Portsmouth, R.I.: Thames & Kosmos.
$99.95. Order from Thames & Kosmos.

Supercharged Science Kits. San Luis Obispo, Calif.: Superchanged Science.
Order kits from Supercharged Science.

Physics Kit. $89.95.
Electricity and Robotics Kit. $89.95.
Laser Show Kit. $119.95.

Supplementary Resources

Adventures in Science kits
$12.99 each. Order from Rainbow Resource Center.
Color and Light.
Electricity.
How Things Work.
Magnetism.

Cassidy, John. *Explorabook: A Kid's Science Museum in a Book.* Palo Alto, Calif.: Klutz Press, 1992.
$21.95. Order from Klutz Press. One hundred pages on seven subjects like light-wave craziness, magnetism, hair-dryer science, and ouchless physics. Bound directly into the book are most of the tools needed; these include a mylar mirror, a magnet, two packets of agar growth medium, a diffraction grating, and a Fresnel lens.

Doherty, Paul, John Cassidy, and Martin Gardner. *The Klutz Book of Magnetic Magic.* Palo Alto, Calif.: Klutz Press, 1994.
$12.95. Order from Klutz Press. Written by an MIT physicist and two magicians (one of whom is a mathematician), this book includes ten magnets and thirty-one magic activities that explore their properties.

Eyewitness Science series. New York: Dorling Kindersley.
$15.99 each.
Burnie, David. *Light.* 1999.
Challoner, Jack. *Energy.* 2000.
Gribbon, Mary, and John R. Gribbon. *Time and Space.* 2000.
Lafferty, Peter. *Force and Motion.* 1999.
Parker, Steve. *Electricity.* 2005.

Horemis, Spyros. *Visual Illusions.* New York: Dover, 1976.
$3.95. Order from Rainbow Resource Center. You won't know whether the lines are straight or curved until you color them. Finished, the designs are spectacular.

Sato, Koichi. *Optical Illusions Coloring Book.* New York: Dover, 1995.
$3.95. Order from Rainbow Resource Center. Mind-bending pictures to color. Eighth-grade level.

Science in a Nutshell series. Nashua, N.H.: Delta Education.
$36.00 each. Order from Delta Education. These kits provide a complete science experiment and activity center, designed for grades 2–6. Consider sharing the cost with a neighbor, since the kits provide materials for two or three students.

Bubble Science.
Variables affecting the size, shape, color, and durability of bubbles.

Charge It! Static Electricity.
Positive and negative charges, static electricity.

Clever Levers.
Build a wheelbarrow, balance a scale, lift weights, and more.

Electrical Connections.
Simple and complex circuits, current, batteries.

Energy and Motion.
Stored energy, motion; weights, marbles, and ramps.

Flight! Gliders to Jets.
Build designes for parachutes, gliders, propeller and jet craft; teaches principles of air pressure and Newton's third law of motion.

Gears at Work.
Gear systems and interaction.

Magnetic Magic.
Magnetic materials, polar strength.

Pulley Power.
Using fixed and movable pulleys to reduce the force needed to lift objects.

Sound Vibrations.
Sound waves and their interaction with various materials.

Work: Plane and Simple.
Inclined planes; force and friction.

Van Cleave, Janice. *Janice Van Cleave's Machines: Mind-Boggling Experiments You Can Turn Into Science Fair Projects.* Boston, Mass.: Jossey-Bass, 1993.
$10.95.

———. *Janice Van Cleave's Magnets: Mind-Boggling Experiments You Can Turn Into Science Fair Projects*. Boston, Mass.: Jossey-Bass, 1993.
$10.95.

———. *Physics for Every Kid*. Boston, Mass.: Jossey-Bass, 1991.
$12.95. Simpler experiments than the Spectacular Science series. Deals with motion, heat, light, machines, and sound.

Alternatives

Exploration Education Science Curriculum. Walnut Creek, Calif.: Exploration Education.
Intermediate Physical Science Course.
$119.95. Order from Exploration Education. Course on CD, Student Logbook, instructor guide, all experiment supplies except for glue gun, scissors, ruler, and pencils.

Real Science-4-Kids, by Rebecca Keller. Albuquerque, N. Mex.: Gravitas Publications, Inc.
Order from Gravitas Publications.
Level 1 Chemistry
Student Text. $29.95
Student Workbook. $21.95
Teacher's Manual. $26.95.
Student/Teacher Bundle (contains all of the above). $100.80.
Level 1 Biology
Student Text. $29.95
Student Workbook. $21.95
Teacher's Manual. $26.95.
Student/Teacher Bundle (contains all of the above). $100.80.
Level 1 Physics
Student Text. $29.95
Laboratory Workbook. $21.95
Teacher's Manual. $26.95.
Student/Teacher Bundle (contains all of the above). $100.80.

19

LOOKING INTO OTHER WORLDS: LATIN AND LANGUAGES

Litterarum radices amarae, fructus dulces.[1]

—Anonymous

SUBJECT: Foreign languages (classical and modern)
TIME REQUIRED: 3 hours or more per week

The middle-grade student learns how her own language works. But that's not the end of her language study. She must also learn how other languages work.

For the middle-grade student, the study of a foreign language becomes an exercise in logic. Every culture puts words together to form thoughts in different ways. Language study is a way to explore these new ways of thinking. To master the syntax (the grammatical structure) of a foreign language is to discover a fresh way of looking at the world. It's become an educational cliché that most European students know several languages, but American

[1]"The roots of language study are bitter, but the fruits are sweet."

students generally learn only their own (if that). The classically educated student isn't limited by knowing only the thought patterns of her own language. She also studies the way other cultures express themselves.

Your goal in the middle grades is to expose the student to both ancient and modern languages. The study of Latin should continue, but the fifth- and sixth-grade years are a fruitful time to introduce the child to a modern spoken language such as Spanish or French. The student is still young enough to develop fluency, but she's already been exposed to grammar and to beginning foreign-language work. (And if you did a modern foreign language instead of Latin in grades 3 and 4, now's the time to start on your Latin study.)

TEACHING OPTIONS

Unless you already know Latin, your fifth grader will rapidly move beyond your ability to teach her. And unless you're already fluent in a modern language, you won't be able to teach that either. You have four basic options for middle-grade language studies.

(1) Use a tutor. If you live near a university, you can call the classics or foreign-language departments and ask the department secretaries to recommend a responsible student tutor.[2] Even if the school doesn't offer Latin classes, several foreign-language majors are bound to have had three or four years of high school Latin. Or one of your local high schools may have a Latin teacher or responsible senior student who would enjoy tutoring. Using a tutor has drawbacks—cost, getting the student to her lesson—as well as advantages: you don't have to keep up with one more subject, and the student gets a break from your teaching style.

(2) Use an online tutorial service. Escondido Tutorial Service maintains a link page for Latin tutorials (www.gbt.org/tut/html); Memoria Press offers online Latin courses (www.memoriapress.com/onlineschool), as does The Potter's School (pottersschool.org).

(3) Use a self-teaching course. This is probably your best at-home option for French, Spanish, or German. The courses we recommend in the Resources

[2]See Chapter 43 for caveats about student tutors and advice on finding a reliable one.

are designed for self-teaching and include pronunciation tapes and conversational practice as well as grammatical instruction and reading drills.

(4) Learn along with your child. If your middle-school student can master this material, so can you.

WHICH LANGUAGES?

We recommend continuing with Latin until the student has mastered a standard (high-school level) second-year Latin course. At that point, the student who's interested in Greek can switch; the student who's not interested at all can quit. Other students should continue on to the reading of actual Latin texts.

Unless you have a personal reason for choosing another language, we suggest Spanish as the first modern language. A good first experience with modern-language learning is important. Since Spanish is full of Latinate vocabulary and structures, the student who has already studied Latin won't struggle. And Spanish is rapidly becoming the unofficial second language of the United States. The beginning Spanish student can easily find Spanish signs, directions, instruction manuals, children's books, Yellow Pages, and more to exercise her growing skills. And she'll have more opportunity to converse in Spanish than in other languages.

If you do choose another language, try to stick with a Romance language—French or Italian. Romance languages are Latin-influenced and easier for the Latin student to understand. Unless your relatives speak Japanese, Chinese, Polish, Russian, and so forth, you're better off saving these languages for high school.

WHICH TEXTS?

The Latin program you choose for the logic-stage years will depend in part on what you decided to use in the grammar stage. If you chose to work through *Prima Latina* or *The Big Book of Lively Latin*, progress on to *Latina Christiana I* and *II*. After completing this sequence, the student can continue on to a standard high-school Latin text—*First Year Latin* by Robert J. Henle, S.J. This text can be completed in two years, or stretched out over a longer period of time; it is a high-school text that provides readings and is used along with a grammar handbook. Memoria Press publishes a curriculum guide to go along with this text; the *Henle Latin Study Guide and Lesson Plan for Units I and II,* designed to help home schoolers get started on higher-level Latin, covers the first one hundred pages of *First Year Latin* and is designed for one year of study. (The authors suggest that you take two or three years to complete *First Year Latin* if you begin it in middle school.) There's also an online support group for Henle users, which you can join by sending an e-mail to HenleLatin-subscribe@yahoogroups.com.[3]

If you are getting ready to begin Latin in fifth or sixth grade, start directly into *Latina Christiana I* and progress on through *Latina Christiana II* and Henle's *First Year Latin.*

If you begin Latin in seventh grade or later, *Latina Christiana* will seem too elementary. Instead, we recommend that you choose *The Latin Road to English Grammar,* a program designed for parents and students who know no Latin. This text makes no assumption about skills and also reviews English grammar. (The curriculum guide claims that you don't have to study English grammar while using the program. We think this is a mistake; the *Latin Road* is an excellent Latin program, but doesn't cover the grammar needed to develop excellent English writing skills.) Start with *The Latin Road to English Grammar, Volume 1* in seventh grade and continue on with *Volume 2* in eighth grade.

Latin Options

Option 1: Following up on grammar stage study:

Third or fourth grade	*Prima Latina or The Big Book of Lively Latin*
Fourth or fifth grade	*Latina Christiana I*
Fifth or sixth grade	*Latina Christiana II*
Sixth or seventh grade	*First Year Latin,* first 100 pages or more (Units 1 and 2)
Seventh or eighth grade	*First Year Latin,* continue on

[3]The first edition of *The Well-Trained Mind* recommended the Canon Press *Latin Primer I, II,* and *III,* followed by Douglas Wilson's *Latin Grammar* and concluding with the high-school level *Wheelock's Latin.* This progression is still a good one, and these are good texts. However, they were originally designed for classrooms and are not the easiest programs for a parent who knows no Latin to use. The Memoria Press programs were developed with home-school parents in mind and are simpler to implement.

Eighth or ninth grade	Finish *First Year Latin* or begin *Second Year Latin*

Option 2: Beginning Latin study in fifth or sixth grade:

Fifth or sixth grade	*Latina Christiana I*
Sixth or seventh grade	*Latina Christiana II*
Seventh or eighth grade	*First Year Latin*
Eighth or ninth grade	*First Year Latin*

Option 3: Beginning Latin study in seventh or eighth grade:

Seventh or eighth grade	*The Latin Road to English Grammar, Volume One*
Eighth or ninth grade	*The Latin Road to English Grammar, Volume Two*

For modern languages, if you're using a tutor, the tutor will no doubt have his own favorite text. For self-teaching, you have a choice of several different resources.

(1) Popular among home schoolers, the Power-Glide courses give the student a role to play—an undercover agent dropped into a foreign country and desperate to communicate with the natives. The courses are in story format so that the student learns familiar phrases first and gradually begins both to speak the language and to translate it. We do wish that Power-Glide grammar were more rigorous, but the courses are conversation-oriented and designed to get the student speaking as quickly as possible. (You can always study the grammar in a more traditional format in high school.) Power-Glide courses are available in Spanish, French, German, Russian, and Japanese. Each course is the equivalent of a two-year language course.

(2) Rosetta Stone is an interactive computer-based language-learning program that uses photos and graphics to encourage the student to think in a foreign language. The program is expensive, but attractive and self-directed; it offers the closest approximation to conversation that you can get without a tutor. The Homeschool Editions offer a computerized "Student Management System" to help the parent and student track progress. Choose from twenty-four languages—not only Spanish, French, and German, but also Dutch, Danish, Portuguese, Russian, Polish, Arabic,

Chinese, Japanese, and many more. See the Rosetta Stone website (www.RosettaStone.com) for a complete list. Each level appears to be the equivalent of one high-school language year; middle-school students will probably need two years to complete each level.

WHEN DO I DO IT?

Ideally, you could study both Latin and a modern foreign language every year, each for three to four hours per week (option 1—see page 420). We realize, though, that a six- to eight-hour commitment per week to foreign-language studies may not be possible.

Instead, you might want to study both languages—for example, Spanish and Latin—but progress more slowly through each (option 2—see pages 420–421). Study Spanish on Mondays and Tuesdays, Latin on Wednesdays and Thursdays; take two years to go through each Latin book and four years to complete an entire Power-Glide or Rosetta Stone course. (If you're using a language tutor, explain that you only want to go at half speed.) You'll probably find that you don't need the full four years to finish the modern-language courses.

If the student finds two languages overwhelming, you can choose option 3: studying only one language each year, alternating your study (see page 421). To do this, begin your modern-language studies in fifth grade; continue with Latin in sixth grade; go back to your modern-language studies in seventh grade; then do Latin again in eighth grade. This works best if you're studying a Romance language (Spanish, French, or Italian) because the similarities between these languages and Latin will prevent the student from forgetting too much during the "year off." Whatever language you choose, be sure to schedule regular review sessions (every two weeks is good; once a month is minimum) for the student to read over the previous year's lessons. If you're studying Spanish in fifth grade, for example, stop every other Friday and review Latin vocabulary and grammar from the fourth-grade Latin book. If you're studying Latin in sixth grade, use every other Friday to listen to the Spanish tapes and/or read through Spanish lessons from the fifth-grade year.

Language skills tend to disappear if they're not constantly used. Don't simply stop Latin for grades 5 and 6 so that you can study a modern language and then try to pick up Latin again in grade 7. The effects of early exposure will fade almost completely.

And don't wait until seventh grade (when the first basic Latin course ends) to introduce the first modern language. Fifth graders can still pick up conversational skills with ease. By seventh grade, the skills are much harder to acquire.

SCHEDULES

Below are the schedules for each of the three options mentioned above.

Option 1: Schedule for Learning Two Languages Quickly

Fifth grade	Modern language	1 hour per day, three to four days per week
	Latina Christiana I	1 hour per day, three to four days per week
Sixth grade	Modern language	1 hour per day, three to four days per week
	Latina Christiana II	1 hour per day, three to four days per week
Seventh grade	Modern language	1 hour per day, three to four days per week
	First Year Latin	1 hour per day, three to four days per week
Eighth grade	Modern language	1 hour per day, three to four days per week
	First Year Latin	1 hour per day, three to four days per week

Option 2: Schedule for Learning Two Languages More Slowly

Fifth grade	Modern language	1 hour per day, two days per week
	Latina Christiana I	1 hour per day, two days per week

Sixth grade	Modern language	1 hour per day, two days per week
	Latina Christiana I	1 hour per day, two days per week
Seventh grade	Modern language	1 hour per day, two days per week
	Latina Christiana II	1 hour per day, two days per week
Eighth grade	Modern language	1 hour per day, two days per week
	Latina Christiana II	1 hour per day, two days per week

Begin Latin I in ninth grade

Option 3: Schedule for Learning Two Languages One at a Time

Fifth grade	Modern language	1 hour per day, three to four days per week; every other week, use the fourth hour to review Latin previously studied
Sixth grade	*Latin Road, Volume 1*	1 hour per day, three to four days per week; every other week, use the fourth hour to review modern-language vocabulary and conversation
Seventh grade	Modern language	1 hour per day, three to four days per week; every other week, use the fourth hour to review *Latin Road, Volume 1* material
Eighth grade	*Latin Road, Volume 2*	1 hour per day, three to four days per week; every other week, use the fourth hour to review modern-language vocabulary and conversation

RESOURCES

For publisher and catalog addresses, telephone numbers, and other information, see Sources (pages 751–778). Latin resources are given first, with modern foreign languages following. Books in a series are listed in order.

Latin

Basic

Beers, Barbara. *The Latin Road to English Grammar, Volume I.* Redding, Calif.: Schola Publications, 1997.

$149.00. Order from Schola Publications, along with all supplementary material.

Teacher Training Videos. Extra parent support for the truly intimidated. $89.00 for DVD. Combination packages are offered at a discount.

———. *The Latin Road to English Grammar, Volume II.* Redding, Calif.: Schola Publications, 1997.

$149.00. Order from Schola Publications, along with all supplementary material.

Teacher Training Videos. Extra parent support for the truly intimidated. $89.00 for DVD. Combination packages are offered at a discount.

Henle, Robert J., S.J. *First Year Latin.* Chicago, Ill.: Loyola Press, 1958.

$16.95 ($18.95 for text plus necessary answer key). Order all resources from Memoria Press (where *First Year Latin* is listed as "Henle I Text & Key"). This text, along with Henle Grammar, serves as the basic text for two years of study: the first year covers Units 1–2, and the second covers Units 3–5.

Henle Latin Study Guide. $14.95. Highly recommended for successful study.

———. *Latin Grammar.* Chicago, Ill.: Loyola Press, 1980.

$9.50. Order from Memoria Press. Necessary to accompany both *First Year Latin* and *Second Year Latin.*

———. *Second Year Latin.* Chicago, Ill.: Loyola Press, 1997.

$15.95 ($17.95 for text plus necessary key). Order from Memoria Press, where it is listed as "Henle II Text with key." Most students will not progress this far during middle school.

Lowe, Cheryl. *Latina Christiana I: An Introduction to Christian Latin.* Louisville, Ky.: Memoria Press, 2001.

$39.95 for the set. Order from Memoria Press.

Student Book. $15.00.

Teacher Manual. $20.00.

Pronunciation CD or Tape. $4.95.

———. *Latina Christiana II. An Introduction to Christian Latin.* Louisville, Ky.: Memoria Press, 2001.

$39.95 for the set. Order from Memoria Press.

Student Book. $15.00.

Teacher Manual. $20.00.

Pronunciation CD or Tape. $4.95.

Latina Christiana Flashcards. Louisville, Ky.: Memoria Press.

$14.95. Order from Memoria Press. Includes the vocabulary for *Latina Christiana.*

Latina Christiana I/Prima Latina Flashcards

Latina Christiana II Flashcards

Supplementary Resources

Lundquist, Joegil. *English from the Roots Up.* Seattle, Wash.: Cune Press, 1996.

$29.95. Order from any bookstore. A vocabulary-building book built around 100 Greek and Latin root words. Each page gives the original definition of the root along with 510 related English words that incorporate the root word. Use this along with Latin to develop English vocabulary (and to teach your student why Latin is important).

———. *Word Cards for English from the Roots Up.* Seattle, Wash.: Cune Press, 1996.

$18.00. Order from Rainbow Resource Center. One hundred already-prepared cards with root words on one side and English definitions on the other.

Schlosser, Franz. *Latine Cantemus: Cantica Popularia Latine Reddita.* Waucona, Ill.: Bolchazy-Carducci Publishers, 1996.

$21.00. Order from Bolchazy-Carducci. A songbook with nursery rhymes, familiar folk songs, and Christmas carols, all translated into Latin; a good way to begin to develop fluency.

Seuss, Dr., Jennifer Morrish Tunberg, and Terence O. Tunberg. *Cattus Petasatus: The Cat in the Hat in Latin.* Waucona, Ill.: Bolchazy-Carducci Publishers, 2003.

$22.95. Order from Bolchazy-Carducci.

———. *Quomodo Invidiosulus Nomine Grinchus: How the Grinch Stole Christmas in Latin.* Waucona, Ill.: Bolchazy-Carducci Publishers, 1998.

$22.95. Order from Bolchazy-Carducci.

———. *Virent Ova! Viret Perna! Green Eggs and Ham in Latin.* Waucona, Ill.: Bolchazy-Carducci Publishers, 2003.

$26.75. Order from Bolchazy-Carducci.

Modern Languages

Power-Glide Language Courses. Provo, Utah: Power-Glide.

Order from Power-Glide. The following courses cost $149.95 each and include all materials for two years of study: workbook, nine audio CDs, a CD-ROM, and a language guide.

Spanish Ultimate Course.
French Ultimate Course.
German Ultimate Course.
Japanese Ultimate Course.
Russian Ultimate Course.

Rosetta Stone Language Learning: Homeschool Edition. Harrisonburg, Va.

$359.00 for complete sets: Level 1 and 2 (probably four to five years of study for a younger student; the program estimates that it offers 800 hours of instruction). Order from Rosetta Stone. An interactive computer-based language-learning program that uses photos and graphics to encourage the student to think in a foreign language. Each Homeschool Edition Level 1 includes a program for keeping track of the student's progress. Many other languages are available at the Rosetta Stone website, www.RosettaStone.com.

Spanish Level I & II Set.

French Level 1& II Set.

German Level I & II Set.

Arabic Level I & II Set.

Japanese Level I & II Set.

Korean Level I & II Set.

Russian Level I & II Set.

Welsh Level I & II Set.

20

AWAY WITH ABUSIVE FALLACIES! RELIGION

Homo sine religione sic ut equus sine freno.[1]
—Medieval saying

In history, your middle-grade student will continually ask why. Why was that war fought? Why did this statesman make this decision? Why did the Crusades dominate the religious life of medieval Europe?

These questions cannot be answered unless you take the role of religion in public life seriously. People of faith have influenced history at every turn. Until the student is willing to examine honestly and soberly the claims of religion in the history of mankind, his study will be incomplete.

In the effort to offend none, the public schools have managed to offend practically everyone—either by leaving religion and ethics out of curricula altogether or by teaching them in a way that satisfies neither believers nor skeptics. In sympathy, we'll say that the public schools are in an impossible situation. They are legally bound to avoid the appearance of promoting one

[1]"Man without religion is like a horse without a bridle."

religion over another. And in a mixed classroom, how can you take one religion seriously without antagonizing those who don't share it? The inevitable result is summed up by a character in P. D. James's mystery *Original Sin:*

> "There were a dozen different religions among the children at Ancroft Comprehensive. We seemed always to be celebrating some kind of feast or ceremony. Usually it required making a noise and dressing up. The official line was that all religions were equally important. I must say that the result was to leave me with the conviction that they were equally unimportant."[2]

When you're instructing your own child, you have two tasks with regard to religion: to teach your own convictions with honesty and diligence, and to study the ways in which other faiths have changed the human landscape.

Only you and your religious community can do the first. As for the second, in high school the student will make a formal study of ethics. For middle school, we suggest you simply keep the following guidelines in mind as you do your history, science, and literature.

(1) Include religious works in your study of primary sources. As you progress through history, stop and read the Old and New Testaments; they are foundational to Western thought and ought to be treated as serious philosophical documents.

(2) Read about major faiths that have shaped our world: Judaism, Buddhism, Christianity, Islam. Compare them. Ask the most basic questions about them: What do these religions say about the nature of man? the nature of God? the purpose of living?

(3) As you choose biographies for history reading, try to seek out works about those who have changed people's minds and ways of living—not only religious figures such as Confucius and Mohammed, but the theologians and prophets who followed them: Augustine, Anselm, Ibn Ezra, Francis of Assisi, Ignatius of Loyola, Martin Luther (just to name a few).

(4) Watch out for logical fallacies. When writers start talking about religion—especially in books for young children—fallacies abound. Keep your eyes open for the three most common errors: chronological snobbery, which

[2]P. D. James, *Original Sin* (New York: Warner, 1994), p. 303.

assumes that people long ago were more stupid than people today ("the Virgin Birth was accepted by theologians of the Middle Ages, but no modern scholar can seriously believe in it"); the black-and-white fallacy, which assumes that there can be no alternatives between extreme positions ("the Catholic Church tried Galileo for heresy because he said the earth wasn't at the center of the universe; therefore the churchmen involved were either blind to the truth, or else hypocritically protecting their own power");[3] and the poisoning-the-well fallacy, which discredits an argument by attacking its source rather than its content ("that legislator is a religious man, so his opinions are obviously biased by his religious beliefs").

(5) Don't ignore the deep religious faith held by many of the West's greatest scientists. The theism of scientists and mathematicians, from Pascal to Einstein, deeply affected their professional and intellectual pursuits.

(6) Finally, discuss the moral and ethical questions of history with your middle-grade student. Don't shy away from the errors made by religious men and women (every faith has mounted its own version of Holy War at some point), but don't identify the mistakes of religious figures with the requirements of faith itself.

You might start by reading together and discussing stories that bring the rewards and costs of ethical behavior to the forefront. *Tending the Heart of Virtue: How Classic Stories Awaken a Child's Moral Imagination* and *Books That Build Character: A Guide to Teaching Your Child Moral Values through Stories* are two useful starting places. Choose an evening once a week to read and talk—as a family—about ethical issues that come up. This will serve as great preparation for the formal study of ethics in high school.

We've also listed a beginning introduction to world religions, *A World of Faith.* This book outlines the beliefs of twenty-eight religious groups. Keep it on hand as a reference while you work through world history.

RESOURCES

These books are easily available through local bookstores, libraries, or online booksellers.

[3]The alternative is that the churchmen were honestly trying to work out a theological picture of the universe that made proper reference to scientific discovery—something they eventually did manage to do.

The Church History TimeLine. Camino, Calif.: Brimwood Press. $27.00. Order from Brimwood Press. Six-foot wall timeline to accompany your regular history timeline; shows the branching off of the Christian church into its multiple denominations as history progresses.

Guroian, Vigen. *Tending the Heart of Virtue: How Classic Stories Awaken a Child's Moral Imagination.* New York: Oxford University Press, 2002.

Kilpatrick, William. *Books That Build Character: A Guide to Teaching Your Child Moral Values through Stories.* New York: Touchstone, 1994.

Stack, Peggy Fletcher, and Kathleen Peterson. *A World of Faith.* Salt Lake City, Utah: Signature Books, 2001.

21

THE HISTORY OF CREATIVITY: ART AND MUSIC

> Music creates order out of chaos; for rhythm imposes unanimity upon the divergent, melody imposes continuity upon the disjointed, and harmony imposes compatibility upon the incongruous.
>
> —Yehudi Menuhin

SUBJECT: Art and music
TIME REQUIRED: 1 to 2 hours, once per week per subject

The classical education is distinguished by its emphasis on fine arts—not necessarily performance (although classical education has traditionally included drawing as a foundational skill), but certainly appreciation and participation.

You started this process in the grammar stage. The young child studied art by looking at it and music by listening to it.

Now, as the student's mind matures, you'll tie this appreciation more closely to history. She'll study artists and musicians when she encounters them in her history readings; she'll enter birth and death dates and the dates of great artistic achievements on the time line.

As with other subjects, art and music will be subjected to analysis during the logic stage. Your middle-grade student will learn about the basic structure of musical pieces, the differences among the instruments of the orchestra, the way paints and other artistic media are used, and the different art movements and their practitioners.

Plan on keeping the same schedule you used during the elementary years. Reserve a one- to two-hour period once a week for music study; reserve the same amount of time on another day for art. In Chapter 12, we suggested the option of scheduling only one period per week and alternating the study of art and music. Now we strongly encourage you to make time for both subjects per week. Remember, much of this work can be done independently by the student. Your job is to supervise and provide resources.

The study of art and music is a good late-afternoon or early-evening project. You might schedule art appreciation for Mondays from 3:30 to 5:00 and music appreciation for Thursdays from 3:30 to 5:00. Or make it an after-dinner assignment, to be completed between 7:00 and 8:30 two evenings per week.

ART

The study of art is twofold: practicing the actual skills of art (drawing, painting, modeling), and learning to understand and appreciate the works of great artists.

You should alternate art skills and art appreciation. During the first week, spend one to one and a half hours on art projects; during the second week, use the time to study paintings and artists.

Art Skills

Art skills fall into three basic categories—drawing, painting, and modeling. During the logic stage, try to spend some time in each category. You can divide each year into three sections (if you're doing art lessons every other week, you'll have approximately eighteen lessons; you'll be able to divide the lessons into six drawing lessons, six painting lessons, and six modeling lessons). Or spend a year on each skill, allowing the child to return in the fourth year to her favorite one. Always begin with drawing, progress to painting, and finish up with modeling.

Your goal isn't to turn out a polished artist. You just want to introduce the child to the basic techniques and possibilities of art. With any luck, her interest will be sparked, and she'll continue working on her own time. But even if this doesn't happen, she'll have gained valuable and increasingly rare skills in a basic human activity.

In Resources, we supply ideas for drawing, painting, and modeling projects. For basic texts, we recommend the following.

Drawing

The *Artistic Pursuits* curriculum suggested for elementary art continues on into middle school, with two books designed for use in grades 4–6, and two more intended for grades 7–8. All four are focused on color and composition, and continue to teach art appreciation and art skills simultaneously.

Another option: you can use the classic *Drawing on the Right Side of the Brain* and its accompanying workbook, both by Betty Edwards. This book teaches logical drawing skills, perfect for the middle-grade student. Work progressively through the lessons in the time that you've scheduled. When you've finished, you can move on to any of the drawing projects (colored pencil, calligraphy, portrait drawing, and so forth) listed at the end of the chapter.

Painting

Start painting with watercolors, which are readily available and easy to clean up. Beginning watercolor books abound. (You can also find instructional videotapes at your library.) A favorite among home schoolers is *Watercolor for the Artistically Undiscovered,* written by children's book illustrator Thacher Hurd with John Cassidy. The book includes the how-to text, forty-eight pages of Italian watercolor paper, a professional-quality six-color box, and a number 5 brush. All you need is water. This will introduce you to all the basics.

Modeling

Fine Art Studio Sculpting, by sculptor Kenneth Watson, introduces the student to basic modeling techniques and also provides tools, clay, instructions, and step-by-step projects.

Art Appreciation

Let your study of history guide your study of art. Whenever the student comes across the name of a great artist during her history readings, she should jot it down. During art-appreciation sessions, she'll follow a four-step process. She will

1. read about the artists she's encountered in history during the previous two weeks,
2. enter the birth and death dates of each artist on the history time line,
3. prepare a brief biographical sketch for each artist and file it in the history notebook under Great Men and Women,
4. spend some time looking at, reading about, and coloring the work of the artists under study.

During this time, the student can use either art books that treat a single artist (such as the Famous Artist Series titles *Michelangelo* or *Cézanne*) or books that cover an entire school (such as the Masters of Art series, which includes *The Impressionists: The Origin of Modern Painting* and *Rembrandt and Seventeenth-Century Holland*). There's no need for the student to write about what she's learning, but she should enter on her time line the dates of famous works of art (the completion of the Sistine Chapel ceiling or the year the *Mona Lisa* was finished). You can be flexible about art appreciation. If the student wants to spend some time learning more about a particular school of painting, don't insist that she read biographies instead.

At the end of this chapter, we've listed a number of art books for young people that include both interesting text and full-color reproductions of paintings. Use them alongside your other historical resources when you study history.

Because artists often go unmentioned in history texts, a reference list follows below. This isn't meant to be exhaustive, merely to provide you with a basic "skeleton" for your study of art history.

Gustave Doré (1832–1883)
Albrecht Dürer (1471–1528)
Tintoretto (1518–1594)
Rembrandt van Rijn (1606–1669)

Jean Francois Millet (1814–1874)
Carl Bloch (1834–1890)
Georges Rouault (1871–1958)
Giorgio Vasari (1511–1574)
John Ruskin (1819–1900)
Giovanni Cimabue (1240–1301)
Giotto di Bondone (1266–1337)
Michelangelo Buonarroti (1475–1564)
Raphael (1483–1520)
Titian (1477–1576)
Peter Brueghel (1525–1569)
Jan Vermeer (1632–1675)
Hierononymus Bosch (1450–1516)
Peter Paul Rubens (1577–1640)
Gerrit Dou (1613–1675)
Antoine Watteau (1684–1721)
Jean Honoré Fragonard (1732–1806)
Jacques-Louis David (1748–1825)
Jean-Auguste-Dominique Ingres (1780–1867)
Honoré Daumier (1808–1879)
Joshua Reynolds (1723–1792)
William Hogarth (1697–1764)
William Blake (1757–1827)
George Stubbs (1724–1806)
John Constable (1776–1837)
Joseph Mallord William Turner (1775–1851)
Claude Monet (1840–1926)
Edgar Degas (1834–1917)
Pierre Auguste Renoir (1841–1919)
Vincent Van Gogh (1853–1890)
Henri Fantin-Latour (1836–1904)
Paul Cézanne (1839–1906)
Benjamin West (1732–1820)
Gilbert Stuart (1755–1828)
John James Audubon (1785–1851)
James Abbott McNeill Whistler (1834–1903)
John Singer Sargent (1856–1925)

Winslow Homer (1836–1910)
Edward Hopper (1882–1967)
Grant Wood (1892–1942)
Frederic Remington (1861–1909)
Charles Marion Russell (1864–1926)
Norman Rockwell (1894–1978)
Edvard Munch (1863–1944)
Emil Nolde (1867–1956)
Kathe Kollwitz (1867–1945)
Henri Matisse (1869–1954)
Raoul Dufy (1877–1953)
André Derain (1880–1954)

MUSIC

Music Skills

If time and your budget make it possible—and if the child shows an interest—private music lessons are great. We think that every student should have two years of piano lessons early in her academic career. After two years, she can quit, switch to another instrument, or keep going. Consult friends and your local newspaper to find private music teachers; if you live near a university or community college, you can call the music department for recommendations.

Jessie adds—from years of experience with kids and music lessons—that forcing a reluctant child to keep taking lessons for more than two years is pointless. If interest hasn't developed after two years of study, let the student change instruments or turn her attention to other things.

Music Appreciation

Whether or not the student is taking music lessons, she should spend one and a half to two hours every week doing music appreciation. This time should involve the study of composers' lives, as well as an introduction to musical instruments and musical forms.

Reading about the lives of composers (and musicians) should be part of the study of history. Composers tend to get shorted in history texts, so we've supplied a reference list below. Make an effort to read biographies of these musical greats at the appropriate point in your chronological history study. (This is not intended to be an exhaustive list, merely a guide; nor do you have to read about everyone on it. Pick and choose.) Specific titles and series are suggested at the end of this chapter, but your library will yield others; look in the Junior Biography section, or ask your librarian for help. If you can't find a biography, at least look the musician up in an encyclopedia and make a brief time-line entry.

John Dunstable (1390–1453)
Guillaume Dufe (1400–1474)
Thomas Tallis (1505–1585)
Giovanni Palestrina (1525–1594)
Michael Praetorius (1571–1621)
Henry Purcell (1659–1695)
Johann Sebastian Bach (1685–1750)
Domenico Scarlatti (1685–1757)
George Frederic Handel (1685–1759)
Antonio Vivaldi (1678–1741)
George Philipp Telemann (1681–1767)
Franz Joseph Hadyn (1732–1809)
Wolfgang Amadeus Mozart (1756–1791)
Ludwig van Beethoven (1770–1827)
Nicolo Paganini (1782–1840)
Antonio Rossini (1792–1868)
Franz Schubert (1797–1828)
Hector Berlioz (1803–1869)
Felix Mendelssohn (1809–1847)
Frederic Chopin (1810–1849)
Robert Schumann (1810–1856)
Franz Liszt (1811–1886)
Richard Wagner (1813–1883)
Guiseppe Verdi (1813–1910)
Anton Bruckner (1824–1896)
Johannes Brahms (1833–1897)
George Bizet (1838–1875)

Piotr Ilyitch Tchaikovsky (1840–1893)
Antonin Dvořák (1841–1904)
Arthur Sullivan (1842–1900)
Edvard Grieg (1843–1907)
Edward William Elgar (1857–1934)
Giacomo Puccini (1858–1924)
Gustav Mahler (1860–1911)
Claude Debussy (1862–1918)
Richard Strauss (1864–1949)
Jean Sibelius (1865–1957)
Ralph Vaughan Williams (1872–1958)
Sergei Vasilievich Rachmaninoff (1873–1943)
Gustav Holst (1874–1934)
Arnold Schoenberg (1874–1951)
Maurice Ravel (1875–1937)
Respighi (1879–1936)
Igor Stravinsky (1882–1971)
Sergei Prokofiev (1891–1953)
Dimitri Shostakovich (1906–1975)
Samuel Barber (1910–1981)
Gian Carlo Menotti (1911–)
John Cage (1912–1992)
Benjamin Britten (1913–1976)
Leonard Bernstein (1918–1990)
Kenneth Leighton (1929–1988)

Because the study of composers' lives will take place mostly in the third and fourth years of history (from 1600 on), plan on spending fifth and sixth grade concentrating on musical instruments and musical forms.

In these years, the student will use *The Young Person's Guide to the Orchestra,* a book-CD set that offers double-page spreads describing the different sections of the orchestra. The accompanying CD offers Benjamin Britten's 1945 composition "The Young Person's Guide to the Orchestra" (variations on a theme by Purcell, written specifically to serve as a guide to the orchestra's instruments), along with narration by Ben Kingsley; each section of the orchestra plays individually and then joins in the finale. During each music-appreciation period, the student should read a double-page spread, and listen to the appropriate track on the CD. Writing about music is difficult, and there's no need for the beginning listener to write a summary unless she wants to.

After this, the student should progress to another engaging orchestra book: *The Story of the Incredible Orchestra: An Introduction to Musical Instruments and the Symphony Orchestra.* This book doesn't have an accompanying CD, but it does pay much more attention to the orchestra's development through history. Now that the student is familiar with the orchestra's sound, she should read through this book at a comfortable pace (it's very easy reading), putting any dates on the time line.

Beginning in sixth grade, the student can also begin to listen to music from the periods studied in history: medieval and early Renaissance music (sixth grade), music of the late Renaissance, Baroque, and Classical periods (seventh grade), and music of the Romantic and modern periods (eighth grade). As in art appreciation, whenever the student encounters a great composer in her history reading, she should jot down the name. During music appreciation, she should record the birth and death dates on the time line, read a brief biography, and spend the rest of her music-appreciation period listening to the composer's works. (Again, plan on making use of your library's collection.)

Although you should generally try to keep music appreciation in step with history reading, don't worry if you get a little behind or ahead. When the student encounters a major musical figure—J. S. Bach, Handel, Mozart, Schubert—on the music time line, she can spend several weeks on each figure, even as she's going forward with her history reading.

SCHEDULES

Sample Schedules

Fifth grade	Mondays, 1–2 hrs.	Alternate art projects with studying ancient art.
	Thursdays, 1–2 hrs.	Study the orchestra and its instruments.
Sixth grade	Mondays, 1–2 hrs.	Alternate art projects with making biographical pages and studying the works of

		medieval and early Renaissance artists; enter dates on time line.
	Thursdays, 1–2 hrs.	Listen to medieval and early Renaissance music; make biographical pages for musicians; enter dates on time line.
Seventh grade	Mondays, 1–2 hrs.	Alternate art projects with making biographical pages and studying the works of artists from the late Renaissance through the early modern periods; enter dates on time line.
	Thursdays, 1–2 hrs.	Listen to late Renaissance, Baroque, and Classical music; make biographical pages for musicians; enter dates on time line.
Eighth grade	Mondays, 1–2 hrs.	Alternate art projects with making biographical pages and studying the works of modern artists; enter dates on time line.
	Thursdays, 1–2 hrs.	Listen to Romantic and modern music, including musical theater and light opera; make biographical pages for musicians; enter dates on time line.

RESOURCES

For publisher and catalog addresses, telephone numbers, and other information, see Sources (pages 751–778). Most books and tapes or CDs can be obtained from any bookstore or library; where we know of a mail-order option, we have provided it.

These resources are divided into three lists: art skills, art appreciation, and music appreciation (at this stage, music skills should be studied with a professional teacher). For each list, we have given basic texts first, followed by supplementary resources (you can pick and choose among these). You can also use many of the resources listed in Chapter 12.

Art Skills

Basic Texts

Edwards, Betty. *The New Drawing on the Right Side of the Brain: A Course in Enhancing Creativity and Artistic Confidence,* rev. and expanded. New York: Tarcher, 1999.
$16.95. Easily available at bookstores or through online booksellers.

———. *New Drawing on the Right Side of the Brain Workbook: Guided Practice in the Five Basic Skills of Drawing.* New York: Tarcher, 2002.
$17.95. Order from any bookstore.

Hurd, Thacher, and John Cassidy. *Klutz Art Book: Watercolor for the Artistically Undiscovered.* Palo Alto, Calif.: Klutz Press, 1992.
$19.95. Order through a bookstore or online bookseller.

Sculpey, Elk Grove Village, Ill.: Polyform Products.
$11.65 for a 1.75-pound pack, $49.99 for an 8-pound pack. Order from Rainbow Resource Center. Sculpey is an easy-to-work clay that fires in a regular oven in twenty minutes without shrinking. Rainbow also sells Sculpey Glaze, in either matte finish or glossy finish, for $3.49 per bottle.

Watson, Kenneth Greg. *Fine Art Studio Sculpting Box Set.* San Diego, Calif.: Silver Dolphin Books, 2005.
$18.95. Order from any bookstore.

Supplementary Resources

Draw Today kits. Laguna Hills, Calif.: Walter Foster Publishing.
Order from Walter Foster directly. The kits offer step-by-step instruction in classical drawing technique. Each kit includes all supplies. Creator Walter Foster includes a toll-free 800 number to call if you have specific questions.

Foster, Walter. *The Cartoon Animation Kit.* 1996. $24.95.

———. *The Oil Painting Kit.* 1998. $19.95.

Foster, Walter, et al. *The Calligraphy Kit.* 1995. $14.95.

Franks, Gene. *The Pencil Drawing Kit.* 1995. $19.95.

Light, Duane R., et al. *Watercolor.* 1995. $19.95.

Iverson, Mary. *Fine Art Studio Painting.* San Diego, Calif.: Silver Dolphin Books, 2005.

$18.95. Order from any bookstore. A beginner's foray into acrylic paints; includes paints, tools, and careful directions.

Smith, Alastair, et al. *The Complete Book of Drawing.* Tulsa, Okla.: E.D.C. Publications, 2002.

$17.99. Buy from an Usborne dealer or through an online bookstore. This is a complete guide to drawing and painting—everything from portraits to cartoons.

Art Appreciation

Basic Texts

Hodge, Susie. *Ancient Egyptian Art,* 2d ed. (Art in History). Chicago, Ill.: Heinemann Library, 2006.

$7.99 each. This series offers a good introduction to the appreciation of ancient art.

———. *Ancient Egyptian Art.*

———. *Ancient Greek Art.*

———. *Ancient Roman Art.*

———. *Prehistoric Art.*

Martin, Mary, and Steve Zorn. *Start Exploring Masterpieces: A Fact-Filled Coloring Book.* Philadelphia, Pa.: Running Press, 2001.

$9.95. Sixty famous paintings, done in detail for you to color. The book includes the story behind each painting. A great way to learn about particular works. The work is best done with good-quality colored pencils.

Peppin, Anthea, and Joseph McEwan. *The Usborne Story of Painting: Cave Painting to Modern Art.* Tulsa, Okla.: E.D.C. Publications, 1980.

$7.95. Order from Rainbow Resource Center. An introduction to painting styles, techniques, and personalities. A good general guide with lots of color reproductions.

Wilkins, David G. *The Collins Big Book of Art: From Cave Art to Pop Art.* New York: Collins Design, 2005.

$39.95. Order from any bookstore. An excellent family reference book: a chronological survey of masterpieces from around the world, with explanations of major movements, styles, and themes. The text may be too difficult for some middle-grade students, but all can benefit from the photographs.

Supplementary Resources

The Famous Artists series. New York: Scholastic, 1994.

$6.95 for each. Order from Greenleaf Press. These provide a neat 32-page introduction to each artist, his life, and his major works. Color reproductions.

Green, Jen, et al. *Michelangelo.*
Hughes, Andrew S. *Van Gogh.*
Mason, Anthony, et al. *Cézanne.*
———. *Leonardo da Vinci.*

The Great Names biography series. Broomball, Pa.: Mason Crest Publishers.

$19.95 each. Try your library for this series, which is written on a higher level than the Getting to Know series listed below.

Bowen, Richard. *Van Gogh.* 2002.
Cook, Diane. *Henri Toulouse-Lautrec.* 2003.
———. *Michelangelo: Renaissance Artist.* 2002.
———. *Paul Gauguin.* 2003.
January, Brendan. *Da Vinci: Renaissance Painter.* 2002.

Krull, Kathleen. *Lives of the Artists: Masterpieces, Messes (and What the Neighbors Thought).* Illus. Kathryn Hewitt. New York: Harcourt, 1995.

$20.00. A fun biography resource full of interesting (and obscure) snippets. (You may want to pre-read, since the lives of some of these artists were, to say the least, colorful.)

Stevenson, Neil. *Architecture Explained,* rev. ed. New York: Dorling Kindersley, 2007.

$15.00. Order from any bookstore. Well-photographed guide to architecture styles from ancient Egypt through the present day.

Strickland, Carol. *The Illustrated Timeline of Art History: A Crash Course in Words & Pictures.* New York: Sterling, 2006.

$12.95. Order from any bookstore. Beautifully illustrated timeline of painting, sculpture, and architecture, from cave paintings all the way up to the present.

Taschen Basic Art series. Los Angeles, Calif.: Taschen.

$9.99 each. Order from any bookstore. This series of 96-page books provides full-page annotated illustrations, guiding readers into an understanding of specific artists and their styles. More difficult than the Getting to Know series listed below.

Baur, Eva Gesine and Ingo F. Walther. *Rococo.* 2007.

Becks-Malorny, Ulrike. *James Ensor, 1860–1949: Masks, Death, and the Sea.* 2001.

———. *Paul Cezanne, 1839–1906: Pioneer of Modernism.* 2001.

Emmerling, Leonhard. *Jackson Pollock, 1912–1956.* 2003.

Hendrickson, Janis. *Roy Lichtenstein, 1923–1997.* 2001.

Hess, Barbara. *Lucio Fontana, 1899–1968.* 2006.

Holzhey, Magdalena. *Giorgio de Chiricio, 1888–1978: The Modern Myth.* 2005.

Kennedy, Ian G. *Titian, 1490–1576.*

Kettenmann, Andrea. *Diego Rivera, 1886–1957: A Revolutionary Spirit in Modern Art.* 2001.

Masanes, Fabrice. *Gustave Courbet, 1819–1877.* 2006.

Neret, Gilles. *Edouard Manet, 1832–1883: The First of the Moderns.* 2003.

———. *Henri Matisse.* 2006.

———. *Peter Paul Rubens, 1577–1640: The Homer of Painting.* 2004.

———. *Rubens.* 2004.

Neret, Gilles, and Gilles Lambert. *Caravaggio, 1571–1610.* 2000.

Scholz-Hansel, Michael. *El Greco, 1541–1614: Domenikos Theotokopoulos.* 2004.

Wolf, Norbert. *Giotto Di Bondone, 1267–1337.* 2006.

———. *Hans Holbein the Younger, 1497/98–1543: The German Raphael.* 2004.

———. *Albrecht Dürer.* 2006.

Venezia, Mike. Getting to Know the World's Greatest Artists series. Danbury, Conn.: Childrens Press.

$6.95 each. Order from any bookstore. Thirty-two-page biographies illustrated with masterpieces, on a simple reading level.

Andy Warhol. 1997.
Botticelli. 1991.
Da Vinci. 1989.
Diego Rivera. 1995.
Edgar Degas. 2001.
Frida Kahlo. 1999.
Georges Seurat. 2003.
Georgia O'Keeffe. 1994.
Giotto. 2000.
Henri Matisse. 1997.
Jackson Pollock. 1994.
Johannes Vermeer. 2002.
Marc Chagall. 2000.
Mary Cassatt. 1991.
Michelangelo. 2992.
Monet. 1990.
Paul Cezanne. 1998.
Paul Klee. 1991.
Picasso. 1988.
Pierre Auguste Renoir. 1996.
Raphael. 2001.
Rembrandt. 1988.
Rene Magritte. 2003.
Roy Lichtenstein. 2002.
Salvador Dali. 1993.
Van Gogh. 1989.

Music Appreciation

Basic Texts

Ganeri, Anita, and Benjamin Britten. *The Young Person's Guide to the Orchestra.* New York: Harcourt, 1996.

$25.00 for book and CD. Order from any bookstore.

Koscielniak, Bruce. *The Story of the Incredible Orchestra: An Introduction to Musical Instruments and the Symphony Orchestra.* Boston: Houghton Mifflin, 2000.

$6.95. Order from any bookstore.

Supplementary Resources

Brownell, David, and Nancy Conkle. *Great Composers I: Bach to Berlioz Coloring Book.* Santa Barbara, Calif.: Bellerophon Books, 1985.

$4.95. Order from Bellerophon. Portraits to color along with biographical sketches for fifteen composers including Bach, Handel, Beethoven, and Mozart.

Brownell, David. *Great Composers II: Chopin to Tchaikovsky Coloring Book.* Santa Barbara, Calif.: Bellerophon Books, 1991.

$4.95. Order from Bellerophon. Twenty-nine composers, including Schumann, Liszt, Wagner, Verdi, Brahms, and Grieg.

———. *Great Composers III: Mahler to Stravinsky Coloring Book.* Santa Barbara, Calif.: Bellerophon Books, 1993.

$4.95. Order from Bellerophon. Twenty-seven composers.

Ganeri, Anita, and Nicola Barber. *The Young Person's Guide to the Opera: Book and CD Set.* New York: Harcourt, 2001.

$25.00. For students who are interested in learning more about opera, this resource, structured like the Ganeri text listed above, covers the music and stagecraft of opera.

The Great Names biography series. Broomball, Pa.: Mason Crest Publishers.

$19.95 each. Try your library for this series, which is written on a higher level than the Getting to Know series listed below.

Carew-Miller, Anne. *Ludwig van Beethoven.* 2002.

Cook, Daien, and Victoria Fomina. *Mozart: World-Famous Composer.* 2002.

January, Brendan. *Louis Armstrong.* 2003.

Krull, Kathleen. *Lives of the Musicians: Good Times, Bad Times (and What the Neighbors Thought).* Illus. Kathryn Hewitt. New York: Harcourt, 2002.

$12.00. A fun biography resource full of interesting (and obscure) snippets.

The Music Masters series.

$2.98 for each CD. Order from Amazon.com. Each contains a narration of the composer's life, with significant events illustrated by selections from the works composed at that time and 18 to 20 minutes of unbroken music at the end. Good introduction to classical music.

The Story of Vivaldi and Corelli.
The Story of Bach.
The Story of Handel.
The Story of Haydn.
The Story of Mozart.
The Story of Beethoven.
The Story of Schubert.
The Story of Berlioz.
The Story of Mendelssohn.
The Story of Schumann and Grieg.
The Story of Chopin.
The Story of Verdi.
The Story of Wagner.
The Story of Strauss.
The Story of Foster and Sousa.
The Story of Brahms.
The Story of Tchaikovsky.
The Story of Dvořák.

O'Brien, Eileen. *The Usborne Story of Music.* Illus. David Cuzik, rev. ed. Tulsa, Okla.: Usborne Books, 2006.

$7.99. A colorful and interesting beginner's guide; good to have on hand for reference.

Tomb, Eric, and Nancy Conkle. *Early Composers Coloring Book.* Santa Barbara, Calif.: Bellerophon Books, 1988.

$3.95. Order from Bellerophon. The first in the Composers Coloring Books series. A detailed coloring book of composers' portraits from Palestrina through Corelli, with a biographical note for each. Also a good guide to early composers.

Venezia, Mike. Getting to Know the World's Greatest Composers series. Danbury, Conn.: Children's Press.

$6.95 each. Order from any bookstore. Thirty-two-page biographies with historical images, on a simple reading level.

Aaron Copland. 1995.
The Beatles. 1997.
Duke Ellington. 1996.
George Gershwin. 1995.
George Handel. 1995.
Igor Stravinsky. 1997.
Leonard Bernstein. 1998.
Ludwig van Beethoven. 1996.
Peter Tchaikovsky. 1995.
Wolfgang Amadeus Mozart. 1996.
Johann Sebastian Bach. 1998.
Johannes Brahms. 1999.
Frederic Chopin. 2000.
John Philip Sousa. 1999.

22

MAGIC BOXES: USING COMPUTERS AND VIDEOS

Computers should work. People should think.

—IBM slogan

All of the cautions we extended in Chapter 10 also apply to the middle-grade student. Software and videos are easier to use than books. They teach through images, not words; they encourage passive reception instead of active engagement. This is directly opposed to the goal of the logic stage. In grades 5 through 8, you're constantly teaching the student to analyze and make connections; software and (especially) videos tend to push the brain into a state of uncritical observation.

Software and videos can be used as careful supplements to a language-based curriculum. They can also serve as constructive entertainment—but always with the recognition that if the student weren't glued to a screen, he'd be doing something more active (making a model? playing Monopoly? shooting hoops? reading a book?). Every time you use the computer or turn on the TV, ask yourself: What am I giving up? What will my child do if I don't turn on the computer or pop in this video?

Having said this, we offer the following cautious recommendations.

SOFTWARE

When choosing software programs, beware of software that reduces complex subjects (science and history) to ten-second flashes of information narrated by constantly animated figures. Educational software is most appropriate for subjects that are largely visual anyway (geography, for example, or anatomy) or for fact-based drills that are being used as an alternative to flash cards. There's not much difference between turning a card over to check the answer to a math fact or clicking an icon to achieve the same effect. (There is, however, a difference between doing a computer math drill and writing the answers to a math drill on a sheet of paper. Don't substitute software for written drills, which engage the muscles as well as the mind—kinesthetic learning.) We've recommended several software resources, popular with home schoolers, at the end of this chapter.

Every middle-grade student should learn to type and to use a word-processing program. You can use a typing program such as the standard *Mavis Beacon Teaches Typing*. Or use *TypingMaster* (you can try a demo at its home page, www.TypingMaster.com) or *Letter Chase Typing Tutor* (www.letterchase.com). Each is available for Windows or for Mac users. Alternatively, you can use a standard typing book such as *Keyboarding Made Simple* (see Resources at the end of this chapter).

Once keyboard skills have been mastered, middle-grade students should learn how to use a standard word-processing program: Microsoft Word, or Pages for Mac users. The best way to learn a word-processing program is to buy it, install it, and work through the tutorial provided. Good typing skills and word-processing fluency will simplify paper preparation and open up entry-level job positions. If you don't have a computer, consider using a friend's or the computers now available at most public libraries.

We think students should do handwritten work through sixth grade. But beginning in seventh grade (the first year of junior high), papers can be prepared on the computer.

THE INTERNET

There's plenty of information online, much of it highly useful. The rest is either garbage or simply a waste of time.

Although reference works are increasingly available online, information accessed through home pages tends to be superficial, untrustworthy, and unedited. If the student can find online versions of respected works (articles from the *Encyclopaedia Britannica*, for example, or from publications such as *Time, Newsweek,* or the *New York Times*), that's fine. But for research papers, he should still use the library for most of his references. Respected scholarly works aren't often posted online for free; publishers pay scholars for it, publish it, and charge for the books. On the Internet, the adage "You get what you pay for" comes to life.

It is important for middle-grade students to understand the difference between *published* material and *self-published* material (blogs and personal web pages). Self-published material may easily be better than published material, but it hasn't been subjected to the checks and balances of the publication process: it hasn't been approved by an outside editor, approved by an editorial board, gone over by a fact-checker, or corrected by a researcher—processes that don't eliminate all errors but certainly catch a good many of them. Susan's freshmen often arrive at college thinking that web page, blog, and Wikipedia citations are perfectly acceptable in papers—which represents some sort of enormous failure in our technological education. (Wikipedia has an open editing process that does manage to weed out the majority of mistakes over time—but because anyone can post to Wikipedia, there's always the chance that your fifth grader will consult an entry just after a bored fifth grader in another state has posted prank information. Wikipedia can be a great starting point, but it should never be the ending place for research.)

Supervise Internet use. Net surfing, like TV watching, can waste hundreds of priceless hours. E-mail is great, but chat rooms tend to be the cyber equivalent of hanging out at the local fast-food joint—and just as intellectually stimulating. And cyber relationships can too easily become substitutes for real friendships—something that is socially (and academically) destructive. Online relationships allow teens to present themselves in carefully edited versions and to control exactly what's said; the relationships offer no chance for adolescents to learn the ins and outs of face-to-face communication—tone of voice, facial expression, body language. Your child won't conduct his adult social life in cyberspace, so don't let him practice all of his social skills via keyboard.

Unsupervised Internet use is the electronic equivalent of allowing your twelve year old to wander alone through a bookstore that has a large X-rated section just off to one side. Keep an eye on computer use, and don't put all your trust in a filter such as CyberPatrol or NetNanny, which can block useful information and let harmful information through. (One recent fuss was over one Net filter's blocking of all Christian websites along with neo-Nazi and white-supremacist sites, claiming that they contain "hate language.")

Be aware that e-mail isn't safe. Online pornographers routinely spam electronic mailboxes with deceptive mail containing hyperlinks to X-rated sites. Your twelve year old can open an e-mail, click once, and enter an adult movie house.

Keep both the television and the computer in a family area. This will prevent mindless use and will make every member of the family accountable for what he or she watches or where he or she surfs. Some TV programs and websites are appropriate for adults but not for children, but we think it is hypocritical for parents to restrict teenage viewing and then indulge in soft- (or hard-)core porn.

DVDs

Rule one for DVD use: never substitute DVDs for bookwork.

Watch DVDs after preparation. Once you've already studied a subject, a program becomes a vehicle for building more connections, rather than one for passive absorption of ideas. After you've read about sea life, a Jacques Cousteau or National Geographic program can not only reinforce, but make vivid the concepts that the student has learned. If you've just studied volcanoes, watching the Mount St. Helens eruption can cement that information in the student's mind forever.

Movies made from classic novels can be great fun—*after* the student has read the book. Filmed versions of *Ivanhoe* or *Pride and Prejudice* can fill in valuable historical details of dress and daily life. But vast areas of plot and character development are, of necessity, eliminated.

The exception to this rule can be filmed versions of plays, which, after all, were written to be seen. The print versions of *Henry V* or *Murder in the Cathedral* will probably be more interesting and easier to understand once the student has seen a performance.

DVDs can always be useful for language acquisition. If the child is studying Spanish, try to find Spanish-language versions of popular programs for him to watch. He'll be able to immerse himself in the language for an hour. But don't substitute this for a regular language course.

RESOURCES

For publisher and catalog addresses, telephone numbers, and other information, see Sources (pages 751–778). This section lists typing programs, other software, online tutorials, and video/software resources.

Typing Programs

Letter Chase Typing Tutor.
$19.55. Download free lessons and try the program out before buying at www.letterchase.com.

Mavis Beacon Teaches Typing Deluxe. Los Angeles, Calif.: Encore Software.
$19.99 on CD-ROM. Order from Amazon, and check publication dates so that you find the most recent version.

TypingMaster.
$39.90. Try the free trial before buying at www.typingmaster.com. TypingMaster Pro is for Windows, TypingMaster for Mac/Linux.

Zeitz, Leigh. *Keyboarding Made Simple. New York:* Random House, 2005.
$12.95. Order from any bookstore.

Other Software

Most software can be ordered through bookstores, but for heavily discounted prices and an enormous supply, try Nothing But Software at www.nothingbutsoftware.com. Software is rapidly outdated; always check for the latest version.

K12 Software carries hundreds of software titles for K–12. Visit their website at www.K12software.com to view the catalog and download demos. The Learning Company (www.learningcompany.com) also carries a well-organized catalog of educational software.

Human 3D. Megasystems.
$49.95. A multimedia human body tour; rotate and move organs, joints, and more so that you can see from any angle.

Liberty's Kids. The Learning Company.
$24.49. Replay events in the American Revolution, create your own newspaper, and investigate interactive exhibits.

Oregon Trail. The Learning Company.
$29.95. Order from The Learning Company. Lay in stores, plan a route, hunt game, and watch out for bears; this strategy game is based on the journey west. Try Yukon Trail too!

Planetarium. Fogware.
$9.99. See the sky at any time, during any season; look up over 250,000 catalogued celestial bodies; see photographs from the Hubble Space Telescope.

Ultimate Math Invaders.
$35.00. Order from The Learning Company. Math drill based on the old Space Invaders model: not only the basic math facts, but also fractions, decimals, percentages, square roots, integers, and powers.

Where in the World Is Carmen Sandiego? The Learning Company/Mindscape.
$19.99. Track stolen items through the world as you advance from a lowly gumshoe to a master detective; builds geography skills.

Zoombinis Logical Journey: An Epic Adventure of Math and Logic.
$19.99. Order from The Learning Company. Wonderful for fifth and sixth graders—and older students might be tempted as well. The Zoombinis have lost their island to the horrible Bloats—and the player has to use logic, reasoning, and systematic testing of theories to help them get it back.

Educational DVDs

The most economical place to find good programs on DVD (and video) is to browse through the shelves at your local library. You can also find scores of good titles at the National Geographic website (channel.nationalgeographic.com), the History Channel site (www.history.com), the Discovery Channel (www.dsc.discovery.com), and PBS (www.pbs.org). You can buy from these sites or make a list of titles for rental. Netflix (www.netflix.com), Blockbuster Online (www.blockbuster.com), and iTunes all provide rental programs that include documentaries.

23

MOVING TOWARD INDEPENDENCE: LOGIC FOR LIFE

What we have to learn to do, we learn by doing.
—Aristotle, *Nicomachean Ethics*

Your middle-grade student is busy learning about logic, cause and effect, valid and invalid arguments, clear thinking. All this knowledge isn't limited to bookwork. Logic applies to daily life as well.

The logic stage is a time of growing independence, both mental and practical. As the student begins to form her own opinions, she also should begin to take responsibility for parts of her daily life.

Educationally, this new independence assumes the form of increased time spent in self-study. As you move through the middle-grade years, you—the parent—should start to step back from minute-to-minute supervision of the child's study. Begin in fifth grade by giving the child a single assignment ("Read these two pages in your history book, and choose which topics you want to study further. Then see me.") If the child completes the assignment responsibly, she enjoys the rewards. ("Now you're done. Take some free time.") If she doesn't, she pays the price. ("It's time for swimming. But you've been lying on your bed reading a comic book instead of doing your history, so you'll need to stay in and finish it instead of going outside.")

This is the practical application of logic. Certain behaviors have certain consequences. And responsibility leads to freedom. If the child does her assignments regularly, you can begin to assign her a week's work at a time and check in with her on Fridays to make sure she's finished. If she doesn't complete the work, supervise more closely.

During the logic stage, the home-educated student should begin to understand the logical relationships of daily living as well the connection between responsibility and freedom—that is, between work and money, preparation and success. During the middle grades, students should begin to manage their own finances and keep their own daily schedules.

We suggest that seventh graders open a checking account at a local bank (many offer free checking without a minimum balance to students). Help the student draw up a budget so that she knows what portion of her money (earned or allowance) is available for spending, what part should be saved for a long-term goal (at least 20 percent), what part should be kept for family responsibilities (clothing, presents), and what part should be given away to charity or the religious community.

We also think that the logic stage is the perfect time for students to learn how to keep to a schedule independently. At the beginning of fifth grade, go together to an office supply store, and buy a daily planning calendar and a large wall calendar with enough space to write on for each day of the month.

In the fall, sit down together and make preliminary plans for the entire year. On the large wall calendar, write down the weeks you plan to spend in school, the weeks you'll take off, family holidays, and other commitments. (Now is a good time to explain to the student that schedules are flexible.)

At the beginning of each month, the two of you should make lists of goals. What do you want to accomplish in each subject? What days will the student "go to school"? What other appointments (library visits, music lessons, sports, doctors' visits, birthday parties, holidays, science fairs) need to be written on the calendar? Keep this calendar in a prominent place, and make it a cardinal rule that the student *must* write all new appointments (baby-sitting jobs, nights out, visits with friends) on both calendars as they come up. *A good rule:* If it isn't on the calendar, it doesn't happen. (If you're schooling two or more children, this rule is necessary for your sanity.)

In her daily calendar, the student should keep a basic daily schedule ("Mondays: up by 7, math 8–9:00, science 9:30–11 . . .") and refer to it. Each week, she should list her responsibilities. What should she complete in each subject? How much time can she spend watching TV, playing on the computer, talking on the phone? She should have her own alarm clock and watch so that she can begin to keep track of her own time.

This basic training in the logic of daily life yields three rewards. First, the student gains structure to her days. We understand that different personalities cope well with different degrees of structure, but we firmly believe that everyone needs a daily schedule of some kind in order to be productive.

Second, the student begins to understand that you, the parent, are not the sole motivating force in her life. She doesn't do her assignments because you're nagging her; she does them because the assignments have to be done by Friday so that she can move on to the next week's lessons because she wants to have enough time over the summer to do no school at all. She doesn't turn off the TV because you ordered her to; she turns off the TV because she's used up her TV quota for the day.

Third, she's getting ready for college and a career. Freshmen who fail classes or get fired from jobs often do so because they've never been responsible for their own schedules. They've always gotten up because Mom called them, changed classes because the bell rang, done homework because the teacher told them to. When they reach the relative freedom of college life, they often flounder.

Your classically trained student won't flounder if she has been well trained—not only for academics, but for the responsibilities of daily life.

PART II

EPILOGUE

The Logic Stage at a Glance

Guidelines to how much time you should spend on each subject are general; parents should feel free to adjust schedules according to the child's maturity and ability.

Fifth Grade

Logic	3 hours per week: do logic puzzles (*Mind Benders, Red Herrings*).
Mathematics	45–60 minutes, four days per week: do fifth-grade math; 60 minutes, once per week: do real-life math.
History	60 minutes, three days per week, or 1½ hours, twice per week: study ancient times (5000 B.C.–A.D. 400), using selected history resources; outline sections (one sentence per paragraph); mark dates on the time line; do map work; prepare written summaries on two topics per week.
Language	15 minutes per day: do *Spelling Workout* books; 40 minutes per day: do formal grammar; 30 minutes or more per day: do structured reading—ancient myths and legends, epics; 60 minutes per day: do free reading.

Writing	30–60 minutes daily: do writing program two or three days per week; do dictation twice per week.
Science	1½ hours, two days per week: study biology—day 1, do reading and prepare a report; day 2, do sketches and experiments.
Latin/foreign language	3 or more hours per week, depending on pace: study Latin and begin a foreign language.
Religion	10–15 minutes per day: learn the basics of personal faith; learn about world religions through the study of history.
Art	1–2 hours, once per week: alternate art projects with studying ancient art.
Music	1–2 hours, once per week: study the instruments of the orchestra.

Sixth Grade

Logic	3 hours per week: do *Critical Thinking, Book One* and *Two*.
Mathematics	45–60 minutes, four days per week: do sixth-grade math; 60 minutes, once per week: do real-life math.
History	60 minutes, three days per week, or 1½ hours, twice per week: study medieval–early Renaissance times (400–1600), using selected history resources; outline each section; mark dates on the time line; do map work; prepare one composition per week.
Language	15 minutes per day: do *Spelling Workout* books; 40 minutes per day: do formal grammar; 40 minutes or more per day: do structured reading—medieval and early Renaissance literature; 60 minutes per day: do free reading.
Writing	30–60 minutes two or three days per week: do writing program; once per week: do essays in history and science; twice per month: write personal letters.
Science	1½ hours, two days per week: study astronomy

	and earth science—day 1, do reading and prepare report; day 2, do sketches and experiments.
Latin/foreign language	3 or more hours per week, depending on pace: study Latin and begin a foreign language.
Religion	10–15 minutes per day: learn the basics of personal faith; learn about world religions through the study of history.
Art	1–2 hours, once per week: alternate art projects with studying medieval and early Renaissance art.
Music	1–2 hours, once per week: listen to medieval and early Renaissance music; read biographies of the composers.

Seventh Grade

Logic	3 hours per week: do *Traditional Logic.*
Mathematics	50–60 minutes per day: do pre-algebra.
History	60 minutes, three days per week, or 1½ hours, twice per week: study late Renaissance–early-modern times (1600–1850), using selected history resources plus the Jackdaw primary-reference packs; outline each section; mark dates on the time line; do map work; prepare one composition per week.
Language	45 minutes, once per week: do *Spelling Workout* books, and, when finished, go to *Vocabulary from Classical Roots A* and *B* (5 minutes, four days per week: review the material); 40 minutes or more per day: do formal grammar; 40 minutes or more per day: do structured reading—late Renaissance through early modern literature; 60 minutes per day: do free reading.
Writing	30–60 minutes, two or three days per week: do writing program; twice per month: write personal letters.
Science	1½ hours, two days per week: study chemistry, using kits and reporting on experiments.
Latin/foreign language	3 or more hours per week, depending on pace:

study Latin and continue with the foreign language.

Religion	10–15 minutes per day: learn the basics of personal faith; learn about world religions through the study of history.
Art	1–2 hours, once per week: alternate art projects with studying art from the late Renaissance through the early-modern periods.
Music	1–2 hours, once per week: listen to Renaissance, Baroque, and Classical music; read biographies of the composers.

Eighth Grade

Logic	3 hours per week: *Traditional Logic II.*
Mathematics	60 minutes per day: do *Algebra I.*
History	60 minutes, three days per week, or 1½ hours, twice per week: study modern times (1850–present), using the selected history resources; outline each section; mark dates on the time line; do map work; prepare one composition per week; schedule oral-history interviews once per month.
Language	45 minutes, once per week: do *Vocabulary from Classical Roots C* and *D* (5 minutes, four days per week: review the material); 40 minutes or more per day: do formal grammar study; 40 minutes or more per day: do structured reading—literature from 1850 to the present; 60 minutes per day: do free reading.
Writing	45–60 minutes, three days per week: do writing program.
Science	1½ hours, two days per week: study physics, using kits and reporting on experiments.
Latin/foreign language	3 or more hours per week, depending on pace: study Latin and continue with the foreign language.
Religion	10–15 minutes per day: learn the basics of personal faith; learn about world religions through the study of history.

Art	1–2 hours, once per week: alternate art projects with studying modern art.
Music	1–2 hours, one day per week: listen to Romantic and modern music; read biographies of the composers.

PART III

THE RHETORIC STAGE

Ninth Grade through Twelfth Grade

24

SPEAKING YOUR MIND: THE RHETORIC STAGE

It is absurd to hold that a man should be ashamed of an inability to defend himself with his limbs, but not ashamed of an inability to defend himself with speech and reason; for the use of rational speech is more distinctive of a human being than the use of his limbs.

—Aristotle, *Rhetoric*

SUBJECT: Rhetoric and debate
TIME REQUIRED: 3 hours per week in grades 9 and 10, plus time spent in extracurricular debate activities

Rhetoric is the art of expression. During the rhetoric stage—grades 9 through 12, the traditional high-school years—the student learns to express herself with fluency, grace, elegance, and persuasiveness.

Since self-expression is one of the greatest desires of adolescence, high-school students should have training in the skills of rhetoric so that they can say, clearly and convincingly, what's on their minds. Without these skills, the desire for self-expression is frustrated. Expression itself becomes inarticulate. External objects—clothes, jewelry, tattoos, hairstyles—assume an exaggerated value as the clearest forms of self-expression possible.[1]

[1]Susan has a completely unscientific theory about this—she believes that students who are skilled in rhetoric will never feel the need for a tongue stud.

"To a certain extent," Aristotle writes in *Rhetoric,* the classic text on the subject, "all men attempt to discuss statements and to maintain them, to defend themselves and to attack others. Ordinary people do this either at random, or through practice and from acquired habit."[2] The study of rhetoric is designed to make success in speech a matter of skill and practice, not accident.

A GENERAL GUIDE TO THE RHETORIC STAGE

Rhetoric is dependent upon the first two stages of the trivium. The grammar stage laid a foundation of knowledge; without knowledge, the rhetorician has nothing of substance to say. The logic stage taught the student to think through the validity of arguments, to weigh the value of evidence. In the rhetoric stage, the student uses knowledge and the skill of logical argument to write and speak about all the subjects in the curriculum.

The last four years of classical education stress expression and flexibility. The student expresses herself by continually writing and speaking about what she's learning. At first, rhetoric is a specific subject for study, just as logic was during the middle grades. But the skills acquired in the study of rhetoric are then exercised in history, science, and literature. In the last two years of schooling, the student will undertake two major writing projects in an area of her own choice, which will show her mastery of rhetoric as well as her skills.

Flexibility becomes paramount as the student pursues her junior and senior writing projects. These demand a great deal of time and effort. When the high schooler decides on the fields she'll study in depth, other subjects in which she has already received a good basic grounding will fade into the background. "Those who are likely never to have any great use or aptitude for mathematics," writes Dorothy Sayers in "The Lost Tools of Learning," "[should] be allowed to rest, more or less, upon their oars."[3] The same can be said for languages and for highly technical aspects

[2]Aristotle, *Rhetoric* I.i.

[3]Dorothy Sayers, "The Lost Tools of Learning," in Douglas Wilson, *Recovering the Lost Tools of Learning* (Wheaton, Ill.: Crossway, 1991), p. 161.

of the sciences. Twelve years of schooling aren't sufficient for a student to complete her studies in a particular field of knowledge anyway. But even though the student may not finish twelfth grade with a comprehensive grasp of science or history, she will know how to learn—a skill that she can use for the rest of her life.

A third distinctive characteristic of the rhetoric stage is its focus on great books. History and literature meld together as the student reads the works of great minds, from ancient Greece to the present day. Great books are rhetoric in action; their persuasion has stood time's test. As the high schooler studies the rhetoric of classic authors, she analyzes the force of their arguments. Great books provide historical perspective on the accepted truths of our own age; they can prevent the student from swallowing the rhetoric of modern-day orators undigested.

THE STUDY OF RHETORIC

During the rhetoric stage, the student will study the principles of self-expression and exercise them in both writing and speech, using modern texts that build on the classical foundations.

The study of rhetoric involves developing skill in five areas, or "canons": *inventio, dispositio, elocutio, memoria,* and *pronuntiatio.* The first three of these apply to both written and spoken rhetoric, while *memoria* and *pronuntiatio* apply specifically to debate and speechmaking.

Inventio, "invention," is the process of formulating an argument and gathering all the supporting evidence. It requires both logic and knowledge. In essay writing, *inventio* occurs when you select a thesis and research it, lining up all the proof needed to make your thesis convincing.

Dispositio is the skill of putting all that information into persuasive order. The way you present an argument depends on a slew of factors—the makeup of the audience, the setting you'll be arguing in, the emotional effect various types of information might produce, and so on. *Dispositio* teaches you to arrange all your evidence in the most convincing way. (The question of whether this is also the best and truest way is a source of tension within the study of rhetoric, which continually brings ethical issues to the fore.)

Elocutio, "elocution," teaches you how to evaluate the words you use when you give your argument. Which words will most clearly reveal the truth? (Alternately, which words will produce the desired emotions in the listener?) Which types of metaphors, parallelisms, figures of speech should you use? How can you structure your sentences for maximum effect?

For debate, you'll also need skills in *memoria* (memorizing important points or entire speeches) and *pronuntiatio* (effective methods of delivering the speech).

Rhetoric, Aristotle tells us, leads to fair-mindedness. The student of rhetoric must be able to argue persuasively on both sides of an issue, not in order to convince his audience of that which is wrong, but "in order that we may see clearly what the facts are."[4] And this is true for every subject in which rhetoric is employed. Rhetoric, Aristotle concludes, is universal.[5]

HOW TO DO IT

During ninth and tenth grades, the student should study rhetoric during those hours previously devoted to logic. Plan on three hours per week, divided into two sessions of one and a half hours each or three sessions of one hour each.

Beginning in ninth grade, the student will work her way through three texts: Anthony Weston's *A Rulebook for Arguments,* an introduction to rhetoric that provides a quick review of logic as applied to written essays;[6] Thomas S. Kane's *The New Oxford Guide to Writing;* and finally Edward Corbett's *Classical Rhetoric for the Modern Student.* This study will cover at least two years, and may occupy all four of the high-school years.

As with other advanced subjects, you can use a tutor or online tutorial for the study of rhetoric. However, good readers should be able to pursue this study independently by following this pattern:

1. Read a section in *A Rulebook for Arguments.*
2. Outline the content of the text.

[4]Aristotle, *Rhetoric* I.1.

[5]Ibid., I.2.

[6]Students who begin the classical pattern later should finish one year of logic before beginning the study of rhetoric.

3. Provide two examples of the text's lesson, either from someone else's rhetoric or of your own creation.

The ninth grader using *A Rulebook for Arguments* will encounter, at the end of Chapter 4, a section entitled "Personal attacks do not disqualify a source." Weston's text reads:

> (17) Personal attacks do not disqualify a source. Supposed authorities may be disqualified if they are *not* informed, impartial, or largely in agreement. *Other* sorts of attacks on authorities are not legitimate. Ludwig von Mises describes a series of illegitimate attacks on the economist Ricardo:
>
> > In the eyes of the Marxians the Ricardian theory is spurious because Ricardo was a bourgeois. The German racists condemn the same theory because Ricardo was a Jew, and the German nationalists because he was an Englishman. . . . Some German professors advanced all three arguments together against the validity of Ricardo's teaching.[7]
>
> This is the "ad hominem" fallacy: attacking the *person* of an authority rather than his or her qualifications. Ricardo's class, religion, and nationality are irrelevant to the possible truth of his theories. To disqualify him as an authority, those "German professors" have to show that his evidence was incomplete—that is, they have to show that his judgments were not fully *informed*—or that he was not impartial, or that other equally reputable economists disagree with his findings. Otherwise, personal attacks only disqualify the *attacker*![8]

A good outline of this passage might look like this:

I. An authority can be attacked for three reasons.
   A. Not being informed.
   B. Not being impartial.
   C. Being out of agreement with most other authorities.
II. An authority cannot be attacked for his *person*.
   A. This is the "ad hominem" fallacy.

[7]L. von Mises, *Human Action* (New Haven: Yale University Press, 1963), p. 75.

[8]Anthony Weston, *A Rulebook for Arguments* (Indianapolis: Hackett, 1992), pp. 35–36.

B. Class, religion, nationality, or other personal attacks are irrelevant.
C. Ad hominem attacks disqualify the attacker.

The student would follow this by finding two examples of ad hominem attacks in a political speech (a depressingly easy exercise) or by writing her own ad hominem refutation of something she's read. Either exercise will show that she understands the concept.

When the student turns to *The New Oxford Guide to Writing,* she'll follow a slightly different pattern. Each chapter is divided into sections with bold-print headings; these sections are then divided further by subheadings in regular type. The student's first step should be to outline the chapter. In most cases, the student should probably construct one outline for each chapter, with bold headings generally treated as major outline points. However, she shouldn't feel obliged to make the subheadings into outline points as well. For example, Chapter 16, "Paragraph Development: Cause and Effect," is divided into the following headings and subheadings:

Cause
Ordering Reasons within a Paragraph
Effects
Multiple Effects
Cause and Effect

A good outline of this chapter might look like this:

I. Cause.
  A. Explaining "why" is a major purpose of writing.
  B. The simplest strategy: ask "Why" and then give the answer.
  C. A writer may also choose to give cause and effect implicitly, without using the word "Why."
II. How to write a paragraph containing reasons for a cause.
  A. Give a single reason and repeat it or expand it.
  B. Arrange several reasons in order.
    1. If each reason causes the next, this is "serial order."
    2. If the reasons are independent of each other, they are "parallel."

a. Parallel reasons that have an order in time should be listed chronologically.
b. Otherwise, they should be listed from least to most important.

III. How to write a paragraph containing the effects or consequences of a cause.
  A. The cause should be found in the topic sentence.
  B. The effects should be found in the rest of the paragraph.
    1. There may be a single effect.
    2. There may be more than one effect.
      a. The effects may be independent of each other.
      b. Or each effect may actually be the cause of the next.

Kane gives clear examples of each kind of paragraph.

After outlining the chapter (an exercise which may take the whole week or perhaps longer, for more detailed chapters), the student should complete the practice exercises at each chapter's end. For example, Chapter 16 ends with several practice exercises, the first involving analysis ("Analyze the cause-effect relationship in the following paragraph") and the next two involving composition ("Compose a single paragraph developing three or four reasons to support one of the following topics: The enormous increase in the cost of housing, the contemporary mania for exercise, the expansion of professional sports in the last twenty-five years . . . ," etc.). While the student should generally do the analysis exercises as written, she should always feel free to substitute her own topics (perhaps drawn from her study of history, science, or another subject) for those suggested by Kane. When completing these exercises, she should make an effort to use all of the different techniques described by Kane in the chapter.

Some of the chapters have no practice exercises. In this case, the student should provide an example for each technique described in the chapter, either from someone else's rhetoric or of her own creation.

After working through Kane, the student will have a good grasp of the basics of written rhetoric. Students who are putting a high level of effort into the study of upper-level mathematics or science may need to end their study of rhetoric here in order to have enough time to specialize. However, most students (and all those interested in the humanities) should go on to the final rhetoric text: Edward Corbett's *Classical Rhetoric for the Modern Student* (4th edition).

Corbett's six-chapter study of rhetoric uses models ranging from Socrates to Rachel Carson to teach students the art of persuasion. The student should begin by simply reading the first chapter, "Introduction," carefully. The second chapter, "Discovery of Arguments," deals with *inventio,* choosing a topic for writing (in Corbett's words, "how to 'discover' something to say on some given subject"). The chapter is quite long (over 200 pages!) and should be outlined, section by section (the sections are set off by bold-print headings). After outlining, the student should either give a written example or (where provided) complete the "Practice" provided by Corbett. For example, after outlining "Formulating a Thesis," the student should choose a general topic, ask three questions about it (Corbett writes that you should define a topic for argument by asking whether you intend to prove that the topic is a fact, to define it, or to show what kind of thing it is—three classic strategies for narrowing the subject of an argument), and then state a thesis in a "single declarative sentence."[9]

Most students will need a month or more to work through this chapter. The following chapters are not quite as lengthy; the student should follow the same basic procedure in working through them. The fifth chapter, "The Progymnasmata," walks students through a set of writing exercises which have long been used in classical tutorials to develop writing skills; the student begins by retelling a folktale and then continues, writing a narrative, explaining an anecdote, arguing for or against a proverb (a "maxim or adage"), and so on through the final step of the progymnasmata, the "legislation," in which the student argues "for or against the goodness of a law." These exercises will ask the student to put into practice all of the skills learned throughout the book, and will give her all the tools needed for the junior and senior projects (see Chapter 33).

The final chapter, "A Survey of Rhetoric," can be simply read for information or can be skipped.

Note: Evaluation of these writing exercises can sometimes present a challenge. The resources suggested earlier (see Chapter 17) can help you; also, remember that writing is a subjective activity and that even expert writing

[9]Edward Corbett and Robert J. Connors, *Classical Rhetoric for the Modern Student,* 4th ed. (Oxford: Oxford University Press, 1999), pp. 27–31.

teachers can differ over whether a particular assignment is well-done or incompetent. Often, there is no "right" answer to a writing assignment. However, if you'd like some additional help in evaluating your high school student's writing, consider one of the following options:

(1) Cindy Marsch's Writing Assessment Services (www.writingassessment.com) offers an online evaluation program for home-school students.

(2) Call your local private or parochial school and ask whether the composition teacher would be willing to evaluate your student's work. Make sure that you take the rhetoric text with you, so that the teacher knows the principles the student is trying to put into place. Generally, offering an honorarium of $40.00–$50.00 for an evaluation session is a nice gesture.

(3) Call the secretary of the English department at your local university or community college and ask whether any of the writing teachers might be willing to evaluate your student's papers; the same honorarium is acceptable.

Note: To complete the above rhetoric study, students should be skilled at outlining. This skill is covered in the grammar programs we recommend in Chapters 17 and 25. If necessary, the rhetoric-stage student can return to these resources.

For Further Study

Students who wish to continue the study of rhetoric as a specialization—and particularly those with an interest in political rhetoric—will benefit from Martin Cothran's *Classical Rhetoric with Aristotle: Traditional Principles of Speaking and Writing*. This thirty-three-week rhetoric course is based on the reading and analysis of Aristotle's *Rhetoric*, a foundational ancient text on the subject. It also includes a useful teacher's key, reading exercises from Mortimer Adler's classic *How to Read a Book*, and exercises to reinforce Latin and logic skills (these are optional). The rhetoric course outlined above is focused more toward preparation for college writing; Cothran's course is a more traditional "ancient rhetoric" course, in that it gives equal preparation for speaking and writing and also focuses on the motivations of the men (and women) who seek to persuade.

Alternatives

The program we've outlined above walks the student through foundational training in rhetoric; the texts we recommend are based on the model of the *progymnasmata,* the training exercises used in classical rhetoric, and the skills covered will equip the high school student to write persuasive essays.

However, some parents may feel the need for a more structured curriculum—a "writing program"—particularly for students who continue to struggle with writing, or who have come out of a classroom situation and are not yet used to working independently. (Students who are not yet writing on a high school level should spend at least two years in one of the curricula recommended for logic-stage writing in Chapter 17 before moving on to our rhetoric-stage recommendations).

If you'd prefer to investigate a structured curriculum, we suggest two options:

1. The Institute for Excellence in Writing (see Chapter 17, page 360) now offers a one-year rhetoric course, *Classical Rhetoric through Structure and Style: Writing Lessons Based on the Progymnasmata.* IEW also offers an Advanced Communication Series DVD set, intended for high school persuasive writing, and a College-Bound Student Package, which includes a seminar on DVD plus a fourteen-week program during which students practice writing SAT-type essays as well as the dreaded "personal experience" essays for college applications.

The courses assume previous experience with the IEW "Teaching Writing: Structure and Style" program. Students and parents who have already completed at least one year of the IEW course could progress through the Advanced Communication Series set, the *Classical Rhetoric through Structure and Style* curriculum, and then the College-Bound Student Package. Depending on the student's ease with writing, this is a two- to three-year progression; the final high school year(s) could then be spent on Anthony Weston's text and the *New Oxford Guide to Writing,* as described above.

Students and parents who have not used IEW before should complete one year of "Teaching Writing: Structure and Style" before beginning the Advanced Communication Series.

2. *Classical Writing* (see Chapter 17, page 361), based on the exercises of the *progymnasmata,* is an option for experienced home-school parents or parents who feel comfortable with the writing process. Students who have not used this program can begin with the first level, *Aesop and Homer for Older Beginners,* and can then move into *Diogenes: Maxim* and *Diogenes: Chreia.*

Although upper levels are not yet available, you can check the Classical Writing website (www.classicalwriting.com) for more information.

The curriculum makes very effective use of classical teaching techniques; imitation of good writers is at the center of the method, students are encouraged to incorporate grammar learning, spelling, and editing skills into the daily lessons, and the program develops the specific writing skills needed to tackle Great Books study. However, the lessons are complex and require the parent to be comfortable with grammar, spelling, vocabulary, and writing; the parent is responsible for planning the sessions and directing the integration of grammar and vocabulary learning into the lessons. You can view sample lessons at the Classical Writing website.

DEBATE

Involvement in a debate club or society provides invaluable, hands-on training in rhetoric. If at all possible, find a local debate society, and enroll your ninth grader in it. Try to pursue debate throughout ninth and tenth grades. If the eleventh grader no longer wants to take part, debate can then be dropped from the curriculum—it has served its purpose.

Your local university or college is a good starting place. Call the theater department, which is generally connected with the debate club because debate is a spoken performance. Ask who coaches the debate team. Once you've found the coach, explain what you're doing, list the rhetoric texts you're using, and ask how your ninth grader can practice debating skills. The coach may invite the student to sit in on the college sessions. At the very least, he should be able to direct you to an age-appropriate debate group nearby.

You can also call a parochial school, if you happen to have a good one nearby. Ask for the debate-team coach, and explain your situation. Some private schools welcome home schoolers to extracurricular clubs.

Finally, you can call your state home-education organization (see pages 724–744) and ask about debate clubs for home schoolers. More and more of these are popping up. The quality of the coaching tends to be mixed—you can end up with anyone from an overworked parent who's never studied rhetoric to a moonlighting university professor. Ask about the qualifications of the coach before you commit. But these groups are often very resourceful, mounting regular competitions and even statewide championships for home schoolers.

SCHEDULES

Ninth grade	3 hours per week	*A Rulebook for Arguments* (9–14 weeks); *The New Oxford Guide to Writing* (remainder of the year).
	Extracurricular	Debate club.
Tenth grade	3 hours per week	Complete *The New Oxford Guide,* begin Corbett, *Classical Rhetoric for the Modern Student.*
	Extracurricular	Debate club.
Eleventh and twelfth grades	3 hours per week	Continue with Corbett until finished.

RESOURCES

For publisher and catalog addresses, telephone numbers, and other information, see Sources (pages 751–778). Most books can be obtained from any bookstore or library; where we know of a mail-order option, we have provided it.

Rhetoric

Corbett, Edward P. J., and Robert J. Connors. *Classical Rhetoric for the Modern Student*. 4th ed. Oxford: Oxford University Press, 1998.

$69.95. Order from any bookstore. This is available only in hardback and is rarely discounted, but you can often find used copies through www.abebooks.com.

Cothran, Martin. *Classical Rhetoric with Aristotle: Traditional Principles of Speaking and Writing*. Louisville, Ky.: Memoria Press, 2002.

$39.95 for coursebook, $4.95 for teacher's key. Order from Memoria Press.

Kane, Thomas S. *The New Oxford Guide to Writing*. Oxford: Oxford University Press, 1994.

$19.95. Order from any bookstore.

Marsch, Cindy. Writing Assessment Services. www.writingassessment.com.

Weston, Anthony. *A Rulebook for Arguments*. 3d ed. Indianapolis, Ind.: Hackett, 2000.

$6.95. Order from any bookstore.

Debate

The National Forensic League (www.nflonline.org) provides manuals, forums, support, and links for debaters and debate societies. 125 Watson Street, Ripon, Wisc. 54971; (920) 748-9478.

The National Christian Forensics and Communications Association (www.ncfca.org) was founded by the Christian home-education advocacy group Home School Legal Defense Association (HSLDA). P.O. Box 212, Mountlake Terrace, Wash. 98043; (425) 776-3620. NCFCA provides coaching and how-to resources for would-be debate teams; see http://www.ncfca.org/resources/books_and_materials.

If you're inspired to start your own debate club, look for these useful titles through any bookstore:

Freeley, Austin J. *Argumentation and Debate,* 12th ed. Boston, Mass.: Wadsworth Publishing, 2008.

$119.95. Comprehensive survey of argumentation and debate, with models, scenarios, and guides for real-life situations.

Oberg, Brent C. *Forensics: The Winner's Guide to Speech Contests.* Colorado Springs, Colo.: Meriwether Publishing, 1995.

$17.95. A guide to debate, specifically geared toward competition skills.

Phillips, Leslie, William S. Hicks, and Douglas R. Springer. *Basic Debate,* 5th ed. New York: Glencoe/McGraw-Hill, 2005.

$50.64. A standard hardcover textbook on the subject.

Alternative Resources

Classical Writing. The Classical Writing website provides an e-mail contact and message board, but no physical address or phone number. You can purchase texts from Classical Writing, through print-on-demand from Lulu.com, or from Rainbow Resource Center. The texts are listed below in order of use; each level is approximately one year's worth of work and consists of a core book and student workbooks or guides. The first two levels also require the purchase of a separate instructor's guide.

Aesop & Homer for Older Beginners.

Aesop core book. $20.95.

Homer core book. $34.95.

Student Workbook for Older Beginners. Visit website for pricing.

Instructor's Guide for Older Beginners. Visit website for pricing.

Diogenes: Maxim.

Diogenes: Maxim core book. $26.96.

Student Guide. $26.95.

Visit the Classical Writing website for pricing information and more information on the following advanced courses:

Diogenes: Chreia.

Diogenes: Chreia core book.

Student Guide.

Herodotus.

Herodotus core book.

Herodotus Student Guide and Answer Key.

Institute for Excellence in Writing series. Atascadero, Calif.: Institute for Excellence in Writing.

Order from IEW.

Advanced Communication Series

$65.00. 3-DVD seminar and student E-book.

Classical Rhetoric through Structure and Style: Writing Lessons Based on the Progymnasmata.

$29.00. Student Text.

College-Bound Student Package

$179.00. Worksheets, text, and DVDs.

Teaching Writing: Structure and Style.

$169.00 Prerequisite to the advanced levels; video seminar instructs parents on how to teach writing. The package includes 10 DVDs and a workbook/syllabus.

25

SKILL WITH WORDS: GRAMMAR AND WRITING

Reading maketh a full man, writing an exact man, and conference a ready man.

—Francis Bacon

SUBJECT: Grammar and writing skills
TIME REQUIRED: 3 hours or more per week

In many classical programs, English as a subject drops out of the schedule by high school. Reading and writing aren't separate "subjects," after all, but skills that cut across the entire curriculum. Reading means coming in contact with the philosophical and creative minds of the past and present, something that occurs in both history and science. Writing takes place every day in every subject. So why do we need English as a subject any more?

Overall, we agree with this point of view. It does assume, though, that the ninth grader has a complete grasp of grammar, syntax, and usage. We haven't found this to be generally true.

The middle-grade language topics—spelling and word study, grammar, reading, and writing—do change in high school. In the rhetoric stage, the student finally begins to put the knowledge and skills he's acquired during the first eight years of education to work. Once mastered, basic skills (such as spelling, constructing paragraphs and essays, and developing logical arguments) can be eliminated as specific subjects of study. The skills acquired during the logic stage don't disappear, but the student's focus is now on using those skills rather than acquiring them. A painter may take a special class in art school on mixing colors. He won't stay in this class for the rest of his painting career, but he will continually mix colors as he creates works of art.

HOW TO DO IT

During the rhetoric stage, we suggest that the student keep a single notebook, the language reference notebook. This notebook will serve not as an exercise book, but as a handbook of basic skills. One notebook should be used for the four years of high school.

Divide the language reference notebook into two sections: Words and Grammar.

Spelling and Word Study

Try to finish *Vocabulary from Classical Roots E* in ninth grade. If necessary, complete books *C* and *D* first.

Ninth graders who have followed the program outlined in Chapter 17 know how to spell. They've already studied the rules of spelling and the principles of word formation. Any new words they encounter can be spelled by comparing them to words they already know. Words that consistently trip them up (and we all have a few) should be kept on a list in the Words section of the language reference notebook. No other formal spelling work is necessary.

The reading and language study done during the middle grades should have developed the student's vocabulary skills so that he can tackle classic works without trouble. Even though his vocabulary will continue to grow for the rest of his life, during the rhetoric stage vocabulary acquisition will come "on the job"—from constant reading (exposure to new words in context) and writing (searching for just the right word to use).

We strongly suggest that you do finish up the *Vocabulary from Classical Roots* series. If you're on track, you finished book *D* at the end of the eighth-grade year; book *E* can be done in the fall of the ninth-grade year. *E* reviews the roots, prefixes, and suffixes already used; continue to keep a record of these on pages headed "Prefixes and Suffixes" and "Word Roots" (see Chapter 17 for a full description). If you're not up to book *D* yet, simply continue with the series until you're finished.

Follow the pattern recommended in Chapter 17 (page 339):

Monday	30–45 minutes	Read through the word roots, definitions, and sample sentences; make 3 × 5-inch flash cards for each Latin root and unfamiliar English word.
Tuesday–Thursday	5–10 minutes	Drill with flash cards.
Friday	10 minutes	Review flash cards; complete exercises; check.

Once you've finished *Vocabulary from Classical Roots E,* no further formal vocabulary and spelling work is required. As the student encounters unfamiliar words in his reading, though, he should copy them into the Words section of the notebook, along with pronunciation (these symbols were taught in the *Spelling Workout* books), origin, definition, and the sentence in which they are used.

When reading *Jane Eyre,* for example, the eleventh-grade student will come across this paragraph:

> In her turn, Helen Burns asked me to explain; and I proceeded forthwith to pour out, in my own way, the tale of my sufferings and resentments. Bitter and truculent when excited, I spoke as I felt, without reserve or softening.

If he's not familiar with the word "truculent," he should look it up in the dictionary and make an entry in his language reference notebook:

> *Truculent.* 'trəkyələnt. From the Latin *truculentus,* wild or fierce. "Feeling or showing savage ferocity, harsh, aggressively self-assertive." *Jane Eyre:* "Bitter and truculent when excited, I spoke as I felt, without reserve or softening."

This word-study exercise will help build both Latin and English vocabulary skills.[1] The student will need some encouragement to stop and do this when he sees an unfamiliar word, rather than skimming over it and going on. As the rhetoric stage continues, though, he'll find himself stopping less often.

During the rhetoric stage, you *must* have two reference works on hand: a dictionary (unabridged, if you can afford it) and *Roget's Thesaurus*. Encourage the student to use the thesaurus continually while writing, choosing the exact word for every occasion.

Grammar

Grammar is the single language-skill area that you should study every year through senior high. Grammar, usage, and mechanics must become completely automatic for truly mature reading and writing to take place. And although the logic-stage student has been exposed to all the grammar skills he needs, the skills haven't yet had time to become part of his mental apparatus. To keep on reinforcing these skills, continue with the Rod & Staff grammar and composition series. The ninth- and tenth-grade levels are a two-book series that lead the student through advanced grammar and composition.

The high-school program ends with tenth grade. For eleventh and twelfth grade, the student simply needs a grammar handbook and regular review of grammatical principles while writing. Rod & Staff publishes an *English Handbook* to follow the tenth-grade level of the program; it covers grammar, usage, sentence structure, argumentative essay construction, and proper documentation.

If you are beginning Rod & Staff for the first time, use this chart:

Beginning	**Use**
Ninth grade	Seventh-grade text
Tenth grade	Eighth-grade text
Eleventh grade	Ninth-grade text
Twelfth grade	Tenth-grade text

[1]A side benefit: excellent performance on the verbal section of the SAT.

If you prefer a nonsectarian program, consider using *Analytical Grammar: A Systematic Approach to Language Mastery* for grades 9 and 10. This program reviews and reinforces all grammatical concepts learned in earlier grades and introduces a few more advanced concepts; it provides exercises and also guides the student in making a grammar notebook which will serve as a handbook (although we do suggest that you purchase a standard handbook reference such as the Rod & Staff *English Handbook* listed above, or Warriner's). *Analytical Grammar* consists of a student workbook, a teacher book, and an additional set of "Review and Reinforcement" worksheets. Divide this course into two and complete half in grade 9 and half in grade 10.

For grades 11 and 12, follow this up with the Stewart English Program, published by Educators Publishing Service. This high-school resource consists of three books: *Principles Plus . . . , Grammar Plus . . . ,* and *Writing Plus.* Complete *Principles Plus . . .* (which will be mostly review) and *Grammar Plus . . .* in eleventh grade and *Writing Plus . . .* in twelfth grade.

Plan on spending around forty-five minutes per day, four to five days a week, or an hour three days a week on grammar skills. Whichever program you select, the student should use the "Grammar" section of the language notebook to keep a running list of grammar rules and principles that consistently trip her up.

Ninth grade	Rod & Staff: *Communicating Effectively, Book One* OR *Analytical Grammar,* first half
Tenth grade	Rod & Staff: *Communicating Effectively, Book Two* OR *Analytical Grammar,* second half
Eleventh grade	*English Handbook* OR Stewart English *Book 1: Principles Plus . . .* and Stewart English *Book 2: Grammar Plus . . .*
Twelfth grade	*English Handbook* OR Stewart *English Book 3: Writing Plus . . .*

Reading

The rhetoric stage is centered around the study of great books of philosophy, politics, religion, poetry, fiction, biography. Rather than studying history and literature as two separate subjects, the classically educated student recognizes that these pursuits are essentially the same.

Because of this, "reading" as such is swallowed up by the great-books study outlined in the next chapter.

Writing

The high school student will be writing continually about history, science, art, great books, and everything else he studies. The study of rhetoric described in Chapter 24 also builds the student's writing skills.

The student using Rod & Staff should complete the composition exercises given in those texts. The final two books of the Writing Strands series, *Writing Strands 7* and *Writing Exposition,* are also valuable for all students; they cover forms used in college writing and offer a valuable introduction to persuasive techniques. Consider taking some time in the eleventh-grade year to complete these resources.

We also suggest that the student buy William Strunk and E. B. White's classic *The Elements of Style.* Keep it on hand as a reference work. Ideally, the student should reread it, taking notes as he reads, at the beginning of each year, and should refer to it constantly as he edits and revises his own writing.

SCHEDULES

Ninth grade	Finish *Vocabulary from Classical Roots* series (books *C, D,* and *E*); choose Rod & Staff OR *Analytical Grammar*; follow rhetoric recommendations from Chapter 24; read *Elements of Style.*
Tenth grade	Choose Rod & Staff OR *Analytical Grammar;* follow rhetoric recommendations from Chapter 24; reread *Elements of Style.*
Eleventh grade	Use *English Handbook* OR Stewart English Program; follow rhetoric recommendations from Chapter 24; reread *Elements of Style.*
Twelfth grade	Use *English Handbook* OR Stewart English Program; follow rhetoric recommendations from Chapter 24; reread *Elements of Style.*

RESOURCES

For publisher and catalog addresses, telephone numbers, and other information, see Sources (pages 751–778). Most books can be obtained from any bookstore or library; where we know of a mail-order option, we have provided it. Books in a series are listed together.

Spelling/Word Study

Kipfer, Barbara Ann, ed. *Roget's International Thesaurus.* 6th ed. New York: HarperCollins, 2002.

$16.95. This is available at most bookstores as well as online.

Fifer, Norma, and Nancy Flowers. *Vocabulary from Classical Roots* series. Cambridge, Mass.: Educators Publishing Service, 1994.

Order from Educators Publishing Service.

Vocabulary from Classical Roots C. $10.80.
Teacher's Guide and Answer Key C. $18.75.
Vocabulary from Classical Roots D. $11.55.
Teacher's Guide and Answer Key D. $18.75.
Vocabulary from Classical Roots E. $11.55.
Teacher's Guide and Answer Key E. $18.75.

Grammar

Finlay, R. Robin. *Analytical Grammar: A Systematic Approach to Language Mastery.* Cary, N.C.: Analytical Grammar, 1996.

$99.95. Includes student workbook and teacher book. Order from Analytical Grammar.

Review and Reinforcement Worksheets and Answer Keys. $19.95. Order from Analytical Grammar.

Rod & Staff Grammar and Composition.

Communicating Effectively, Book One: English 9. Crockett, Ky.: Rod & Staff, 2003.

Order from Rod & Staff.

Pupil Textbook. $14.95.
Teacher's Manual. $18.95.
Tests and Editing Sheets. $2.55.

Communicating Effectively, Book Two: English 10. Crockett, Ky.: Rod & Staff, 2001.

Order from Rod & Staff.

Pupil Textbook. $14.95.

Teacher's Manual. $18.95.

Tests and Editing Sheets. $2.55.

English Handbook. $15.00.

Stewart, Donald S. The Stewart English Program. Cambridge, Mass.: Educators Publishing Service, 1998.

Order from Educators Publishing Service.

Book 1, Principles Plus . . . $9.30.

Teacher's Guide, Book 1. $6.10.

Book 2, Grammar Plus . . . $10.75.

Teacher's Guide, Book 2. $8.05.

Book 3, Writing Plus . . . $9.05.

Teacher's Guide, Book 3. $8.05.

Warriner, John, et al. *Elements of Language: Sixth Course.* New York: Holt, Rinehart & Winston, 2000.

$92.25. You don't need the in-print edition; many copies of older editions, titled *Warriner's English Grammar and Composition, Complete Course* (published by Harcourt Brace Jovanovich) are available used for a very economical price. Search the used-book portals at amazon.com and www.abebooks.com for copies.

Writing

Strunk, William, and E. B. White. *The Elements of Style.* 4th ed. New York: Pearson, Allyn & Bacon, 1999.

$15.95. Buy at any bookstore.

Writing Strands. Challenging Writing Programs for Homeschoolers series. Niles, Mich.: National Writing Institute, 1999.

The Writing Strands program can be purchased directly from the National Writing Institute or, at a small discount, from Rainbow Resource Center. The books aren't consumable; you do all the assignments on notebook paper, so you can reuse these books for another child.

Writing Strands 7. $20.00.

Writing Exposition. $20.00.

Evaluating Writing. $20.00.

This booklet for parents/teachers reviews common problems and how to fix them. It also includes an IBM PC program to improve your editing. A good parent resource.

26

GREAT BOOKS: HISTORY AND READING

Reading is to the mind what exercise is to the body.
—Richard Steele, *The Tatler*

SUBJECT: History and reading
TIME REQUIRED: 10 hours per week

If grammar-stage learning is fact-centered and logic-stage learning is skill-centered, then rhetoric-stage learning is idea-centered. During the rhetoric stage, the student actively engages with the ideas of the past and present—not just reading about them, but evaluating them, tracing their development, and comparing them to other philosophies and opinions.

This sounds abstract, but fortunately there's a very practical way to engage in this conversation of ideas: read, talk about, and write about the great books of the world.

To some extent, the division between history and literature has always been artificial; we know about history from archaeology and anthropology, but our primary source of historical knowledge is the testimony of those who lived in the past. Without the books written by Aristotle, Homer,

Plato, Virgil, and Caesar, we would know very little about the politics, religion, culture, and ideals of Greece and Rome.

By ninth grade, the student has already traveled twice through the story of mankind; she's already been exposed to the major writers and thinkers of each historical period. Although the student will record dates and read summaries of historical events, the focus of rhetoric-stage history is on ideas rather than on facts. The study of great books allows the past to speak for itself, combining history, creative writing, philosophy, politics, and ethics into a seamless whole.

The goal of the rhetoric stage is a greater understanding of our own civilization, country, and place in time, stemming from an understanding of what has come before us. "The old books," writes classical schoolmaster David Hicks, "lay a foundation for all later learning and life."[1] The student who has read Aristotle and Plato on human freedom, Thomas Jefferson on liberty, Frederick Douglass on slavery, and Martin Luther King, Jr., on civil rights will read Toni Morrison's *Beloved* with an understanding denied to the student who comes to the book without any knowledge of its roots.

Remember, again, that the goal of classical education is not an exhaustive exploration of great literature. The student with a well-trained mind continues to read, think, and analyze long after classes have ended.

We have supplied lists of great books for each year of study, the ninth-grade list being the shortest, the twelfth-grade list the longest and most complex. A few words about list making:

1. The lists are flexible. Depending on speed of reading and comprehension, the student might read eight books or fifteen or twenty. No one will read all the books listed.
2. If the student finds a work impossible to understand after she's had a good try at it, let her move on.
3. The lists are made up of books that are from the historical period being studied; the date of composition or publication of each entry follows in parentheses. Read the titles in chronological order—as they appear on the lists.
4. List making is dangerous. We've left important books off this list.

[1]David Hicks, *Norms and Nobility: A Treatise on Education* (New York: Praeger, 1981), p. 138.

We've put titles on it that you may find trivial. You will encounter many lists of important books as you home-school, created by people of different ideologies; and those lists inevitably reflect those ideologies. You can always add or drop titles from our list.

HOW TO DO IT

Once again, you'll be dividing your study into four years: Ancients (5000 B.C.–A.D. 400) in ninth grade; medieval–early Renaissance (400–1600) in tenth grade; late Renaissance–early modern (1600–1850) in eleventh grade; modern (1850–present) in twelfth grade.

For each year of study, the student should keep a large three-ringed binder, labeled "History and the Great Books." Each binder should be divided into four sections: The History Foundation, Book Contexts, Book Notes, and Compositions.

Half of each week's study time will be devoted to laying a foundation of historical knowledge; the second half, to the study of the Great Books.

The History Foundation

Half of each week's study time will be devoted to laying the history foundation. The student begins by once again progressing through the story of history, as he did in the grammar stage and logic stages of learning. In this third journey through time, his reading sets the stage for his encounter with the Great Books.

We suggest the following texts:

Ancient Times	*The History of the Ancient World,* Susan Wise Bauer
Middle Ages/ Early Renaissance	*The Civilization of the Middle Ages,* Norman F. Cantor *A History of Asia,* Rhoads Murphey
Late Renaissance/ Early Modern	*The Renaissance: A Short History,* Paul Johnson *America: A Narrative History,* George B. Tindall (read sections dealing with America up until 1850) *A History of Asia,* Rhoads Murphey (read sections dealing with Asia 1600–1850)

Modern	*Modern Times*, Paul Johnson *America: A Narrative History*, George B. Tindall (read sections dealing with America 1850–present) *A History of Asia*, Rhoads Murphey (read sections dealing with Asia 1850–present)

The student's task, over the course of each year, is simply to read each one of these books in the order listed above.

Your lesson planning is straightforward: count the total number of chapters assigned for the year and divide by the number of weeks you intend to do school—36 weeks is a useful benchmark. Fast readers should have no difficulty completing the work. For slower readers, you may choose to eliminate some of the chapters.

At the end of each chapter, the student should stop and record the following on a sheet of notebook paper:

1. A list of the important dates in the chapter, and why they stand out.
2. The names of the two or three most important individuals in the chapter.
3. Three or four events that stand out in the chapter.
4. Two events, people, or ideas he'd like to investigate further.

Note: George Tindall's *America: A Narrative History* has "thought questions" at the end of each chapter; answering these briefly in writing can replace the assignment above.

Study of the Great Books

The second half of each week's study will be devoted to reading, thinking about, and writing about the Great Books. You'll want to keep two additional reference books on hand: *The Timetables of History*, a big paperback reference book listing historical events, birth and death dates of important people, books, painting, inventions, and other facts from 4500 B.C. until the end of the twentieth century; and the Dorling Kindersley *History of the World*, a simple but highly visual survey of world history that covers people and events and all continents.

Try to make a realistic assessment of how many books the student will be able to cover in the course of a year. Eight books is a minimum; twelve is better; eighteen is stellar. Choose eight (or twelve, or eighteen) titles from the lists that follow, and read them in chronological order over the course of the year.

As he reads each book, the student will add a page to each of the remaining three sections of the notebook.

Book Contexts

For each book on this personalized list, the student should follow this pattern:

1. Check the birth and death dates of the author, and the date of the book's composition.
2. Look up the year of the book's publication in *The Timetables of History;* you should also look ten to fifty years on either side of this date to find out what happened just before and just after it was published. Make a note of events that seem significant (or interesting). Read the corresponding section in the Dorling Kindersley *History of the World,* paying particular interest to non-Western civilizations. Note any important events.
3. Write a one-page summary of this historical information, setting the book in historical perspective. Give basic information about the author, major historical events taking place during the author's lifespan, the author's country, and the author's purposes in writing; summarize great events going on in the rest of the world. File this page in the Contexts section of the notebook. As you progress through the lists in chronological order, this section will begin to resemble a one-volume world chronology in its own right.[2]

Book Notes

Now the student should prepare to read the first Great Book on the list.

1. Determine the book's genre. Is it a novel, an autobiography, a work of history, a play, or a poem? Take the time to read the history of this genre and the instructions on how to read it in *The Well-Educated Mind.*

[2]Create a context page only for the great books themselves, not for the history books we've included on the list. The ninth grader should make a Book Context page for Cicero's *De republica,* written around 54 B.C., but not for William Davis's history book *A Day in Old Rome.*

Take notes on this reading and keep the notes in the Book Notes section of the notebook. (If the book is political, like *Utopia* or *The Prince,* categorize it as history; if it is a work of philosophy or theology, you'll need to skip this step and continue on to step 2. We've suggested a couple of additional reference works on these books in the Resources.) *Note:* The student should repeat this reading the first time he encounters each genre in each year of study. That means he'll read the sections on poetry, drama, and history each year; he'll read the section on autobiography for the first time in tenth grade, when he encounters the *Confessions,* and will probably repeat this reading in eleventh and twelfth grades; he'll read the section on the novel for the first time when he reaches *Don Quixote* on the eleventh-grade list, and again in the twelfth-grade year. This repetition will continue to build the student's reading skills.[3]

2. If *The Well-Educated Mind* provides an annotation for the book, read it. Then read through the text, pencil in hand, following the suggestions outlined in *The Well-Educated Mind.* File all the notes you take on the book in the Book Notes section of the great-books notebook.

Compositions

1. Discuss the text. Talk about its purposes, its strengths, its weaknesses. Have a conversation about the ideas and whether or not they are valid. (This step is discussed in the "Rhetoric-Stage Reading" sections of *The Well-Educated Mind;* also see pages 500–502 for additional guidance.)
2. Write about the text. This is a flexible assignment; the student can write a book report, an evaluation, an argumentative essay proving some point about the book, or an analysis of the book's ideas. All of these forms have been taught in the writing programs recommended in Chapters 17 and 25 and in the rhetoric programs recommended in Chapter 24. Put the finished composition (at least two pages) in the Compositions section of the notebook.

We offer the following lists of great books as general guides for the high-

[3]*The Well-Educated Mind,* which is a guide to self-education in the classical tradition, recommends that the mature reader choose one genre at a time and read chronologically through it. Although this is probably ideal for building reading skills, the high-school student is completing history requirements as well as literature requirements in this Great Books Course, and so should read chronologically regardless of genre.

school student. Although she isn't obliged to read everything on this list, what she does read should be read in chronological order, as has been organized here.

Ninth Grade

Bible: Genesis—Book of Job
Epic of Gilgamesh (c. 2500 B.C.)
Homer, *Iliad* and *Odyssey* (c. 850 B.C.)
Sophocles, *Oedipus the King* (490 B.C.)
Aeschylus, *Agamemnon* (c. 458 B.C.)
Herodotus, *The Histories* (c. 441 B.C.)
Euripides, *Medea* (c. 431 B.C.)
Aristophanes, *The Birds* (c. 400 B.C.)
Thucydides, *The History of the Peloponnesian War* (c. 400 B.C.)
Plato, *The Republic* (c. 375 B.C.)
Aristotle, *On Poetics* (350 B.C.)
Aristotle, *Rhetoric* (c. 350 B.C.)
Bible: Book of Daniel (c. 165 B.C.)
Horace, *Odes* (c. 65 B.C.)
Lucretius, *On the Nature of Things* (c. 60 B.C.)
Cicero, *De republica* (54 B.C.)
Virgil, *Aeneid* (c. 30 B.C.)
Ovid, *Metamorphoses* (c. A.D. 5)
Bible: Corinthians 1 and 2 (c. A.D. 58)
Josephus, *Wars of the Jews* (c. A.D. 68)
Plutarch, *The Lives of the Noble Greeks and Romans* (c. A.D. 100)
Tacitus, *Annals* (c. A.D. 117)
Athanasius, *On the Incarnation* (c. A.D. 300)

Tenth Grade

Augustine, *Confessions* (c. 411)
Augustine, *City of God*, Book 8 (c. 426)
Boethius, *The Consolation of Philosophy* (524)
Koran (selections) (c. 650)
Bede, *The Ecclesiastical History of the English People* (731)
Beowulf (c. 1000)

Mabinogion (c. 1050)
Anselm, *Cur Deus Homo* (c. 1090)
Robert Goodwin, ed., *Aquinas: Selected Writings* (c. 1273)
Dante, *The Inferno* (1320)
Everyman (14th century)
Sir Gawain and the Green Knight (c. 1400)
Chaucer, *The Canterbury Tales* (selections) (c. 1400)
Margery Kempe, *The Book of Margery Kempe* (1430)
Malory, *Le Morte d'Arthur* (selections) (c. 1470)
Erasmus, *Education of a Christian Prince* (selections) (1510)
Machiavelli, *The Prince* (1513)
Thomas More, *Utopia* (1516)
Martin Luther, *Commentary on Galatians* (c. 1520)
John Calvin, *Institutes of the Christian Religion* (selections) (1536)
Christopher Marlowe, *Faustus* (1588)
Teresa of Avila, *The Life of Saint Teresa of Avila by Herself* (1588)
Edmund Spenser, *The Faerie Queene* (1590)
William Shakespeare, *Julius Caesar* (1599)
William Shakespeare, *Hamlet* (1600)
William Shakespeare, any other plays (c. 1592–1611)

Eleventh Grade

Miguel de Cervantes, *Don Quixote* (abridged) (1605)
King James Bible, *Psalms* (1611)
John Donne, *Divine Meditations* (c. 1635)
Rene Descartes, *Meditations* (1641)
John Milton, *Paradise Lost* (selections) (1644)
Moliere, *Tartuffe* (1669)
Blaise Pascal, *Pensees* (1670)
John Bunyan, *The Pilgrim's Progress* (1679)
John Locke, "An Essay Concerning Human Understanding" or "On the True End of Civil Government" (1690)
Jonathan Swift, *Gulliver's Travels* (1726)
Jean-Jacques Rousseau, "The Social Contract" (1762)
Edmund Burke, "On American Taxation" (1774)
The Declaration of Independence (1776)
Thomas Paine, *Common Sense* (1776)

Immanuel Kant, "Critique of Pure Reason" (1781)
Alexander Hamilton et al., *The Federalist* (1787–1788)
Constitution of the United States (ratified 1788)
William Blake, *Songs of Innocence and Experience* (1789)
Benjamin Franklin, *The Autobiography* (1791)
Thomas Paine, "The Rights of Man" (1792)
Mary Wollstonecraft, *A Vindication of the Rights of Women* (1792)
William Wordsworth and Samuel Taylor Coleridge, *Lyrical Ballads* (1798)
Jane Austen, *Pride and Prejudice* (1815)
Mary Shelley, *Frankenstein* (1818)
John Keats, "Ode to a Nightingale" and other poems (1820s)
James Fenimore Cooper, *The Last of the Mohicans* (1826)
Alfred, Lord Tennyson, "The Lady of Shalott" and other poems (1832)
Charles Dickens, *Oliver Twist* (1838)
Edgar Allan Poe, "The Fall of the House of Usher" and other stories (1839)
Ralph Waldo Emerson, "Self-Reliance" (1844)
Charlotte Bronte, *Jane Eyre* (1847)
Nathaniel Hawthorne, *The Scarlet Letter* (1850)
Herman Melville, *Moby-Dick* (1851)

Twelfth Grade

Emily Dickinson, *Final Harvest* (1830–1886)
Alexis de Tocqueville, *Democracy in America* (1835)
Karl Marx and Friedrich Engels, *Communist Manifesto* (1848)
Harriet Beecher Stowe, *Uncle Tom's Cabin* (1851)
Henry David Thoreau, *Walden* (1854)
Walt Whitman, *Leaves of Grass* (1855)
Fyodor Dostoyevsky, *Crime and Punishment* (1856)
Charles Darwin, *On the Origin of the Species* (1859)
Charles Dickens, *Great Expectations* (1861)
Harriet Jacobs, *Incidents in the Life of a Slave Girl, Written By Herself* (1861)
Abraham Lincoln, Gettysburg Address (1863)
Leo Tolstoy, *Anna Karenina* (1877)
Thomas Hardy, *The Return of the Native* (1878)
Henrik Ibsen, *A Doll's House* (1879)
Frederick Douglass, *The Life and Times of Frederick Douglass* (1881)
Friedrich Nietzsche, *Thus Spake Zarathustra* (1883)

Mark Twain, *Huckleberry Finn* (1884)
W. B. Yeats, *Selected Poems* (1895)
Stephen Crane, *The Red Badge of Courage* (1895)
Oscar Wilde, *The Importance of Being Earnest* (1899)
Sigmund Freud, *The Interpretation of Dreams* (1900)
Booker T. Washington, *Up From Slavery* (1901)
Joseph Conrad, *Heart of Darkness* (1902)
W. E. B. DuBois, *The Souls of Black Folk* (1903)
Edith Wharton, *The House of Mirth* (1905)
G. K. Chesterton, "The Innocence of Father Brown" (1911)
Wilfrid Owen, *Selected Poems* (1918)
Lytton Strachey, *Queen Victoria* (1921)
Robert Frost, "A Poem with Notes and Grace Notes" (Pulitzer, 1924)
Franz Kafka, *The Trial* (1925)
F. Scott Fitzgerald, *The Great Gatsby* (1925)
T. S. Eliot, *Murder in the Cathedral* (1935)
Zora Neale Hurston, *Their Eyes Were Watching God* (c. 1937)
George Orwell, *The Road to Wigan Pier* (1937)
Thornton Wilder, *Our Town* (1938)
John Steinbeck, *The Grapes of Wrath* (1939)
Adolf Hitler, *Mein Kampf* (1939)
George Orwell, *Animal Farm* (1945)
Tennessee Williams, *A Streetcar Named Desire* (1947)
Ralph Ellison, *Invisible Man* (1952)
C. S. Lewis, *Mere Christianity* (1952)
Arthur Miller, *The Crucible* (1953)
Saul Bellow, *Seize the Day* (1956)
Robert Bolt, *A Man for All Seasons* (1962)
Martin Luther King, Jr., "Why We Can't Wait" (1964)
Tom Stoppard, *Rosencrantz and Guildenstern Are Dead* (1967)
Aleksandr Solzhenitsyn, *The Gulag Archipelago* (1974)
Toni Morrison, *Beloved* (1988)
Philip Larkin, *Collected Poems* (1991)
Elie Wiesel, *All Rivers Run to the Sea: Memoirs* (1995)

The ninth grader, for example, would prepare to read Aristophanes' *The Birds* by first identifying the historical period under study: 450 B.C.–387 B.C., the lifespan of Aristophanes. She'll then look up 450–387 B.C. in the

Timetables of History. The *Timetables* reveal that during this period, several important law systems (the Torah and the Twelve Tables of the Roman law) were codified; Greek architecture flourished (the Acropolis was rebuilt along with several other important Greek buildings); the plague swept through Athens; Greece fought its way through a series of important battles, including the Peloponnesian War; and Ezra and Nehemiah rebuilt the wall of Jerusalem. According to the Dorling Kindersley *History of the World,* Darius of Persia rose to power as well; the Paracus culture flourished in Peru; and in Ohio, the Adena people reached the peak of their civilization.

Using this information plus knowledge gathered from her history reading, the student would go on to create a Context page—one or two pages summarizing the most significant historical events between 450 and 387 B.C. Since *The Birds* is a Greek work, the summary should begin by focusing on events in Greece—the Peloponnesian War, the renaissance in architecture, Greece's form of government—and should then go on to explain events in other countries. (Don't worry about having a "topic sentence" in this composition, or about putting it into essay format; although it should be grammatically correct and spelled properly, these Context pages are likely to sound list-like. "Meanwhile, over in Asia . . .")

This summary page is not meant to be an exhaustive study of ancient history between 450 and 387 B.C. Rather, the student should choose to focus on one series of events during this time. She'll write more than one summary about this period, after all; as she reads Herodotus or Sophocles or Plato, she'll come back to these years again and write yet another Context page, focusing on a different series of events. But even if she doesn't return to this period of history, don't worry. As in every part of the classical education, you're not aiming for a total mastery of history. You're teaching methods of learning—in this case, how to read historical documents and put them into context. The student who masters this process will go on "doing history" for the rest of her life. When this summary page is done, the student should file it in the Book Contexts section of the notebook.

The Birds is a play, so the student will now read the brief history of drama and the tips on how to read drama from *The Well-Educated Mind* (Chapter 8, "The World Stage: Reading through History with Drama"). She'll take notes, paying special attention to the development of Greek drama. She'll then read the annotation for *The Birds,* which outlines the basic plot. Finally, she'll crack open her volume of Aristophanes and read *The Birds* for herself, taking notes as *The Well-Educated Mind* directs. When she's finished, she'll head these notes "*The Birds* by Aristophanes" and put them in the Book Notes section of the great-books notebook.

Once this is done, she'll sit down with you (or a tutor; see pages 688–689) and talk about the play. Why was it written? What's Aristophanes' main point? Does it succeed as a drama? Which parts were interesting? Which were boring? Why? What is the play's structure? How might it be staged? *The Well-Educated Mind* provides discussion questions for each kind of literature in the "Third Level of Inquiry: Rhetoric-Stage Reading" section of each chapter; *Reading Strands*, published by the National Writing Institute, will also give you a pattern for this kind of Socratic dialogue.

When the conversation is over, the student is ready to write. She can do a standard "book report," summarizing the plot of *The Birds* and giving a brief evaluation of the play. She can answer one of the discussion questions in *The Well-Educated Mind.* She can explain what Aristophanes is saying about the nature of man and either agree or disagree. She can write about some technical aspect of Greek drama and how it applies to a scene in the play (this might require some additional research about the staging of Greek drama). This finished composition—which will give her a chance to exercise some of the skills taught in the writing and rhetoric programs recommended in Chapters 17, 24, and 25—should be filed in the Compositions section of the notebook.

How much should you do?

Rather than holding rigidly to a schedule of how much to complete per week, you should instead devote two hours per day to reading and taking notes on history, and to reading, talking about, and writing about the Great Books. You can choose to spend the first hour of each day on history, the second on Great Books; or the first five hours of each week on history, the second five on Great Books; or one week on history, one on Great Books; or the first semester of each year on history, the second on Great Books. Don't worry about keeping history reading and Great Books reading somehow parallel; the two areas of study will fall within the same historical period, but the student will progress through them at different rates. And the time spent on any particular Great Book can vary widely. If the ninth grader isn't stirred by Greek drama, she'll probably finish the Aristophanes assignment in a week. If she decides to write about a technical aspect of staging Greek drama, though, she'll need to do extra reading and research, and the *Birds* assignment could easily cover two or three weeks.

As a parent, it's your responsibility to make sure that those two hours are actually spent in reading and writing, rather than in daydreaming or creating doodles on notebook paper. Especially in the early years of high school, you should supervise this process, rather than allowing the student to disappear into the family room alone with her books. Great Books study in particular is demanding. It requires the student to work hard, to abandon simple question-and-answer learning in favor of a struggle with ideas. Often, the material isn't immediately appealing. The philosophies may be unfamiliar; the opinions are complex; the vocabulary is challenging. Put the student at the kitchen table (or wherever you're planning to be) so that you can encourage her to keep working.

Where do you get the books?

Classical education, as Douglas Wilson notes, isn't a package deal: "No one supplier or textbook publisher will provide you with everything you need in a fifty-pound box delivered by UPS."[4] High-school students will need to do some bookstore hunting and library scouring to find these texts (think of this as a class in advanced reference skills). However, the resurgence of interest in great-books curricula has produced affordable reprints of most of these books. Where we know of a particularly good edition, we've listed it, along with ordering information, at the end of this chapter. But finding the books is part of the process of education.

The sets of Norton anthologies described in Resources at the end of the chapter are wonderful reference works. These contain many difficult-to-find texts (such as the *Epic of Gilgamesh*) and a nice sampling of poetry. We suggest that you find "real books" (stand-alone texts) when possible because anthologies are awkward to handle and the print is very small. Also, they're hard to read in bed and impossible to handle in the bathtub.

HOW TO TALK ABOUT THE GREAT BOOKS

Talking is a necessary part of learning; a student can't write well about the great books until she's had an opportunity to converse about them. But many parents feel intimidated by the thought of carrying on a conversation about Aristophanes or *Moby-Dick*.

If you can read some of these great books along with your student, the

[4]Douglas Wilson, Wesley Callihan, and Douglas Jones, *Classical Education and the Home School* (Moscow, Idaho: Canon Press, 1995), p. 6.

discussion questions in *The Well-Educated Mind* will give you plenty of material for conversation. (Remember, there aren't necessarily "right" answers to most of these questions; what's more important is the process of talking the ideas through.) If you can't read the books, don't hesitate to make use of *Cliffs Notes,* which supply not only plot summaries, but also biographical notes, cultural background, discussion questions, and bibliographies for further reading. *Pink Monkey Notes,* which can be read online at www.pinkmonkey.com, are comparable in quality.

However, you don't have to shoulder the responsibility of this study alone. When you home-educate a high-school student, you organize her curriculum—but you can always outsource teaching responsibilities for those subjects for which you feel unprepared. The student still benefits from the personalized programs and individual attention that are so characteristic of home schooling when you use a tutor.

What options do you have for great-books study? First, ask around your community: colleagues, home-schooling friends, religious community. You might find an ex-English major who wrote a thesis on *Pride and Prejudice,* or an ex-classics major who studied Plato at Harvard twenty-five years ago and would be *delighted* to discuss the *Republic* with your high school student. Asking a friend to tutor your student for a year would be an imposition. Asking a friend to have a two-hour conversation about one book isn't. Remember: your student is working on a very basic level during this first introduction to the classics. She doesn't necessarily need a Ph.D. candidate to discuss the book with her.

If you live near a university or community college, call the secretary of the appropriate department (English for British or American literature, classics for Greek or Latin, comparative literature for modern works in translation, drama or theater for all plays) and ask whether any member of the faculty is interested in meeting with your student. You can also use graduate students and responsible seniors for this sort of tutoring; a good prep school might also supply you with a tutor.

At the end of this chapter, we have provided a list of universities that offer varying types of great-books curricula. These will prove especially valuable to those who live nearby. Most of the universities will also supply you with copies of their great-books reading lists and curricula on request; some may even allow you to join in online discussion groups or e-mail lists.

Online tutorials and discussion groups not connected to universities may also help your high-school student begin her study of great books.

Paid great-books tutorials for high-school students are offered by Escondido Tutorial Services (www.gbt.org), a classical tutoring service with a Reformed Protestant emphasis, and several other online tutorial services; a list is provided at the end of this chapter.

The American Classical League (www.aclclassics.org) has information about Greek and Latin texts, local teachers, and more; ACL also sponsors the National Junior Classical League (www.njcl.org) for high-school students studying the classics. Western Canon Great Books University (www.westerncanon.com) provides discussion forums (moderated by volunteer tutors) and links to other forums, lists, and online lectures centered on the great books of the Western tradition. More discussion forums can be found at www.welltrainedmind.com.

WRITING PROJECTS

The student should plan on writing a research paper in the spring of the ninth- and tenth-grade years. These research papers—six to eight pages in ninth grade, seven to ten pages in tenth grade—explore a historical topic. The ninth- and tenth-grade research papers should attempt to prove a theory about some historical event or series of events, using three to eight history resources, both primary (the works of Plato) and secondary (a critic's book *about* the works of Plato). These papers will put the techniques of rhetoric now being learned into use in writing and will prepare the student for the junior and senior projects described in Chapter 33.

Research-paper forms and procedures are covered in all of the grammar and composition texts we recommend. But because the very term *research paper* seems to terrify many parents (and students), we offer the following brief guide to preparing the first two research papers.

Preparation

Classically educated students don't need to suffer from "paper phobia," since the ongoing study of grammar and composition from early on and the continual writing of short papers have prepared them for the writing of longer papers. Along with mechanics, style, paragraph organization, and the development of arguments—all taught in the texts we recommend—the student must know how to outline.

In a proper outline, each subpoint supports the point that comes before:

I.
  A.
    1.
      a.

Correct outlining is taught in the Rod & Staff grammar books. If you're using a grammar text that doesn't cover outlining, consider ordering *Study Is Hard Work*, an excellent guide to study skills written by William H. Armstrong. Chapter Six, "Putting Ideas in Order," covers outlining skills. The entire guide is valuable, but it's written on a senior high/early college level, and many ninth graders may find its tone (not to mention the scary title) a little daunting. For simpler outlining resources, see page 367.

Inventio

Classical rhetoric divides writing into three stages: *inventio, dispositio,* and *elocutio. Inventio,* formulating an argument, involves picking the subject, deciding on a specific topic, and writing a thesis statement. Think of *inventio* as a three-step process.

1. Prereading. The student shouldn't begin by trying to write a thesis statement. Nor should she start making note cards immediately. Rather, she should begin by spending three or four weeks reading about the general topic she's decided to write on. Begin this process sometime in January. If, for example, the ninth grader decides to write about the Greek Empire after the death of Alexander the Great, she shouldn't try to come up with an exact subject for her paper right away. If she does, she'll more than likely end up with an unworkable subject—one that's too broad or too vague. Instead, she should plan to skim through plenty of books, reading the sections that deal with the Greeks after Alexander. She shouldn't make notes yet, but should put bookmarks (strips of notebook paper are fine) on any pages she finds particularly interesting or informative. As she reads, she should brainstorm, jotting down on a pad of paper thoughts that come to mind, questions that her reading brings up, and comments on what she's finding out. These jottings don't need to be connected in any way. The student is simply exploring all the branches of her topic.

2. Settling on an exact subject. After the student has done plenty of pre-reading—covering ten books or more—she should gather together all her jottings and look for a particular theme that keeps popping up. If she finds, for example, that she has continually written "The Seleucids came after Alexander in Syria. Syria was important because of the trade routes. Antiochus the Great ruled Syria. Antiochus thought he was the sun god. The Seleucids took over Israel," this suggests that that she should narrow her topic to "The Rulers of Syria after Alexander the Great."

This is a narrower and more manageable topic, but the student still isn't ready to write. Now she needs to settle on a thesis statement.

3. Developing a thesis statement is tricky. Fortunately, all the curricula we recommend carefully develop this skill. As the parent/teacher, you should remember this simple definition: a thesis is a statement that requires proof. "Alexander's successors in Syria" or "Syria under Antiochus the Great" aren't thesis statements—they're simply phrases; neither needs to be proved. "Alexander's successors shared his megalomania" or "Antiochus the Great's insanity caused him to lose control of Syria" are thesis statements. Both require the student to explain, using examples from history to support these conclusions.

Bad thesis statements tend to have two problems: either they're not specific enough, or they're so obvious that they don't require support. "Antiochus the Great was a bad ruler" is a bad thesis because it isn't specific—you could say this about any number of ancient potentates ("Nero was a bad ruler," "Akhenaton was a bad ruler"). "Alexander's empire was divided among his generals" doesn't work either. This is perfectly obvious. What's left to say?

"Antiochus's religious obsessions ruined his hold on his empire" is a good thesis statement because it leaves the student something to prove. She's suggesting a specific cause for the decline of the Seleucid Empire. Now she has to defend this conclusion, using historical evidence.

Dispositio

Once the student settles on a topic, she has to arrange supporting information in proper order for a persuasive argument—*dispositio*.

The student should begin by glancing back over the notes she's taken on her reading. From this information, she should make an outline covering the main points of her argument. These are the facts her reader will have to believe in order to be convinced. The outline should be very basic, only three or four points long, each point assigned a Roman numeral. The ninth grader's outline might look like this:

I. Antiochus suffered from religious delusions.
II. These delusions kept him from paying attention to his borders.
III. These delusions caused him to treat his subjects with unnecessary cruelty.

The student should then write each major point at the top of a separate sheet of paper.

Now she's ready to start making note cards. The classic way of collecting information for a research paper is to write down quotes and general information on 3 × 5 cards, each card marked with the title of the book used and the author's last name. The student should go back through the books she used for prereading. In each place where she put a marker, she should evaluate whether or not the information supports one of her main points. If so, she should jot down on the note card either a paraphrase of the idea in the book or an exact quote. And she should indicate on each card where the information belongs by marking it with a Roman numeral that corresponds to a numeral on the outline.

There's no reason why the student shouldn't do this on a computer. Note cards have traditionally been used because the student can shuffle them around as she works on the flow of her argument. But since the cut-and-paste function on a word processor has the same effect, she can input her quotes and paraphrases instead.

Once the student has collected information (four to six sources for a ninth-grade paper, six to ten for a tenth-grade paper), she should put the cards for each Roman numeral into a pile and use this information to develop a more detailed outline:

I. Antiochus suffered from religious delusions.
    A. He thought he was the god Zeus.
        1. He retreated to his estate to practice being divine.
        2. He demanded that his courtiers worship him.

Each of these points is based on a fact discovered while reading and jotted onto a card.

Elocutio

When the outline is complete, the student is ready to write. *Elocutio,* the final stage of written rhetoric, involves the words, phrases, figures of speech, and writing techniques used in persuasive writing. The student should sit down with the outline and note cards, and write one well-structured paragraph about each point in the outline. The paper should always conclude with a summary paragraph, restating the student's thesis and main supporting points. Each book consulted must be placed on a bibliography page, arranged alphabetically by author. We highly recommend keeping a standard research-paper guide on hand throughout this process. *Schaum's Quick Guide to Writing Great Research Papers,* by Laurie Rozakis, is an excellent and straightforward manual covering all of the above steps, and it offers guidance on how to properly document all research.

WHAT ABOUT AMERICAN GOVERNMENT?

A course in American government is a requirement for high-school graduation in most states. Traditionally, American government is offered as a separate one-credit course. However, there's no reason to artificially separate the study of America's present government from its historical development.

As you study through the final two years of history, you'll cover American history from its foundation to the present. The great-books list includes the foundational texts of America's government: The Declaration of Independence, *The Federalist,* and the Constitution of the United States (check to see that your copy includes the Bill of Rights and amendments). Make sure that these classics, along with Burke's "On American Taxation," Thomas Paine's "The Rights of Man," and Alexis de Tocqueville's *Democracy in America,* are on the student's final reading list. The student who reads and understands these books has grasped the core principles of American civics.

However, you'll probably want to supplement these with a guide to United States government. Although you can use a standard high-school government text (such as *Holt American Government*), you can also use a slightly more engaging text such as *The Complete Idiot's Guide to American Government* (which covers all the government required for standard exams such as the AP or CLEP). Read the appropriate sections of the government text as part of history reading; after the student reads the Constitution, for example, she would read from the *Timetables of History,* and Part 1 of *The Complete Idiot's Guide* (this covers the Constitutional Convention, the Constitution, the Bill of Rights, and the Amendments) or Unit 1 of *Holt American Government.* Read Units 7 and 8 of *Holt American Government* when you read *The Federalist* (state and local government); read Parts 2, 3, and 6 of *The Complete Idiot's Guide* or Units 2, 3, and 4 of Holt when you read "On American Taxation" (this covers the branches of government); read Part 5 of *The Complete Idiot's Guide* or Units 5 and 6 of *Holt American Government* when you read "The Rights of Man" (individual rights and the political system). These are merely suggestions, and you should feel free to divide up the student's government reading in another way if it seems to make more sense.

If the student has time, she will also benefit from working through the Critical Thinking Press resource *You Decide: Applying the Bill of Rights to Real Cases,* which presents the student with clear retellings of seventy-five Supreme Court cases and invites her to judge them, using the Bill of Rights as a guide.

When the student has finished this reading, has marked essential dates in the development of the United States government on a time line, and has written about each of these foundational texts, give her a credit on her transcript for American Government (see Chapter 39 for a fuller explanation). When planning out the student's reading list for the years that cover American history (1600–1850 and 1850–present), be sure to allow some extra time for this government study.

STARTING IN THE MIDDLE

Although this chapter describes beginning the study of the ancients in ninth grade and moving through the medieval/early Renaissance, late Renaissance/early modern, and modern lists in grades 10, 11, and 12, this pattern can be adjusted to fit your own needs. A student who has begun the chronological study of history in middle school may begin ninth grade having just finished the ancients, or ready to move into the late Renaissance/early modern years. Whenever your student reaches ninth grade, move him to whichever great-books list corresponds to the period he would naturally study next (see pages 277–278 in Chapter 16 for more detailed directions).

If you're just beginning this for the first time with a high-school student who only has a couple of years left, you have several choices:

1. Begin with whatever great-books list corresponds to the student's grade year and move forward; don't worry too much about what you've skipped. High-school standards in the United States mandate the study of American literature and history, but are much less likely to insist on the study of ancient classics.
2. Condense the first two years of study into one list, attempting to pick half of the year's books from the ancients list and half from the medieval/early Renaissance list.
3. Use a standard high-school history textbook, but fold the reading and writing about great books into this textbook study at the appropriate points (the student will read the *Odyssey* when studying Greece, *Moby-Dick* when studying nineteenth-century America) and give the student a literature credit for this work.

UNIVERSITY SOURCES FOR GREAT-BOOKS CURRICULA

Alabama

Auburn University, Auburn, Alabama: 334-844-4000 general, for great books program; www.media.cla.auburn.edu/english.

The Department of English offers "World Literature at Auburn."

Faulkner University, Montgomery, Alabama; 800-879-9816 general; 334-386-7313 for honors college. www.faulkner.edu/o/academics/honors/gbhc/index.htm.

A Protestant school that offers great-books study through the Great Books Honors College.

California

Seaver College, Pepperdine University, Malibu, California; 310-506-7654; www.seaver.pepperdine.edu/humanities/programs/greatbooks.htm.

The Great Books Colloquium is a five-course sequence offered by the Humanities/Teacher Education Division.

Thomas Aquinas College, Santa Paula, California; 800-634-9797; www.thomasaquinas.edu.

The entire curriculum is centered on great books and Socratic teaching.

Canada

Brock University, St. Catherines, Ontario; 905-688-5550; www.brocku.ca.

Carleton University, Ottawa, Ontario; 613-520-7400; www.carleton.ca.

Concordia University, Montreal, Quebec; 514-848-2424; www.concordia.ca.

Malaspina University, Nanaimo, British Columbia; 250-753-3245; www.mala.ca (general university website).

The Malaspina website offers lists of great books, time lines, links, and more at www.malaspina.org.

Connecticut

Wesleyan University, Middletown, Connecticut; 860-685-3700; www.wesleyan.edu/col.

The College of Letters is an interdisciplinary major centered on great books from ancient times to the twentieth century.

Georgia

Mercer University, Macon, Georgia; 800-MERCER-U; www.mercer.edu/gbk.

Offers a core Great Books program in the College of Liberal Arts.

Idaho

New St. Andrews College, Moscow, Idaho; 208-882-1566; www.nsa.edu.

A Reformed Protestant school where the entire curriculum is focused around the study of great books.

Illinois

Shimer College, Waukegan, Illinois; 312-235-3500; www.shimer.edu.

The college uses no textbooks—all original source readings.

The University of Chicago: William B. and Catherine V. Graham School of General Studies, Chicago, Illinois; 773-702-1722; www.grahamschool.uchicago.edu.

The Basic Program of Liberal Education for Adults is a noncredit discussion program—a four-year sequence of classics.

Wilbur Wright College, Chicago, Illinois; 773-481-8014; faculty.ccc.edu/colleges/wright/greatbooks/home.htm.

Indiana

University of Notre Dame, South Bend, Indiana; 574-631-7172; www.nd.edu/~pls.

The Program of Liberal Studies is a three-year sequence centered on great books.

Louisiana

Northwestern State University of Louisiana, Natchitoches, Louisiana; 800-838-2208 general; 318-357-6011 for the Scholars' College; www.nsula.edu/scholars_college.

The Louisiana Scholars' College offers a great-books program, from classics to moderns.

Maryland

St. John's College, Annapolis, Maryland; 410-263-2371; www.stjohnscollege.edu.

A four-year program of reading, discussion, and writing.

Massachusetts

Boston University, Boston, Massachusetts; 617-353-5404; www.bu.edu/core. The "Core Curriculum" centers on the discussion of great books and writing skills.

Minnesota

Saint Olaf College, Northfield, Minnesota; 507-786-3201; www.stolaf.edu/depts/great-conversation.

New Hampshire

Saint Anselm College, Manchester, New Hampshire; 603-641-7000; www.anselm.edu, www.dbanach.com/gbs.htm.

Offers the Liberal Studies in the Great Books program.

New Mexico

St. John's College, Santa Fe, New Mexico; 505-984-6000; www.sjcsf.edu.

A four-year program of reading, discussion, and writing.

New York

Columbia College, Columbia University, New York, New York; 212-854-2453; www.college.columbia.edu/core/classes/lh.php.

Offers a year-long Masterpieces of Western Literature and Philosophy course.

Oregon

Gutenberg College, Eugene, Oregon; 541-683-5141; www.gutenberg.edu.

A Christian school with a great-books program.

Pennsylvania

Temple University, Philadelphia, Pennsylvania; 215-204-5625; http://temple.edu/ih.

The Intellectual Heritage Program is a great-books sequence; the core curriculum focuses on great books in eight different areas.

Texas

College of Arts and Sciences, University of North Texas, Denton, Texas; 940-565-2107; www.engl.unt.edu.

Offers a great-books series through the English department.

Virginia

Emory & Henry College, Emory, Virginia; 276-944-4121; www.ehc.edu/academic/libarts.htm.

Methodist affiliation; offers great-books courses as part of the liberal arts curriculum.

Lynchburg College, Lynchburg, Virginia; 434-544-8652; www.lynchburg.edu/symposium.xml.

The Lynchburg College Symposium Readings Program reaches outside the college to encourage reading, writing, and discussion focused on the classics.

Washington

Central Washington University, Ellensburg, Washington; 509-963-1445; www.cwu.edu/~dhc/books.html.

The William O. Douglas Honors College offers a four-year great-books program.

Whitman College, Walla Walla, Washington; 509-527-05111; www.whitman.edu/general_studies.

The General Studies Program offers courses on great books and their world views.

Wisconsin

The University of Wisconsin-Milwaukee, Milwaukee, Wisconsin; 414-229-1122; www.uwm.edu/Dept/Great_Books.

Offers an undergraduate Great Books Program.

SCHEDULES

Ninth through twelfth grade	2 hrs. per day	Read, discuss, write about history and great books.

RESOURCES

For publisher and catalog addresses, telephone numbers, and other information, see Sources (pages 751–778). Most books can be obtained from any bookstore or library; where we know of a mail-order option, we have provided it.

Basic texts for the four-year rhetoric stage are listed first. A great-books section follows. The list for each year of study is in chronological order. Most of these book are available in standard editions, but where we think a specific edition is particularly good, we have recommended it.

Many of the resources recommended in Chapter 16 are still suitable for high-school students, particularly the Jackdaw portfolios of primary sources. We suggest that you call Jackdaw for a catalog and order any of the packs that look particularly interesting to your student. Check Resources at the end of Chapter 16 for details.

Basic Texts

Armstrong, William H. *Study Is Hard Work: The Most Accessible and Lucid Text Available on Acquiring and Keeping Study Skills Through a Lifetime*, 2d ed. Boston, Mass.: David R. Godine, 1998.

$11.95.

Bauer, Susan Wise. *The History of the Ancient World: From the Earliest Accounts to the Fall of Rome.* New York: W. W. Norton, 2007.

———. *The Well-Educated Mind: A Guide to the Classical Education You Never Had.* New York: W. W. Norton, 2003.
$27.95. Order from any bookstore or from Peace Hill Press.

Bundy, George. *You Decide: Applying the Bill of Rights to Real Cases.* Pacific Grove, Calif.: Critical Thinking Press, 1992.
$26.99 ($14.99 additional for the teacher's guide, which is necessary because it contains the Supreme Court decisions). Order from Critical Thinking Press.

Cantor, Norman F. *The Civilization of the Middle Ages: A Completely Revised and Expanded Edition of Medieval History.* New York: HarperPerennial, 1994.
$18.95.

Fry, Plantagenet Somerset. *History of the World,* 3d ed., rev. and updated. New York: Dorling Kindersley, 2007.
$39.99. Order from any bookstore.

Grun, Bernard, and Daniel J. Boorstin. *The Timetables of History.* 4th rev. ed. New York: Touchstone, 2005.
$25.00.

Holt American Government. Austin, Tex.: Holt, Rinehart and Winston, 2002.
$100.75. Order from any bookstore. A high-school standard (you may be able to buy a used 1998 edition, which is not significantly different, for a lower price).

Johnson, Paul. *Modern Times: The World from the Twenties to the Nineties,* rev. ed. New York: HarperPerennial, 2001.
$21.00.

———. *The Renaissance: A Short History.* New York: Modern Library, 2002.
$12.95.

Murphey, Rhoads. *A History of Asia,* 5th ed. New York: Longman, 2005.
$88.67.

Rozakis, Laurie. *Schaum's Quick Guide to Writing Great Research Papers.* New York: McGraw-Hill, 1999.
$10.85.

Shaffrey, Mary, and Melanie Fonder. *The Complete Idiot's Guide to American Government*, 2d ed. New York: Alpha Books, 2005.

$18.95. Order from any bookstore. An engaging and sometimes irreverent "text" that nevertheless covers all the bases.

Tindall, George, and David Shi. *America: A Narrative History, Brief Seventh Edition (Single Volume)*. New York: W. W. Norton, 2007.

$50.00. This book comes in various volumes and editions; for high-school students, get the one-volume brief edition.

For Additional History Reading

Daugherty, James. *The Magna Carta.* Sandwich, Mass.: Beautiful Feet Books, 1998.

$11.95. Order from American Home-School Publishing.

Davis, William S. *A Day in Old Athens.* Minneapolis, Minn.: University of Minnesota Press, 1960.

$18.00. Order from American Home-School Publishing.

———. *A Day in Old Rome.* New York: Biblo & Tannen, 1963.

$25.00. Order from American Home-School Publishing.

———. *Life in Elizabethan Days.* New York: Biblo & Tannen, 1994.

$25.00. Order from American Home-School Publishing.

———. *Life in a Medieval Barony.* New York: Biblo & Tannen, 1990.

$25.00. Order from American Home-School Publishing.

Fairbank, John King, and Merle Goldman. *China: A New History*, 2d enlarged ed. New York: Belknap Press, 2006.

$21.00. Order from any bookstore.

Howarth, David. *1066: The Year of Conquest.* New York: Viking Penguin, 1981.

$14.00. Order from any bookstore.

Johnson, Paul. *A History of the American People.* New York: HarperCollins, 1999.

$20.00. Order from any bookstore.

Keay, John. *India: A History.* New York: Grove Press, 2001.
$19.95. Order from any bookstore.

Lee, Ki-Baik. *A New History of Korea.* Trans. Edward W. Wagner. Boston, Mass.: Harvard University Press, 1984.
$19.95. Order from any bookstore.

Marrin, Albert. *America and Vietnam: The Elephant and the Tiger.* Sandwich, Mass.: Beautiful Feet Books, 2002.
$13.95. Order from The Book Peddler. Marrin's history books are excellent for beginning historians; they offer readable overviews of complex events, driven by a strong narrative style.

———. *Empires Lost and Won: The Spanish Heritage in the Southwest.* New York: Simon & Schuster, 1997.
$19.00. Order from any bookstore.

———. *George Washington and the Founding of a Nation.* Dutton, 2003.
$14.99. Order from American Home-School Publishing.

———. *Stalin: Russia's Man of Steel.* Sandwich, Mass.: Beautiful Feet Books, 2002.
$13.95. Order from The Book Peddler.

Meyer, Milton W. *Japan: A Concise History,* 3d ed. Lanham, Md.: Littlefield Adams, 1992.
$16.95. Order from any bookstore.

Morgan, Kenneth O., ed. *The Oxford Illustrated History of Britain,* rev. ed. Oxford: Oxford University Press, 2001.
$31.95. Order from any bookstore.

Roberts, John Morris. *The New Penguin History of the World.* 5th ed., rev. and updated. New York: Penguin, 2007.
$22.00. Order from any bookstore.

Additional Great-Books Resources

Cliffs Notes. New York: Wiley Publishing.
Most bookstores stock these distinctive yellow paperbacks, which offer

summaries and brief critical analyses. Visit www.cliffsnotes.com for a complete list of available notes.

Guinness, Os, and Louise Cowan. *Invitation to the Classics.* Grand Rapids, Mich.: Baker Book House, 1998.

$34.99. Offers historical background on fifty Western classics and evaluates them from a Protestant Christian perspective.

Pink Monkey Notes. www.pinkmonkey.com.

This online alternative to *Cliffs Notes* offers good summaries and critical considerations.

Online Resources

Escondido Tutorial Service. 2634 Bernardo Avenue, Escondido, Calif. 92029; www.gbt.org.

Offers year-long tutorials in the great books from a Reformed Protestant perspective; also serves as a gateway to a number of other tutorial services and courses.

Oxford Tutorials. 6500 NE 192nd Place, Kenmore, Wash. 98028; 425-402-9624; www.oxfordtutorials.com.

Courses in Shakespeare, Latin, and logic, as well as in the core great books.

Schola Tutorials. P.O. Box 546, Potlatch, Idaho 83855; 208-301-2637; www.schola-tutorials.org.

Great books as well as Latin, Greek, rhetoric, and other subjects; taught from a Reformed Protestant perspective.

Great Books

Any titles listed without mentioning a specific edition can be easily located in standard editions. We've supplied ordering information where possible, but texts can also be bought through bookstores or online book services. In addition, public libraries should carry almost all of these titles.

The easiest way to read great books is to buy a Norton anthology—the standard collection of classic works between two covers, all properly annotated. These are great reference works, but, like all reference works, they are unwieldy and have very small print. Your student won't read these in bed or in the car, only at a desk or table. We think you should use individual texts where possible because they're easier to read and more fun. Also, some works that you'll want to read in full are only excerpted in the anthologies. But consider investing in the Norton anthologies to fill in the gaps. You can also buy instructor's manuals with discussion questions and guides—an extremely valuable resource.

Baym, Nina, gen. ed., et al. *The Norton Anthology of American Literature,* 6th ed. New York: Norton, 2002.

$62.50 per package. Order from W. W. Norton or through any bookstore. This anthology is divided into five volumes (A–E) but ships in two packages, each of which has its own ISBN.

Package 1 (Volumes A, B): *Literature to 1865*. From the explorers and settlers through Whitman; includes the American Founding Fathers.

Package 2 (Volumes C, D, E): *1865 to Present*. From Clemens through the modern poets.

Greenblatt, Stephen, gen. ed. *The Norton Anthology of English Literature,* 8th ed. New York: W. W. Norton, 2005.

$62.50 for each volume. Order from W. W. Norton or through any bookstore.

Volume 1: *The Middle Ages through the Restoration and the Eighteenth Century.*

Volume 2: *The Romantic Period through the Twentieth Century.*

Lawall, Sarah, et al. *The Norton Anthology of Western Literature,* 8th ed. New York: W. W. Norton, 2005.

$62.50 for each volume. Order from W. W. Norton or through any bookstore.

Previous editions, called *The Norton Anthology of World Masterpieces,* can be bought used.

Volume 1.

Volume 2.

Ancients, 5000 B.C.–A.D. 400 (Ninth Grade)

Bible: Genesis—Book of Job.

Use a modern version for clarity. The New International Version is colloquial and clear; the New American Standard Bible is more stilted and also more literal.

Epic of Gilgamesh (c. 2500 B.C.).

Gilgamesh: A New Rendering in English Verse. Trans. David Ferry. New York: Farrar, Straus and Giroux, 1993.

Homer, *Iliad* and *Odyssey* (c. 850 B.C.).

Homer. *The Iliad*. Trans. Robert Fagles. New York: Penguin Books, 1998.
Homer. *The Odyssey*. Trans. Robert Fagles. New York: Penguin Books, 1999.

Sophocles, *Oedipus the King* (490 B.C.).

Sophocles. *The Oedipus Cycle*. Trans. Robert Fitzgerald and Dudley Fitts. San Diego: Harvest Books, 2002.

Aeschylus, *Agamemnon* (c. 458 B.C.).

Aeschylus. *Aeschylus I: The Oresteia*. Trans. David R. Slavitt. Philadelphia: University of Pennsylvania Press, 1997.

Herodotus, *The Histories* (c. 441 B.C.).

Trans. Robin Waterfield. Oxford: Oxford University Press, 1998.

Euripides, *Medea* (c. 431 B.C.).

Euripides. *Euripides: Medea, Hippolytus, Electra, Helen*. Trans. James Morwood. Oxford: Oxford University Press, 1998.

Aristophanes, *The Birds* (c. 400 B.C.).

Aristophanes. *Aristophanes I: Clouds, Wasps, Birds*. Trans. Peter Meineck. Indianapolis: Hackett, 1998.

Thucydides, *The History of the Peloponnesian War* (c. 400 B.C.).

The Landmark Thucydides. Trans. Richard Crawley. New York: Free Press, 1998.

Plato, *The Republic* (c. 375 B.C.).

Trans. Desmond Lee. New York: Viking Press, 1976.

Aristotle, *On Poetics* (350 B.C.).

Aristotle. *Aristotle on Poetics.* Trans. Seth Benardete. South Bend, Ind.: St. Augustine Press, 2002.

Aristotle, *Rhetoric* (c. 350 B.C.).

Bible: Book of Daniel (c. 165 B.C.).

Horace, *Odes* (c. 65 B.C.).

New Translations by Contemporary Poets. Ed. J. D. McClatchy. Princeton, N.J.: Princeton University Press, 2005.

Lucretius, *On the Nature of Things* (c. 60 B.C.).

Cicero, *De republica* (54 B.C.).

Virgil, *Aeneid* (c. 30 B.C.).

Ovid, *Metamorphoses* (c. A.D. 5).

Bible: Corinthians 1 and 2 (c. A.D. 58).

Josephus, *Wars of the Jews* (c. A.D. 68).

Plutarch, *The Lives of the Noble Greeks and Romans* (c. A.D. 100).

Plutarch. *Roman Lives: A Selection of Eight Lives.* Trans. Robin Waterfield. Oxford: Oxford University Press, 2000.

Plutarch. *Greek Lives: A Selection of Nine Lives.* Trans. Robin Waterfield. Oxford: Oxford University Press, 1999.

Tacitus, *Annals* (c. A.D. 117).

Athanasius, *On the Incarnation* (c. A.D. 300).

Medieval/Early Renaissance, 400–1600 (Tenth Grade)

Augustine, *Confessions* (c. 411).

Trans. Henry Chadwick. Oxford: Oxford University Press, 1998.

Augustine, *City of God,* Book 8 (c. 426).

Abridged ed. Trans. Marcus Dods. New York: Modern Library, 2000.

Boethius, *The Consolation of Philosophy* (524).

Koran (selections) (c. 650).

Bede, *The Ecclesiastical History of the English People* (731).

Eds. Judith McClure and Roger Collins. Oxford: Oxford University Press, 1999.

Beowulf (c. 1000).

Beowulf: A New Verse Translation. Trans. Seamus Heaney. New York: W. W. Norton, 2001.

Mabinogion (c. 1050).

Anselm, *Cur Deus Homo* (c. 1090).

Thomas Aquinas, *Selected Writings* (c. 1273).

Thomas Aquinas. *Selected Writings of St. Thomas Aquinas*. Trans. Ralph McInerny. New York: Penguin, 1999.

Dante, *The Inferno* (1320).

Trans. Robert Pinsky. New York: Farrar, Straus and Giroux, 1997.

Everyman (14th century).

Sir Gawain and the Green Knight (c. 1400).

Sir Gawain and the Green Knight, Patience, Pearl: Verse Translations. Trans. Marie Boroff. New York: W. W. Norton, 2001.

Chaucer, *The Canterbury Tales* (selections) (c. 1400).

Trans. Nevill Coghill. New York: Penguin Books, 2003 (rev. ed.).

Margery Kempe, *The Book of Margery Kempe* (1430).

Margery Kempe. *The Book of Margery Kempe: A New Translation, Contexts, Criticism*. Trans. and ed. Lynn Staley. New York: W. W. Norton, 2001.

Malory, *Le Morte d'Arthur* (selections) (c. 1470).

Erasmus, *Education of a Christian Prince* (selections) (1510).

Machiavelli, *The Prince* (1513).

2d ed. Trans. Harvey C. Mansfield. Chicago: University of Chicago Press, 1998.

Thomas More, *Utopia* (1516).

Trans. Robert M. Adams. New York: W. W. Norton, 1991.

Martin Luther, *Commentary on Galatians* (c. 1520).

John Calvin, *Institutes of the Christian Religion* (selections) (1536).

Christopher Marlowe, *Faustus* (1588).

Teresa of Avila, *The Life of Saint Teresa of Avila by Herself* (1588).

Trans. J. M. Cohen. New York: Penguin, 1988.

Edmund Spenser, *The Faerie Queene* (1590).

William Shakespeare, *Julius Caesar* (1599).
William Shakespeare. *Julius Caesar: Oxford School Shakespeare.* 3d ed. Ed. Roma Gill. Oxford: Oxford University Press, 2001.

William Shakespeare, *Hamlet* (1600).
William Shakespeare. *Hamlet: Oxford School Shakespeare.* Rev. ed. Ed. Roma Gill. Oxford: Oxford University Press, 2002.

William Shakespeare, any other plays (c. 1592–1611).

Late Renaissance/Early Modern, 1600–1850 (Eleventh Grade)

Miguel de Cervantes, *Don Quixote* (1605).
Abridged. Trans. Walter Starkie. New York: Signet, 1987.

King James Bible, *Psalms* (1611).
John Donne, *Divine Meditations* (c. 1635).
Rene Descartes, *Meditations* (1641).
John Milton, *Paradise Lost* (selections) (1644).
Moliere, *Tartuffe* (1669).

Blaise Pascal, *Pensées* (1670).
The *Pensées* are lengthy. If you'd prefer an edited version, try Peter Kreeft's *Christianity for Modern Pagans: Pascal's Pensees Edited, Outlined, and Explained* (Fort Collins, Col.: Ignatius Press, 1997). This picks out the most relevant of the *Pensées* for today's student and provides discussion.

John Bunyan, *The Pilgrim's Progress* (1679).

John Locke, "An Essay Concerning Human Understanding" or "On the True End of Civil Government" (1690).
Jonathan Swift, *Gulliver's Travels* (1726).
Edmund Burke, "On American Taxation" (1774).

Jean-Jacques Rousseau, "The Social Contract" (1762).
Trans. Maurice Cranston. New York: Penguin, 1968.

The Declaration of Independence (1776).
Thomas Paine, *Common Sense* (1776).
Immanuel Kant, "Critique of Pure Reason" (1781).

Alexander Hamilton et al., *The Federalist* (1787–1788).
Constitution of the United States (ratified 1788).
William Blake, *Songs of Innocence and Experience* (1789).
Benjamin Franklin, *The Autobiography* (1791).
Thomas Paine, "The Rights of Man" (1792).
Mary Wollstonecraft, *A Vindication of the Rights of Women* (1792).
William Wordsworth and Samuel Taylor Coleridge, *Lyrical Ballads* (1798).
Jane Austen, *Pride and Prejudice* (1815).
Mary Shelley, *Frankenstein* (1818).
John Keats, "Ode to a Nightingale" and other poems (1820s).
James Fenimore Cooper, *The Last of the Mohicans* (1826).
Alfred, Lord Tennyson, "The Lady of Shalott" and other poems (1832).
Charles Dickens, *Oliver Twist* (1838).
Edgar Allan Poe, "The Fall of the House of Usher" and other stories (1839).
Ralph Waldo Emerson, "Self-Reliance" (1844).
Charlotte Bronte, *Jane Eyre* (1847).
Nathaniel Hawthorne, *The Scarlet Letter* (1850).
Herman Melville, *Moby-Dick* (1851).

Modern, 1850–Present Day (Twelfth Grade)

Alexis de Tocqueville, *Democracy in America* (1835).
Trans. Manfield and Winthrop; edited and abridged by Richard D. Heffner. New York: Signet, 2001.

Karl Marx and Friedrich Engels, *Communist Manifesto* (1848).
Harriet Beecher Stowe, *Uncle Tom's Cabin* (1851).
Henry David Thoreau, *Walden* (1854).
Walt Whitman, *Leaves of Grass* (1855).
Emily Dickinson, *Final Harvest* (1830–1886).

Fyodor Dostoyevsky, *Crime and Punishment* (1856).
Trans. Richard Pevear and Larissa Volokhonsky. New York: Random House, 2008.

Charles Darwin, *On the Origin of the Species* (1859).
Charles Dickens, *Great Expectations* (1861).
Harriet Jacobs, *Incidents in the Life of a Slave Girl, Written By Herself* (1861).
Abraham Lincoln, Gettysburg Address (1863).

Leo Tolstoy, *Anna Karenina* (1877).

Trans. Constance Garnett, rev. Leonard J. Kent and Nina Berberova. New York: Barnes and Noble, 2004.

Thomas Hardy, *The Return of the Native* (1878).

Henrik Ibsen, *A Doll's House* (1879).

Trans. Frank McGuinness. New York: Faber & Faber, 1997.

Frederick Douglass, *The Life and Times of Frederick Douglass* (1881).
Friedrich Nietzsche, *Thus Spake Zarathustra* (1883).
Mark Twain, *Huckleberry Finn* (1884).

W. B. Yeats, *Selected Poems* (1895).

W. B. Yeats. *The Collected Poems of W. B. Yeats.* 2d rev. ed.. Ed. Richard J. Finneran. New York: Scribner's, 1996.

Stephen Crane, *The Red Badge of Courage* (1895).
Oscar Wilde, *The Importance of Being Earnest* (1899).
Sigmund Freud, *The Interpretation of Dreams* (1900).
Booker T. Washington, *Up From Slavery* (1901).
Joseph Conrad, *Heart of Darkness* (1902).
W. E. B. DuBois, *The Souls of Black Folk* (1903).
Edith Wharton, *The House of Mirth* (1905).
G. K. Chesterton, "The Innocence of Father Brown" (1911).
Wilfrid Owen, *Selected Poems* (1918).
Lytton Strachey, *Queen Victoria* (1921).
Robert Frost, "A Poem with Notes and Grace Notes" (Pulitzer, 1924).

Franz Kafka, *The Trial* (1925).

Trans. Breon Mitchell. New York: Schocken Books, 1999.

F. Scott Fitzgerald, *The Great Gatsby* (1925).
T. S. Eliot, *Murder in the Cathedral* (1935).
Zora Neale Hurston, *Their Eyes Were Watching God* (c. 1937).
George Orwell, *The Road to Wigan Pier* (1937).
Thornton Wilder, *Our Town* (1938).
John Steinbeck, *The Grapes of Wrath* (1939).

Adolf Hitler, *Mein Kampf* (1939).

Trans. Ralph Manheim. New York: Mariner Books, 1998.

George Orwell, *Animal Farm* (1945).
Tennessee Williams, *A Streetcar Named Desire* (1947).
Ralph Ellison, *Invisible Man* (1952).
C. S. Lewis, *Mere Christianity* (1952).
Arthur Miller, *The Crucible* (1953).
Saul Bellow, *Seize the Day* (1956).
Robert Bolt, *A Man for All Seasons* (1962).
Martin Luther King, Jr., "Why We Can't Wait" (1964).
Tom Stoppard, *Rosencrantz and Guildenstern Are Dead* (1967).

Aleksandr Solzhenitsyn, *The Gulag Archipelago* (1974).
Aleksandr Solzhenitsyn. *The Gulag Archipelago: An Authorized Abridgement.* Ed. Edward E. Erickson, Jr. New York: HarperCollins, 2002.

Toni Morrison, *Beloved* (1988).

Philip Larkin, *Collected Poems* (1991).
Ed. Anthony Thwaite. New York: Farrar, Straus and Giroux, 2004.

Elie Wiesel, *All Rivers Run to the Sea: Memoirs* (1995).

27

COMFORT WITH NUMBERS: MATH

The cumulative and coherent study of mathematics is, in fact, a microcosm of the entire curriculum and reflects in its expanding field the workings of the scholarly mind in a manner analogous to that which we examined in the field of arts and letters.

—David Hicks, *Norms and Nobility*

SUBJECT: Higher mathematics
TIME REQUIRED: 5 hours per week for each year of study

A classical education considers competency in higher-math skills—algebra, plane geometry, and geometrical proofs—to be part of basic literacy. The classically educated student will complete courses in geometry, first-year algebra, and second-year algebra. This coincides with the bare minimum demanded by most colleges for admission.

Most classical educators suggest that students who have no particular bent for mathematics and no plans for a career in science be allowed to "rest on their oars" after completing basic upper-level mathematics requirements. Ideally, the student would take at least one additional mathematics course after Algebra II; this will give him an edge both in college admissions and in general mathematical and scientific literacy. If this is impossible or if the student has spent extra years struggling to reach the Algebra II level, the additional mathematics course can be eliminated. Generally, students who don't plan to use advanced mathematics in later life and who aren't trying for selective college admissions can aim for math-free junior and senior years (grades 11 and 12).

Of the math programs described in Chapters 6 and 15, four—A Beka Book, Saxon, Math-U-See, and Singapore—extend through the high-school years. *Developmental Math* is not advanced enough to stand alone as a high-school math program, but the books can be very useful for providing extra practice and checking comprehension. In addition, the Teaching Textbooks and Chalk Dust Math programs described in Chapter 15 offer high-school courses.

The A Beka program includes *Algebra I* (ninth grade), *Plane Geometry* (tenth grade), *Algebra II* (eleventh grade), and a two-semester advanced elective course that covers trigonometry in the first semester and analytical geometry in the second. As in the early grades, the presentation is clear and drill-intensive.

Saxon, which began its algebra sequence with pre-algebra (*Algebra 1/2*) in the middle-grade years, continues with *Algebra I, Algebra II,* and *Advanced Mathematics.* Rather than separating geometry out into a different course (a custom peculiar to American mathematics), Saxon covers geometry over the three years of this sequence. By the end of *Advanced Mathematics,* the student has mastered a full geometry course. Saxon then offers three upper-level electives: calculus, physics, or trigonometry.

Math-U-See is a good option for parents who feel the need for step-by-step teaching but don't plan on using a tutor. This manipulative-based curriculum presents concepts on video and then asks the student to complete workbook exercises. *Algebra I* is designed for ninth grade; *Geometry,* for tenth grade; *Algebra II* for eleventh grade. A trigonometry elective is available for the twelfth grade.

The Singapore high-school math sequence, designed to run from grades 7 through 10, consists of a four-book sequence: *New Elementary Mathematics 1–4.* These four books cover introductory, intermediate, and advanced algebra and geometry. Unless you've been using Singapore all along, this would not be a good program to start with; it doesn't follow a standard U.S. math sequence, and it depends on problem-solving methods taught in the primary and middle-school books. You would probably want to list these four years as *Algebra I, Algebra II, Geometry,* and *Trigonometry/Pre-Calculus* on the high school transcript, to show that the student has met U.S. college admissions requirements. (*NEM* covers some, but not all, trigonometry concepts.)

Teaching Textbooks, described on page 255, offers interactive math instruction from Pre-algebra on through Algebra 1, Algebra 2, Geometry, and Pre-Calculus. Chalk Dust Math, another program that makes use of lectures on CD/DVD, also offers these courses, as well as Trigonometry and Calculus 1.

As with junior-high courses, the program you choose will depend on the student's learning style and your own preferences. If you intend to use a tutor or are comfortable with high-school math, Saxon, A Beka, or Singapore may suit you; if you need a course that provides the student with more tutorial support, Math-U-See, Teaching Textbooks, or Chalk Dust may be a better fit.

Whichever program you use, continue to give the student problems from a second program (as suggested in earlier chapters) to check comprehension. If she can transfer skills learned in one program to problems presented in a different way, she's thinking mathematically, rather than learning by rote.

The entertaining narrative math series Life of Fred (pages 96–97) can still provide a valuable supplement to the high-school math student. The volumes *Beginning Algebra* and *Geometry* are followed by *Advanced Algebra, Trigonometry, Calculus,* and *Statistics*; even students who do not intend to go on through a full math course in these advanced topics can benefit by working through these books.

POSSIBLE SEQUENCES

The Ideal Saxon Sequence

In Chapter 15, we outlined several possible tracks for the home-educated student. If you're using the Saxon home-education courses, you've probably followed this sequence:

Seventh grade	*Algebra 1/2*
Eighth grade	*Algebra I*
Ninth grade	*Algebra II*

The student who's been on this schedule should now continue with the Saxon *Advanced Mathematics* course in tenth grade. This program weaves together topics in algebra, geometry, trigonometry, discrete mathematics, and Euclidean geometry. Any student who has managed to finish *Algebra II* by ninth grade should take this course. Because Saxon integrates geometry into the algebra programs, the student will not have completed a full geometry course until he finishes *Advanced Mathematics.* A full geometry course is important to fulfill college admission requirements. Students who want to do well on the PSATs (which also serve as the National Merit Scholarship qualifying test), taken in the fall of the eleventh-grade year, should have completed *Advanced Mathematics* before taking the test; both the PSATs and SATs are heavy on geometry.

After *Advanced Mathematics,* the student can drop math or continue with Advanced Placement options. Saxon also offers an eleventh-grade calculus course designed to prepare home-educated students for the Advanced Placement examination.

The mathematically gifted twelfth grader can elect to take the Saxon physics course, a mathematically focused program for Advanced Placement students. Or he could take a trigonometry course. Saxon doesn't offer trigonometry, but the student can take a course at a local university or community college. Alternately, he can enroll in one of the correspondence or online courses that we discuss later in this chapter.

The sequence for high school, then, becomes

(Eighth grade)	*(Algebra I)*
Ninth grade	*Algebra II*
Tenth grade	*Advanced Mathematics*
Eleventh grade	*Calculus* (elective)
Twelfth grade	*Physics* (elective) or *trigonometry* (elective)

The Saxon advanced-math course covers the trigonometry necessary to do well on the SATs. If the student chooses to take an SAT II subject test in math, an advanced, full course in trigonometry should be taken rather than (or before) physics (use the A Beka program or a community-college class).

The Slightly Slower Saxon Sequence

Some students using Saxon math take an extra year to begin algebra, as we outlined in Chapter 15. These students will follow this pattern:

(Seventh grade)	(*Math 8/7,* the extra drill book for those who aren't quite ready to move on to pre-algebra)
(Eighth grade)	(*Algebra 1/2*)
Ninth grade	*Algebra I*
Tenth grade	*Algebra II*
Eleventh grade	*Advanced Mathematics*
Twelfth grade	*Calculus* (elective)

You might also find yourself on this schedule if you've pulled your high-school student out of a public or private school. Although this is a good college prep program, it has one drawback: the student doesn't finish *Advanced Mathematics* until the end of eleventh grade, which means that he will not have full knowledge of geometry when he takes the PSATs.

Should you worry about this? The PSATs have two functions: they serve as practice for the SATs taken in the senior year, and they also qualify students for the National Merit Scholarship program. If your high-school student consistently tests above the 90th percentile, a National Merit Scholarship is within the realm of possibility. In this case, you should plan on doing a catch-up course in geometry the summer before the eleventh-grade year so that he'll be fully prepared for the test.

You can use the A Beka geometry text and work through it with a tutor, or use an online tutorial or correspondence course (see pages 532–533 for details).

A Beka Book Sequence

If you find Saxon frustrating or if you've been using A Beka all along and are happy with it, use the A Beka upper-level math program. If you follow the suggested sequence, you will be a year behind the full-speed Saxon program. The *Basic Mathematics I* text provides a review of arithmetic topics and introduces a few advanced concepts. A strong mathematics student could skip this level and go into pre-algebra in seventh grade, which would accelerate the Beka program to match the Saxon program. You may also wish to use a tutor, since A Beka was designed for classroom use and includes little in the way of teacher guidance.

Grade 7	*Basic Mathematics I*
Grade 8	*Pre-Algebra*

Grade 9 *Algebra I*
Grade 10 *Plane Geometry*
Grade 11 *Algebra II*
Grade 12 *Trigonometry with Tables*, one semester/*Analytic Geometry*, one semester

Remember, you should plan on completing geometry by the end of the tenth-grade year in order to score well on the PSATs.

Math-U-See

The Math-U-See program is excellent for visual learners and parents who need extra teaching support. The student should have finished the two-year *Advanced Mathematics* course, which covers seventh and eighth grades (see Chapter 15 for a full explanation of this level).

Grade 9 *Algebra I*
Grade 10 *Geometry*
Grade 11 *Algebra II*
Grade 12 *Trigonometry*

This suggested sequence isn't for students who wish to specialize in math, since it leaves no room for physics, calculus, or other advanced math electives. However, it provides a good, solid knowledge of high school mathematics for the non-specialist.

Singapore Sequence

Students who have already used Singapore should be on the following sequence:

Grade 7 *New Elementary Mathematics 1*
Grade 8 *New Elementary Mathematics 2*
Grade 9 *New Elementary Mathematics 3*
Grade 10 *New Elementary Mathematics 4*

This leads the student through all algebra, geometry, beginning trigonometry, and pre-calculus skills. A calculus or full trigonometry course from another program could be added for students who wish to do upper-level electives.

If the student is on a slower sequence (beginning *NEM 1* later than seventh grade), she'll run into the same difficulty as the student on the slower Saxon sequence: standardized testing will begin before she has covered all of the required mathematics. Consider supplementing with a focused geometry course from another program before the test.

Chalk Dust Sequence

Students who began the Chalk Dust pre-algebra in seventh grade will follow this sequence:

Grade 7 *Pre-algebra*
Grade 8 *Algebra 1*
Grade 9 *Geometry*
Grade 10 *Algebra II*

with the option of moving on to:

Grade 11 *Trigonometry*
Grade 12 *Precalculus with Limits*

Students who move more quickly also have the option of finishing the sequence with the Calculus of a Single Variable course.

Teaching Textbooks Sequence

Because Teaching Textbooks allows students to complete a seventh-grade year of arithmetic before moving on to pre-algebra, students can follow this sequence:

Grade 8 *Pre-algebra*
Grade 9 *Algebra 1*
Grade 10 *Geometry*
Grade 11 *Algebra 2*
Grade 12 *Pre-calculus*

OUTSIDE HELP

Online Resources

No matter what program you use, you may find yourself needing help. Cornell University sponsors a website with links to all the best online math resources: Ask Dr. Math (a free question-answering service staffed by Swarthmore College students and faculty), Calculus Help, Math Homework Help, Interactive Online Geometry, software tutoring packages, and more. Go to www.tc.cornell.edu/Edu/MathSciGateway to explore the options. You can also check out the University of Pennsylvania math help site at www.math.upenn.edu/MathSources.html. The Living Math website offers articles, reviews of programs, and links to reference and information sites. You can access the site at www.livingmath.net.

Correspondence Options

Seton Home Study School offers both Saxon algebra and a standard Houghton Mifflin geometry course by correspondence. You pay the tuition fee; they provide explanations, lesson plans, tests, and the final grade. Seton is Catholic-oriented and academically demanding. See Resources for contact information.

The most extensive high-school correspondence program is offered by the University of Nebraska at Lincoln. Their Independent Study High School is used both by home schoolers and by small rural schools that want to broaden their range of courses. Over 130 courses are available, including a full range of mathematics classes. See Resources for contact information.

The University of Oklahoma offers by correspondence Algebra 1 and Algebra 2, using the Saxon texts. Other high-school math courses include modern geometry, trigonometry, pre-calculus, and analytic geometry. These will provide the student with more feedback than the Saxon home-study kits.

Keystone National High School offers a full range of high-school courses, including AP courses, by traditional correspondence or through online instruction; you can view the course options at www.keystonehighschool.com.

A number of other colleges and universities offer correspondence courses that are open to high-school students. For a full list, see Chapter 43.

For advanced mathematics, you can also enroll your high-school student in a local college or university introductory math course. This is known as "concurrent enrollment" and has the advantage of proving that the student is capable of college-level work. Consider this option for eleventh- and twelfth-grade math electives.

ADVANCED PLACEMENT

Students completing calculus and trigonometry as advanced electives may qualify for Advanced Placement credit. The standard Advanced Placement test is given every year in March. The College Board offers Advanced Placement credit in both calculus and physics. To qualify for credit, all you have to do is score well on the exam. For detailed descriptions of the exams, you can call the College Board AP information line at 212-713-8066 or visit their website at www.collegeboard.com (search the site for "AP"). According to the College Board, home schoolers are permitted to take Advanced Placement exams at their local school; call your nearest high school, and ask to speak to the person in charge of the exams.

For further discussion of standardized tests, see Chapter 40.

SCHEDULES

All college-bound students should complete two years of algebra plus a geometry course. This sequence should begin in eighth or ninth grade.

Saxon Sequence

Algebra I
Algebra II
Advanced Mathematics
Elective: *Calculus*

Standard Sequence

Algebra I
Geometry
Algebra II
Electives: *Pre-calculus, Calculus, Trigonometry, Statistics*

Singapore Sequence

NEM 1 (algebra, geometry)
NEM 2 (algebra, geometry)
NEM 3 (algebra, geometry, basic trigonometry, pre-calculus)
NEM 4 (algebra, geometry, basic trigonometry, pre-calculus)

RESOURCES

For publisher and catalog addresses, telephone numbers, and other information, see Sources (pages 751–778). We suggest that you contact these publishers of math materials and examine their catalogs closely before deciding on a curriculum. Most publishers will help you place your child at the most appropriate level. We have listed basic curricula first and other resources (online tutorials and correspondence schools) second.

Math Curricula

A Beka Book Traditional Arithmetic series. Pensacola, Fla.: A Beka Book. Order from A Beka Book. A Beka Book also offers a wide range of mathematics teaching aids. Ask for a copy of their home-school catalog. Parents don't need the curriculum/lesson-plan books for each level; these give tips for classroom teaching.

Basic Mathematics I (seventh grade/optional). $20.25.
Basic Mathematics I Teacher Key. $25.00.
Student Test and Quiz Book. $6.75.
Teacher Test/Quiz Key. $9.50.
Pre-Algebra (seventh/eighth grades). $20.25.
Pre-Algebra Teacher Key. $25.00.
Student Test and Quiz Book. $6.75.
Teacher Test/Quiz Key. $9.50.
Algebra I (eighth/ninth grades). $23.75.
Algebra I Solution Key. $42.00.
Algebra I Student Test and Quiz Book. $10.50.
Algebra I Teacher Edition. $42.00.
Algebra I Teacher Test and Quiz Key. $11.50.
Plane Geometry (ninth/tenth grades). $23.75.

Plane Geometry Solution Key. $58.75.

Plane Geometry Student Test and Quiz Book. $10.50.

Plane Geometry Teacher Test and Quiz Key. $11.50.

Algebra II (tenth/eleventh grades). $23.50.

Algebra II Solution Key. $43.00.

Algebra II Student Test and Quiz Book. $10.50.

Algebra II Teacher Test and Quiz Key. $11.50.

Trigonometry with Tables (eleventh/twelfth grades, one semester). $20.00.

Trigonometry Answer Key. $11.75.

Trigonometry Solution Key, Selected Problems. $37.00.

Trigonometry Student Test and Quiz Book. $6.50.

Trigonometry Teacher Test and Quiz Key. $9.50.

Analytic Geometry (eleventh/twelfth grades, one semester). $20.00.

Analytic Geometry Solution Key, Selected Problems. $37.00.

Analytic Geometry Student Test and Quiz Book. $6.50.

Analytic Geometry Teacher Test and Quiz Key. $9.50.

Chalk Dust Math. Sugar Land, Tex.: Chalk Dust Company.

Order from Chalk Dust Company.

Algebra 1. 6 DVDs, textbook, and solutions guide. $354.00.

Geometry. 9 DVDs, textbook, and solutions guide. $299.00.

Algebra 2. 8 DVDs, textbook, and solutions guide. $429.00.

Precalculus. 14 DVDs, textbook, and solutions guide. $534.00.

Calculus. 11 DVDs, textbook, and solutions guide. $429.00.

Trigonometry. 9 DVDs, textbook, and solutions guide. $419.00.

Developmental Math: A Self-Teaching Program. Halesite, N.Y.: Mathematics Programs Associates.

Each level includes a workbook and teacher's edition. Buy from Mathematics Programs Associates. Good for reinforcement and comprehension testing. A full description of the twenty levels available can be obtained by calling 888-MPA-MATH or visiting www.mathplace.com.

Level 13. Decimals, Fractions, and the Metric System: Concepts and Basic Skills. $20.00.

Level 14. Fractions: Concepts and Skills. $20.00.

Level 15. Fractions: Advanced Skills. $20.00.

Level 16. Special Topics: Ratio, Percent, Graphs and More. $20.00.

Level 17. Algebra 1: Signed Numbers. $20.00.
Level 18. Algebra 2: Equations. $20.00.
Level 19. Geometry 1: Foundations of Geometry. $30.00.
Level 20. Geometry 2: Two-Dimensional Figures. $30.00.

Life of Fred. Reno, Nev.: Polka Dot Publishing.
Order from Polka Dot Publishing.
Beginning Algebra. $29.00.
Fred's Home Companion: Beginning Algebra. $14.00.
Advanced Algebra. $29.00.
Fred's Home Companion: Advanced Algebra. $14.00.
Geometry. $39.00.
Geometry Answer Key. $6.00.
Trigonometry. $29.00.
Fred's Home Companion: Trigonometry. $14.00.
Calculus. $39.00.
Calculus Answer Key. $6.00.
Statistics $39.00.
Statistics Answer Key. $6.00.

Math-U-See.
This program has a number of different levels and workbook/video/DVD/manipulative combinations. For prices, explanatory material, and brochures, call the Math-U-See national number (888-854-6284), which will transfer you to a local representative; or visit the website at www.mathusee.com. Each teacher kit includes an instructional video or DVD and a manual; each student kit contains a text and test booklet. The manipulative blocks are the same set required for earlier Math-U-See curricula. New "Honors Enhancement" books are offered for each level, $10.00 per book.
Pre-Algebra.
Teacher Kit. $50.00.
Student Kit. $20.00.
Algebra/Decimal Inserts. $20.00.
Manipulative Blocks. $30.00.
Algebra 1.
Teacher Kit. $50.00.
Student Kit. $20.00.

Geometry.

Teacher Kit. $50.00.

Student Kit. $20.00.

Algebra 2.

Teacher Kit. $70.00.

Student Kit. $20.00.

Trigonometry.

Teacher Kit. $70.00.

Student Kit. $20.00.

Saxon Secondary Mathematics. Orlando, Fla.: Harcourt Achieve.

Order from Saxon. Prices are for the Saxon Home Study Kits. Visit the Saxon website (www.saxonhomeschool.harcourtachieve.com) for other combinations and options.

Math 8/7. $84.50.

This is the transitional book for seventh-grade students who aren't ready to begin pre-algebra. If your sixth grader went through *Math 7/6* without unusual difficulty, you can skip *Math 8/7* and go straight into *Algebra 1/2*.

Algebra 1/2. $99.00.

Pre-algebra for seventh grade; also used by eighth graders who did the *Math 8/7* book in seventh grade.

Algebra 1. $102.00.

For eighth grade; also used by ninth graders who did *Algebra 1/2* in eighth grade.

Algebra II. $99.00.

For ninth grade. Used by tenth graders who did *Algebra I* in ninth grade.

Advanced Mathematics. $108.00.

For tenth grade. Used by eleventh graders who did *Algebra II* in tenth grade.

Calculus. $74.50.

For eleventh or twelfth grade. Treats the topics covered in an Advanced Placement AB-level program as well as some of the topics required for a BC-level program.

Physics. $69.50.

For any student who has completed *Algebra 2*.

Singapore Math, U.S. edition.

Singapore Math workbooks and textbooks can be ordered from Singapore Math (an independent dealer, not the program publisher). The U.S. edition uses American weights and money (the previous edition for sale in the U.S. does not). Visit singaporemath.com for additional options, combinations, and courses.

New Elementary Mathematics 1 (seventh grade)

Textbook. $21.50.

Workbook. $8.30.

Teacher's Manual. $9.00.

Solution Manual. $27.00.

Handbook for Secondary Math Teachers (7–10). $29.00.

New Elementary Mathematics 2 (eighth grade).

Textbook. $21.50.

Workbook. $8.30.

Teacher's Manual. $9.00.

Solution Manual. $27.00.

New Elementary Mathematics 3 (ninth grade).

Math Textbook 3A. $12.50.

Teacher's Manual 3A. $6.50.

Math Textbook 3B. $12.50.

Teacher's Manual 3B. $6.50.

New Elementary Mathematics 4 (tenth grade).

Math Textbook 4A. $12.50.

Math Textbook 4B. $12.50.

Teacher's Manual 4. $15.00.

Teaching Textbooks. Oklahoma City, Okla.: Teaching Textbooks.

$184.90 for each course. Order from Teaching Textbooks.

The Pre-Algebra Teaching Textbook.

The Algebra 1 Teaching Textbook.

The Geometry Teaching Textbook.

The Algebra 2 Teaching Textbook.

The Pre-Calculus Teaching Textbook.

Online Tutorials and Correspondence Schools

Cornell University website with links to online math resources: www.tc.cornell.edu/Edu/MathSciGateway.

Keystone National High School, 920 Central Road, Bloomsburg, Pa. 17815; 866-382-1228; www.keystonehighschool.com.

Living Math: www.livingmath.net.

Saxon Math online help: www.saxonpub.com.

Seton Home Study School, 1350 Progress Drive, P.O. Box 396, Front Royal, VA 22630. Call: 540-636-9990. Web: www.setonhome.org.

$175.00 plus book fee for a single course. Offers Saxon *Algebra 1* through AP Calculus.

University of Nebraska–Lincoln Independent Study High School. P.O. Box 888400, Lincoln, NE 68588-8400. Call them at 866-700-4747. Or visit the website at www.nebraskahs.unl.edu.

The University of Oklahoma Center for Independent and Distance Learning, University of Oklahoma High School, 1600 Jenkins, Room 101, Norman, OK 73072-6507. Call them at 800-942-5702, or visit the website at www.ouhigh.ou.edu.

Also see the full list of correspondence-course resources in Chapter 43.

28

PRINCIPLES AND LAWS: SCIENCE

Science without conscience is the death of the soul.
—François Rabelais

SUBJECT: High-school science (biology, astronomy, chemistry, physics)
TIME REQUIRED: 4 or more hours per week

How does the classical approach to the study of science differ from science taught in schools across the country?

Two distinctive characteristics set rhetoric-stage science apart. First, science studies are rigorous and intellectually demanding, like all classical subjects. The student is encouraged to study science for all four years of high school, passing again through biology, astronomy,[1] chemistry, and physics. She'll study the principles and laws of each science, finishing high school with a sound grasp of foundational scientific ideas. As in all stages of classical education, she will read and write about science as well as per-

[1]In high school, earth science gives way to a more intensive study of astronomy.

form experiments. And she'll be encouraged to explore science resources, rather than filling in workbooks and answering comprehension questions.

But rigorous science education can be found in any number of nonclassical curricula. "Classical" science is further distinguished by its demand that the student do science *self-consciously*—not simply learn about the world, but ask what the implications of each discovery might be. What does this theory say about my existence? What does that principle imply about human beings and their place in the universe? What are the implications for the human race?

As a whole, then, rhetoric-stage science is taught in the context of the student's broader study of ideas. The student isn't merely learning abstract principles; she's seeing how they fit into the Great Conversation she's having with the great books of the classical curriculum.

AN OVERVIEW OF RHETORIC-STAGE SCIENCE

Rhetoric-stage science study falls into three parts.

1. ***The study of principles*** This is "standard science." Using texts and experiment books, the student will learn the laws of each scientific field. As she did in the logic stage, she'll do this by reading, writing, and experimentation.
2. ***Source readings*** Each year, the student will read from primary scientific sources—the reflections of contemporary scientists on the work being done in their own day. She'll start with Hippocrates and end with Michael J. Behe, writing a brief book report/analysis of each text. These readings are not meant to crowd out science or the other great books. Rather, they are meant to give historical perspective to the study of science and its ongoing debates.
3. ***Joining the Great Conversation*** Each year, the science student will write a paper tracing the history and development of some new technology or knowledge. This paper should be centered around the field being studied. The ninth grader, for example, could write on the changing ideas about origins, on the problems of extinction, on the rise of new diseases

or the development of antibiotic-resistant strains, on the developments in reproductive technology such as cloning or in vitro fertilization techniques that allow sixty-year-old women to become mothers, on the effects of the body on the mind and vice versa. The tenth grader could write about the changing paradigms of the universe—the earth's move from the center of the universe to its edge—and the effect this shift had on our view of ourselves. The eleventh grader can research the development of various types of fuels and how they changed the landscape of work and daily life. High-school students could choose any twentieth-century technology, from the splitting of the atom to the development of the Internet, and write about its history and future.

HOW TO DO IT

As in the previous two stages, the student will keep her work in a science notebook. Each should have three sections: Principles, Source Readings, and Papers.

We suggest studying science two days each week for two hours per day. Six to eight weeks should be devoted to the reading of source materials; four to six weeks should be given to the writing of the science paper; the rest of the time will be spent in studying the principles of science.

The Study of Principles

For the study of science principles, we suggest following the same general procedure as in the middle grades. The student should read from her science text, write a brief composition summarizing the information, make sketches of any diagrams, and do any experiments and record the results. Compositions should be more detailed than in the logic stage—the ninth grader can write one and a half to two pages about the function of a cell, whereas the fifth grader wrote two or three paragraphs. All of this work should be filed under Principles in the science notebook.

These compositions should draw their information not only from the primary science texts we recommend, but also from other general reference works. We suggest that you keep on hand *The Usborne Illustrated Dictionary of Science*. Other specific resources may be found in Resources, at the end of this chapter.

Generally, the student should use the first science period of every week to read and make notes applying the techniques learned in *The Well-Educated Mind* (see Chapter 26).[2] She should supplement these notes by looking up in other science books, kept on a nearby shelf, those subjects that interest her or that seem unclear. Make use of the library—stock up on the popular and colorful science books written for young adults. At this time, the student should also sketch any diagrams (cell structure, atomic structure, trajectories) and label them.

In the second period of every week, the student should write a composition of one and a half to two pages, referring to her notes. She should also do experiments, recording the results in the form suggested in Chapter 18. All of this material—the notes along with diagrams, the composition, and the results of experiments—should be filed in the Principles section of the science notebook.

For high-school texts, we like Wiley's *Self-Teaching Guides,* a series of clear, well-written books designed for independent college preparation:

Ninth grade	*Biology: A Self-Teaching Guide,* by Steven D. Garber
Tenth grade	*Astronomy: A Self-Teaching Guide,* by Dinah L. Moche
Eleventh grade	*Chemistry: Concepts and Problems—a Self-Teaching Guide,* by Clifford C. Houk and Richard Post
Twelfth grade	*Basic Physics: A Self-Teaching Guide,* by Karl F. Kuhn (principles-focused), or *Saxon Physics Home Study Kit,* a more technical and math-focused physics course leading to Advanced Placement credit.[3]

You'll want to supplement these by picking and choosing from the following experiment guides. For lab equipment, visit Tobin's Lab at www.tobinslab.com and Carolina Biological Supply at www.carolina.com.

[2]Additional guidance in reading science can be found in Chapter 17 of *How to Read a Book,* a classic text on how to read, written by Mortimer Adler and Charles Van Doren (Touchstone, 1972).

[3]If you use the Saxon physics program, you'll need to do physics five days per week, rather than following the schedule we suggest at the end of this chapter. However, if you do Saxon physics, you can drop advanced math electives. Saxon physics should be considered a math course; continue to do the source readings and composition assignments, as outlined in this chapter, two days per week.

Biology	*Plant Biology Science Projects,* by David R. Hershey
	Ecosystem Science Fair Projects, by Pam Walker and Elaine Wood
	Cell and Microbe Science Fair Projects, by Kenneth G. Rainis
	Genetics and Evolution Science Fair Projects, by Robert G. Gardner
	Janice VanCleave's A+ Projects in Biology, by Janice VanCleave
Astronomy	*Planet Earth Science Fair Projects,* by Robert Gardner
	Janice VanCleave's A+ Projects in Astronomy, by Janice VanCleave
Chemistry	*Chemistry Science Fair Projects,* by Robert Gardner
	Plastics and Polymers Science Fair Projects, by Madeleine P. Goodstein
	Janice VanCleave's A+ Projects in Chemistry, by Janice VanCleave
	Hands-On Chemistry with Real-Life Applications, by Norman Herr and James Cunningham
Physics	*Science Fair Projects About the Properties of Matter,* by Robert Gardner
	Electricity and Magnetism Science Fair Projects, by Robert Gardner
	Forces and Motion Science Fair Projects, by Robert Gardner
	Light, Sound, and Waves Science Fair Projects, by Robert Gardner
	Hands-On Physics Activities with Real-Life Applications, by Norman Herr and James Cunningham

A word about basic high-school science: This is a difficult subject to do at home unless the parent is knowledgeable and enthusiastic. The Wiley guides will provide a good solid foundation in science principles, but they're not very exciting. And many of the other texts we looked at assume that the student has access to a full range of high-school lab equipment (this is also true of some of the experiments in the experiment guides listed above, although others are easily done at home).

If you live near a community college or university, consider enrolling your high school student in an introductory college science course.

Generally, one semester of college study is considered the equivalent of a year of high-school study; the student can then use the following semester to complete the source reading requirement described later in this chapter. Enrolling your student in a college class allows her to fulfill lab requirements and also gives her the opportunity to learn from someone who is enthusiastic about science—perhaps awakening new interest in her.

We've listed other options below that may suit individual family needs.

Alternative Curricula

Gravitas Publications, publisher of Real Science-4-Kids, has followed up their well-done middle-grade courses with the first level of a high-school program: Level 2 Chemistry. Although additional subjects are not yet available, this program provides you with at least one year of planned-out science. Visit the publisher's website, www.gravitaspublications.com, to view sample lessons.

For Christian Home-School Families

The Apologia Science series, by Jay Wile, is written for home schoolers; it explains concepts clearly, includes experiments designed to be done at home, and comes with companion lab materials and instructional CD-ROMs. The series assumes Christian belief. The courses are also offered online in cooperation with the Potter's School (www.pottersschool.org). In Susan's opinion, the weakest book in the series is the introductory text, *Exploring Creation with Biology;* although the sections dealing with biological functions are well-done, the sections that discuss origins contain rhetorical excesses and do not treat all aspects of the subject. The Apologia science series does not include an astronomy course, but does include advanced texts in biology, chemistry, and physics; students who wish to do a fourth year of science would need to do an additional year in one of these topics, rather than studying astronomy.

For Families with Financial Resources

The Teaching Company offers videotaped courses taught by college professors from all over the country. Their offerings include: a biology course (*Understanding the Human Body: An Introduction to Anatomy and Physiology*); two physics courses (*Einstein's Relativity and the Quantum Revolution: Modern Physics for Non-Scientists,* as well as *Particle Physics for Non-Physicists: A Tour of the*

Microcosmos); an astronomy course, *Understanding the Universe: An Introduction to Astronomy*; and a chemistry course, *Chemistry—High School Level.*

Although these courses are designed for nonspecialists, they are targeted for adults (with the exception of the chemistry course) and require a student whose comprehension skills are reasonably mature. The courses are also expensive; the tapes provide a full year's worth of lectures, but the sticker prices are in the $400 to $600 range. (However, they often go on sale for $100 to $200, so if you can plan ahead and wait for a sale, they may become more affordable.) This is a very good at-home option if circumstances allow. Visit www.theteachingcompany.com for more information.

Source Readings

The student should begin to explore the development of scientific thought by reading three or four original works of science each year. This study promotes critical thought; the student learns to view science not as an unerring oracle, but as a human endeavor, limited by time and culture. Even great scientists suffer from bias and ignorance. The reading of source works each year makes science human.

The following titles are suggestions; you can add to or change this list, depending on the student's interests and capabilities. *The Timetables of History* (see page 491) offers a full list of scientific publications by year, from 500 B.C. until the present.

The student should read her selected text and write a summary/evaluation. Each source reading will take a couple of weeks to complete; during this time, source reading replaces the study of science principles (see the schedules at the end of this chapter).

Ninth Grade

Hippocrates, *Aphorisms* (c. 420 B.C.)
Euclid, *Elements of Geometry* (380 B.C.)
Aristotle, *Physics* (c. 380 B.C.)

Tenth Grade

Nicholas Copernicus, *On the Revolutions of the Heavenly Spheres* (1543)
Johannes Kepler, *Harmonies of the World* (1619)
Galileo Galilei, *Dialogues Concerning the Two Chief World Systems* (1632)

Eleventh Grade

Robert Boyle, *The Sceptical Chymist* (1661)
Isaac Newton, *Principia Mathematica* (1687)
Antoine Lavoisier, *Elements of Chemistry* (1790)

Twelfth Grade

Albert Einstein, *Relativity: The Special and the General Theory* (trans. Robert W. Lawson) (1915)
Stephen Hawking, *A Brief History of Time* (1988)
Michael J. Behe, *Darwin's Black Box* (1998)

The titles suggested above are just that: suggestions. If you prefer, you can choose titles from the fuller "Rhetoric of Science" list below. As in the study of great books, read any titles chosen in chronological order.

Hippocrates, *Aphorisms* (c. 420 B.C.)
Aristotle, *Physics* (c. 380 B.C.)
Aristotle, *The History of Animals* (c. 380 B.C.)
Euclid, *Elements of Geometry* (380 B.C.)
Theophrasteus, *On the History of Plants* (abridged) (c. 300 B.C.)
Archimides, *On the Sphere and the Cylinder* (c. 220 B.C.)
Lucretius, *De Rerum Natura* (c. 70 B.C.)
Pliny the Elder, *Natural History* (selections), (c. 60)
Andreas Vesalius, *De Humani Corporis Fabrica* (1543)
Nicolaus Copernicus, *On the Revolutions of the Heavenly Spheres (De Revolutionibus Orbium Coelestium)* (1543)
Johannes Kepler, *Harmonies of the World* (1619)
Francis Bacon, *Novum Organum* (1620)
William Harvey, *De Motu Cordis* (1628)
Galileo Galilei, *Dialogue Concerning the Two Chief World Systems* (1632)
Robert Boyle, *The Sceptical Chymist* (1661)
Isaac Newton, *Principia Mathematica* (1687)
Antoine Lavoisier, *Elements of Chemistry* (1790)
Charles Darwin, *Origin of the Species* (1864)
Gregor Mendel, "Experiments with Plant Hybrids" (1866)
Albert Einstein, *Relativity: The Special and General Theories* (1915)

Erwin Schrodinger, *What Is Life?* (1944)
Ernst Nagel and James R. Newman, *Godel's Proof* (1958)
Werner Carl Heisenberg, *Physics and Philosophy* (1962)
Rachel Carson, *Silent Spring* (1962)
George Gamow, *Thirty Years That Shook Physics: The Story of Quantum Physics* (1966)
James D. Watson, *The Double Helix* (1968)
Edward O. Wilson, *Sociobiology* (1975)
Richard Dawkins, *The Selfish Gene* (1976)
Stephen J. Gould, *Ever Since Darwin* (1977)
Douglas R. Hofstadter, *Godel, Escher, Bach* (1979)
Robert Jastrow, *Red Giants and White Dwarfs* (1980)
Richard Feynmann, *QED: The Strange Theory of Light of Matter* (1985)
James Gleick, *Chaos: Making a New Science* (1987)
Stephen Hawking, *A Brief History of Time* (1988)
Paul Davies, *The New Physics* (1989)
Michael Behe, *Darwin's Black Box* (1998)
Freeman Dyson, *Origins of Life* (1999)
Ray Kurzweil, *The Singularity Is Near: When Humans Transcend Biology* (2005)

The Great Conversation: Writing Papers

Each year, the student should write one paper (four to six pages in ninth grade, five to eight pages in tenth, six to ten in eleventh, eight to twelve pages in twelfth), discussing some scientific discovery or technological innovation. These papers should trace the historical development of the topic, mentioning the ethical issues raised. A ninth-grade paper might begin with the plague and progress through the 1917 influenza epidemic, the discovery of antibiotics, and the development of antibiotic-resistent "superbugs." The ninth grader should then conclude by answering the following: What overall effect has the use of antibiotics had on the war against disease? What defenses against the superbugs remain? Don't expect the student to solve these dilemmas; do encourage her to consider them.

In *The End of Education,* Neil Postman suggests that any student who has truly studied science and technology will consider certain questions, including:

1. Any technology offers both advantages and disadvantages. What are they?
2. These advantages and disadvantages aren't evenly spread throughout the population; some will benefit, others will be injured. Who are they?
3. All technologies come complete with a philosophy about what is important about human life and what is unimportant. What parts of life does the technology exalt? What parts does it ignore?
4. Every technology competes with an old technology for time, money, and attention. What technology is being replaced or squeezed out?
5. Every technology favors a certain type of intellectual expression, a certain type of emotional expression, a certain type of political system, a certain type of sensory experience. What are these?[4]

These questions will serve as thought starters for the student as she studies science and considers paper topics. Postman further proposes the following two possibilities for a hypothetical final exam. They would serve equally well as topics for the eleventh- and twelfth-grade papers:

> Part I: Choose one pre-twentieth century technology—for example, the alphabet, the printing press, the telegraph, the factory—and indicate what were the main intellectual, social, political, and economic advantages of the technology, and why. Then indicate what were the main intellectual, social, political, and economic disadvantages of the technology, and why.
>
> Part II: Indicate, first, what you believe are or will be the main advantages of computer technology, and why; second, indicate what are or will be the main disadvantages of computer technology, and why.[5]

This paper should be written in the spring of each year (see the discussion of the research paper on pages 502–506 for specific guidelines). Allow four to six weeks for this paper.

[4]Neil Postman, *The End of Education: Redefining the Value of School* (New York: Knopf, 1995), pp. 192–93. For a full explanation that will help both you and the student think through these issues, we highly recommend reading Postman's essay on the necessity of "technological education."

[5]Postman, p. 193.

OUTSIDE HELP

Correspondence Options

The student who wants to pursue a standard high-school science course can elect to use a correspondence course instead of studying science independently. The University of Nebraska offers standard and advanced high-school science courses by correspondence in biology, chemistry, and physics; chemistry may be taken with or without lab. The University of Oklahoma offers high-school biology, chemistry, and physics, as well as a college course in astronomy. Keystone National High School offers both regular and AP high-school science courses with lab components, both by traditional correspondence and through online tutorials. Visit www.keystonehighschool.com for the catalog of available courses. We've provided a full list of correspondence-school resources in Chapter 43. These courses will be textbook- and question-and-answer-focused rather than centered on reading and writing, and the student may or may not be able to manage source readings and the spring science paper while using them.

However, if you'd feel more comfortable with a structured correspondence course or if the student flounders without a textbook-type approach, investigate the correspondence option. Call the schools listed in Chapter 43, and look through their catalogs for courses in biology, astronomy, chemistry, and physics. Teachers are available for consultation. Levels of involvement can vary from materials only to complete grading and transcript service.

Online Resources

Whether you use correspondence courses or not, make use of online science resources. Cornell University sponsors a math and science website with links to dozens of fantastic science sites, including Human Anatomy Online; Chickscope (an online MRI of a developing chick in an egg); Cornell's Lab of Ornithology; Interactive Frog Dissection (sponsored by the University of Virginia, this site allows you to dissect a virtual frog—you can reach them at http://frog.edschool.virginia.edu); DNA molecular modeling; microscopy of living cells; the latest pictures from the Mars Global

Surveyor, the *Galileo* probe, and the *Pathfinder* mission; online planetariums; an online tour of the Fermilab high-energy physics laboratory; virtual chemistry textbooks and experiment sites; and more. Go to www.tc.cornell.edu/Services/Education/Gateways/Math_and_Science.

SAMPLE SCHEDULES

We suggest you schedule two weeks per source reading and four to six weeks for the writing of each science paper. The remaining weeks should be devoted to the study of science principles. This means that ninth, eleventh, and twelfth graders will spend six weeks on source readings; tenth graders will spend eight weeks. Allot four to six weeks for the writing of the spring science paper. In a thirty-six-week school year, you'll be left with twenty-two to twenty-six weeks to study the science text. Don't attempt to cover the entire text. Decide with your student how many pages she can reasonable cover each week, and try to hold to this schedule.

Ninth grade	Weeks 1–6	*Biology: A Self-Teaching Guide*
	Weeks 7–8	Hippocrates, medical treatises
	Weeks 9–15	*Biology: A Self-Teaching Guide*
	Weeks 16–17	Euclid, *Elements*
	Weeks 18–24	*Biology: A Self-Teaching Guide*
	Weeks 25–26	Aristotle, *Physics*
	Weeks 27–32	*Biology: A Self-Teaching Guide*
	Weeks 33–36	Paper on life-science topic
Tenth grade	Weeks 1–7	*Astronomy: A Self-Teaching Guide*
	Weeks 8–10	Copernicus, *On the Revolutions of the Heavenly Spheres*
	Weeks 11–14	*Astronomy: A Self-Teaching Guide*
	Weeks 15–16	Kepler, *Epitome of Copernican Astronomy* and *Harmonies of the World* (first half)
	Weeks 17–19	*Astronomy: A Self-Teaching Guide*
	Weeks 20–21	Kepler, *Epitome* . . . (second half)
	Weeks 22–26	*Astronomy: A Self-Teaching Guide*

	Weeks 27–28	Galileo, *Dialogues Concerning Two New Sciences*
	Weeks 29–32	*Astronomy: A Self-Teaching Guide*
	Weeks 33–36	Paper on astronomy topic
Eleventh grade	Weeks 1–6	*Chemistry: Concepts and Problems—a Self-Teaching Guide*
	Weeks 7–8	Boyle, *The Sceptical Chemist*
	Weeks 9–15	*Chemistry: Concepts and Problems—a Self-Teaching Guide*
	Weeks 16–17	Newton, *Principia*
	Weeks 18–24	*Chemistry: Concepts and Problems—a Self-Teaching Guide*
	Weeks 25–26	Lavoisier, *Elements of Chemistry*
	Weeks 27–32	*Chemistry: Concepts and Problems—a Self-Teaching Guide*
	Weeks 33–36	Paper on technology topic
Twelfth grade	Weeks 1–6	*Basic Physics: A Self-Teaching Guide*
	Weeks 7–8	Einstein, *Relativity: The Special and the General Theory*
	Weeks 9–15	*Basic Physics: A Self-Teaching Guide*
	Weeks 16–17	Hawking, *A Brief History of Time*
	Weeks 18–24	*Basic Physics: A Self-Teaching Guide*
	Weeks 25–26	Behe, *Darwin's Black Box*
	Weeks 27–32	*Basic Physics: A Self-Teaching Guide*
	Weeks 33–36	Paper on technology topic

RESOURCES

For publisher and catalog addresses, telephone numbers, and other information, see Sources (pages 751–778). Most books can be obtained from any bookstore or library; where we know of a mail-order option, we have provided it. Reference materials for the entire four years of the rhetoric stage are listed first. Resources for each year are listed next, with each list divided into basic texts and optional supplementary materials. You can still use some of the resources listed in Chapter 18, particularly the experiment kits and the CD-ROMs.

Reference Materials for All Four Years

Adler, Mortimer, and Charles Van Doren. *How to Read a Book*. New York: Touchstone, 1972.

$16.00. Order from any bookstore. Chapter 17 gives specific guidance about how to read scientific nonfiction.

Bauer, Susan Wise. *The Well-Educated Mind: A Guide to the Classical Education You Never Had*. New York: W. W. Norton, 2003.

$27.95. Order from any bookstore. Recommended in Chapter 26 of this book for developing reading skills in nonfiction and fiction.

Brock Magiscope. Maitland, Fla.: Brock Optical, Inc.

$119.00 and up. Order from Brock. A selection of good-quality microscopes can be viewed at www.magiscope.com.

Eyewitness Encyclopedia of Science CD-ROM. New York: Dorling Kindersley, 1997.

$29.99. Order from any bookstore. The current version is 2.0; check for any update. This CD-ROM encyclopedia contains articles in mathematics, physics, chemistry, and life sciences, as well as many definitions, animations, video illustrations, magnified and cutaway views, and much more.

Stockley, Corinne, et al. *The Usborne Illustrated Dictionary of Science*. Tulsa, Okla.: Usborne Publishing, 2007.

$29.99. Detailed facts in physics, chemistry, and biology.

Science Equipment

For an overwhelmingly complete (over 1,200 print pages) catalog of high-quality school science supplies, visit the Carolina Biological Supply Company website at www.carolina.com. Although much of what Carolina sells is packaged in large quantities, it carries some materials that are unavailable elsewhere.

You can also buy a wonderful selection of lab materials and science supplies from Science Stuff. Visit their website at www.sciencestuff.com.

Biology (Ninth Grade)

Basic Texts

Aristotle. *Physics.* Ed. Robin Waterfield and David Bostock. Oxford: Oxford University Press, 1999.

$12.95. Order through a bookstore or online bookseller, or check your library.

Euclid. *Thirteen Books of Euclid's Elements, Vol. 1.* Ed. Thomas L. Heath. 2d ed. New York: Dover, 1989.

$14.95. Order through a bookstore or online bookseller, or check your library.

Garber, Steven D. *Biology: A Self-Teaching Guide.* 2d ed. New York: Wiley, 2002.

$19.95. Order through a bookstore or online bookseller.

Gardner, Robert. *Genetics and Evolution Science Fair Projects.* Berkeley Heights, N.J.: Enslow, 2005.

$26.60. Order from any bookstore.

Hershey, David R. *Plant Biology Science Projects.* Hoboken, N.J.: Jossey-Bass, 1995.

$16.95. Order from any bookstore.

Hippocrates. *Hippocrates: Places in Man, General Nature of Glands, Fleshes, Use of Liquids, Ulcers, Fistulas, Haemorrhoids, Vol. 8.* Trans. Paul Potter. Loeb Classical Library, no. 482. Cambridge, Mass.: Harvard University Press, 1995.

$24.00. Order through a bookstore or online bookseller, or check your library.

Rainis, Kenneth G. *Cell and Microbe Science Fair Projects.* Berkeley Heights, N.J.: Enslow, 2005.

$26.60. Order from any bookstore.

VanCleave, Janice. *Janice VanCleave's A+ Projects in Biology.* Hoboken, N.J.: Jossey-Bass, 1993.

$12.95. Order from any bookstore.

Walker, Pam, and Elaine Wood. *Ecosystem Science Fair Projects.* Berkeley Heights, N.J.: Enslow, 2005.
$26.60. Order from any bookstore.

Supplementary Resources

A.D.A.M.: The Inside Story, Complete. Atlanta, Ga.: A.D.A.M. Software.
$87.95. Order from A.D.A.M. Software. This is an award-winning interactive CD-ROM that guides you through the human body.

Burnie, David. *Eyewitness: Life.* New York: Dorling Kindersley, 1999.
$15.99. A good basic reference work for biology; covers everything from cell structure to classification.

Eyewitness Books. New York: Dorling Kindersley, 2000.
$15.99 each. Designed by Dorling Kindersley, these are museums in a book—photos, reference text, definitions, all beautifully done.
Burnie, David, and Peter Chadwick. *Bird.*
———. *Tree.*
Parker, Steve, and Philip Dowell. *Pond and River.*
———. *Skeleton.*
Whalley, Paul, et al. *Butterfly and Moth.*

Kapit, Wynn, and Lawrence M. Elson. *Anatomy Coloring Book.* 3d ed. Paramus, N.J.: Pearson Education, 2001.
$21.80. Order from Rainbow Resource Center. Even more detailed than the *Gray's Anatomy* coloring book (see below). Covers, in 400 pages, all major body systems. Revised to include information on AIDS.

Pollock, Steve. *Eyewitness: Ecology.* New York: Dorling Kindersley, 2005.
$15.99. This is a particularly good guide for students trying to come up with paper topics. Examines cause and effect in the natural world.

Stark, Fred. *Start Exploring Gray's Anatomy: A Fact-Filled Coloring Book.* Philadelphia, Pa.: Running Press, 2001.
$8.95. Order from Greenleaf Press. Detailed drawings to color, with descriptions from the classic anatomy text.

Astronomy (Tenth Grade)

Basic Texts

Copernicus, Nicholas. *On the Revolutions of the Heavenly Spheres.* Trans. Charles G. Wallis. New York: Prometheus, 1995.
$14.95. Order through a bookstore or online bookseller.

Galilei, Galileo. *Dialogues Concerning Two New Sciences.* Trans. Alfonso De Salvio and Henry Crew. New York: Prometheus, 1991.
$12.95. Order through a bookstore or online bookseller.

Gardner, Robert. *Planet Earth Science Fair Projects.* Berkeley Heights, N.J.: Enslow, 2005.
$26.60. Order from any bookstore. Includes astronomy projects.

Kepler, Johannes. *Epitome of Copernican Astronomy and Harmonies of the World.* Trans. Charles Glenn Wallis. New York: Prometheus, 1995.
$13.00. Order through a bookstore or online bookseller.

Moche, Dinah L. *Astronomy: A Self-Teaching Guide.* New York: Wiley, 2004.
$19.95. Order through a bookstore or online bookseller.

VanCleave, Janice. *Janice VanCleave's A+ Projects in Astronomy.* Hoboken, N.J.: Jossey-Bass, 2001.
$12.95. Order from any bookstore.

Supplementary Resources

Lippincott, Kristen. *Eyewitness: Astronomy.* New York: Dorling Kindersley, 2008.
$15.99. Order from Dorling Kindersley. Reviews the history of astronomy along with recent discoveries.

Luminous Star Finder. Skokie, Ill.: Rand McNally.
$5.00. Order from Science Stuff. This big wheel turns to the appropriate month, day, and time. Has glow-in-the-dark stars.

Ridpath, Ian, and Wil Tirion. *Stars and Planets: Princeton Field Guides.* Princeton, N.J.: Princeton University Press, 2001.
$19.95. Order from any bookstore. Photos, diagrams, and lots of information.

Chemistry (Eleventh Grade)

Basic Texts

Boyle, Robert. *The Sceptical Chymist.* New York: Dover, 2003.
$14.95. Order from any bookstore or online bookseller.

Gardner, Robert. *Chemistry Science Fair Projects.* Berkeley Heights, N.J.: Enslow, 2004.
$26.60. Order from any bookstore.

Goodstein, Madeleine P. *Plastics and Polymers Science Fair Projects.* Berkeley Heights, N.J.: Enslow, 2004.
$26.60. Order from any bookstore.

Herr, Norman, and James Cunningham. *Hands-On Chemistry Activities with Real Life Applications.* New York: Jossey-Bass, 1999.
$32.95. Order from any bookstore.

Houk, Clifford C., and Richard Post. *Chemistry: Concepts and Problems—A Self-Teaching Guide.* 2d ed. New York: Wiley, 1996.
$19.95. Order from any bookstore or online bookseller.

Lavoisier, Antoine. *Elements of Chemistry.* New York: Dover, 1984.
$19.95. Order from any bookstore or online bookseller.

Newton, Isaac. *Principia.* Trans. Andrew Motte. New York: Prometheus, 1995.
$17.00. Order from any bookstore or online bookseller.

VanCleave, Janice. *Janice VanCleave's A+ Projects in Chemistry.* Hoboken, N.J.: Jossey-Bass, 1993.
$12.95. Order from any bookstore.

Supplementary Resources

CHEM C3000 Chemistry Kit. Portsmouth, R.I.: Thames & Kosmos.
$239.95. Order from Thames & Kosmos; the company makes two lower-priced sets as well, but this one contains all necessary high-school materials.

ElementO.
$34.95. Order from Rainbow Resource Center. In this Monopoly-type

game, players collect elements and pay each other with proton and neutron certificates. Keep track with the Periodic Table of Elements in the middle of the board. A great way to memorize the basic properties of chemistry.

Knapp, Brian. ChemLab series. Danbury, Conn.: Grolier Educational Corporation, 1997.

This is an excellent twelve-volume series covering all the major areas of chemistry with illustrations, experiments, and definitions. You should be able to find these at your local library.

Volume 1: *Gases, Liquids, and Solids.*
Volume 2: *Elements, Compounds, and Mixtures.*
Volume 3: *The Periodic Table.*
Volume 4: *Metals.*
Volume 5: *Acids, Bases, and Salts.*
Volume 6: *Heat and Combustion.*
Volume 7: *Oxidation and Reduction.*
Volume 8: *Air and Water Chemistry.*
Volume 9: *Carbon Chemistry.*
Volume 10: *Energy and Chemical Change.*
Volume 11: *Preparations.*
Volume 12: *Tests.*

Periodic Table of Elements Chartlet.

$1.99. Order from Rainbow Resource Center. A 17 × 22-inch reference chart of the table of elements.

Trombley, Linda, and Thomas G. Cohn. *Mastering the Periodic Table: Exercises on the Elements.* Portland, Me.: J. Weston Walch, 2002.

$22.99. Order from J. Weston Walch or from Rainbow Resource Center.

Physics (Twelfth Grade)

Basic Texts

Behe, Michael. *Darwin's Black Box.* New York: Touchstone, 2006.

$15.00. Order through any bookstore or online bookseller.

Cunningham, James, and Norman Herr. *Hands-On Physics Activities with Real-*

Life Applications: Easy-to-Use Labs and Demonstrations for Grades 8–12. New York: Jossey-Bass, 1994.
$32.95. Order from any bookstore.

Einstein, Albert. *Relativity: The Special and the General Theory.* Trans. Robert W. Lawson. New York: Dover, 2005.
$6.99. Order through any bookstore or online bookseller.

Gardner, Robert. *Electricity and Magnetism Science Fair Projects.* Berkely Heights, N.J.: Enslow, 2004.
$26.60. Order from any bookstore.

———. *Forces and Motion Science Fair Projects.* Berkeley Heights, N.J.: Enslow, 2004.
$26.60. Order from any bookstore.

———. *Light, Sound, and Waves Science Fair Projects.* Berkeley Heights, N.J.: Enslow, 2004.
$26.60. Order from any bookstore.

———. *Science Fair Projects About the Properties of Matter.* Berkeley Heights, N.J.: Enslow, 2004.
$26.60. Order from any bookstore.

Hawking, Stephen. *A Brief History of Time: From the Big Bang to Black Holes.* 10th anniversary ed. New York: Bantam, 1998.
$18.00. Order through any bookstore or online bookseller.

Kuhn, Karl F. *Basic Physics: A Self-Teaching Guide.* 2d ed. New York: Wiley, 1996.
$19.95. Order through any bookstore or online bookseller.

Supplementary Resources

Adams, Richard C., et al. *Energy Projects for Young Scientists,* rev. ed. New York: Franklin Watts, 2003.
$9.95. Order from any bookstore. Experiments in power.

Physics Projects Kits. Riverside, N.Y.: Educational Designs.
$10.00 each. Order from Rainbow Resource Center. Each kit is complete with all materials.

Crystal Radio.
A working crystal radio.
Electric Bell.
Build a bell-buzzer-telegraph.
Electric Motor.
Electro-Magnetix.
Electromagnetic motor to build.

Alternative Science Courses

Real Science-4-Kids, by Rebecca Keller. Albuquerque, N.Mex.: Gravitas Publications, Inc.
Order from Gravitas Publications.
Level 2 Chemistry
Student Text. $72.95
Student Workbook. $21.95
Teacher's Manual. $26.95.
Student/Teacher Bundle (contains all of the above). $121.85.

The Teaching Company.
Order these courses from the Teaching Company. Check the site regularly for sales, which lower prices by as much as 70 percent. Prices include tapes plus transcript book.
Chemistry—High School Level.
$254.95. Taught by Frank Cardulla, Niles North High School (Chicago).
Einstein's Relativity and the Quantum Revolution: Modern Physics for Non-Scientists, 2d Edition.
$254.95. Taught by Richard Wolfson, Middlebury College.
Particle Physics for Non-Physicists: A Tour of the Microcosmos.
$254.95. Taught by Steven Pollock, University of Colorado.
Understanding the Human Body: An Introduction to Anatomy and Physiology.
$519.95. Taught by Dr. Anthony Goodman, Cornell.
Understanding the Universe: An Introduction to Astronomy
$799.95. Taught by Alex Filippenko, UC-Berkeley.

Wile, Jay. Apologia Science. Anderson, Ind.: Apologia Educational Ministries.

Order from Tobin's Lab, Rainbow Resource Center, or directly from Apologia. Visit apologia.com to view more ordering options and supplies.

Exploring Creation with Biology.

$85.00 for two-volume set: text and solution manual.

Multimedia CD-ROM. $15.00.

Full course CD. $65.00.

Dissection Lab Supplies. $36.00.

Biology Lab Supplies. $85.00.

Biology Lab Supplies w/Microscope. $260.00.

Exploring Creation with Chemistry

$79.00 for two-volume set: text and solution manual.

Multimedia CD-ROM. $15.00.

Full course CD. $ 65.00.

Chemistry Lab Supplies. $55.00.

Exploring Creation with Physics.

$75.00 for two-volume set: text and solution manual.

Advanced Biology: The Human Body: Fearfully and Wonderfully Made

$85.00 for two-volume set: text and solution manual

Advanced Biology Dissection Specimens. $32.00.

Full course CD. $65.00.

Human Body Slide Set. $56.00.

Advanced Chemistry in Creation.

$75.00 for two-volume set: text and solution manual.

Advanced Chemistry Lab Set. $45.00.

Advanced Physics in Creation.

$75.00 for two-volume set: text and solution manual.

29

LEARNING OTHER WORLDS: FOREIGN LANGUAGES

> We are greatly helped to develop objectivity of taste if we can appreciate the work of foreign authors, living in the same world as ourselves, and expressing their vision of it in another great language.
>
> —T. S. Eliot

SUBJECT: Classical and modern languages
TIME REQUIRED: 3 to 6 hours per week

When it comes to rhetoric-stage foreign-language study, you have two goals. One is to fulfill the standard college-prep high-school requirement—two years of a foreign language studied during the high-school years (grades 9–12).[1] Students who have followed our suggested middle-grade program will be in good shape. Two years of high-school language study should lead to at least basic fluency as well as the ability to read popular-level foreign-language literature.

This two-year requirement is a minimum. The classically educated stu-

[1]Languages studied before ninth grade generally don't count in the eyes of college admissions officers; they assume that this study was on a lower level.

dent has other purposes in mind: the mastery of one foreign language (the equivalent of four years of study, resulting in the ability to read literature fluently), and the beginning study at the high-school level (two years) of another. Ideally, one of these languages should be ancient Greek or Latin, while the other should be a modern spoken language.

Why this more ambitious program?

During the rhetoric stage, the student is continually dealing with words—how they should be put together, how they express emotions and ideas, how they can be arranged for greatest effect. Study of two foreign languages teaches the student how writers from other cultures, thinking in different ways, deal with words. This expands the student's grasp of language, raising questions about the relationship between language and thought.

In his 1892 essay "The Present Requirements for Admission to Harvard College," James Jay Greenough writes that reading in a foreign language forces the student to look at each thought from two points of view: that of the original language and that of the English translation he is producing. This gives the student "a clearer conception of the thought than he could possibly get by looking at it from the English side only. . . . He grows accustomed to clear thinking, and therefore expresses his own thoughts more clearly both in speech and in writing." Language study is central to the skills of expression being worked on during the rhetoric stage.

WHICH LANGUAGES?

For the four-year language requirement, we suggest that most students keep studying Latin, completing the equivalent of Latin IV during the high-school years. The student who truly loathes Latin could be permitted to drop it after completing Latin II, but he should plan on studying a modern foreign language through the fourth-year level. The modern language resources listed in Chapter 19 only take you through second-year studies. As you continue, you should choose a tutor, a community-college or a beginning university course, or a correspondence course for the third and fourth levels of study.

The student with a strong interest in the classics could substitute Greek I and Greek II for a modern foreign language, while continuing with the study of Latin through Latin IV.

Since the study of modern languages was begun in the middle grades, the rhetoric-stage student who applies himself for an additional two years of high-school study will progress much further than students who come into high school unprepared. As mentioned before, we strongly recommend the study of Spanish for the modern-foreign-language requirement; French, Italian, German, Russian, Japanese, Chinese, and Hebrew are also possibilities. T. S. Eliot, in his essay "The Man of Letters," suggests that scholars with "very exceptional linguistic ability" will benefit from studying a language that is "more remote" from our own. He mentions Hebrew and Chinese, but Japanese or Arabic (and, to a lesser degree, Russian) would have the same effect.[2]

TEXTS AND COURSES

Ancient Languages

If the student has already begun the study of Latin as recommended in Chapter 19, you'll want to continue on with the same resources: Henle's Latin texts or *The Latin Road to English Grammar.*

The student who began with *Latina Christiana* and progressed to the Henle *First Year Latin* will continue in this same pattern:

Option 1: Following up on grammar stage study:

Third or fourth grade	*Prima Latina*
Fourth or fifth grade	*Latina Christiana I*
Fifth or sixth grade	*Latina Christiana II*
Sixth or seventh grade	*First Year Latin,* first 100 pages or more (Units 1 and 2)
Seventh or eighth grade	*First Year Latin,* continue on
Eighth or ninth grade	Finish *First Year Latin* or begin *Second Year Latin*
Ninth or tenth grade	Begin *Second Year Latin* or finish *Second Year Latin*

[2] T. S. Eliot, *The Classics and the Man of Letters* (Brooklyn, N.Y.: Haskell House, 1974), p. 22.

Tenth or eleventh grade	Finish *Second Year Latin* or begin *Third Year Latin* (Cicero)
Eleventh or twelfth grade	*Third Year Latin* or *Fourth Year Latin* (Virgil)
Twelfth grade	*Fourth Year Latin* or year off from Latin studies

As long as the student is able to pick up the pace of Latin study so that he is completing one Latin book per year by eleventh grade, he will finish a full high-school Latin course—and you can give him four years of high-school Latin credit.

The texts by Robert Henle (*Second Year Latin, Third Year Latin, Fourth Year Latin,* with accompanying keys) are used along with Henle's *Latin Grammar.* The student will probably need a tutor, either online or from a local parochial school or university, to meet with once a week and go over any translation issues. (See Chapter 43 for more guidance on selecting a tutor.) Online classes based on Henle are offered at Memoria Press's online academy (www.memoriapress.com); The Potter's School (pottersschool.org) and Schola Tutorials (www.scholatutorials.org) also offer Latin courses. Visit www.gbt.org for links to other tutorial services.

The student who began Latin study in fifth or sixth grade can follow a similar pattern, but will have to pick up his pace slightly earlier if he wants to finish all four years of study:

Option 2: Beginning Latin study in fifth or sixth grade:

Fifth grade	*Latina Christiana I*
Sixth grade	*Latina Christiana II*
Seventh grade	Begin *First Year Latin*
Eighth grade	Finish *First Year Latin*
Ninth grade	Begin *Second Year Latin*
Tenth grade	Finish *Second Year Latin*
Eleventh grade	*Third Year Latin* (Cicero)
Twelfth grade	*Fourth Year Latin* (Virgil)

Or

Sixth grade	*Latina Christiana I*
Seventh grade	*Latina Christiana II*

Eighth grade	Begin *First Year Latin*
Ninth grade	Finish *First Year Latin*
Tenth grade	*Second Year Latin*
Eleventh grade	*Third Year Latin*
Twelfth grade	*Fourth Year Latin* (Virgil)

Remember that the student can also choose to stop Latin after the second-year book is finished. At that point, you can award two years of high-school credit.

The student who begins Latin later will need to follow a slightly different course:

Option 3: Beginning Latin study in seventh or eighth grade:

Seventh or eighth grade	*The Latin Road to English Grammar, Volume One*
Eighth or ninth grade	*The Latin Road to English Grammar, Volume Two*
Ninth or tenth grade	*The Latin Road to English Grammar, Volume Three*
Tenth or eleventh grade	*Oxford Latin Course, Part III*
Eleventh or twelfth grade	*Oxford Latin Reader*

The three years of the *Latin Road* program are equivalent to two years of high-school Latin, so when the student has finished this program, you can give him credit for Latin I and Latin II on his high-school credit. If he would then like to continue on and do the two additional years of Latin literature, he should use the third- and fourth-year texts from another Latin course: the *Oxford University Latin Course. Part III* is a reader built around the life of Horace; the fourth year of the course is called the *Latin Reader, Part IV* and is an anthology of selections from Caesar, Cicero, Catullus, Virgil, Livy, and Ovid. He should also buy *Part II,* the last year of grammar, and keep it on hand for reference so that he can review any skills not covered in the *Latin Road* program.

If the student begins Latin for the first time in high school, he can work through the entire four-year Oxford course with the help of a tutor, or he can use the *Latin Road* followed by the third and fourth books of the Oxford course. If he wants to do a four-year study, he'll need to cover all three volumes of the *Latin Road* in two years. He can choose instead to complete one volume per year, but he can only earn two years total of high-school credit for this work, even if he does it over a three-year period. If he then goes on to do the third Oxford book, he can earn a total of three years of high-school credit in Latin.

If the student wishes to begin Greek, we suggest Oxford University Press's *Athenaze*. This two-year program supplies a full introduction to Greek grammar and syntax, essays on Greek history and culture, plenty of exercises, and an extensive teacher's edition. Greek is not a difficult language to learn, but you'll want to find a tutor to help with the introduction to the alphabet (it's different from the Latin alphabet) and pronunciation. Try a local church. Almost all seminaries require ministers-in-training to take two years of New Testament Greek in order to graduate. Although New Testament (Koine) Greek is different in structure and vocabulary from classical Greek, the alphabet and pronunciation are the same. With a few weeks of introductory help, most students who have mastered the first two years of Latin can continue Greek studies independently.

If the student is interested in Koine Greek itself, a self-teaching course called *Elementary Greek: Koine for Beginners* is available from Open Texture; the three-workbook course will lead older students through the basics of Greek, equal in content to about a one-year seminary course. Visit the publisher's website, www.opentexture.com, to see samples of the program.

Modern Languages

If you haven't yet studied a modern foreign language, complete one of the courses described in Chapter 19. These courses take the student through second-year modern language. A Power-Glide or Rosetta Stone course plus Latin III and IV will fulfill the classical requirements for foreign language (and impress college admissions officers). If you already finished both levels of a modern language course in the middle grades, you have two options: you can learn a second modern language in high school (you need to have those two high-school years for the sake of college admissions), or you can continue to study the language you are learning for two additional years.

For the latter option, you'll need to "outsource"—find a teacher or class. Modern foreign-language literature should be read with a teacher who's enthusiastic and knowledgeable about both the culture and the language. You may be able to locate a tutor who would be willing to do a two-year reading course with a student who's already had the language basics—try the language department of your local college, or call a good private school and ask for options. Or you can enroll your high-school student in a class at your local university or community college (see Chapter 43 for a full discussion of concurrent enrollment). We suggest that you and your child talk to the instructor, who will want to evaluate the student's readiness. In most cases, two years of high-school study is considered the equivalent of one year of college study, so a student who's finished two years of French or Spanish will probably be placed in a second-year class. After this two-semester class, you'll advance to a literature class. These two years of study (French II and French literature, Spanish II and Spanish literature, and so forth) are the equivalent of four high-school years of study (French I–IV, Spanish I–IV, and so on).

Another option is a correspondence course offered by either the University of Nebraska or one of the other schools listed in Chapter 43 (call for catalogs). The University of Oklahoma offers high-school Latin, French, German, and Spanish. The student could also enroll in one of that university's college-level courses (Russian, Spanish, German, Greek, Japanese, French, Chinese), which takes the student through literature study. Finally, Keystone National High School offers a wide range of both regular and AP language classes.

SCHEDULES

The basic goals of grades 9 through 12 are

- two years of study in one language (which completes the learning of basic grammar and conversational vocabulary),
- four years of study in another language (grammar, vocabulary, plus two years of developing reading competency).

One of these languages should be modern, the other, ancient.

The choices you make concerning foreign-language study depend, in part, on your seventh- and eighth-grade preparation. There are a number of different ways to arrange language study; here are a few sample schedules for you to play with and adjust.

Maximum language option: 4 years each, modern and ancient:

Sixth grade	*First Year Latin,* first 100 pages or more (Units 1 and 2)
Seventh grade	*First Year Latin,* continue on; Power-Glide or Rosetta Stone, Level 1
Eighth grade	Finish *First Year Latin;* Power-Glide or Rosetta Stone, Level 2
Ninth grade	Begin *Second Year Latin*; modern language: enroll in a second-year college course
Tenth grade	Finish *Second Year Latin* and begin *Third Year Latin* (Cicero); modern language: read with a tutor or enroll in one semester of a college modern-language literature course
Eleventh grade	*Third Year Latin*
Twelfth grade	*Fourth Year Latin*

High-school credits awarded: 4 Latin, 4 modern language (each credit = 1 year of study).

Ancient language concentration for student beginning Latin in middle school:

Fifth grade	*Latina Christiana I*
Sixth grade	*Latina Christiana II*; Power-Glide or Rosetta Stone, Level 1
Seventh grade	Begin *First Year Latin*; Power-Glide or Rosetta Stone, Level 1
Eighth grade	Finish *First Year Latin*
Ninth grade	Begin *Second Year Latin; Athenaze, Book I*
Tenth grade	Finish *Second Year Latin; Athenaze, Book 2*
Eleventh grade	*Third Year Latin* (Cicero)
Twelfth grade	*Fourth Year Latin* (Virgil)

High-school credits awarded: 4 Latin, 2 Greek.

Modern language focus for student beginning Latin in middle school:

Sixth grade	*Latina Christiana I*
Seventh grade	*Latina Christiana II*
Eighth grade	Begin *First Year Latin*
Ninth grade	Finish *First Year Latin*; Power-Glide or Rosetta Stone, Level 1
Tenth grade	*Second Year Latin*; Power-Glide or Rosetta Stone, Level 2
Eleventh grade	Finish *Second Year Latin*, if necessary; enroll in a second-year college modern language course (the ninth- and tenth-grade years of study are equal to the first year of college study)
Twelfth grade	Read with a tutor or enroll in a modern language reading course

High-school credits awarded: 2 Latin, 4 modern language.

Two-language option for student beginning language study in high school:

Ninth grade	*The Latin Road to English Grammar, Volume One*; begin *Latin Road, Volume Two*
Tenth grade	Finish *The Latin Road to English Grammar, Volume Two; Latin Road, Volume Three*
Eleventh grade	*Oxford Latin Course, Part III*, Rosetta Stone or Power-Glide, Level 1
Twelfth grade	*Oxford Latin Reader*; Rosetta Stone or Power-Glide, Level 2

High-school credits awarded: 4 Latin, 2 modern language.

Modern language concentration for student beginning language study in high school:

Ninth grade	*The Latin Road to English Grammar, Volume One*; Begin *Latin Road, Volume Two*; Rosetta Stone or Power-Glide, Level 1
Tenth grade	Finish *The Latin Road to English Grammar, Volume Two*; *Latin Road, Volume Three*; Rosetta Stone or Power-Glide, Level 2

Eleventh grade	Enroll in second-year college modern language course
Twelfth grade	Read with a tutor or enroll in a modern language reading course

High-school credits awarded: 2 Latin, 4 modern language.

This still fulfills the classical language requirements—two years of Latin and four years of a modern language, leading to reading proficiency.

RESOURCES

For publisher and catalog addresses, telephone numbers, and other information, see Sources (pages 751–778). Latin resources are given first, with Greek second and modern foreign languages following. Books in a series are listed in order. See Chapter 19 for additional foreign-language resources and more supplementary Latin readings.

Latin

Basic Texts

Beers, Barbara. *The Latin Road to English Grammar, Vol. I.* Redding, Calif.: Schola Publications, 1997.

———. *The Latin Road to English Grammar, Vol. II.* Redding, Calif.: Schola Publications, 1997.

$149.00 each. Order from Schola Publications, along with all supplementary material.

Teacher Training Videos. Extra parent support for the truly intimidated. $89.00 for DVD. Combination packages are offered at a discount.

Henle, Robert J., S.J. *First Year Latin.* Chicago, Ill.: Loyola Press, 1958.

$16.95; $18.95 along with answer key (necessary). Order all resources from Memoria Press (where *First Year Latin* is listed as "Henle I Text & Key"). This text, along with Henle Grammar, serves as the basic text for two years of study: the first year covers Units 1–2, and the second covers Units 3–5.

Henle Study Guide. Highly recommended for successful study. $14.95

———. *Latin Grammar.* Chicago, Ill.: Loyola Press, 1980.
$9.50. Order from Memoria Press. Necessary to accompany both *First Year Latin* and *Second Year Latin.*

________. *Second Year Latin.* Chicago, Ill.: Loyola Press, 1997.
$15.95 ($17.95 for text plus necessary key). Order from Memoria Press, where it is listed as "Henle II Text with key."

Morwood, James, and Maurice G. Balme. *Oxford University Latin Course.* Oxford: Oxford University Press.
Order from American Home-School Publishing.
Oxford University Latin Course, Part I. 2d ed. 1996.
(May be useful for reference; necessary if doing this course with a tutor)
Student Text. $23.00.
Teacher's Book. $25.00.
Oxford University Latin Course, Part II. 2d ed. 1997.
Student Text. $23.00.
Teacher's Book. $25.00.
Oxford University Latin Course, Part III. 2d ed. 1997.
Student Text. $25.00.
Teacher's Book. $27.00.
Oxford University Latin Course Reader. 2d ed. 1997.
Fourth year in the course. $24.00.

Supplementary Resources

Hammond, Mason, and Anne R. Amory. *Aeneas to Augustus: A Beginning Latin Reader for College Students.* Cambridge, Mass.: Harvard University Press, 1967.
$31.00. Order from any bookstore. A standard introduction to great Latin writers.

Lenard, Alexander, and A. A. Milne. *Winnie Ille Pu: A Latin Version of A. A. Milne's Winnie-the-Pooh.* New York: Puffin, 1991.
Order from any bookstore.

Rowling, J. K. *Harrius Potter et Philosophi Lapis.* New York: Bloomsbury USA, 2003.
You'll have to guess what this one is. Order from any bookstore.

Russell, D. A. *An Anthology of Latin Prose.* Oxford: Oxford University Press, 1990.

$49.50. Order from any bookstore. A standard reader that may be simpler than the Hammond/Amory reader for home use, since it doesn't include poetry (which is extremely difficult).

Greek

Basic Texts

Lawall, Gilbert, and Maurice G. Balme. *Athenaze: An Introduction to Ancient Greek.* 2d ed. Oxford: Oxford University Press, 2003.

Order from American Home-School Publishing or from Oxford University Press.

Book 1. $34.95.

Workbook to Accompany Athenaze, Book 1. $19.95.

Teacher's Handbook for Athenaze, Book 1. $24.95.

Book 2. $32.95.

Workbook to Accompany Athenaze, Book 2. $19.95.

Teacher's Handbook for Athenaze, Book 2. $24.95.

Supplementary Resources

Betts, Gavin, and Alan Henry. *Teach Yourself Ancient Greek.* New York: McGraw-Hill, 2002.

$17.95. If *Athenaze* proves too challenging, you can use this mass-market self-teaching guide as a supplement or even a substitute. It isn't as complete, but you may find it easier to use.

Gatchell, Christine. *Elementary Greek: Koine for Beginners.* Highlands Ranch, Colo.: Open Texture.

$149.95 for the complete course.

Pharr, Clyde, and John Henry Wright. *Homeric Greek: A Book for Beginners,* rev. ed. Norman, Okla.: University of Oklahoma Press, 1986.

$29.95. A good complement to *Athenaze.* This book, designed for students who know no Greek, plunges you into the reading of Homer almost straightaway. A good motivator for the first-year Greek student.

Modern Languages

Basic Texts

Power-Glide Language Courses. Provo, Utah: Power-Glide.

Order from Power-Glide. High-school courses come in three price ranges: $159.99 for a one-year course, $259.99 for a one-year course along with accredited proof of high-school credit; or $509.99 for course, credit, and support from a tutor. Visit power-glide.com for more options and sample lessons.

Spanish. 1, 2, 3, and *AP.*
French. 1, 2, 3, and *AP.*
German. 1 and 2.
Latin 1.
Mandarin 1.

Rosetta Stone Language Learning: Homeschool Edition. Harrisonburg, Va.

$349.00 for sets of Level 1 and 2 (probably 4–5 years of study for a younger student; the program estimates that it offers 800 hours of instruction). Order from Rosetta Stone. An interactive computer-based language learning program that uses photos and graphics to encourage the student to think in a foreign language. Each Homeschool Edition Level 1 includes a program for keeping track of the student's progress. Many other languages are available at the Rosetta Stone website, www.rosettastone.com.

Spanish, Level I & II Set.
French, Level 1& II Set.
German, Level I & II Set.
Arabic, Level I & II Set.
Japanese, Level I & II Set.
Korean, Level I & II Set.
Russian, Level I & II Set.
Welsh, Level I & II Set.

Supplementary Resources

Calvez, Daniel J. *French Grammar: A Complete Reference Guide.* 2d ed. New York: McGraw-Hill, 2004.

$18.95. A useful grammatical supplement to the spoken-language courses recommended above, which tend to be light on grammar.

Parish, Peggy, et al. *Amelia Bedelia (Ya See Leer)*. New York: HarperCollins, 1996.

$4.95. A children's standard, for fun Spanish reading; see how the puns work in another language.

Saint-Exupery, Antoine de. *Le Petit Prince*. French ed. San Diego, Calif.: Harvest Books, 2001.

$10.00. A good first excursion into French literature.

Viorst, Judith, and Alma F. Ada. *Alexander Y El Dia Terrible, Horrible, Espantoso, Horrorosa*. Illus. Ray Cruz. New York: Aladdin, 1989.

$5.99. Another children's favorite in Spanish, just for fun.

Wiley Self-Teaching Guides. New York: John Wiley Publishers.

$18.95 apiece. Order from any bookstore. These paperbacks, designed for independent study, will fill in the grammar "holes" left by the conversation-focused programs recommended above. Good to have on hand for reference.

Hershfield-Haims, Suzanne A. *French: A Self-Teaching Guide*. 2d ed. 2000.
Lebano, Edoardo A. *Italian: A Self-Teaching Guide*. 2d ed. 2000.
Prado, Marcial. *Practical Spanish Grammar: A Self-Teaching Guide*. 1997.
Taylor, Heimy, and Werner Haas. *German: A Self-Teaching Guide*. 1997.

Correspondence Courses

University of Nebraska-Lincoln
Independent Study High School
P.O. Box 888400
Lincoln, NE 68588-8400
402-472-2175
Fax: 402-472-1901
Web: nebraskahs.unl.edu
E-mail: extservice@unl.edu

Offers high-school courses, including foreign languages, by correspondence.

University of Oklahoma
Distance and Online Programs
Independent Study for College and High School Courses
1600 Jenkins, Room 101
Norman, OK 73073-6507
800-942-5702 or 405-325-1921
Fax: 405-325-7687
Web: isd.ou.edu
E-mail: cidl@ou.edu

The University of Oklahoma has good language correspondence courses, complete with texts and audiotapes. The catalog includes both high-school and college courses.

Keystone National High School
920 Central Road
Bloomsburg, PA 17815
866-376-8534 or 570-784-5220
Web: keystonehighschool.com
E-mail: info@keystonehighschool.com

Offers a full range of regular and AP classes, both by correspondence and online.

30

MASTERING THE MAGIC BOX: COMPUTER SKILLS

People are flooding the Internet like the lava from Vesuvius flooded Pompeii.

—Tom Lichty, *America Online's Internet*

SUBJECT: Basic computer programming
TIME REQUIRED: 3 to 5 hours per week for one year (eleventh or twelfth grade)

GENERALLY SPEAKING

Throughout Part III of this book, we referred the high-school student to computer resources—CD-ROMs, online tutorials, reference websites. So we're certainly not antitechnology. Computers are marvelous tools; word processing beats typewriting; e-mail is more convenient (and cheaper) than the postal service. We live in the country. Before Internet access, we had to make the hour-long round-trip drive to the public library in order to look up information about books we wanted to recommend. Now we can sign on, search the library catalog, and be off in three minutes.

In the spirit of classical education, though, we approach this new technology with great caution. In Chapter 28, we suggested that the student use questions outlined by Neil Postman in *The End of Education* to evaluate scientific discovery and innovation better. These should be applied first and foremost to computer technology.

Postman says, in essence: Any technology offers both advantages and disadvantages. What are they?[1]

The Internet floods cyberspace with information. Yet only some of this information is filtered in any way—fact-checked, read through for general accuracy, edited. Scholarly books, on the other hand, have been *mediated*—passed through a number of tests before publication. They may still be bad scholarship, but they generally won't contain libelous statements, out-and-out lies, or intentional distortions. It is relatively easy to publish on the Internet; libel, lies, and distortions abound. The student who uses the Internet for information needs to check everything carefully, applying to the task all her skills in logic and analysis.

In other words, Internet information doesn't make the book obsolete. It doesn't remove the need for the student to be trained in critical thought. It should not take the place of library trips, magazine subscriptions, or any of the mediated ways to gain information. When Internet resources become primary, the student herself becomes the mediator of knowledge—and no high-school student can match the experience of an editor at a university press who's been working with scholars and their manuscripts for many years.

Now, consider this:

> All technologies come complete with a philosophy about what is important about human life and what is unimportant. What parts of life does the technology exalt? What parts does it ignore?[2]

Constructing a philosophy of the Internet is a complex job, but one part of that philosophy is immediately obvious: the Internet exalts intellectual

[1]Neil Postman, *The End of Education: Redefining the Value of School* (New York: Knopf, 1995), p. 192.

[2]Postman, p. 192.

experience over sensory experience. The Internet is body-neutral. Physical sensations—touch, smell, taste, balance—are irrelevant.

What are the implications of that? At least two stand out.

First, because we're physical beings, our intellectual pursuits affect our bodies. Numerous studies have been done on how different experiences change the physical makeup of the brain. Specifically, the brain of the student who spends eight hours per day in front of the computer looks different than the brain of the student who spends an hour in front of the computer, four hours in front of books, and the other three hours doing outside activities. Any constantly repeated activity develops some neural pathways at the expense of others. In other words, balance computer use with paper-and-pencil work and active learning. Otherwise, you'll be developing certain parts of the brain while ignoring others. Don't let this form of modern technology dominate your child's spare time; think long and hard about what you're agreeing to when you allow your adolescent to roam the Net for five hours in the evening instead of building models, reading Plato, playing a musical instrument, cutting the grass, drawing, keeping a journal, eating, sleeping, or staring into space and thinking about what life means.

A second implication is especially important for high-school students. Any normal adolescent—by which we mean one who is insecure, struggling to face others with both grace and confidence, self-conscious about skin and hair and weight—prefers to communicate via chat room. Electronic friends are much safer than flesh-and-blood companions. We've met teenagers who spend almost all their recreation time in chat rooms or e-mailing. Although computer friendships can be productive, any computer friendship may take the place of real, live give-and-take between people who are physically present.

For high school, we're not laying down hard-and-fast rules. We are encouraging you to realize that computers, like all technologies, put priorities on some types of experience and relegate others to the background. Know what kind of bargain you and your teen are making when dealing with computer use. As a matter of fact, simply to maintain balance, we think that every high-school student ought to read at least one neo-Luddite work on the computer age (for example, *Data Smog, Resisting the Virtual Life,* or one of the other titles listed at the end of this chapter) to balance out the techno-ravings of software executives and Internet providers.

PRACTICALLY SPEAKING

High-school students should be familiar with basic computer use (how to navigate through Windows), Internet access, and a common word-processing program such as Pages or Microsoft Word. Knowledge of a desktop-publishing program such as QuarkXPress or PageMaker and a spreadsheet program such as Quicken will boost the student's employability. The best way to learn any of these programs is to buy, install, and use it with one eye on the computer, the other on the manual. Let the rhetoric-stage student prepare her paper on a word processor, keep her checkbook on Quicken, and write the family newsletter on PageMaker. Then she can add to her résumé: "Computer skills: Microsoft Word, PageMaker, Quicken."

Every high-school student should be introduced to basic computer programming. This is a way to take the mystery out of computers and put them in their place—as powerful tools, not as dictators of culture. The student who can program has asserted her control over the computer genie.

We suggest that during eleventh or twelfth grade, you schedule at least a year of beginning computer programming into the student's curriculum. Computer programming traditionally takes the place of an advanced mathematics elective or a language elective (anything beyond the four years of one language and two of another outlined in Chapter 29).

One of the most straightforward starting places for beginners is Visual Basic. We suggest several self-teaching courses in the Resources list at the end of this chapter. With the proper equipment, the student should be able to work through these independently for a good grasp of programming principles. Computer languages slide into obsolescence faster than fresh produce spoils. So before you plunge into the study of Visual Basic, you might call a friend who programs (or consult the computer-science department at a local college, or talk to the technology-education teacher at a good private school) and ask whether another language (suitable for beginners) has already trumped it.

As always in high school, you can also enroll your student in a programming course at a local college or find her a tutor. Adult-education classes offered by colleges and libraries often include basic computer skills and programming.

SCHEDULE

Grade 11 or 12: a one-year course in beginning computer programming for three to five hours per week

RESOURCES

For publisher and catalog addresses, telephone numbers, and other information, see Sources (pages 751–778). Most books and tapes or CDs can be obtained from any bookstore or library; where we know of a mail-order option, we have provided it.

Skeptical Reflections on Technology

Meadows, Mark Stephen. *I, Avatar: The Culture and Consequences of Having a Second Life*. Berkeley, Calif.: New Riders Press, 2008.

Part memoir, part analysis, this book asks us to reflect about what the existence of virtual worlds (primarily in role-playing games) means for existence in the real thing. (Best for older students and their parents.)

Postman, Neil. *Technopoly: The Surrender of Culture to Technology*. New York: Vintage, 1993.

Technology, Postman insists, is "a branch of moral philosophy"; it demands that we assume certain moral positions, and we should know what they are.

Sale, Kirkpatrick. *Rebels Against the Future: The Luddites and Their War on the Industrial Revolution: Lessons for the Computer Age*. New York: Perseus, 1996.

Like Postman, Sale argues that technology isn't morally neutral; to prove his point, he goes back in time and makes connections between steam and computer technology. Fascinating reading.

Shenk, David. *Data Smog: Surviving the Information Glut*. San Francisco, Calif.: Harper San Francisco, 1998.

Shenk argues that the huge amount of unfiltered information available in society contributes to social fragmentation, lowered educational standards, religious extremism, and political bickering.

Slouka, Mark. *War of the Worlds: Cyberspace and the High-Tech Assault on Reality.* New York: Basic Books, 1996.

Fascinating essays on how cyberspace changes the rest of reality.

Stoll, Clifford. *Silicon Snake Oil: Second Thoughts on the Information Highway.* New York: Anchor, 1996.

Although it's easier to poke holes in Stoll's argument than in the arguments of the other authors we recommend, he offers some provocative ideas: that computers change the way we think, isolate us, and tie us to a cycle of constant spending and updating.

Basic Computer Knowledge

Common Word-Processing Programs

Pages (Mac)
Microsoft Word

Common Spreadsheet Program

Quicken

Other Common Programs

QuarkXPress
PageMaker
Photoshop
Adobe Illustrator

Acquiring Programming Skills

We offer this as a tentative and extremely rudimentary list. You would do well to call a local computer-science teacher or the computer-science department of the college where your child hopes to apply, and ask what titles they would recommend for beginning programming skills.

If you're a beginner (still looking for the power switch), start with one of these:

Rathbone, Andy. *Windows Vista for Dummies.* Foster City, Calif.: IDG Books Worldwide, 2006.

Order directly from Dummies. Use this if you have Windows and an

IBM-compatible system. It is written for novice users and provides a very easy start for the intimidated. (If you still have XP, you're one of the lucky ones—try *XP for Dummies* instead.)

Levitus, Bob. *Mac OS X Leopard for Dummies.* Foster City, Calif.: IDG Books Worldwide, 2007.

Order directly from Dummies. Use this if you have a Macintosh with the OS X Leopard operating system. This guide to the latest Mac operating system begins with "What you should see after turning the power on" and progresses to more advanced concepts.

If you're already familiar with your computer's operating system, you're ready to move on to programming. There are many websites that offer up-to-date insights into coding and programming. One of the best is www.webmonkey.com. If you prefer to begin with books, you can start with one of the following titles:

Hillegass, Aaron. *Cocoa (R) Programming for Mac (R) OS X.* 3d ed. Boston, Mass.: Pearson Addison-Wesley, 2008.

A solid introduction to the Cocoa programming language for the Mac.

Halvorson, Michael. *Microsoft Visual Basic 2008 Step by Step.* Redmond, Wash.: Microsoft Press, 2008.

This book introduces users to the fundamentals of programming in Visual Basic, and then moves on to some of the more advanced aspects of coding. Comes with a CD.

Goodman, Danny. *JavaScript & DHTML Cookbook.* 2d ed. Sebastopol, Calif.: O'Reilly & Associates, 2007.

Use this if you are interested in coding websites at a higher level. With competent technical writing and an engaging writing style, this book covers a wide range of suggestions and solutions for web programmers.

31

APOLOGIZING FOR FAITH: RELIGION

> It is upon this that our whole Western culture has been built: The universe had a personal beginning—a personal beginning on the high order of the Trinity.
>
> —Francis Schaeffer

One goal of rhetoric is the apologia, the articulate and well-reasoned defense of belief. During the rhetoric stage, the student should certainly learn to defend his own faith without resorting to rhetorical abuses—ad hominem attacks, abusive fallacies, black-and-white fallacies, or any of the other illegitimate arguments forbidden by both logic and rhetoric. And the study of rhetoric should protect the student from abuse of his own beliefs by others.

Religion and rhetoric have an even deeper relationship, though. Classical rhetoric cannot be pursued apart from the considerations of faith. In *Rhetoric,* Aristotle writes that the man who wishes to master rhetoric must be able

> (1) to reason logically, (2) to understand human character and goodness in their various forms, and (3) to understand the emotions—that is, to name them and describe them, to know their causes and the way in which they are excited.[1]

[1]Aristotle, *Rhetoric* I.2.

The ability to reason logically is learned during the logic stage; rhetoric itself aims to name and describe human emotions. But an understanding of human character and goodness in its various forms cannot be separated from our belief about who human beings are, where they came from, and what they are essentially like. Goodness itself cannot be defined without making serious faith decisions: either goodness resides in a Being, or it exists as a social construct.

This is the foundation of ethics.

Nor can ethics be discussed in some sort of "neutral" fashion. If you are a theist, you believe that human character comes from a Creator and reflects some of the Creator's qualities. If you are a materialist, you believe that human character is primarily the result of biological factors, some of which can be controlled, some of which can't. If you are a Christian, you believe that moral absolutes are binding upon every human being. If you are an agnostic, you believe that moral absolutes are unknowable and that making pronouncements about moral absolutes thus reaches the height of arrogance.

What sort of neutral ground can these views meet on?

None. Rhetoric involves an intensive discussion of social ethics, the nature of good and evil, individual responsibility, and the extent to which the manipulation of emotions is morally acceptable. None of these issues can be tackled without a grasp of ethics. And ethics is, itself, inseparable from our view of God, our belief about the nature of humankind, and our expectations of society.

The rhetoric exercises we recommend—evaluating the ideas and philosophies of the great books, writing about the moral and ethical implications of technology—have to be done in the context of faith. Tolerance for the faith of others doesn't mean that the student simply throws open his arms and says, "We're *all* right"; that makes nonsense of five thousand years of deeply held and contradictory beliefs. The tolerance taught by rhetoric involves the student's holding on to his own deep, well-reasoned convictions, while simultaneously treating others with respect. Respect doesn't mean admitting that someone else is right. It does mean refraining from resorting to abusive fallacies and the rhetoric of propaganda so that those of different faiths can seriously and peacefully argue about ideas.

We think that every rhetoric-stage student should make at least a preliminary study of ethics. Since ethics is related to belief, we can't (obviously) recommend an ethics text that will satisfy all home schoolers. The texts we recommend are those we've used ourselves—as Protestant Christians. We encourage you, as you work through the rhetoric stage with your high-school student, to formulate your own beliefs. Use logic and rhetoric to extract what you really believe from the cloudy ideas that may be swirling around you. And then base your own discussions of ethics—right and wrong—self-consciously on those beliefs.

RESOURCES

Consult your own religious or intellectual community, or make use of the following resources:

Christian Ethics

Schaeffer, Francis. *How Should We Then Live?* Wheaton, Ill.: Good News Books, 2005.

$19.99. Order from any bookstore. An outline of Western history and the place of Christian morality within it. Special emphasis on art and philosophy.

Wilkens, Steve. *Beyond Bumper Sticker Ethics: An Introduction to Theories of Right and Wrong*. Downers Grove, Ill.: InterVarsity Press, 1995.

$16.00. Order from any bookstore. The basics of cultural relativism, emotivism, utilitarianism, situation ethics, and deontology, with an evaluation of each.

Jewish Ethics

Gittelsohn, Roland B. *How Do I Decide? A Contemporary Jewish Approach to What's Right and What's Wrong*. West Orange, N.J.: Behrman House, 1989.

$11.95. Order directly from Behrman House, which also offers other titles on ethics.

Grishaver, Joel Lurie. *You Be the Judge: A Collection of Ethical Cases and Jewish Answers*. Los Angeles, Calif.: Torah Aura Publications, 2000.

$9.95. Order directly from Torah Aura, which also offers other titles on ethics.

32

APPRECIATING THE ARTS: ART AND MUSIC

Art is the imposing of a pattern on experience, and our aesthetic enjoyment is recognition of the pattern.

—A. N. Whitehead

SUBJECT: Art and music
TIME REQUIRED: 2 hours, twice per week

The rhetoric student recognizes both art and music as types of expression that are as valid as words. Just as words, spoken and written, are governed by the rules of rhetoric, so art and music are governed by conventions. The study of art and music during the final four years of classical education will center on those conventions—how they are used, how they are altered, how and when they are discarded.

Logic-stage study of art and music was tied chronologically to the study of history. The student was attempting to establish logical connections between artists and musicians and their times. Rhetoric-stage art and music study doesn't need to be connected quite so closely to the historical periods under study. Rather, the study focuses on art and music as the means by which ideas are expressed, just as the study of great books centers on writing as the expression of ideas in words. Pablo Picasso was a philosopher; Cubism embraced an ethical system; Ludwig van Beethoven and John Cage subscribed to widely different world views, and their compositions express this difference. Gothic cathedrals were built to demonstrate God's place at the center of existence; fifteen hundred years later, London artist Francis Bacon painted a screaming pope surrounded by sides of beef to show that "we are all carcasses."

Art *is* rhetoric.

Keep roughly to the same schedule you've been using all along—one one- to two-hour period per week for music study, another for art study. The student will keep two notebooks, one for art and the other for music. These notebooks should last for the entire four years of the rhetoric stage.

ART

The high-school student should continue to study both art skills and art appreciation. As in middle school, the student can alternate art projects one week with art appreciation the next. Or she can choose to study drawing, painting, and modeling one semester and art appreciation the following semester.

Art Skills

The high-school student can continue to divide art-project days among drawing, painting, and modeling (as in the middle grades). Or she can focus on one of these skills, developing a real mastery. For an artistically gifted student, you may want to consider "outsourcing"—hiring a tutor for her (most artists are accustomed to teaching for bread-and-butter money) or enrolling her in a college or adult-education art class. Call your local art association (check your Yellow Pages), and ask for a recommendation. Art museums and galleries often offer art classes, taught by professionals, that are appropriate for students who've already mastered basic skills.

Drawing and Painting

The high-school student can use any of the drawing and painting resources listed at the end of Chapter 21. A slightly more advanced course, good for anyone who's finished Edwards's *Drawing on the Right Side of the Brain,* is the Basic Techniques series published by North Lights Books, designed to teach basic skills in drawing. Drawing was once considered to be an essential skill for any educated man or woman; if you'd like to recapture this attitude, complete *Basic Drawing Techniques* and *Basic Figure Drawing Techniques.*

Students who wish to continue on to explore other media can use *Watercolor Basics: Let's Get Started* as well as choosing from another series, the Dorling Kindersley Art School books; these teach techniques and materials for a range of drawing and painting skills. Titles include:

Watercolor Still Life.
An Introduction to Acrylics.
An Introduction to Oil Painting.

The student can also use an introduction to pastels such as the *Pastel Workbook* (see Resources).

Modeling

The high-school student can either use the titles we list at the end of this chapter—*Sculpture: Principles and Practice, Modeling the Head in Clay,* and *Modeling the Figure in Clay*—or devote that time to painting and drawing, using the Dorling Kindersley series.

Art Appreciation

The high-school student is ready for a full art-history course, one that covers techniques, the philosophies of individual artists, and the rise of the various schools.

For a base text, we like *The Annotated Mona Lisa: A Crash Course in Art History from Prehistoric to Postmodern.* This survey, written by Carol Strickland, walks the beginner through art history in a brisk, nontechnical manner. It summarizes schools, periods, artists, and techniques in architecture, painting, and sculpture, from prehistoric times through postmodernism.

In a thirty-six-week school year, the student will spend eighteen weeks studying art history. In each of these eighteen weeks, she should read from the *Annotated Mona Lisa* and use additional resources to study the artists and works of art discussed (we suggest keeping the Eyewitness art series and *The Story of Painting,* by Sister Wendy Beckett, on hand). She should then record something she's learned, either writing briefly about it, or using the distinctive characteristics of the artist or school under discussion to sketch something in that style. These notebook pages and sketches should be kept in the art notebook.

If the ninth grader, for example, is studying the Italian Renaissance, she'll read through the appropriate pages in the textbook and pick one of the subjects discussed (the life of Leonardo da Vinci, the composition of the *Mona Lisa* or *The Last Supper,* Michelangelo's accomplishments, Raphael as a representative of the High Renaissance, Titian's methods of painting textures, or the four R's of Renaissance architecture (Rome, rules, reason, and 'rithmetic). Whatever subject she chooses, she'll look at any relevant paintings in the Eyewitness art series and in *The Story of Painting* and read any relevant background material. Then she'll write briefly (three-quarters of a page to a full page is fine), summarizing the information. If suitable, she could also sketch her report; if she were studying the composition of the *Mona Lisa* or *The Last Supper,* for example, she could simply draw the layout, adding annotations that contain the information she's learned (the diagonal lines all converge on Christ's head; Mona Lisa sits in an innovative, three-quarter pose). Creativity in reflection should be encouraged during the rhetoric stage of art-historical study.

Divide *The Annotated Mona Lisa* as follows:

Ninth grade	"The Birth of Art" through "The Renaissance: The Beginning of Modern Painting"
Tenth grade	"Baroque: The Ornate Age" through "Birth of Photography"
Eleventh grade	"Impressionism: Let There Be Color and Light" through "Expressionism"
Twelfth grade	"Mondrian: Harmony of Opposites" through "The New Breed: Post-Modern Art"

Since these divisions contain approximately eighteen sections each, the student can plan on studying one per week. The ninth grader, for example, will begin with "Prehistoric Art: The Beginning," progress through "Egypt:

The Art of Immortality," "African Art: The First Cubists," and "Gothic Art: Height and Light," and will finally end up with "The Spanish Renaissance."

MUSIC

Music Skills

By high school, those students who are not interested in playing an instrument will have dropped lessons, while those who are interested will have developed some proficiency and will know whether they want to keep on.

Music Appreciation

Whether or not the student is taking music lessons, she should continue to spend one and a half to two hours every week doing music appreciation.

For a basic text, we like *The Classical Music Experience: Discover the Music of the World's Greatest Composers,* by Julius H. Jacobson. This book and CD set covers forty-two composers; the book gives brief chapters with biographical information, definitions, photos, and dates, while the CDs offer selections from each composer, with narration by Kevin Kline. This is a wonderful beginner's introduction to music.

After finishing this book, the student can then move on to a more detailed study of classical music, Fred Plotkin's *Classical Music 101*. Rather than progressing chronologically, Plotkin organizes his discussion by instrument and musical form. This book will allow the student to dig deeper, moving beyond the "greatest hits" presented in *The Classical Music Experience.*

Rather than charging through these books at a set number of pages per week, the student should progress through them in a relaxed manner, taking plenty of time to borrow (or buy) CDs and listen to them. It's fine to take all four years to cover these resources. Follow these guidelines:

1. Write a short biographical sketch (one to two pages long) for each composer encountered. Try to focus not just on facts (birth and death dates, training, posts held), but on the development of each composer as an artist. Did he ever express his purpose for compos-

ing? What were his musical models? What did he consider to be his greatest work? Why? Did he hold to his early training or break away from it?

2. Whenever *The Classical Music Experience* or *Classical Music 101* describes a certain school of composition, write a couple of paragraphs discussing the school's characteristics and its major followers. Then make a brief list of important world events and philosophical movements going on at the same time (*The Timetables of History* will provide this information).
3. For each composer studied, keep a list of works that you've listened to. Before you move on to another composer, write a couple of paragraphs describing the quality of this composer's work (this is a creative assignment). What effect does the music have on you? Do you like it? dislike it? Are you excited by it? bored? Be sure to give specific reasons.

The student encountering Chopin, for example, could linger on this section until she's listened to several weeks worth of Chopin's music. When she's ready to move on, she should (1) write a biographical sketch of Chopin, (2) briefly describe the Romantic movement and list major world events and philosophical shifts (for example, the Romantic movement in literature), and (3) list the works of Chopin listened to and write a couple of paragraphs about the effects of Chopin's music on her. She should file all these papers in the music notebook.

SCHEDULES

Sample Schedules

Ninth grade	Mondays, 2 hrs.	Alternate art projects with studying about 50 pages of *The Annotated Mona Lisa.*
	Thursdays, 2 hrs.	Listen to *The Classical Music Experience* whenever you move on to a new topic, write biographies, descriptions of musical schools, and reactions to compositions.

Tenth grade	Mondays, 2 hrs.	Alternate art projects with studying about 50 pages of *The Annotated Mona Lisa.*
	Thursdays, 2 hrs.	Listen to *The Classical Music Experience* whenever you move on to a new topic, write biographies, descriptions of musical schools, and reactions to compositions.
Eleventh grade	Mondays, 2 hrs.	Alternate art projects with studying about 50 pages of *The Annotated Mona Lisa.*
	Thursdays, 2 hrs.	Listen to *The Classical Music Experience* whenever you move on to a new topic, write biographies, descriptions of musical schools, and reactions to compositions.
Twelfth grade	Mondays, 2 hrs.	Alternate art projects with studying about 50 pages of *The Annotated Mona Lisa.*
	Thursdays, 2 hrs.	Listen to *The Classical Music Experience* whenever you move on to a new topic, write biographies, descriptions of musical schools, and reactions to compositions.

RESOURCES

For publisher and catalog addresses, telephone numbers, and other information, see Sources (pages 751–778). Most books and tapes or CDs can be obtained from any bookstore or library; where we know of a mail-order option, we have provided it. These resources are divided into three lists: art skills (including art supplies), art appreciation, and music appreciation (at this stage, music skills should be studied with a professional teacher). For each list, we have given basic texts first, followed by supplementary resources (you can pick and choose among these). You can also use many of the resources listed in Chapter 21, particularly the art-skills books and materials.

Art Skills

Basic Texts

Basic Techniques series. Cincinnati, Ohio: North Light Books.
$17.99. Order from North Light Books.
———. *Basic Drawing Techniques.* 1992.
———. *Basic Figure Drawing Techniques.* 1994.
Reid, Jack. *Watercolor Basics: Let's Get Started.* 1998. $19.99.
Wolf, Rachel. *Basic Flower Painting Techniques in Watercolor.* 1996.

Dorling Kindersley Art School series. New York: Dorling Kindersley.
$18.55 in hardback; $10.00 in paperback. Check these titles out from the library, order from Dorling Kindersley (hardbacks only), or buy through a bookstore or online bookseller.
Lloyd, Elizabeth Jane. *Watercolor Still Life.* 2001.
Smith, Ray. *An Introduction to Acrylics.* 1998.
———. *An Introduction to Oil Painting.* 1998.

Lucchesi, Bruno, and Margit Malmstrom. *Modeling the Figure in Clay.* New York: Watson-Guptill, 1996.
$19.95. Order from a bookstore or online bookseller.

———. *Modeling the Head in Clay.* New York: Watson-Guptill, 1996.
$19.95. Order from a bookstore or online bookseller.

Simmonds, Jackie. *Pastel Workbook: A Complete Course in 10 Lessons.* New York: David & Charles, 2007.
$19.99. Order from any bookstore. A good introduction to pastels.

Slobodkin, Louis. *Sculpture: Principles and Practice.* New York: Dover, 1983.
$14.95. An introduction to the theory of sculpture, along with projects.

Art Supplies

Sculpey. Elk Grove Village, Ill.: Polyform Products.
$11.65 for a 1.75-pound pack, $49.99 for an 8-pound pack. Order from Rainbow Resource Center. Sculpey is an easy-to-work clay that fires in a regular oven in twenty minutes without shrinking. Rainbow also sells Sculpey Glaze, in either matte finish or glossy finish, for $3.75 per bottle.

Visit an art supply store, or call for art supply catalogs to browse through available materials:

Cheap Joe's, 800-227-2788, www.cheapjoes.com.

Jerry's Artarama, 800-827-8478, www.jerrysartorama.com.

Rainbow Resource Center, 888-841-3456, www.rainbowresource.com.

Supplementary Resources

North Lights Books publishes additional high-quality titles aimed at developing particular skills. Choose from the following (see www.artistsnet work.com/artbooks for a complete list of titles):

Borgeson, Bet. *Basic Colored Pencil Techniques*. $17.99.

Leville, Paul. *Drawing Expressive Portraits*. $19.99.

Metzger, Phil. *Watercolor Basics: Perspective Secrets*. $19.99.

Nice, Claudia. *Painting with Watercolor, Pen & Ink*. $26.99.

Roddon, Guy. *Pastel Painting Techniques*. $23.99.

Smith, Stan. *Oil Painting Workbook*. $19.99.

Webber, Mark Christopher. *Brushwork Essentials*. $28.99.

Wolf, Rachel. *The Acrylic Painter's Book of Styles & Techniques*. $19.99.

Art Appreciation

Basic Texts

Strickland, Carol. *The Annotated Mona Lisa: A Crash Course in Art History from Prehistoric to Postmodern*. Kansas City, Mo.: Andrews McMeel, 1992.
$22.95. Order from Rainbow Resource Center.

Supplementary Resources

Beckett, Sister Wendy. *The Story of Painting: The Essential Guide to the History of Western Art*. 2d ed. New York: Dorling Kindersley, 2000.
$50.00. Order through a bookstore or online bookseller, or try your library. Contains more than 450 full-color paintings spanning 800 years.

Eyewitness Art series. New York: Dorling Kindersley.
$15.99 each. Order from any bookstore, or check your library. These

books present not only artists, but also their times and the "schools" they belonged to.

Bernard, Bruce. *Van Gogh.* 2000.
Clarke, Michael. *Watercolor.* 2000.
Cole, Alison. *Perspective.* 2000.
———. *The Renaissance.* 2000.
Langley, Andrew. *Da Vinci and His Times.* 2006.
Welton, Jude. *Impressionism.* 2000.
———. *Monet.* 1999.

Music Appreciation

Basic Texts

Johnson, Julius H., II. *The Classical Music Experience: Discover the Music of the World's Greatest Composers.* Naperville, Ill: Sourcebooks, 2002.
$39.95. Order this book-CD combination from any bookstore.

Plotkin, Fred. *Classical Music 101: A Complete Guide to Learning and Loving Classical Music.* New York: Hyperion, 2002.
$18.95. Organized around instruments and musical forms rather than by composer or history.

Supplementary Resources

Copland, Aaron. *What to Listen for in Music.* New York: Signet, 2002.
$7.95. Order from any bookstore; a reprint of the classic jargon-free guide by composer Aaron Copland.

The Illustrated Lives of the Great Composers series. London: Omnibus Press.
$19.95 for each of these nicely done, engaging biographies. Order from any bookstore or check your library.

Dowly, Tim. *Bach.* 1987.
Gammond, Peter. *Offenbach.* 1986.
Headington, Christopher. *Britten.* 1998.
James, Burnett. *Ravel.* 1983.
Layton, Robert. *Grieg.* 1998.
Mundy, Simon. *Elgar.* 2001.

———. *Tchaikovsky.* 1995.

Ortega, Ates. *Chopin.* 1983.

Seckerson, Edward. *Mahler.* 1983.

Thompson, Wendy. *Handel.* 1994.

Wenborn, Neil. *Stravinsky.* 1990.

Woodford, Peggy. *Mozart.* 1990.

———. *Schubert.* 1978.

Libbey, Theodore. *The NPR Guide to Building a Classical CD Collection: The 350 Essential Works.* 2d ed. New York: Workman Publishing, 1999.

$15.95. This wonderfully useful book will help you follow up on the excerpts presented in *The Classical Music Experience* by guiding you toward the full works on CD. Libbey evaluates performances and labels and makes specific buying recommendations. The first edition was revised after five years; check to see whether the 1999 edition has been replaced by a newer revision.

33

THE SPECIALIST

> Any child who already shows a disposition to specialize should be given his head: for, when the use of the tools has been well and truly learned, it is available for any study whatever. It would be well, I think, that each pupil should learn to do one, or two, subjects really well, while taking a few classes in subsidiary subjects so as to keep his mind open to the inter-relations of all knowledge.
>
> —Dorothy Sayers, "The Lost Tools of Learning"

SUBJECT: Junior and senior project
TIME REQUIRED: 2 to 3 hours or more per week in grades 11 and 12

In the preceding chapters, you will have noticed that the number of subjects studied are reduced in the junior and senior years of high school. For example, math and language study can be completed in tenth or eleventh grade; the formal study of writing ends. By the junior year in high school, the typical student of rhetoric is spending two hours per day studying great books, an additional hour and a half two days per week studying science, and a couple of hours twice a week dealing with art and music. He's also pursuing an elective—computer programming, advanced language, or Advanced Placement math. This schedule leaves time for the junior and senior writing projects. Eleventh and twelfth graders should choose a major research project in a field that interests them and carry this project out. This is the equivalent of a high-school "honors" program.

During the high-school years, most students begin to develop a "speciality," a skill or branch of learning in which they have a particular talent and interest. Computer programming, Victorian novels, ancient Britain, Renaissance art, French poetry, piano performance, gymnastics, baseball, writing fiction—whatever the student chooses to spend his time doing can become a speciality.

The junior and senior projects give the student an opportunity to exercise all his hard-learned skills in writing and reasoning on a subject that excites him. The opportunity to do in-depth reading and writing on these subjects may steer him toward (or away from) a college major.

GENERAL GUIDELINES

The junior and senior projects are wider in scope than the ninth- and tenth-grade research papers. Research papers focus on a topic that can be summarized in a thesis statement; they tend to deal with a single time and place (that is, they are *synchronic*—they examine a particular point in time). The junior and senior projects should be more complex—they should be *diachronic* (moving through history, examining the origins and historical development of the topic under study).

Any subject, Neil Postman observes, can be given scholarly value if the student traces its historical development, reflects on its origins, and theorizes about its future.[1] Every topic treated in this way sheds insight on human endeavor—the way we live. Baseball, for example, becomes a fascinating and fruitful study if the student follows it back to its beginnings and traces it from there. Bat-and-ball games were played as far back as the Aztecs; baseball became a popular child's game in the nineteenth century; the mutation of baseball into a professional sport parallels the general shift in American culture from rural-centered to urban-centered; baseball clubs, first formed in the 1870s, were plagued by corruption; in the twentieth century, baseball heroes were carefully shielded by the media, which felt they had a duty to protect the hero status of baseball players by not reporting on their misdeeds; baseball players evolved into "celebrities"; and so

[1]Neil Postman, *The End of Education: Redefining the Value of School* (New York: Knopf, 1995), p. 112.

forth. This study pinpoints a number of cultural shifts in American life—amateur to professional, rural to urban, hero to celebrity. Any student who completes this project will have a better understanding not only of baseball, but of his own culture and history.

The student should keep these questions in mind while developing his topic of study:

- When did this begin? What was its original form? What cultural purpose did it serve?
- Who performed this activity? What cultural place did they occupy? How were they regarded by others?
- What prior historical events did this event/activity resemble? Is this coincidental? Did this event/activity model itself on something that came before? What philosophy does this reveal? (The Olympics, for example, obviously owe a great deal to the ancient Greeks and their ideas about what makes an ideal human being.)
- What ideal picture of human beings does this activity/event hold up?
- How did this activity develop from its beginnings to the present day?
- What effects did this event have on its surroundings? On the generation directly after? Five hundred years later? The present day?
- How did this activity/event change the way people viewed nature? How did it change the way they thought about God?
- What current cultural trends are reflected in this activity? What cultural trends resulted from this event?

Not all of these questions will be applicable to every topic. But if the student can answer some form of these queries, his paper will begin to take shape.

For example, suppose the high-school junior loves the novels of Jane Austen. If he decides to do a project on Austen's novels, he needs to think widely about the origins of the novel, its development, Austen's use of it, and the effects of Austen's work on present-day readers. His questions, then, might take the following form:

- When were the first novels written? What were the first novels? (*Don Quixote* is widely regarded as the first European novel.) What cultural shifts around the time of Cervantes led him to create this new form?

- Who originally wrote novels? (Men.) What cultural place did they occupy? (They were thinkers and philosophers.) How were they regarded by others?
- What is the relationship between the historical forms that came before the novel (the epic poem, the fable) and the novel itself? How do novels differ from epic poems and fables? How are they the same? What can a novel do that a poem or fable can't?
- How did novel reading develop from Cervantes to Austen? (This is an immensely fruitful area—novels were viewed with suspicion by the Church; novel reading became a silly, "female" activity and thus was considered trivial and a waste of time; the "lady novelist" was a figure of fun.)
- How did novel reading develop from Austen to the present? (Novels slowly regained their position as serious reflections on the human condition, paralleling in some ways the rise in status of women in society.)
- What effects did Austen's novels have on novel writing in general? (The "novel of manners"—a new genre—was created.) What is the twentieth-century equivalent of the novel of manners?
- What is the relationship of "women's fiction" in the twentieth century to Austen's novels? Have certain types of novel become (once more) the province of "lady novelists"?
- What does the current popularity of Austen's novels say about our own culture? (Quite a bit has been written about the postmodern longing for a return to proper etiquette and manners.)

As in preparation for writing the research papers for ninth and tenth grades, the student should plan on doing a great deal of prereading (the entire fall semester can be spent prereading). Extensive reading in criticism, history, and theory can clarify which of the questions can be answered and which don't apply.

After prereading, the student can follow the general guidelines for preparing the research paper, given in Chapter 26. We suggest that you buy and use *Schaum's Quick Guide to Writing Great Research Papers*, the text recommended in that chapter.

The junior paper should be fifteen to twenty pages long; the senior paper, twenty or more pages long.

FLEXIBILITY

Allow some room for creativity. At least one of the projects (ideally, the junior project) should be in standard research-paper form. But permit the second to vary. A student with an interest in creative writing could research the novel in the junior year and write part of a novel for the senior project. The junior with an interest in physics can write a historical study of some development in physics during the junior year; in the senior year, he could perform a complex experiment and document it. The musical student could write a music-history paper in the junior year and give a recital (or compose a piece) for the senior project. The gymnast can write a history of gymnastics in the junior year and prepare for a serious competition to take place the year after.

Just keep the following guideline in mind: whatever creative project is undertaken for the senior year must be documented—it must involve *writing*. The high-school scientist can perform experiments, but he must then write an article about his findings—just as practicing scientists do. The gymnast must write an account of his preparation and competition. The musician must write an essay explaining his choice of recital pieces or analyzing the form of his composition. If the senior writing project is combined with some other activity, it can be shorter (ten pages is a good rule of thumb), but it can't disappear entirely. These writing projects force the student to evaluate what he's doing. They also serve as documentation of the senior project for school boards and college admissions officers.

SPECIFIC GUIDELINES

During the rhetoric stage, as Dorothy Sayers writes in "The Lost Tools of Learning," all subjects tend to run together; knowledge is interrelated.[2] The student writing a history paper will find himself discussing scientific developments; the physicist will have to deal with the religious implica-

[2]Dorothy Sayers, "The Lost Tools of Learning," in Douglas Wilson, *Recovering the Lost Tools of Learning* (Wheaton, Ill.: Crossway Books, 1991), p. 161.

tions of discoveries in physics (something that occupied Einstein); the musician will find himself studying philosophy. However, projects in each area of knowledge should follow specific guidelines.

History

The student who chooses to research a historical event or era should be careful not to get "stuck in the past." He should deal with the event's relationship to similar prior events, its effect on the surrounding cultures, and any effects that stretch to the present day. The student working on a historical topic should always conclude his paper by answering the question: What does this tell me about my own day and culture?

Research on the lost continent of Atlantis, for example, should deal with early stories of lost civilizations, early volcanic eruptions and other natural disasters that wiped out entire groups of people, the specific events surrounding the loss of Atlantis, the stories of the lost continent told by different cultures (each one varies slightly, depending on the culture that tells it), and the theme of a lost country in twentieth-century American science fiction, fantasy, and folklore. You might answer the question "What does Atlantis tell me about my own day and culture?" by saying: "We have a constant longing to find an 'unspoiled' country, free from the problems we see around us."

For a shining example of this sort of history, read Thomas Cahill's *How the Irish Saved Civilization,* in which the author relates the copying activities of a group of Irish monks to both ancient culture and the preservation of Western civilization in our own day. (He also points out eerie parallels between the descent of darkness in the Middle Ages and the "new barbarism" of our own times.)

Literature

The student working on literature should always treat the development of the genre under study, from its roots to the present day. This will yield a number of insights, as is illustrated by the Jane Austen example, above. Why was novel reading considered a female activity? Why has the epic poem fallen out of favor? Why was philosophy first written in verse and then in prose? These sorts of questions will widen the study of literature.

Mathematics

Mathematics projects can take two forms: the historical development of a type of mathematics (from Pythagoras and Euclid to the present) and the application of mathematics to specific scientific problems. Generally, the junior mathematics project should trace historical development. The senior project can involve the solving of problems, as long as the student writes up his findings as though for publication.

Science

Scientific projects should follow the same guidelines as those given in "Mathematics," above. A historical survey in the junior year can be followed by experimentation or projects in the senior year, providing everything is properly documented.

Foreign Languages

The language student can write a paper on the literature of another country, following the "Literature" guidelines, above. For a more challenging project, he can write a literature, history, or creative paper *in* the foreign language of his choice. Like the science student, the language student can do a project for the senior year (teaching a language class to other home schoolers; going abroad to the country where that language is spoken). This project should be summarized in a ten-page essay.

Computer Programming

Any student planning to specialize in computers *must* write a junior or senior paper following Neil Postman's guidelines:

> Indicate, first, what you believe are or will be the main advantages of computer technology, and why; second, indicate what are or will be the main disadvantages of computer technology, and why.[3]

[3]Postman, p. 93.

This will help prevent "Computer Programmer's Disease"—the belief that computers are the center of existence.

The second project can be a programming one, which must be properly documented. A manual to accompany the project could fulfill this requirement.

Religion

A paper on religion will resemble a history paper in that it will trace the development of a certain aspect of faith and practice and will reflect on present-day effects and applications. Ethics papers should follow the same general guidelines. Any paper treating the ethical aspect of some behavior (assisted suicide or cloning, for example) must examine the history of the issue as well as proposing present guidelines.

The Arts: Painting, Sculpture, Theater, Music

As in science and math, the junior project should be a historical survey (of a painting or sculptural style or school, the development of a particular theatrical convention, the performance history of one of Shakespeare's plays, the development over time of a particular musical form or style, the development of an instrument). The senior project can be a recital, an art exhibit, or a theatrical performance. A ten-page essay should document and explain this project.

Sports

As demonstrated in the discussion of baseball, sports can provide great cultural insight if studied historically. Sports are a type of performance, and, as with the performing arts, the student should write one historical study. The senior year can be devoted to a sports performance, properly documented with a ten-page essay.

EVALUATION

We strongly suggest that you find someone to evaluate the junior and senior projects. Enlist local college faculty members or experts in the student's field. You can also write to authors, musicians, and scholars, asking them to evaluate the junior and senior papers and projects. If you can afford it, you should offer to pay for these evaluations. (If you can't, the student has the chance to write a persuasive essay, explaining why he's worthy of the scholar's time and energy.)

If the expert will agree, the student should follow this pattern:

1. Preread.
2. Make an appointment to discuss the topic with the expert, either in writing or by phone, on the Internet or in person. The expert will have additional suggestions, clarifying questions, and resources for the student to investigate.
3. Write or perform the project.
4. Submit the project for evaluation. Ask the expert to comment on and evaluate it.
5. Rewrite the project according to suggestions made by the expert.
6. Resubmit the completed, revised project.

Since this will take a fair amount of time and effort on the part of the expert, you should offer him or her a one-hundred-dollar honorarium, a small but acceptable token of good faith (it shows that you're not just wasting his or her time).

This evaluation has two purposes. (1) The student is submitting his work to an expert, who can help him to sharpen and improve his knowledge in the specific area. (2) The expert is now in a position to write letters of reference for the student when the student applies to colleges.

SCHEDULE

Eleventh grade	Allow 2–3 hours or more per week in the fall for prereading, 2–3 hours or more per week in the spring for writing.
Twelfth grade	Allow 2–3 hours or more per week in the fall for prereading or preparation, 2–3 hours or more per week for writing or performance.

RESOURCE

Rozakis, Laurie. *Schaum's Quick Guide to Writing Great Research Papers.* New York: McGraw-Hill, 1999.

34

SOME PEOPLE HATE HOMER

> Tomorrow's economy will be volatile and dependent on flexible workers with a high level of intellectual skills. Thus, the best vocational education will be . . . in the use of one's mind.
>
> —Theodore R. Sizer, *Horace's Compromise*

Classical education's fine for the college-bound. Homer and Plato might be fun for intellectuals. But what about the student who isn't interested in college? What about the student who doesn't really care about scholarship? What about the student who wants to finish high school, get out, and work?

A classical education is valuable even for people who hate Homer.

At a recent conference on education in Richmond, Virginia, a top executive from a car manufacturer let fly in frustration: Why are you asking me how to prepare students for the job market? Most of the high-school graduates who apply for jobs with us can't write, don't read well, can't think through a problem. We spend an unbelievable amount of money retraining these graduates in basic academic skills *before* we can teach them how to do their jobs. Don't bring more vocational training into the high-school curriculum. Teach them how to read, to write, to do math, and to think. *We'll* train them in the specific job skills they need.

A well-trained mind is a necessity for any job—from car repair person to university teacher. The mechanic with a classical education will be more successful than her untrained counterparts; she'll know how to plan her business, how to relate to her customers, how to organize her responsibilities, how to *think*. A classical education is the best possible preparation for the job market.

Throughout this book, we've maintained that the classical education is not intended to teach all subjects comprehensively—history, science, math, language. The classical education *is* designed to teach the student how to learn. In its constant demand that the student read and then analyze and write about what she's read, the classical education trains the mind to gather, organize, and use information. And the student who knows how to learn—and has had practice in independent learning—can successfully do any job.

In their book *Teaching the New Basic Skills: Principles for Educating Children to Thrive in a Changing Economy,* authors Richard J. Murnane and Frank Levy analyze the hiring practices of several large companies. They conclude that while employers look for certain basic skills—the ability to do math, to read well, to communicate effectively in writing and in speech, to use computers for simple tasks—the primary quality that makes students employable is the ability to "raise performance continually" by learning on the job.[1] Such ability follows the Platonic definition of *knowledge*—an activity, a continual process of learning, not some sort of static body of information.

Gene Edward Veith points out that the Greeks would have viewed with suspicion education that trains the student for a highly specific job. Such training creates "a slave mentality, making the learner an obedient worker utterly dependent upon his masters."[2] In an economy where the average worker has held five different jobs over the space of a career, only the flexible can survive (and be free).

A classical education is useful.

But to a certain extent, to ask "What's the use?" is itself antithetical to

[1]Richard J. Murnane and Frank Levy, *Teaching the New Basic Skills: Principles for Educating Children to Thrive in a Changing Economy* (New York: Free Press, 1996), p. 32.

[2]Gene Edward Veith, "Renaissance, Not Reform," an essay posted at the Philanthropy, Culture and Society website, August 1996; www.capitalresearch.org. See also Gene Edward Veith, Jr., and Andrew Kern, *Classical Education: Towards the Revival of American Schooling* (Washington, D.C.: Capital Research Center, 1997), p. 78.

the goals of the classical education. "The practical life," writes David Hicks, in a paraphrase of Plato, "falls short of completeness. The wealth one acquires in business is a useful thing, but as such, it exists for the sake of something else."[3] The classically educated student aims for more than a life of comfort; she aims for a "life that knows and reveres, speculates and acts upon the Good, that loves and re-produces the Beautiful, and that pursues excellence and moderation in all things."

The classical education, with its emphasis on the life of the mind, on reading and writing about ideas, is aimed at producing a student who pursues excellence and moderation in all things. This is Plato's "virtuous man" (who, parenthetically, is generally highly employable—a side effect).

There's yet another reason for classical education, which has to do with the nature of a democracy. From ancient times through recent centuries, only a small, elite segment of the population received the kind of education we've outlined in these chapters. Because only a fraction of society was equipped to think through ideas and their consequences, only that fraction was qualified to govern—an act that demands that the governing members of society look past the immediate, the popular, and the simplistic in order to evaluate long-range consequences and complex cause and effect.

But in a democracy, all citizens have a part in government. They should be able to look past immediate gratification, rhetorical flourishes, and simplistic solutions in order to understand which course of action is the right one to take. In a healthy democracy, the casting of a vote is the act of a well-trained mind.

Every citizen in a democracy takes on the responsibilities that were once reserved for the well-educated aristocratic segment of society. And so every citizen, college-bound or not, should receive the type of education that will develop the life of the mind.

What happens if this is neglected?

"The average citizen," David Hicks writes, "will begin to doubt the soundness of his own judgments. He will surrender his fundamental democratic right to ideas and to decision making to a few experts. . . . [He will] grow lazy in his demand for a high quality of public thought and information. He will doubt his ability to decide the issues shaping his life, and he

[3]David Hicks, *Norms and Nobility: A Treatise on Education* (New York: Praeger, 1981), p. 20.

will take another step beyond representative government in relinquishing the privilege of self-government by putting himself at the mercy of a few experts. At last, abandoning his Western classical heritage, he will resign himself and his children to . . . a democracy in name only."[4]

It's a chilling scenario, but already these tendencies are visible in America in the beginning of the twenty-first century. The classical education—for all students, not just for some college-bound "elite"—is the best preventive.

And you don't have to wait for your local school to come to this conclusion. You can train your child's mind yourself.

[4]Hicks, p. 83.

PART III

EPILOGUE

The Rhetoric Stage at a Glance

Guidelines to how much time you should spend on each subject are general; parents should feel free to adjust schedules according to the child's maturity and ability.

Ninth Grade

(Vocabulary)	(2 hours per week: finish the *Vocabulary from Classical Roots* series.)
(Writing)	(60 minutes, three days per week: finish up the writing program.)
Rhetoric	3 hours per week: study and summarize *A Rulebook for Arguments,* followed by *The New Oxford Guide to Writing.*
Language	45 minutes per day: work on a formal grammar workbook; read *The Elements of Style.*
Great books	2 hours per day: work through *The Well-Educated Mind;* read, discuss, and write about great books; work on the research paper in the spring.
Mathematics	60 minutes, five days per week: Algebra I, Geometry, or Algebra II.
Science	4 hours per week: study biology.
Latin/foreign language	3–6 hours per week (depending on pace): Latin, modern language or Greek.

Religion	Discuss ethics as appropriate when reading great books; work on apologia for your faith during "family time."
Art	2 hours per week: alternate art projects with studying *The Annotated Mona Lisa.*
Music	2 hours per week: work through music-appreciation texts, and listen to music.
Extracurricular activity	Debate club.

CLASS TIME SPENT: 36–40 hours per week (typical high-school week: 35 hours in class, plus homework and transportation time)

Tenth Grade

Rhetoric	3 hours per week: study and summarize *The New Oxford Guide,* begin *Classical Rhetoric*
Language	45 minutes per day: work on a formal grammar workbook; read *The Elements of Style.*
Great books	2 hours per day: read, discuss, and write about great books; work on the research paper in the spring.
Mathematics	60 minutes, five days per week: Geometry, Algebra II, or advanced mathematics.
Science	4 hours per week: study astronomy.
Latin/foreign language	3–6 hours per week (depending on pace): Latin, modern language or Greek.
Religion	Discuss ethics as appropriate when reading great books; work on apologia for your faith during "family time."
Art	2 hours per week: alternate art projects with studying *The Annotated Mona Lisa.*
Music	2 hours per week: work through music-appreciation texts, and listen to music.
Extracurricular activity	Debate club.
PSAT/SAT prep	1 hour per day, five days per week.

CLASS TIME SPENT: 36–40 hours per week (typical high-school week: 35 hours in class, plus homework and transportation time)

Eleventh Grade

Rhetoric	Continue to read and summarize *Classical Rhetoric.*
Language	45–60 minutes per day: do formal grammar; read *The Elements of Style.*
Great books	2 hours per day: read, discuss, and write about great books.
Mathematics	60 minutes, five days per week: Algebra II, advanced mathematics, or an Advanced Placement elective.
Science	4 hours per week: study chemistry.
Latin/foreign language	3–6 hours per week (depending on pace): Latin, modern language or Greek.
(Computer programming)	(3–5 hours per week for one year: this is a substitute for advanced math or language study.)
Religion	Discuss ethics as appropriate when reading great books; work on apologia for your faith during "family time."
Art	2 hours per week: alternate art projects with studying *The Annotated Mona Lisa.*
Music	2 hours per week: work through music-appreciation texts, and listen to music.
Junior project	2–3 hours or more per week.

CLASS TIME SPENT: 36–40 hours per week (typical high-school week: 35 hours in class, plus homework and transportation time)

Twelfth Grade

Language	45–60 minutes per day: do formal grammar; read *The Elements of Style.*
Great books	2 hours per day: read, discuss, and write about great books.
Mathematics	60 minutes, five days per week: advanced mathematics or an optional advanced elective.
Science	4 hours per week: study physics (5–6 hours per

	week, if Saxon course is used as an advanced elective).
Latin/foreign language	3–6 hours per week (depending on pace): Latin, Greek, or modern language.
(Computer programming)	(3–5 hours per week for one year: this is a substitute for advanced math or language study.)
Religion	Discuss ethics as appropriate when reading great books; work on apologia for your faith during "family time."
Art	2 hours per week: alternate art projects with studying *The Annotated Mona Lisa.*
Music	2 hours per week: work through music-appreciation texts, and listen to music.
Senior project	2–3 hours or more per week.

CLASS TIME SPENT: 36–40 hours per week (typical high-school week: 35 hours in class, plus homework and transportation time)

PART IV

COMING HOME

How to Educate Your Child at Home

35

THE KITCHEN-TABLE SCHOOL: WHY HOME-EDUCATE?

Over the next decade, up to 2 million children, or 5% of the total student population, could be home schooled.

—Denise G. Masters

The perfect school is a myth. Rather than trying to do the impossible by attempting to duplicate the perfect (and imaginary) school experience, be realistic and diligent about what you can do well. Offer personal, individual tutoring; use your time efficiently; control the child's social and moral environment until she's mature enough to make wise decisions. Your aim is education, not the duplication of an institution.

Remember, you aren't alone. Home schooling is now legal in all fifty states for one reason—parent activism. The beginning of the modern home-school movement can be traced to the alternative schools founded in the 1960s and 1970s by parents who defended their right to choose from among educational alternatives.

These alternative schools tended to be politically liberal and activist.[1]

[1]Shawn Callaway, "Home Education, College Admission, and Financial Aid," *Journal of College Admission* (Spring 1997): 8.

Parents without access to these schools or who saw themselves as more conservative followed the trend of parent involvement by choosing instead to home-school their children quietly. By the 1980s, increasing numbers of Christian Protestants were taking their children out of the public school systems, which they saw as culturally and spiritually alien to their values. Catholic families had done this years before, as had orthodox Jewish families; now there are Jewish, Muslim, Mormon, and secularist home-school support organizations as more and more parents decide to exercise their option to choose an alternative to the public school system.

The reasons for making this choice are varied: unhappiness with academic standards, a wish to avoid negative social pressures, frustration with oversized classes, disagreement with the philosophy of education held by local schools. What all these parents have in common is a single belief: the right of all parents to choose how to educate their children. And all of them are actively, not passively, involved in helping their children learn.

WHY SHOULD YOU HOME-SCHOOL?

Over the years, we've heard a number of reasons why parents choose to take their children out of school. They include

- Boredom.
- Fatigue caused by long bus rides or unreasonable schedules.
- Frustration and academic failure.
- Lack of academic challenge.
- Constant travel.
- Health problems that prevent the child from taking part in a regular school-day program.
- School pressure for conformity, rather than flexible programs that enable children to develop their own strengths and solve their own problems.
- The need for one-on-one instruction, individual attention, time, and encouragement to develop special talents or strengths.
- Negative peer pressure. The child starts to adopt the standards of her peer group and reject those of her family.

- The need for quiet. The child doesn't mentally operate well where there is confusion and noise.
- Learning problems that aren't being solved. The child isn't being challenged to overcome weaknesses.
- Peer or faculty intimidation. The child is being intimidated, teased, or abused verbally or physically by classmates or teachers.
- The need for more or less time per subject. The rate of instruction (too fast, too slow) doesn't match the child's rate of learning.
- Too much emphasis on nonacademic activities. Extracurricular activities usurp necessary time from academic excellence.
- The waste of a gifted student's time. The gifted child is used by the teacher to tutor slower students, rather than being challenged to press forward.
- An emphasis on popularity rather than on academic achievement. The child becomes popular, but not productive and literate.
- The "pariah" status of the gifted student. The quick student feels discriminated against because of giftedness—often jealousy and resentment from classmates, sometimes even from teachers.
- The ostracization of the student who is different. The child with a mild problem or difference (lisp, shyness, or even slowness in doing work because she's unusually careful) often gets placed in a special-education class and is then negatively labeled by both classmates and teachers for the rest of her school career.[2]
- Conflicting family schedules. The parent may have a work situation that doesn't allow him to spend time with the child except during school hours.
- Loss of academic self-esteem. The child is losing confidence in her ability to learn. (Jessie once worked with a sixteen-year-old girl who was unresponsive and discouraged. Jessie kept on with one-on-one instruction, basic phonics, remedial math and writing, and lots of encouragement. Eventually the girl returned to regular school, grad-

[2]Students with mild speech impediments are often placed in special-education classes. According to an article in the *New York Times,* financial incentives encourage schools to keep these children in special education, a situation that often yields "isolation and failure." These children often never return to mainstream classes, and many do not graduate with a regular diploma. ("Fresh Thinking on Special Education," *New York Times,* 26 November 1996, sec. A, p. 20.)

uated, and completed nursing school. She came back for a visit after she had worked as a nurse for several years. "Thank you," she said, "for making me believe that I *could* learn.")

- The parent is shut out of the educational system and wants back in. A December 8, 1996, article in the *New York Times* tells of a peer intervention program in the New York City public schools. Instead of being dismissed, incompetent teachers are allowed to enroll in a remedial program for poor teachers "in which a teaching coach works one-on-one in the classroom for as long as a year. . . . Parents who ask," the article continues, "are generally given the impression that the extra adult in class is a teacher's assistant."[3] In other words, these parents aren't told the truth. The article goes on to describe a first-grade teacher who yells at the children and humiliates them. The teaching coach corrects him privately, but the parents are never told what's going on in the classroom.

These are reasons to home-educate.

ENCOURAGEMENT FOR PARENTS

Don't be intimidated because you can't reproduce a classroom environment or school activity. Remember, programs, multiple aids, and group activities are designed for groups. Tutoring is probably the most efficient method of education since the teaching is tailored to the individual child's needs and rate of learning. You can supply this.

And as teaching progresses, parents can teach not only academic subjects, but life experiences as well. Home schooling allows time and space for the teaching of practical skills; older students especially have the flexibility to learn painting, papering, carpentry, woodworking, electrical and plumbing repair, food preparation, car repair, gardening, yard care, and so on. We've listed a few high-school electives to help you teach these practical skills at the end of this chapter.

Parents also serve as models and guides for acceptable, productive

[3]Pam Belluck, "Poor Teachers Get Coaching, Not Dismissal," *New York Times*, 8 December 1996, sec. A, pp. 1 and 46.

behavior. When you teach your child at home, you're training her to work hard and to be disciplined. Help her set goals with a plan for reaching those goals—this gives a reason for the hard work. Teach her how to manage time and schedule tasks. Work on gradual improvement, keeping records of progress and planning rewards for increments of achievement. Don't spend time only on the tasks you like, but form a plan to improve weaknesses. Take rest and recreation breaks when you become nonproductive. All of these are principles for success in any endeavor, not just in home education.

In classical education, the teacher isn't a never-ceasing fount of information from which students continually drink up answers. Instead, the model of the classical teacher and students is that of leader and "disciples," meaning that the teacher and students are united together in the same task, learning an inherited body of knowledge together. "The teacher's true competence," writes classical headmaster David Hicks, "is not in his mastery of a subject, but in his ability to provoke the right questions and . . . [in his] peculiar eagerness to explore new subjects and new ideas with his students."[4]

Given the time and the resources we suggest, any dedicated parent can do this.

Plan ahead, of course, but don't panic, when your child is in first grade, that you won't be able to do eighth-grade algebra. Take one year at a time. You'll study and grow and learn with your child. Jessie says that she learned more when she was home-educating her children than she did in college.

The home-school environment prepares children for the "real world" better than identification with age-segregated peer groups. After all, the typical workplace contains a number of different ages and abilities, not a single peer group. The home, with its mixed-age, mixed-ability environment, is much more like this workplace than the single-grade classroom.

A special encouragement to the parents of high-school students: you don't have to teach everything. If your child were enrolled in a large, well-equipped high school that offered many courses, time would still allow only so many selections. Jessie has observed that in larger schools with

[4]David Hicks, *Norms and Nobility: A Treatise on Education* (New York: Praeger, 1981), p. 129.

more courses, students often end up with less-than-desirable schedules—courses fill up, guidance counselors are overworked, students are given too much freedom to take easy courses. We know of one student at a big, prosperous high school who was allowed to sign up for four art courses—not because he was interested, but because he thought they would be easy. By the time his mother saw his schedule, he wasn't able to sign up for a better-balanced year because the other classes were full.

FIRST STEPS

If you have decided to home-school, start by contacting your state home-schooling organization. It can give you information about the laws in your state. (Different states require different types of notification: some want you to submit a general plan of study; others are happy with a photocopied college diploma.) We've provided a list at the end of this chapter. They'll also give you advice on the best way to remove your child from public or private school, if she's already enrolled there.

Look at all the material out there. Write for catalogs. Gather together what you'll need to start the year.

Plan schedules for your family. (See Chapter 38 for suggestions.)

Visit a home-school support group. Your state organization will give you a list of local groups.

Two cautions. Jessie has found that for ongoing support and a social outlet for yourself and your children, you may choose not to join the group closest to you. Local support groups, of necessity, take on the personality and philosophy of the leadership. Some are inclusive; some are exclusive and make those who don't agree uncomfortable. You have to find the one that best suits you.

Also, you may find that your local home-school group is populated mostly by "unschoolers." Classical education is not easily compatible with "unschooling," which is immensely popular among many home schoolers. "Unschooling" is child-centered. It assumes that the child will learn all that she needs to know by following her natural impulses and that any learning that is "imposed" on the child by an authority figure will prove unproductive.

Classical education is knowledge-focused, not child-focused. It attempts to teach knowledge in a way that awakens the child's interest, but the child's interest is not the sole determining factor in whether or not a subject should be followed. How does a child know whether something will interest and excite her unless she works at unfamiliar (and perhaps intimidating) material to find out what it's all about?

Unschoolers may also tend to denigrate "book" learning in favor of "real" learning. Many unschoolers claim that the day-to-day realities of family life provide plenty of opportunities for learning. For these unschoolers, taking care of the house, grocery shopping, cooking, car repair, working in the family business, writing thank-you notes, and so on provide enough opportunity for children to learn real-life skills without "doing school" in a formal way.

While this may be true, a child's education shouldn't be limited to "real-life skills." Classically educated children should be able to cook, write thank-you notes, and tie their shoes. They also know where their country came from, how to construct a logical argument, and what *puella* means.

Unschoolers sometimes claim that students who aren't forced to learn the mathematics tables in third grade can pick them up in a day once they hit sixth or seventh grade and get interested on their own. In our experience, the student who doesn't learn the math tables in third grade will never be comfortable enough with math to get interested in sixth or seventh grade.

If you end up in a local group of unschoolers and you want to follow the curriculum we've outlined in this book, you may need to switch groups.

TAKING YOUR CHILD OUT OF SCHOOL

If your child has been in a bad situation—destructive peer relationships, discouraging classroom experiences—and you've brought her home to rescue her, expect a period of adjustment. Be understanding but firm in your decision. Fully explain what you are doing and why. Your confidence in the decision that what you are doing is best for her will be communicated. So will indecision, which will make her resist the change even more.

Any radical change can cause "culture shock." Children generally prefer a known situation, no matter how flawed, to an unknown one—structure and routine are always comforting. Expect a period of adjustment.

But use common sense. If you see depression and anger that doesn't adjust in six weeks or so, take your child to a trusted counselor so that you can both talk out the problems.

LEARNING CHALLENGES

More and more frequently, parents of children with learning challenges—ranging from mild dyslexia all the way to severe autism—are deciding to bring their children home for school. While some of these children do well with the extra stimulation and expertise of school-provided therapists, others flourish and progress more rapidly at home.

In the decade since the first publication of *The Well-Trained Mind,* we have talked to many parents who are home schooling children with dyslexia, processing difficulties, seizure disorders, autism, Asperger's, and other difficulties. Many of these parents have chosen to use classical methods. From them, we've heard scores of success stories. We've also heard one message loud and clear: *I wish someone had told me I was working on a different timeline than everyone else.* Too often, they've told us, they pushed children too quickly from one stage to the next, feeling that they would fail to be "classical" educators if they didn't move into critical thinking or into rhetoric during the age windows that we've described in this book.

Each learning challenge has its own set of difficulties, and we encourage you to make use of the specialists who can offer you specific teaching help with your child. But one principle holds true for almost all struggling learners: You will need to spend *more time* in the grammar stage before introducing critical thinking, and *more time* in the critical thinking stage before gently pushing the student toward rhetoric-level skills. Severely autistic or developmentally disabled children may never reach the rhetoric level—but they can benefit enormously from careful, patient instruction in the first two stages of classical education. Although this subject is obviously beyond the scope of this book, we encourage you to examine the grammar- and logic-stage methods of teaching and think about stretching them out over longer periods of time—six years, eight years, or even more. Teach patiently, within the child's own time frame, and you will begin to hear them move forward.

Many parents of learning-challenged kids post on the Special Needs forum at welltrainedmind.com/forums. Visitors are welcome to read their stories and ask questions.

THE REALITIES OF HOME SCHOOLING

While we think home education is wonderful—we've seen children and parents thrive at home, we've heard hundreds of success stories—you must go into it with your eyes open.

- Home schooling is time-consuming, hard work.
- Housework suffers. Books and science experiments and papers are all over the house.
- Everyone wants to quit at some point during the school year.
- The kids aren't always perfect, and you can't blame it on school or on their friends.
- Academic schedules are frequently interrupted by sickness, family needs, and life in general.
- Children often "just don't get it"—that is, they may experience plateaus or have difficulty with a new concept.
- Grandparents may think you're ruining your children.
- The neighbors will probably tell you that you're crazy.

A PERSONAL WORD FROM JESSIE

I was often tired and sometimes felt overwhelmed by what I had undertaken—that is, home-educating my children. And if I'd had a perfect school available, I would have enrolled my children in it. But I looked at the academic and social options, and concluded that, in spite of my failures, my children were doing better under my tutoring than they would have done in a group situation.

Personally, I decided to put on hold some of my goals. But I held on to the wise counsel given me when my children were toddlers: "Live your life in chapters. You don't have to do everything you want to do in life during this chapter of rearing children." This advice provided the cornerstone of my plans for personal goals.

I wanted to write. I wanted to make a hand-braided early American–style rug. When my three children were toddlers, I had a whole stash of wool, all stripped in preparation for braiding. Since toddlerhood wasn't the right time to start such a large project, I stored it in boxes "until the children are in school." Instead of sending them off each morning while I quietly braided the rug, I was even more busy with home schooling than I had been with three preschoolers.

I have time to write now. My rug-in-waiting is still in boxes, although I can almost see the time approaching to start it—thirty years later! But my children are the most creative project I have been involved in. I can't compare the relationship I have with them to a relationship with a rug, no matter how beautifully hand-crafted. And my crafting of their education has been life-enriching to all of us.

There were times when I longed for a magazine-beautiful house instead of a house with "projects" all over it. Housework wasn't always done on time. Every October and March, I wanted to quit. (I learned to take a week off when that feeling came over me. Rest and change of pace renewed my focus.) When my children needed correction, I had to take the responsibility and not blame it on bad friends. Academic schedules were sometimes interrupted by life. My father had a brain tumor. My son had allergies. But looking back, I can see that even when we took off from school for the necessities of family life, we had a long-range goal in mind. We were able to get back on track and continue with our plan, taking up where we left off.

The most discouraging thing I encountered was the lack of support from family and neighbors. When I started home schooling, I worried a lot. I worried I wouldn't be able to keep up with my children's grade levels. I worried that their social development would suffer. The neighbors said, "They'll never get into college." The grandparents cried.

But as I look back, none of the worries materialized. My children did get into college. They have careers and relationships. And even the grandparents, seeing the academic progress and the better-than-normal social development, eventually admitted that they had been mistaken.

RESOURCES

For a list of home-education organizations, see Appendix 2.

Resources for Practical Skills

These high-school practical courses are produced by Christian Light Education, a Mennonite company, but are usable by all home schoolers. Order from Christian Light Education.

Beginning Woodworking.
Textbook. $42.00.
Student pack (workbook and study guide). $15.00.
Teacher pack (guide and answer key). $3.00.

Car Care.
Textbook. $77.00.
Student pack (workbook and study guide). $15.00.
Teacher pack (guide and answer key). $5.00.

Carpentry.
Textbook. $83.00.
Student pack (workbook and study guide). $38.00.
Teacher pack (guide and answer key). $5.00.

Home Repair and Maintenance.
Textbook. $59.00.
Student pack (workbook and study guide). $13.00.
Teacher pack (guide and answer key). $3.00.

Modern Residential Wiring.
Textbook. $53.00.
Student pack (workbook and study guide). $25.00.
Teacher pack (guide and answer key). $3.00.

Small Gas Engines.
Textbook. $56.00.
Student pack (workbook and study guide). $22.00.
Teacher pack (guide and answer key). $4.00.

Magazines and Newspapers

Home Education Magazine treats home schooling as a lifestyle; it tends to lean toward unschooling and to be somewhat anti-curricula, but has much of value (even for parents who *like* curricula). Write them at P.O. Box 1083, Tonasket, WA 98855-1083; visit their website at www.homeedmag.com; or call 800-236-3728.

The Link is a national home-schooling newspaper designed to be nonsectarian—accessible to home educators of every persuasion. Articles, reviews, and ads for dozens of home-school resources in every issue. It's a free publication. Write them at 741 Lakefield Road, STEJ, Westlake Village, CA 91361, visit the website at www.homeschoolnewslink.com, or call 804-497-3311.

The Old Schoolhouse Magazine is a comprehensive home-school publication: reviews, ads, interviews, and articles that appeal to a wide variety of homeschooling philosophies. Visit their site, www.thehomeschoolmagazine.com, or call 888-718-HOME.

36

THE CONFIDENT CHILD: SOCIALIZATION

> The Smithsonian Institution's recipe for genius and leadership: (1) children should spend a great deal of time with loving, educationally minded parents; (2) children should be allowed a lot of free exploration; and (3) children should have little to no association with peers outside of family and relatives.
>
> —H. McCurdy, "The Childhood Pattern of Genius"

"But what about socialization?" If you haven't asked this question already, a neighbor or grandparent certainly will.

The most convincing proof that home-educated children develop normally is a conversation with a home-educated child who's bright, engaged, polite, interesting, and outgoing. Home-school graduates get into college and do fine; they get jobs and excel.

But it's important to understand what socialization means. According to the dictionary, *socialization* is "the process by which a human being, beginning in infancy, acquires the habits, beliefs, and accumulated knowledge of his society." In other words, you're being socialized when you learn habits, acquire beliefs, learn about the society around you, develop character traits, and become competent in the skills you need to function properly in society.

Who teaches all of this? Agents of socialization include the family (both immediate and extended), the religious community, neighborhoods, tutors and mentors, the media (TV, radio, films, books, magazines all tell the child what's expected of him, for better or worse), clubs (social or academic), the arts (both in observation and participation), travel, jobs, civic participation. And formal schooling in an institution.

Taking the child out of school doesn't mean that you're going to remove him from the other "agents of socialization" that surround him. Furthermore, think about the type of socialization that takes place in school. The child learns how to function in a specific environment, one where he's surrounded by thirty children his own age. This is a very specific type of socialization, one that may not prove particularly useful. When, during the course of his life, will he find himself in this kind of context? Not in work or in family life or in his hobbies. The classroom places the child in a peer-dominated situation that he'll probably not experience again.

And this type of socialization may be damaging. Thirty years ago, Cornell Professor of Child Development Urie Bronfenbrenner warned that the "socially-isolated, age-graded peer group" created a damaging dependency in which middle-school students relied on their classmates for approval, direction, and affection. He warned that if parents, other adults, and older children continued to be absent from the active daily life of younger children, we could expect "alienation, indifference, antagonism, and violence on the part of the younger generation."[1]

Peer dependence is dangerous. When a child is desperate to fit in—to receive acceptance from those who surround him all day, every day—he may defy your rules, go against his own conscience, or even break the law.

We live in an age in which people think a great deal about peers, talk about them constantly, and act as if a child's existence will be meaningless if he isn't accepted by his peer group. But the socialization that best prepares a child for the real world can't take place when a child is closed up in a classroom or always with his peer group. It happens when the child is living with people who vary widely in age, personality, background, and circumstance.

The antidote for peer-centered socialization is to make the family the basic unit for socialization—the center of the child's experience. The fam-

[1]Urie Bronfenbrenner, *Two Worlds of Childhood* (London: George Allen & Unwin, 1971), p. 105.

ily should be the place where real things happen, where there is a true interest in each other, acceptance, patience, and peace, as far as is possible.

Socialization in the family starts when very young children learn that they can trust adults to give them answers, to read books to them, to talk to them, to listen to music with them. Socialization continues as the child learns to fit into the lives of his parents and siblings, to be considerate and thoughtful of other people, to be unselfish instead of self-centered. A two year old can learn to play alone for a few minutes while the parent teaches a ten year old; an eight year old can learn not to practice the piano during the baby's nap time. It's the *real* world when a child learns to play quietly because Daddy is working on his income taxes. (We still talk about "the year we couldn't go into the living room" because Dad was being audited and his tax papers were spread throughout the living room for weeks.)

In our society, children, taught by their peer groups, learn to survive, not to live with kindness and grace. Exclusive peer groups—cliques—start forming around age five. Even in kindergarten, children are accepted or rejected on the basis of what they wear, what toys they own, what TV programs they watch. Even when adults are supervising, these cliques survive—and strengthen—as children grow. And only the strongest flourish.

The trend in our culture is to devalue—even bypass—the family as a basic unit of socialization. But it's within the family that children learn to love by seeing love demonstrated; learn unselfishness both through teaching and through example (choosing to teach a child at home is unselfishness at work); learn conflict resolution by figuring out how to get along with parents and with each other.

The family unit—this basic agent of socialization—is itself a place to communicate with people of different ages. But socialization doesn't stop there. As a family, you should make a wide range of friends of various ages. Home-school parent and lawyer Christopher Klicka points out that home-educated children are continually socialized through community activities, Little League, Scouts, band, music lessons, art classes, field trips, and the numerous events sponsored by local home-school support groups.[2]

By means of these activities, parents teach children how to live in society and how to relate to others. In contrast, peer groups teach a child either

[2]Christopher Klicka, *The Case for Home Schooling,* 4th rev. ed. (Gresham, Ore.: Noble, 1995), p. 13.

to take direction from the most popular kid in school or to transform himself into the most popular kid at school, often sacrificing intelligence and character in the process.

What about high school?

High-school students demonstrate what sociologist Charles Horton Cooley describes as "the looking-glass self"—they evaluate their worth by looking at themselves in the mirror held up by their peers.[3] Unfortunately, the qualities that lead to high-school success—such as peer popularity and athletic prowess—are precisely those that may be of least use during later life. In contrast, the home-style classical education develops and rewards skills (perseverance, dedication, patience) that will be useful in later life. Is it more important that the high-school years be ones of dizzying social success followed by a lifetime of nostalgia or a time of preparation for a successful life?

Of course, high school isn't a "dizzying social success" for most people.

> At a reception for students at Cornell University, a ring of young women closes around Jane [Goodall], who is describing how adolescent chimp females often leave their community to join another. Kimberly Phillips, a graduate student in genetics, asks what kind of welcome a female can expect from the new community.
>
> "Well, the males are delighted," Jane says. "But the females beat her up. They don't want the competition. One strategy the newcomer can use, however, is to attach herself to a high-ranking female, even if she is treated badly by that female. The others will eventually accept her."
>
> "God, it sounds just like high school," Kimberly says.[4]

By the time the student reaches high school, he's looking at a future that will probably be spent in family life, work, and community involvement. Doesn't it make sense to spend your training time with these emerging young adults preparing them for the real life they're getting ready to enter? There is life after high school. (There is even life after college and graduate school.)

[3]Charles Horton Cooley, *Human Nature and the Social Order* (New York: Scribner's, 1902), pp. 184–185.

[4]Peter Miller, "Jane Goodall," *National Geographic,* December 1995, p. 121.

In this day of endemic family breakup, teaching your high schooler to live peacefully in a family is probably the most important feat of socialization you can accomplish. Teach skills of resolving conflict, habits of doing for others instead of self, truthfulness, loyalty, sensitivity.

What about dating?

We'll brave the collective wrath of American high-school students by suggesting that exclusive dating in high school is a waste of time. After all, what are you going to do if you fall deeply in love at seventeen? Get married? Break up? Have sex? We believe that sex without commitment is damaging at any age (we're pro-marriage). But it's even worse for teens, who are uncertain, vulnerable, and unsure of their own attraction. Sex can be a powerful, manipulative tool even for supposedly mature adults. It's even more devasting when wielded by the unready. We have yet to find an adult who remembers high-school dating as rewarding and life-enriching.

Not that you should ignore the opposite sex (a practical impossibility). Lots of family-oriented socializing—parties that include not just teens, but people of all ages—give teens plenty of practice in relating to the opposite sex in an atmosphere that isn't fraught with sexual tension, the pain of uncertainty, and the possibility of rejection. Look at the general state of peace, joy, and sexual fulfillment at the average high school and ask: Is this what I want my teen to be socialized to?

Positive socialization is all about living in your world responsibly, fulfilling your potential, taking advantage of opportunity, making the lives of others around you better. You don't need the institutional school to teach these values to your child.

Practically speaking, you provide positive socialization through family-based and interest-based activities. The Red Cross offers CPR and babysitting instruction. Museums offer special classes. Church and community teams offer sports participation. Clubs for every hobby from photography to stamp collecting meet regularly. Science fairs, debate clubs, swimming lessons—all of these provide opportunities for social interaction.

Nor should you be afraid of being alone. A measure of solitude can develop creativity, self-reliance, and the habit of reflective thought. Socialize, but don't crowd your schedule so full that the child has no time to think, to sit and stare at the walls, to lie in the backyard and watch ants crawl by.

RESOURCE

Sande, Ken, with Tom Raabe. *Peacemaking for Families: A Biblical Guide to Managing Conflict in Your Home*. Wheaton, Ill.: Tyndale House, 2002.
$12.99. Order from any bookstore. Visit the author's website, www.peacemakerministries.org, for more information on conflict resolution. For those working from a Christian worldview, this is an invaluable guide to handling and resolving family conflict.

37

THE CHARACTER ISSUE: PARENTS AS TEACHERS

> Becoming a responsible human being is a path filled with potholes and visited constantly by temptations. Children need guidance and moral road maps, and they benefit immensely with the examples of adults who speak truthfully and act from moral strength.
>
> —Vigen Guroian, *Tending the Heart of Virtue*

Schools have tried to implement "character training," an enterprise that's bound to fail because it's been taught in a theological and philosophical vacuum. Moral issues are discussed, but no one moral standard can be settled on since someone might disagree and the beliefs of all must be respected. Right and wrong can't be asserted with too much vigor because "we want our children to be tolerant, and we sometimes seem to think that a too sure sense of right and wrong only produces fanatics."[1]

Character training isn't some sort of subject, like algebra or spelling, that can be packaged into a curriculum and taught to everyone, regardless of belief. The definition of character is tied to standards of right and wrong, which in turn are tied to religious belief; the training of character is done through example and teaching—not in a classroom, but in daily life.

[1]Vigen Guroian, *Tending the Heart of Virtue: How Classic Stories Awaken a Child's Moral Imagination* (New York: Oxford University Press, 1998), p. 3.

What is character? Character is the possession of moral qualities that have become habits of life. As a partial list, we offer:

Boldness	Honesty
Compassion	Humility
Creativity	Initiative
Dependability	Patience
Determination	Perseverance
Diligence	Responsibility
Endurance	Self-control
Enthusiasm	Sincerity
Fairness	Thoroughness
Forgiveness	Tolerance
Gratefulness	Truthfulness

While we can't imagine anyone arguing about the components of this list, we also can't figure out how to teach them in the abstract without some sort of philosophical, theological underpinning (taboo in public schools).

Be diligent, the teacher of the character curriculum says.

The student yawns: I'm bored with the subject. I don't see what good it's doing me. So why be diligent?

As parents, we answer: Because we believe that this subject *will* do you good down the road, and that's what we're aiming you toward. (Schools don't really have the right—or the authority—to make career plans for students. Parents do.) And even if you don't see this, we have the responsibility of planning for your future and the authority to tell you how to prepare for it.

This is our approach—yours might be different. The point is that the parent and child share a context—a worldview—within which certain qualities of character can be explained in a way that makes sense. Without this shared context, character training becomes a matter of following pointless rules. And this sort of character building lasts only until the student reaches the age of independence.

When it comes to the more demanding virtues—tolerance, forgiveness, humility—that shared context is even more vital. The Christian believes in a forgiveness that is modeled after God's—it doesn't expire after a number of offenses. A secular, Muslim, Buddhist, or Scientologist definition of forgiveness might be expressed differently. The unfortunate teacher, honor-bound not to step on anyone's toes, has to allow the class to evolve a lowest-common-denominator definition of *forgiveness* from the students' shared consciousness. By the time this is done, the moral quality under discussion—supposedly a yardstick for the students to measure themselves against—has become a loosely worded definition of what everyone is prepared to accept.

To define *character* properly may be nearly impossible for schools, but to build character is even further out of the realm of possibility. These moral qualities have to become habits, and habits are often achieved by going against the immediate short-term desire of the child. This is a parent's job, not a teacher's.

If these moral qualities are to become habits of life, they must be reinforced by both observation and practice. As you supervise your child's education, you can encourage him to read books and watch movies that demonstrate admirable character. Be careful of the character content of teen or young-adult books. Some are excellent, some aren't. Jessie remembers her sixth-grade son picking up a book full of sexual obsession with no encouragement of positive morality. The author of that book has said in interviews that any experience children have is a valid theme for literature. But the whole enterprise of teaching character assumes that some experiences are worth dwelling on and striving for, while others aren't.

You must also be a model of these qualities every day. When you forgo your own wants to tutor your child through fifth-grade math, you're demonstrating self-control. When you patiently go through a lesson several times until the child figures it out, you're showing perseverance. When you introduce a history lesson, complete with coloring books, paper models, and interesting books that you've collected, you're showing enthusiasm. When you turn off the TV because a program you want to watch wouldn't be good for the child, you're showing self-discipline. These qualities have to be internalized by the child, and this will only happen if she continually sees them being practiced by you.

As you work with her every day, you're helping her to put good character into practice. To develop character, a child has to learn obedience. Obviously, strict obedience changes as the child grows older and shows herself to be responsible. But it is impossible to teach a child over whom you have no control (ask any public-school teacher). Currently, obedience is a virtue that isn't popular since it's at odds with the autonomy now touted as being essential to proper development. But autonomy—what *I* want supersedes any consideration for family, community, or government—can ultimately turn into disregard for laws or restrictions.

It's an expression of intelligent, loving care to teach a child that disregarding certain rules brings unpleasant consequences. You can't live in the real world without structure and authority: every day, we stop at stop signs, drive on the right side of the road, refrain from stealing food at the grocery store. The child with character has learned to thrive within structure.

Requiring a child to work and study hard in the early years develops the moral qualities of industry and perseverance. This doesn't mean that the child has a cheerless education. Many of the subjects studied *are* enjoyable, fascinating, immediately engrossing. But others won't be instantly fun. Some will require hard work so that the student can acquire skills she'll need in the future. The reality of life is that disciplined people usually accomplish more and can achieve their goals.

Powerful models of character are found in stories. Read them together. Talk about them. The joy of home education is that all of this learning takes place in the context of the family. You're not just teaching hard principles. You're also living them out. Thus, education becomes entwined with the living of life—together.

RESOURCES

Guroian, Vigen. *Tending the Heart of Virtue: How Classic Stories Awaken a Child's Moral Imagination.* New York: Oxford University Press, 2002.

A fantastic book about good, evil, friendship, redemption, faith, and courage. Read it together, and read the books Guroian discusses. At bookstores.

Kilpatrick, William, Gregory Wolfe, and Suzanne M. Wolfe. *Books That Build Character: A Guide to Teaching Your Child Moral Values through Stories.* New York: Touchstone, 1994.

An introduction to morality, along with descriptions of dozens of stories for families to read together. At bookstores.

38

AND JUST WHEN DO I DO ALL THIS? SCHEDULES FOR HOME SCHOOLERS

To choose time is to save time.
—Francis Bacon

Home education is a family commitment. We've noticed that in many families the entire responsibility for teaching the kids is shifted to one overworked parent. If one parent works full-time while the other teaches, that's a fine arrangement. But the job of planning lessons, investigating curricula, taking trips, reviewing progress, going to conventions, and generally talking about what goes on in home school needs to be shared by both parents.

Life is made up of hard but rewarding choices. It isn't possible for both parents to pursue demanding full-time careers while home-educating. Flex-time, part-time, or semester-oriented jobs (like teaching) can be worked around home schooling. A full-time criminal lawyer and a practicing obstetrician, married to each other, won't be able to manage.

We know of families that home-educate almost entirely in the evenings because of job schedules; we know of families that do school in the summer because the parents teach during the school year; we know families with home businesses and telecommuting jobs who set up school right in the home office and do it, on and off, throughout the day; we know single parents who home-school when they're not working. Although it takes organization, energy, and determination, combining home school with work can be done. And if you're able to do this, the child will be involved in a great part of your life—and you in his.

Susan and her husband, Peter, both work at home. Susan also teaches at the university during the school year. In the mornings, Peter works while Susan does grammar, writing and spelling, and history or science with the boys. At 2:00 P.M., they swap shifts, Susan goes to work, and Peter does math with the boys and takes them to appointments (swimming, doctor's visits, grocery store). Art and music fit into the evenings and weekends. Sundays and Mondays are family days for housework, museums, zoo visits, worship, and doing nothing.

An important, sanity-preserving part of every home-school day ought to be the "afternoon nap." Jessie scheduled an afternoon nap for all three of her children up until the time they finished high school. For two hours, everyone went to his or her room and pursued a quiet activity alone, while Jessie put her feet up. Bedtime was also strictly enforced—no one went wandering through the house after the lights were off.

Susan, following the same principles, had her preschoolers go from taking naps to a two-hour rest period, even though they stopped sleeping. The boys had toys, coloring books, other books, and tape recorders with good books on tape to listen to. If they got out of bed (except to go to the bathroom, of course), they lost a privilege (like the tape recorder). They've never gotten accustomed to skipping the nap; it's a regular part of every day. Susan keeps certain books, tapes, and craft supplies just for naptime use. This middle-of-the-day break period is necessary for everyone. The children need it after studying hard all morning; the baby needs it; and parents certainly need the chance to sit down, rest, have a cup of coffee, and catch up on business. The boys also go to bed early—between 8:00 and 8:30—and are allowed to have lights on for an hour for quiet reading and play before going to sleep.

Home-educating parents like their children's company. They don't want to send the kids off for most of every day. But they need a break in the middle of the day, someone to share the job of teaching, and quiet evenings.

And in terms of parental sanity, the younger the children, the more important these rest times and early bedtimes.

HOW MUCH TIME DOES IT TAKE?

After having taught in a classroom, Jessie found that she could accomplish as much instructing—and a great deal more one-on-one interacting—in less time at home. The children didn't spend time on a bus or in lines. And with immediate detection of errors and on-the-spot correction, instruction time is more efficient and progress is faster.

For kindergarten, intensive instruction in reading, writing, and math can be done in about an hour, gradually increasing to five to six hours per day in high school. If the foundations are properly laid in basic reading, writing, spelling, and math, the student becomes more independent and less in need of direct instruction.

Jessie found that by high school, her role became one of "chief of accountability" and encourager. She helped her high-school children keep in mind their long-range goals (college) as well as their daily and weekly goals. Education took place continually, not just in a "sit at the desk" format. Discussion occurred around the table, during snacks and meals. We listened to tapes and had conversations in the car, going to the library or to music lessons or on field trips. We played classical music while cleaning. Books were everywhere in the house (we took the TV out). The children read all the time—while waiting, in the car, at bedtime, during rest periods. And while she polished shoes, Susan even read the newspaper that was under them.

As the children got older, Jessie taught them how to prepare meals. In the beginning, this was time-consuming; but when Susan was thirteen, she asked, and was permitted, to prepare a full-course dinner for an extended family birthday celebration (Jessie has pictures of a very tired but accomplished cook). In his teens, Susan's brother, Bob, hand-kneaded and made all the family bread. Her sister, Deborah, became the expert pie baker and did much of the general cooking. These are not only time-savers for the parent-teacher, but life skills that have been mastered by the children.

Jessie still remembers her surprise when a group of Susan's college friends came home for the weekend. One girl didn't even know how to break lettuce and make a salad. She was a good student, with a traditional institutional education, but had never been allowed in the kitchen.

Read through time-management books for hints, both corporate (how to handle paperwork) and domestic (freedom from unnecessary housework). We've listed Jessie's favorites on page 655.

Douglas Wilson, founder of a national classical-school organization, writes that education "is the process of selling someone on books."[1] The home-schooling parent must make time for reading. Read at night, at lunch, in the bathroom, while waiting, and whenever else you can squeeze in the time. Turn off the TV, and reclaim those hours.

YEARLY PLANNING

There's no particular reason why you should home-school every day for nine months and then take the summer off. The children burn out during the year and get bored (and forget all their math) over the long summer break. We advise going year round, taking vacations throughout the year.

Here are plans that are time-equivalent to the traditional nine-month school year. You can adjust your time off for family vacations, company, illness, a new baby, or whatever else you have planned.

Option 1

School	September, October, November
Break	December
School	January, February, March
Break	April
School	May, June, July
Break	August

Option 2

School for three weeks and break for one week, year round.

[1]Douglas Wilson, in Douglas Wilson, Wesley Callihan, and Douglas Jones, *Classical Education and the Home School* (Moscow, Idaho: Canon Press, 1995), p. 19.

Option 3

Adjust breaks around holidays and times when everyone is growing tired of school.

School	September through mid-October
Break	Week off
School	Late October until Thanksgiving
Break	Week off
School	Early December
Break	Three weeks off for Christmas and New Year's
School	Mid-January until late February or early March
Break	Two weeks (Everyone gets tired of school by late February!)
School	March, April
Break	Two weeks off
School	Late April, May, on through summer
Breaks	Anytime during the summer, whenever you're vacationing, visiting, entertaining, etc.

For each year, set goals ("Finish the whole math book," "Read through the Renaissance in history," "Teach my five year old to read"). Then, as you divide your year into monthly, weekly, and daily segments, ask: What am I doing to achieve this goal? Be specific. The math book is divided into daily lessons; you need to do 140 days of math to finish the book. Your school year is nine months long, and you have 200 history pages to cover; that's around 22 pages per month or 6 pages per week. In ten minutes per day of phonics, the five year old can learn to read.

Set goals for each subject, and chart out the pace you would like to keep. If you're using a textbook, you can divide the number of pages by the number of days or weeks you plan to study. Write down the master plan. You can accelerate or slow down as you progress, but you have this general guide to keep you on target. You may want to have a master-plan notebook to record goals for each subject; checking periodically will give you a feeling for the progress you've made. Also, there are courses, like Saxon Math, that have daily plans for you. Try to follow whatever plan you choose, but be flexible. If the child needs to work more slowly or wants to work faster, accommodate him.

With the older child who is studying more independently, check on his progress weekly. When Susan was in eighth grade, she was generally responsible and studied hard, so Jessie didn't check on her progress in accounting for several months. By the time Jessie did check, Susan was far behind; since she was doing the course by correspondence, she had a huge amount of work to do to catch up.

In spring—preferably by June—read through the next year's suggested work, write and call for information, and try to place orders. The earlier you order books, the quicker they'll arrive. Remember that since by midsummer everyone's buying books, you can expect a six- to eight-week delay in the processing of your order.

In his book *How to Get Control of Your Time and Your Life,* Alan Lakein suggests setting A, B, and C priorities. Do the A's first, the B's next, and let the C's fall off your schedule, if you don't have time for them.[2]

WEEKLY PLANNING

Many home schoolers are able to accomplish in four days what would normally take five days in a classroom setting. The fifth day can be used for library trips, tutoring, lessons, field trips, or other "off-campus" learning. Jessie did four-day school weeks and was still able to take off three months every year; she also took a week off in October and February, when everyone was feeling stressed. If she could do it over again, she would follow Option 3 given earlier, but she says, "I wasn't courageous enough to break out of the school mold!"

We sometimes found it less crowded and more convenient to take "Saturday trips" during the week, when most other children are in school, and to use Saturday as a school day.

Start the year with a disciplined approach, following a preplanned, written schedule. If the plan is too strenuous, you can adjust and ease up, which is much easier than starting out with a relaxed approach and then finding that you are not accomplishing your goals or that your child is becoming lazy.

Don't panic about illness or doctors' appointments. The child would

[2]Alan Lakein, *How to Get Control of Your Time and Your Life* (New York: Signet, 1974), pp. 28–29.

miss those days from school anyway. And Jessie found that a bored, mildly sick or recovering child welcomed "something to do." If there was no TV allowed, he continued to do some schoolwork.

Don't be upset over unavoidable interruptions. Remember, schools have interruptions, too: the teacher is sick and the substitute doesn't follow her lesson plan; weather or mechanical problems close down the school; violence or lack of discipline sometimes disrupts teaching; strikes or political demonstrations interfere with instruction. In the midst of interruptions, teach children to be flexible. And don't worry about your child lagging behind the rest of the class. Simply take up where you left off.

Jessie's Weekly Schedule

4 days	"In-house" teaching
1 day	"Off-campus" learning—library, tutoring, lessons, short trips
1 day	Major projects (household, yard, shopping) or family trips
1 day	Rest, worship, relaxation

DAILY PLANNING

Plan a schedule for daily life, and stick to it. If you can, go to bed early and get up early—mind and body are fresher in the morning. Get up at the same time every day.

Plan how much time you'll spend on each lesson. Always leave some "wiggle room" by scheduling in a little more time than you think you'll need. Schedules reduce indecision and arguing because everyone knows what to do and is able to get on with the job at hand.

Have a specific time each day for each class, and try to keep to this. Math, spelling, and writing are skills that need daily practice and feedback in a predictable routine.

Be flexible. Schedules will change as children grow. And a new baby or suddenly mobile toddler can wreck the most carefully put-together schedule. You have the freedom to change activities around. If a small child becomes interested in earthworms, you'd still do basic skills—phonics, reading, writing, math—every day, but you might not do history for a week while he learns about earthworms. A high-school student might suddenly develop an interest in some research project. You should keep up with the daily lesson in math because it's an incremental skill. But he can spend a week on just history or just science and catch up on his other work later. The key is the *intentional* use of flexibility for an educational goal, rather than allowing students to do what they "feel like" doing.

Write down all family activities on a chart. Once a week, we filled out a wall chart that had a column for each member of the family. On it were the unchangeables: outside work, appointments, deadlines for lessons or hobbies, meetings. If Mom and Dad were taking a child to a recital, that went on all three columns (Mom's, Dad's, and the child's). Then we scheduled school lessons, meals, naps, practices, chores, housework, and free time. This way, Jessie could assign subjects with an eye to her availability: Susan didn't need help practicing the piano, but Bob needed help with grammar, so Mom put Bob's grammar lesson on her schedule at the same time Susan practiced.

JESSIE'S METHOD OF ORGANIZING: A PERSONAL ACCOUNT

I started with a 3 × 5-inch notebook to carry in my purse, but soon I needed more space. I went to the 5 × 8-inch size, which is the size of many daily business organizers available at office-supply stores. Calendars, paper, and plastic zip cases are easy to find for this size.

I put a plastic zip case containing a 2½ × 4-inch pocket calculator in the front of this notebook (handy for figuring shopping bargains).

I kept a Month At-A-Glance, tabbed, yearly planning calendar just behind the plastic zip case. All appointments, meetings, birthdays, deadlines, holiday celebrations, and so forth were kept in here, colored with highlighters.

I bought a set of blank 5 × 8-inch notebook dividers and made the following personal divisions in the notebook:

Daily Plan Here I put in blank sheets of paper, each one dated at the top, and outlined the family activities for that day. I kept a week ahead and threw sheets away as I transferred unfinished items to the next page. I kept one page separate and wrote a list of large projects to plan for.

Shop In this division, I kept current shopping lists (except the grocery list, which I kept on the refrigerator until grocery day). Clothes, hardware, office supplies—all this was available whenever we shopped or had the chance to run into a store.

Household Information Here I kept all the notes useful for running the household: printer and typewriter model numbers, sizes of household items (like the dining-room table's dimensions for tablecloth shopping), paint shades, appliance model numbers.

Clothes I kept current sizes of all family members here and their current needs in case I saw a sale.

Business Here I kept Social Security numbers of family members, contents of the safety deposit boxes, frequently used phone numbers, account numbers, and so forth.

Books I kept a running list of books, videos, tapes, and music to look for at libraries, stores, and sales.

Directions Because we live out in the country, I kept a typed-up set of directions to the house so that service companies could find us. (You might not want to do this for security reasons.)

Gifts Here I jotted down ideas for gifts for all family members.

Miscellaneous Notes Just what it sounds like—recipes I read in magazines at the doctor's office, notes about people I met, addresses, things to think about.

Make your own personal dividers according to the information you need at your fingertips. I was never able to buy a preprinted plan book that could satisfy my needs.

GOOD USE OF TIME

Read in the evenings, instead of watching TV.

For once-a-week family entertainment, go to the public library together instead of to the mall or movies. Read books together; go to evening story time with younger children; check out CDs and books. Get all the books for the next week's study.

Take control of the telephone. Take it off the hook, turn off the ringer, get an answering machine—but don't answer it when you're home schooling. And tell family and frequent callers not to call when you're teaching. Jessie's father had a long and serious illness at one point when the children were still studying; she put in a second line and gave that number only to family.

Limit outside commitments. You don't have to meet all personal goals while you are home educating your children. As a family, discuss, decide, and keep in mind your long-term goals. Balance other responsibilities with these goals.

Simplify life. Jessie's lifestyle while home educating didn't require formal entertainment. So she put away silver that needed polishing, chose not to buy clothes that required special care, put time-consuming hobbies on hold. Instead of entertaining, the family shared meals with friends.

Try to set aside a place for learning, not playing. If you don't have a separate room, the kitchen table is fine. When you get ready to do school, clear off the table. Don't allow toys or other distracting objects to co-exist with the books and papers.

Remember that everything costs either money, time, or energy, all of which are in limited supply. If you have more money than time or energy, buy your teaching aids. If you have more time and energy, make them.

HOME SCHOOLING WITH BABIES AND TODDLERS

Try these ideas to keep babies and toddlers occupied:

- Do something with the youngest children first. Then give them independent activities or toys that are only brought out at "schooltime."
- Make a "job" chart for toddlers, with pictures of activities.
- Don't ask, "What do you want to do?" or "Do you want to color?" Children always choose to do something else. State what the toddler can do, leaving no options. (Unless, of course, he's ill or fatigued and needs special attention.)
- Let a baby or toddler sit on your lap during some of the instruction. Children can be taught to sit still in a lap if it is made a habit. (Jessie's two year olds learned to sit through hour-long religious services because the small church didn't have a nursery. They slept, listened, or looked at picture books.)

- Hire an older sibling (or use a grandparent) to babysit. Be careful not to use older children as unpaid labor; however, a seven year old can earn extra pocket money by babysitting (and can get in some good job practice).
- Start actual instruction with toddlers—simple repetition, with no pressure. Susan's eighteen month old learned to say his letters when Daddy held up the wooden blocks, and her toddlers drew frantically with a pencil when the older children were doing writing. Jessie's oldest, Bob, learned his alphabet by playing with refrigerator magnets. *B* was on the refrigerator until he learned it; then Jessie added other letters one at a time.
- Don't let the baby's morning nap disappear. (A home-schooling friend of Susan's told her to keep on putting the baby in his crib with plenty of toys, even when he gave up sleeping. She did. Now he "takes a crib break" for half an hour every midmorning. Susan uses this time to do intensive, one-on-one instruction in math.)
- Don't worry if toys and books get spread all over the house. Schedule a daily fifteen-minute pickup before lunch and dinner, and put everything back in its place.
- Susan has put the toddler at the sink and allowed him to play with water, even though some got on the floor; has hidden Cheerios around the house for the baby to find; has made suds in the tub with Ivory soap; has turned the living room into a set of connected forts made with blankets; and has generally allowed him to make a mess so that she can tutor the older two.

SCHEDULES FOR HOME SCHOOLERS

At the beginning of every school year, we make out a schedule. We adhere slavishly to it for about two weeks—and then we loosen up.

You must have a schedule to start with. You need some idea of how much time each subject should take, how often to take breaks, when to start, when to stop. But once you've worked with your child for several weeks, you'll know how to adjust the schedule to suit yourself. You'll find that math may take less time and grammar more time than scheduled (or vice versa). You'll discover that your child can do certain tasks on his own, allowing you to rearrange the schedule so that these tasks coincide with putting the baby to bed or making phone calls. Or, if you're a working parent, you'll change the schedule so that the child is schooled when you're there.

Make sure that evenings are free to do some schoolwork and reading since the student doesn't have "homework" in addition to his regular study.

One Family's Schedule

Susan and her family have a master "week plan" that tells everyone where they need to be on what day (Susan and Peter make a new one at the beginning of every week). They find it easier not to have set times for each subject, since their days are subject to interruption. The children always get up at the same time every day, do chores before school, have a naptime/rest time/play alone period from 1:00 to 3:00 P.M., and go to bed on a regular schedule (7:30 for the todder, 8:00 for the younger children, 8:30 for the almost-teen). Since Peter does a good portion of the home schooling, their lists are divided into two columns; Peter supervises the left-hand side of each page, while Susan does the right-hand subjects. Saturday is a workday, but the family takes Mondays off for recreation.

This schedule reflects the assignments for Christopher (eleven), Benjamin (nine), and Daniel (just turned six, doing some first grade and some kindergarten work, since he's actually kindergarten age):

Tuesday

Christopher	Trumpet	________	Grammar	________
	Math	________	History	________
	Latin Cards	________	Writing	________
	Geography	________	Reading	________
	Science		Latin	________
	Experiment	________	Logic	________
Benjamin	Drum	________	Grammar	________
	Latin Cards	________	History	________
	Spelling	________	Writing	________

	Geography	________	Reading	________
	Science		Latin	________
	Experiment	________	Piano	________
Daniel	Math	________	Spelling	________
	Reading	________	First Language	
	Geography	________	Lessons	________
			Piano	________

Wednesday

Christopher	Trumpet	________	Writing	________
	Math	________	Latin	________
	Latin Cards	________	Music Theory	________
	Spelling	________	Library	________
	Geography	________		
	Handwriting	________		
Benjamin	Drum	________	Music Theory	________
	Math	________	Reading	________
	Latin Cards	________	Piano	________
	Spelling	________	Library	________
	Geography	________		
	Handwriting	________		
Daniel	Math	________	Spelling	________
	Reading	________	Piano	________
	Geography	________	Library	________

Thursday

Christopher	Trumpet	________	Grammar	________
	Spelling	________	History	________
	Latin Cards	________	Writing	________
	Choir	________	Reading	________
	Handwriting	________	Logic	________
			Piano	________

Benjamin	Drum	________	Grammar	________
	Math	________	History	________
	Choir	________	Writing	________
	Handwriting	________	Reading	________
			Spanish	________
			Piano	________
Daniel	Math	________	Spelling	________
	Choir	________	First Language Lessons	________
			Spanish	________

Friday

Christopher	Trumpet	________	Grammar	________
	Math	________	History	________
	Latin Cards	________	Writing	________
	Piano	________	Reading	________
	Science Reading	________	Latin	________
			Logic	________
Benjamin	Drum	________	Grammar	________
	Math	________	History	________
	Latin Cards	________	Writing	________
	Spelling	________	Reading	________
	Science Reading	________	Latin	________
			Piano	________
Daniel	Math	________	Spelling	________
	Science Reading	________	First Language Lessons	________
			Piano	________

Saturday

Christopher	Trumpet	________	Piano	________
	Math	________	Science Report	________
	Spelling	________	Reading	________
	Handwriting	________	Latin	________
			Music Theory	________

Benjamin	Drum	________	Grammar	________
	Math	________	Science Report	________
	Handwriting	________	Writing	________
	Spelling	________	Spanish	________
			Music Theory	________
Daniel	Reading	________	Science Report	________
	Spelling	________	Spanish	________
			Piano	________

RESOURCES

For publisher and catalog addresses, telephone numbers, and other information, see Sources (pages 751–778). Most books can be obtained from any bookstore or library.

Lakein, Alan. *How to Get Control of Your Time and Your Life*. New York: Signet, 1989.
A guide to setting priorities for work and home jobs.

McCullough, Bonnie. *Bonnie's Household Organizer: The Essential Guide for Getting Control of Your Home.* 2d rev. ed. New York: St. Martin's, 1983.
Strategies for spending a minimum amount of time on household jobs.

McCullough, Bonnie, and Susan Monson. *401 Ways to Get Your Kids to Work at Home.* New York: St. Martin's, 2003.
Tips for training children to work.

39

PAPER PROOF: GRADES AND RECORD KEEPING

> The purpose . . . is to communicate his nontraditional education in the traditional terms outsiders will understand.
>
> —Debra Bell

Ironically, a classical education is now considered "nontraditional" because it doesn't fit into the neat credits-per-subject pattern of the average high school. Home education is nontraditional as well. Your task is to record what your student is doing in a way that makes sense to school administrators and college admissions officers.

Fortunately, many people have walked this road before you. Your state home-school organization can send you a packet of information covering state requirements for home schoolers, the awarding of grades and diplomas, and the keeping of an appropriate transcript. As a home-educating parent, you'll be doing paperwork in three areas: notification, portfolio keeping for elementary-school and middle-school students, and transcript preparation for high-school students.

NOTIFICATION

When you begin home schooling, you'll need to notify your local school system. Contact your state organization for the exact way to do this. In some states, if you have a college diploma, you simply fill out an "Intent to Home School" form and send a copy of your diploma. If you don't have a diploma, the state may require you to submit an outline of study, which is simply a list of the books you plan to cover each year in each subject. Only basic texts need be listed.

ELEMENTARY SCHOOL AND MIDDLE SCHOOL: PORTFOLIOS

In elementary school and middle school, you must keep track of each subject taught each year. Since no one but you and the local school district will ever see the grades for school years K–8, you should check with your school administrators. Most schools will happily accept portfolios of work as proof that you're doing what you're supposed to do; the notebooks you create for each subject fulfill this requirement. Keep these notebooks filed where you can get to them, and offer them when you need to document your child's work at home.

The only reason for you to issue the child a letter or number grade for K–8 is (1) if the school district demands it (very rare) or (2) if you think the child might want to transfer into a school that requires transcripts. In most cases, schools are content with portfolios—which, in any case, offer a much better picture of the child's achievements. If you do want to issue a grade, you can keep a K–8 transcript like the one we've suggested you use for high school (see below). But in most situations, this is unnecessary.

A word about testing. We don't think there's much point in administering tests in grades 1 through 4. During those years, you should be evaluating rather than testing. Watch the child's work to see what errors she makes again and again. Then reteach those concepts.

In middle grades, you should start giving tests in the "skills" areas—math, grammar, spelling—just to accustom the student to the testing process. You can do this with the tests supplied in the teacher's editions and test booklets that accompany your texts. But in history, science, and reading—the "content" areas—the child is continually reading, writing, and talking about what she's learning. There's no need to create some kind of test for this material.

HIGH SCHOOL: TRANSCRIPTS

For grades 9 through 12, issuing grades and filling out a transcript form is necessary. The transcript records subjects studied, years of study, units of credit, and final grades. Transcripts ought to be kept on permanent file. Although some colleges are happy to accept portfolios for home-school applications (see Chapter 44), others insist on a regular transcript. Employers and educational institutions will often request a high-school transcript. (Occasionally, a potential employer will still call Jessie and ask for the high-school transcript of a student she tutored ten years ago.) That piece of paper is important!

At a minimum, you should record each subject studied, the traditional end-of-semester grades—A, B, C, and so forth—and achievement test scores. Having taught in traditional schools, Jessie knows that many factors influence a final course grade, among them attendance, participation, application, attitude, projects and activities. We also know of some classrooms where an A equals 95 to 100, and other classrooms where an A equals 90 to 100. Failing scores are always determined by the teacher and can range from 60 to 75. The home-school teacher is allowed to exercise the same flexibility of judgment as the traditional school teacher. Taking all of the above factors into account, Jessie awarded an A for excellent work and application, a B for above-average work that could have been a little better, a C for meeting-the-grade work, and a D for performance that was much less than the child was capable of doing.

Because, in a home situation, Jessie continually evaluated and tested for mastery before testing to award a grade, the grades were usually high. She also tried to match the grades to achievement scores (see Chapter 40 for more on testing). A transcript with all A's and low standardized test scores won't appear credible (although a standardized test doesn't necessarily test the material taught and shouldn't be used to determine a course grade).

Even if your school system allows a portfolio assessment instead of traditional grades, you must keep this official transcript for high school. You might be asked for it at the most unexpected times.

The student needs to fulfill a minimum number of credits in order to graduate from high school. Traditionally, 1 credit in high school equals 120 hours of class work, or 160 45-minute periods. Labs and projects, field trips, and independent reading can all count as class work.

Check with your support group, state home-school organization, or local school-board office on graduation requirements. Remember, they do change from time to time and from state to state. Typically, 20 credits are required for graduation:

Language arts	4
Mathematics	2
Science	2
American history	1
American government	1
Physical education	2
Electives	8

A college-preparation course is more extensive, ordinarily requiring the following 21 to 29 credits:

Language arts	4
Mathematics	3–4
Foreign language	2–4
World history	1
American history	1
American government	1
Science	3–4
Physical education	2
Electives	4–8

The student who follows the classical curriculum outlined in Part III and holds to a basic 36-week school year will spend, on average, the following hours in study every year (this is adjusted to allow for illness, field trips, and other skipped days of school):

Ninth Grade	
Grammar	120 hours
Rhetoric	90 hours
Great books	320 hours
Math	120 hours
Science	108 hours
Foreign language	108–216 hours
Art and music appreciation	108 hours

Tenth Grade	
Grammar	120 hours
Rhetoric	90 hours
Great books	320 hours
Math	120 hours
Science	108 hours
Foreign language	108–216 hours
Art and music appreciation	108 hours

Eleventh Grade	
Grammar	120 hours
Great books	320 hours
Math	120 hours
Science	108 hours
Foreign language	108–216 hours
Art and music appreciation	108 hours
Junior thesis	100–150 hours
(Computer programming)	(150 hours)

Twelfth Grade	
Grammar	120 hours
Great books	320 hours
Math	120 hours
Science	108 hours (more like 180 hours, if Saxon physics is elected)

Foreign language	108–216 hours
Art and music appreciation	108 hours
Senior thesis	100–150 hours
(Computer programming)	(150 hours)

How does this fit into a transcript? If you keep to this schedule, you award 1 English credit per year for the study of grammar (that's the language-arts requirement). You also award 1 math credit each year that a math course is completed. After the ninth- and tenth-grade years, math courses can be counted toward the eight required electives.

Science courses are slightly below the normal class hours, but don't forget that home study tends to be more concentrated than classroom work. Also, the 108 hours of science is supplemented by the works on science read in the great-books course and by extra time spent on science-fair projects and outside reading. If the junior and senior projects are science-oriented, the number of hours climbs even more. So it's perfectly legitimate for you to award 1 science credit for each year of study. And if, by the end of the year, you don't feel that the child has done the equivalent of a year's study, simply continue into the summer until that extra 12 hours are completed (it's only 4 extra weeks—less if you do more than 3 hours per week). Use common sense and look at what the student has completed when deciding to award the credit.

We suggest you award 1 fine-arts elective credit for every year's work in art and music appreciation combined. Award 1 foreign-language credit for each one-year course in foreign language completed. For physical education, award the student 1 credit for a full year's involvement in organized physical activity—aerobics classes, tennis lessons, karate lessons, community softball or basketball leagues. Alternately, the student can just keep a year-long log of the time spent in regular physical activities such as walking, jogging, and bike riding. When she reaches 120 hours, award her 1 physical-education credit (everyone who does the exercise gets A's in physical education). This will encourage the child to exercise regularly, which will help her overall health.

The great-books study is the equivalent of considerably more than 2 high-school courses. Add the study of rhetoric in ninth and tenth grades, and the junior and senior theses in eleventh and twelfth grades, and you've got more credits than needed for graduation. The study of great books encompasses world history, world literature (although the study of grammar provides the necessary language-arts credit, you can give elective credit in world literature for every year of great-books study), American history, and American government (it includes source readings from all the texts required in a government course plus the background readings in ancient political theory that most high-school courses simply can't cover). If you do debate, count rhetoric and debate club together as 1 speech elective. Computer programming is another elective. Furthermore, in the junior and senior years, the senior-thesis requirement can be counted as an honors elective course in independent research.

The transcript is not the place to explain that you've done rhetoric and great books instead of traditional textbook courses. The transcript will show that you've met and exceeded the minimum state requirements; the portfolio, that you've met those requirements in a challenging, creative way—it accompanies your transcript when you apply to college (see Chapter 44).

The transcript values, then, look like this:

High-School Credits

Curriculum		**What you put on transcript**	
Course	**Hours**	**Course**	**Units**
		Ninth grade	
Grammar	120	English 1	1 language arts
Rhetoric	90	Speech 1	1 elective
Great books	320	World lit. 1	1 elective
		World hist. 1	1 history
Math	120	Algebra	1 math
Science	108	Biology	1 science
Foreign lang.	108–216	Latin/modern	1–2 foreign lang.
Art and music	108	Fine arts 1	1 elective
		Tenth grade	
Grammar	120	English 2	1 language arts
Rhetoric	90	Speech 2	1 elective

Great books	320	World lit. 2	1 elective
		World hist. 2	1 history
Math	120	Algebra	1 math
Science	108	Earth science	1 science
Foreign lang.	108–216	Latin/modern	1–2 foreign lang.
Art and music	108	Fine arts 2	1 elective

Eleventh grade

Grammar	120 hours	English 3	1 language arts
Great books	320 hours	Victorian lit.	1 elective
		American hist.	1 history
Math	120 hours	Advanced math	1 math
Science	108 hours	Chemistry	1 science
Foreign lang.	108–216 hours	Latin/modern	1–2 foreign lang.
Art and music	108 hours	Fine arts 3	1 elective
Junior thesis	100–150 hours	Junior honors	1 elective
(Computer prog.)	(150 hours)	(Computer prog.)	(1 elective)

Twelfth grade

Grammar	120 hours	English 4	1 language arts
Great books	320 hours	Modern lit.	1 elective
		American gov.	1 government
(Math, elective)	(120 hours)	(Elective)	(1 math)
Science	108 hours	Physics	1 science
Foreign lang.	108–216 hours	Latin/modern	1–2 foreign lang.
Art and music	108 hours	Fine arts 4	1 elective
Senior thesis	100–150 hours	Senior honors	1 elective
(Computer prog.)	(150 hours)	(Computer prog.)	(1 elective)

The student who follows this curriculum ends up with these credits:

Language Arts	4
Mathematics	3–4
Foreign language	4–8

World history	2
American history	1
American government	1
Science	4
Electives	10–14

Add 2 credits in physical education, and this goes far beyond the average college prep high-school track.

As can be seen, it's acceptable (especially for the student who isn't college-bound) to simplify the high-school curriculum. The fine-arts electives aren't necessary either for graduation or for the college track. One to two years of science could be eliminated as well as several years of foreign language and at least one year of mathematics.

But a rigorous high-school program prepares the student for the unexpected—a future change in employment, a sudden desire to go to college or graduate school, a growing home business that requires a high level of intellectual competency. We recommend as vigorous a curriculum as the child's mental ability allows. Jessie also feels that every student, even those who don't plan on college, ought to take the PSAT and SAT (see Chapter 40). If, two or three years later, the high-school graduate decides to go to college, the standardized scores already exist; she doesn't have to take tests on material that's been partially forgotten.

Any courses taken through correspondence, a community college, or a concurrent program at a local university should be listed on the high-school transcript along with the grade earned. These courses also count toward high-school graduation credits.

The high-school transcript also includes space for extracurricular activities. Record all the student's nonacademic activities (teams, hobbies that she puts significant time into, athletic pursuits, music lessons, competitions, volunteer work, jobs, all memberships in any kind of organization, any leadership positions at church or in community groups, all participation in regular community activities). You'll probably have to list these on a separate sheet of paper or fit them into a margin on the transcript since most transcripts have a preset list of extracurricular activities ("Offices Held" or "Band"). Just make sure these activities appear with the transcript wherever it is submitted.

DIPLOMA

If your state home-school association has a graduation ceremony that awards high-school diplomas (as Virginia does), take advantage of it. And if your state allows your home school to operate as a private school, you can design and present your own diploma with the name you have selected for your institution. Home-school diplomas can be designed and purchased at homeschooldiploma.com. The transcript form, not the diploma, proves that your student has completed the necessary work for graduation.

Many home-schooling organizations suggest that students take the GED. We're not sure this is a good idea, especially for classically educated students. The GED really only requires a mastery of tenth-grade material, and taking it tends to lump highly accomplished, academically oriented students together with those who couldn't or wouldn't finish eleventh grade.

We suggest calling the admissions offices of colleges you might be interested in and asking them how they view a home-schooled transcript and whether they require a diploma. Many colleges are now formulating specific policies for home schoolers.

If the student is thinking about joining the military, talk to a local recruiter about the high-school graduation requirement and how you can best document graduation. If the recruiter seems uncooperative, contact HSLDA for advice.

Your transcript (and portfolio) plus achievement scores are much more valuable than a diploma. Schools all across the United States vary so widely in the skills required to gain a diploma that the piece of paper itself has lost much of its meaning. Again, the most important thing you can do is *call* any of the institutions requiring a diploma and ask what they prefer for home schoolers.

RESOURCES

For publisher and catalog addresses, telephone numbers, and other information, see Sources (pages 751–778). Most books can be obtained from any bookstore or library; where we know of a mail-order option, we have provided it.

Instructor Daily Planner. New York: Scholastic, 1999.

$4.95. Order from Rainbow Resource. This basic record book supplies space to keep track of dates, assignments, field trips, and grades in K–12.

Diploma.

$30.00–$50.00, depending on features. Order from HomeschoolDiploma.com.

Edu-Track Home School Software.

$59.00. Order from Edu-Track. Generates lesson plans, progress reports, transcripts, report cards, certificates, diplomas, and other forms. For PC and for Mac.

High-school transcript form.

$1.50. Order from Debra Bell's Home School Resource Center. This standard high-school transcript form is published by the National Association of Secondary School Principals. Get several in case you make a mistake.

Home School Cumulative Record.

$2.95. Order from Rainbow Resource. Cardstock folder for keeping important papers has a transcript draft form on the back and on the inside.

Homeschooler's High School Journal.

$9.25. Order from Rainbow Resource Center. Highly recommended, this spiral-bound journal gives the student sections for recording test scores, daily logs for recording time spent on each subject and time spent on field trips or research, library list forms to keep track of what you've read, a chart to keep track of weekly hours spent on each subject, and a grade record.

TranscriptPro Home School Transcript Generator. Taylors, S.C.: Education+Plus.

$49.00. Order from Education+Plus. This software, developed by Inge Cannon, helps parents generate personalized, official-appearing transcripts.

40

THE YARDSTICK: STANDARDIZED TESTING

In some ways, parents who educate at home are in better shape because of the sanctity of modern testing. It's not that hard to teach a child to do well on a standardized test, and since the tests are sacred, good results command respect.

—Mary Pride, *The New Big Book of Home Learning*

Standardized tests are necessary evils. On the negative side, they don't necessarily measure the child's knowledge or skill; they may not coincide with what you've been working on; and they require specific test-taking skills that your child will have to practice when he could be doing something else. On the positive side, standardized tests are a great equalizer. Because grading standards vary so much from school to school, standardized tests scores have become the ultimate proof that you're doing a good job educating your child. High Scholastic Aptitude Test (SAT) scores will open dozens of doors for high-school seniors. Advanced Placement (AP) tests give college credit to the well prepared. Students with a good grounding in the foundational skills of reading, writing, and mathematics generally test well; students who read widely almost always score highly.

YEARLY TESTING

If you're home educating, you may need to have your child tested every year. Although this is a pain in the neck, look on the bright side: children who are accustomed to taking timed standardized tests inevitably score well on college admissions exams. Jessie, paranoid about academic achievement back when no one else she knew was home schooling, had her children tested every year. As a result, when they took their PSATs and SATs, they were relaxed and confident, and came out with high scores.

There are a slew of standardized skills tests for grades K–12. The only way to negotiate the maze is to follow these steps:

1. Call your state home-school organization, and ask what your state regulations are. When does the child need to be tested? What tests are acceptable? (In Virginia, home-schooled students are allowed to use any nationally standardized achievement test, not only the test that happens to be used by the local school district.)

2. Decide how you want the test to be administered. You have several options:

   a. If you want to, and if you have a well-ordered, friendly private school nearby, call and ask whether your children can take the standardized test on test day.[1] You will have to register ahead of time and pay a nominal fee, show up with the children on test day for the test, and take them home. This is especially good for older children (seventh grade and up) since it exposes them to the conditions that will surround SAT testing. Younger home schoolers are better off taking the test in a familiar setting, preferably from an administrator they know. At the very least, go to the test site before the test date, and wander around.

   b. Administer the test yourself. A number of the standardized basic

[1]Jessie doesn't recommend that elementary-age home schoolers take tests with public-school students unless the state requires this. The confusion and unfamiliar chaos of a big class sometimes prevents the child from concentrating on the test. We have also heard of an occasional case where hostility to home schoolers has made a child uncomfortable.

tests—including the California Achievement Test and the Comprehensive Test of Basic Skills—can be given by the parent and sent back for grading. Information about each test can be found at the end of this chapter. This is the best option for K–4 students. Jessie thinks that at this stage the parent should give the test and then teach the child what he needs to know about taking tests.

c. Take your children to a professional testing site for private test administration. Your state organization can tell you where to find a local test site. The education department of a local college or university should also have this information.

3. Prepare for the test. A good basic guide to standardized test taking is found in *Dr. Gruber's Essential Guide to Test Taking for Kids.* The guide is published in two volumes, *Grades 3, 4, 5* and *Grades 6, 7, 8, 9.* These contain basic content, guides to the specific types of tests offered, practice in specific test-taking skills, and anxiety-reduction strategy. Jessie spent time prior to standardized test time teaching each child how to take the tests. They practiced taking sample tests so that the techniques of test taking became familiar and they could focus on content.

The best way to reduce anxiety, though, is for you to accept the status of the test as "no big deal." If you're agitated because you feel that your success as a parent and teacher is resting on this standardized test, your child will pick up on your urgency.

4. Take sample tests. SRA/McGraw-Hill publishes sample tests for most of the basic series. You can also order sample tests from some of the testing centers listed at the end of this chapter.

Make sure you tell the child, before he takes the test, that it will contain material beyond his grade level. For example, a test for grades 1 through 3 typically contains material from the fourth, fifth, and sixth grade in order to identify highly gifted or advanced third graders. But if the student doesn't know that some of the material is purposely designed to be too hard, he might panic and stop thinking clearly.

What if the child doesn't do well? Perhaps the child was sick or was upset about an unrelated matter or was suffering from text anxiety. Or perhaps you didn't cover the material emphasized on the test.

In most cases, you're given a second year to show substantial progress—something you'll need for a child who's doing remedial work. Spend extra time before the next test working on test skills.

A great advantage to administering the test yourself or having it done privately is that you can schedule the test three to four months before the deadline your state requires. Then, if the child doesn't score well, you can prepare again and retest.

You can also appeal for a different form of testing: an individual, portfolio-based assessment of the student's progress. Your state organization can help you with the appeal and steer you toward a professional assessment service. Portfolios are made up of samples of the child's work, arranged chronologically to demonstrate achievement in different areas. They include information that can't be tested—art talent, engineering projects, community-service award. These are valuable for showing reasonable progress for a child who's testing below grade level. Contact your portfolio evaluator (recommended by your home-school state organization) at the beginning of each year to see what materials you should include.

Even if you use portfolios to satisfy the school system, you should keep on taking standardized tests. Tests are a reality of educational and professional life (you even have to take a test to get a driver's license), and constant practice will eventually dull test anxiety. You can give these tests privately, without forwarding the results to school officials.

Use the test results to target weak areas that need more study, as well as to praise the child when scores show that he has made progress. If the child consistently tests poorly in a particular skill, you might want to consult a professional evaluator to see whether the child has a learning problem or simply needs more time in that area. At its best, standardized testing is a tool for evaluating instruction. It should be used to plan the next step in the educational process. *Never make an important educational decision on the basis of one test.*

Note that a fairly new development on the scene are tests such as Performance Assessment in Mathematics (PAM) and Performance Assessment in Language (PAL). These require the student to explain in writing why he chose the answer he did. Because these answers are open to wide interpretation by the test scorer, Jessie recommends avoiding this type of testing unless it is required by law. If you do have to take these tests, call Continental Press (800-233-0759) or visit their website at www.continentalpress.com and ask for a testing catalog. Then talk to a customer-service representative at Continental and ask for advice on the product that will best prepare the student for your state's specific test. These tests will require more preparation time than standard multiple-choice tests. So start getting ready at the beginning of the year, and practice periodically until the child is comfortable with the format.

AP AND CLEP EXAMS

High-school students who take advanced electives can earn college credit through the Advanced Placement and College Level Examination Program exams administered by the College Board. High scores on these exams don't mean that you'll actually get credit on a college transcript. (This depends on the college to which you apply—some will give you credit, others simply allow you to skip low-level classes and go into more advanced work.) But high scores from home schoolers demonstrate that you have, indeed, mastered the material on your transcript. AP and CLEP scores, according to the College Board, improve the admission appeal of home schoolers "by demonstrating college-level knowledge."[2]

The College Board offers thirty-four CLEP exams as well as AP exams in twenty areas of study. For online information on both types of exams, visit the College Board website at www.collegeboard.com. The website offers online test reviews and an evaluation service as well as information about all the exams. Ideally, you should get this information in ninth grade to help you plan your high-school electives.

AP exams are given at local high schools. As long as they have studied the subject in depth, home-school students can take AP exams without enrolling in the school-offered AP course. You can obtain practice AP exams from the College Board. To get specific AP information, call 888-CALL-4-AP or 609-771-7300; or go to www.collegeboard.com/ap/students/index.html.

CLEP exams determine placement in a number of subjects—most notably foreign languages—and show achievement. Call CLEP at 800-257-9558, e-mail clep@info.collegeboard.com, or visit the CLEP section of the

[2]"Getting College Credit before College," College Board Online, www.collegeboard.com/parents/csearch/know-the-options/21298.html.

College Board website, www.collegeboard.com/student/testing/clep/about.html.

If you plan to take an AP or CLEP exam, get a review book from Barron's, the College Board, or Princeton Review. During the semester before the exam, spend several hours per week preparing for the test.

PSAT, SAT, AND ACT

The PSAT, the SAT, and the ACT (American College Test) are all standardized high-school achievement/skill-evaluation tests used by colleges to sort through and rank applicants. If you're planning to attend college, take these tests seriously. Finish as much math as possible before the junior year. The Latin and vocabulary programs as well as *The Well-Educated Mind* will thoroughly prepare you for the vocabulary and reading-comprehension sections of the test. Logic will help with the analytical sections.

However, you should also study directly for the tests. Beginning in tenth grade, spend at least an hour a day working through one of the review guides published by Barron's, the College Board, or the Princeton Review. All tests have their peculiarities, and the types of problems may not be familiar if you don't prepare. Study regularly, and take at least three practice tests under test conditions—timed, sitting in one place without getting up for water or cookies. Susan scored above the 90th percentile in all college admissions tests by studying Latin, finishing Algebra II and geometry, and working through review books every day for over a year before taking the tests. The effort paid off in scholarship money and admission to every program she applied to.

Find out what format the test will be in. Currently, standardized tests are in the middle of a shift from paper-and-pencil administration to computerized administration, but as of this writing the SATs are still taken with paper and pencil. If you'll be taking a traditional exam, use a book to prepare for it instead of the review software sold by the College Board or Princeton Review. There's enough of a difference in the way the problems are presented via computer to throw you off when you sit down with the test booklet.

The PSAT/NMSQT (Preliminary SAT/National Merit Scholarship Qualifying Test) is administered by the College Board. It not only offers practice for the SATs, but serves as a qualifying exam for scholarships offered by the National Merit Scholarship Corporation. The PSAT is generally taken during the sophomore or junior year of high school. Students who take it in the fall of the junior year generally score higher and have a better chance of qualifying for National Merit scholarships. Questions about National Merit scholarships should be directed to the National Merit Scholarship Corporation at 847-866-5100, or www.nationalmerit.org.

Home-school students register for the PSAT/NMSQT through the local high school. Note that, unlike the SAT, the PSAT is given *only* in October—and if you miss it, it's gone. Call your local public or private high school in the spring of the freshman or sophomore year, and arrange to take the test the following October. Ask to speak to the PSAT administrator. Find out the day and time the test is being given. Ask about the fee (if you can't afford it, ask how you can apply for a fee waiver) and how to register. Home-school students use a College Board home-school code when filling out the registration forms. Call PSAT General Information (866-433-7728) for the appropriate code, e-mail psat@info.collegeboard.org, or visit www.collegeboard.com/student/testing/psat/about.html.

The College Board suggests that, if the school seems resistant, you contact another public high school or try a private school. PSAT scores for home schoolers are sent directly to your home.

The SAT, the standard college admissions test, has two parts. SAT I is the test everyone takes; it lasts three hours and thirty-five minutes. Students receive three scores: mathematics, critical reading, and writing. SAT II, or subject, tests are optional, but home schoolers should strongly consider taking as many of them as they feel prepared for. The tests are one-hour multiple-choice exams that measure knowledge in specific areas. Good scores on the SAT II tests will validate your high-school transcript.

You should plan to take the SAT no later than January of the senior year (if you think you might want to take it more than once, take it in the spring of the junior year or the fall of the senior year). Register online at collegeboard.com/student/testing/sat/about.html. Home-schooled students will be given instructions about what code to use during registration. The College Board recommends that you ask for their free publications *Taking the SAT I: Reasoning Test* and *Taking the SAT II: Subject Test;* these have test-taking tips and practice test questions. As in the PSAT, you can request a fee waiver if the SAT test fees are too much for your budget.

When you fill out the form, you'll choose three test centers close to you. When your registration is confirmed, you'll be informed about where and when to take the test. Specific questions about the SAT should be directed to SAT Customer Service, either by way of the College Board website, or by phone (866-756-7346).

The most useful (and hard to find) page on the College Board website is www.collegeboard.com/html/communications000.html; it has phone numbers, addresses, and links for every single Board-related standardized test and screening.

The ACT is widely, although not universally, accepted for college admissions—check with the college you want to attend. However, if you have to choose between the SAT and the ACT, pick the SAT.

The four ACT tests cover English, mathematics, reading, and science reasoning. The test is three and a half hours long, is given five times—in October, December, February, April, and June—and costs $30.00 ($44.50 for ACT Plus Writing). For information about the ACT, visit their online site at www.act.org. You should take the ACT in the spring of your junior year. For registration and location information, call 319-337-1270 or visit www.actstudent.org.

RESOURCES

For publisher and catalog addresses, telephone numbers, and other information, see Sources (pages 751–778). Most books can be obtained from any bookstore or library; where we know of a mail-order option, we have provided it. Resources for yearly standardized testing and test preparation are listed first, followed by PSAT, SAT, ACT, AP, and CLEP resources.

Test Ordering Information

Check with your state home-education organization to find out which of these is accepted by your state. The following tests can be administered by parents under certain conditions:

California Achievement Test.

Order through the Independent Test Service of Christian Liberty Academy. This national test can be given by the parent. The test has to be mailed back to CLA, where it will be scored and returned. See www.class-homeschools.org/class/itsform_clp.htm.

Comprehensive Test of Basic Skills.
Order from Seton School, and mail back to Seton for scoring and evaluation. Adds science, social science, and reference skills to the material tested by the other exams. See www.setonhome.org/testing/.

Bob Jones University offers home-school parents assistance with administering a range of standardized tests, including the Stanford Achievement Test and the Iowa Test of Basic Skills. Contact Bob Jones University Press customer service at 800-845-5731 (www.bjup.com), and ask for their Testing Catalog and Order Form, or visit www.bjupress.com/services/testing.

Test Preparation

Achieve Test Preparation Series. Austin, Tex.: Steck-Vaughn, 2008.
Order directly from Steck-Vaughn at steckvaughn.harcourtachieve.com. The series offers individual test prep books for the following state assessment tests:

Arizona—AIMS DPA.
Florida—FCAT.
Hawaii—HAS.
Maryland—MSA.
Massachusetts—MCAS.
Michigan—MEAP.
New Jersey—GEPA.
New York—NYS.
Pennsylvania—PSSA.
Texas—TAKS.

Continental Press Testing Resources.
Continental Press offers test prep resources coded to the test of each individual state. Visit http://www.continentalpress.com/pages/subjects/testprep_states_1.html and click on your state to locate the best materials for your family.

Gruber, Gary R. *Dr. Gruber's Essential Guide to Test Taking for Kids.* 2d ed. Naperville, Ill.: Sourcebook, 2008.

Available in two volumes. *Grades 3–5* and *Grades 6–9*. Order through any bookstore or online bookseller. Includes reviews and practice questions for all widely used achievement tests.

Scoring High series. New York: McGraw-Hill.

Order from SRA/McGraw-Hill. These booklets cover the skills needed for the major achievement tests. Call for the most recent titles: each series has a number of levels, so when you call, tell the customer-service representative which test you're preparing for and what grade child you're working with. Or visit sraonline.com to locate the correct booklets for your student.

Scoring High on the California Achievement Tests. 2007.
Scoring High on the Iowa Test of Basic Skills. 2007.
Scoring High on the Metropolitan Achievement Test. 2007.

PSAT Preparation

For PSAT information, visit www.collegeboard.com. For National Merit Scholarship information, contact the National Merit Scholarship Corporation at 1560 Sherman Avenue, Suite 200, Evanston, IL 60201-4897, call 847-866-5100, or visit www.nationalmerit.org.

Cracking the PSAT/NMSQT, 2009 Edition. Princeton, N.J.: Princeton Review, 2008.

$13.95. Order from any bookstore or online—be sure to check for the most recent edition.

Kaplan PSAT/NSQT, 2009 Edition. New York: Kaplan, 2007.

$17.00. Order from any bookstore or online—be sure to check for the most recent edition.

SAT Preparation

For the SAT Registration Bulletin or questions, visit the College Board website at www.collegeboard.com.

Green, Sharon Weiner, et al. *Barron's How to Prepare for the SAT I.* Hauppauge, N.Y.: Barron's Educational Series.

The Barron's SAT series is Susan's favorite. It's complete, affordable, and scores on the practice tests are generally close reflections of the real thing. The books are revised yearly; the most recent versions can be ordered online or found in the reference section of your local bookstore. Barron's also offers an SAT II preparation series with one title for almost every high-school subject. These are valuable for students who are planning to take an SAT subject exam.

Princeton Review Staff. *Cracking the SAT with CD-ROM.* Princeton, N.J.: Princeton Review.

This guide has a long history of success. Princeton Review also publishes a Cracking the SAT II series, which covers most high-school subjects.

ACT Preparation

For ACT information, contact ACT at www.act.org.

Ehrenhaft, George, et al. *Barron's Pass Key to the ACT.* Hauppauge, N.Y.: Barron's Educational Series.

———. *How to Prepare for the ACT.* Hauppauge, N.Y.: Barron's Educational Series.

Both books are updated regularly. Buy at any bookstore.

AP Preparation

For College Board resources and information about Advanced Placement exams, visit their website at www.collegeboard.com.

Advanced Placement series. Piscataway, N.J.: Research and Education Association.

This series offers titles in almost every AP subject area.

Best Test Preparation AP series. Piscataway, N.J.: Research and Education Association.

This series offers titles in almost every AP subject area.

Barron's How to Prepare for the AP series. Hauppauge, N.Y.: Barron's Educational Series.

This series, covering all the subjects in which AP exams are offered, includes reviews, test tips, lots of practice, and sample tests.

CLEP Preparation

For College Board resources and information about CLEP exams, visit their website at www.collegeboard.com.

Best Test Preparation CLEP series. Piscataway, N.J.: Research and Education Association.

The titles in this series offer general practice for taking the CLEP exams as well as information about the specific subject exams available (one for almost every high-school subject).

41

WHERE'S THE TEAM? ATHLETICS AT HOME

> Serious sport has nothing to do with fair play. It is bound up with hatred, jealousy, boastfulness, disregard of all rules . . . it is war minus the shooting.
>
> —George Orwell, "The Sporting Spirit"

Can home schoolers play team sports? It depends on what you mean. If your teenager has a good chance of becoming a professional basketball or football player, home schooling probably isn't a good option. There's simply no foolproof way to plug a home-schooled student into the pro-sports assembly line that starts in high school. If the student wants to participate in college sports, though, the Home School Legal Defense Association provides a packet that helps home schoolers validate the initial eligibility requirements for the National Collegiate Athletic Association (NCAA). (Call HSLDA, 540-338-5600, or visit hslda.org for details.)

But players who are serious contenders for a professional team sports career make up a very small segment of the total high-school population. For the average, academically inclined teenager, we think the question of organized team sports has gotten too much emphasis. How many students will find that team sports make up an important part of life after high school? And even in a regular school, very few players are actually able to play regularly on official teams.

However, home schoolers can make arrangements to take part in team sports. Church and community leagues often welcome home schoolers—call your local Parks and Recreation office for information on community leagues. Check the bulletin boards at local sports stores to find out about special-interest sports groups and small clubs; many of these are family-oriented and welcome all ages. Youth groups such as Little League, 4-H, Scouts, Camp Fire, and Civil Air Patrol sponsor sports teams.

Home-school support groups, particularly in areas where home schooling is popular, sponsor teams especially for home schoolers. Call several local support groups (your state organization can give you names and numbers), and find out whether any of them has put a basketball, baseball, or soccer team together. (If no one has, you can always start your own.) Your state organization may also know of home-school teams; some states have organized statewide home-school leagues.

Private schools, especially smaller ones, are often willing to allow home schoolers to play on school teams. If no one's ever asked to do this before, suggest that your child try it for a few weeks on a trial basis.

As in other high-school subjects, use your community-college resources for older students. A teenaged home schooler can enroll for physical-education (or kinesiology) classes. This can lead to team participation once the student becomes familiar with the coaches and sports staff.

Some states make specific provisions for home-schooled students to participate in public-school sports. Call your state organization, and ask what the existing policy is. In many states, there's no official policy—you'll simply need to approach your school district and ask whether your child can participate. However, if you've taken your child out of school to avoid a destructive social environment, this obviously is not a good choice.

A more relaxed approach to physical education is simply making sure that your children exercise every day, from kindergarten through twelfth grade. In elementary and middle school, play games together at least twice a week (we've suggested two good books on children's games in the Resources at the end of this chapter). Jessie concentrated on general physical fitness and on sports skills that could be honed either individually or without a large team of people: running (Susan ran a half marathon at thirteen), cycling (her brother trained alone or with Mom "drafting" him in the station wagon), horseback riding, tennis, golf, handball, swimming. All are suitable for individual recreation as well as for competition, if the student enjoys the challenge.

Walking is free (except for good shoes) and can be done alone or with a friend or sibling. Aerobics can be done in a regular class or with a home video. Pickup games of basketball, softball, and soccer with family and friends teach basic games-playing skills. Activities such as hiking, karate, skating, skiing, swimming, dancing (folk, ethnic, ballroom, classical, modern), and weight training can be learned privately. Investigate classes at your local community recreation center; generally, these are offered for a wide range of ages and levels. Clubs and gyms offer instruction in martial arts, gymnastics, fencing, and other sports or skills.

As described in Chapter 39, the high-school student should, for at least two years, keep a log of hours spent doing physical activity, including in the log brief descriptions of the activity itself and the skills practiced and mastered. These logs can serve as the basis of credits awarded for physical education. The student must devote 120 hours per year to doing physical activity in order to earn 1 unit of credit; 2 units are required for high-school graduation.

Another kind of physical activity that is often overlooked is physical work, which builds muscles as well as character. Jessie's home schoolers cut grass, gardened, took care of animals (carrying feed and water in freezing weather as well as cleaning their living quarters), and hired themselves out to trusted friends and neighbors for housework and yardwork.

RESOURCES

For publisher and catalog addresses, telephone numbers, and other information, see Sources (pages 751–778). Most books can be obtained from any bookstore or library; where we know of a mail-order option, we have provided it.

Bailey, Guy. *The Ultimate Homeschool Physical Education Game Book*. Columbus, Ohio: Educator's Press, 2003.

$19.95. Order from any bookstore.

Maguire, Jack. *Hopscotch, Hangman, Hot Potato, and Ha, Ha, Ha: A Rulebook of Children's Games.* New York: Fireside, 1992.

$15.00. Order from any bookstore or online bookseller. A classic with rules for all the active kids' games your child would play in elementary and middle-school PE.

Marini, Alexander D. *We Win: A Complete Non-Competitive Physical Education Program for the Entire Family.* Gresham, Ore.: Noble, 1995.

$21.95. Order from Noble Publishing. This is a good guide to physical fitness and family games put out by a Christian publisher. It has an introduction aimed at Christian home schoolers, but the rest of the book is simply about fitness.

Wise, Debra. *Great Big Book of Children's Games.* New York: McGraw-Hill, 2003.

$14.95. Order from any bookstore. Dozens more games.

42

THE LOCAL SCHOOL: DEALING WITH YOUR SCHOOL SYSTEM

Out of sight, out of mind.
—Proverb

Most home schoolers find that the easiest way to deal with their local school system is simply to stay out of sight once the legal formalities have been completed. Many local schools are cooperative and friendly to home schoolers. But we've also heard of instances where local school systems, in cooperation with social-services personnel, have interfered in family life, taken away parental authority, and sometimes even removed children from homes even though no abuse has occurred—only differences in philosophy or opinion over how a child should be educated.

For this reason, many home-schooling parents are wary of using public-school facilities and programs. When a home-schooled child becomes part of a public-school class or activity, he's placed under the jurisdiction of public-school authorities, who may take the opportunity to investigate the home-based part of the child's education.

Be careful, but don't assume the worst about your local schools. Assume what is most frequently the truth—that your local school officials want to make sure that you're providing a quality education at home. The best way to avoid any trouble is to comply fully with all state laws about notification, testing, and record keeping. Although some states offer a "religious exemption" clause for home schoolers—this excuses you from any accountability to the state on the ground that such accountability will violate your conscience—we do not encourage you to take this option unless you join the Home School Legal Defense Association (HSLDA) for legal advice. It is possible that you may have to prove in court that your definition of "religious exemption" is the same as that of your school authorities. (The HSLDA is listed in the Resources, at the end of this chapter.) Comply with the laws as far as your convictions allow.

Don't draw attention to yourself or encourage retaliation by openly attacking and criticizing your local schools. If you want to change your school, you need to keep your child enrolled and bring about change from the inside. But if you've decided to invest your own time in educating your child, make the transition from public school to home school as quietly as possible. Be polite and respectful. Realize that public schools provide a valuable service to the community and to those who can't home-school. Your energies should now go toward creating an excellent education at home and not toward establishing an adversarial relationship with your school system.

School systems in areas where home schooling is common will be well acquainted with the law. In other places, schools may simply be unaware of the legal right to home-school. If your officials protest that you can't home-school, or if they tell you that public-school authority extends to all children of school age whether they're enrolled or not, they may be operating from a position of ignorance. Get a copy of your state law from your state home-school organization, and bring it to all meetings.

School officials need to see that you're using a good curriculum, that you're having your child properly tested, that the child is involved in outside activities, and that you're keeping decent academic records. You'll save yourself trouble if you create a "founding document" for your home school—a brief paper with the following sections:

1. Your educational background and any teaching experience or professional capabilities that support your ability to tutor your child at home.

2. Your philosophy of education—in other words, an explanation of why you're teaching at home. If you're convinced that your child needs a religious education that the school can't provide, say so. If you're working toward academic excellence in a one-on-one, tutorial-based environment, put that down, too. You can use our explanation of the three stages of the trivium in Chapter 2 as part of your educational-philosophy statement.
3. The legal requirements of the state—notification, record keeping, testing—and how you plan to meet them.

Every year, write up a summary of your educational plans, complete with titles of texts. (You may not need this, but if you're questioned, having it on hand will add to your credibility.) You can use the "At a Glance" sections we've provided, which summarize the program of study and the time spent on each subject. Add specific basic text titles, and you have a summary that should satisfy any school system. Be faithful about keeping the notebooks we describe. These prove that your child is doing good, continual work in every subject.

Some school systems happily allow parents to home school, even encouraging home schoolers to take part in the system's programs, labs, and sports. If you want to participate in selected school activities, approach the local school. If no home schooler has ever made such a request, the school might not have a policy in place. Suggest participation on a trial basis. If the arrangement works out, the school will probably create a policy favorable to home schoolers. Be aware, though, that using your public-school system for anything invariably opens the rest of your home program to closer scrutiny.

It's an unfortunate truth that some school systems attempt to exclude parents from the educational process because they view education as the sole responsibility of the state. Other schools may be afflicted by a single zealous social worker out to prove that home-schooled kids are socially deprived. Join your state home-school organization for support and good advice. Parents experienced in home schooling unanimously agree that you should not allow social workers or school officials to tour your home even if they show up at the door. Sometimes, one phone call from a neighbor who notices your kids in the backyard will trigger a social-services visit. Even in states where legal restrictions on home schoolers are relaxed, a home visit from a social worker can land you in a morass of legal problems. You're not legally required to let anyone into your home who doesn't have a search warrant. Furthermore, denying access won't prejudice any legal system against you.

But these situations are rare. In most cases, diplomacy and good record keeping will resolve any difficulties. Collect any favorable newspaper and magazine reports about home schooling, and use them for PR when you talk to your local officials. If you can, get to know your school-board members. And always ask for access as though you're requesting a privilege, not demanding a right.

RESOURCE

Home School Legal Defense Association
P.O. Box 3000
Purcellville, VA 20134
540-338-5600
Fax: 540-338-2733
Web: www.hslda.org
E-mail: info@hslda.org

43

YELLING FOR HELP: TUTORS, ONLINE RESOURCES, CORRESPONDENCE SCHOOLS, COOPERATIVE CLASSES, AND COLLEGES AND UNIVERSITIES

Two heads are better than one.
—Proverb

In the early grades, parents serve as the child's primary teacher. Any literate parent can master the basics of an academic subject well enough to teach it to an elementary or middle-school child.

Parents are accustomed to using private teachers for music, gymnastics, or any other subject that requires a high degree of accomplishment. Upper-level academic subjects are no different. When your home-schooled student develops proficiency in a field of study, you may want to enlist help for further work.

"Outsourcing" is one of the secrets of success for high school at home. Tutors, online services, and correspondence courses all preserve the strengths of home schooling—flexibility, one-on-one attention, expertise above and beyond that permitted by a normal high-school curriculum—while eliminating its one weakness—parental ignorance of the subject at hand. Cooperative and college classes give the student a chance to get used to the classroom environment, while still following a home-based program. And the student also gets a needed break from working with Mom and Dad.

TUTORS

Throughout Parts I through III, we've mentioned the use of a private tutor for certain subjects. You can employ a tutor for one-on-one work in a subject you're not comfortable teaching or simply to give yourself (and the student) a change of pace. Jessie used tutors for high-school math, foreign language, art, and music. She suggests the following for finding tutors and for supervising the work:

- Local colleges are a good source of help. Don't advertise for a tutor. Instead, call the department of the subject you want tutored, and ask for student recommendations. Make sure that the person you speak to (the chairman of the department or the departmental secretary) knows the age of the student you want tutored. Accomplished scholars aren't always good teachers, and you want someone who's patient and comfortable with your child's skill level. Also, ask what the going rate for private tutoring is. Expect to pay an hourly rate of $10.00 for a student to $20.00 or more for a professor. Schedule sessions for once a week, and make sure the tutor gives the child assignments to complete before the next session.
- If you use a college student, make sure your tutor is the same sex as the child. This eliminates the embarrassment factor between child and tutor (especially as the child moves into adolescence).
- Supervise tutorials. Any time a child is in an intimate, one-on-one setting with an older person who has a measure of authority, the potential for abuse exists. Jessie always made sure that tutorials took place in a public setting (the university student center), and she stayed in sight (sitting on the side of the room and catching up on paperwork or reading while the tutorial took place). Don't leave a child at the tutor's house; wait in an adjoining room instead. This provides protection for the student as well as the tutor.

- Private schools are another good source for tutors. Private-school teachers are often happy to supplement their income by tutoring home schoolers. Expect to pay a little more than you would for a college student.
- Junior- and senior-high-school students (recommended by their teachers) are quite capable of tutoring elementary and middle-grade students.
- If you're in an active home-school community, older home schoolers may also be willing to work with younger students. Our advice about supervision still applies.
- Continue to keep an eye on the child's work. You're still responsible for issuing a grade (for high-school students) or for proving to your local school superintendent that reasonable progress has been made in the subject being studied.

ONLINE RESOURCES

In recent years, the availability of online resources has exploded. Online tutorials should never take up the majority of the child's time—limit them to one or two subjects per semester, if possible. But online tutors can be invaluable for Latin, logic, rhetoric, or other subjects that you may have difficulty finding a local tutor for.

Currently, most online classical tutorials for secondary students are Christian-oriented (Christian home schoolers have been on the cutting edge of the classical-education movement). Escondido Tutorial Service (ETS), at www.gbt.org, is one of the best-established classical tutorials on the web. Tutor Fritz Hinrichs offers demanding courses (100 pages of reading per week with e-mailed papers for one great-books tutorials). The tutorial meets for two hours weekly and includes online discussions with other enrolled students. The www.gbt.org website also maintains links to other tutorial sites.

Schola Tutorials, at scholatutorials.com; Talisker Tutorials at www.taliskertutorials.com; and Oxford Tutorial Service at www.oxfordtutorials.com offer tutorials in great books, logic, rhetoric, Latin, and other subjects. Visit the sites for classes, schedules, tutor qualifications, and costs. Online classes are also offered by the Potter's School at www.pottersschool.org.

The Institute for Study of the Liberal Arts and Sciences (ISLAS) is located at www.islas.org. ISLAS is a cooperative project of Scholars' Online Academy (SOLA) and the Catholic school Regina Coeli Academy (RCA). It offers college-prep classes on a number of levels: Scholars' Online Academy and Regina Coeli Online Academy are taught on a high-school/adult level, while the Agnus Dei Junior Program and the Regina Coeli Junior Program are geared for ages ten through thirteen.

Explore the web on your own, and you'll find any number of resources. Try these starting places:

- Our website, www.welltrainedmind.com, supplies articles, links to many other resource sites, and a very active set of message boards with thousands of posts from parents who are home schooling by classical methods.
- A good general-reference classical site is the Perseus Project, designed by the Tufts University classics department: www.perseus .tufts.edu.
- The About.com page homeschooling.about.com includes links to magazines, other home-school websites, publishers, and vendors.
- An extensive home-school website, which includes home schoolers of all persuasions, is Jon's Homeschool Resource Page at www.mid nightbeach.com/hs. If you want to join mailing lists, check out other websites, and generally inform yourself, visit this page.
- The Homeschool Web Ring is a connected map of home-school sites. A web ring directory, pointing you toward sites on topics from education, literature, computing, games, religion, and more, can be found at www.webring.org.
- The best way to find online resources is to surf, using a good browser. If you're new to the Internet, we recommend *The Internet for Dummies*, a good introduction to getting online. If you're already online, visit www.google.com, the best search engine on the web.

We strongly feel that the computer should be a family tool. It's easy to access graphic pornography—even by accident—and online predators often target young users. Put the computer in a family area so that web surfing is open to general view.

CORRESPONDENCE SCHOOLS

A number of universities and private schools offer correspondence courses in dozens of subjects. The advantage of correspondence is that your student gets a detailed outline, course information, step-by-step instruction, and an official grade. The disadvantage is that correspondence courses lock you into inflexible schedules and particular texts. The best way to decide whether you want to use correspondence courses is to call for a number of catalogs and examine each school's philosophy and offerings. A detailed listing is found in the Resources list at the end of this chapter.

COOPERATIVE CLASSES

In many areas, home-school groups have set up cooperative classes taught by parents with particular knowledge or skills. Parents of home schoolers include doctors, lawyers, aerospace engineers, diplomats, and university teachers, and these parents often organize cooperative classes in their areas of expertise. In larger cities, home schoolers have even set up "academies," where students can enroll for one, two, or three courses in exchange for a time donation from student and parent. Contact your local and state home-school organizations, and ask what resources are already in place.

Even if you don't find a formal group, don't overlook the possibility of swapping with another home-school parent. If you were a math major in college but hated grammar, you can probably find a parent with a degree in English but few math skills and teach each other's children in your respective areas of expertise. This works best when the children are of similar age and ability. And if you can make this arrangement with another home-school family you trust, you can reduce the workload for both sets of parents since each of you will be faced with preparing one class rather than two.

COMMUNITY COLLEGES AND LOCAL UNIVERSITIES

Community colleges and university classes are usually open to home schoolers. Community colleges are the easiest to deal with. Just call the Office of the Registrar, and ask about enrolling your high-school student in one or two classes. Universities often offer a "concurrent" program, which allows high-school students to take a class or two per semester for high-school credit. The Registrar will be able to steer you toward the proper contact.

Do remember, though, that high-school students on a college campus are vulnerable—they're younger than the other students and more uncertain. Supervise attendance. You don't have to sit in on the class, but it's probably not a good idea to leave a high-school student on campus for hours alone. Also, try to make an appointment with the professor before classes start so that the student can meet the instructor face to face. This will reduce nervousness and give the instructor a chance to evaluate your student's readiness for college work.

RESOURCES

For publisher and catalog addresses, telephone numbers, and other information, see Sources (pages 751–778). Most books can be obtained from any bookstore or library; where we know of a mail-order option, we have provided it.

Guide to the Internet

Levine, John R., et al. *The Internet for Dummies.* 11th ed. Hoboken, N.J.: For Dummies, 2007.

$21.99. Order through any bookstore. A good guide to all the tasks you'll need to do on the Internet: shopping, joining mailing lists, searching, using your browser properly, and so on.

Correspondence Schools

For a listing of accredited correspondence schools, write the Distance Education and Training Council, 1601 Eighteenth Street, NW, Washington, DC 20009-2529, call 202-234-5100, or visit the council's home page at www.detc.org. We suggest you investigate the following schools; call or write for catalogs. All of them offer courses by correspondence in the K–12 area. Some also offer college-level work.

A Beka Academy
P.O. Box 17600
Pensacola, FL 32522-7750
800-874-3592
www.abekaacademy.org
Conservative Christian, K–12.

BYU Independent Study
206 Harman Continuing Education Building
Provo, UT 84602-1514
800-914-8931
ce.byu.edu/is

The Calvert School
10713 Gilroy Road STE B
Hunt Valley, MD 21031
888-487-4652 or 410-785-3400
www.calvertschool.org
Traditional K–8 correspondence program, academically thorough and rigorous.

Home Study International
12501 Old Columbia Pike
Silver Spring, MD 20914-4437
800-782-4769
www.hsi.edu
Christian orientation.

Indiana University
School of Continuing Studies

Owen Hall, 790 East Kirkwood Avenue
Bloomington, IN 47405-7107
800-334-1011
www.scs.indiana.edu
Ask for their *Homeschooling* brochure.

Keystone National High School
920 Central Road
Bloomsburg, PA 17815
866-376-6160 or 570-784-5220
www.keystonehighschool.com

Laurel Springs School
P.O. Box 1440
Ojai, CA 93024-1440
805-646-2473 or 800-377-5890
www.laurelsprings.com
A well-respected private school, academically rigorous, with a full range of correspondence courses for K–12.

Seton Home School
1350 Progress Drive
Front Royal, VA 22630
540-636-9990
www.setonhome.org
K–12 Catholic correspondence school.

University of Arkansas
Division of Continuing Education
Department of Independent Study
#2 East Center
Fayetteville, AR 72701
800-952-1165
www.uacted.uark.edu

University of Nebraska—Lincoln
Independent Study High School
P.O. Box 888400
Lincoln, NE 68588-8400

402-472-2175 or 866-700-4747
www.nebraskahs.unl.edu

University of Oklahoma High School
Center of Independent and Distance Learning
1600 Jenkins, Room 101
Norman, OK 73072-6507
800-942-5702 or 405-325-1921
http://ouilhs.ou.edu

44

GOING TO COLLEGE: APPLICATIONS FOR HOME SCHOOLERS

We favor well-prepared students wherever they attend school.

—Stanford Admissions Office

The education we describe in Parts I through III is college-preparatory. College isn't for everyone, but a student who plans on a white-collar or intellectual job should go to college. The possession of a college degree has risen in importance over the last decades as the value of a high-school diploma has dropped.

According to the National Center for Home Education, 93 percent of colleges polled in a recent study were willing to accept course descriptions or portfolios instead of a high-school diploma.[1] Some universities will always look at nontraditional work with suspicion; state universities will occasionally take an inflexible stand. But as the home-schooling wave con-

[1]Christopher J. Klicka, *Home Students Excel in College,* rev. ed. (Washington, D.C.: National Center for Home Education, 1998), p. 1.

tinues to swell, more and more colleges are growing accustomed to home-school applications.

Generally, we favor small private schools over large public universities. Although this isn't always financially feasible, we've noticed that home schoolers do better in a more intimate environment in their first two years away from home. Small schools are also more likely than large schools to extend a welcome to home schoolers, with their nontraditional preparation and nonstandardized transcripts. But more and more universities are admitting home schoolers—Stanford and Swarthmore, among many others, now have an admissions procedure geared specifically for home-educated students.

PLANNING FOR COLLEGE

Many parents and students don't think about a high-school program until eighth grade. But if college is a goal for your child, you should begin preparation for a college-track program in middle school (grades 5 and 6). Critical-thinking courses, research projects, elementary Latin, and modern foreign language—all of these are college-readiness courses. Ideally, the college-bound student will begin Algebra I no later than eighth grade in preparation for the SAT and ACT. The minimum math requirement for a college-prep program is Algebra I, completed in ninth grade, and a course in geometry, completed before the PSATs given in the fall of the eleventh-grade year (see Chapter 27 for a full explanation). Latin increases vocabulary scores and general reading and grammar skills. Since students who do well on the SATs have read widely for the previous ten years, the middle-grade student should develop the habit of reading, rather than constantly watching TV or playing computer games.

Although the program outlined in Part III should be more than adequate for any set of college admission requirements, you should still get a catalog from prospective colleges before ninth grade in order to find out their requirements and to make sure that your high-school program includes these courses.

Jessie suggests the following timetable for parents and students thinking of college:

Grades 5–6	Plan a math sequence that will finish up Algebra II and geometry by PSAT time. Also plan to complete the *Vocabulary from Classical Roots* series, the courses in logic, and at least two years of Latin before taking the PSAT.
Grades 7–8	Start writing for college catalogs to find out what high-school requirements you must fulfill in grades 9–12. (See "Choosing a College," page 699.)
Grade 9	Ask prospective colleges what form they prefer home-school admissions to take—a transcript, a portfolio, and so forth. That way, you can start to keep your high-school records in an orderly manner. If you're not sure, just keep good records so that you can be flexible when application time comes. *Keep a transcript, even if your colleges don't require it.* You never know when you might need one.
Grade 10	Find out from a local public- or private-school guidance counselor when the PSAT will be given (in the fall of the eleventh-grade year) and how to preregister. You can take the PSAT any time from eighth grade on and as many times as you wish. But if you're interested in a National Merit scholarship, take it only once—in the eleventh-grade year. Start working daily through an SAT preparation guide as though you were taking an extra course.
Grade 11	Register for the SAT, which will be taken in the fall of the twelfth-grade year. Continue working daily through the SAT preparation guide. Visit colleges, and zero in on choices. Call admissions offices; find out when they start taking applications for early decision and regular admissions, and how to apply for financial aid. Early applications produce better aid than last-minute submissions. Investigate taking classes for college credit. Some colleges allow students who take college courses during their senior year to apply these credits to the freshman year. Also, these classes prove that you're capable of doing college work.
Grade 12	Take the SATs. Complete the application forms for the colleges of your choice. Submit these forms and the financial-aid forms as soon as possible. If the college con-

ducts interviews, practice role-play interviews. Use a guide to job interviews to check on basic skills (dress nicely, make eye contact, shake hands).

CHOOSING A COLLEGE

After sending her own children to college—and after years of counseling other home schoolers—Jessie strongly advises parents to exercise their judgment (and economic leverage) to steer high-school students away from making college decisions that might sabotage their mental, physical, social, or spiritual health. Your shy eleventh grader may think that he wants to live in a freshman dorm at a 20,000-student state university. But if you believe he should spend two years at a smaller school and then transfer, limit the child's options to those that are acceptable to you. One of the saddest statements we ever heard was from a mother who told Jessie, "I spent forty thousand dollars to ruin my daughter's life." She had let her daughter make all the choices about college, despite serious misgivings.

Over the last fifteen years, Jessie has observed that home-schooled students who flourish both academically and personally keep close ties with family, make dear and valuable friends, and adjust well to the demands of college. These students invariably attend small colleges that have a moral and religious climate similar to that found at home. Many large universities have big, unrestricted dormitories, where bedlam reigns and there is no check on adolescent behavior. Your student may be both mature and responsible. But if he's forced to live on a floor filled with noisy, immature students who stay up until 2:00 A.M. dropping firecrackers down the toilets or having all-night concerts in the hall (as in the freshman dorm that Susan's brother lived in), he probably won't flourish.

Don't let financial need scare you off. Private universities often have better financial-aid packages than large state universities. Small religious schools can dig up funds for worthy students from unexpected places. And the student who cannot complete a desired major at a small school can always transfer after the sophomore year. If you think this might be the way to go, call the college that the student is thinking of transferring to, and find out which courses will transfer.

Start the college search by talking to friends, relatives, and other home schoolers about college experiences, both positive and negative. Consult the most recent guides to colleges (see Resources at the end of the chapter) to narrow your search to the colleges with the academic specialties, geographic location, and campus climate that you're looking for.

Write to the National Center for Home Education, P.O. Box 3000, Purcellville, VA 20134, or visit their website at http://nche.hslda.org and ask for the following: the list of colleges that have accepted home schoolers (there were 698 on the most recent list, including Ivy League schools) and the brochure *Home Students Excel in College* by Christopher J. Klicka, which details various admissions procedures and lists colleges that actively recruit home schoolers.

For a full list of colleges that have accepted home-schooled students, along with links to college home pages, visit Karl Bunday's School Is Dead, Learn in Freedom site at learninfreedom.org. Since Bunday is generally anti-institutional, his site appears to encourage its audience not to go to college at all. But the list and links are invaluable.

THE APPLICATION PROCESS

Some college admissions officers aren't familiar with home schooling. Others actively recruit home-educated students because of their excellent past performance. So contact the admissions office of each prospective school. Some want transcripts; others ask for a listing of courses, projects, and books read; still others will examine a complete portfolio. Find out whether financial aid requires a diploma or GED (financial-aid forms and admissions applications generally go to two different offices). It's always good to take at least two subject tests in addition to the SAT, especially if the student tests well.

According to the College Board, a transcript isn't necessary for college admissions. Nevertheless, many of the college admissions officers we spoke to were overworked and didn't want to plow through portfolios. "Send us a standard transcript form," one admissions office told us. So take that transcript seriously. A good transcript plus standardized scores will serve as the foundation of your college application.

An application will give you room to describe your areas of interest, extracurricular activities, and any special research projects you've done.

Maximize your application by using the lines set aside for interests, activities, and clubs to emphasize your language accomplishments and great-books studies. Make sure you describe the junior and senior thesis projects, which will set you apart from most high-school students. List all community-service projects—anything you've volunteered for that benefits others.

Many colleges have an "early decision" process where you agree to enroll in that college if you're accepted. You would then go ahead and finish your senior year of high school with an assured fall acceptance. If you're interested in early decision, make sure you ask about the deadline (it differs from the regular deadline).

If you're interested in college sports, call the Home School Legal Defense Association, and ask for the packet that assists home schoolers in validating their completion of all initial eligibility requirements for the National Collegiate Athletic Association.

THE PORTFOLIO

If the college agrees to look at a portfolio (and many do), this will be your most persuasive tool.

What should you include in your portfolio?

1. A narrative description of your high-school studies. This is the place to explain your great-books program.
2. A list of all significant books read (from about seventh grade on).
3. At least one writing sample.
4. A description of any academic contests and honors.
5. Descriptions of any apprenticeships, interesting work experiences, and internships.
6. A brief description of any special area of expertise.

ONE SUCCESSFUL APPLICATION

Home schooler Peggy Ahern's daughter was admitted to an Ivy League college. As well as the standard application, admissions essay, and SAT scores (including four SAT II subject-area tests), Peggy and her daughter submitted a thirty-two-page portfolio with the following eight sections:

1. *School Philosophy* A one-page statement written by Peggy about why she taught her daughter at home, including her summary of their use of the trivium.
2. *Character Profile* A brief assessment written by Peggy, using comments from teachers, friends, relatives, and siblings.
3. *Student Assessment of Home Schooling* A one-page critique written by Peggy's daughter of her home-school experience, including both positives and negatives.
4. *Curriculum Description* A narrative description of each course done in high school, written by Peggy. According to Peggy, this turned out to be thirteen pages long—much longer than necessary for most home schoolers.
5. *Teacher Evaluations* Copies of evaluations given to Peggy by some of her daughter's other tutors.
6. *Sample Papers* Three papers written by Peggy's daughter. One is sufficient for most portfolios.
7. *Reading List* All the books read by Peggy's daughter since eighth grade.
8. *Music Achievement* Details of competitions, master classes, recitals, and a tape. You could use this section for any major achievement.

Although Peggy and her daughter were successful in their Ivy League applications, Peggy isn't sure that a portfolio of this length will continue to be read by admissions officers—particularly if home-school applications continue to rise. We suggest that you follow Peggy's pattern, but make each section as brief as possible. And always call first to make sure that a portfolio submission is acceptable and what length is preferred.

Peggy adds these words on college preparation:

> I realized that outside substantiation of her work was going to be particularly helpful when it came time to put together that transcript, and that good teacher recommendations would be invaluable. So for all four years, I actively sought out teachers for at least one or two subjects each year. I never found any locally, but did find some through correspondence and then later on through the internet, all of whom developed enough of a relationship with her that they could have written recommendations. I

think it is very wise for homeschoolers to actively seek out and cultivate relationships with a few teachers. Further, if possible, I would recommend seeking out college-level teachers and courses for the student, even if it is not-for-credit, for several reasons:

1) A teacher who can vouch for the student's ability to handle college level work and to contribute in a meaningful way to class discussion will go a long way toward allaying certain admissions concerns.

2) A teacher who has been a part of the collegiate community will hopefully have a good idea of what sort of issues are typically addressed in these recommendations, how they're written and so forth, and therefore will do an effective job of it.

By the end of her four years, my daughter had a number of choices as to from whom she would seek her two recommendations. She and I really strategized at this point. We knew that any of these teachers would highly recommend her. But several of them had stand-out writing skills as well as long-term experience in higher education, and we knew that their high recommendations would likely be far more effective than those of her other options. I think it is a fair conclusion that these two recommendations played a very major role in her acceptance.

TRANSCRIPT HELP

Keeping a transcript is simply a matter of entering the subjects studied each semester, along with a final grade, onto a transcript form. However, since this is an important piece of paper, many parents feel the need for some extra help in preparing the form properly. The cassette tape/booklet set "Creating Transcripts and Issuing Diplomas: What Every Parent Should Know," by Inge P. Cannon, goes along with the TranscriptPro software recommended in Chapter 39. This set will guide you through the process of transcript creation.

A WORD ABOUT EARLY ADMISSIONS

Many home schoolers finish their high-school studies early. It's been our experience that students are better off spending the extra time before college by studying and reading while working at an internship, apprenticeship, or other meaningful job. Maturity can't be forced—students who go to college early are more likely to flounder socially, academically, or spiritually. There's no rush. So stay at home. Read, work, write, study, enjoy life. And go to college with everyone else your age. You'll be that much better prepared.

RESOURCES

For publisher and catalog addresses, telephone numbers, and other information, see *Sources (pages 751–778).* *Most books can be obtained from any bookstore or library; where we know of a mail-order option, we have provided it. College guides are listed first, followed by guides to the application procedure itself.*

College Guides

Barron's Profiles of American Colleges. Hauppauge, N.Y.: Barron's Educational Series.

Book and CD. Colleges organized by geography (Northeast, Southeast, and so forth). Regularly revised.

CollegeConfidential.com.

A web source for finding college rankings, admissions guidelines, reviews of books, information about financial aid, and more.

The College Board College Handbook. New York: College Board.

Includes admission policies, requirements, and deadlines; ACT and SAT test dates; enrollment figures and majors; campus life, including sports and student services; and more. Updated annually.

Fiske, Edward B. *The Fiske Guide to Colleges.* Naperville, Ill.: Sourcebooks, Inc.

According to *USA Today*, it's "the best college guide you can buy." Updated annually.

Petersons.com

An online source for test preparation information, financial aid updates, and essay editing; here you can pay tutors to help you revise admissions essays, resumes, and personal statements.

Peterson's Competitive Colleges. Princeton, N.J.: Peterson's.

This guide lists colleges that admit high achievers, based largely on SAT scores and grades. Regularly revised.

Peterson's Two-Year Colleges. Four-Year Colleges. Book and CD-ROM.

Good standard annual guide to colleges. The CD-ROM makes it possible to search the information electronically.

Guides to Application Procedures

Cannon, Inge. *TranscriptPro Home School Transcript Generator.* Taylors, S.C.: Education+Plus.

$49.00. Order from Education+Plus. Software to produce personalized transcripts.

Creating Your High School Portfolio, 2d ed. Indianapolis, Id.: Jist Works, 2003.

$8.95. Order from any bookstore or from Rainbow Resource. A useful workbook that leads students through many of the steps involved in writing essays, choosing a major, and making up a resume.

Gelb, Alan. *Conquering the College Admissions Essay in 10 Steps: Crafting a Winning Personal Statement.* Berkeley, Calif.: Ten Speed Press, 2008.

Metcalfe, Linda. *How to Say It to Get into the College of Your Choice: Application, Essay, and Interview Strategies to Get You the Big Envelope.* Upper Saddle River, N.J.: Prentice Hall, 2007.

$15.95. Order from any bookstore. The problem with most books about college applications—including this one—is that they cultivate an unnecessary sense of panic; getting into any particular college is partly (sometimes almost entirely) a matter of luck, and it is a huge mistake to spend too much time fretting and planning instead of learning. However, there are good tips in this book. Just don't get sucked into the panic.

45

WORKING: APPRENTICESHIPS AND OTHER JOBS

Employment is nature's physician, and is essential to human happiness.
—Galen

Because of their flexibility of schedule, home-educated students have more opportunity to work at meaningful jobs. They're not limited to the typical after-school and summer routine of fast-food and retail service.

We encourage you to think of high-school employment not as jobs, but as apprenticeships—preparation for a career. If financial pressures allow, it's always better for a student to take a low-paying or nonpaying apprenticeship or internship that gives her training and experience in important job skills than for her to make more money waiting tables. The classical approach to education emphasizes long-range goals over short-term satisfactions. The student who is so busy making money that she can't prepare for worthwhile work as an adult is substituting quick pleasure for long-term gain.

Of course, many students need to make money for college. But if you can involve your child in training and apprenticeship work early, you can improve the money-making skills she'll need for college summers. The student who takes an unpaid position at a computer firm, learning consulting, will make much more money in the summer after her freshman year than the student who works a paying retail job in high school.

Be creative when looking for job opportunities. Network with friends and relatives. Do you know a computer consultant, a newspaper editor, or an electrician? Ask whether your teen can do a six-week internship to learn about the business. When the internship is over, if the student has an interest, ask whether she can stay for three more months. If she becomes substantially more skilled and begins to contribute to the business, that's the time to broach the subject of pay.

Even before beginning this process, encourage your young teen to ask questions about the jobs that relatives and neighbors have. What do you like about your work? What do you dislike? What's the most important skill you have? What skills do you wish you had? How did you get this job? What preparation would I need to get it? What's your daily schedule like? These questions will help the thirteen or fourteen year old begin to think of her own interests and skills in terms of employment.

Also assign the fourteen or fifteen year old regular reading in the career and employment books written for young people. Ask your local librarian to guide you toward career books for the appropriate age. Reading through these books now, before work has become a pressing issue for the student, makes career planning a fun exercise in thinking through possibilities.

For older teens, look for series such as Careers in Focus and Career Opportunities. Most teens don't have any idea of the variety of jobs that are available. The classic job-hunter's manual *What Color Is Your Parachute? A Practical Manual for Job Hunters and Career Changers,* by Richard Bolles, has sections on developing interests, looking for specific jobs, interviews, and more. Your library will also have the most recent guides to internships for junior- and senior-high-school students.

Every high-school student should also spend some time reading through newspaper and magazine want ads. These provide a valuable look at the sorts of job that are available and the qualifications needed to land them.

A crucial part of skill development is learning to do home chores responsibly. Prepare your student for successful internships and apprenticeships by assigning regular work at home and allowing her to work for neighbors and friends as soon as you feel that she's mature enough to do a good job.

Volunteer work is also important. It develops skills and experience, and often opens the door to paid jobs later on.

If your high-school senior has no particular interest in a field of study and no burning career plans, don't push her straight into college. Let her take a year or two off to work. College will still be there when she's ready to go. And she may discover, through an apprenticeship or internship, a career that doesn't require a college degree.

RESOURCES

For publisher and catalog addresses, telephone numbers, and other information, see Sources (pages 751–778). Most books can be obtained from any bookstore or library; where we know of a mail-order option, we have provided it.

Bolles, Richard. *What Color Is Your Parachute? 2008: A Practical Manual for Job Hunters and Career Changers.* Berkeley, Calif.: Ten Speed Press, 2007.
Directed at adults and older teens. One of the most popular resources for job-seekers.

———. *What Color Is Your Parachute for Teens: Discovering Yourself, Defining Your Future.* Berkeley, Calif.: Ten Speed Press, 2006.

Career Opportunities in . . . series. New York: McGraw-Hill.
Each book describes a number of career paths open to students who have particular skills.

Ferguson's Careers in Focus series. Chicago, Ill.: Ferguson Publishing.
A whole range of books, each describing the aspects of a single career.

Sher, Barbara. *I Could Do Anything if I Only Knew What It Was: How to Discover What You Really Want and How to Get It.* New York: Dell, 1995.
Written for adults, but helpful for older teens who are beginning to think through their options.

46

MORE STUFF: THE ANNOTATED CATALOG LIST

Of the making of many books, there is no end.
—Ecclesiastes

When you start to home-educate, you'll order a book or two. You'll get a catalog, and then another, and then another. Soon you'll have a stack of resource catalogs for home schoolers as high as your table. Go to a state home-education conference, and you'll find yourself surrounded by books, materials, aids, curricula, learning guides, posters, software, supplies, and so forth.

In this chapter, we've listed some of our favorite catalogs and resources. If you're thinking about home schooling, start by calling and asking for all these catalogs. You'll be surprised to find how wide your options are.

Enjoy exploring these catalogs. Use them as guides to books you might want to check out of your local library (yes, we know that's not what they're meant for, but who can afford all those books?). Order what will suit your family and your budget, and make the learning-at-home experience as rich as possible.

GENERAL

American Home-School Publishing, P.O. Box 570, Cameron, MO 64429; call 800-684-2121; www.ahsp.com; e-mail booklovers@ahsp.com.

History, Latin, Greek, and reading resources.

Book Peddler, P.O. Box 1960, Elyria, OH 44036-1960; call 440-284-6654 or 800-928-1760 (orders only); fax 440-323-9494; www.bookpeddler.us.

A wide selection of literature, history, and home-school-planning resources, all at a discount.

Children's Books, P.O. Box 239, Greer, SC 29652; call 800-344-3198 (orders only) or 864-968-0392 (questions about orders); www.homeschooldiscount products.com.

A wide selection of home-school resources.

Rainbow Resource Center, Route 1 Box 159A, 50 North 500 East Road, Toulon, IL 61483; call 309-695-3200 or 888-841-3456; fax 800-705-8809; www.rainbowresource.com.

A home business that hit the big time. The catalog has everything you need—books, resources, games, and more—with a huge art section. All the selections are described in detail by home schoolers, and all books are discounted. A must-have.

Timberdoodle. 1510 E. Spencer Lake Road, Shelton, WA 98584; call 800-478-0672 or 360-426-0673; fax 360-427-5625; www.timberdoodle.com.

Well-laid out site and catalog with wonderful resources across the curriculum; Timberdoodle also carries a whole range of learning and life-skills materials for autistic students (timberdoodleautismcenter.com) and has trained many employees to help parents select curricula for these special children.

Tree of Life, 106 Main Street, Suite 518, Houlton, ME 04730-9001; Canadian address, 443 Weston Road, Weston, New Brunswick E7K 1B1; call 506-328-6781; fax 506-328-9506; www.treeoflifeathome.com.

A Canadian-based supplier of classical resources.

ELEMENTARY GRADES

Gryphon House, Inc., P.O. Box 207, Beltsville, MD 20704-0207; 800-638-0928; fax 301-595-0051; www.ghbooks.com.

A small catalog full of hands-on, exploration-based science, art, and more. For parents and young children.

HISTORY

Greenleaf Press Catalog, Rob and Cyndy Shearer, 3761 Highway 109N, Lebanon, TN 37087; call 615-449-1617 or 800-311-1508 (orders only); fax 615-449-4018; www.greenleafpress.com.

History resources and history-project stuff—models, coloring books, and more.

Peace Hill Press: Products for a Well-Trained Mind, 18021 The Glebe Lane, Charles City, VA 23030; call 877-322-3445 or 804-829-5043; www.peacehillpress.com.

Our own classical-history company.

CLASSICS, LATIN, LOGIC

The Critical Thinking Company (formerly Critical Thinking Books and Software), P.O. Box 1610, Seaside, CA 93955-1610 call 800-458-4849; www.criticalthinking.com.

Not only logic puzzles, but critical-thinking workbooks for every area of the curriculum. We particularly like the history-based workbooks (the science and math ones are okay, but not all that important).

Memoria Press, 4605 Poplar Level Rd., Louisville, KY 40213; call 877-862-1097 or 502-966-9115; www.memoriapress.com.

A growing company with well-designed language and logic resources.

SHAKESPEARE

The Writing Company, Shakespeare catalog, 10200 Jefferson Boulevard, Room K4, P.O. Box 802, Culver City, CA 90232-0802; call 310-839-2436 or 800-421-4246; fax 310-839-2249; www.writingco.com/shakespeare.

Contains movies, the Oxford series we recommend for student use, Advanced Placement course material, background information, everything you'll need.

LANGUAGE: READING, WRITING, GRAMMAR, AND SO FORTH

Blackstone Audiobooks Catalog, P.O. Box 969, Ashland, OR 97520; call 800-729-2665; www.blackstoneaudio.com.

Has every unabridged book-on-tape you'll ever need plus a rental program. An invaluable language development tool. Everything from Homer to Primary Colors.

Greathall Productions, P.O. Box 5061, Charlottesville, VA 22905-5061; call 800-477-6234; fax 434-296-4490; www.greathall.com.

Sells story tapes from Jim Weiss, the award-winning storyteller of classic tales.

Perfection Learning Corporation Books Catalog, Covercraft & Paperback, PreK-8; 1000 North Second Avenue, P.O. Box 500, Logan, IA 51546-1099; call 800-831-4190; fax 800-543-2745; www.perfectionlearning.com.

Hundreds of affordable literature titles for kids.

Zaner-Bloser, 1201 Dublin Road, Columbus, OH 43215-1026; call 800-421-3018; www.zaner-bloser.com

Essential for handwriting and penmanship.

SCIENCE

Carolina Biological Supply Company, 2700 York Road, Burlington, NC 27125; U.S. customers call 800-334-5551; U.S. customers fax 800-222-7112; Canadian customers call 800-387-2474; Canadian customers fax 800-374-6714; international customers call 336-584-0381; www.carolina.com.

An overwhelming 1,200-page catalog of supplies for biology, physics, chemistry, mathematics, earth science, and space science for K–12. You can get every possible dissection specimen, already dead and pickled in formaldehyde. Some chemicals and resources are sold only in class-sized lots; buy those from Science Supplies (see below). A smaller K–6 catalog is free and contains 134 pages of activities, materials, kits, models, projects, and equipment for all branches of elementary science.

ETA/Cuisenaire: Materials for Learning Math and Science, 500 Greenview Court, Vernon Hills, IL 60061; call 800-445-5985 or 847-816-5050; fax 800-875-9643 or 847-816-5066; www.etacuisenaire.com.

Hands-on resources for grades K–9. Science kits and manipulatives from a well-respected company; good for earth science, physics, and life science.

Delta Education Hands-On Science, 80 Northwest Boulevard, P.O. Box 3000, Nashau, NH 03061-3000; call 800-442-5444 or 800-258-1302; fax 800-232-9560; international customers call 603-579-3454; international customers fax 603-886-4632; www.delta-education.com.

Good physics and astronomy projects, labs, and experiment kits for elementary and middle school. Classroom-oriented so some of the equipment is expensive.

Home Training Tools, 665 Carbon Street, Billings, MT 59102; call 800-860-6272; fax 888-860-2344; www.hometrainingtools.com.

Hands-on resources and kits from popular curriculum suppliers; everything from rocks to robots. For grades K–12.

Pitsco and Lego Dacta catalog, Box 1707, Pittsburg, KS 66762; call 800-362-4308; www.legoeducation.com.

A necessary catalog full of physics and engineering materials, K–12. We really like the Lego machine sets.

Tobin's Lab, P.O. Box 725, Culpeper, VA 22701; call 540-829-6906; www.tobinslab.com.

The best astronomy and rocket-construction resource around. Also good biology projects, lots of books, posters, and kits.

MATHEMATICS

Activity Resources Catalog, 20655 Hathaway Avenue, Hayward, CA 94541; call 510-782-1300; www.activityresources.com.

All manipulatives, math aids, and games for K–8; heavier on visual aids than hands-on.

Delta Education Hands-On Math, 80 Northwest Boulevard, P.O. Box 3000, Nashau, NH 03061-3000; call 800-442-5444 or 800-258-1302; fax 800-282-9560; International customers call 603-579-3454; international customers fax 603-886-4632; www.delta-education.com.

The best math manipulatives around, including the ones you'll want for primary Saxon math.

USED-CURRICULA AND -BOOK VENDORS

The Back Pack, P.O. Box 125, Ernul, NC 28527; call or fax 252-244-0728; www.thebackpack.com.

A good way to save money and still build your home library.

Laurelwood Books, 1639 Ebenezer Road, Bluemont, VT 20135; call 540-554-2670; fax 540-554-2938; www.laurelwoodbooks.com.

An extensive collection of reasonably priced used books, along with new books popular with homeschoolers.

47

THE FINAL WORD: STARTING IN THE MIDDLE

Finally, what if you're starting to home-educate a third grader or fifth grader or tenth grader? Generally speaking, it's better to go quickly through foundational materials (such as basic grammar, pre-algebra, or beginning logic) than to start using material that will frustrate a student. The following are some general guidelines to help you find your child's place in the classical curriculum. Check the Resources section of the appropriate chapters for information on the teaching/learning apparatuses mentioned here. Throughout this book, we have given suggestions for how to start history, science, languages, and other subjects "in the middle." Refer to each chapter for these detailed directions. In addition, keep the following principles in mind:

Reading — If a student is having difficulty reading, *start at the beginning*. Use *The Ordinary Parent's Guide to Teaching Reading* or another beginning primer to review basic phonetic reading. When it comes to reading, many children stumble because they've never been taught the principles of phonics. As a matter of fact, phonics is often used remedially even by those school systems that take a whole-language approach in the classroom. Jessie has done beginning phonics with eighth graders; the earlier pages are easy and build confidence, while the later pages improve both reading and spelling skills. After finishing phonics, the student should continue with *Spelling Workout B* or *C*.

Spelling Any student who begins spelling in fourth grade or sooner should start with *Spelling Workout B*. Fifth or sixth graders can begin with *Spelling Workout C*. Seventh graders and older can go straight into *Spelling Workout D* and continue from there.

Grammar Most grammar programs can be begun on grade level; the texts we recommend all start with a detailed review of material that should have been learned in previous years.

Writing An older student who begins the Writing Strands program should start with book 4. This will be easy, but he can progress quickly to the more difficult material. Book 4 teaches basic paragraph construction skills, which the program then builds upon. Other programs can be started on grade level.

Vocabulary Always start with the first of the *Vocabulary from Classical Roots* series, no matter how old the student is.

Math If you know your child's grade level, the chapters on mathematics should give you the information you need to select a text. If you're not sure what level your child is working on, most programs offer a diagnostic test.

Logic Always begin the Canon Press logic program with the first book. With an older student (grade 10 or above), you can skip Critical Thinking Press's warm-up books and go straight to *Traditional Logic or The Art of Argument*.

Languages Unless a student has a particular interest in a modern language, we always recommend doing at least a year of Latin as the first foreign language. It greatly simplifies

	the learning of other languages.
History	Begin history with whichever year you please. Use whichever resources are age-appropriate, and continue forward chronologically from that point. See Chapters 7 and 16 for more details.
Science	Although the science sequence we suggest (biology, earth science/astronomy, chemistry, physics) meshes nicely with the four-year history cycle, it isn't vital that you follow this order. You can choose whichever science fits into your curriculum.
Great books	As with history, begin the great-books curriculum in any year and progress up to the present. See Chapter 26.
Research paper	Do *not* begin a research paper with a student who isn't ready. Before doing the research paper, the student should complete at least a year of systematic grammar and short writing assignments; he should also be comfortable with the outlining process. It's fine to wait until eleventh (or even twelfth) grade for the research paper, if you have catch-up work to do.

What if you're home-schooling two children or more? We suggest that you keep each child doing individual, grade-level work in mathematics, grammar, writing, spelling, and vocabulary. The content areas—history, science, reading—can be done simultaneously with children of different ages. If you have a fifth grader and an eighth grader, don't drive yourself insane by doing ancient history, ancient readings, modern history, modern readings, biology, and physics. Synchronize their schedules so that both students are doing ancient history, ancient readings, and biology. You'll still have to get two sets of books, each differing in complexity and reading level, but at least you'll be covering the same basic material with each child. The same is true of a first grader and a third grader, or a seventh grader and a ninth grader. Require more writing, a higher level of difficulty in reading and experimentation, and more complex outlines from the older student. If one student goes through the four-year history cycle two and a quarter times, while the other goes through it three times, it will affect neither their academic achievement nor the quality of their lives.

APPENDICES

APPENDIX 1

TAKING AN ORAL HISTORY

This is a simplified version of the "Oral History Interview Outline" developed by Judith Ledbetter for the Charles City County Historical Society. Thanks to them for their help.

1. Record the name of the interviewer, the date, the time, and the place of the interview.
2. Record the name, and the general description of the interview subject.
3. When and where were you born?
   a. Names of parents, parents' occupations.
   b. Siblings?
   c. Birth assisted by doctor or midwife?
4. What are your earliest memories about food and meals?
5. What do you remember about school?

a. Transportation to school.
b. School buildings.
c. Subjects taught.
d. Teachers.
e. Discipline, sports, extracurricular activities.

6. How did you spend time outside of school? What kinds of games did you play? What chores did you do?
7. Were you sick in childhood? What illnesses did you have? Who was your doctor, and what was he like?
8. How did you travel (foot, horse, wagon, auto, bus, train, airplane)?
9. Tell me about holidays when you were small—birthdays, Christmas, Thanksgiving. Did your family have any special days?
10. What religion did your family observe? How did you observe it?
11. Do you remember going fishing/hunting, farming, gardening, or getting food in other ways?
12. What stores were near you? What were post offices like? How about banks? Where did people go for entertainment?
13. What stories do you remember your parents, grandparents, or other elderly persons telling?
    a. Slavery, Civil War, Reconstruction.
    b. Bootleggers, stills, illegal activities, Prohibition.
    c. Woman's suffrage.
    d. World War I.
    e. The flu epidemic of 1917–1918.
    f. Ghosts.
    g. Sensational crimes (lynchings, murders, fires, etc.).
    h. Racial relations—white/black, white/Indian, black/Indian, etc.
14. What do you remember about the Great Depression?
15. What do you remember about segregation in schools and other public places? How about other kinds of discrimination?
16. Do you remember when electricity/telephone service first came to your house?
17. What do you remember about World War II?
    a. Service in the armed forces.
    b. Friends or relatives who lost lives.
    c. Rationing.
    d. Precautions.

   e. News stories about the war.
   f. Letters to and from home.
18. When did you get married? What was your courtship like? How was it different from modern traditions?
19. When were your children born? Where? Were they born in a hospital or at home?
20. What do you remember about the Korean conflict? Were you affected by it?
21. What do you remember about the Civil Rights movement?
    a. *Brown v. Board of Education.*
    b. Passage of the Voting Rights Act.
    c. Passage of the Fair Housing Act.
    d. The death of Martin Luther King, Jr.
22. What do you remember about the assassination of President Kennedy?
23. What do you remember about the Vietnam War? Did it have an effect on your hometown?
24. Could you describe the jobs you've held during your lifetime—your responsibilities, skills, the working conditions, the pay and benefits?
25. How has life changed the most since you were a child?

APPENDIX 2

HOME-EDUCATION ORGANIZATIONS

UNITED STATES: STATE ORGANIZATIONS

Many of these are Christian in orientation. Where possible we have also listed nonsectarian state organizations, but not every state has one. (They also tend to be much smaller.) Although we have tried to keep this list up to date, phone numbers change and groups disband. Because most of these groups are run by volunteer parents, many have a "home office" in someone's kitchen and do not publish phone numbers; visit the group's website and use the "Contact" button or e-mail address to ask for information.

Alabama
Christian Home Education Fellowship of Alabama
P.O. Box 20208
Montgomery, AL 36120
334-288-7229
www.chefofalabama.org

Alaska
Alaska Private and Home Educator's Association
P.O. Box 14764
Anchorage, AK 99514
907-376-9382
www.aphea.org

Arizona
Arizona Families for Home Education
P.O. Box 2035
Chandler, AZ 85244-2035
602-235-2673
www.afhe.org

Eastside Explorers
homeschool-life.com/az/eastsideexplorers

Arkansas
Home Educators of Arkansas
P.O. Box 192455
Little Rock, AR 72219
www.geocities.com/heartland/garden/4555/hear.html

Live and Learn
www.geocities.com/live-and-learn.geo

California
Christian Home Educators Association of California
P.O. Box 2009
Norwalk, CA 90651-2009
562-864-2432
www.cheaofca.org

Homeschool Association of California
P.O. Box 77873
Corona, CA 92877-0128
888-472-4440
www.hsc.org

Colorado

Christian Home Educators of Colorado
10431 South Parker Road
Parker, CO 80134
877-842-2432
www.chec.org

Secular Homeschool Support Group
719-572-5645
shssg.com

Connecticut

The Education Association of Christian Homeschoolers of Connecticut
10 Mooschorn Road
West Granby, CT 06090
863-435-2890
www.teachct.org

Delaware

Delaware Home Education Association
P.O. Box 268
Hartly, DE 19953
www.dheaonline.org

Florida

Florida Parent-Educators Association
www.fpea.com
800-ASK-FPEA

Georgia

Georgia Home Education Association

141 Massengale Road
Brooks, GA 30205
770-461-3657
www.ghea.org

Home Education Information Resource
P.O. Box 1128
Tucker, GA 30085-1128
www.heir.org

Hawaii

Christian Home Educators of Hawaii
344 Kaumakani Street
Honolulu, HI 96825

Hawaii Homeschool Association
P.O. Box 970811
Waipahu, HI 06797
www.hawaiihomeschoolassociation.org

Idaho

Christian Homeschoolers of Idaho State
P.O. Box 45062
Boise, ID 83711
208-424-6685
www.chois.org

Southeast Idaho Homeschool Association
www.eyedocgreg.com/homeschool

Illinois

Grassroots Homeschoolers
grassrootshomeschoolers.com

Illinois Christian Home Educators
P.O. Box 307
Russell, IL 60075-0307
847-603-1259
www.iche.org

Indiana

Indiana Association of Home Educators
320 East Main Street
Greenfield, IN 46140
317-467-6244
www.inhomeeducators.org

Life Education and Resource Network
P.O. Box 6351
Bloomington, IN 47407-6351
www.bloomington.in.us/~learn

Iowa

Network of Iowa Christian Home Educators
Box 158
Dexter, IA 50070
800-723-0438 (in Iowa)
515-830-1614 (all other areas)
www.the-niche.org

Kansas

Christian Home Educators Confederation of Kansas
P.O. Box 1332
Topeka, KS 66601
913-397-9506
www.kansashomeschool.org

Kentucky

Christian Home Educators of Kentucky
691 Howardstown Road
Hodgenville, KY 42748
270-358-9270
www.chek.org

Louisiana

Christian Home Educators Fellowship of Louisiana
P.O. Box 226
Maurice, LA 70555

888-876-CHEF
www.chefofla.org

Louisiana Home Education Network
PMB 700
602 West Prien Lake Road
Lake Charles, LA 70601
www.la-home-education.com

Maine

Homeschoolers of Maine
P.O. Box 159
Camden, ME 04843-0159
207-763-2880
www.homeschoolersofmaine.org/index.htm

Maine Home Education Association
www.geocities.com/mainehomeed

Maryland

Maryland Association of Christian Home Educators
P.O. Box 417
Clarksburg, MD 20871
301-607-4284
www.machemd.org

Maryland Home Education Association
9085 Flamepool Way
Columbia, MD 21045
410-730-0073
www.MHEA.com (Address is case-sensitive.)

Massachusetts

Massachusetts Homeschool Organization of Parent Educators
46 South Road
Holden, MA 01520
508-829-0973
www.masshope.org

Michigan
Information Network for Christian Homes
4934 Cannonsburg Road
Belmont, MI 49306-9614
616-874-5656
www.inch.org

Minnesota
Minnesota Association of Christian Home Educators
P.O. Box 32308
Fridley, MN 55432
763-717-9070 (metro area), 866-717-9070 (outside metro area)
www.mache.org

Minnesota Homeschoolers' Alliance
P.O. Box 40486
St. Paul, MN 55104
612-288-9662 or 1-888-346-7622
www.homeschoolers.org

Mississippi
Mississippi Home Educator's Association
662-494-1999
www.mhea.net

Missouri
Missouri Association of Teaching Christian Homes
www.match-inc.org

Montana
Montana Coalition of Home Educators
Box 43
Gallatin Gateway, MT 59730
www.mtche.org

Nebraska
Nebraska Christian Home Educators Association

P.O. Box 57041
Lincoln, NE 68505-7041
402-423-4297
www.nchea.org

Nevada

Nevada Homeschool Network
P.O. Box 1212
Carson City, NV 89702
www.nevadahomeschoolnetwork.com

Northern Nevada Home Schools
P.O. Box 18652
Reno, NV 89511
775-852-NNHS
www.nnhs.org

New Hampshire

Christian Home Educators of New Hampshire
P.O. Box 961
Manchester, NH 03105
www.chenh.org

New Hampshire Homeschooling Coalition
P.O. Box 2224
Concord, NH 03302
603-437-3547
www.nhhomeschooling.org

New Jersey

Education Network of Christian Home-Schoolers of New Jersey
P.O. Box 308
Atlantic Highlands, NJ 07716
732-291-7800
www.enochnj.org

New Jersey Homeschool Association
P.O. Box 1386

Medford, NJ 08055
609-346-2060
www.geocities.com/jerseyhome

New Mexico
Christian Association of Parent Educators of New Mexico
P.O. Box 25046
Albuquerque, NM 87125
505-898-8548

New York
Actively and Positively Parenting and Lovingly Educating
P.O. Box 2036
North Babylon, NY 11703
www.APPLEnetwork.US/ny/apple.html

New York City Home Educators Alliance
c/o Charissa Martin
1816 Cornelia Street
Ridgewood, NY 11385
www.nychea.org

North Carolina
Families Learning Together
fltnc.cjb.net

North Carolinians for Home Education
4326-A Bland Road
Raleigh, NC 27609
919-790-1100
www.nche.com

North Dakota
North Dakota Home School Association
1854 107th Street NE
Bottineau, ND 58318
701-263-3727
www.ndhsa.org

Ohio

Christian Home Educators of Ohio
616 Hebron Road, Suite E
Heath, OH 43056-1444
740-522-2460
www.cheohome.org

Ohio Home Educators Network
www.ohiohomeeducators.net

Oklahoma

Christian Home Educators Fellowship of Oklahoma
P.O. Box 471363
Tulsa, OK 74147-1363
918-583-7323
www.chefok.org

Home Educators' Resource Organization
12725 Breckinridge Road
Enid, OK 73701
www.oklahomahomeschooling.org

Oregon

Oregon Christian Home Education Association Network
17985 Falls City Road
Dallas, OR 97338
503-288-1285
www.oceanetwork.org/lowres.cfm

Oregon Home Education Network
P.O. Box 1386
Beaverton, OR 97075-0218
503-321-5166
www.ohen.org

Pennsylvania

Christian Homeschool Association of Pennsylvania
231 North Chestnut Street

Palmyra, PA 17078
www.chapboard.org/Home.html

Pennsylvania Home Education Network
952 Peach Street
Ellwood City, PA 16117
412-922-8344
www.phen.org

Rhode Island

Rhode Island Guild of Home Teachers
www.rihomeschool.com

South Carolina

Palmetto Homeschool Association
P.O. Box 486
Lancaster, SC 29721
803-285-3916
www.palmettoha.org

South Carolina Association of Independent Home Schools
930 Knox Abbott Drive
Cayce, SC 29033
803-454-0427
www.scaihs.org

South Dakota

South Dakota Christian Home Educators
P.O. Box 9571
Rapid City, SD 57709-9571
605-348-2001
www.sdche.org

South Dakota Home School Association
P.O. Box 882
Sioux Falls, SD 57101
www.sdhsa.org

Tennessee

Tennessee Home Education Association

P.O. Box 681652
Franklin, TN 37068
888-854-3407
www.tnhea.org

Texas

Christian Home Educators Association of Central Texas
P.O. Box 141998
Austin, TX 78714-1998
512-450-0070
www.cheact.org

North Texas Home Educators' Network
P.O. Box 1071
Allen, TX 75013
214-495-9600
www.nthen.org

Southeast Texas Home School Association
10592-A Fuqua #503
Houston, TX 77089
281-756-9792
www.sethsa.org

Texas Home School Coalition
P.O. Box 6747
Lubbock, TX 79493
806-744-4441
www.thsc.org

Utah

Utah Christian Home School Association
P.O. Box 3942
Salt Lake City, UT 84110-3942
801-296-7198
www.utch.org

Utah Home Education Association
www.uhea.org

Vermont

Vermont Home Education Network
www.vhen.net

Virginia

Home Educators Association of Virginia
1900 Byrd Avenue, Suite 201
Richmond, Virginia 23230
804-288-1608
www.heav.org

Northern Virginia Home Education Conference
www.novaconference.net

Washington

Teaching Parents Association
P.O. Box 1934
Woodinville, WA 98072-1934
206-654-5658
www.washtpa.org

Washington Association of Teaching Christian Homes
P.O. Box 14122
Mill Creek, WA 98082
425-956-3282
www.watchhome.org

Washington Homeschool Organization
6627 South 191st Place, Suite F-109
Kent, WA 98032-2117
425-251-0439
www.washhomeschool.org

West Virginia

Christian Home Educators of West Virginia
P.O. Box 8770
South Charleston, WV 25303-0770
877-802-1773
www.chewv.org

West Virginia Home Educators Association
P.O. Box 3707
Charleston, WV 25337-3707
800-736-9843
www.wvhea.org

Wisconsin

Wisconsin Christian Home Educators Association
P.O. Box 320458
Franklin, WI 53132
www.wisconsinchea.com

Wisconsin Parents Association
P.O. Box 2502
Madison, WI 53701-2502
608-283-3131
www.homeschooling-wpa.org

Wyoming

Homeschoolers of Wyoming
4859 Palmer Canyon Road
Wheatland, WY 82201
www.homeschoolersofwy.org

UNITED STATES: NATIONAL ORGANIZATIONS

Adventist Home Educator
P.O. Box 836
Camino, CA 95709-0836
www.adventisthomeducator.org

African-American Homeschoolers Network
www.aahnet.org

American Homeschool Association
P.O. Box 3142

Palmer, AK 99645
800-236-3278
www.americanhomeschoolassociation.org

Catholic Family Expo
P.O. Box 27
Woodstock, MD 21163
443-539-4140
catholicfamilyexpo.org

Catholic Home School Network of America
P.O. Box 6343
River Forest, IL 60305-6343
www.geocities.com/Heartland/8579/chsna.html

Family Unschoolers Network
Dept. W
1688 Belhaven Woods Court
Pasadena, MD 21122-3727
410-360-7330
www.unschooling.org

Home School Legal Defense Association
P.O. Box 3000
Purcellville, VA 20134-9000
540-338-5600
Fax 540-338-2733
www.hslda.org

Muslim Home School Network and Resource
282 County Street #531
Attleboro, MA 02703
www.muslimhomeschool.com

National African-American Homeschoolers Alliance
www.naaha.com

National Black Home Educators
13434 Plank Road PMB 110
Baker, LA 70714
www.nbhera.org

National Challenged Homeschoolers Associated Network
P.O. Box 310
Moyie Springs, ID 83845
208-267-6246
www.nathhan.com

National Home Education Network
P.O. Box 1652
Hobe Sound, FL 33475-1652
www.nhen.org

National Home Education Research Institute
P.O. Box 13939
Salem, OR 97309
503-364-1490
www.nheri.org

Native Americans for Home Education
P.O. Box 464
Bostic, NC 28018

CANADA: PROVINCIAL ORGANIZATIONS

Alberta
Alberta Home Education Organization
www.ahea.online.com

British Columbia
British Columbia Home Learners Association
c/o 6132 Killarney Drive
Surrey, BC V35 5W9
604-543-5025
www.bchla.bc.ca

British Columbia Home School Association
6225-C 136 Street
Surrey, BC V3X 1H3
604-572-7817
www.bchomeschool.net

Manitoba
Manitoba Association of Christian Home Schools
P.O. Box 283 RPO SO St. Vital
Winnipeg, MB R2N 3X9
www.machs.mb.ca

New Brunswick
Home Educators of New Brunswick
c/o 44 Marks Street
St. Stephen's, NB ESL 2B3
www.henb.org

Ontario
Ontario Christian Home Educators' Connection
49430 Mapleton Line RR2
Springfield, ON N0L 2J0
519-764-2841
www.ochec.org

Ontario Federation of Teaching Parents
416-410-5218
800-704-0448
www.ontariohomeschool.org

Saskatchewan
Saskatchewan Home Based Educators
Box 8541
Saskatoon, SK 57K 6K6
www.shbe.info

CANADA: NATIONAL ORGANIZATIONS

Afrocentric Homeschoolers Association
geocities.com/blackhomeschool

Canadian Home Based Learning Resource Page
www.flora.org/homeschool-ca/achbe/index.html

Home School Legal Defence Association of Canada
32B-980 Adelaide Street SO
London, Ontario N6E IR3
519-913-0318
www.hsldacanada.org

INTERNATIONAL ORGANIZATIONS

Australia
Home Education Association, Inc.
4 Bruce Street
Stanmore, NSW 2048
1300 72 99 91
www.hea.asn.au/hea

China
Homeschooling International Group of Hong Kong, China
GPO Box 12114
Central, Hong Kong, China
www.geocities.com/homeschoolinghk

England
Education Otherwise
P.O. Box 325
Kings Lynn PE34 3XW
www.education-otherwise.org

Home Education Advisory Service
P.O. Box 98
Welwyn Garden City
Herts, AL8 6AN
44 (0)1707 371854
www.heas.org.uk

Home Service
48 Heaton Moor Road
Heaton Moor

Stockport SK4 4NX
44(0) 161 432 3782
www.home-service.org

Germany

Kaiserslautern Military Community Christian Home Educators
kmc.homeschool.org

Stuttgart Area Homeschoolers Association
stuttgarthomeschoolers.com

Schulunterricht zu Hause (School Instruction At Home)
Buchwaldstr. 16
D-63303, Dreieich
+49-(0)1805-724894
www.schuzh.de

Ireland

Home Education Network
henireland.org

Israel

Israel Home Education Association
02 993 4762
www.israelhomeschool.org

Japan

Homeschooling in Japan
www.asahi-net.or.jp/~ja8i-brtl

New Zealand

Home Education Foundation
P.O. Box 9064
Palmerston North
New Zealand
www.hef.org.nz
(06)354 7699

Puerto Rico

Christian Home Educators Association of Puerto Rico
Luchetti 7
Ramon Fdz.
Manati PR 00674
787-854-0167

Christian Home Educators of the Caribbean
Calle 10, E-19
Villa Universitavia, Humacao PR00791
787-852-5672

Scotland

Schoolhouse Home Education Association
P.O. Box 18044
Glenrothes, Fife KY7 9AD
0 1307 463120
www.schoolhouse.org.uk

South Africa

Western Cape Home Schooling Association
www.wchsa.org.za

Pestalozzi Trust (Legal Defence for Home Education)
www.pestalozzi.org

Spain

Association for Freedom in Education
www.educacionlibre.org

Sweden

Mitt Alternativ Till Skolan (My Alternative to School)
c/o Vairagi
Växjövägen 4
360 24 Linneryd, Sverige
0470-344 48
hem.passagen.se/matshem/index.htm

Switzerland

Home Schooling Association of Switzerland
Bildung zu Hause Schweiz
CH-3000 Bern
www.bildungzuhause.ch

Taiwan

Resource Center of Self-Directed Learning
7F, #113, San-Chung 1st Road
Chu-Dung, Hsin-Chu 310
Taiwan
03-582-3842
www.rcsdl.ngo.org.tw

APPENDIX 3

NATIONAL SCIENCE COMPETITIONS

FOR ELEMENTARY STUDENTS

Exploravision
Toshiba/NSTA ExploraVision Awards
1840 Wilson Boulevard
Arlington, VA 22201-3000
703-243-7100 or 800-EXPLOR9
www.toshiba.com/tai/exploravision
Divisions for grades K–3 and 4–6
Submission deadline: February
Submit an application, abstract, project description, bibliography, and five web page graphics. Choose an aspect of current technology, analyze it, and project its usage in 20 years.

Science Olympiad
2 Trans Am Plaza Drive, STE 415
Oakbrook Terrace, IL 60181
630-792-1251
Fax: 630-792-1287
www.soinc.org
Competition: May
Solve problems in biology, earth science, chemistry, physics, computers, and technology in teams

Young America Horticulture Project
National Junior Horticultural Association
Carol S. Norden (Project Chairperson)
Wake County Center
North Carolina Cooperative Extension Service
4001-E Carya Drive
Raleigh, NC 27610-2914
919-250-1098
www.ces.ncsu.edu/depts/hort/hil/expermt.html
Divisions for children 8 or younger and 9–11 years old.
Competition: October 15
Contests in gardening, environmental beautification, plant propagation, and experimental horticulture.

FOR MIDDLE-GRADE STUDENTS

Discovery Channel Young Scientist Challenge
Discovery Education
One Discovery Place
Silver Spring, MD 20910
800-323-9084
school.discovery.com/sciencefaircentral/dysc
Open to grades 5–8
Submission deadline: June
Complete a science fair project and win a state or regional International Science and Engineering Fair.

Exploravision
Toshiba/NSTA ExploraVision Awards
1840 Wilson Boulevard
Arlington, VA 22201-3000
800-EXPLOR9
www.exploravision.org
Divisions for grades 4–6 and 7–9
Submission deadline: February
Submit an application, abstract, project description, bibliography, and five web page graphics. Choose an aspect of current technology, analyze it, and project its usage in 20 years.

Invent America! Contest
P.O. Box 26065
Alexandria, VA 22313
703-684-1836
Fax: 410-489-2852
www.inventamerica.com/contest.cfm
Open to K-8 students enrolled in their program; may submit one entry per grade.
Contest: Entry must be postmarked by June 15.
Submit any creative inventions.

Science Olympiad
2 Trans Am Plaza Drive, STE 415
Oakbrook Terrace, IL 60181
630-792-1251
Fax: 630-792-1287
www.soinc.org
Competition: May
Solve problems in biology, earth science, chemistry, physics, computers, and technology in teams or individually.

Young America Horticulture Contest
National Junior Horticultural Association
Carol S. Norden (Project Chairperson)
Wake County Center
North Carolina Cooperative Extension Service

4001-E Carya Drive
Raleigh, NC 27610-2914
919-250-1098
www.ces.ncsu.edu/depts/hort/hil/expermt.html
Divisions for children 9–11 and 12–14 years old
Competition: October 15
Contests in gardening, environmental beautification, plant propagation, and experimental horticulture.

FOR HIGH-SCHOOL STUDENTS

Exploravision
Toshiba/NSTA ExploraVision Awards
1840 Wilson Boulevard
Arlington, VA 22201-3000
800-EXPLOR9
www.exploravision.org
Divisions for grades 7–9 and 10–12
Submission deadline: February
Submit an application, abstract, project description, bibliography, and five web page graphics. Choose an aspect of current technology, analyze it, and project its usage in 20 years.

Intel International Science and Engineering Fair Science Service
1719 North Street, NW
Washington, DC 20036
202-785-2255
www.sciserv.org/isef
Open to grades 9–12
Competition: May
Complete Research Plan and Approval Form; submit a 250-word abstract; display a project notebook and research paper. A student must win a regional or state science fair to be eligible.

Intel Science Talent Search
Science Service

1719 North Street, NW
Washington, DC 20036
202-785-2255
www.intel.com/education/sts
Open to high-school seniors
Submission deadline: November
Complete an independent research project in the physical sciences, behavioral and social sciences, engineering, mathematics, or biological sciences.

Junior Science and Humanities Symposium
Academy of Applied Science
24 Warren Street
Concord, NH 03301
603-228-4520
Fax: 603-228-4730
www.jshs.org
Open to high-school students
Competition: April
Conduct an original research investigation in the sciences, engineering, or mathematics.

National Science Bowl
United States Department of Energy
University and Science Education
Sue Ellen Walbridge (Coordinator)
Office of Science (SC-27)
U.S. Dept. of Energy
1000 Independence Avenue, SW
Washington, DC 20585
202-586-7231
www.scied.science.doe.gov/nsb/default.htm
Open to grades 9–12
Competition: May
Double-elimination competition, question-and-answer format: astronomy, biology, chemistry, mathematics, physics, earth, computer, and general science.

Science Olympiad
2 Trans Am Plaza Drive, STE 415
Oakbrook Terrace, IL 60181
630-792-1251
www.soinc.org
Division B is open to grades 6–9; Division C is open to grades 10–12
Competition: May
Solve problems in biology, earth science, chemistry, physics, computers, and technology in teams.

Siemens Westinghouse Competition in Math, Science & Technology
Siemens Foundation
170 Wood Avenue South
Iselin, NJ 08830
877-822-5233
Fax 732-603-5890
For information about the competition, contact:
College Board
800-626-9795, ext. 5930
www.siemens-foundation.org
Open to high-school students
Submission deadline: October
Complete individual or team research projects in science, mathematics, engineering, and technology, or combinations of these disciplines.

APPENDIX 4

SOURCES

A Beka Book, Inc.
P.O. Box 19100
Pensacola, FL 32523-9100
877-223-5226
Fax: 800-874-3590
Web: www.abeka.com

Publishes the *Little Owl* and *Little Book* readers as well as grammar texts and math books for grades 3-12.

A.D.A.M. Software, Inc.
1600 RiverEdge Parkway, Suite 100
Atlanta, Georgia 30328
770-980-0888
Fax: 770-955-3088

Web: www.adam.com

Sells *The Inside Story* and other anatomy-exploration software.

American Home School Publishing
P.O. Box 570
Cameron, MO 64429
800-684-2121
Fax: 800-557-0234
E-mail: booklovers@ahsp.com
Web: www.ahsp.com

Analytical Grammar
3810-201 Lunceston Way
Raleigh, NC 27613
919-783-0795
Web: www.analyticalgrammar.com

Sells the *Analytical Grammar* workbook.

Anatomy Warehouse
227 Dempster Street
Evanston, IL 60201
312-242-1650
Web: www.anatomywarehouse.com

Apologia Educational Ministries
1106 Meridian Plaza, Suite 220
Anderson, IN 46016
888-524-4724
Fax: 765-608-3290
Web: www.apologia.com

Publishes science courses for Christian home-school families.

Are You Game?
2030 Harrison Street
San Francisco, CA 94110
800-471-0641
Web: www.areyougame.com

Aristoplay/Talicor
Talicor, Inc.
901 Lincoln Parkway
Plainwell, MI 49080
800-433-GAME
Web: www.aristoplay.com
Sells educational games in math, science, and history.

Artistic Pursuits, Inc.
10142 West 69th Avenue
Arvada, CO 80004
303-467-0504
Web: www.artisticpursuits.com

Astromax
P.O. Box 7981
Dallas, TX 75209-0981
Web: www.astromax.com

Audible
One Washington Park
Newark, NJ 07102
888-283-5051
Web: www.audible.com

Audiobooks Alive
Web: audiobooksalive.com

Audio Memory
501 Cliff Drive
Newport Beach, CA 92663
800-365-SING
Web: www.audiomemory.com
Sells memory tapes in math and history.

The Back Pack
P.O. Box 125

Ernul, NC 28527
252-244-0728
Web: www.thebackpack.com
General home-school resources.

Behrman House
11 Edison Place
Springfield, NJ 07081
800-221-2755
Fax: 973-379-7280
Web: www.behrmanhouse.com
Publishes titles on Jewish ethics and history.

Bellerophon Books
P.O. Box 21307
Santa Barbara, CA 93121
800-253-9943
Fax: 805-965-8286
E-mail: sales@bellerophonbooks.com
Web: www.bellerophonbooks.com
Publishes coloring books based on actual historical images.

Blackstone Audiobooks
P.O. Box 969
Ashland, OR 97520
800-729-2665
Fax: 800-482-9294
Web: www.blackstoneaudio.com
Sells and rents books on tape.

Blister Microscope
General Science Service Co.
3547 Holmes Avenue S.
Minneapolis, MN 55408
612-822-7937
Web: blistermicroscope.com

Bolchazy-Carducci Publishers, Inc.
1000 Brown Street, Unit 101
Wauconda, IL 60084
800-392-6453
Fax: 847-526-2867
Web: www.bolchazy.com
Sells the *Artes Latinae* program and other Latin and Greek resources.

The Book Peddler
P.O. Box 1960
Elyria, OH 44036-1960
440-284-6654
Fax: 440-323-9494
Orders only: 800-928-1760
Web: www.bookpeddler.us
Sells literature and history resources and many other home-school products.

Books in Motion
9922 East Montgomery, STE 31
Spokane Valley, WA 99206
800-752-3199
Web: www.booksinmotion.com
E-mail: sales@booksinmotion.com
Sells and rents books on tape.

Brimwood Press
1941 Larsen Drive
Camino, CA 95709
530-644-7538
Web: www.brimwoodpress.com

Brock Optical, Inc.
414 Lake Howell Road
Maitland, FL 32751
407-647-6611 or 800-780-9111
Fax: 407-647-1811

Web: www.magiscope.com
E-mail: magiscope@aol.com
Sells microscopes and supplies.

Calvert School
10713 Gilroy Road, STE B
Hunt Valley, MD 21031
888-487-4652 or 410-785-3400
Web: www.calvertschool.org
E-mail: inquiry@calvertservices.org
A well-respected correspondence school that offers full-grade curricula as well as a separate math course.

Capstone Press
P.O. Box 669
Mankato, MN 56002-0669
Phone 800-747-4992
Fax: 888-262-0705
Web: www.capstone-press.com
Sells the *Photo-Illustrated Biography* series.

Carolina Biological Supply Company
2700 York Road
Burlington, NC 27215-3398
800-334-5551
Web: www.carolina.com

Castlemoyle Books
The Hotel Revere Building
7th and Main Street
Pomeroy, WA 99347-0520
888-773-5586
Fax: 509-843-3183
Web: www.castlemoyle.com
E-mail: orders@castlemoyle.com
Sells *Spelling Power.*

Chalk Dust Company
3506 Highway 6 South
Sugar Land, TX 77478-4401
800-588-7564
Web: www.chalkdust.com

Children's Books
Orders:
P.O. Box 239
Greer, SC 29652
Store location:
557 Hammett Store Road
Lyman, SC 29365
864-968-0391 or 800-344-3198
Web: www.childsbooks.com

Christian Liberty Academy
502 Euclid Avenue
Arlington Heights, IL 60004
847-259-4444
Fax: 847-259-9972
Web: www.christianlibertyacademy.com
Supplies the California Achievement Test.

Christian Light Education
1050 Mt. Clinton Pike
P.O. Box 1212
Harrisonburg, VA 22803-1212
800-776-0478 or 540-434-1003
Fax: 540-433-8896
Web: www.clp.org
E-mail: orders@clp.org
Sells high school courses in practical skills.

Classical Academic Press
3920 Market Street

Camp Hill, PA 17011
866-730-0711
Web: www.classicalacademicpress.com

Classical Writing
Web: www.classicalwriting.com

Cobblestone Publishing
30 Grove Street, Suite C
Peterborough, NH 03458
800-821-0115
Fax: 603-924-7380
Web: www.cobblestonepub.com
Publishes *Calliope* and *Cobblestone* magazines.

College Board Publications
Educational Testing Services
45 Columbus Avenue
New York, NY 10023-6917
866-630-9305
Web: www.collegeboard.com
College Board publications can most easily be ordered through a bookstore or from the online store at the College Board website.

Common Sense Press
8786 Highway 21
Melrose, FL 32666
352-475-5757
Web: www.commonsensepress.com

Continental Press
520 East Bainbridge Street
Elizabethtown, PA 17022
800-233-0759
Fax: 888-834-1303
Web: www.continentalpress.com
Sells the *On Target for Tests* series.

The Critical Thinking Company
(formerly Critical Thinking Books and Software)
P.O. Box 1610
Seaside, CA 93955-1610
800-458-4849
Web: www.criticalthinking.com
Sells logic and critical-thinking resources across the curriculum.

Curriculum Connection
614 East 8th Street
Moscow, ID 83843
208-882-2477
Web: www.curriculumconnection.net
E-mail: info@curriculumconnection.net
Sells biographies and other history books.

Debra Bell's Home School Resource Center
P.O. Box 67
Palmyra, PA 17078
Orders only: 800-937-6311
Web: www.hsrc.com
Sells standard high-school transcripts and home-school books and supplies.

Delta Education
80 Northwest Boulevard
Nashua, NH 03061-3000
800-258-1302
Orders: 800-442-5444
Fax: 800-282-9560
Web: www.delta-education.com
E-mail: customerservice@delta-education.com
Publishes Science in a Nutshell kits (www.delta-education.com/teachers/science/nutshellclusters.html) and other science materials.

Didax Educational Resources
395 Main Street

Rowley, MA 01969
800-458-0024
Fax: 800-350-2345
Web: www.didaxinc.com
E-mail: info@didaxinc.com
Sells wooden pattern blocks and other mathematics resources.

Discover This
P.O. Box 1791
Clackamas, OR 97015
866-438-8697
Web: www.discoverthis.com

Dover Publications
Customer Care
31 East 2d Street
Mineola, NY 11501-3852
Fax: 516-742-6953
Web: www.doverpublications.com
Publishes coloring books, paper dolls, and economy editions of the classics.

Ebaru Publishing
2085 Burnice Drive
Clearwater, FL 33764-4803
727-442-6828
Web: www.theviolinebook.com
Publishes *The Violin Book* series.

Education+Plus
2 Cobblestone Road
Greenville, SC 29615
864-286-6492
Web: www.edplus.com
Produces the TranscriptPro transcript-generating software.

Education Works
850 Harford Turnpike

Waterford, CT 06385
800-211-9443
Web: www.educationworks.com
Carries floor puzzles, manipulatives.

Educators Publishing Service
P.O. Box 9031
Cambridge, MA 02139-9031
800-225-5750
Web: www.epsbooks.com
Publishes *Explode the Code,* the *Vocabulary from Classical Roots* series and the *Stewart English Program.*

Edu-Track
1753 West State Hwy J
Ozark, MO 65721
866-682-3025
Web: www.edu-track.net

Emmanuel Books
P.O. Box 321
New Castle, DE 19720
800-871-5598
Fax: 302-325-4336
Web: www.emmanuelbooks.com
E-mail: email@emmanuelbooks.com
Sells *The First Whole Book of Diagrams* and resources for Catholic home schoolers.

Exploration Education
31 El Camino Terrace
Walnut Creek, CA 94596
925-324-4504
Web: www.explorationeducation.com

Fat Brain Toys
20285 Wirt Street

Elkhorn, NE 68022
800-590-5987
Web: www.fatbraintoys.com

Figures in Motion
6278 Clive Avenue
Oakland, CA 94611
510-482-8500
Web: www.figuresinmotion.com

Flyleaf Publishing
c/o IDS
400 Bedford Street, STE 322
Manchester, NH 03101
800-449-7006
Web: www.flyleafpublishing.com
Sells the *Books to Remember* early reading series.

For Dummies
10475 Crosspoint Boulevard
Indianapolis, IN 46256
877-762-2974
Web: www.dummies.com
Sells the *For Dummies* series.

Geography Matters
P.O. Box 92
Nancy, KY 42544
606-636-4678
E-mail: info@geomatters.com
Web: www.geomatters.com
Publishes outline maps and resources.

Glencoe-McGraw Hill
1221 Avenue of the Americas
New York, NY 10020
800-334-7344
Fax: 614-755-5682

Web: www.glencoe.com
E-mail: customer.service@mcgraw-hill.com
Publishes the *Writer's Choice* grammar series.

Gravitas Publications
P.O. Box 4790
Albuquerque, NM 87196-4790
888-466-2761
Web: www.gravitaspublications.com

Greathall Productions
P.O. Box 5061
Charlottesville, VA 22905
800-477-6234
Web: www.greathall.com
Sells storytelling tapes by Jim Weiss.

Greenleaf Press
3761 Highway 109 North
Lebanon, TN 37087
615-449-1617
Orders only: 800-311-1508
Web: www.greenleafpress.com
Specializes in history resources.

Grolier Publishing
A division of Scholastic Library Publishing
90 Sherman Turnpike
Danbury, CT 06816
800-621-1115
Web: store.scholastica.com

The Hedge School
24934 478th Avenue
Garretson, SD 57030
Web: hedgeschool.homestead.com
Publishes *The First Whole Book of Diagrams* and accompanying worktext.

Holt, Rinehart and Winston
Order Fulfillment Department
6277 Sea Harbor Drive
Orlando, FL 32887-0001
800-225-5425
Web: www.hrw.com
Publishes the Holt grammar series.

Home School Legal Defense Association
P.O. Box 3000
Purcellville, VA 20134-9000
540-338-5600
Fax 540-338-2733
Web: www.hslda.org
Sells high-school diploma forms.

The Institute for Excellence in Writing
P.O. Box 6065
Atascadero, CA 93423
800-856-5815
Fax 603-925-5123
Web: www.excellenceinwriting.com
Publishes the Institute for Excellence in Writing program.

Jackdaw Publications
P.O. Box 503
Amawalk, NY 10501
800-789-0022 or 914-962-6911
Fax: 800-962-9101 or 914-962-0034
Web: www.jackdaw.com
Sells facsimiles of historical documents for primary-source historical study.

J. L. Hammett Co.
P.O. Box 859057
Braintree, MA 02185-9057
800-955-2200
Fax: 888-262-1054

Web: www.hammett.com
E-mail: info@hammett.com
Sells paper and art supplies.

J. W. Pepper
2480 Industrial Boulevard
Paoli, PA 19301
800-345-6296
Web: www.jwpepper.com

K12 Software
8 West Broad Street, STE 302
Hazleton, PA 18201
866-K12-SOFT
Web: www.k12software.com

Klutz Press
455 Portage Avenue
Palo Alto, CA 94306
800-737-4123
Fax: 650-857-9110
Web: klutz.com
Sells activity book/kits for science, art, and other subjects.

Knowledge Quest
P.O. Box 789
Boring, OR 97009
877-697-8611
Web: www.knowledgequestmaps.com
Publishes maps for history.

La Clase Divertida
1703 Anniston Avenue
Holly Hill, FL 32117
386-677-0421
Web: www.funclase.com
Publishes *La Clase Divertida* Spanish program.

Lawrence Hall of Science Museum Store
University of California, Berkeley
#5200
Berkeley, CA 94720-5200
510-642-7771
Web: store.yahoo.com/lawrencehallofscience
Sells the *Family Math* books and other math and science resources.

Learning Express
Devens Business Community
29 Buena Vista Street
Devens, MA 01434
978-889-1000
Fax: 978-889-1010
Web: www.learningexpress.com
E-mail: info@learningexpress.com
Sells Smithsonian learning kits and toys.

Lively Latin
Web: www.livelylatin.com

Loyola Press
3441 North Ashland Avenue
Chicago, IL 60657
800-621-1008
Fax: 773-281-0555
Web: www.loyolapress.com
E-mail: customerservice@loyolapress.com
Publishes *Voyages in English.*

McGraw-Hill/SRA
A Division of the McGraw-Hill Companies
220 East Danieldale Road
DeSoto, TX 75115-2490
888-772-4543
Fax: 972-228-1982
Web: sraonline.com

Maps.com
120 Cremona Drive, STE H
Santa Barbara, CA 93117
800-430-7532
Web: www.maps.com

Math on the Level
9461 Vinecrest Road
Windsor, CA 95492
Web: www.mathonthelevel.com

Mathematics Programs Associates
P.O. Box 2118
Halesite, NY 11743
Web: www.mathplace.com
Purchase through www.gpasmartstore.com.
Sells the *Developmental Mathematics* program.

Math-U-See
1378 River Road
Drumore, PA 17518
888-854-6284 (directs you to a local representative)
(800-255-6654 in Canada)
Web: www.mathusee.com
Sells the Math-U-See program by directing you to a local representative (you can go straight to the list at www.mathusee.com/reps.html#1001).

Memoria Press
4605 Poplar Level Road
Louisville, KY 40213
877-862-1097
Web: www.memoriapress.com
Email: magister@memoriapress.com
Publishes *Classical Rhetoric, Prima Latina, Latina Christiana.*

Metropolitan Museum Store
800-468-7386
Web: www.metmuseum.org

Modern Curriculum Press
Pearson Learning Group
145 South Mount Zion Road
P.O. Box 2500
Lebanon, IN 46052
800-321-3106
Web: www.pearsonlearning.com/mcp/mcp_default.cfm
Sells *Spelling Workout,* phonics materials, and other language arts resources.

National Forensic League
125 Watson Street
P.O. Box 38
Ripon, WI 54971
920-748-6206
Web: www.nflonline.org

National Geographic Maps
212 Beaver Brook Canyon Road
Evergreen, CO 80439
(800) 962-1643
Web: www.natgeomaps.com
Up-to-date globes and world maps for online purchase.

National Writing Institute
624 West University, Suite 248
Denton, TX 76201-1889
800-688-5375
Fax: 888-663-7855
Web: www.writingstrands.com
Publishes the Writing Strands program.

Noble Publishing Associates
1311 NE 134th Street Suite 2A

Vancouver, WA 98685
800-225-5259
Web: www.noblepublishing.com

North Lights Books
c/o Consumer Books Direct
P.O. Box 5009
Iola, WI 54945
800-258-0929
Web: www.fwbookstore.com/category/north-light
Publishes the *Basic Techniques* art skills series.

Nothing But Software
37207 Colorado Avenue
Avon, OH 44011
800-755-4619
Web: www.nothingbutsoftware.com
Sells typing and other software.

Nothing New Press
P.O. Box 1109
La Porte, CO 80535
Web: www.nothingnewpress.com
E-mail: info@nothingnewpress.com
Republishes old resources, including the H.A. Guerber history series.

Open Texture
9457 S. University Boulevard #409
Highlands Ranch, CO 80130
866-546-6459
Web: www.opentexture.com
Publishers Koine Greek program.

Oxford University Press
198 Madison Avenue
New York, NY 10016
800-445-9714
Web: www.oup.com/us/

Parent Child Press, Inc.
P.O. Box 675
Hollidaysburg, PA 16648-0675
866-727-3683
Fax: 814-696-7510
Web: www.parentchildpress.com
E-mail: info@parentchildpress.com
Publishes the *Child-size Masterpieces* series.

Pathfinders Design and Technology
925 Clapham Drive
Victoria, VC V9C 4G7
250-478-2677
Web: www.pathfindersdesignandtechnology.com

PBS Home Video
P.O. Box 751089
Charlotte, NC 28275
800-531-4727
Web: www.shop.pbs.org
Sells the David Macaulay videos.

Peace Hill Press
18021 The Glebe Lane
Charles City, VA 23030
804-829-5043 or 877-322-3445 (toll-free) for questions and information
Fax: 804-829-5704
Web: www.peacehillpress.com
E-mail: info@peacehillpress.com
Publishes *The Story of the World, First Language Lessons,* and other resources for history and language arts.

Pemblewick Press
Box 321
Lincoln, MA 01773
Fax: 781-259-8832

Web: www.pemblewickpress.com
E-mail: pemblewick@aol.com
Sells Suzanne Strauss Art's middle-grade histories.

Perfection Learning Corporation
1000 North Second Avenue
P.O. Box 500
Logan, IA 51546-0500
800-831-4190
Fax: 800-543-2745
Web: www.perfectionlearning.com
Sells all manner of books for children.

Polka Dot Publishing
3799 Portland Drive
Reno, NV 89511-6036
775-852-2690
Web: www.polkadotpublishing.com

Power-Glide, Inc.
1682 West 820 North
Provo, UT 84601
800-596-0910
Fax: 801-343-3912
Web: www.power-glide.com
Publishes foreign-language resources.

Rainbow Resource Center
Route 1 Box 159A
50 North 500 East Road
Toulon, IL 61483
888-841-3456
Fax: 800-705-8809
Web: www.rainbowresource.com
Sells many of the books we recommend at a significant discount.

Recorded Books Productions, Inc.
LLC 270 Skipjack Road
Prince Frederick, MD 20678
800-638-1304
Fax: 410-535-5499
Web: www.recordedbooks.com
Sells and rents unabridged books on tape.

Remedia Publications
15887 North 76th Street, Suite 120
Scottsdale, AZ 85260
800-826-4740
Web: www.rempub.com

Right Start Math
Activities for Learning, Inc.
321 Hill Street
P.O. Box 468
Hazelton, ND 58544
888-272-3291
Web: www.alabacus.com

Rio Grande Games
P.O. Box 45715
Rio Rancho, NM 87174
Web: www.riograndegames.com

Rod & Staff Publishers, Inc.
P.O. Box 3
Highway 172
Crockett, KY 41413-0003
606-522-4348
Fax: 800-643-1244
Publishes grammar and language textbooks.

Rosetta Stone
Fairfield Language Technologies

135 West Market Street
Harrisonburg, VA 22801
800-280-8172
Web: www.RosettaStone.com

Saxon Publishers
Harcourt Achieve
6277 Sea Harbor Drive
Orlando, FL 32887
800-284-7019
Web: www.saxonpublishers.com

Schola Publications
1698 Market Street, Suite 162
Redding, CA 96001
530-275-2064
Fax: 530-275-9151
Web: www.thelatinroad.com
Sells *The Latin Road to English Grammar.*

Scholastic, Inc.
557 Broadway #1
New York, New York 10012
212-431-0350
Web: www.scholastic.com.

School Specialty Publishing
3195 Wilson Drive NW
Grand Rapids, MI 49534
800-417-3261
Web: www.schoolspecialtypublishing.com

The Science Fair
P.O. Box 934
St. Augustine, FL 32085
904-824-9323
Web: www.thesciencefair.com

Science Stuff
1104 Newport Avenue
Austin, TX 78753-4019
800-795-7315 or 512-323-6002
Web: www.sciencestuff.com
Sells lab materials and other science supplies.

Seton School
1350 Progress Drive
Front Royal, VA 22630
540-636-9990
Web: www.seton-school.org
Supplies the *Comprehensive Test of Basic Skills* and correspondence courses.

Shurley Instructional Materials, Inc.
366 SIM Drive
Cabot, AR 72023
800-566-2966
Web: www.shurley.com
Sells *Shurley English.*

Simply Audiobooks
P.O. Box 4112
Buffalo, NY 14240-9709
877-554-4332
Web: www.simplyaudiobooks.com

Singapore Math, Inc.
404 Beavercreek Road #225
Oregon City, OR 87045
503-557-8100
Fax: 503-557-8103
Web: www.singaporemath.com
Sells the *Singapore Math* program.

Social Studies School Service
10200 Jefferson Boulevard, Box 802

Culver City, CA 90232
800-421-4246 or 310-839-2436
Fax: 800-944-5432 or 310-839-2249
Web: www.socialstudies.com
Sells Jackdaw primary resource portfolios, *Teaching Students to Read Nonfiction,* and other history materials.

Sonlight Curriculum Ltd.
8042 South Grant Way
Littleton, CO 80122-2705
303-730-6292
Fax: 303-795-8668
Web: www.sonlight.com

Steck-Vaughn Publishing Company
Harcourt Achieve
6277 Sea Harbor Drive
Orlando, FL 32887
800-531-5015
Web: www.steck-vaughn.harcourtachieve.com
Sells the *Test Best* series for standardized test preparation.

Supercharged Science
Web: www.superchargedscience.com

The Teaching Company
4151 Lafayette Center Drive, Suite 100
Chantilly, VA 20151-1232
800-832-2412
Fax: 703-378-3819
Web: www.teachco.com
Offers filmed courses in a wide variety of fields.

Teaching Planet
93 Mill Plain Road
Danbury, CT 06811
800-307-6278
Web: Teachingplanet.com

Teaching Textbooks
P.O. Box 60529
Oklahoma City, OK 73146-0529
866-867-6284
Web: www.teachingtextbooks.com

Thames & Kosmos
207 High Point Avenue
Portsmouth, RI 02871
800-587-2872
Web: www.thamesandkosmos.com

Timberdoodle
1510 East Spencer Lake Road
Shelton, WA 98584
800-478-0672
Web: www.timberdoodle.com
E-mail: mailbag@timberdoodle.com
General supplier of history, literature, and other materials.

Tobin's Lab
P.O. Box 725
Culpeper, VA 22701
540-829-6906
Web: www.tobinslab.com
Sells science supplies.

Torah Aura Publications
4423 Fruitland Avenue
Los Angeles, CA 90058
800-689-0793
Fax: 323-585-0327
Web: www.torahaura.com
Publishes titles on Jewish ethics.

Trigger Memory System
Web: www.triggermemorysystem.com

Usborne Publishing
Educational Development Corporation
P.O. Box 470663
Tulsa, OK 74147-0663
800-475-4522
Web: www.edcpub.com
Publishes history and science titles.

Ventura Educational Systems
P.O. Box 1622
Arroyo Grande, CA 93421-1622
800-336-1022
Web: www.venturaes.com
Sells A.D.A.M. software such as *The Inside Story* and other educational titles.

J. Weston Walch, Publisher
40 Walch Drive
Portland, ME 04103-1286
800-341-6094 for orders
Fax: 207-772-3105 or 888-991-5755
Web: www.walch.com
Sells *Practical Chemistry Labs* and other science materials.

Walter Foster Publishing
23062 La Cadena Drive
Laguna Hills, CA 92653
800-426-0099
Fax: 949-380-7575
Web: www.walterfoster.com
Sells art kits and materials.

Wayside Publishing
11 Jan Sebastian Way, Suite 5
Sandwich, MA 02563
888-302-2519 or 508-833-5096
Fax: 508-833-6284

Web: www.waysidepublishing.com
Publishes Suzanne Strauss Art's history titles.

Wiley Publishing
10475 Crosspoint Boulevard
Indianapolis, IN 46256
Phone: 877-762-2974
Fax: 800-597-3299
Web: www.wiley.com
Publishes the *For Dummies* series, the *Self-Teaching Guides*, and other books.

The Writing Company
10200 Jefferson Boulevard
Box 802
Culver City, CA 90232-0802
800-421-4246
800-944-5432 (fax)
Web: www.writingco.com
E-mail: access@writingco.com
Publishes the Shakespeare catalog.

Young Explorers
P.O. Box 3338
Chelmsford, MA 01824-0938
800-239-7577
Web: www.youngexplorers.com

Zaner-Bloser
1201 Dublin Road
Columbus, OH 43215-3018
800-421-3018
Fax: 800-992-6087
Web: www.zaner-bloser.com

APPENDIX 5

PREVIOUS RECOMMENDATIONS

Resources which do not appear on this list are out of print or supplementary.

Recommendation	Reason for Change
A Beka Grammar and Composition	Rod & Staff extended their program into high school; the Rod & Staff books are simpler to use and the design of the composition lessons is better.
English for the Thoughtful Child	Parents needed additional help in teaching the concepts; the book also moved too quickly for many elementary students.
G.U.M. (Grammar, Usage, Mechanics)	After the 1999 edition of *The Well-Trained Mind* came out, Loyola Press published a

	nonsectarian version of their Catholic school program, *Voyages in English. VIE* is more complete and provides more drill than *G.U.M.*
How to Read a Book (Adler)	A wonderful book and an enduring classic—but better for adult readers than for high-school students. The new recommendations are more age-appropriate.
Introductory Logic and *Intermediate Logic* (Canon Press)	The Memoria Press logic is simpler to use at home; the Canon Press program was designed for classrooms.
Latin Primer and *Latin Grammar* (Canon Press)	The Memoria Press Latin course is simpler to use at home; the Canon Press program was designed for classrooms.
Phonics Pathways	An excellent phonics program, but many parents found that they needed more guidance in how to teach the skills.
The Usborne Book of World History	Many parents found the encyclopedic presentation choppy and hard to follow; the book did not lend itself to narration practice.
Western Civilization (Spielvogel)	Adequate but not engaging reading for high-school students; we have suggested more attractive narratives.
Wheelock's Latin	Still a very sound program, but not designed for home educators; other programs intended for home-schooling parents are simpler to use.

SELECTED BIBLIOGRAPHY

Beechick, Ruth. *A Strong Start in Language.* Pollock Pines, Calif.: Arrow Press, 1993.

Eliot, T. S. *Classics and the Man of Letters.* New York: Haskell House Publishers, 1974.

Flesch, Rudolph. *Why Johnny Can't Read and What You Can Do about It.* 1955. New York: Perennial Library, 1986.

Guroian, Vigen. *Tending the Heart of Virtue: How Classic Stories Awaken a Child's Moral Imagination.* Oxford: Oxford University Press, 1998.

Healy, Jane, Ph.D. *Endangered Minds: Why Our Children Don't Think and What We Can Do about It.* New York: Touchstone, 1990.

Hicks, David. *Norms and Nobility: A Treatise on Education.* New York: Praeger, 1981.

Kilpatrick, William, and Gregory and Suzanne M. Wolfe. *Books That Build Character: A Guide to Teaching Your Child Moral Values through Stories.* New York: Touchstone, 1994.

Murnane, Richard J., and Frank Levy. *Teaching the New Basic Skills: Principles for Educating Children to Thrive in a Changing Economy.* New York: Free Press, 1996.

Postman, Neil. *The End of Education: Redefining the Value of School.* New York: Knopf, 1995.

Sayers, Dorothy. "The Lost Tools of Learning." Paper delivered at Oxford University, 1947. Reprinted in Douglas Wilson. *Recovering the Lost Tools of Learning.* Wheaton, Ill.: Crossway Books, 1991.

Veith, Gene Edward, Jr., and Andrew Kern. *Classical Education: Towards the Revival of American Schooling.* Washington, D.C.: Capital Research Center, 1997.

Wilson, Douglas. *Recovering the Lost Tools of Learning.* Wheaton, Ill: Crossway Books, 1991.

Wilson, Douglas, Wesley Callihan, and Douglas Jones. *Classical Education and the Home School.* Moscow, Idaho: Canon Press, 1995.

INDEX